CYPHER SYSTEM RULEBOOK

CREDITS

Writer/Designer: Monte Cook
Additional Designers: Bruce R. Cordell, Robert J. Schwalb, Shanna Germain
Creative Director: Shanna Germain
Editor/Proofreader: Ray Vallese
Graphic Designer: Bear Weiter
Cover Artist: Roberto Pitturru

Artists

Jacob Atienza, Marco Caradonna, Milivoj Ćeran, chrom, Florian Devos, Dreamstime.com, Jason Engle, Erebus, David Hueso, Baldi Konijn, Guido Kuip, Brandon Leach, Eric Lofgren, Patrick McEvoy, Jeremy McHugh, Brynn Metheney, Grzegorz Pedrycz, Mike Perry, John Petersen, Roberto Pitturru, Scott Purdy, Nick Russell, Joe Slucher, Lee Smith, Matt Stawicki, Cyril Terpent, Cory Trego-Erdner, Tiffany Turrill, Shane Tyree, Chris Waller, Cathy Wilkins, Ben Wootten, Danar Worya, Kieran Yanner

Printed in Canada

TABLE OF CONTENTS

CHAPTER 1

INTRODUCTION

A cypher is a secret. It's something that not everyone understands. It holds potential. Promise.

The *Cypher System Rulebook* came about because we published a game called Numenera, and then another called The Strange. These were quite popular, both for their settings and for their rules. They shared the same basic game engine: the Cypher System. So it occurred to us, what if gamers want to use the system for fantasy, horror, or something else? Wouldn't it be nice if they could have the system material from Numenera and The Strange with all the setting-specific material stripped out?

And doing that would be easy, right? We'd just need to grab stuff from both games, already finished, and cram it all into one book. No problem.

Of course, once I started working on it, I realized that the way both games handled character types was entirely idiosyncratic to those settings. You can't take a Numenera nano and plop her down in any genre. And if you tried to make the type fit more into a fantasy setting, it wouldn't fit into a science fiction one. Oh, and superheroes—those throw a big wrench into things.

In other words, while the *Cypher System Rulebook* is partially a compilation of game material from both Numenera and The Strange, it also has a whole lot of new stuff. New descriptors and foci to make different genres work, along with four new character types. New creatures and NPCs. New cyphers. Lots of new rules for handling everything from starship battles to the rising dread of horror. And rules for superheroes—characters who break all the other rules.

In the Cypher System, the story is king, and thus you can't really get the rules wrong. If it works for your game, then it works!

What you'll take away from this book depends on your context.

If you're already a fan of both Numenera and The Strange, many of the specifics here will be familiar. Still, you'll find new descriptors, foci, types, creatures, cyphers, artifacts, and rules. Mostly, though, you'll see how to use the game system you already love in any setting and any genre. Use the material in this book to supplement your current games, or start a new game set in a fantasy land of elves and fae creatures, a science fiction setting spanning the galaxy, or a modern slasher horror game, different from anything you've played before.

If you're a fan of Numenera *or* The Strange, but not both, you'll find a ton of material here that is new to you. Again, this can supplement your existing game, or it can be used to stretch the system into any genre you wish when you're finished with your current campaign.

Fans of Numenera and The Strange should check out the rules for Insights (page 216) and the optional genre rules in addition to the descriptors, types, and foci that are brand new to this book.

If you're new to the Cypher System entirely, you're really in for a lot of great information and advice. The rules are simple, but this book includes plenty of character and setting options. It might seem overwhelming at first. But remember that in the Cypher System, the story is king, and thus you can't really get the rules wrong. If it works for your game, then it works!

Chapter 2

ANYTHING GOES

For just a moment, I'm talking directly to the game masters out there. Both players and GMs will use this book, but more than likely the GM will look at it first.

What you hold in your hands is a guidebook. A how-to. You can't just sit down and start playing, because the *Cypher System Rulebook* is not meant to be used that way. You have to put something of your own into it first. There is no setting or world here. The system is designed to help you portray any world or setting you can dream up.

Think of this book as a chest of toys. You can pull out whatever you want and play with it however you want. You won't use everything in it, at least not all at once. You'll use parts of it to build the game you want to play. Pull out some pieces and give them a try. Put back the ones that don't suit you, and try different ones. Use some now and save others for your next game. You have all the freedom in the world (many worlds, actually).

Speaking of worlds, you get to decide what setting to use, based on what genre you want. It can be anything. Pick your favorite book or movie, or just design something from scratch.

GENRES

Take a look at Part 3: Genres, which has a number of chapters devoted to genres. These are broad categories, and I use them in this book as a starting point. Those categories are: fantasy, modern, science fiction, horror, and superheroes.

With those broad strokes, I cover most (but probably not all) of the kinds of games you can run with the Cypher System. Some of these genres require unique equipment, artifacts, or descriptors. Some need new rules to convey the experience you're after.

I say "experience" because in many ways, that's what a genre is. If you want to capture the experience of being terrified by zombies swarming around a character's home, you want horror. If you want to convey the experience of being extremely powerful and using those powers to protect the world from aliens, you want superheroes (maybe with a dash of science fiction).

So really, what you're choosing here is the experience you want to have—and that you want the players to have. This is such a fundamental decision that perhaps the whole group should be in on it. Ask the other players what genre they like and what kinds of experiences they want to have. This is vital because it ensures that everyone gets what they want out of the game.

Of course, not everything in this book is suitable for every genre. You, the GM, will need to read through it once you've chosen a genre and pick types, foci, and so forth.

Part 3: Genres, page 235

Genre categories are difficult. Sometimes they can be constricting when they should be liberating. Don't worry too much about being a genre purist. Just have a fun game.

Campaign Design Worksheet, page 412

You'll find a lot of help throughout the book, and first and foremost is the Campaign Design Worksheet in part 5. Use it to let the players know what material you've chosen to be available so they can create characters that fit the genre.

SETTINGS

Bears a Halo of Fire, page 98

Flavor, page 50

Chapter 5: Character Type, page 22

Chapter 6: Character Descriptor, page 64

Chapter 7: Character Focus, page 90

Chapter 19: Running the Cypher System, page 366

If you like the Cypher System but don't want to create your own setting, check out Numenera or The Strange. Both games offer complete settings as well as the rules you need to play. Neither requires any customization if you don't want to do that.

While genres are useful categories to organize your thoughts, what you're actually going to create is a setting. Labels like "science fiction" or "space opera" are fine, but in the end what is important is the specific setting that you create.

Your setting—whether it's your original creation or adapted from something else—is yours to do with as you will. Don't worry about what anyone else might think is appropriate for the genre. Once you start putting together the setting, you might want to go through the character creation material in the book again. Just because something is appropriate for the fantasy genre, it might not work for *your* fantasy setting. For example, you might have designed it such that fire magic is always evil and in the hands of demon-possessed priests, and thus Bears a Halo of Fire is not an appropriate focus for your PCs, even though it's fine in other fantasy games.

The more specific details you have about your setting, the easier this is to do, and the more distinct your setting is from genre tropes, the more you'll *have* to do it. But that's okay. Specific, distinct settings are usually the most fun, the most memorable, and the most likely to engage your players. They're worth the extra work.

TAILORING THE RULES

Sometimes you have to alter things to make them into what you need and want. Take, for example, the magic flavor that you can give to any of the types in chapter 5. It's called "magic" and has a lot of the trappings of magic, but it would be simple to change the name to "psionics," "mutant powers," or whatever your setting needs.

In other words, picking and choosing material from this book might not be enough. You might have to tweak things here and there. Fortunately, most of the material is made to be changed or manipulated. In fact, because the core mechanics of the Cypher System are so simple, tweaking things here and there is a breeze. This is not the kind of game where changing one thing creates a domino effect that has a lot of unintended consequences. In chapter 6, you'll find guidelines for creating new descriptors. In chapter 7, you'll find specific ideas for swapping out new foci abilities, which can help you create new ones if need be. And the character types in this book are designed to be tailored and reshaped.

When making alterations, worry less about game balance and more about telling the stories you want to tell and allowing the players to create and play the characters they want to play. If you successfully do both of those things, everyone will be happy. And that's really what game balance is all about.

You can also look at Chapter 19: Running the Cypher System for further insights into changing the mechanics. But mostly, that chapter will tell you the same thing that you're reading now: it's your game to do with as you will.

Chapter 3

HOW TO PLAY THE CYPHER SYSTEM

The rules of the Cypher System are quite straightforward at their heart, as all of gameplay is based around a few core concepts.

This chapter provides a brief explanation of how to play the game, and it's useful for learning the game. Once you understand the basic concepts, you'll likely want to reference Chapter 9: Rules of the Game, for a more in-depth treatment.

The Cypher System uses a twenty-sided die (1d20) to determine the results of most actions. Whenever a roll of any kind is called for and no die is specified, roll a d20.

The game master sets a difficulty for any given task. There are ten degrees of difficulty. Thus, the difficulty of a task can be rated on a scale of 1 to 10.

Each difficulty has a target number associated with it. The target number is always three times the task's difficulty, so a difficulty 4 task has a target number of 12. To succeed at the task, you must roll the target number or higher. See the Task Difficulty table (page 8) for guidance in how this works.

Character skills, favorable circumstances, or excellent equipment can decrease the difficulty of a task. For example, if a character is trained in climbing, she turns a difficulty 6 climb into a difficulty 5 climb. This is called decreasing the difficulty by one step. If she is specialized in climbing, she turns a difficulty 6 climb into a difficulty 4 climb. This is called decreasing the difficulty by two steps.

A skill is a category of knowledge, ability, or activity relating to a task, such as climbing, geography, or persuasiveness. A character who has a skill is better at completing related tasks than a character who lacks the skill. A character's level of skill is either trained (reasonably skilled) or specialized (very skilled).

If you are trained in a skill relating to a task, you decrease the difficulty of that task by one step. If you are specialized, you decrease the difficulty by two steps. A skill can never decrease a task's difficulty by more than two steps.

Anything else that reduces difficulty (help from an ally, a particular piece of equipment, or some other advantage) is referred to as an asset. Assets can never decrease a task's difficulty by more than two steps.

You can also decrease the difficulty of a given task by applying Effort. (Effort is described in more detail in Chapter 9: Rules of the Game.)

To sum up, three things can decrease a task's difficulty: skills, assets, and Effort.

If you can decrease a task's difficulty to 0, you automatically succeed and don't need to make a roll.

You don't earn XP for killing foes or overcoming standard challenges in the course of play. Discovery is the soul of the Cypher System.

Chapter 9: Rules of the Game, page 188

Difficulty, page 8

Effort, page 192

Decrease the difficulty, page 192

Skill, page 20

TASK DIFFICULTY

Task Difficulty	Description	Target No.	Guidance
0	Routine	0	Anyone can do this basically every time.
1	Simple	3	Most people can do this most of the time.
2	Standard	6	Typical task requiring focus, but most people can usually do this.
3	Demanding	9	Requires full attention; most people have a 50/50 chance to succeed.
4	Difficult	12	Trained people have a 50/50 chance to succeed.
5	Challenging	15	Even trained people often fail.
6	Intimidating	18	Normal people almost never succeed.
7	Formidable	21	Impossible without skills or great effort.
8	Heroic	24	A task worthy of tales told for years afterward.
9	Immortal	27	A task worthy of legends that last lifetimes.
10	Impossible	30	A task that normal humans couldn't consider (but one that doesn't break the laws of physics).

For some people, combat will be an important part of the Cypher System. However, this is your choice; a Cypher System game doesn't have to be about combat.

WHEN DO YOU ROLL?

Any time your character attempts a task, the GM assigns a difficulty to that task, and you roll a d20 against the associated target number.

When you jump from a burning vehicle, swing an axe at a mutant beast, swim across a raging river, identify a strange device, convince a merchant to give you a lower price, craft an object, use a power to control a foe's mind, or use a blaster rifle to carve a hole in a wall, you make a d20 roll.

However, if you attempt something that has a difficulty of 0, no roll is needed—you automatically succeed. Many actions have a difficulty of 0. Examples include walking across the room and opening a door, using a special ability to negate gravity so you can fly, using an ability to protect your friend from radiation, or activating a device (that you already understand) to erect a force field. These are all routine actions and don't require rolls.

Using skill, assets, and Effort, you can decrease the difficulty of potentially any task to 0 and thus negate the need for a roll. Walking across a narrow wooden beam is tricky for most people, but for an experienced gymnast, it's routine. You can even decrease the difficulty of an attack on a foe to 0 and succeed without rolling.

Armor, page 184

If there's no roll, there's no chance for failure. However, there's also no chance for remarkable success (in the Cypher System, that usually means rolling a 19 or 20; see Special Rolls on page 10 and in Chapter 9: Rules of the Game).

COMBAT

Making an attack in combat works the same way as any other roll: the GM assigns a difficulty to the task, and you roll a d20 against the associated target number.

The difficulty of your attack roll depends on how powerful your opponent is. Just as tasks have a difficulty from 1 to 10, creatures have a level from 1 to 10. Most of the time, the difficulty of your attack roll is the same as the creature's level. For example, if you attack a level 2 bandit, it's a level 2 task, so your target number is 6.

It's worth noting that players make all die rolls. If a character attacks a creature, the player makes an attack roll. If a creature attacks a character, the player makes a defense roll.

The damage dealt by an attack is not determined by a roll—it's a flat number based on the weapon or attack used. For example, a spear always does 4 points of damage.

Your Armor characteristic reduces the damage you take from attacks directed at you. You get Armor from wearing physical armor (such as a leather jacket in a modern game or chainmail in a fantasy setting) or from special abilities. Like weapon damage, Armor is a flat number, not a roll. If you're attacked, subtract your Armor from the damage you take. For example, a leather jacket gives you +1 to Armor, meaning that you take 1 less point of damage from attacks. If a mugger hits you with a knife for 2 points of damage while you're wearing a leather jacket, you take only 1 point of damage. If your Armor reduces the damage from an attack to 0, you take no damage from that attack.

When you see the word "Armor" capitalized in the game rules (other than in the name of a special ability), it refers to your Armor characteristic—the number you subtract from incoming damage. When you see the word "armor" with a lowercase "a," it refers to any physical armor you might wear.

Typical physical weapons come in three categories: light, medium and heavy.

Light weapons inflict only 2 points of damage, but they reduce the difficulty of the attack roll by one step because they are fast and easy to use. Light weapons are punches, kicks, clubs, knives, handaxes, rapiers, small pistols, and so on. Weapons that are particularly small are light weapons.

Medium weapons inflict 4 points of damage. Medium weapons include swords, battleaxes, maces, crossbows, spears, pistols, blasters, and so on. Most weapons are medium. Anything that could be used in one hand (even if it's often used in two hands, such as a quarterstaff or spear) is a medium weapon.

Heavy weapons inflict 6 points of damage, and you must use two hands to attack with them. Heavy weapons are huge swords, great hammers, massive axes, halberds, heavy crossbows, blaster rifles, and so on. Anything that must be used in two hands is a heavy weapon.

BONUSES

Rarely, an ability or piece of equipment does not decrease a task's difficulty but instead adds a bonus to the die roll. Bonuses always add together, so if you get a +1 bonus from two different sources, you have a +2 bonus. If you get enough bonuses to add up to a +3 bonus for a task, treat it as an asset: instead of adding the bonus to your roll, decrease the difficulty by one step. Therefore, you never add more than +1 or +2 to a die roll.

For more on the types of weapons that characters can use, see Chapter 8: Equipment.

SPECIAL ROLLS

For more information on special rolls and how they affect combat and other interactions, see page 193.

When you roll a natural 19 (the d20 shows "19") and the roll is a success, you also have a minor effect. In combat, a minor effect inflicts 3 additional points of damage with your attack, or, if you'd prefer a special result, you could decide instead that you knock the foe back, distract him, or something similar. When not in combat, a minor effect could mean that you perform the action with particular grace. For example, when jumping down from a ledge, you land smoothly on your feet, or when trying to persuade someone, you convince her that you're smarter than you really are. In other words, you not only succeed but also go a bit further.

When you roll a natural 20 (the d20 shows "20") and the roll is a success, you also have a major effect. This is similar to a minor effect, but the results are more remarkable. In combat, a major effect inflicts 4 additional points of damage with your attack, but again, you can choose instead to introduce a dramatic event such as knocking down your foe, stunning him, or taking an extra action. Outside of combat, a major effect means that something beneficial happens based on the circumstance. For example, when climbing up a cliff wall, you make the ascent twice as fast. When a roll grants you a major effect, you can choose to use a minor effect instead if you prefer.

In combat (and only in combat), if you roll a natural 17 or 18 on your attack roll, you add 1 or 2 additional points of damage, respectively. Neither roll has any special effect options—just the extra damage.

Rolling a natural 1 is always bad. It means that the GM introduces a new complication into the encounter.

RANGE AND SPEED

Distance is simplified into three categories: immediate, short, and long.

Immediate distance from a character is within reach or within a few steps. If a character stands in a small room, everything in the room is within immediate distance. At most, immediate distance is 10 feet (3 m).

Short distance is anything greater than immediate distance but less than 50 feet (15 m) or so.

Long distance is anything greater than short distance but less than 100 feet (30 m) or so. Beyond that range, distances are always specified—500 feet (152 m), a mile (2 km), and so on.

The idea is that it's not necessary to measure precise distances. Immediate distance is right there, practically next to the character. Short distance is nearby. Long distance is farther off.

All weapons and special abilities use these terms for ranges. For example, all melee weapons have immediate range—they are close-combat weapons, and you can use them to attack anyone within immediate distance. A thrown knife (and most other thrown weapons) has short range. A bow has long range. An adept's Onslaught ability also has short range.

A character can move an immediate distance as part of another action. In other words, he can take a few steps over to the control panel and activate a switch. He can lunge across a small room to attack a foe. He can open a door and step through.

A character can move a short distance as his entire action for a turn. He can also try to move a long distance as his entire action, but the player might have to roll to see if the character slips, trips, or stumbles as the result of moving so far so quickly.

For example, if the PCs are fighting a group of cultists, any character can likely attack any cultist in the general melee—they're all within immediate range. Exact positions aren't important. Creatures in a fight are always moving, shifting, and jostling, anyway. However, if one cultist stayed back to fire his pistol, a character

Adept, page 29

Onslaught, page 31

Many rules in this system avoid the cumbersome need for precision. Does it really matter if the ghost is 13 feet away from you or 18? Probably not. That kind of needless specificity only slows things down and draws away from, rather than contributes to, the story.

GLOSSARY

Game Master (GM): The player who doesn't run a character, but instead guides the flow of the story and runs all the NPCs.

Nonplayer Character (NPC): Characters run by the GM. Think of them as the minor characters in the story, or the villains or opponents. This includes any kind of creature as well as people.

Party: A group of player characters (and perhaps some NPC allies).

Player Character (PC): A character run by a player rather than the GM. Think of the PCs as the main characters in the story.

Player: The players who run characters in the game.

Session: A single play experience. Usually lasts a few hours. Sometimes one adventure can be accomplished in a session. More often, one adventure is multiple sessions.

Adventure: A single portion of the campaign with a beginning and an end. Usually defined at the beginning by a goal put forth by the PCs and at the end by whether or not they achieve that goal.

Campaign: A series of sessions strung together with an overarching story (or linked stories) with the same player characters. Often, but not always, a campaign involves a number of adventures.

Character: Anything that can act in the game. Although this includes PCs and human NPCs, it also technically includes creatures, aliens, mutants, automatons, animate plants, and so on. The word "creature" is usually synonymous.

In the Cypher System, players make all die rolls. If a character attacks a creature, the player makes an attack roll. If a creature attacks a character, the player makes a defense roll.

might have to use her entire action to move the short distance required to attack that foe. It doesn't matter if the cultist is 20 feet (6 m) or 40 feet (12 m) away—it's simply considered short distance. It does matter if he's more than 50 feet (15 m) away because that distance would require a long move.

Chapter 4: Creating Your Character, page 14

EXPERIENCE POINTS

Experience points, page 219

GM intrusion, page 193

Cypher, page 340

Experience points (XP) are rewards given to players when the GM intrudes on the story (this is called GM intrusion) with a new and unexpected challenge. For example, in the middle of combat, the GM might inform the player that he drops his weapon. However, to intrude in this manner, the GM must award the player 2 XP. The rewarded player, in turn, must immediately give one of those XP to another player and justify the gift (perhaps the other player had a good idea, told a funny joke, performed an action that saved a life, and so on).

Alternatively, the player can refuse the GM intrusion. If he does so, he doesn't get the 2 XP from the GM, and he must also spend 1 XP that he already has. If the player has no XP to spend, he can't refuse the intrusion.

A d6 is used most often for recovery rolls (page 202) and to determine the level of cyphers (page 340).

The GM can also give players XP between sessions as a reward for making discoveries during an adventure. Discoveries are interesting facts, wondrous secrets, powerful artifacts, answers to mysteries, or solutions to problems (such as where the kidnappers are keeping their victim or how the PCs repair the starship). You don't earn XP for killing foes or overcoming standard challenges in the course of play. Discovery is the soul of the Cypher System.

Experience points are used primarily for character advancement (for details, see Chapter 4: Creating Your Character), but a player can also spend 1 XP to reroll any die roll and take the better of the two rolls.

CYPHERS

Cyphers are abilities that have a single use. A character can carry cyphers and use them during the game. The form they take depends on the setting. In a fantasy world they might be spells or potions, but in a science fiction game they could be alien crystals or just inspirations.

Characters will find new cyphers frequently in the course of play, so players shouldn't hesitate to use their cypher abilities. Because cyphers are always different, the characters will always have new special powers to try.

OTHER DICE

In addition to a d20, you'll need a d6 (a six-sided die). Rarely, you'll need to roll a number between 1 and 100 (often called a d100 or d% roll), which you can do by rolling a d20 twice, using the last digit of the first roll as the "tens" place and the last digit of the second roll as the "ones" place. For example, rolling a 17 and a 9 gives you 79, rolling a 3 and an 18 gives you 38, and rolling a 20 and a 10 gives you 00 (also known as 100). If you have a d10 (a ten-sided die), you can use it instead of the d20 to roll numbers between 1 and 100.

PART 1

CHARACTERS

CHAPTER 4

CREATING YOUR CHARACTER

This chapter explains how to create characters to play in a Cypher System game. This involves a series of decisions that will shape your character, so the more you understand what kind of character you want to play, the easier character creation will be. The process involves understanding the values of three game statistics and choosing three aspects that determine your character's capabilities.

CHARACTER STATS

Every player character has three defining characteristics, which are typically called "statistics" or "stats." These stats are Might, Speed, and Intellect. They are broad categories that cover many different but related aspects of a character.

Might could be thought of as Might/Health because it governs how strong you are and how much physical punishment you can take.

Speed could be thought of as Speed/Agility because it governs your overall swiftness and reflexes.

MIGHT

Might defines how strong and durable your character is. The concepts of strength, endurance, constitution, hardiness, and physical prowess are all folded into this one stat. Might isn't relative to size; instead, it's an absolute measurement. An elephant has more Might than the mightiest tiger, which has more Might than the mightiest rat, which has more Might than the mightiest spider.

Might governs actions from forcing doors open to walking for days without food to resisting disease. It's also the primary means of determining how much damage your character can sustain in a dangerous situation. Physical characters, tough characters, and characters interested in fighting should focus on Might.

SPEED

Speed describes how fast and physically coordinated your character is. The stat embodies quickness, movement, dexterity, and reflexes. Speed governs such divergent actions as dodging attacks, sneaking around quietly, and throwing a ball accurately. It helps determine whether you can move farther on your turn. Nimble, fast, or sneaky characters will want good Speed stats, as will those interested in ranged combat.

INTELLECT

This stat determines how smart, knowledgeable, and likable your character is. It includes intelligence, wisdom, charisma, education, reasoning, wit, willpower, and charm. Intellect governs solving puzzles, remembering facts, telling convincing lies, and using mental powers. Characters interested in communicating effectively, being learned scholars, or wielding supernatural powers should stress their Intellect stat.

POOL, EDGE, AND EFFORT

Each of the three stats has two components: Pool and Edge. Your Pool represents your raw, innate ability, and your Edge represents knowing how to use what you have. A third element ties into this concept: Effort. When your character really needs to accomplish a task, you apply Effort.

POOL

Your Pool is the most basic measurement of a stat. Comparing the Pools of two creatures will give you a general sense of which creature is superior in that stat. For example, a character who has a Might Pool of 16 is stronger (in a basic sense) than a character who has a Might Pool of 12. Most characters start with a Pool of 9 to 12 in most stats—that's the average range.

When your character is injured, sickened, or attacked, you temporarily lose points from one of your stat Pools. The nature of the attack determines which Pool loses points. For example, physical damage from a sword reduces your Might Pool, a poison that makes you clumsy reduces your Speed Pool, and a psionic blast reduces your Intellect Pool. You can also spend points from one of your stat Pools to decrease a task's difficulty (see Effort, below). You can rest to recover lost points from a stat Pool, and some special abilities or cyphers might allow you to recover lost points quickly.

EDGE

Although your Pool is the basic measurement of a stat, your Edge is also

Intellect could be thought of as Intellect/Personality because it governs both intelligence and charisma.

Recovering points in a Pool, page 202

Your stat Pools, as well as your Effort and Edge, are determined by the character type, descriptor, and focus that you choose. Within those guidelines, however, you have a lot of flexibility in how you develop your character.

When applying Effort to melee attacks, you have the option of spending points from either your Might Pool or your Speed Pool. When making ranged attacks, you may spend points only from your Speed Pool. This reflects that with melee you sometimes use brute force and sometimes use finesse, but with ranged attacks, it's always about careful targeting.

important. When something requires you to spend points from a stat Pool, your Edge for that stat reduces the cost. It also reduces the cost of applying Effort to a roll.

For example, let's say you have a mental blast ability, and activating it costs 1 point from your Intellect Pool. Subtract your Intellect Edge from the activation cost, and the result is how many points you must spend to use the mental blast. If using your Edge reduces the cost to 0, you can use the ability for free.

Your Edge can be different for each stat. For example, you could have a Might Edge of 1, a Speed Edge of 1, and an Intellect Edge of 0. You'll always have an Edge of at least 1 in one stat. Your Edge for a stat reduces the cost of spending points from that stat Pool, but not from other Pools. Your Might Edge reduces the cost of spending points from your Might Pool, but it doesn't affect your Speed Pool or Intellect Pool. Once a stat's Edge reaches 3, you can apply one level of Effort for free.

A character who has a low Might Pool but a high Might Edge has the potential to perform Might actions consistently better than a character who has a Might Edge of 0. The high Edge will let her reduce the cost of spending points from the Pool, which means she'll have more points available to spend on applying Effort.

EFFORT

When your character really needs to accomplish a task, you can apply Effort. For a beginning character, applying Effort requires spending 3 points from the stat Pool appropriate to the action. Thus, if your character tries to dodge an attack (a Speed roll) and wants to increase the chance for success, you can apply Effort by spending 3 points from your Speed Pool. Effort lowers the difficulty of the task by one step. This is called applying one level of Effort.

You don't have to apply Effort if you don't want to. If you choose to apply Effort to a task, you must do it before you attempt the roll—you can't roll first and then decide to apply Effort if you rolled poorly.

Applying more Effort can lower a task's difficulty further: each additional level of Effort reduces the difficulty by another step. Applying one level of Effort lowers the

difficulty by one step, applying two levels lowers the difficulty by two steps, and so on. However, each level of Effort after the first costs only 2 points from the stat Pool instead of 3. So applying two levels of Effort costs 5 points (3 for the first level plus 2 for the second level), applying three levels costs 7 points (3 plus 2 plus 2), and so on.

Every character has an Effort score, which indicates the maximum number of levels of Effort that can be applied to a roll. A beginning (first-tier) character has an Effort of 1, meaning you can apply only one level of Effort to a roll. A more experienced character has a higher Effort score and can apply more levels of Effort to a roll. For example, a character who has an Effort of 3 can apply up to three levels of Effort to reduce a task's difficulty.

When you apply Effort, subtract your relevant Edge from the total cost of applying Effort. For example, let's say you need to make a Speed roll. To increase your chance for success, you decide to apply one level of Effort, which will reduce the difficulty of the task by one step. Normally, that would cost 3 points from your Speed Pool. However, you have a Speed Edge of 2, so you subtract that from the cost. Thus, applying Effort to the roll costs only 1 point from your Speed Pool.

What if you applied two levels of Effort to the Speed roll instead of just one? That would reduce the difficulty of the task by two steps. Normally, it would cost 5 points from your Speed Pool, but after subtracting your Speed Edge of 2, it costs only 3 points.

Once a stat's Edge reaches 3, you can apply one level of Effort for free. For example, if you have a Speed Edge of 3 and you apply one level of Effort to a Speed roll, it costs you 0 points from your Speed Pool. (Normally, applying one level of Effort would cost 3 points, but you subtract your Speed Edge from that cost, reducing it to 0.)

Skills and other advantages also decrease a task's difficulty, and you can use them in conjunction with Effort. In addition, your character might have special abilities or equipment that allow you to apply Effort to accomplish a special effect, such as knocking down a foe with an attack or affecting multiple targets with a power that normally affects only one.

EFFORT AND DAMAGE

Instead of applying Effort to reduce the difficulty of your attack, you can apply Effort to increase the amount of damage you inflict with an attack. For each level of Effort you apply in this way, you inflict 3 additional points of damage. This works for any kind of attack that inflicts damage, whether a sword, a crossbow, a mind blast, or something else.

When using Effort to increase the damage of an area attack, such as the explosion created by an adept's Flash ability, you inflict 2 additional points of damage instead of 3 points. However, the additional points are dealt to all targets in the area. Further, even if one or more of the targets resist the attack, they still take 1 point of damage.

MULTIPLE USES OF EFFORT AND EDGE

If your Effort is 2 or higher, you can apply Effort to multiple aspects of a single action. For example, if you make an attack, you can apply Effort to your attack roll and apply Effort to increase the damage.

The total amount of Effort you apply can't be higher than your Effort score. For example, if your Effort is 2, you can apply up to two levels of Effort. You could apply one level to an attack roll and one level to its damage, two levels to the attack and no levels to the damage, or no levels to the attack and two levels to the damage.

You can use Edge for a particular stat only once per action. For example, if you apply Effort to a Might attack roll and to your damage, you can use your Might Edge to reduce the cost of one of those uses of Effort, not both. If you spend 1 Intellect point to activate your mind blast and one level of Effort to decrease the difficulty of the attack roll, you can use your Intellect Edge to reduce the cost of one of those things, not both.

STAT EXAMPLES

A beginning character is fighting a giant rat. She stabs her spear at the rat, which is a level 2 creature and thus has a target number of 6. The character stands atop a boulder and strikes downward at the beast, and the GM rules that this helpful tactic is an asset that decreases the difficulty by one step (to difficulty 1). That lowers the

For information on additional types of damage, see Damage Track, page 202, and Special Damage, page 203.

Flash, page 33

target number to 3. Attacking with a spear is a Might action; the character has a Might Pool of 11 and a Might Edge of 0. Before making the roll, she decides to apply a level of Effort to decrease the difficulty of the attack. That costs 3 points from her Might Pool, reducing the Pool to 8. But they appear to be points well spent. Applying the Effort lowers the difficulty from 1 to 0, so no roll is needed—the attack automatically succeeds.

Another character is attempting to convince a guard to let him into a private office to speak to an influential noble. The GM rules that this is an Intellect action. The character is third tier and has an Effort of 3, an Intellect Pool of 13, and an Intellect Edge of 1. Before making the roll, he must decide whether to apply Effort. He can choose to apply one, two, or three levels of Effort, or apply none at all. This action is important to him, so he decides to apply two levels of Effort, decreasing the difficulty by two steps. Thanks to his Intellect Edge, applying the Effort costs only 4 points from his Intellect Pool (3 points for the first level of Effort plus 2 points for the second level minus 1 point for his Edge). Spending those points reduces his Intellect Pool to 9. The GM decides that convincing the guard is a difficulty 3 (demanding) task with a target number of 9; applying two levels of Effort reduces the difficulty to 1 (simple) and the target number to 3. The player rolls a d20 and gets an 8. Because this result is at least equal to the target number of the task, he succeeds. However, if he had not applied some Effort, he would have failed because his roll (8) would have been less than the task's original target number (9).

Skills are a broad category of things your character can learn and accomplish. For a list of sample skills, see the Skills sidebar on page 20.

CHARACTER TIERS AND BENEFITS

Every character starts the game at the first tier. Tier is a measurement of power, toughness, and ability. Characters can advance up to the sixth tier. As your character advances to higher tiers, you gain more abilities, increase your Effort, and can improve a stat's Edge or increase a stat. Generally speaking, even first-tier characters are already quite capable. It's safe to assume that they've already got some experience under their belt. This is not a "zero to hero" progression, but rather an instance of competent people refining and honing their capabilities and knowledge. Advancing to higher tiers is not really the goal of Cypher System characters, but rather a representation of how characters progress in a story.

To progress to the next tier, characters earn experience points (XP) by going on adventures and discovering new things—the system is about discovery and exploration as much as or more than anything else. Experience points have many uses, and one use is to purchase character benefits. After your character purchases four character benefits, he or she advances to the next tier. Each benefit costs 4 XP, and you can purchase them in any order, but you must purchase one of each kind of benefit (and then advance to the next tier) before you can purchase the same benefit again. The four character benefits are as follows.

Increasing Capabilities: You gain 4 points to add to your stat Pools. You can allocate the points among the Pools however you wish.

Moving Toward Perfection: You add 1 to your Might Edge, your Speed Edge, or your Intellect Edge (your choice).

Extra Effort: Your Effort score increases by 1.

Skills: You become trained in one skill of your choice, other than attacks or defense. As described in Chapter 9: Rules of the Game, a character trained in a skill treats the difficulty of a related task as one step lower than normal. The skill you choose for this benefit can be anything you wish, such as climbing, jumping, persuading, or sneaking. You can also choose to be knowledgeable in a certain area of lore, such as history or geology. You can even choose a skill based on your character's special abilities. For example, if your character can make an Intellect roll to blast an enemy with mental force, you can become trained in using that ability, treating its difficulty as one step lower than normal. If you choose a skill that you are already trained in, you

become specialized in that skill, reducing the difficulty of related tasks by two steps instead of one.

Players can also spend 4 XP to purchase other special options in lieu of gaining a new skill. Selecting any of these options counts as the skill benefit necessary to advance to the next tier. The special options are as follows:

- Reduce the cost for wearing armor. This option lowers the Speed cost for wearing armor by 1.
- Add 2 to your recovery rolls.
- Select a new type-based ability from your tier or a lower tier.

CHARACTER DESCRIPTOR, TYPE, AND FOCUS

To create your character, you build a simple statement that describes him or her. The statement takes this form: "I am a [fill in an adjective here] [fill in a noun here] who [fill in a verb here]."

Thus: "I am an *adjective noun* who *verbs*." For example, you might say, "I am a Rugged warrior who Controls Beasts" or "I am a Charming explorer who Focuses Mind over Matter."

In this sentence, the adjective is called your descriptor.

The noun is your character type.

The verb is called your focus.

Even though character type is in the middle of the sentence, that's where we'll start this discussion. (Just as in a sentence, the noun provides the foundation.)

Your character type is the core of your character. In some roleplaying games, it might be called your character class. Your type helps determine your character's place in the world and relationship with other people in the setting. It's the noun of the sentence "I am an *adjective noun* who *verbs*."

You can choose from four character types in chapter 5: warriors, adepts, explorers, and speakers.

Your descriptor defines your character—it colors everything you do. Your descriptor places your character in the situation (the first adventure, which starts the campaign) and helps provide motivation. It's the adjective of the sentence "I am an *adjective noun* who *verbs*."

Descriptor, page 64

Type, page 22

Focus, page 90

Recovery roll, page 202

Warrior, page 22

Adept, page 29

Explorer, page 38

Speaker, page 44

You can use flavors (page 50) to slightly modify character types to customize them for different genres.

SKILLS

Sometimes your character gains training in a specific skill or task. For example, your focus might mean that you're trained in sneaking, in climbing and jumping, or in social interactions. Other times, your character can choose a skill to become trained in, and you can pick a skill that relates to any task you think you might face.

The Cypher System has no definitive list of skills. However, the following list offers ideas:

Astronomy	Leatherworking
Balancing	Lockpicking
Biology	Machinery
Botany	Metalworking
Carrying	Perception
Climbing	Persuasion
Computers	Philosophy
Deceiving	Physics
Disguise	Pickpocketing
Escaping	Piloting
Geography	Repairing
Geology	Riding
Healing	Smashing
History	Sneaking
Identifying	Stealth
Initiative	Swimming
Intimidation	Vehicle driving
Jumping	Woodworking

You could choose a skill that incorporates more than one of these areas (interacting might include deceiving, intimidation, and persuasion) or that is a more specific version of one (hiding might be sneaking when you're not moving). You could also make up more general, professional skills, such as baker, sailor, or lumberjack. If you want to choose a skill that's not on this list, it's probably best to run it past the GM first, but in general, the most important aspect is to choose skills that are appropriate to your character.

Remember that if you gain a skill that you're already trained in, you become specialized in that skill. Because skill descriptions can be nebulous, determining whether you're trained or specialized might take some thinking. For example, if you're trained in lying and later gain an ability that grants you skill with all social interactions, you become specialized in lying and trained in all other types of interactions. Being trained three times in a skill is no better than being trained twice (in other words, specialized is as good as it gets).

Only skills gained through character type abilities or other rare instances allow you to become skilled with attack or defense tasks.

If you gain a special ability through your type, your focus, or some other aspect of your character, you can choose it in place of a skill and become trained or specialized in that ability. For example, if you have a mind blast, when it's time to choose a skill to be trained in, you can select your mind blast as your skill. That would reduce the difficulty every time you used it. Each ability you have counts as a separate skill for this purpose. You can't select "all mind powers" or "all spells" as one skill and become trained or specialized in such a broad category.

In most campaigns, fluency in a language is considered a skill. So if you want to speak French, that's the same as being trained in biology or swimming.

Unless your GM says otherwise, you can choose from any of the character descriptors in chapter 6.

Focus is what your character does best. Focus gives your character specificity and provides interesting new abilities that might come in handy. Your focus also helps you understand how you relate with the other player characters in your group. It's the verb of the sentence "I am an *adjective noun* who *verbs*."

There are many character foci in chapter 7. The ones you choose from will probably depend on the setting and genre of your game.

SPECIAL ABILITIES

Character types and foci grant PCs special abilities at each new tier. Using these abilities usually costs points from your stat Pools; the cost is listed in parentheses after the ability name. Your Edge in the appropriate stat can reduce the cost of the ability, but remember that you can apply Edge only once per action. For example, let's say an adept with an Intellect Edge of 2 wants to use his Onslaught ability to create a bolt of force, which costs 1 Intellect point. He also wants to increase the damage from the attack by using a level of Effort, which costs 3 Intellect points. The total cost for his action is 2 points from his Intellect Pool (1 point for the bolt of force, plus 3 points for using Effort, minus 2 points from his Edge).

Sometimes the point cost for an ability has a + sign after the number. For example, the cost might be given as "2+ Intellect points." That means you can spend more points or more levels of Effort to improve the ability further, as explained in the ability description.

Many special abilities grant a character the option to perform an action that she couldn't normally do, such as projecting rays of cold or attacking multiple foes at once. Using one of these abilities is an action unto itself, and the end of the ability's description says "Action" to remind you. It also might provide more information about when or how you perform the action.

Some special abilities allow you to perform a familiar action—one that you can already do—in a different way. For example, an ability might let you wear heavy armor, reduce the difficulty of Speed defense rolls, or add 2 points of fire damage to your weapon damage. These abilities are called enablers. Using one of these abilities is not considered an action. Enablers either function constantly (such as being able to wear heavy armor, which isn't an action) or happen as part of another action (such as adding fire damage to your weapon damage, which happens as part of your attack action). If a special ability is an enabler, the end of the ability's description says "Enabler" to remind you.

Some abilities specify a duration, but you can always end one of your own abilities anytime you wish.

Because this book covers so many genres, not all of the descriptors, types, and foci might be available for players. The GM will decide what's available in her particular game and whether anything is modified, and she'll let the players know.

Onslaught, page 31

CHAPTER 5

CHARACTER TYPE

In some roleplaying games, your character type might be called your character class.

Flavor, page 50

Some Cypher System games, like The Strange or Numenera, have highly specific types designed to fit those settings perfectly.

Character type is the core of your character. Your type helps determine your character's place in the world and relationship with other people in the setting. It's the noun of the sentence "I am an *adjective noun* who *verbs*."

You can choose from four character types: warrior, adept, explorer, and speaker. However, you may not want to use these generic names for them. This chapter offers a few more specific names for each type that might be more appropriate to various genres. You'll find that particularly in games set in modern times, names like "warrior" or "explorer" don't feel right. As always, you're free to do as you wish.

Since the type is the basis upon which your whole character is built, it's important to consider how the type relates to the chosen setting. To help with this, types are actually general archetypes. A warrior, for example, might be anyone from a knight in shining armor to a cop on the streets to a grizzled cybernetic veteran of a thousand futuristic wars.

To further massage the four types for better use in various settings, different methods called flavors are presented at the end of this chapter to help slightly tailor the types toward fantasy, science fiction, or other genres (or just to address different character concepts).

WARRIOR

Fantasy: warrior, fighter, swordsman, knight, barbarian, soldier, myrmidon, valkyrie
Modern/Horror: police officer, soldier, watchman, detective, guard, brawler, tough, athlete
Science fiction: security officer, warrior, trooper, soldier, merc
Superhero: hero, brick, bruiser

You're a good ally to have in a fight. You know how to use weapons and defend yourself. Depending on the genre and setting in question, this might mean wielding a sword and shield in the gladiatorial arena, an AK-47 and a bandolier of grenades in a savage firefight, or a blaster rifle and

powered armor when exploring an alien planet.

Individual Role: Warriors are physical, action-oriented people. They're more likely to overcome a challenge using force than by other means, and they often take the most straightforward path toward their goals.

Group Role: Warriors usually take and deal the most punishment in a dangerous situation. Often it falls on them to protect the other group members from threats. This sometimes means that warriors take on leadership roles as well, at least in combat and other times of danger.

Societal Role: Warriors aren't always soldiers or mercenaries. Anyone who is ready for violence, or even potential violence, might be a warrior in the general sense. This includes guards, watchmen, police officers, sailors, or people in other roles or professions who know how to defend themselves with skill.

Advanced Warriors: As warriors advance, their skill in battle—whether defending themselves or dishing out damage—increases to impressive levels. At higher tiers, they can often take on groups of foes by themselves or stand toe to toe with anyone.

Your type is who your character is. You should use whatever name you want for your type, as long as it fits both your character and the setting.

Background Connection: Your type helps determine the connection you have to the setting. Roll a d20 or choose from the following list to determine a specific fact about your background that provides a connection to the rest of the world. You can also create your own fact.

Roll	Background
1	You were in the military and have friends who still serve. Your former commander remembers you well.
2	You were the bodyguard of a wealthy woman who accused you of theft. You left her service in disgrace.
3	You were the bouncer in a local bar for a while, and the patrons there remember you.
4	You trained with a highly respected mentor. He regards you well, but he has many enemies.
5	You trained in an isolated monastery. The monks think of you as a brother, but you're a stranger to all others.
6	You have no formal training. Your abilities come to you naturally (or unnaturally).
7	You spent time on the streets and even were in prison for a while.
8	You were conscripted into military service, but you deserted before long.
9	You served as a bodyguard to a powerful criminal who now owes you his life.
10	You worked as a police officer or constable of some kind. Everyone knows you, but their opinions of you vary.
11	Your older sibling is an infamous character who has been disgraced.
12	You served as a guard for someone who traveled extensively. You know a smattering of people in many locations.
13	Your best friend is a teacher or scholar. She is a great source of knowledge.
14	You and a friend both smoke the same kind of rare, expensive tobacco. The two of you get together weekly to chat and smoke.
15	Your uncle runs a theater in town. You know all the actors and watch all the shows for free.
16	Your craftsman friend sometimes calls on you for help. However, he pays you well.
17	Your mentor wrote a book on martial arts. Sometimes people seek you out to ask about its stranger passages.
18	A man you fought alongside in the military is now the mayor of a nearby town.
19	You saved the lives of a family when their house burned down. They're indebted to you, and their neighbors regard you as a hero.
20	Your old trainer still expects you to come back and clean up after her classes, but when you do, she occasionally shares interesting rumors.

WARRIOR STAT POOLS

Stat	Pool Starting Value
Might	10
Speed	10
Intellect	8

You get 6 additional points to divide among your stat Pools however you wish.

FIRST-TIER WARRIOR

First-tier warriors have the following abilities:

Effort: Your Effort is 1.

Physical Nature: You have a Might Edge of 1 and a Speed Edge of 0, or you have a Might Edge of 0 and a Speed Edge of 1. Either way, you have an Intellect Edge of 0.

Cypher Use: You can bear two cyphers at a time.

Practiced With All Weapons: You can use any weapon. Enabler.

Your character's starting equipment is as important as his starting skills. Learn more about what you carry and how it's used in Chapter 8: Equipment.

Starting Equipment: Appropriate clothing and two weapons of your choice, plus one expensive item, two moderately priced items, and up to four inexpensive items.

Special Abilities: Choose four of the abilities described below. You can't choose the same ability more than once unless its description says otherwise.

Bash (1 Might point): This is a pummeling melee attack. Your attack inflicts 1 less point of damage than normal, but dazes your target for one round, during which time the difficulty of all tasks it performs is modified by one step to its detriment. Action.

Control the Field (1 Might point): This melee attack inflicts 1 less point of damage than normal, but regardless of whether you hit the target, you maneuver it into a position you desire within immediate range. Action.

Extra Edge: Your physical nature grants you an Edge of 1 in both Speed and Might, rather than one or the other.

No Need for Weapons: When you make an unarmed attack (such as a punch or kick), it counts as a medium weapon instead of a light weapon. Enabler.

Overwatch (1 Intellect point): You use a ranged weapon to target a limited area (such as a doorway, a hallway, or the eastern side of the clearing) and make an attack against the next viable target to enter that area. This works like a wait action, but you also negate any benefit the target would have from cover, position, surprise, range, illumination, or visibility. Further, you inflict 1 additional point of damage with the attack. You can remain on overwatch as long as you wish, within reason. Action.

Physical Skills: You are trained in two skills in which you are not already trained. Choose two of the following: balancing, climbing, jumping, running, or swimming. You can select this ability multiple times. Each time you select it, you must choose two different skills. Enabler.

Pierce (1 Speed point): This is a well-aimed, penetrating ranged attack. You make an attack and inflict 1 additional point of damage if your weapon has a sharp point. Action.

Practiced in Armor: You can wear armor for long periods of time without tiring and can compensate for slowed reactions from wearing armor. You can wear any kind of armor. You reduce the Speed cost for wearing armor by 1. You start the game with a type of armor of your choice. Enabler.

Quick Draw (2 Speed points): After using a thrown light weapon, you draw another light weapon and make another thrown attack against the same target or a different one. Action.

Swipe (1 Speed point): This is a quick, agile melee attack. Your attack inflicts 1 less point of damage than normal but dazes your target for one round, during which time the difficulty of all tasks it performs is modified by one step to its detriment. Action.

Thrust (1 Might point): This is a powerful melee stab. You make an attack and inflict 1 additional point of damage if your weapon has a sharp edge or point. Action.

Trained Without Armor: You are trained in Speed defense actions when not wearing armor. Enabler.

SECOND-TIER WARRIOR

Choose two of the abilities described below (or from a lower tier) to add to your repertoire. In addition, you can replace one of your lower-tier abilities with a different one from a lower tier.

Chop (2 Might points): This is a heavy, powerful slice with a bladed weapon, probably overhand. You must grip your weapon with two hands to chop. When making this attack, you take a –1 penalty to the attack roll, and you inflict 3 additional points of damage. Action.

Wait action, page 209

Cover, page 204

Surprise, page 204

Illumination, page 205

Remember that at higher tiers, you can choose special abilities from lower tiers. This is sometimes the best way to ensure that you have exactly the character you want. This is particularly true with abilities that grant skills, which can usually be taken multiple times.

Practiced in Armor, page 25

Defense tasks are when a player makes a roll to keep something undesirable from happening to his PC. The type of defense task matters when using Effort.

Might defense: *Used for resisting poison, disease, and anything else that can be overcome with strength and health.*

Speed defense: *Used for dodging attacks and escaping danger. This is by far the most commonly used defense task.*

Intellect defense: *Used for fending off mental attacks or anything that might affect or influence one's mind.*

Crush (2 Might points): This is a powerful pummeling attack with a bashing weapon, probably overhand. You must grip your weapon with two hands to crush. (If fighting unarmed, this attack is made with both fists or both feet together.) When making this attack, you take a –1 penalty to the attack roll, and you inflict 3 additional points of damage. Action.

Mighty Blow (2 Might points): You strike two foes with a single blow. Make separate attack rolls for each foe, but both attacks count as a single action in a single round. You remain limited by the amount of Effort you can apply on one action. Anything that modifies your attack or damage applies to both of these attacks. Action.

Reload (1 Speed point): When using a weapon that normally requires an action to reload, such as a heavy crossbow, you can reload and fire (or fire and reload) in the same action. Enabler.

Skill With Attacks: Choose one type of attack in which you are not already trained: light bashing, light bladed, light ranged, medium bashing, medium bladed, medium ranged, heavy bashing, heavy bladed, or heavy ranged. You are trained in attacks using that type of weapon. You can select this ability multiple times. Each time you select it, you must choose a different type of attack. Enabler.

Skill With Defense: Choose one type of defense task in which you are not already trained: Might, Speed, or Intellect. You are trained in defense tasks of that type. You can select this ability up to three times. Each time you select it, you must choose a different type of defense task. Enabler.

Successive Attack (2 Speed points): If you take down a foe, you can immediately make another attack on that same turn against a new foe within your reach. The second attack is part of the same action. You can use this ability with melee attacks and ranged attacks. Enabler.

THIRD-TIER WARRIOR

Choose three of the abilities described below (or from a lower tier) to add to your repertoire. In addition, you can replace one of your lower-tier abilities with a different one from a lower tier.

Deadly Aim (3 Speed points): For the next minute, all ranged attacks you make inflict 2 additional points of damage. Action to initiate.

Experienced With Armor: The cost reduction from your Practiced in Armor ability improves. You now reduce the Speed cost for wearing armor by 2. Enabler.

Expert Cypher Use: You can bear three cyphers at a time. Enabler.

Fury (3 Might points): For the next minute, all melee attacks you make inflict 2 additional points of damage. Action to initiate.

Lunge (2 Might points): This ability requires you to extend yourself for a powerful stab or smash. The awkward lunge increases the difficulty of the attack roll by one step. If your attack is successful, it inflicts 4 additional points of damage. Action.

Reaction: If a creature you attacked on your last turn with a melee attack uses its action to move out of immediate range, you gain an action to attack the creature as a parting blow, even if you have already taken a turn in the round. Enabler.

Seize the Moment (4+ Speed points): If you succeed on a Speed defense roll to resist an attack, you gain an action. You can use the action immediately even if you have already taken a turn in the round. You don't take an action during the next round, unless you apply a level of Effort when you use Seize the Moment. Enabler.

Slice (2 Speed points): This is a quick attack with a bladed or pointed weapon that is hard to defend against. The difficulty of the attack roll is decreased by one step. If the attack is successful, it deals 1 less point of damage than normal. Action.

Spray (2 Speed points): If a weapon has the ability to fire rapid shots without reloading (usually called a rapid-fire weapon, such as the submachine gun), you can spray multiple shots around your target to increase the chance of hitting. This ability uses 1d6 + 1 rounds of ammo (or all the ammo in the weapon, if it has less than the number rolled). The difficulty of the attack roll is decreased by one step. If the attack is successful, it deals 1 less point of damage than normal. Action.

Trick Shot (2 Speed points): As part of the same action, you make a ranged attack against two targets that are within immediate range of each other. Make a separate attack roll against each target. The difficulty of each attack roll is increased by one step. Action.

FOURTH-TIER WARRIOR

Choose two of the abilities described below (or from a lower tier) to add to your repertoire. In addition, you can replace one of your lower-tier abilities with a different one from a lower tier.

Capable Warrior: Your attacks deal 1 additional point of damage. Enabler.

Experienced Defender: When wearing armor, you gain +1 to Armor. Enabler.

Feint (2 Speed points): If you spend one action creating a misdirection or diversion, in the next round you can take advantage of your opponent's lowered defenses. Make a melee attack roll against that opponent. The difficulty of the roll is decreased by one step. If your attack is successful, it inflicts 4 additional points of damage. Action.

Minor to Major: You treat rolls of natural 19 as rolls of natural 20 for Might attack rolls or Speed attack rolls (your choice when you gain this ability). This allows you to gain a major effect on a natural 19 or 20. Enabler.

Momentum: If you use an action to move, your next attack made using a melee weapon before the end of the next round inflicts 2 additional points of damage. Enabler.

Opening Gambit (4 Might points): Your melee attack shreds the defenses of a target. Any energy-based defenses it has (such as a force field or mental ward) are negated for 1d6 + 1 rounds. If the target has no energy-based defenses, its Armor is reduced by 2 for one minute. If it has no energy-based defenses or Armor, the difficulty of all attacks made against the target is lowered by one step for one minute. Action.

Snipe (2 Speed points): If you spend one action aiming, in the next round you can make a precise ranged attack. The difficulty of the attack roll is decreased by one step. If your attack is successful, it inflicts 4 additional points of damage. Action.

Tough As Nails: When you are impaired or debilitated on the damage track, the difficulty of Might-based tasks and defense rolls you attempt is decreased by one step. If you also have Ignore the Pain, make a difficulty 1 Might defense roll when you reach 0 points in all three of your Pools to immediately regain 1 Might point and avoid dying. Each time you attempt to save yourself with this ability before your next ten-hour recovery roll, the difficulty increases by one step. Enabler.

FIFTH-TIER WARRIOR

Choose three of the abilities described below (or from a lower tier) to add to your repertoire. In addition, you can replace one of your lower-tier abilities with a different one from a lower tier.

Adroit Cypher Use: You can bear four cyphers at a time. Enabler.

Arc Spray (3 Speed points): If a weapon has the ability to fire rapid shots without reloading (usually called a rapid-fire weapon, such as the submachine gun), you can fire your weapon at up to three targets (all next to one another) at once. Make a separate attack roll against each target. The difficulty of each attack is increased by one step. Action.

Greater Skill With Attacks: Choose one type of attack, even one in which you are already trained: light bashing, light bladed, light ranged, medium bashing, medium bladed, medium ranged, heavy bashing, heavy bladed, or heavy ranged. You are trained in attacks using that type of weapon. If you're already trained in that type of attack, you instead are specialized in that type of attack. Enabler.

Improved Success: When you roll a 17 or higher on an attack roll that deals damage, you deal 1 additional point of damage. For instance, if you roll a natural 18, which normally deals 2 extra points of damage, you deal 3 extra points instead. If you roll a natural 20 and choose to deal damage instead of achieve a special major effect, you deal 5 extra points of damage. Enabler.

Jump Attack (5 Might points): You attempt a difficulty 4 Might action to jump high into the air as part of your melee attack. If you succeed, your attack inflicts 3 additional points of damage and knocks the foe down. If you fail, you still make your normal attack roll, but you don't inflict the extra damage or knock down the opponent if you hit. Action.

Ignore the Pain, page 154

A character can't apply Effort or other abilities to any task he accomplishes using Tough As Nails.

Damage track, page 202

Mastery With Armor: The cost reduction from your Practiced in Armor ability improves. When you wear any armor, you reduce the armor's Speed cost to 0. If you select this ability and you already have the Experienced With Armor ability, replace Experienced With Armor with a different third-tier ability because Mastery With Armor is better. Enabler.

Experienced With Armor, page 26

Mastery With Defense: Choose one type of defense task in which you are trained: Might, Speed, or Intellect. You are specialized in defense tasks of that type. You can select this ability up to three times. Each time you select it, you must choose a different type of defense task. Enabler.

Seize the Moment, page 26

Parry (5 Speed points): You can deflect incoming attacks quickly. For the next ten rounds, the difficulty of all Speed defense rolls is reduced by one step. Enabler.

SIXTH-TIER WARRIOR

Choose two of the abilities described below (or from a lower tier) to add to your repertoire. In addition, you can replace one of your lower-tier abilities with a different one from a lower tier.

Finishing Blow (5 Might points): If your foe is prone, stunned, or somehow helpless or incapacitated when you strike, you inflict 8 additional points of damage on a successful hit. Enabler.

Magnificent Moment: If you make an attack or attempt a task with the immediate action you gain by using Seize the Moment, the difficulty is reduced by one step. Enabler.

Shooting Gallery (5 Speed points): You stand still and make ranged attacks against up to five foes within range, all as part of the same action in one round. Make a separate attack roll for each foe. You remain limited by the amount of Effort you can apply on one action. Anything that modifies your attack or damage applies to all of these attacks. Action.

Slayer (3 Might points): When you successfully strike a foe of level 5 or lower, make another roll (using whichever stat you used to attack). If you succeed on the second roll, you kill the target outright. If you use this ability against a PC of any tier and you succeed on the second roll, the character moves down one step on the damage track. Enabler.

Spin Attack (5 Speed points): You stand still and make melee attacks against up to five foes within reach, all as part of the same action in one round. Make a separate attack roll for each foe. You remain limited by the amount of Effort you can apply on one action. Anything that modifies your attack or damage applies to all of these attacks. Action.

Weapon and Body (5 Speed points): After making a melee weapon or ranged weapon attack, you follow up with a punch or kick as an additional attack, all as part of the same action in one round. The two attacks can be directed at different foes.

Make a separate attack roll for each attack. You remain limited by the amount of Effort you can apply on one action. Anything that modifies your attack or damage applies to both attacks, unless it is tied specifically to your weapon. Action.

WARRIOR EXAMPLE

Ray wants to create a warrior character for a modern campaign. He decides that the character is an ex-military fellow who is fast and strong. He puts 3 of his additional points into his Might Pool and 3 into his Speed Pool; his stat Pools are now Might 13, Speed 13, Intellect 8. As a first-tier character, his Effort is 1, his Might Edge is 1, and his Speed Edge and Intellect Edge are both 0. His character is not particularly smart or charismatic.

He wants to use a large combat knife (a medium weapon that inflicts 4 points of damage) and a .357 Magnum (a heavy pistol that inflicts 6 points of damage but requires the use of both hands). Ray decides not to wear armor, as it's not really appropriate to the setting, so for his first ability, he chooses Trained Without Armor so he reduces the difficulty of Speed defense actions. For his second ability, he chooses Thrust so he can inflict extra damage with his big knife if he spends 1 point of Might. Since he has a Might Edge of 1, he can use Thrust for free if he doesn't use his Might for anything else in that action.

Ray wants to be fast as well as tough, so he selects Extra Edge. This gives him a Speed Edge of 1. He rounds out his character with Physical Skills and chooses swimming and running.

The warrior can bear two cyphers. The GM decides that Ray's first cypher is a pill that restores 6 points of Might when swallowed, and his second is a small, easily concealed grenade that explodes like a firebomb when thrown, inflicting 3 points of damage to all within immediate range.

Ray still needs to choose a descriptor and a focus. Looking ahead to the descriptor rules, Ray chooses Strong, which increases his Might Pool to 17. He also becomes trained in jumping and breaking inanimate objects. (If he had chosen jumping as one of his physical skills, the Strong descriptor would have made him specialized in jumping instead of trained.) Being Strong also gives Ray an extra medium or heavy weapon. He chooses a baseball bat that he'll use in a pinch. He keeps it in the trunk of his car.

For his focus, Ray chooses Masters Weaponry. This gives him yet another weapon of high quality. He chooses another combat knife and asks the GM if he could use it in his left hand—not to make attacks, but as a shield. This will reduce the difficulty of his Speed defense rolls if he has both knives out (the "shield" counts as an asset). The GM agrees. During the game, Ray's warrior will be hard to hit—he is trained in Speed defense rolls, and his extra knife decreases the difficulty by another step.

Thanks to his focus, he also inflicts 1 additional point of damage with his chosen weapon. Now he inflicts 5 points of damage with his blade. Ray's character is a deadly combatant, likely starting the game with a reputation as a knife fighter.

Masters Weaponry, page 148

Trained Without Armor, page 25

Thrust, page 25

Extra Edge, page 25

Physical Skills, page 25

Strong, page 85

ADEPT

Fantasy: wizard, mage, sorcerer, cleric, druid, seer, diabolist, fey-touched
Modern/Horror: psychic, occultist, witch, practitioner, medium, fringe scientist
Science fiction: psion, psionicist, telepath, seeker, master, scanner, ESPer, abomination
Superhero: mage, sorcerer, power-wielder, master, psion, telepath

You master powers or abilities outside the experience, understanding, and sometimes belief of others. They might be magic, psychic powers, mutant abilities, or just a wide variety of intricate devices, depending on the setting.

Individual Role: Adepts are usually thoughtful, intelligent types. They often think carefully before acting and rely heavily on their supernatural abilities.

Group Role: Adepts are not powerful in straightforward combat, although they often wield abilities that provide excellent combat support, both offensively and defensively. They sometimes possess abilities that facilitate overcoming challenges. For example, if the group must get through a locked door, an adept might be able to destroy it or teleport everyone to the other side.

Adepts are almost always emblematic of the paranormal or superhuman in some way—wizards, psychics, or something similar. If the game you're playing has absolutely none of that, an adept could be a charlatan mimicking such abilities with tricks and hidden devices, or a gadgeteer character with a "utility belt" full of oddments. Or a game like that might not have adepts. That's okay too.

"Magic" here is a term used very loosely. It's a catch-all for the kinds of wondrous, possibly supernatural things that your character can do that others cannot. It might actually be an expression of technological devices, channeling spirits, mutations, psionics, nanotechnology, or any number of other sources.

Adept abilities require at least one free hand unless the GM says otherwise.

Societal Role: In settings where the supernatural is rare, strange, or feared, adepts are likely rare and feared as well. They remain hidden, shadowy figures. When this is not the case, adepts are more likely to be common and forthright. They might even take leadership roles.

Advanced Adepts: Even at low tiers, adept powers are impressive. Higher-tier adepts can accomplish amazing deeds that can reshape matter and the environment around them.

Background Connection: Your type helps determine the connection you have to the setting. Roll a d20 or choose from the following list to determine a specific fact about your background that provides a connection to the rest of the world. You can also create your own fact.

ADEPT STAT POOLS

Stat	Pool Starting Value
Might	7
Speed	9
Intellect	12

You get 6 additional points to divide among your stat Pools however you wish.

FIRST-TIER ADEPT

First-tier adepts have the following abilities:

Effort: Your Effort is 1.

Genius: You have an Intellect Edge of 1, a Might Edge of 0, and a Speed Edge of 0.

Expert Cypher Use: You can bear three cyphers at a time.

Roll	Background
1	You served as an apprentice for an adept respected and feared by many people. Now you bear his mark.
2	You studied in a school infamous for its dark, brooding instructors and graduates.
3	You learned your abilities in the temple of an obscure god. Its priests and worshippers, although small in number, respect and admire your talents and potential.
4	While traveling alone, you saved the life of a powerful person. He remains indebted to you.
5	Your mother was a powerful adept while she lived, helpful to many locals. They look upon you kindly, but they also expect much from you.
6	You owe money to a number of people and don't have the funds to pay your debts.
7	You failed disgracefully at your initial studies with your teacher and now proceed on your own.
8	You learned your skills faster than your teachers had ever seen before. The powers that be took notice and are paying close attention.
9	You killed a well-known criminal in self-defense, earning the respect of many and the enmity of a dangerous few.
10	You trained as a warrior, but your adept predilections eventually led you down a different path. Your former comrades don't understand you, but they respect you.
11	While studying to be an adept, you worked as an assistant for a bank, making friends with the owner and the clientele.
12	Your family owns a large vineyard nearby known to all for its fine wine and fair business dealings.
13	You trained for a time with a group of influential adepts, and they still look upon you with fondness.
14	You worked the gardens in the palace of an influential noble or person of wealth. She wouldn't remember you, but you made friends with her young daughter.
15	An experiment you conducted in the past went horribly awry. The locals remember you as a dangerous and foolhardy individual.
16	You hail from a distant place where you were well known and regarded, but people here treat you with suspicion.
17	People you meet seem put off by the strange birthmark on your face.
18	Your best friend is also an adept. You and she share discoveries and secrets readily.
19	You know a local merchant very well. Since you give him so much business, he offers you discounts and special treatment.
20	You belong to a secretive social club that gathers monthly to drink and talk.

Starting Equipment: Appropriate clothing, plus two expensive items, two moderately priced items, and up to four inexpensive items of your choice.

Special Abilities: Choose four of the abilities described below. You can't choose the same ability more than once unless its description says otherwise.

Distortion (2 Intellect points): You modify how a willing creature within short range reflects light for one minute. The target rapidly shifts between its normal appearance and a blot of darkness. The target has an asset on Speed defense rolls until the effect wears off. Action to initiate.

Erase Memories (3 Intellect points): You reach into the mind of a creature within immediate range and make an Intellect roll. On a success, you erase up to the last five minutes of its memory. Action.

Far Step (2 Intellect points): You leap through the air and land some distance away. You can jump up, down, or across to anywhere you choose within long range if you have a clear and unobstructed path to that location. You land safely. Action.

Hedge Magic (1 Intellect point): You can perform small tricks: temporarily change the color or basic appearance of a small object, cause small objects to float through the air, clean a small area, mend a broken object, prepare (but not create) food, and so on. You can't use hedge magic to harm another creature or object. Action.

Magic Training: You are trained in the basics of magic and can attempt to understand and identify its properties (including the operation of magic artifacts and cyphers). Enabler.

Onslaught (1 Intellect point): You attack a foe within short range using energies that assail either his physical form or his mind. In either case, you must be able to see your target. If the attack is physical, you emit a force blast: a ray of force that inflicts 4 points of damage. If the attack is mental, you focus your mental energy into a mindslice that disrupts the creature's thought processes, inflicting 2 points of Intellect damage (ignores Armor). Some creatures without minds (such as robots or zombies) might be immune to a mindslice. Action.

Practiced With Light Weapons: You can use light weapons without penalty. If you wield a medium weapon, increase the difficulty of the attack by one step. If you wield a heavy weapon, increase it by two steps. You also start with one light weapon of your choice. Enabler.

Push (2 Intellect points): You push a creature or object an immediate distance in any direction you wish. You must be able to see the target, which must be your size or smaller, must not be affixed to anything, and must be within short range. The push is quick, and the force is too crude to be manipulated. For example, you can't use this to pull a lever or close a door. Action.

Your character's starting equipment is as important as his starting skills. Learn more about what you carry and how it's used in Chapter 8: Equipment.

Resonance Field (1 Intellect point): Faint lines in a color you choose form a tracery over your entire body and emit faint light. The effect lasts for one minute. Whenever a creature within immediate range makes an attack against you, the pattern energizes to block the attack. You can make an Intellect defense roll in place of the defense roll you would normally make. If you do so and you get a minor effect, the creature attacking you takes 1 point of damage. If you get a major effect, the creature attacking you takes 4 points of damage. Action to initiate.

Cautious adepts rely on Ward. Depending on what you work out with your GM, the energy shield might be completely invisible, visible only when you are attacked, always visible as a faint glimmer surrounding you, and so on.

Scan (2 Intellect points): You scan an area equal in size to a 10-foot (3 m) cube, including all objects or creatures within that area. The area must be within short range. Scanning a creature or object always reveals its level (a measure of how powerful, dangerous, or difficult it is). You also learn whatever facts the GM feels are pertinent about the matter and energy in that area. For example, you might learn that the wooden box contains a device of metal and synth. You might learn that the glass cylinder is full of poisonous gas, and that its metal stand has an electrical field running through it that connects to a metal mesh in the floor. You might learn that the creature standing before you is a mammal with a small brain. However, this ability doesn't tell you what the information means. Thus, in the first example, you don't know what the metal and synth device does. In the second, you don't know if stepping on the floor causes the cylinder to release the gas. In the third, you might suspect that the creature is not very intelligent, but scans, like looks, can be deceiving. Many materials and energy fields prevent or resist scanning. Action.

Sculpt Flesh (2 Intellect points): You cause a willing creature's fingers to lengthen into claws and her teeth to grow into fangs. The effect lasts for ten minutes. The damage dealt by the target's unarmed strikes increases to 4 points. Action.

Shatter (2 Intellect points): You interrupt the fundamental force holding normal matter together for a moment, causing the detonation of an object you choose within long range. The object must be a small, mundane item composed of homogeneous matter (such as a clay cup, an iron ingot, a stone, and so on). The object explodes in an immediate radius, dealing 1 point of damage to all creatures and objects in the area. Because this is an area attack, adding Effort to increase your damage works differently than it does for single-target attacks: for each level of Effort applied in this way, the explosion deals 2 additional points of damage to each target, and even if you fail your attack roll, all targets in the area still take 1 point of damage. Action.

Ward: You have a shield of energy around you at all times that helps deflect attacks. You gain +1 to Armor. Enabler.

SECOND-TIER ADEPT

Choose one of the abilities described below (or from a lower tier) to add to your repertoire. In addition, you can replace one of your lower-tier abilities with a different one from a lower tier.

Adaptation (2+ Intellect points): You adapt to a hostile environment for twenty-four hours. As a result, you can breathe safely, the temperature doesn't kill you (though it might be extremely uncomfortable or debilitating), crushing gravity doesn't incapacitate or harm you (though, again, you might be seriously hindered), and so on. In extreme environments, the GM might increase the cost of activating this ability to a maximum cost of 10 Intellect points. Roughly speaking, the cost should equal the amount of damage you would sustain in a given round. For example, if you enter a hostile environment that would normally deal 6 points of damage per round, using Adaptation to avoid that damage costs 6 points. You can protect other creatures in addition to yourself, but each additional creature costs the same number of Intellect points as it costs to protect you. Thus, if it costs 6 points to protect yourself, it costs 12 more to protect two other people. This ability never protects against quick, instantaneous threats, like an attack with a weapon or a sudden explosion of fire. Action to initiate.

Cutting Light (2 Intellect points): You emit a thin beam of energized light from your hand. This inflicts 5 points of damage to a single foe in immediate range. The beam is even more effective against immobile, nonliving targets, slicing up to 1 foot (30 cm) of any material that is level 6 or lower. The material can be up to 1 foot thick. Action.

Flash (4 Intellect points): You create an explosion of energy at a point within close range, affecting an area up to immediate range from that point. You must be able to see the location where you intend to center the explosion. The blast inflicts 2 points of damage to all creatures or objects within the area. Because this is an area attack, adding Effort to increase your damage works differently than it does for single-target attacks: for each level of Effort applied in this way, the explosion deals 2 additional points of damage to each target, and even if you fail your attack roll, all targets in the area still take 1 point of damage. Action.

Hover (2 Intellect points): You float slowly into the air. If you concentrate, you can control your movement to remain motionless in the air or float up to a short distance as your action; otherwise, you drift with the wind or with any momentum you have gained. This effect lasts for up to ten minutes. Action to initiate.

Mind Reading (4 Intellect points): You can read the surface thoughts of a creature within short range, even if the target doesn't want you to. You must be able to see the target. Once you have established contact, you can read the target's thoughts for up to one minute. If you or the target move out of range, the connection is broken. Action to initiate.

Retrieve Memories (3 Intellect points): You touch the remains of a recently killed creature and make an Intellect-based roll to restore its mind to life long enough to learn information from it. The GM sets the difficulty based on the amount of time that has passed since the creature died. A creature that has been dead for only a few minutes is a difficulty 2 task, one that has been dead for an hour is a difficulty 4 task, and one that has been dead for a few days is a difficulty 9 task. If you succeed, you awaken the corpse, causing its head to animate and perceive things as if it were alive. This enables communication for about one minute, which is how long it takes for the creature to realize that it's dead. The creature is limited to what it knew in life, though it cannot recall minor memories, only big events of importance to it. When the effect ends, or if you fail the roll, the creature's brain dissolves to mush and cannot be awakened again. Action.

Reveal (2+ Intellect points): You adjust a creature's eyesight so that it can see normally in areas of dim light and darkness. You can affect one willing creature within immediate range for one hour. Instead of applying Effort to decrease the difficulty, you can use it to affect more targets; each level of Effort applied affects two additional targets. You must touch additional targets to affect them. Action to initiate.

Stasis (3 Intellect points): You surround a foe of your size or smaller with scintillating energy, keeping it from moving or acting for one minute, as if frozen solid. You must be able to see the target, and it must be within short range. While in stasis, the target is impervious to harm, cannot be moved, and is immune to all effects. Action.

THIRD-TIER ADEPT

Choose two of the abilities described below (or from a lower tier) to add to your repertoire. In addition, you can replace one of your lower-tier abilities with a different one from a lower tier.

Adroit Cypher Use: You can bear four cyphers at a time. Enabler.

Barrier (3+ Intellect points): You create an opaque, stationary barrier of solid energy within immediate range. The barrier is 10 feet by 10 feet (3 m by 3 m) and of negligible thickness. It is a level 2 barrier and lasts for ten minutes. It can be placed anywhere it fits, whether against a solid object (including the ground) or floating in the air. Each level of Effort you apply strengthens the barrier by one level. For example, applying two levels of Effort creates a level 4 barrier. Action.

Countermeasures (4 Intellect points): You immediately end one ongoing magical effect within immediate range. Alternatively, you can use this as a defense action to cancel any incoming magical ability targeted at you, or you can cancel any magic device or the effect of any magic device for 1d6 rounds. You must touch the effect or device to cancel it. Action.

Energy Protection (3+ Intellect points): Choose a discrete type of energy that you have experience with (such as heat, sonic, electricity, and so on). You gain +10 to Armor against damage from that type of energy for ten minutes. Alternatively, you gain +1 to Armor against damage from that energy for twenty-four hours. You must be familiar with the type of energy; for example, if you have no experience with a certain kind of extradimensional energy, you can't protect against it. Instead of applying Effort to decrease the difficulty of this ability, you can use it to protect more targets; each level of Effort applied affects up to two additional targets. You must touch additional targets to protect them. Action to initiate.

Onslaught, page 31

Fire and Ice (4 Intellect points): You cause a target within short range to become either very hot or very cold (your choice). The target suffers 3 points of ambient damage (ignores Armor) each round for up to three rounds, although a new roll is required each round to continue to affect the target. Action to initiate.

Sensor (4 Intellect points): You create an immobile, invisible sensor within immediate range that lasts for twenty-four hours. At any time during that duration, you can concentrate to see, hear, and smell through the sensor, no matter how far you move from it. The sensor doesn't grant you sensory capabilities beyond the norm. Action to create; action to check.

Targeting Eye: You are trained in any physical ranged attack that is a special ability or comes from a cypher or an artifact. For example, you are trained when using an Onslaught force blast because it's a physical attack, but not when using an Onslaught mindslice because it's a mental attack. Enabler.

FOURTH-TIER ADEPT

Choose one of the abilities described below (or from a lower tier) to add to your repertoire. In addition, you can replace one of your lower-tier abilities with a different one from a lower tier.

Exile (5 Intellect points): You send a target that you touch hurtling into another random dimension or universe, where it remains for ten minutes. You have no idea what happens to the target while it's gone, but at the end of ten minutes, it returns to the precise spot it left. Action.

Invisibility (4 Intellect points): You become invisible for ten minutes. While invisible, you are specialized in stealth and Speed defense tasks. This effect ends if you do something to reveal your presence or position—attacking, using an ability, moving a large object, and so on. If this occurs, you can regain the remaining invisibility effect by taking an action to focus on hiding your position. Action to initiate or reinitiate.

Matter Cloud (5 Intellect points): Pebbles, dirt, sand, and debris rise into the air around you to form a swirling cloud. The cloud extends out to immediate range, moves with you, and lasts for one minute. When it ends, all the materials fall to the ground around you. The cloud makes it harder for other creatures to attack you, giving you an asset on Speed defense rolls. In addition, while the cloud is around you, you can use an action to whip the material so that it abrades everything within immediate range, dealing 1 point of damage to each creature and object in the area. Action to initiate.

Mind Control (6+ Intellect points): You control the actions of another creature you touch. This effect lasts for ten minutes. The target must be level 2 or lower. Once you have established control, you maintain mental contact with the target and sense what it senses. You can allow it to act freely or override its control on a case-by-case basis. Instead of applying Effort to decrease the difficulty, you can apply Effort to increase the maximum level of the target. Thus, to control the mind of a level 5 target (three levels above the normal limit), you must apply three levels of Effort. Smart adepts use the Scan ability on a creature to learn its level before trying to control its mind. When the effect ends, the creature doesn't remember being controlled or anything it did while under your command. Action to initiate.

Projection (4 Intellect points): You project an image of yourself to any location you have seen or previously visited. Distance does not matter as long as the location is on the same world as you. The projection copies your appearance, movements, and any sounds you make for the next ten minutes. Anyone present at the location can see and hear you as if you were there. However, you do not perceive through your projection. Action to initiate.

Rapid Processing (6 Intellect points): You or a target you touch experiences a higher level of mental and physical reaction time for about a minute. During that period, the difficulty of all Speed tasks (including Speed defense rolls) is reduced by one step. In addition, the target can take one extra action at any time before the ability's duration expires. Action.

Regeneration (6 Intellect points): You restore points to a target's Might Pool or Speed Pool in one of two ways: either the chosen Pool regains up to 6 points, or it is restored to a total value of 12. You make this decision when you initiate this ability. Points are restored at a rate of 1 point each round. You must maintain contact with the target the whole time. In no case can this ability raise a Pool higher than its normal maximum. Action.

Reshape (5 Intellect points): You reshape matter within short range in an area no larger than a 5-foot (1 m) cube. If you spend only one action on this ability, the changes you make are crude at best. If you spend at least ten minutes and succeed at an appropriate crafting task (with a difficulty at least one step higher than normal, due to the circumstances), you can make complex changes to the material. You can't change the nature of the material, only its shape. Thus, you can make a hole in a wall or floor, or you can seal one up. You can fashion a rudimentary sword from a large piece of iron. You can break or repair a chain. With multiple uses of this ability, you could bring about large changes, making a bridge, a wall, or a similar structure. Action.

Slay (6 Intellect points): You gather disrupting energy in your fingertip and touch a creature. If the target is an NPC or a creature of level 3 or lower, it dies. If the target is a PC of any tier, he moves down one step on the damage track. Action.

Wormhole (6 Intellect points): You create a doorway through time and space. The shortcut manifests as a hole in reality large enough to accommodate you and creatures of your size or smaller. One side of the doorway appears anywhere within immediate range, and the other side opens at a spot you choose anywhere within long range. Any character or object moving into one side exits from the other. The door remains open for one minute or until you use an action to close it. Action to initiate.

FIFTH-TIER ADEPT

Choose two of the abilities described below (or from a lower tier) to add to your repertoire. In addition, you can replace one of your lower-tier abilities with a different one from a lower tier.

Absorb Energy (7 Intellect points): You touch an object and absorb its energy, if any. If you touch a cypher, you render it useless. If you touch an artifact, roll for its depletion. If you touch another kind of powered machine or device, the GM determines whether its power is fully drained. In any case, you absorb energy from the object touched and regain 1d10 Intellect points. If this would give you more Intellect than your Pool's maximum, the extra points are lost, and you must make a Might defense roll with a difficulty equal to the number of extra points you absorbed. If you fail the roll, you take 5 points of damage and are unable to act for one round. You can use this ability as a defense action when you're the target of an incoming

Scan, page 32

Crafting, page 217

energy-based attack. Doing so cancels the incoming attack, and you absorb the energy as if it were a device. Action.

Concussion (7 Intellect points): You cause a pulse of concussive force to explode out from a point you choose within long range. The pulse extends up to short range in all directions, dealing 5 points of damage to everything in the area. Even if you fail the attack roll, targets in the area take 1 point of damage. Action.

Conjuration (7 Intellect points): You produce, as if from thin air, a level 5 creature of a kind you have previously encountered. The creature remains for one minute and then returns home. While present, the creature acts as you direct, but this requires no action on your part. Action.

Create (7 Intellect points): You create something from nothing. You can create any item you choose that would ordinarily have a difficulty of 5 or lower (using the crafting rules). Once created, the item lasts for a number of hours equal to 6 minus the difficulty to create it. Thus, if you create a motorbike (difficulty 5), it would last for one hour. Action.

Crafting, page 217

Divide Your Mind (7 Intellect points): You split your consciousness into two parts. For one minute, you can take two actions on each of your turns, but only one of them can be to use a special ability. Action.

Dust to Dust (7 Intellect points): With a touch, you disintegrate one nonliving object that is smaller than you and whose level is less than or equal to your tier. If the GM feels it appropriate to the circumstances, you can disintegrate a portion of an object (the total volume of which is smaller than you) rather than the entire thing. Action.

Knowing the Unknown (6 Intellect points): Tapping into a source of information beyond yourself, you can ask the GM one question and get a general answer. The GM assigns a level to the question, so the more obscure the answer, the more difficult the task. Generally, knowledge that you could find by looking somewhere other than your current location is level 1, and obscure knowledge of the past is level 7. Gaining knowledge of the future is impossible. Action.

Master Cypher Use: You can bear five cyphers at a time. Enabler.

Teleportation (6+ Intellect points): You instantaneously transmit yourself to any location that you have seen or been to, no matter the distance, as long as it is on the same world as you. Instead of applying Effort to decrease the difficulty, you can apply Effort to bring other people with you; each level of Effort affects up to three additional targets. You must touch additional targets to teleport them. Action.

True Senses: You can see in complete darkness up to 50 feet (15 m) as if it were dim light. You recognize holograms, disguises, optical illusions, sound mimicry, and other such tricks (for all senses) for what they are. Enabler.

SIXTH-TIER ADEPT

Choose one of the abilities described below (or from a lower tier) to add to your repertoire. In addition, you can replace one of your lower-tier abilities with a different one from a lower tier.

Control Weather (10 Intellect points): You change the weather in your general region. If performed indoors, this creates minor effects, such as mist, mild temperature changes, and so on. If performed outside, you can create rain, fog, snow, wind, or any other kind of normal (not overly severe) weather. The change lasts for a natural length of time, so a storm might last for an hour, fog for two or three hours, and snow for a few hours (or for ten minutes if it's out of season). For the first ten minutes after activating this ability, you can create more dramatic and specific effects, such as lightning strikes, giant hailstones, twisters, hurricane-force winds, and so on. These effects must occur within 1,000 feet (305 m) of your location. You must spend your turn concentrating to create an effect or to maintain it in a new round. These effects inflict 6 points of damage each round. Action.

Earthquake (10 Intellect points): You trigger an earthquake centered on a spot you can see within 1,000 feet (305 m). The ground within 250 feet (76 m) of that spot heaves and shakes for five minutes, causing widespread damage to structures and terrain in the area. Buildings made of wood, stone, or brick collapse; walls topple; cliffs crumble; ceilings cave in; some areas of ground rise up; and other areas sink. Creatures inside collapsed buildings or beneath a crumbling cliff or falling wall are subject to a crush (3 points of damage) or a huge crush (6 points of damage) and may have to dig themselves free, as the GM decides. Furthermore, the force of the quake is sufficient to knock creatures to the ground and prevent them from standing until the shaking stops. Action to initiate.

Move Mountains (9 Intellect points): You exert a tremendous amount of physical force within 250 feet (76 m) of you. You can push up to 10 tons (9 t) of material up to 50 feet (15 m). This force can collapse buildings, redirect small rivers, or perform other dramatic effects. Action.

Traverse the Worlds (8+ Intellect points): You instantaneously transmit yourself to another planet, dimension, plane, or level of reality. You must know that the destination exists; the GM will decide if you have enough information to confirm its existence and what level of difficulty is required to reach it. Instead of applying Effort to decrease the difficulty, you can apply Effort to bring other people with you; each level of Effort affects up to three additional targets. You must touch additional targets to transmit them. Action.

Usurp Cypher: You destroy one cypher that you bear and gain its power, which then functions for you continuously. The cypher must have an effect that is not instantaneous. You can choose a cypher when you gain this ability, or you can wait and make the choice later. However, once you usurp a cypher's power, you cannot later switch to a different cypher—the ability works only once. Action to initiate.

ADEPT EXAMPLE

Jen wants to create an adept—a sorcerer for a fantasy campaign. She decides to be somewhat well rounded, so she puts 2 of her additional points into each stat Pool, giving her a Might Pool of 9, a Speed Pool of 11, and an Intellect Pool of 14. Her adept is smart and quick. She has an Intellect Edge of 1, a Might Edge of 0, and a Speed Edge of 0. As a first-tier character, her Effort is 1. As her initial abilities, she chooses Onslaught and Ward, giving her a strong offense and defense. She also chooses Magic Training and rounds out her character with Scan, which she hopes will be useful in gaining insight and information. For this character, Onslaught, Ward, and Scan are all spells she has mastered through years of training and study.

She can bear three cyphers. The GM gives her a potion that acts as a short-range teleporter, a small charm that restores 5 points to her Intellect Pool, and a fluid-filled flask that explodes like a fiery bomb. Jen's sorcerer has no skill with physical weapons, so she doesn't bother with them.

For her descriptor, Jen chooses Graceful, which adds 2 points to her Speed Pool, bringing it to 13. That descriptor means she is trained in balancing and anything requiring careful movements, physical performing arts, and Speed defense tasks. Perhaps she is a dancer. In fact, she begins to develop a backstory that involves graceful, lithe movements that she incorporates into her spells.

For her focus, she chooses Leads. This gives her training in social interactions, which again helps round her out—she's good in all kinds of situations. Moreover, she has the Good Advice ability, which enables her to be a focal point of her group.

Her spells and focus abilities cost Intellect points to activate, so she's glad to have a lot of points in her Intellect Pool. In addition, her Intellect Edge will help reduce those costs. If she uses her Onslaught force blast without applying Effort, it costs 0 Intellect points and deals 4 points of damage. Likewise, using her Good Advice ability without applying Effort costs 0 Intellect points. Her Intellect Edge will allow her to save points to devote toward applying Effort for other purposes, perhaps to boost the accuracy of Onslaught.

Magic Training, page 31

Scan, page 32

Graceful, page 74

Leads, page 143

GMs are always free to pre-select a type's special abilities at a given tier to reinforce the setting. In the fantasy setting of Jen's sorcerer, the GM might have just said that all sorcerers (adepts) start with Magic Training as one of their tier 1 abilities. This doesn't make the character any less powerful or special, but it says something about her role in the world and expectations in the game.

Onslaught, page 31

Ward, page 32

Your character's starting equipment is as important as his starting skills. Learn more about what you carry and how it's used in Chapter 8: Equipment.

EXPLORER

Fantasy: explorer, adventurer, delver, mystery seeker
Modern/Horror: athlete, explorer, adventurer, drifter, detective, scholar, spelunker, trailblazer, investigative reporter
Science fiction: explorer, adventurer, wanderer, planetary specialist, xenobiologist
Superhero: adventurer, crimefighter

You are a person of action and physical ability, fearlessly facing the unknown. You travel to strange, exotic, and dangerous places, and discover new things. This means you're physical but also probably knowledgeable.

Individual Role: Although explorers can be academics or well studied, they are first and foremost interested in action. They face grave dangers and terrible obstacles as a routine part of life.

Group Role: Explorers sometimes work alone, but far more often they operate in teams with other characters. The explorer frequently leads the way, blazing the trail. However, she's also likely to stop and investigate anything intriguing she stumbles upon.

Societal Role: Not all explorers are out traipsing through the wilderness or poking about an old ruin. Sometimes, an explorer is a teacher, a scientist, a detective, or an investigative reporter. In any event, an explorer bravely faces new challenges and gathers knowledge to share with others.

Advanced Explorers: Higher-tier explorers gain more skills, some combat abilities, and a number of abilities that allow them to deal with danger. In short, they become more and more well-rounded, able to deal with any challenge.

Background Connection: Your type helps determine the connection you have to the setting. Roll a d20 or choose from the following list

Roll	Background
1	You were a star high school athlete. You're still in great shape, but those were the glory days, man.
2	Your brother is the lead singer in a really popular band.
3	You have made a number of discoveries in your explorations, but not all opportunities to capitalize on them have panned out yet.
4	You were a cop, but you gave it up after encountering corruption on the force.
5	Your parents were missionaries, so you spent much of your young life traveling to exotic places.
6	You served in the military with honor.
7	You received assistance from a secretive organization, which paid for your schooling. Now they seem to want a lot more from you.
8	You went to a prestigious university on an athletic scholarship, but you excelled in class as well as on the field.
9	Your best friend from your youth is now an influential member of the government.
10	You used to be a teacher. Your students remember you fondly.
11	You worked as a small-time criminal operative until you were caught and served some time in jail, after which you tried to go straight.
12	Your greatest discovery to date was stolen by your arch-rival.
13	You belong to an exclusive organization of explorers whose existence is not widely known.
14	You were kidnapped as a small child under mysterious circumstances, although you were recovered safely. The case still has some notoriety.
15	When you were young, you were addicted to narcotics, and now you are a recovering addict.
16	While exploring a remote location, you saw something strange you've never been able to explain.
17	You own a small bar or restaurant.
18	You published a book about some of your exploits and discoveries, and it has achieved some acclaim.
19	Your sister owns a store and gives you a hefty discount.
20	Your father is a high-ranking officer in the military with many connections.

to determine a specific fact about your background that provides a connection to the rest of the world. You can also create your own fact.

EXPLORER STAT POOLS

Stat	Pool Starting Value
Might	10
Speed	9
Intellect	9

You get 6 additional points to divide among your stat Pools however you wish.

FIRST-TIER EXPLORER

First-tier explorers have the following abilities:

Effort: Your Effort is 1.

Physical Nature: You have a Might Edge of 1, a Speed Edge of 0, and an Intellect Edge of 0.

Cypher Use: You can bear two cyphers at a time.

Practiced With Light and Medium Weapons: You can use light and medium weapons without penalty. If you wield a heavy weapon, increase the difficulty of the attack by one step. Enabler.

Starting Equipment: Appropriate clothing and a weapon of your choice, plus two expensive items, two moderately priced items, and up to four inexpensive items.

Special Abilities: Choose four of the abilities described below. You can't choose the same ability more than once unless its description says otherwise.

Block (3 Speed points): You automatically block the next melee attack made against you within the next minute. Action to initiate.

Danger Sense (1 Speed point): The difficulty of your initiative roll is reduced by one step. Enabler.

Initiative, page 197

Decipher (1 Intellect point): If you spend one minute examining a piece of writing or code in a language you do not understand, you can make an Intellect roll of difficulty 3 (or higher, based on the complexity of the language or code) to get the gist of the message. Action to initiate.

Endurance: Any duration dealing with physical actions is either doubled or halved, whichever is better for you. For example, if the typical person can hold his breath for thirty seconds, you can hold it for one

minute. If the typical person can march for four hours without stopping, you can do so for eight hours. In terms of harmful effects, if a poison paralyzes its victims for one minute, you are paralyzed for thirty seconds. The minimum duration is always one round. Enabler.

Extra Edge: You have a Might Edge of 1 and a Speed Edge of 1.

Fleet of Foot: If you succeed at a difficulty 2 Speed roll to run, you can move a short distance and take an action in the same round. Enabler.

Knowledge Skills: You are trained in two skills in which you are not already trained. Choose two areas of knowledge such as history, geography, paleontology, archeology, and so on. You can select this ability multiple times. Each time you select it, you must choose two different skills. Enabler.

Muscles of Iron (2 Might points): For the next ten minutes, the difficulty of all Might-based actions other than attack rolls that you attempt is reduced by one step. Enabler.

No Need for Weapons: When you make an unarmed attack (such as a punch or kick), you can choose whether it is considered a medium weapon or a light weapon. Enabler.

Physical Skills: You are trained in two skills in which you are not already trained. Choose two of the following: balancing, climbing, jumping, running, or swimming. You can select this ability multiple times. Each time you select it, you must choose two different skills. Enabler.

Practiced in Armor: You can wear armor for long periods of time without tiring and can compensate for slowed reactions from wearing armor. You can wear any kind of armor. You reduce the Speed cost for wearing armor by 1. You start the game with armor of your choice. Enabler.

Practiced With All Weapons: You can use any weapon. Enabler.

Surging Confidence (1 Might point): When you use an action to make your first recovery roll of the day, you immediately gain another action. Enabler.

Trained Without Armor: You are trained in Speed defense actions when not wearing armor. Enabler.

SECOND-TIER EXPLORER

Choose four of the abilities described below (or from a lower tier) to add to your repertoire. In addition, you can replace one of your lower-tier abilities with a different one from a lower tier.

Enable Others: You can use the helping rules to provide a benefit to another character attempting a physical task. This requires no action on your part. Enabler.

Helping, page 211

Escape (2 Speed points): You slip your restraints, squeeze through the bars, break the grip of a creature holding you, pull free from sucking quicksand, or otherwise get loose from whatever is holding you in place. Action.

Eye for Detail (2 Intellect points): When you spend five minutes or so thoroughly exploring an area no larger than a typical room, you can ask the GM one question about the area, and she must answer you truthfully. You cannot use this ability more than one time per area per twenty-four hours. Enabler.

Hand to Eye (2 Speed points): This ability provides an asset to any tasks involving manual dexterity, such as pickpocketing, lockpicking, games involving agility, and so on. Each use lasts up to a minute; a new use (to switch tasks) replaces the previous use. Action to initiate.

Investigative Skills: You are trained in two skills in which you are not already trained. Choose two of the following: identifying, perception, lockpicking, assessing danger, or tinkering with devices. You can select this ability multiple times. Each time you select it, you must choose two different skills. Enabler.

Quick Recovery: Your second recovery roll (usually requiring ten minutes) is only a single action, just like the first roll. Enabler.

Range Increase: Ranges for you increase by one step. Immediate becomes short, short becomes long, and long becomes 200 feet (61 m). Enabler.

Skill With Defense: Choose one type of defense task in which you are not already trained: Might, Speed, or Intellect. You are trained in defense tasks of that type. You can select this ability up to three times. Each time you select it, you must choose a different type of defense task. Enabler.

Stand Watch (2 Intellect points): While standing watch (mostly remaining in place for an extended period of time), you unfailingly remain awake and alert for up to eight hours. During this time, you are trained in perception tasks as well as stealth tasks to conceal yourself from those who might approach. Action to initiate.

Travel Skills: You are trained in two skills in which you are not already trained. Choose two of the following: navigation, riding, running, piloting, or vehicle driving. You can select this ability multiple times. Each time you select it, you must choose two different skills. Enabler.

Wreck: Using two hands, you wield a weapon or a tool with a powerful swing. (If fighting unarmed, this attack is made with both fists or both feet together.) When using this as an attack, you take a –1 penalty to the attack roll, and you inflict 3 additional points of damage. When attempting to damage an object or barrier, you are trained in the task. Action.

THIRD-TIER EXPLORER

Choose three of the abilities described below (or from a lower tier) to add to your repertoire. In addition, you can replace one of your lower-tier abilities with a different one from a lower tier.

Controlled Fall: When you fall while you are able to use actions and within reach of a vertical surface, you can attempt to slow your fall. Make a Speed roll with a difficulty of 1 for every 20 feet (6 m) you fall. On a success, you take half damage from the fall. If you reduce the difficulty to 0, you take no damage. Enabler.

Experienced With Armor: The cost reduction from your Practiced in Armor ability improves. You now reduce the Speed cost by 2. Enabler.

Practiced in Armor, page 40

Expert Cypher Use: You can bear three cyphers at a time.

Ignore the Pain: You do not feel the detrimental effects of being impaired on the damage track, and when you are debilitated, you ignore those effects and experience the effects normally associated with being impaired instead. (Dead is still dead.) Enabler.

Damage track, page 202

Resilience: You have +1 to Armor against any kind of physical damage, even damage that normally ignores Armor. Enabler.

Run and Fight (4 Might points): You can move a short distance and make a melee attack that inflicts 2 additional points of damage. Action.

Damage track, page 202

Ignore the Pain, page 41 (type ability) or page 154 (focus ability)

A character can't apply Effort or other abilities to any task he accomplishes using Tough As Nails.

GM intrusion, page 193

A character can't apply Effort or other abilities to any task he accomplishes using the Expert ability.

Seize Opportunity (4 Speed points): If you succeed on a Speed defense roll to resist an attack, you gain an action. You can use it immediately even if you have already taken a turn in the round. If you use this action to attack, the difficulty of your attack is reduced by one step. You don't take an action during the next round. Enabler.

Skill With Attacks: Choose one type of attack in which you are not already trained: light bashing, light bladed, light ranged, medium bashing, medium bladed, medium ranged, heavy bashing, heavy bladed, or heavy ranged. You are trained in attacks using that type of weapon. Enabler.

Stone Breaker: Your attacks against objects inflict 4 additional points of damage when you use a melee weapon that you wield in two hands. Enabler.

Think Your Way Out: When you wish it, you can use points from your Intellect Pool rather than your Might Pool or Speed Pool on any noncombat action. Enabler.

Wrest From Chance: If you roll a natural 1 on a d20, you can reroll the die. If you reroll, you avoid a GM intrusion—unless you roll a second 1—and might succeed on your task. Once you use this ability, it is not available again until after you make a ten-hour recovery roll. Enabler.

FOURTH-TIER EXPLORER

Choose two of the abilities described below (or from a lower tier) to add to your repertoire. In addition, you can replace one of your lower-tier abilities with a different one from a lower tier.

Capable Warrior: Your attacks deal 1 additional point of damage. Enabler.

Expert: Instead of rolling a d20, you can choose to automatically succeed on a task you're trained in. The task must be difficulty 4 or lower, and it can't be an attack roll or a defense roll. Enabler.

Increased Effects: You treat rolls of natural 19 as rolls of natural 20 for either Might actions or Speed actions (your choice when you gain this ability). This allows you to gain a major effect on a natural 19 or 20. Enabler.

Read the Signs (4 Intellect points): You examine an area and learn precise, useful details about the past (if any exist). You can ask the GM up to four questions about the immediate area; each requires its own roll. Action.

Runner: Your standard movement distance becomes long. Enabler.

Tough As Nails: When you are impaired or debilitated on the damage track, the difficulty of Might-based tasks and defense rolls you attempt is decreased by one step. If you also have Ignore the Pain, make a difficulty 1 Might defense roll when you reach 0 points in all three of your Pools to immediately regain 1 Might point and avoid dying. Each time you attempt to save yourself with this ability before your next ten-hour recovery roll, the difficulty increases by one step. Enabler.

FIFTH-TIER EXPLORER

Choose three of the abilities described below (or from a lower tier) to add to your repertoire. In addition, you can replace one of your lower-tier abilities with a different one from a lower tier.

Adroit Cypher Use: You can bear four cyphers at a time.

Jump Attack (5 Might points): You attempt a difficulty 4 Might action to jump high into the air as part of your melee attack. If you succeed, your attack inflicts 3 additional points of damage and knocks down the foe. If you fail, you still make your normal attack roll, but you don't inflict the extra damage or knock down the opponent. Action.

Mastery With Defense: Choose one type of defense task in which you are trained: Might, Speed, or Intellect. You are specialized in defense tasks of that type. You can select this ability up to three times. Each time you select it, you must choose a different type of defense task. Enabler.

Parry (5 Speed points): You can deflect incoming attacks quickly. For the next ten rounds, the difficulty of all Speed defense rolls is reduced by one step. Enabler.

Physically Gifted: Any time you spend points from your Might Pool or Speed Pool on an action for any reason, if you roll a 1 on the associated die, you reroll, always taking the second result (even if it's another 1). Enabler.

Take Command (3 Intellect points): You issue a specific command to another character. If that character chooses to listen, the difficulty of any attack he attempts is reduced by one step, and a hit deals 3 additional points of damage. If your command is to perform a task other than an attack, the difficulty of the task is reduced by two steps. Action.

Vigilant (5 Might points): When you would normally be dazed or stunned, you are not dazed or stunned. Enabler.

SIXTH-TIER EXPLORER

Choose three of the abilities described below (or from a lower tier) to add to your repertoire. In addition, you can replace one of your lower-tier abilities with a different one from a lower tier.

Again and Again (8 Speed points): You can take an additional action in a round in which you have already acted. Enabler.

Greater Skill With Attacks: Choose one type of attack, even one in which you are already trained: light bashing, light bladed, light ranged, medium bashing, medium bladed, medium ranged, heavy bashing, heavy bladed, or heavy ranged. You are trained in attacks using that type of weapon. If you're already trained in that type of attack, you instead are specialized in that type of attack. Enabler.

Mastery With Armor: The cost reduction from your Practiced in Armor ability improves. When you wear any armor, you reduce the armor's Speed cost to 0. If you select this ability and you already have the Experienced With Armor ability, replace Experienced With Armor with a different third-tier ability because Mastery With Armor is better. Enabler.

Spin Attack (5 Speed points): You stand still and make melee attacks against up to five foes within reach, all as part of the same action in one round. Make a separate attack roll for each foe. You remain limited by the amount of Effort you can apply on one action. Anything that modifies your attack or damage applies to all of these attacks. Action.

Wild Vitality (4 Intellect points): You attune with the life force of a natural creature (your size or bigger) within long range that you can see. This is a level 2 Intellect task. If you succeed, the creature is not harmed, but through resonance with its wild vitality, you gain several benefits for up to one minute: an asset to all your Might-based tasks (including attacks and defenses), +2 to your Might Edge and Speed Edge, and 2 additional points of damage on all successful melee attacks. Action to initiate.

EXPLORER EXAMPLE

Dave decides to create an explorer character for a science fiction (space opera) campaign. This character will be a hardy soul who explores alien worlds. He puts 3 of his additional points into his Might Pool, 2 into his Speed Pool, and 1 into his Intellect Pool; his stat Pools are now Might 13, Speed 11, Intellect 10. As a first-tier character, his Effort is 1, his Might Edge is 1, and his Speed Edge and Intellect Edge are 0. His character is fairly well-rounded so far.

Dave immediately leaps in and starts choosing abilities. He picks Danger Sense and Surging Confidence, thinking they will be generally useful in his activities. He also chooses Practiced in Armor, reasoning that he wears high-tech medium armor on his explorations. Last, he chooses Knowledge Skills and selects geology and biology to help in his interplanetary explorations.

Dave's explorer can bear two cyphers, which in this setting involve nanotechnology. The GM decides that one is a nanite injector that grants a +1 bonus to Might Edge when used, and the other is a device that can create one simple handheld object the user wishes.

Dave's explorer is not really geared toward fighting, but sometimes the universe is a dangerous place, so he notes that he's carrying a medium blaster as well.

Dave still needs a descriptor and a focus. Looking to the descriptor chapter, he chooses Hardy, which increases his Might Pool to 17. He also heals more quickly and can operate better when injured. He's trained in Might defense but has an inability with initiative; however, it's effectively canceled out by his Danger Sense (and vice versa). He could go back and select something else instead of Danger Sense, but he likes it and decides to keep it. Overall, the descriptor ends up making him tough but a little slow.

For his focus, Dave chooses Explores Dark Places (in his case, weird ruins of alien civilizations). This gives him a bunch of additional skills: searching, listening, climbing, balancing, and jumping. He's quite the capable explorer.

Dazed, page 203

Stunned, page 203

Danger Sense, page 39

Surging Confidence, page 40

Knowledge Skills, page 40

Practiced in Armor, page 40

Experienced With Armor, page 41

Hardy, page 74

Inability, page 63

Explores Dark Places, page 123

Your character's starting equipment is as important as his starting skills. Learn more about what you carry and how it's used in Chapter 8: Equipment.

SPEAKER

Fantasy: bard, speaker, skald, emissary, priest, advocate
Modern/Horror: diplomat, charmer, face, spinner, manipulator, minister, mediator, lawyer
Science fiction: diplomat, empath, glam, consul, legate
Superhero: charmer, mesmerist, puppet master

You're good with words and good with people. You talk your way past challenges and out of jams, and you get people to do what you want.

Individual Role: Speakers are smart and charismatic. They like people and, more important, they understand them. This helps speakers get others to do what needs to be done.

Group Role: The speaker is often the face of the group, serving as the person who speaks for all and negotiates with others. Combat and action are not a speaker's strong suits, so other characters sometimes have to defend the speaker in times of danger.

Societal Role: Speakers are frequently political or religious leaders. Just as often, however, they are con artists or criminals.

Roll	Background
1	One of your parents was a famous entertainer in his or her early years and hoped you would excel in the same medium.
2	When you were a teenager, one of your siblings went missing and is presumed dead. The shock rent your family, and it's something you've never gotten over.
3	You were inducted into a secret society that claims to hold and protect esoteric knowledge opposing the forces of evil.
4	You lost one of your parents to alcoholism. He or she may still be alive, but you'd be hard pressed to find forgiveness.
5	You have no memory of anything that happened to you before the age of 18.
6	Your grandparents raised you on a farm far from bustling urban centers. You like to think the instruction they gave you prepared you for anything.
7	As an orphan, you had a difficult childhood, and your entry into adulthood was challenging.
8	You grew up in extreme poverty, among criminals. You still have some connections with the old neighborhood.
9	You served as an envoy for a powerful and influential woman in the past, and she still looks upon you with favor.
10	You have an annoying rival who always seems to get in your way or foil your plans.
11	You've worked yourself into the position of spokesperson for an organization or company of some importance.
12	Your neighbors were murdered, and the mystery remains unsolved.
13	You have traveled extensively, and during that time you accumulated quite a collection of strange souvenirs.
14	Your childhood sweetheart ended up with your best friend (now your ex-best friend).
15	You are part of a maligned minority, but you work to bring the injustice of your status to public attention.
16	You're part owner of a local bar, where you're something of a whiz in creating specialty cocktails.
17	You once ran a con that cheated important people out of money, and they want revenge.
18	You used to act in a traveling theater, and they remember you fondly (as do people in the places you visited).
19	You are in a close romantic relationship with someone in local politics.
20	Someone out there tries to pose as you, using your identity, often for nefarious ends. You've never met the culprit, but you'd certainly like to.

Advanced Speakers: Higher-tier speakers use their abilities to control and manipulate people as well as aid and nurture their friends. They can talk their way out of danger and even use their words as weapons.

Background Connection: Your type helps determine the connection you have to the setting. Roll a d20 or choose from the list on page 44 to determine a specific fact about your background that provides a connection to the rest of the world. You can also create your own fact.

SPEAKER STAT POOLS

Stat	Pool Starting Value
Might	8
Speed	9
Intellect	11

You get 6 additional points to divide among your stat Pools however you wish.

FIRST-TIER SPEAKER

First-tier speakers have the following abilities:

Effort: Your Effort is 1.

Physical Nature: You have an Intellect Edge of 1, a Might Edge of 0, and a Speed Edge of 0.

Cypher Use: You can bear two cyphers at a time.

Practiced With Light Weapons: You can use light weapons without penalty. If you wield a medium weapon, increase the difficulty of the attack by one step. If you wield a heavy weapon, increase it by two steps. You also start with one light weapon of your choice. Enabler.

Starting Equipment: Appropriate clothing and a light weapon of your choice, plus two expensive items, two moderately priced items, and up to four inexpensive items.

Special Abilities: Choose four of the abilities described below. You can't choose the same ability more than once unless its description says otherwise.

Aggression (2 Intellect points): Your words twist the mind of a character within short range who is able to understand you, unlocking her more primitive instincts. As a result, she gains an asset on her Might-based attack rolls for one minute. Action to initiate.

Encouragement (1 Intellect point): While you maintain this ability through ongoing inspiring oration, your allies within short range modify the difficulty of one of the following task types (your choice) by one step to their benefit: defense tasks, attack tasks, or tasks related to any skill that you are trained or specialized in. Action.

Enthrall (1 Intellect point): While talking, you grab and keep another creature's attention, even if the creature can't understand you. For as long as you do nothing but speak (you can't even move), the other creature takes no actions other than to defend itself, even over multiple rounds. If the creature is attacked, the effect ends. Action.

Erase Memories (3 Intellect points): You reach into the mind of a creature within immediate range and make an Intellect roll. On a success, you erase up to the last five minutes of its memory. Action.

Fast Talk (1 Intellect point): When speaking with an intelligent creature who can understand you and isn't hostile, you convince that creature to take one reasonable action in the next round. A reasonable action must be agreed upon by the GM; it should not put the creature or its allies in obvious danger or be wildly out of character. Action.

Interaction Skills: You are trained in two skills in which you are not already trained. Choose two of the following: deceiving, persuading, public speaking, seeing through deception, or intimidating. You can select this ability multiple times. Each time you select it, you must choose two different skills. Enabler.

Practiced With Light and Medium Weapons: You can use light and medium weapons without penalty. If you wield a heavy weapon, increase the difficulty of the attack by one step. Enabler.

Spin Identity (2+ Intellect points): You convince all intelligent creatures who can see, hear, and understand you that you are someone or something other than who you actually are. You don't impersonate a specific individual known to the victim. Instead, you convince the victim that you are someone they do not know belonging to a certain category of people. "We're from the government." "I'm just a simple farmer from the next town over." "Your commander sent me." A disguise isn't necessary, but a good disguise will almost certainly be an asset to the roll involved. If you attempt to convince more than one creature, the Intellect cost increases by 1 point per additional victim. Fooled creatures remain so for up to an hour, unless your actions or other circumstances reveal your true identity earlier. Action.

Some speaker abilities, like Mind Reading or True Senses, imply a supernatural element. If this is inappropriate to the character or the setting, these abilities can be replaced with something from the stealth flavor, or the GM can slightly modify them so they are based in extraordinary talents and insight rather than the supernatural.

Stealth flavor, page 51

Terrifying Presence (2+ Intellect points): You convince one intelligent target of level 3 or lower that you are its worst nightmare. The target must be within short range and be able to understand you. For as long as you do nothing but speak (you can't even move), the target is paralyzed with fear, runs away, or takes some other action appropriate to the circumstances. Instead of applying Effort to decrease the difficulty of the roll, you can apply Effort to increase the maximum level of the target. Thus, to terrorize a level 5 target (two levels above the normal limit), you must apply two levels of Effort. Action.

Understanding (2 Intellect points): You observe or study a creature or object. The next time you interact with it, the difficulty of the related task is reduced by one step. Action.

SECOND-TIER SPEAKER

Choose two of the abilities described below (or from a lower tier) to add to your repertoire. In addition, you can replace one of your lower-tier abilities with a different one from a lower tier.

Babel: After hearing a language spoken for a few minutes, you can speak it and make yourself understood. If you continue to use the language to interact with native speakers, your skills improve rapidly, to the point where you might be mistaken for a native speaker after just a few hours of speaking the new language. Enabler.

Impart Ideal (3 Intellect points): After interacting for at least one minute with a creature who can hear and understand you, you can attempt to temporarily impart an ideal to it that you could not otherwise convince it to adopt. An ideal is different than a specific suggestion or command; an ideal is an overarching value such as "all life is sacred," "my political party is the best," "children should be seen, not heard," and so on. An ideal influences a creature's behavior but doesn't control it. The imparted ideal lasts for as long as befits the situation, but usually at least a few hours. The ideal is jeopardized if someone friendly to the creature spends a minute or more bringing it back to its senses. Action.

Practiced in Armor: You can wear armor for long periods of time without tiring and can compensate for slowed reactions from wearing armor. You can wear any kind of armor. You reduce the Speed cost for wearing armor by 1. You start the game with armor of your choice. Enabler.

Skills: You are trained in one task of your choosing (other than attacks or defense). If you choose a task you're already trained in, you become specialized in that task. You can't choose a task you're already specialized in.

Speed Recovery (3 Intellect points): Your words enhance the normal regenerative

ability of a character within short range who is able to understand you. When he makes a recovery roll, he must spend only half the normal amount of time required to do so (minimum one action). Action.

Unexpected Betrayal: Within a round or two of successfully using Enthrall, Fast Talk, or a similar ability on a target within short range, the difficulty of the first attack you make on that target is decreased by two steps. Once you use Unexpected Betrayal on a target, the difficulty of using your abilities or attempting simple persuasion on that target is permanently increased by two steps. Enabler.

THIRD-TIER SPEAKER

Choose three of the abilities described below (or from a lower tier) to add to your repertoire. In addition, you can replace one of your lower-tier abilities with a different one from a lower tier.

Accelerate (4+ Intellect points): Your words imbue the spirit of a character within immediate range who is able to understand you, accelerating her so that she gains an asset on initiative tasks and Speed defense rolls for ten minutes. Instead of applying Effort to decrease the difficulty, you can use it to affect more targets; each level of Effort affects one additional target. You must speak to additional targets to accelerate them, one target per round. Action per target to initiate.

Blend In (4 Intellect points): When you blend in, creatures still see you, but they attach no importance to your presence for about a minute. While blending in, you are specialized in stealth and Speed defense tasks. This effect ends if you do something to reveal your presence or position—attacking, using an ability, moving a large object, and so on. If this occurs, you can regain the remaining period of effect by taking an action to focus on seeming innocuous and as if you belong. Action to initiate or reinitiate.

Discerning Mind: You have +3 to Armor against damaging attacks and damaging effects that target your mind and Intellect. The difficulty of defense rolls you make against attacks that attempt to confuse, persuade, frighten, or otherwise influence you is decreased by one step. Enabler.

Expert Cypher Use: You can bear three cyphers at a time.

Enthrall, page 45

Fast Talk, page 46

A speaker with Discerning Mind has practiced swaying the minds of others so much that she's gained a measure of protection against others attempting the same on her.

Grand Deception (3 Intellect points): You convince an intelligent creature that can understand you and isn't hostile of something that is wildly and obviously untrue. Action.

Mind Reading (4 Intellect points): You can read the surface thoughts of a creature within short range, even if it doesn't want you to. You must be able to see the target. Once you have established contact, you can read the target's thoughts for up to one minute. If you or the target moves out of range, the connection is broken. Action to initiate.

Oratory (4 Intellect points): When speaking with a group of intelligent creatures that can understand you and aren't hostile, you convince them to take one reasonable action in the next round. A reasonable action must be agreed upon by the GM; it should not put the creatures or their allies in obvious danger or be wildly out of character. Action.

Telling (2 Intellect points): This ability provides an asset to any tasks attempting to deceive, persuade, or intimidate. Each use lasts up to a minute; a new use (to switch tasks) replaces the previous use. Action to initiate.

FOURTH-TIER SPEAKER

Choose two of the abilities described below (or from a lower tier) to add to your repertoire. In addition, you can replace one of your lower-tier abilities with a different one from a lower tier.

Anticipate Attack (4 Intellect points): You can sense when and how creatures attacking you will make their attacks. The difficulty of Speed defense rolls is reduced by one step for one minute. Action.

Confounding Banter (4 Intellect points): You spew a stream of nonsense to distract a foe within immediate range. On a successful Intellect roll, the difficulty of your defense roll against the creature's next attack before the end of the next round is reduced by one step. Action.

Feint (2 Speed points): If you spend one action creating a misdirection or diversion, in the next round you can take advantage of your foe's lowered defenses. Make a melee attack against that foe; the difficulty of the attack is decreased by one step, and a hit inflicts 4 additional points of damage. Action.

Heightened Skills: You are trained in two tasks of your choosing (other than attacks or defense). If you choose a task you're already trained in, you instead become specialized in that task. You can't choose a task you're already specialized in.

Psychosis (4 Intellect points): Your words inflict a destructive psychosis in the mind of a target within long range that can understand you, dealing 6 points of Intellect damage (ignores Armor) per round. The psychosis can be dispersed if a target spends an action doing nothing but calming and centering itself. Action to initiate.

Quick Wits: When performing a task that would normally require spending points from your Intellect Pool, you can spend points from your Speed Pool instead. Enabler.

Read the Signs (4 Intellect points): You examine an area and learn precise, useful details about the past (if any exist). You can ask the GM up to four questions about the immediate area; each requires its own roll. Action.

Suggestion (4 Intellect points): You suggest an action to another creature (level 2 or lower) within immediate range. If the action doesn't seem completely at odds with the creature's nature, it follows your suggestion for up to a minute. Instead of applying Effort to decrease the difficulty, you can apply it to increase the maximum level of the target by 1. When the effect ends, the creature remembers following the suggestion, but believes that it chose to do so willingly. Action to initiate.

FIFTH-TIER SPEAKER

Choose three of the abilities described below (or from a lower tier) to add to your repertoire. In addition, you can replace one of your lower-tier abilities with a different one from a lower tier.

Adroit Cypher Use: You can bear four cyphers at a time.

Experienced With Armor: The cost reduction from your Practiced in Armor ability improves. You now reduce the Speed cost by 2. Enabler.

Flee (6 Intellect points): All non-allies within short distance who can hear your dreadful, intimidating words flee from you at top speed for one minute.

Font of Inspiration: With your approval, characters within immediate range can use an action to gain inspiration from your presence; the difficulty of one action they take in the following round is reduced by one step. This inspiration costs each affected character 2 Intellect points. Once this ability is used, others can't gain inspiration from you again until after you make a recovery roll. Enabler.

Foul Aura (5+ Intellect points): Your words, gestures, and touch invest an object no larger than yourself with an aura of doom, fear, and doubt for one day. Creatures that can hear and understand you feel an urge to move at least a short distance away from the object. If a creature does not move away, the difficulty of all tasks, attacks, and defenses it attempts while within the aura is increased by one step. The duration of the aura is extended by one day per level of Effort applied. The aura is temporarily blocked while the object is covered or contained. Action to initiate.

Skill With Attacks: Choose one type of attack in which you are not already trained: light bashing, light bladed, light ranged, medium bashing, medium bladed, medium ranged, heavy bashing, heavy bladed, or heavy ranged. You are trained in attacks using that type of weapon. Enabler.

Stimulate (6 Intellect points): Your words encourage a target you touch who can understand you. The difficulty of the next action it takes is decreased by three steps. Action.

SIXTH-TIER SPEAKER

Choose two of the abilities described below (or from a lower tier) to add to your repertoire. In addition, you can replace one of your lower-tier abilities with a different one from a lower tier.

Battle Management (4 Intellect points): As long as you spend your action each round giving orders or advice, the difficulty of attack and defense actions by your allies within short range is decreased by one step. Action.

Inspiring Success (6 Intellect points): When you succeed on a roll to perform a task related to the stat that you choose upon selecting this ability, and you applied at least one level of Effort, you may choose another character within short range. That PC has an asset on the next task she attempts using that stat on her next turn. Enabler.

Shatter Mind (7+ Intellect points): Your words reverberate destructively in the brain of an intelligent level 1 target within short range that can understand you. They destroy tissue, memories, and personality, triggering a vegetative state. Instead of applying Effort to decrease the difficulty of the attack, you can apply Effort to increase the maximum level of the target. Thus, to shatter the mind of a level 5 target (four levels above the normal limit), you must apply four levels of Effort. Action.

True Senses: You can see in complete darkness up to 50 feet (15 m) as if it were dim light. You recognize holograms,

Practiced in Armor, page 46

The vegetative state created by Shatter Mind can be healed by advanced magic or science, or by a condition remover cypher that cures psychosis.

Condition remover, page 347

disguises, optical illusions, sound mimicry, and other such tricks (for all senses) for what they are. Enabler.

Word of Command (6 Intellect points + level 6 cypher): You utter a word so powerful that to fully invest it, you sacrifice a cypher in your possession that is level 6 or higher. You issue the word to one creature within long range that you can see. The affected target must obey the command for several hours before it is free to act as it wishes. Targets that are attacked while under the effect of the command can defend themselves. Typical commands include "retreat," "calm," "come," and "stay." The GM decides how the target acts once a command is given. Action.

SPEAKER EXAMPLE

Mary wants to create a speaker for a Lovecraftian horror campaign. She puts 3 of her additional stat points into her Intellect Pool and 3 into her Speed Pool; her stat Pools are now Might 8, Speed 12, Intellect 14. As a first-tier character, her Effort is 1, her Might Edge and Speed Edge are 0, and her Intellect Edge is 1. She's smart and charismatic but not particularly tough.

Mary chooses Fast Talk and Spin Identity to help get into places and learn things she wants to know. She's a bit of a con artist. She's good to her friends, however, and chooses Encouragement as well. Mary rounds out her first-tier abilities with Interaction Skills (deceiving and persuading).

A speaker normally starts with two cyphers, but the GM rules that characters in this campaign start with only one—something creepy relating to their background. Mary's cypher is an odd pocket watch given to her by her grandfather. She doesn't know how or why, but when activated, it allows her to take twice as many actions for three rounds.

Mary's character carries a small knife hidden in her bag in case of trouble. As a light weapon, it inflicts 2 points of damage but reduces the difficulty of attacks by one step.

Mary chooses Driven for her descriptor and decides that she's driven to learn the truth behind some of the strange things that she's heard might be going on. Maybe she can even publish her findings. Driven increases her Might Pool to 10. She's trained in Intellect defense actions and can choose a skill each day to help her reach her goals. At first, Mary is sad that her descriptor gives her an inability in perception tasks, but then she realizes that the flaw fits her character well—she's better at getting people to tell her what she needs to know than at finding the information herself.

For her focus, Mary chooses Moves Like a Cat, granting her a final Speed Pool of 15 and training in balance. In the end, she's graceful and quick, charismatic, and hardier than she initially thought thanks to her drive. She's ready to investigate the weird.

Inability, page 63

Moves Like a Cat, page 150

Flavoring is not mandatory. You can always use a type as is.

Fast Talk, page 46

Spin Identity, page 46

Encouragement, page 45

Interaction Skills, page 46

Unless otherwise noted, you cannot choose the same ability twice, even if you get it from both your type and a flavor.

You should never give a type more than one flavoring.

Driven, page 71

FLAVORS

Flavors are groups of special abilities the GM and players can use to alter a character type to make it more to their liking or more appropriate to the genre or setting. For example, if a player wants to create a magic-using thief character, she could play an adept with stealth flavoring. In a science fiction setting, a warrior might also have knowledge of machinery, so the character could be flavored with technology.

At a given tier, abilities from a flavor are traded one for one with standard abilities from a type. So to add the Danger Sense stealth flavor ability to a warrior, something else—perhaps Bash—must be sacrificed. Now that character can choose Danger Sense as he would any other first-tier warrior ability, but he can never choose Bash.

The GM should always be involved in flavoring a type. For example, she might know that for her space opera game, she wants a type called a "glam," which is a speaker flavored with certain technology abilities—specifically those that make the character a flamboyant starship pilot. Thus, she exchanges the first-tier abilities Spin Identity and Aggression for the tech flavor abilities Datajack and Tech Skills so the character can plug into the ship directly and can take piloting and computers as skills.

In the end, flavor is mostly a tool for the GM to easily create campaign-specific types by making a few slight alterations to the four base types. Although players may wish to use flavors to get the characters they want, remember that they can also shape their PCs with descriptors and foci very nicely.

The flavors available are stealth, technology, magic, combat, and skills and knowledge.

STEALTH FLAVOR

Characters with the stealth flavor are good at sneaking around, infiltrating places they don't belong, and deceiving others. They use these abilities in a variety of ways, including combat. An explorer with stealth flavor might be a thief, while a warrior with stealth flavor might be an assassin. An explorer with stealth flavor in a superhero setting might be a crimefighter who stalks the streets at night.

FIRST-TIER STEALTH ABILITIES

Danger Sense (1 Speed point): The difficulty of your initiative roll is reduced by one step. Enabler.

Fleet of Foot: If you succeed at a difficulty 2 Speed roll to run, you can move a short distance and take an action in the same round. Enabler.

Goad (2 Might points): After you successfully attack a creature, the difficulty of Speed defense rolls by all others against the creature's attacks is decreased by one step until the end of the next round. Enabler.

Legerdemain (1 Speed point): You can perform small but seemingly impossible tricks. For example, you can make a small object in your hands disappear and move into a desired spot within reach (like your pocket). You can make someone believe that he has something in his possession that he does not have (or vice versa). You can switch similar objects right in front of someone's eyes. Action.

Opportunist: You have an asset on any attack roll you make against a creature that has already been attacked at some point during the round and is within immediate range. Enabler.

Stealth Skills: You are trained in your choice of two of the following skills: disguise, deception, lockpicking, pickpocketing, seeing through deception, sleight of hand, or stealth. You can choose this ability multiple times, but you must select different skills each time. Enabler.

SECOND-TIER STEALTH ABILITIES

Contortionist (2 Speed points): You can wriggle free from bindings or squeeze through a tight spot. You are trained in escaping. When you use an action to escape or move through a tight area, you can immediately use another action. You may use this action only to move. Enabler.

Find an Opening (1 Intellect point): You use trickery to find an opening in your foe's defenses. If you succeed on a Speed roll against one creature within immediate range, the difficulty of your next attack against that creature before the end of the next round is reduced by one step. Action.

Get Away (2 Speed points): After your action on your turn, you move up to a short distance or get behind or beneath cover within immediate range. Enabler.

Impersonate (2 Intellect points): You alter your voice, posture, and mannerisms, whip together a disguise, and gain an asset on an attempt to impersonate someone else, whether it is a specific individual (Bob the

Initiative, page 197

Of course, you can "flavor" a character in the Cypher System in many ways. To make a character more stealthy, for example, you can also choose the Stealthy descriptor or any number of foci, including Works the Back Alleys.

Stealthy, page 85

Works the Back Alleys, page 179

cop) or a general role (a police officer). Action to initiate.

Sense Ambush: You are never surprised by an attack. Enabler.

Surprise Strike (3 Speed points): When you attack a creature you have surprised, the difficulty of your attack roll is reduced by one step, and, on a success, you deal 1 additional point of damage. Enabler.

THIRD-TIER STEALTH ABILITIES

Daring Escape (5 Speed points): You dodge an attack. If you succeed on a Speed defense roll, you can trick your attacker into accidentally attacking a different creature within immediate range. Enabler.

Evanesce (3 Speed points): You step into shadows or behind cover, and everyone who was observing you completely loses track of you. Although you're not invisible, you can't be seen until you reveal yourself again by moving out of the shadows or from behind cover (or by making an attack). Action.

From the Shadows: If you successfully attack a creature that was previously unaware of your presence, you deal 3 additional points of damage. Enabler.

Gambler: Each day, choose two different numbers from 2 to 16. One number is your lucky number, and the other is your unlucky number. Whenever you make a roll that day and get a number matching your lucky number, the difficulty of your next task is reduced by one step. Whenever you make a roll that day and get a number matching your unlucky number, the difficulty of your next task is increased by one step. Enabler.

Inner Defense: You are trained in any task to resist another creature's attempt to discern your true feelings, beliefs, or plans. You are likewise trained in resisting torture, telepathic intrusion, and mind control. Enabler.

Seize Opportunity (4 Speed points): If you succeed on a Speed defense roll to resist an attack, you gain an action. You can use it immediately even if you have already taken a turn in the round. If you use this action to attack, the difficulty of your attack is reduced by one step. You don't take an action during the next round. Enabler.

Stab and Run (4 Might points): You make a melee attack and move a short distance. The attack inflicts 2 additional points of damage. Action.

Subterfuge: When you move no more than a short distance, you can move without making a sound, regardless of the surface you move across. Enabler.

FOURTH-TIER STEALTH ABILITIES

Ambusher: When you attack a creature that has not yet acted during the first round of combat, the difficulty of your attack is reduced by one step. Enabler.

Debilitating Strike (4 Speed points): You make an attack to deliver a painful or debilitating strike. The difficulty of the attack is increased by one step. If it hits, the creature takes 2 additional points of damage at the end of the next round, and the difficulty of defense rolls to resist its attacks is decreased by one step until the end of the next round. Action.

Outwit: When you make a Speed defense roll, you can use your Intellect in place of your Speed. Enabler.

Preternatural Senses: While you are conscious and able to use an action, you cannot be surprised. In addition, you are trained in initiative actions. Enabler.

Tumbling Moves (5 Speed points): When you use an action to move, the difficulty of Speed defense rolls is reduced by one step until the end of your next turn. Enabler.

FIFTH-TIER STEALTH ABILITIES

Assassinate (5 Intellect points): If you successfully attack a creature that was previously unaware of your presence, you deal 9 additional points of damage. Enabler.

Mask (5 Intellect points): You transform your body to become someone else. You can change any physical characteristic you wish, including coloration, height, weight, gender, and distinguishing markings. You can also change the appearance of whatever you are wearing or carrying. Your stats, as well as the stats of your items, do not change. You remain in this form for up to twenty-four hours or until you use an action to resume your normal appearance. Action to initiate.

Riposte (6 Speed points): When you succeed on a Speed defense roll against an attack from a creature within immediate range, you can immediately make an attack on that creature, or you can gain an asset on the next attack you make on it before the end of the next round. Enabler.

Uncanny Luck (4 Speed points): When you roll for a task and succeed, roll again. If the second number rolled is higher than the first, you get a minor effect. If you roll the same number again, you get a major effect. Enabler.

Minor effect, page 10

Major effect, page 10

SIXTH-TIER STEALTH ABILITIES

Exploit Advantage: Whenever you have an asset for a roll, the difficulty of the roll is reduced by another step. Enabler.

Spring Away (5 Speed points): Whenever you succeed on a Speed defense roll, you can immediately move up to a short distance. You cannot use this ability more than once in a given round. Enabler.

Thief's Luck: Luck is not the chaotic ocean of random chance most people believe it to be. If you fail on a task (including an attack roll or a defense roll), you can change the die result to a natural 20. That still might not be enough to succeed if the difficulty is higher than 6. Once you use this ability, it is not available again until after you make a ten-hour recovery roll. (Thief's Luck doesn't work if a character rolls a natural 1 for an attempted task, unless she also has and uses the third-tier explorer ability Wrest From Chance.) Enabler.

Wrest From Chance, page 42

Twist of Fate: When you roll a 1, you can reroll. You must use the new result, even if it's another 1. Enabler.

TECHNOLOGY FLAVOR

Characters with a flavor of technology typically are from science fiction or at least modern-day settings (although anything is possible). They excel at using, dealing with, and building machines. An explorer with technology flavor might be a starship pilot, and a speaker flavored with technology could be a techno-priest.

Some of the less computer-oriented abilities might be appropriate for a steampunk character, while a modern-day character could use some of the abilities that don't involve starships or ultratech.

FIRST-TIER TECHNOLOGY ABILITIES

Datajack (1 Intellect point): With computer access, you jack in instantly and learn a bit more about something you can see. You get an asset on a task involving that person or object. Action.

Hacker (2 Intellect points): You gain quick access to a desired bit of information in a computer or similar device, or you access one of its primary functions. Action.

Machine Interface (2 Intellect points): The difficulty of discerning the level, function, and activation of technological devices that you touch is decreased by one step for one minute. Enabler.

Scramble Machine (2 Intellect points): You render one machine within short range unable to function for one round. Alternatively, you can increase the difficulty of any action by the machine (or by someone attempting to use the machine) by one step for one minute. Action.

Tech Skills: You are trained in two skills in which you are not already trained. Choose two of the following: crafting, computers, identifying, machines, piloting, repairing, or vehicle driving. You can select this ability multiple times. Each time you select it, you must choose two different skills. Enabler.

Tinker (1 Intellect point): You make a device do something different from its original purpose. For example, a blaster becomes a bomb. A scanner becomes a signal booster for a radio transmitter. A music player becomes a battery for another device. The effective level of the modified device is 1 lower than normal, and the device is rendered unusable until repaired. Action to initiate.

SECOND-TIER TECHNOLOGY ABILITIES

Distant Interface (2 Intellect points): You can activate and control a machine at long range as if you were next to it. If you have never interacted with the particular device before, it is treated as 2 levels higher than normal. Action.

Machine Efficiency (3 Intellect points): You can make a blaster shoot farther, coax more speed from a skycycle, improve the clarity of a camera, jury-rig a light to be brighter, speed up a network connection, and so on. You increase an object's level by 2 for one minute, or you treat the object as an asset that reduces an associated task's difficulty by two steps for one minute (your choice). Action to initiate.

Overload Machine (3+ Intellect points): Through your Serv-0, you infuse a powered device of level 3 or lower with more energy than it can handle. If affected, the device is destroyed or disabled for at least one minute, depending on its size and complexity. The GM may rule that the disabling effect lasts until the device is repaired. Instead of applying Effort to decrease the difficulty, you can apply Effort to increase the maximum level of the target. Thus, to overload a level 5 device (two levels above the normal limit), you must apply two levels of Effort. Action.

Serv-0: You build a tiny robot assistant. It is level 1 and cannot take independent actions or leave your immediate area. In truth, it's more an extension of you than a separate being. Any time you use a device outside of combat and the Serv-0 is next to you, it serves as an asset. This benefit doesn't include repairing, modifying, or building devices, only using them. Enabler.

Serv-0 Defender: Your Serv-0 aids you in combat by blocking attacks. Whenever it is next to you, you get an asset on Speed defense rolls. Enabler.

Serv-0 Repair: Your Serv-0 aids you in repairing other devices. Whenever it is next to you, you get an asset on all repair tasks. Enabler.

Tool Mastery: When you have an asset from using a tool, the time required to perform the task is cut in half (minimum one round). Enabler.

THIRD-TIER TECHNOLOGY ABILITIES

Mechanical Telepathy (3 Intellect points): By touching a thinking machine, you gain access to its surface "thoughts." Action.

Serv-0 Scanner (2 Intellect points): Through your Serv-0, you scan an area equal in size to a 10-foot (3 m) cube, including all objects or creatures within that area. The area must be within short range. Scanning a creature or object always reveals its level (a measure of how powerful, dangerous, or difficult it is). You also learn whatever facts the GM feels are pertinent about the matter and energy in that area. For example, you might learn that the wooden box contains a device of metal and plastic. You might learn that the glass cylinder is full of poisonous gas, and that its metal stand has an electrical field running through it that connects to a metal mesh in the floor. You might learn that the creature standing before you is a mammal with a small brain. However, this ability doesn't tell you what the information means. Thus, in the first example, you don't know what the metal and plastic device does. In the second, you don't know if stepping on the floor causes the cylinder to release the gas. In the third, you might suspect that the creature is not very intelligent, but scans, like looks, can be deceiving. Many materials and energy fields resist or prevent scanning. Action.

Ship Footing (3 Speed points): For ten minutes, the difficulty of all tasks you attempt while on a spaceship is decreased by one step. Action to initiate.

To use Serv-0 Defender, Serv-0 Repair, and similar abilities, you must have a Serv-0 assistant.

Of course, you can "flavor" a character in the Cypher System in many ways. To make a character more technological, for example, you can choose the Mechanical descriptor or any number of foci, including Builds Robots.

Shipspeak: You can make basic maneuvers from a planetary distance with a starship that you have bonded with. You can send it to a designated place, call it to you, have it land, allow or deny entrance, and so on, even if you are not on board. Bonding is a process that requires twenty-four hours of meditation while jacked into the ship. Action.

Spray (2 Speed points): If a weapon has the ability to fire rapid shots without reloading (usually called a rapid-fire weapon, such as a submachine gun), you can spray multiple shots around your target to increase the chance of hitting. Spray uses 1d6 + 1 rounds of ammo (or all the ammo in the weapon, if it has less than the number rolled). The difficulty of the attack roll is decreased by one step. If the attack is successful, it deals 1 less point of damage than normal. Action.

A creature's level determines its target number, health, and damage, unless otherwise stated. So a level 3 machine companion has a target number of 9 and a health of 9, and it inflicts 3 points of damage.

FOURTH-TIER TECHNOLOGY ABILITIES

Machine Bond: From long range, you can activate and control a device that you have bonded with. For example, you can fire a blaster even when it is held by someone else, or direct someone's scanner to where you want it. Bonding is a process that requires twenty-four hours of meditation in the presence of the device. Action.

Robot Fighter: When fighting an automaton or intelligent machine, you are trained in attacks and defense. Enabler.

Serv-o Aim: Your Serv-o aids you in combat. Whenever it is next to you, you get an asset on ranged attack rolls. Enabler.

Serv-o Brawler: Your Serv-o aids you in combat. Whenever it is next to you, you get an asset on melee attack rolls. Enabler.

Serv-o Spy (3 Intellect points): You can send your Serv-o up to a long distance away for up to ten minutes and see and hear through it as though its senses were your own. You direct its movement. Action to initiate.

Of course, you can "flavor" a character in the Cypher System in many ways. To make a character more magical, for example, you can choose the Mystical descriptor or any number of foci, including Casts Spells.

Mystical, page 81

Casts Spells, page 103

FIFTH-TIER TECHNOLOGY ABILITIES

Control Machine (6 Intellect points): You can control the functions of any machine, intelligent or otherwise, within short range. This effect lasts for ten minutes. Action.

Jury-Rig (5 Intellect points): You quickly create an object using what would seem to be entirely inappropriate materials. You can make a bomb out of a tin can and household cleaners, a lockpick out of aluminum foil, or a sword out of broken furniture. The level of the item determines the difficulty of the task, but the appropriateness of the materials modifies it as well. Generally, the object can be no larger than something you can hold in one hand, and it functions once (or, in the case of a weapon or similar item, is essentially useful for one encounter). If you spend at least ten minutes on the task, you can create an item of level 5 or lower. You can't change the nature of the materials involved. For example, you can't take iron rods and make a pile of gold coins or a wicker basket. Action.

Machine Companion: You create a level 3 animate, intelligent machine that accompanies you and acts as you direct. If the machine is destroyed, it takes you one month to create a new one. Enabler.

SIXTH-TIER TECHNOLOGY ABILITIES

Information Gathering (6 Intellect points): You speak telepathically with any or all machines within 1 mile (2 km). You can ask one basic question about themselves or anything happening near them and receive a simple answer. For example, while in an area with many machines, you could ask "Where is the ravage bear?" and if the creature is within a mile of you, one or more machines will probably provide the answer. Action.

Master Machine (8 Intellect points): You can control the functions of any machine, intelligent or otherwise. If you spend an action to concentrate on a machine, you are aware of what is going on around it (you see and hear as if you were standing next to it, no matter how far away you are). You must touch the machine to create the bond, but afterward, there is no range limitation. This effect lasts for one week. You can master only one machine at a time. Action to initiate.

MAGIC FLAVOR

You know a little about magic. You might not be a wizard, but you know the basics—how it works, and how to accomplish a few wondrous things. Of course, in your setting, "magic"

might actually mean psychic powers, mutant abilities, weird alien tech, or anything else that produces interesting and useful effects.

An explorer flavored with magic might be a wizard-hunter, and a speaker with magical flavor might be a sorcerer-bard. Although an adept flavored with magic is still an adept, you might find that swapping some of the type's basic abilities with those given here tailors the character in desirable ways.

FIRST-TIER MAGIC ABILITIES

Closed Mind: You are trained in Intellect defense tasks and have +2 to Armor against damage that selectively targets your Intellect Pool (which normally ignores Armor). Enabler.

Entangling Force (1+ Intellect point): A target within short range is subject to a snare constructed of semi-tangible lines of force for one minute. The force snare is a level 2 construct. A target caught in the force snare cannot move from its position, but it can attack and defend normally. The target can also spend its action attempting to break free. You can increase the level of the force snare by 1 per level of Effort applied. Action to initiate.

Hedge Magic (1 Intellect point): You can perform small tricks: temporarily change the color or basic appearance of a small object, cause small objects to float through the air, clean a small area, mend a broken object, prepare (but not create) food, and so on. You can't use hedge magic to harm another creature or object. Action.

Magic Training: You are trained in the basics of magic (including the operation of magic artifacts and cyphers) and can attempt to understand and identify its properties. Enabler.

Mental Link (1+ Intellect point): You open a pathway to another creature's mind via a light touch, which allows you to transmit thoughts and images to each other. The mental link remains regardless of distance and lasts for one hour. Instead of applying Effort to decrease the difficulty of this ability, you can extend the duration by one hour for each level of Effort applied. Action to initiate.

Premonition (2 Intellect points): You learn one random fact about a creature or location that is pertinent to a topic you designate. Alternatively, you can choose to learn a creature's level; however, if you do so, you cannot learn anything else about it later with this ability. Action.

SECOND-TIER MAGIC ABILITIES

Concussive Blast (2 Intellect points): You release a beam of pure force that smashes into a creature within short range, inflicting 5 points of damage and moving it back an immediate distance. Action.

Damage track, page 202

Fetch (3 Intellect points): You cause an object to disappear and reappear in your hands or somewhere else nearby. Choose one object that can fit inside a 5-foot (2 m) cube and that you can see within long range. The object vanishes and appears in your hands or in an open space anywhere you choose within immediate range. Action.

Force Field (3 Intellect points): You create an invisible energy barrier around a creature or object you choose within short range. The force field moves with the creature or object and lasts for ten minutes. The target has +1 to Armor until the effect ends. Action.

Repair Flesh (3 Intellect points): When you touch an impaired or debilitated character, you can move him up one step on the damage track (for example, a debilitated PC becomes impaired, and an impaired one becomes hale). Alternatively, if you use this ability on a PC during a rest, you grant him a +2 bonus to his recovery roll. Action.

THIRD-TIER MAGIC ABILITIES

Distance Viewing (5 Intellect points): An observer with the ability to revise reality knows that space and distance are illusions. You concentrate to create an invisible, immobile sensor at a location you have previously visited or viewed (at the GM's discretion, you may have to succeed at an Intellect task if the location is warded). The sensor lasts for one hour. Once it is created, you can concentrate to see, hear, and smell through the sensor. It doesn't grant you sensory capabilities beyond the norm. Action to create; action to check.

Fling (4 Intellect points): You violently launch a creature or object about your size or smaller within short range and send it flying a short distance in any direction. This is an Intellect attack that inflicts 4 points of damage to the object being flung when it lands or strikes a barrier. If you aim the primary target at another creature or object (and succeed on a second attack), the secondary target also takes 4 points of damage. Action.

Force at Distance (4+ Intellect points): You temporarily bend the fundamental law of gravity around a creature or object (up to twice your mass) within short range. The target is caught in your telekinetic grip, and you can move it up to a short distance in any direction each round that you retain your hold. A creature in your grip can take actions, but it can't move under its own power. Each round after the initial attack, you can attempt to keep your grip on the target by spending 2 additional Intellect points and succeeding at a difficulty 2 Intellect task. If your concentration lapses, the target drops back to the ground. Instead of applying Effort to decrease the difficulty, you can apply Effort to increase the amount of mass you can affect. Each level allows you to affect a creature or object twice as massive as before. For example, applying one level of Effort would affect a creature four times as massive as you, two levels would affect a creature eight times as massive, three levels would affect a creature sixteen times as massive, and so on. Action to initiate.

FOURTH-TIER MAGIC ABILITIES

Ignition (4 Intellect points): You designate a creature or flammable object you can see within short range to catch fire. This is an Intellect attack. The target takes 6 points of ambient damage per round until the flames are extinguished, which a creature can do by dousing itself in water, rolling on the ground, or smothering the flames. Usually, putting out the flames takes an action. Action to initiate.

Pry Open (4 Intellect points): You tear apart the defenses of a creature within long range. Any energy-based defenses it has (such as a force field or a Ward ability) are negated for 1d6 + 1 rounds. If the creature has no energy defenses, its Armor is reduced by 2 for one minute. If it has no energy-based defenses or Armor, the difficulty of all attacks made against the creature is modified by one step to its detriment for one minute. Action.

FIFTH-TIER MAGIC ABILITIES

Create (7 Intellect points): You create something from nothing. You can create any item you choose that would ordinarily have a difficulty of 5 or lower (using the crafting rules). Once created, the item lasts for a number of hours equal to 6 minus the difficulty to create it. Thus, if you create a set of sturdy manacles (difficulty 5), it would last for one hour. Action.

Fast Travel (7 Intellect points): You warp time and space so that you and up to ten other creatures within immediate distance travel overland at ten times the normal rate for up to eight hours. At this speed, most dangerous encounters or regions of rough terrain are ignored, though the GM may declare exceptions. Outright barriers still present a problem. Action to initiate.

True Senses: You can see in complete darkness up to 50 feet (15 m) as if it were dim light. You recognize holograms, disguises, optical illusions, sound mimicry, and other such tricks (for all senses) for what they are. Enabler.

SIXTH-TIER MAGIC ABILITIES

Relocate (7 Intellect points): Choose one creature or object within immediate range. You instantly transport it to a new position within long range that you can see. The new position can be any direction from you, but it cannot be inside a solid object. Action.

Traverse the Worlds (8+ Intellect points): You instantaneously transmit yourself to another planet, dimension, plane, or level of reality. You must know that the destination exists; the GM will decide if you have enough information to confirm its existence and what level of difficulty is required to reach it. Instead of applying Effort to decrease the difficulty, you can apply Effort to bring other people with you; each level of Effort affects up to three additional targets. You must touch additional targets to transmit them. Action.

COMBAT FLAVOR

Combat flavor makes a character more martial. A speaker with combat flavor in a fantasy setting would be a battle bard. An explorer with combat flavor in a historical game might be a pirate. An adept flavored with combat in a science fiction setting could be a veteran of a thousand psychic wars.

There's really very little to gain by flavoring a warrior with combat.

FIRST-TIER COMBAT ABILITIES

Danger Sense (1 Speed point): The difficulty of your initiative roll is reduced by one step. Enabler.

Crafting, page 217

Initiative, page 197

Practiced in Armor: You can wear armor for long periods of time without tiring and can compensate for slowed reactions from wearing armor. You can wear any kind of armor. You reduce the Speed cost for wearing armor by 1. You start the game with a type of armor of your choice. Enabler.

Practiced With Light and Medium Weapons: You can use light and medium weapons without penalty. If you wield a heavy weapon, increase the difficulty of the attack by one step. Enabler.

Of course, you can "flavor" a character in the Cypher System in many ways. To make a character more combat oriented, for example, you can choose the Tough descriptor or any number of foci, including Masters Weaponry.

Tough, page 87

Masters Weaponry, page 148

SECOND-TIER COMBAT ABILITIES

Bash (1 Might point): This is a pummeling melee attack. Your attack inflicts 1 less point of damage than normal but dazes your target for one round, during which time the difficulty of all tasks it performs is modified by one step to its detriment. Action.

Bloodlust (3 Might points): If you take down a foe, you can move a short distance, but only if you move toward another foe. You don't need to spend the points until you know that the first foe is down. Enabler.

Pierce (1 Speed point): This is a well-aimed, penetrating ranged attack. You make an attack and inflict 1 additional point of damage if your weapon has a sharp point. Action.

Thrust (1 Might point): This is a powerful melee stab. You make an attack and inflict 1 additional point of damage if your weapon has a sharp edge or point. Action.

Trained Without Armor: You are trained in Speed defense actions when not wearing armor. Enabler.

THIRD-TIER COMBAT ABILITIES

Practiced With All Weapons: You can use any weapon. Enabler.

Skill With Attacks: Choose one type of attack in which you are not already trained: light bashing, light bladed, light ranged, medium bashing, medium bladed, medium ranged, heavy bashing, heavy bladed, or heavy ranged. You are trained in attacks using that type of weapon. You can select this ability multiple times. Each time you select it, you must choose a different type of attack. Enabler.

Skill With Defense: Choose one type of defense task in which you are not already trained: Might, Speed, or Intellect. You are trained in defense tasks of that type. You can select this ability up to three times. Each time you select it, you must choose a different type of defense task. Enabler.

Successive Attack (2 Speed points): If you take down a foe, you can immediately make another attack on that same turn against a new foe within your reach. The second attack is part of the same action. You can use this ability with melee attacks and ranged attacks. Enabler.

FOURTH-TIER COMBAT ABILITIES

Capable Warrior: Your attacks deal 1 additional point of damage. Enabler.

Daring Escape (5 Speed points): You dodge an attack. If you succeed on a Speed defense roll, you can trick your attacker into accidentally attacking a different creature within immediate range. Enabler.

Deadly Aim (3 Speed points): For the next minute, all ranged attacks you make inflict 2 additional points of damage. Action to initiate.

Fury (3 Might points): For the next minute, all melee attacks you make inflict 2 additional points of damage. Action to initiate.

Spray (2 Speed points): If a weapon has the ability to fire rapid shots without reloading (usually called a rapid-fire weapon, such as a submachine gun), you can spray multiple shots around your target to increase the chance of hitting. This ability uses 1d6 + 1 rounds of ammo (or all the ammo in the weapon, if it has less than the number rolled). The difficulty of the attack roll is decreased by one step. If the attack is successful, it deals 1 less point of damage than normal. Action.

FIFTH-TIER COMBAT ABILITIES

Experienced Defender: When wearing armor, you gain +1 to Armor. Enabler.

Hard Target: If you move a short distance or farther on your turn, the difficulty of all Speed defense rolls is reduced by one additional step. Enabler.

Parry (5 Speed points): You can deflect incoming attacks quickly. For the next ten rounds, the difficulty of all Speed defense rolls is reduced by one step. Enabler.

SIXTH-TIER COMBAT ABILITIES

Greater Skill With Attacks: Choose one type of attack, even one in which you are already trained: light bashing, light bladed, light ranged, medium bashing, medium bladed, medium ranged, heavy bashing, heavy bladed, or heavy ranged. You are trained in attacks using that type of weapon. If you're already trained in that type of attack, you instead are specialized in that type of attack. Enabler.

Mastery With Armor: The cost reduction from your Practiced in Armor ability improves. When you wear any armor, you reduce the armor's Speed cost to 0. If you select this ability and you already have the Experienced With Armor ability, replace Experienced With Armor with a different ability from the same tier because Mastery With Armor is better. Enabler.

Mastery With Defense: Choose one type of defense task in which you are trained: Might, Speed, or Intellect. You are specialized in defense tasks of that type. You can select this ability up to three times. Each time you select it, you must choose a different type of defense task. Enabler.

SKILLS AND KNOWLEDGE FLAVOR

This flavor is for characters in roles that call for more knowledge and more real-world application of talent. It's less flashy and dramatic than supernatural powers or the ability to hack apart multiple foes, but sometimes expertise or know-how is the real solution to a problem.

A warrior flavored with skills and knowledge might be a military engineer. An explorer flavored with skills and knowledge could be a field scientist. A speaker with this flavor might be a teacher.

FIRST-TIER SKILLS AND KNOWLEDGE ABILITIES

Interaction Skills: You are trained in two skills in which you are not already trained. Choose two of the following: deceiving, persuading, public speaking, seeing through deception, or intimidating. You can select this ability multiple times. Each time you select it, you must choose two different skills. Enabler.

Investigative Skills: You are trained in two skills in which you are not already trained. Choose two of the following: perception, identifying, lockpicking, assessing danger, or tinkering with devices. You can select this ability multiple times. Each time you select it, you must choose two different skills. Enabler.

Knowledge Skills: You are trained in two skills in which you are not already trained. Choose two areas of knowledge such as history, geography, paleontology, archeology, and so on. You can select this ability multiple times. Each time you select it, you must choose two different skills. Enabler.

Physical Skills: You are trained in two skills in which you are not already trained.

Practiced in Armor, page 59

Choose two of the following: balancing, climbing, jumping, running, or swimming. You can select this ability multiple times. Each time you select it, you must choose two different skills. Enabler.

Travel Skills: You are trained in two skills in which you are not already trained. Choose two of the following: navigation, riding, running, piloting, or vehicle driving. You can select this ability multiple times. Each time you select it, you must choose two different skills. Enabler.

SECOND-TIER SKILLS AND KNOWLEDGE ABILITIES

The skills and knowledge flavor is particularly useful in shaping character types to fit modern and futuristic science fiction settings, where characters are more likely to be defined by what they know more than anything else. This flavor can distinguish a scientist and a medical doctor, for example, who both might be explorers at their core.

Extra Skill: You are trained in one skill of your choice (other than attacks or defense) in which you are not already trained. You can select this ability multiple times. Each time you select it, you must choose a different skill. Enabler.

Tool Mastery: When you have an asset from using a tool, the time required to perform the task is cut in half (minimum one round). Enabler.

Understanding (2 Intellect points): You observe or study a creature or object. The next time you interact with it, the difficulty of the related task is reduced by one step. Action.

THIRD-TIER SKILLS AND KNOWLEDGE ABILITIES

Flex Skill: At the beginning of each day, choose one task (other than attacks or defense) on which you will concentrate. For the rest of that day, you're trained in that task. You can't use this ability with a skill in which you're already trained.

Improvise (3 Intellect points): When you perform a task in which you are not trained, you can improvise to gain an asset on the task. The asset might be a tool you cobble together, a sudden insight into overcoming a problem, or a rush of dumb luck. Enabler.

FOURTH-TIER SKILLS AND KNOWLEDGE ABILITIES

Multiple Skills: You are trained in two skills of your choice in which you are not already trained. You can select this ability multiple times. Each time you select it, you must choose two different skills. Enabler.

Quick Wits: When performing a task that would normally require spending points from your Intellect Pool, you can spend points from your Speed Pool instead. Enabler.

Specialization: You are specialized in a skill of your choice in which you are already trained. You can select this ability multiple times. Each time you select it, you must choose a different skill. Enabler.

FIFTH-TIER SKILLS AND KNOWLEDGE ABILITIES

Multiple Skills: You are trained in three skills of your choice in which you are not already trained. You can select this ability multiple times. Each time you select it, you must choose three different skills. Enabler.

Practiced With Light and Medium Weapons: You can use light and medium weapons without penalty. If you wield a heavy weapon, increase the difficulty of the attack by one step. Enabler.

Read the Signs (4 Intellect points): You examine an area and learn precise, useful details about the past (if any exist). You can ask the GM up to four questions about the immediate area; each requires its own roll. Action.

SIXTH-TIER SKILLS AND KNOWLEDGE ABILITIES

Skill With Attacks: Choose one type of attack in which you are not already trained: light bashing, light bladed, light ranged, medium bashing, medium bladed, medium ranged, heavy bashing, heavy bladed, or heavy ranged. You are trained in attacks using that type of weapon. Enabler.

Skill With Defense: Choose one type of defense task in which you are not already trained: Might, Speed, or Intellect. You are trained in defense tasks of that type. You can select this ability up to three times. Each time you select it, you must choose a different type of defense task. Enabler.

FURTHER CUSTOMIZATION OF CHARACTER TYPES

The rules in this section are more advanced and always involve the GM. They can be used by the GM to tailor a type to better fit the genre or setting, or by a player and a GM to tweak a character to fit a concept.

MODIFYING TYPE ASPECTS

The following aspects of the four character types can be modified at character creation. Other abilities should not be changed.

Stat Pools: Each character type has a starting stat Pool value. A player can exchange points between his Pools on a one-for-one basis. For example, he can trade 2 points of Might for 2 points of Speed. However, no starting stat Pool should be higher than 20.

Edge: A player can start with an Edge of 1 in whichever stat he wishes.

Cypher Use: If a character gives up the ability to bear one cypher, he gains an additional skill of his choice.

Practiced With Weapons: Some types have static first-tier abilities that grant them practice with certain weapons. Warriors have Practiced With All Weapons, explorers have Practiced With Light and Medium Weapons, and speakers have Practiced With Light Weapons. Any one of these abilities can be sacrificed to gain training in one skill of the player's choice.

DRAWBACKS AND PENALTIES

In addition to other customization options, a player can choose to take drawbacks or penalties to gain further advantages.

Weakness: A weakness is, essentially, the opposite of Edge. If you have a weakness of 1 in Speed, all Speed actions that require you to spend points cost 1 additional point from your Pool. At any time, a player can give his character a weakness in one stat and, in exchange, gain +1 to his Edge in one of the other two stats. So a PC can take a weakness of 1 in Speed to gain +1 to his Might Edge.

Normally, you can have a weakness only in a stat in which you have an Edge of 0. Further, you can't have more than one weakness, and you can't have a weakness greater than 1 unless the additional weakness comes from another source (such as a disease or disability arising from actions or conditions in the game).

Inabilities: Inabilities are like "negative skills." They make one type of task harder by increasing the difficulty by one step. If a character chooses to take an inability, he gains a skill of his choice. Normally, a character can have only one inability unless the additional inability comes from another source (such as a descriptor or a disease or disability arising from actions or conditions in the game).

CHAPTER 6

CHARACTER DESCRIPTOR

Charming, page 66

Graceful, page 74

Inability, page 63

Your descriptor defines your character—it flavors everything you do. The differences between a Charming explorer and a Graceful explorer are considerable. The descriptor changes the way those characters go about every action. Your descriptor places your character in the situation (the first adventure, which starts the campaign) and helps provide motivation. It is the adjective of the sentence "I am an *adjective noun* who *verbs*."

Descriptors offer a one-time package of extra abilities, skills, or modifications to your stat Pools. Not all of a descriptor's offerings are positive character modifications. For example, some descriptors have inabilities—tasks that a character isn't good at. You can think of inabilities as "negative skills"—instead of being one step better at that kind of task, you're one step worse. If you become skilled at a task that you have an inability with, they cancel out. Remember that characters are defined as much by what they're *not* good at as what they *are* good at.

Descriptors also offer a few brief suggestions of how your character got involved with the rest of the group on their first adventure. You can use these, or not, as you wish.

This section details fifty descriptors. Choose one of them for your character. You can pick any descriptor you wish regardless of your type.

APPEALING

You're attractive to others, but perhaps more important, you are likeable and charismatic. You've got that "special something" that draws others to you. You often know just the right thing to say to make someone laugh, put them at ease, or spur them to action. People like you, want to help you, and want to be your friend.

You gain the following characteristics:

Charismatic: +2 to your Intellect Pool.

Skill: You are trained in pleasant social interactions.

Resistant to Charms: You're aware of how others can manipulate and charm people, and you notice when those tactics are used on you. Because of this awareness, you are trained in resisting any kind of persuasion or seduction if you wish it.

Initial Link to the Starting Adventure: From the following list of options, choose how you became involved in the first adventure.

1. You met a total stranger (one of the other PCs) and charmed him so much that he invited you to come along.
2. The PCs were looking for someone else, but you convinced them that you were the perfect person to join them instead.
3. Pure happenstance—because you just go along with the flow of things and everything usually works out well.
4. Your charismatic ways helped get one of the PCs out of a difficult spot a long time ago, and she always asks you to join her on new adventures.

BRASH

You're a self-assertive sort, confident in your abilities, energetic, and perhaps a bit irreverent toward ideas that you don't agree with. Some people call you bold and brave, but those you've put in their place might call you puffed up and arrogant. Whatever. It's not in your nature to care what other people think about you, unless those people are your friends or family. Even someone as brash as you knows that friends sometimes have to come first.

You gain the following characteristics:

Energetic: +2 to your Speed Pool.

Skill: You are trained in initiative.

Initiative, page 197

Bold: You are trained in all actions that involve overcoming or ignoring the effects of fear or intimidation.

Initial Link to the Starting Adventure: From the following list of options, choose how you became involved in the first adventure.

1. You noticed something weird going on, and without much thought, you jumped in with both feet.

DESCRIPTORS

Appealing	Exiled	Learned	Spiritual
Brash	Fast	Lucky	Stealthy
Calm	Foolish	Mad	Strong
Charming	Graceful	Mechanical	Strong-Willed
Clever	Guarded	Mysterious	Swift
Clumsy	Hardy	Mystical	Tongue-Tied
Craven	Hideous	Naive	Tough
Creative	Honorable	Noble	Vengeful
Cruel	Impulsive	Perceptive	Virtuous
Dishonorable	Inquisitive	Resilient	Wealthy
Doomed	Intelligent	Rugged	Weird
Driven	Jovial	Sharp-Eyed	
Empathic	Kind	Skeptical	

2. You showed up when and where you did on a dare because, hey, you don't back down from dares.

3. Someone called you out, but instead of walking into a fight, you walked into your current situation.

4. You told your friend that nothing could scare you, and nothing you saw would change your mind. She brought you to your current point.

Calm is a great descriptor for characters who never intended to have adventures but were thrust into them, a trope that occurs often in modern games and particularly in horror games.

CALM

You've spent most of your life in sedentary pursuits—books, movies, hobbies, and so on—rather than active ones. You're well versed in all manner of academia or other intellectual pursuits, but nothing physical. You're not weak or feeble, necessarily (although this is a good descriptor for characters who are elderly), but you have no experience in more physical activities.

You gain the following characteristics:

Bookish: +2 to your Intellect Pool.

Skills: You are trained in four nonphysical skills of your choice.

Trivia: You can come up with a random fact pertinent to the current situation when you wish it. This is always a matter of fact, not conjecture or supposition, and must be something you could have logically read or seen in the past. You can do this one time, although the ability is renewed each time you make a recovery roll.

Inability: You're just not a fighter. The difficulty of all physical attacks is increased by one step.

Inability: You're not the outdoorsy type. The difficulty of all climbing, running, jumping, and swimming tasks is increased by one step.

Initial Link to the Starting Adventure: From the following list of options, choose how you became involved in the first adventure.

1. You read about the current situation somewhere and decided to check it out for yourself.

2. You were in the right (wrong?) place at the right (wrong?) time.

3. While avoiding an entirely different situation, you walked into your current situation.

4. One of the other PCs dragged you into it.

CHARMING

You're a smooth talker and a charmer. Whether through seemingly supernatural means or just a way with words, you can convince others to do as you wish. Most likely, you're physically attractive or at least highly charismatic, and others enjoy listening to your voice. You probably pay attention to your appearance, keeping yourself well groomed. You make friends easily. You play up the personality facet of your Intellect stat; intelligence is not your strong suit. You're personable, not necessarily studious or strong-willed.

You gain the following characteristics:

Personable: +2 to your Intellect Pool.

Skill: You're trained in all tasks involving positive or pleasant social interaction.

Skill: You're trained when using special abilities that influence the minds of others.

Contact: You have an important contact who is in an influential position, such as a minor noble, the captain of the town guard/police, or the head of a large gang of thieves. You and the GM should work out the details together.

Inability: You were never good at studying or retaining facts. The difficulty of any task involving lore, knowledge, or understanding is increased by one step.

Inability: Your willpower is not one of your strong points. Whenever you try to resist a mental attack, the difficulty is increased by one step.

Additional Equipment: You've managed to talk your way into some decent discounts and bonuses in recent weeks. As a result, you have enough cash jangling in your pocket to purchase a moderately priced item.

Initial Link to the Starting Adventure: From the following list of options, choose how you became involved in the first adventure.

1. You convinced one of the other PCs to tell you what he was doing.
2. You instigated the whole thing and convinced the others to join you.
3. One of the other PCs did a favor for you, and now you're repaying that obligation by helping her with the task at hand.
4. There is reward involved, and you need the money.

CLEVER

You're quick-witted, thinking well on your feet. You understand people, so you can fool them but are rarely fooled. Because you easily see things for what they are, you get the lay of the land swiftly, size up threats and allies, and assess situations with accuracy. Perhaps you're physically attractive, or maybe you use your wit to overcome any physical or mental imperfections.

You gain the following characteristics:

Smart: +2 to your Intellect Pool.

Skill: You're trained in all interactions involving lies or trickery.

Skill: You're trained in defense rolls to resist mental effects.

Skill: You're trained in all tasks involving identifying or assessing danger, lies, quality, importance, function, or power.

Inability: You were never good at studying or retaining trivial knowledge. The difficulty of any task involving lore, knowledge, or understanding is increased by one step.

CUSTOMIZING DESCRIPTORS

Under the normal rules, each descriptor is based on some modification of the following guidelines:

Some descriptors offer +4 to one stat Pool and either two narrow skills or one broad skill.

Other descriptors offer +2 to one stat Pool and either three narrow skills or one narrow skill and one broad skill.

A broad skill covers many areas (such as all interactions). A narrow skill covers fewer areas (such as deceptive interactions). Combat-related skills, such as defense or initiative, are considered broad skills in this sense.

Regardless, you can add an additional skill if it is balanced by an inability. You can add other nonskill abilities by eyeballing them and trying to equate them to the value of a skill, if possible. If the descriptor seems lacking, add a moderately priced item as additional equipment to balance things out.

With this general information, you can customize a descriptor, but keep in mind that a heavily customized descriptor isn't a descriptor if it no longer says one thing about a character. It's better to use this information to create a new descriptor that fits exactly how the player wants to portray the character.

Additional Equipment: You see through the schemes of others and occasionally convince them to believe you—even when, perhaps, they should not. Thanks to your clever behavior, you have an additional expensive item.

Initial Link to the Starting Adventure: From the following list of options, choose how you became involved in the first adventure.

1. You convinced one of the other PCs to tell you what he was doing.
2. From afar, you observed that something interesting was going on.
3. You talked your way into the situation because you thought it might earn some money.
4. You suspect that the other PCs won't succeed without you.

Some players may not want to be defined by a "negative" quality like Clumsy, but in truth, even this kind of descriptor has enough advantages that it makes for capable and talented characters. What negative descriptors really do is make more interesting and complex characters that are often great fun to play.

GM intrusion, page 193

CLUMSY

Graceless and awkward, you were told that you'd grow out of it, but you never did. You often drop things, trip over your own feet, or knock things (or people) over. Some people get frustrated by this quality, but most find it funny and even a little charming.

You gain the following characteristics:

Butterfingers: −2 to your Speed Pool.

Thick-Muscled: +2 to your Might Pool.

Inelegant: You have a certain lovable charm. You are trained in all pleasant social interactions when you express a lighthearted, self-deprecating manner.

Dumb Luck: The GM can introduce a GM intrusion on you, based on your clumsiness, without awarding you any XP (as if you had rolled a 1 on a d20 roll). However, if this happens, 50% of the time, your clumsiness works to your advantage. Rather than hurting you (much), it helps, or it hurts your enemies. You slip, but it's just in time to duck an attack. You fall down, but you trip your enemies as you crash into their legs. You turn around too quickly, but you end up knocking the weapon from your foe's hand. You and the GM should work together to determine the details. The GM can use GM intrusions based on your clumsiness normally (awarding XP) if she desires.

Skill: You've got a certain bull-like quality. You are trained in tasks involving breaking things.

Inability: The difficulty of any task that involves balance, grace, or hand-to-eye coordination is increased by one step.

Initial Link to the Starting Adventure: From the following list of options, choose how you became involved in the first adventure.

1. You were in the right place at the right time.

2. You had a piece of information that the other PCs needed to make their plans.

3. A sibling recommended you to the other PCs.

4. You stumbled into the PCs as they were discussing their mission, and they took a liking to you.

Descriptors like Craven, Cruel, and Dishonorable might not be appropriate for every group. These are villainous traits and some people want their PCs to be entirely heroic. But others don't mind a little moral greyness thrown into the mix. Still others see things like Craven and Cruel as traits to overcome as their characters develop (probably earning them different descriptors).

CRAVEN

Courage fails you at every turn. You lack the willpower and resolve to stand fast in the face of danger. Fear gnaws at your heart, chewing away at your mind, driving you to distraction until you cannot bear it. Most times, you back down from confrontations. You flee from threats and vacillate when faced with difficult decisions.

Yet for all that fear dogs you and possibly shames you, your cowardly nature proves to be a useful ally from time to time. Listening to your fears has helped you escape danger and avoid taking unnecessary risks. Others may have suffered in your place, and you might be the first to admit this fact, but secretly you feel intense relief from having avoided an unthinkable and terrible fate.

You gain the following characteristics:

Furtive: +2 to your Speed Pool.

Skill: You're trained in stealth-based tasks.

Skill: You're trained in running actions.

Skill: You're trained in any action taken to escape danger, flee from a dangerous situation, or wheedle your way out of trouble.

Inability: You do not willingly enter dangerous situations. The difficulty of any initiative actions (to determine who goes first in combat) is increased by one step.

Inability: You fall to pieces when you have to undertake a dangerous task alone. The difficulty of any potentially dangerous task you undertake alone (such as attacking a creature by yourself) is increased by one step.

Additional Equipment: You have a good luck charm or protective device to keep you out of harm's way.

Initial Link to the Starting Adventure: From the following list of options, choose how you became involved in the first adventure.

1. You believe that you're being hunted, and you have hired one of the other PCs as your protector.

2. You seek to escape your shame and take up with capable individuals in the hopes of repairing your reputation.

3. One of the other PCs bullied you into coming along.

4. The group answered your cries for help when you were in trouble.

CREATIVE

Maybe you have a notebook where you write down ideas so you can develop them later. Perhaps you email yourself ideas that strike you out of the blue so you can sort them in an electronic document. Or maybe you just sit down, stare at your screen and, by indomitable force of will, produce something from nothing. However your gift works, you're creative—you code, write, compose, sculpt, design, direct, or otherwise create narratives that enthrall other people with your vision.

You gain the following characteristics:

Inventive: +2 to your Intellect Pool.

Original: You're always coming up with something new. You're trained in any task related to creating a narrative (such as a story, play, or scenario). This includes deception, if the deception involves a narrative you're able to tell.

Skill: You are naturally inventive. You are trained in one specific creative skill of your choice: writing, computer coding, music composition, and so on.

Skill: You love solving riddles and the like. You are trained in puzzle-solving tasks.

Skill: To be creative requires that you always be learning. You are trained in any task that involves learning something new, such as when you're digging through a library, data bank, news archive, or similar collection of knowledge.

Inability: You're inventive but not charming. The difficulty of all tasks related to pleasant social interaction is one step higher for you.

Initial Link to the Starting Adventure: From the following list of options, choose how you became involved in the first adventure.

1. You were doing research for a project and convinced the PCs to bring you along.
2. You're looking for new markets for the results of your creative output.
3. You fell in with the wrong crowd, but they grew on you.
4. A creative life is often one beset with financial hurdles. You joined the PCs because you hoped it would be profitable.

CRUEL

Misfortune and suffering do not move you. When another endures hardship, you find it hard to care, and you may even enjoy the pain and difficulty the person experiences. Your cruel streak may derive from bitterness brought about by your own struggles and disappointments. You might be a hard pragmatist, doing what you feel you must even if others are worse for it. Or you could be a sadist, delighting in the pain you inflict.

Being cruel does not necessarily make you a villain. Your cruelty may be reserved for those who cross you or other people useful to you. You might have become cruel as the result of an intensely awful experience. Abuse and torture, for example, can strip away compassion for other living beings.

As well, you need not be cruel in every situation. In fact, others might see you as personable, friendly, and even helpful. But when angered or frustrated, your true nature reveals itself, and those who have earned your scorn are likely to suffer for it.

You gain the following characteristics:

Cunning: +2 to your Intellect Pool.

Cruelty: When you use force, you can choose to maim or deliver painful injuries to draw out your foe's suffering. Whenever you inflict damage, you can choose to inflict 2 fewer points of damage to decrease the difficulty of the next attack against that foe by one step.

Skill: You're trained in tasks related to deception, intimidation, and persuasion when you interact with characters experiencing physical or emotional pain.

Inability: You have a hard time connecting with others, understanding their motives, or sharing their feelings. The difficulty of any task to ascertain another character's motives, feelings, or disposition is increased by one step.

Additional Equipment: You have a valuable memento from the last person you destroyed. The memento is moderately priced, and you can sell it or trade it for an item of equal or lesser value.

Initial Link to the Starting Adventure: From the following list of options, choose how you became involved in the first adventure.

1. You suspect that you might gain a long-term advantage from helping the other PCs and may be able to use that advantage against your enemies.
2. By joining the PCs, you see an opportunity to grow your personal power and status at the expense of others.
3. You hope to make another PC's life more difficult by joining the group.
4. Joining the PCs gives you an opportunity to escape justice for a crime you committed.

DISHONORABLE

There is no honor among thieves—or betrayers, backstabbers, liars, or cheats. You are all of these things, and either you don't lose any sleep over it, or you deny the truth to others or to yourself. Regardless, you are willing to do whatever it takes to get your own way. Honor, ethics, and principles are merely words. In your estimation, they have no place in the real world.

You gain the following characteristics:

Sneaky: +4 to your Speed Pool.

Just Desserts: When the GM gives another player an experience point to award to someone for a GM intrusion, that player cannot give it to you.

Skill: You are trained in deception.

Skill: You are trained in stealth.

Skill: You are trained in intimidation.

Inability: People don't like or trust you. The difficulty of pleasant social interactions is increased by one step.

Initial Link to the Starting Adventure: From the following list of options, choose how you became involved in the first adventure.

1. You are interested in what the PCs are doing, so you lied to them to get into their group.
2. While skulking about, you overheard the PCs' plans and realized that you wanted in.
3. One of the other PCs invited you, having no idea of what you're truly like.
4. You bullied your way in with intimidation and bluster.

DOOMED

You are quite certain that your fate is leading you, inextricably, toward a terrible end. This fate might be yours alone, or you might be dragging along the others closest to you.

You gain the following characteristics:

Jumpy: +2 to your Speed Pool.

Skill: Always on the lookout for danger, you are trained in perception-related tasks.

Skill: You are defense minded, so you are trained in Speed defense tasks.

Skill: You are cynical and expect the worst. Thus, you are resistant to mental shocks. You are trained in Intellect defense tasks having to do with losing your sanity.

Doom: Every other time the GM uses GM intrusion on your character, you cannot refuse it and do not get an XP for it (you still get an XP to award to another player). This is because you are doomed. The universe is a cold, uncaring place, and your efforts are futile at best.

GM intrusion, page 193

Initial Link to the Starting Adventure: From the following list of options, choose how you became involved in the first adventure.

1. You attempted to avoid it, but events seemed to conspire to draw you to where you are.
2. Why not? It doesn't matter. You're doomed no matter what you do.
3. One of the other PCs saved your life, and now you're repaying that obligation by helping her with the task at hand.
4. You suspect that the only hope you have of avoiding your fate might lie on this path.

DRIVEN

You have set your sights on a goal, and everything you do is in pursuit of that objective. The thing you seek defines you—it shapes your decisions, colors your outlook, and impels you to take action even when your body and mind scream for you to give up and set the task aside, at least for a while. No matter the hardships you face along the way, you believe in your purpose and will let nothing stop you from achieving it.

When you choose this descriptor, choose a goal that is possible to attain. You might set a goal of finding a lost parent, making a sacrifice at a rumored temple, learning how to perform a particular task, or gaining the funds to pay for medical treatment for a loved one. Once you achieve this goal, you may choose a new one.

You probably talk about your mission all the time, bringing it up even when it's only tangentially connected to the conversation. You usually consider other pursuits in the context of whether or not they advance your own agenda.

You gain the following characteristics:

Determined: +2 to your Might Pool.

Skill: You're trained in Intellect defense actions.

Skill: Each day, choose one skill that you believe will clearly help you reach your goal. You are trained in tasks related to that skill.

Inability: Your commitment to your goals makes it hard to relate to others who don't share your objectives or to notice things that don't pertain to your present mission. The difficulty of all perception tasks is increased by one step.

Initial Link to the Starting Adventure: From the following list of options, choose how you became involved in the first adventure.

1. You saw that the other PCs were pursuing the same goal as you, and you believed that joining forces would improve both of your chances at attaining your objectives.
2. One of the PCs gave you information or other assistance in your mission, and you now repay the favor.
3. Helping the PCs may put key resources you need to complete your mission into your hands.
4. One of the other PCs found you when you were wounded and nursed you back to health.

Driven characters can be "one note" in some respect, and that can be dull. Some people may want to use Driven as a temporary descriptor that lasts until their mission is done, and then choose a different descriptor (see page 233).

EMPATHIC

Other people are open books to you. You may have a knack for reading a person's tells, those subtle movements that convey an individual's mood and disposition. Or you may receive information in a more direct way, feeling a person's emotions as if they were tangible things, sensations that lightly brush against your mind. Your gift for empathy helps you navigate social situations and control them to avoid misunderstandings and prevent useless conflicts from erupting.

The constant bombardment of emotions from those around you likely takes a toll. You might move with the prevailing mood, swinging from giddy happiness to bitter sorrow with little warning. Or you might close yourself off and remain inscrutable to others out of a sense of self-preservation or an unconscious fear that everyone else might learn how you truly feel.

You gain the following characteristics:

Open Mind: +4 to your Intellect Pool.

Skill: You're trained in tasks involving sensing other emotions, discerning dispositions, and getting a hunch about people around you.

Skill: You're trained in all tasks involving social interaction, pleasant or otherwise.

Inability: Being so receptive to others' thoughts and moods makes you vulnerable to anything that attacks your mind. The difficulty of Intellect defense rolls is increased by one step.

Initial Link to the Starting Adventure: From the following list of options, choose how you became involved in the first adventure.

1. You sensed the commitment to the task the other PCs have and felt moved to help them.

2. You established a close bond with another PC and can't bear to be parted from him or her.

3. You sensed something strange in one of the PCs and decided to join the group to see if you can sense it again and uncover the truth.

4. You joined the PCs to escape an unpleasant relationship or negative environment.

EXILED

You have walked a long and lonely road, leaving your home and your life behind. You might have committed a heinous crime, something so awful that your people forced you out, and if you dare return, you face death. You might have been accused of a crime you didn't commit and now must pay the price for someone else's wicked deed. Your exile might be the result of a social gaffe—perhaps you shamed your family or a friend, or you embarrassed yourself in front of your peers, an authority, or someone you respect. Whatever the reason, you have left your old life behind and now strive to make a new one.

You probably have a memento from your past—an old picture, a locket with a few strands of hair inside, or a lighter given to you by someone important. You keep the object close at hand and pull it out to help you remember better times.

You gain the following characteristics:

Self-Reliant: +2 to your Might Pool.

Loner: You gain no benefit when you get help with a task from another character who is trained or specialized in that task.

Skill: You're trained in all tasks involving sneaking.

Skill: You're trained in all tasks involving foraging, hunting, and finding safe places to rest or hide.

Inability: Living on your own for as long as you have makes you slow to trust others and awkward in social situations. The difficulty of any task involving social interactions is increased by one step.

Initial Link to the Starting Adventure: From the following list of options, choose how you became involved in the first adventure.

1. The other PCs earned your trust by helping you when you were in need. You accompany them to repay their aid.

2. While exploring on your own, you discovered something strange. When you traveled to a settlement, the PCs were the only ones who believed you, and they have accompanied you to help you deal with the problem.

3. One of the other PCs reminds you of someone you used to know.

4. You have grown weary of your isolation. Joining the other PCs gives you a chance to belong.

FAST

You're fleet of foot. Because you're quick, you can accomplish tasks more rapidly than others can. You're not just quick on your feet, however—you're quick with your hands, and you think and react quickly. You even talk quickly.

You gain the following characteristics:

Energetic: +2 to your Speed Pool.

Skill: You are trained in running.

Fast: You can move a short distance and still take another action in the same round, or you can move a long distance as your action without needing to make any kind of roll.

Inability: You're a sprinter, not a long-distance runner. You don't have a lot of stamina. The difficulty of any Might defense roll is increased by one step.

Initial Link to the Starting Adventure: From the following list of options, choose how you became involved in the first adventure.

1. You jumped in to save one of the other PCs who was in dire need.
2. One of the other PCs recruited you for your unique talents.
3. You're impulsive, and it seemed like a good idea at the time.
4. This mission ties in with a personal goal of your own.

FOOLISH

Not everyone can be brilliant. Oh, you don't think of yourself as stupid, and you're not. It's just that others might have a bit more . . . wisdom. Insight. You prefer to barrel along headfirst through life and let other people worry about things. Worrying's never helped you, so why bother? You take things at face value and don't fret about what tomorrow might bring.

People call you "idiot" or "numbskull," but it doesn't faze you much.

You gain the following characteristics:

Unwise: −4 to your Intellect Pool.

Carefree: You succeed more on luck than anything. Every time you roll for a task, roll twice and take the higher result.

Intellect Weakness: Any time you spend points from your Intellect Pool, it costs you 1 more point than usual.

Inability: The difficulty of any Intellect defense task is increased by one step.

Inability: The difficulty of any task that involves seeing through a deception, an illusion, or a trap is increased by one step.

Initial Link to the Starting Adventure: From the following list of options, choose how you became involved in the first adventure.

1. Who knows? Seemed like a good idea at the time.
2. Someone asked you to join up with the other PCs. They told you not to ask too many questions, and that seemed fine to you.
3. Your parent (or a parental/mentor figure) got you involved to give you something to do and maybe "teach you some sense."
4. The other PCs needed some muscle that wouldn't overthink things.

It can be liberating and really fun to play a foolish character. In some ways, the pressure to always do the right, smart thing is off. On the other hand, if you play such a character as a bumbling moron in every situation, that can become annoying to everyone else at the table. As with everything, moderation is the key.

GRACEFUL

You have a perfect sense of balance, moving and speaking with grace and beauty. You're quick, lithe, flexible, and dexterous. Your body is perfectly suited to dance, and you use that advantage in combat to dodge blows. You might wear garments that enhance your agile movement and sense of style.

You gain the following characteristics:

Agile: +2 to your Speed Pool.

Skill: You're trained in all tasks involving balance and careful movement.

Skill: You're trained in all tasks involving physical performing arts.

Skill: You're trained in all Speed defense tasks.

Initial Link to the Starting Adventure: From the following list of options, choose how you became involved in the first adventure.

1. Against your better judgment, you joined the other PCs because you saw that they were in danger.
2. One of the other PCs convinced you that joining the group would be in your best interests.
3. You're afraid of what might happen if the other PCs fail.
4. There is reward involved, and you need the money.

GUARDED

You conceal your true nature behind a mask and are loath to let anyone see who you really are. Protecting yourself, physically and emotionally, is what you care about most, and you prefer to keep everyone else at a safe distance. You may be suspicious of everyone you meet, expecting the worst from people so you won't be surprised when they prove you right. Or you might just be a bit reserved, careful about letting people through your gruff exterior to the person you really are.

No one can be as reserved as you are and make many friends. Most likely, you have an abrasive personality and tend to be pessimistic in your outlook. You probably nurse an old hurt and find that the only way you can cope is to keep it and your personality locked down.

You gain the following characteristics:

Suspicious: +2 to your Intellect Pool.

Skill: You are trained in all Intellect defense tasks.

Skill: You are trained in all tasks involving discerning the truth, piercing disguises, and recognizing falsehoods and other deceptions.

Inability: Your suspicious nature makes you unlikeable. The difficulty of any task involving deception or persuasion is increased by one step.

Initial Link to the Starting Adventure: From the following list of options, choose how you became involved in the first adventure.

1. One of the PCs managed to overcome your defenses and befriend you.
2. You want to see what the PCs are up to, so you accompany them to catch them in the act of some wrongdoing.
3. You have made a few enemies and take up with the PCs for protection.
4. The PCs are the only people who will put up with you.

HARDY

Your body was built to take abuse. Whether you're pounding down stiff drinks while holding up a bar in your favorite watering hole or trading blows with a thug in a back alley, you keep going, shrugging off hurts and injuries that might slow or incapacitate a lesser person. Neither hunger nor thirst, cut flesh nor broken bone can stop you. You just press on through the pain and continue.

As fit and healthy as you are, the signs of wear show in the myriad scars crisscrossing your body, your thrice-broken nose, your cauliflower ears, and any number of other disfigurements you wear with pride.

You gain the following characteristics:

Mighty: +4 to your Might Pool.

Fast Healer: You halve the time it takes to make a recovery roll (minimum one action).

Unstoppable: While you are impaired on the damage track, you function as if you were hale. While you are debilitated, you function as if you were impaired. In other words, you don't suffer the effects of being impaired until you become debilitated, and you never suffer the effects of being debilitated. You still die if all your stat Pools are 0.

Damage track, page 202

Skill: You are trained in Might defense actions.

Inability: Your big, strong body is slow to react. The difficulty of any task involving initiative is increased by one step.

Ponderous: When you apply Effort when making a Speed roll, you must spend 1 extra point from your Speed Pool.

Initial Link to the Starting Adventure: From the following list of options, choose how you became involved in the first adventure.

1. The PCs recruited you after learning about your reputation as a survivor.
2. You join the PCs because you want or need the money.
3. The PCs offer you a challenge equal to your physical power.
4. You believe the only way the PCs will succeed is if you are along to protect them.

HIDEOUS

You are physically repugnant by almost any human standard. You might have had a serious accident, a harmful mutation, or just poor genetic luck, but you are incontrovertibly ugly.

You've more than made up for your appearance in other ways, however. Because you had to hide your appearance, you excel at sneaking about unnoticed or disguising yourself. But perhaps most important, being ostracized while others socialized, you took the time growing up to develop yourself as you saw fit—you grew strong or quick, or you honed your mind.

You gain the following characteristics:

Versatile: You get 4 additional points to divide among your stat Pools.

Skill: You are trained in intimidation and any other fear-based interactions.

Skill: You are trained in disguise and stealth tasks.

Inability: The difficulty of all tasks relating to pleasant social interaction is increased by one step.

Initial Link to the Starting Adventure: From the following list of options, choose how you became involved in the first adventure.

1. One of the other PCs approached you while you were in disguise, recruiting you while believing you were someone else.
2. While skulking about, you overheard the other PCs' plans and realized you wanted in.
3. One of the other PCs invited you, but you wonder if it was out of pity.
4. You bullied your way in with intimidation and bluster.

HONORABLE

You are trustworthy, fair, and forthright. You try to do what is right, to help others, and to treat them well. Lying and cheating are no way to get ahead—these things are for the weak, the lazy, or the despicable. You probably spend a lot of time thinking about your personal honor, how best to maintain it, and how to defend it if challenged. In combat, you are straightforward and offer quarter to any foe.

You were likely instilled with this sense of honor by a parent or a mentor. Sometimes

the distinction between what is and isn't honorable varies with different schools of thought, but in broad strokes, honorable people can agree on most aspects of what honor means.

You gain the following characteristics:

Stalwart: +2 to your Might Pool.

Skill: You are trained in pleasant social interactions.

Skill: You are trained in discerning people's true motives or seeing through lies.

Initial Link to the Starting Adventure: From the following list of options, choose how you became involved in the first adventure.

1. The PCs' goals appear to be honorable and commendable.
2. You see that what the other PCs are about to do is dangerous, and you'd like to help protect them.
3. One of the other PCs invited you, hearing of your trustworthiness.
4. You asked politely if you could join the other PCs in their mission.

IMPULSIVE

Impulsive characters get into trouble. That's their thing, and that's fine. But if you're constantly dragging your fellow PCs into trouble (or worse, getting them seriously hurt or killed), that will be annoying, to say the least. A good rule of thumb is that impulsiveness doesn't always mean a predilection for doing the wrong thing. Sometimes it's the urge to do the right thing.

You have a hard time tamping down your enthusiasm. Why wait when you can just do it (whatever it is) and get it done? You deal with problems when they arise rather than plan ahead. Putting out the small fires now prevents them from becoming one big fire later. You are the first to take risks, to jump in and lend a hand, to step into dark passages, and to find danger.

Your impulsiveness likely gets you into trouble. While others might take time to study the items they discover, you use such items without hesitation. After all, the best way to learn what something can do is to use it. When a cautious explorer might look around and check for danger nearby, you have to physically stop yourself from bulling on ahead. Why fuss around when the exciting thing is just ahead?

You gain the following characteristics:

Reckless: +2 to your Speed Pool.

Skill: You're trained in initiative actions (to determine who goes first in combat).

Skill: You're trained in Speed defense actions.

Inability: You'll try anything once or twice. The difficulty of any task that involves patience, willpower, or discipline is increased by one step.

Initial Link to the Starting Adventure: From the following list of options, choose how you became involved in the first adventure.

1. You heard what the other PCs were up to and suddenly decided to join them.
2. You pulled everyone together after you heard rumors about something interesting you want to see or do.
3. You blew all of your money and now find yourself strapped for cash.
4. You're in trouble for acting recklessly. You join the other PCs because they offer a way out of your problem.

INQUISITIVE

The world is vast and mysterious, with wonders and secrets to keep you amazed for several lifetimes. You feel the tugging on your heart, the call to explore the wreckage of past civilizations, to discover new peoples, new places, and whatever bizarre wonders you might find along the way. However, as strongly as you feel the pull to roam the world, you know there is danger aplenty, and you take precautions to ensure that you are prepared for any eventuality. Research, preparation, and readiness will help you live long enough to see everything you want to see and do everything you want to do.

You probably have a dozen books and travelogues about the world on you at any time. When not hitting the road and looking around, you spend your time with your nose in a book, learning everything you can about the place you're going so you know what to expect when you get there.

You gain the following characteristics:

Smart: +4 to your Intellect Pool.

Skill: You are eager to learn. You are trained in any task that involves learning something new, whether you're talking to a local to get information or digging through old books to find lore.

Skill: You have made a study of the world. You are trained in any task involving geography or history.

Inability: You tend to fixate on the details, making you somewhat oblivious to what's going on around you. The difficulty of any task to hear or notice dangers around you is increased by one step.

Inability: When you see something interesting, you hesitate as you take in all

the details. The difficulty of initiative actions (to determine who goes first in combat) is increased by one step.

Additional Equipment: You have three books on whatever subjects you choose.

Initial Link to the Starting Adventure: From the following list of options, choose how you became involved in the first adventure.

1. One of the PCs approached you to learn information related to the mission, having heard you were an expert.
2. You have always wanted to see the place where the other PCs are going.
3. You were interested in what the other PCs were up to and decided to go along with them.
4. One of the PCs fascinates you, perhaps due to a special or weird ability she has.

INTELLIGENT

You're quite smart. Your memory is sharp, and you easily grasp concepts that others might struggle with. This aptitude doesn't necessarily mean that you've had years of formal education, but you have learned a great deal in your life, primarily because you pick things up quickly and retain so much.

You gain the following characteristics:

Smart: +2 to your Intellect Pool.

Skill: You're trained in an area of knowledge of your choice.

Skill: You're trained in all actions that involve remembering or memorizing things you experience directly. For example, instead of being good at recalling details of geography that you read about in a book, you can remember a path through a set of tunnels that you've explored before.

Initial Link to the Starting Adventure: From the following list of options, choose how you became involved in the first adventure.

1. One of the other PCs asked your opinion of the mission, knowing that if you thought it was a good idea, it probably was.
2. You saw value in what the other PCs were doing.
3. You believed that the task might lead to important and interesting discoveries.
4. A colleague requested that you take part in the mission as a favor.

JOVIAL

You're cheerful, friendly, and outgoing. You put others at ease with a big smile and a

Your descriptor matters most when you are a beginning character. The benefits (and perhaps drawbacks) that come from your descriptor will eventually be overshadowed by the growing importance of your type and focus. However, the influence of your descriptor will remain at least somewhat important throughout your character's life.

joke, possibly one at your own expense, though lightly ribbing your companions who can take it is also one of your favorite pastimes. Sometimes people say you never take anything seriously. That's not true, of course, but you have learned that to dwell on the bad too long quickly robs the world of joy. You've always got a new joke in your back pocket because you collect them like some people collect bottles of wine.

You gain the following characteristics:

Witty: +2 to your Intellect Pool.

Skill: You're convivial and set most people at ease with your attitude. You are trained in all tasks related to pleasant social interaction.

Skill: You have an advantage in figuring out the punch lines of jokes you've never heard before. You are trained in all tasks related to solving puzzles and riddles.

Initial Link to the Starting Adventure: From the following list of options, choose how you became involved in the first adventure.

1. You solved a riddle before realizing that answering it would launch you into the adventure.
2. The other PCs thought you'd bring some much-needed levity to the team.
3. You decided that all fun and no work was not the best way to get through life, so you joined up with the PCs.
4. It was either go with the PCs or face up to a circumstance that was anything but jovial.

KIND

It's always been easy for you to see things from the point of view of other people. That ability has made you sympathetic to what they really want or need. From your perspective, you're just applying the old proverb that "it's easier to catch flies with honey than with vinegar," but others simply see your behavior as kindness. Of course, being kind takes time, and yours is limited. You've learned that a small fraction of people don't deserve your time or kindness—true sadists, narcissists, and similar folk will only waste your energy. So you deal with them swiftly, saving your kindness for those who deserve it and can benefit from your attention.

You gain the following characteristics:

Emotionally Intuitive: +2 to your Intellect Pool.

Skill: You know what it's like to go a mile in someone else's shoes. You're trained in all tasks related to pleasant social interaction and discerning the dispositions of others.

Karma: Sometimes, strangers just help you out. To gain the aid of a stranger, you must pay 1 XP to the GM, and the GM determines the nature of the aid you gain. Usually, the act of kindness isn't enough to turn a bad situation completely around, but it may moderate a bad situation and lead to new opportunities. For example, if you are captured, a guard loosens your bonds slightly, brings you water, or delivers a message.

Inability: Being kind comes with a few risks. The difficulty of all tasks related to detecting falsehoods in the speech and mannerisms of other creatures is increased by one step.

Initial Link to the Starting Adventure: From the following list of options, choose how you became involved in the first adventure.

1. A PC needed your help, and you agreed to come along and add your expertise.
2. You gave the wrong person access to your money, and now you need to make some back.
3. You're ready to take your benevolence on the road and help more people than you could if you didn't join the PCs.
4. Your job, which seemed like it would be personally rewarding, is the opposite. You join the PCs to escape the drudgery.

LEARNED

You have studied, either on your own or with an instructor. You know many things and are an expert on a few topics, such as history, biology, geography, mythology, nature, or any other area of study. Learned characters typically carry a few books around with them and spend their spare time reading.

You gain the following characteristics:

Smart: +2 to your Intellect Pool.

Skill: You're trained in three areas of knowledge of your choice.

Inability: You have few social graces. The difficulty of any task involving charm, persuasion, or etiquette is increased by one step.

Additional Equipment: You have two additional books on topics of your choice.

Initial Link to the Starting Adventure: From the following list of options, choose how you became involved in the first adventure.

1. One of the other PCs asked you to come along because of your knowledge.
2. You need money to fund your studies.
3. You believed that the task might lead to important and interesting discoveries.
4. A colleague requested that you take part in the mission as a favor.

LUCKY

You rely on chance and timely good luck to get you through many situations. When people say that someone was born under a lucky star, they mean you. When you try your hand at something new, no matter how unfamiliar the task is, as often as not you find a measure of success. Even when disaster strikes, it's rarely as bad as it could be. More often, small things seem to go your way, you win contests, and you're often in the right place at the right time.

You gain the following characteristics:

Luck Pool: You have one additional Pool called Luck that begins with 3 points, and it has a maximum value of 3 points. When spending points from any other Pool, you can take one, some, or all the points from your Luck Pool first. When you make a recovery roll, your Luck Pool is one additional Pool to which you can add recovered points. When your Luck Pool is at 0 points, it does not count against your damage track. Enabler.

Advantage: When you use 1 XP to reroll a d20 for any roll that affects only you, add 3 to the reroll.

Initial Link to the Starting Adventure: From the following list of options, choose how you became involved in the first adventure.

1. Knowing that lucky people notice and take active advantage of opportunities, you became involved in your first adventure by choice.
2. You literally bumped into someone else on this adventure through sheer luck.
3. You found a briefcase lying alongside the road. It was battered, but inside you found a lot of strange documents that led you here.
4. Your luck saved you when you avoided a speeding car by a fortuitous fall through an open manhole. Beneath the street, you found something you couldn't ignore.

MAD

You have delved too deeply into subjects people were not meant to know. You are knowledgeable in things beyond the scope of most, but this knowledge has come at a terrible price. You are likely in questionable physical shape and occasionally shake with nervous tics. You sometimes mutter to yourself without realizing it.

You gain the following characteristics:

Knowledgeable: +4 to your Intellect Pool.

Fits of Insight: Whenever such knowledge is appropriate, the GM feeds you information although there is no clear explanation as to how you could know such a thing. This is up to the GM's discretion, but it should happen as often as once each session.

Erratic Behavior: You are prone to acting erratically or irrationally. When you are in the presence of a major discovery or subjected to great stress (such as a serious physical threat), the GM can use GM intrusion that directs your next action without awarding XP. You can still pay 1 XP to refuse the intrusion. The GM's influence is the manifestation of your madness and thus is always something you would not likely do otherwise, but it is not directly, obviously harmful to you unless there are extenuating circumstances. (For example, if a foe suddenly leaps out of the darkness, you might spend the first round babbling incoherently or screaming the name of your first true love.)

Skill: You are trained in one area of knowledge (probably something weird or esoteric).

Inability: Your mind is quite fragile. Whenever you try to resist a mental attack, the difficulty is increased by one step.

Initial Link to the Starting Adventure: From the following list of options, choose how you became involved in the first adventure.

GM intrusion, page 193

Damage track, page 202

1. Voices in your head told you to go.

2. You instigated the whole thing and convinced the others to join you.

3. One of the other PCs obtained a book of knowledge for you, and now you're repaying that favor by helping her with the task at hand.

4. You feel compelled by inexplicable intuition.

MECHANICAL

You have a special talent with machines of all kinds, and you're adept at understanding and, if need be, repairing them. Perhaps you're even a bit of an inventor, creating new machines from time to time. You get called "techie," "tech," "mech," "gear-head," "motor-head," or any of a number of other nicknames. Mechanics usually wear practical work clothes and carry around a lot of tools.

You gain the following characteristics:

Smart: +2 to your Intellect Pool.

Skill: You're trained in all actions involving identifying or understanding machines.

Skill: You're trained in all actions involving using, repairing, or crafting machines.

Additional Equipment: You start with a variety of machine tools.

Initial Link to the Starting Adventure: From the following list of options, choose how you became involved in the first adventure.

1. While repairing a nearby machine, you overheard the other PCs talking.

2. You need money to buy tools and parts.

3. It was clear that the mission couldn't succeed without your skills and knowledge.

4. Another PC asked you to join them.

MYSTERIOUS

The dark figure lurking silently in the corner? That's you. No one really knows where you came from or what your motives are—you play things close to the vest. Your manner perplexes and confounds others, but that doesn't make you a poor friend or ally. You're just good at keeping things to yourself, moving about unseen, and concealing your presence and identity.

You gain the following characteristics:

Skill: You are trained in all stealth tasks.

Skill: You are trained in resisting interrogation or tricks to get you to talk.

Confounding: You pull talents and abilities seemingly out of nowhere. You can attempt one task in which you have no training as if you were trained. This ability refreshes every time you make a recovery roll, but the uses never accumulate.

Inability: People never know where they stand with you. The difficulty of any task involving getting people to believe or trust you is increased by one step.

Initial Link to the Starting Adventure: From the following list of options, choose how you became involved in the first adventure.

1. You just showed up one day.

2. You convinced one of the other PCs that you had invaluable skills.

3. Some equally mysterious figure told you where to be and when (but not why) to join the group.

4. Something—a feeling, a dream—told you where to be and when to join the group.

MYSTICAL

You think of yourself as mystical, attuned with the mysterious and the paranormal. Your true talents lie with the supernatural. You likely have experience with ancient lore, and you can sense and wield the supernatural—though whether that means "magic," "psychic phenomena," or something else is up to you (and probably up to those around you as well). Mystical characters often wear jewelry, such as a ring or an amulet, or have tattoos or other marks that show their interests.

You gain the following characteristics:

Smart: +2 to your Intellect Pool.

Skill: You're trained in all actions involving identifying or understanding the supernatural.

Sense Magic: You can sense whether the supernatural is active in situations where its presence is not obvious. You must study an object or location closely for a minute to get a feel for whether a mystical touch is at work.

Spell: You can perform the following spell when you have a free hand and can pay the Intellect point cost.

Hedge Magic (1 Intellect point): You can perform small tricks: temporarily change the color or basic appearance of a small object, cause small objects to float through the air, clean a small area, mend a broken object, prepare (but not create) food, and so on. You can't use hedge magic to harm another creature or object. Action.

Inability: You have a manner or an aura that others find a bit unnerving. The difficulty of any task involving charm, persuasion, or deception is increased by one step.

Initial Link to the Starting Adventure: From the following list of options, choose how you became involved in the first adventure.

1. A dream guided you to this point.
2. You need money to fund your studies.
3. You believed the mission would be a great way to learn more about the supernatural.
4. Various signs and portents led you here.

NAIVE

You've lived a sheltered life. Your childhood was safe and secure, so you didn't get a chance to learn much about the world—and even less chance to experience it. Whether you were training for something, had your nose in a book, or just were sequestered in a secluded place, you haven't done much, met many people, or seen many interesting things so far. That's probably going to change soon, but as you go forward into a larger world, you do so without some of the understanding that others possess about how it all works.

You gain the following characteristics:

Fresh: You add +1 to your recovery rolls.

Incorruptible: You are trained in Intellect defense tasks and all tasks that involve resisting temptation.

Skill: You're wide-eyed. You are trained in perception tasks.

Inability: The difficulty of any task that involves seeing through deceptions or determining someone's secret motive is increased by one step.

Initial Link to the Starting Adventure: From the following list of options, choose how you became involved in the first adventure.

1. Someone told you that you should get involved.
2. You needed money, and this seemed like a good way to earn some.
3. You believed that you could learn a lot by joining the other PCs.
4. Sounded like fun.

NOBLE

You are of noble birth. You are not of the common people. Your family has a title and the prestige and (probably) the wealth that goes along with it.

The world can be a classist place, and in that structure you are in the top echelon. Often, laws don't apply to you, you enjoy special treatment, and sometimes people do as you command. You probably dress in finery and walk with a noble bearing, but sometimes the nobility must conceal their station to keep themselves safe—from brigands, thieves, protestors, or aristocratic enemies and their servants.

You gain the following characteristics:

Respect: People who are not of noble

station often treat you with deference. A few, however, secretly treat you with contempt. The difficulty of interactions with non-nobles is decreased by one step 75% of the time, and increased by one step 25% of the time.

Retainer or Mount: You start with a level 2 servant or mount that serves you faithfully. You and the GM should work out the details.

Contact: You have a contact among the nobility who helps you and treats you well. You and the GM should work out the details.

Skill: You are trained in etiquette and interacting with the nobility.

Additional Equipment: You begin the game with an additional expensive item.

Initial Link to the Starting Adventure: From the following list of options, choose how you became involved in the first adventure.

1. It seemed like a lark.
2. You're on the run from an enemy, and joining the PCs seemed like a good way to hide among the common folk.
3. The mission involves somehow redeeming or helping your family.
4. Your parent(s) forced you into it, hoping the experience would be good for you.

Is there really much difference between a character who is Hardy, one who is Resilient, and another who is Tough? The descriptors are indeed close, but the differences will become apparent in play. Players should choose the one they like best.

PERCEPTIVE

You miss little. You pick out the small details in the world around you and are skilled at making deductions from the information you find. Your talents make you an exceptional sleuth, a formidable scientist, or a talented scout.

As adept as you are at finding clues, you have no skill at picking up on social cues. You overlook an offense that your deductions give or how uncomfortable your scrutiny can make the people around you. You tend to dismiss others as being intellectual dwarfs compared to you, which avails you little when you need a favor.

You gain the following characteristics:

Smart: +2 to your Intellect Pool.

Skill: You have an eye for detail. You are trained in any task that involves finding or noticing small details.

Skill: You know a little about everything. You are trained in any task that involves identifying objects or calling to mind a minor detail or bit of trivia.

Skill: Your skill at making deductions can be imposing. You are trained in any task that involves intimidating another creature.

Inability: Your confidence comes off as arrogance to people who don't know you. The difficulty of any task involving positive social interactions is increased by one step.

Additional Equipment: You have a bag of light tools.

Initial Link to the Starting Adventure: From the following list of options, choose how you became involved in the first adventure.

1. You overheard the other PCs discussing their mission and volunteered your services.
2. One of the PCs asked you to come along, believing that your talents would be invaluable to the mission.
3. You believe that the PCs' mission is somehow related to one of your investigations.
4. A third party recruited you to follow the PCs and see what they were up to.

RESILIENT

You can take a lot of punishment, both physically and mentally, and still come back for more. It takes a lot to put you down. Neither physical nor mental shocks or damage have a lasting effect. You're tough to faze. Unflappable. Unstoppable.

You gain the following characteristics:

Resistant: +2 to your Might Pool, and +2 to your Intellect Pool.

Recover: You can make an extra recovery roll each day. This roll is just one action. So you can make two recovery rolls that each take one action, one roll that takes ten minutes, a fourth roll that takes one hour, and a fifth roll that requires ten hours of rest.

Skill: You are trained in Might defense tasks.

Skill: You are trained in Intellect defense tasks.

Inability: You're hardy but not necessarily strong. The difficulty of any task involving moving, bending, or breaking things is increased by one step.

Inability: You have a lot of willpower and mental fortitude, but you're not necessarily smart. The difficulty of any task involving knowledge or figuring out problems or puzzles is increased by one step.

Initial Link to the Starting Adventure: From the following list of options, choose how you became involved in the first adventure.

1. You saw that the PCs clearly need someone like you to help them out.

2. Someone asked you to watch over one of the PCs in particular, and you agreed.

3. You are bored and desperately in need of a challenge.

4. You lost a bet—unfairly, you think—and had to take someone's place on this mission.

RUGGED

You're a nature lover accustomed to living rough, pitting your wits against the elements. Most likely, you're a skilled hunter, gatherer, or naturalist. Years of living in the wild have left their mark with a worn countenance, wild hair, or scars. Your clothing is probably much less refined than the garments worn by city dwellers.

You gain the following characteristics:

Skill: You're trained in all tasks involving climbing, jumping, running, and swimming.

Skill: You're trained in all tasks involving training, riding, or placating natural animals.

Skill: You're trained in all tasks involving identifying or using natural plants.

Inability: You have no social graces and prefer animals to people. The difficulty of any task involving charm, persuasion, etiquette, or deception is increased by one step.

Additional Equipment: You carry an explorer's pack with rope, two days' rations, a bedroll, and other tools needed for outdoor survival.

Initial Link to the Starting Adventure: From the following list of options, choose how you became involved in the first adventure.

1. Against your better judgment, you joined the other PCs because you saw that they were in danger.

2. One of the other PCs convinced you that joining the group would be in your best interests.

3. You're afraid of what might happen if the other PCs fail.

4. There is reward involved, and you need the money.

SHARP-EYED

You're perceptive and well aware of your surroundings. You notice the little details and remember them. You can be difficult to surprise.

You gain the following characteristics:

Skill: You're trained in initiative actions.

Skill: You're trained in perception actions.

Find the Flaw: If an opponent has a straightforward weakness (takes extra damage from fire, can't see out of his left eye, and so on), the GM will tell you what it is.

Initial Link to the Starting Adventure: From the following list of options, choose how you became involved in the first adventure.

1. You heard about what was going on, saw a flaw in the other PCs' plan, and joined up to help them out.
2. You noticed that the PCs have a foe (or at least a tail) they weren't aware of.
3. You saw that the other PCs were up to something interesting and got involved.
4. You've been noticing some strange things going on, and this all appears related.

SKEPTICAL

You possess a questioning attitude regarding claims that are often taken for granted by others. You're not necessarily a "doubting Thomas" (a skeptic who refuses to believe anything without direct personal experience), but you've often benefited from questioning the statements, opinions, and received knowledge presented to you by others.

You gain the following characteristics:

Insightful: +2 to your Intellect Pool.

Skill: You're trained in identifying.

Skill: You're trained in all actions that involve seeing through a trick, illusion, rhetorical ruse designed to evade the issue, or lie. For example, you're better at keeping your eye on the cup containing the hidden ball, sensing an illusion, or realizing if someone is lying to you (but only if you specifically concentrate and use this skill).

Initial Link to the Starting Adventure: From the following list of options, choose how you became involved in the first adventure.

1. You overheard other PCs holding forth on a topic with an opinion you were quite skeptical about, so you decided to approach the group and ask for proof.
2. You were following one of the other PCs because you were suspicious of him, which brought you into the action.
3. Your theory about the nonexistence of the supernatural can be invalidated only by your own senses, so you came along.
4. You need money to fund your research.

SPIRITUAL

A sense of awe washes over you when you appreciate a new facet of your religion or a scientific discipline. When a stranger does something kind for someone he's never met before, it's spiritual. However you meditate—whether by taking in breathtaking scenery, reading a book, or repeating mental syllables in a quiet space—it's spiritual. Your spirituality isn't necessarily about religion, though it could be. The main thing is that you're a person who appreciates and even thrills to the positive aspects of existence, and you may help other people do the same.

You gain the following characteristics:

Meditative: +2 to your Intellect Pool.

Likeable: People and animals just seem to like you. You are trained in all tasks related to pleasant social interaction.

Skill: With maturity comes good judgment. You're trained in Intellect defense tasks and all tasks that involve resisting temptation.

Helpful: When you help someone with a task, he adds 1 to his roll (this bonus is in addition to the regular benefits of helping someone).

Inability: When you encounter something novel, you hesitate as you take in all the details. The difficulty of initiative actions (to determine who goes first in combat) is increased by one step.

Initial Link to the Starting Adventure: From the following list of options, choose how you became involved in the first adventure.

1. You heard the PCs would be visiting someplace amazing and wanted to share the experience.
2. You have a message of hope, and going along with the PCs might allow you to get that message across to a larger number of people.
3. The mission involves helping others, and you couldn't say no.
4. You were asked by a different organization to keep tabs on the PCs and help them if they got into trouble.

STEALTHY

You're sneaky, slippery, and fast. These talents help you hide, move quietly, and pull off tricks that require sleight of hand. Most likely, you're wiry and small. However, you're not much of a sprinter—you're more dexterous than fleet of foot.

You gain the following characteristics:

Quick: +2 to your Speed Pool.

Skill: You're trained in all stealth tasks.

Skill: You're trained in all interactions involving lies or trickery.

Skill: You're trained in all special abilities involving illusions or trickery.

Inability: You're sneaky but not fast. The difficulty of all movement-related tasks is one step higher for you.

Initial Link to the Starting Adventure: From the following list of options, choose how you became involved in the first adventure.

1. You attempted to steal from one of the other PCs. That character caught you and forced you to come along with her.
2. You were tailing one of the other PCs for reasons of your own, which brought you into the action.
3. An NPC employer secretly paid you to get involved.
4. You overheard the other PCs talking about a topic that interested you, so you decided to approach the group.

STRONG

You're extremely strong and physically powerful, and you use these qualities well, whether through violence or feats of prowess. You likely have a brawny build and impressive muscles.

Helping, page 211

You gain the following characteristics:

Very Powerful: +4 to your Might Pool.

Skill: You're trained in all actions involving breaking inanimate objects.

Skill: You're trained in all jumping actions.

Additional Equipment: You have an extra medium weapon or heavy weapon.

Initial Link to the Starting Adventure: From the following list of options, choose how you became involved in the first adventure.

1. Against your better judgment, you joined the other PCs because you saw that they were in danger.
2. One of the other PCs convinced you that joining the group would be in your best interests.
3. You're afraid of what might happen if the other PCs fail.
4. There is reward involved, and you need the money.

STRONG-WILLED

You're tough-minded, willful, and independent. No one can talk you into anything or change your mind when you don't want it changed. This quality doesn't necessarily make you smart, but it does make you a bastion of willpower and resolve. You likely dress and act with unique style and flair, not caring what others think.

You gain the following characteristics:

Willful: +4 to your Intellect Pool.

Skill: You're trained in resisting mental effects.

Skill: You're trained in tasks requiring incredible focus or concentration.

Inability: Willful doesn't mean brilliant. The difficulty of any task that involves figuring out puzzles or problems, memorizing things, or using lore is increased by one step.

Initial Link to the Starting Adventure: From the following list of options, choose how you became involved in the first adventure.

1. Against your better judgment, you joined the other PCs because you saw that they were in danger.
2. One of the other PCs convinced you that joining the group would be in your best interests.
3. You're afraid of what might happen if the other PCs fail.
4. There is reward involved, and you need the money.

SWIFT

You move quickly, able to sprint in short bursts and work with your hands with dexterity. You're great at crossing distances quickly but not always smoothly. You are likely slim and muscular.

You gain the following characteristics:

Fast: +4 to your Speed Pool.

Skill: You're trained in initiative actions (to determine who goes first in combat).

Skill: You're trained in running actions.

Inability: You're fast but not necessarily graceful. The difficulty of any task involving balance is increased by one step.

Initial Link to the Starting Adventure: From the following list of options, choose how you became involved in the first adventure.

1. Against your better judgment, you joined the other PCs because you saw that they were in danger.
2. One of the other PCs convinced you that joining the group would be in your best interests.
3. You're afraid of what might happen if the other PCs fail.
4. There is reward involved, and you need the money.

TONGUE-TIED

You've never been much of a talker. When forced to interact with others, you never think of the right thing to say—words fail you entirely, or they come out all wrong. You often end up saying precisely the wrong thing and insult someone unintentionally. Most of the time, you just keep mum.

This makes you a listener instead—a careful observer. It also means that you're better at doing things than talking about them. You're quick to take action.

You gain the following characteristics:

Actions, Not Words: +2 to your Might Pool, and +2 to your Speed Pool.

Skill: You are trained in perception.

Skill: You are trained in initiative (unless it's a social situation).

Inability: The difficulty of all tasks relating to social interaction is increased by one step.

Inability: The difficulty of all tasks involving verbal communication or relaying information is increased by one step.

Initial Link to the Starting Adventure: From the following list of options, choose how you became involved in the first adventure.

1. You just tagged along and no one told you to leave.

2. You saw something important the other PCs did not and (with some effort) managed to relate it to them.

3. You intervened to save one of the other PCs when he was in danger.

4. One of the other PCs recruited you for your talents.

TOUGH

You're strong and can take a lot of physical punishment. You might have a large frame and a square jaw. Tough characters frequently have visible scars.

You gain the following characteristics:

Resilient: +1 to Armor.

Healthy: Add 1 to the points you regain when you make a recovery roll.

Skill: You're trained in Might defense actions.

Additional Equipment: You have an extra light weapon.

Initial Link to the Starting Adventure: From the following list of options, choose how you became involved in the first adventure.

1. You're acting as a bodyguard for one of the other PCs.

2. One of the PCs is your sibling, and you came along to watch out for her.

3. You need money because your family is in debt.

4. You stepped in to defend one of the PCs when that character was threatened. While talking to him afterward, you heard about the group's task.

VENGEFUL

One moment changed everything for you. One dreadful encounter, one betrayal, or one horrific tragedy altered your course and made you who you are today. Looking back at that time, you often wonder how your life would have unfolded if not for the event that ruined everything. The life you imagine you should have had haunts you and feeds your appetite for revenge until vengeance is the only thing you have left.

To be vengeful, you must have someone or something you want revenge against and someone or something to avenge. Work with your GM to determine what happened that affected you so strongly. Maybe a group of bandits wiped out your family. A corrupt official stole your family's savings or otherwise brought ruin to you and your loved ones. Perhaps a rival destroyed your romance by sullying your name. Death, finances, love: any of these can support your motivation.

In addition, consider to what extent your character will go to gain vengeance. Will you compromise your values to destroy the ones who wronged you? Will you sacrifice your companions to get what you want? Can you imagine a life after you get revenge, or will you throw yours away to punish the people who wronged you?

You gain the following characteristics:

Skill: The fires of your hatred make you an imposing figure. You're trained in any task that involves intimidation, threats, or inflicting pain through torture.

Skill: You will follow your enemies to the ends of the earth. You're trained in any task that involves finding and following tracks.

Skill: You're trained in Speed defense actions.

Additional Equipment: You have an additional medium weapon.

Initial Link to the Starting Adventure: From the following list of options, choose how you became involved in the first adventure.

1. You and the other PCs are headed in the same direction.

2. You believe that one of the PCs knows something about your enemy. You accompany the group to find out what that character knows.

3. One of the PCs survived the event that caused you to become vengeful. You travel with that character to protect him or her.

4. You drew everyone together to help you get revenge on your enemies.

VIRTUOUS

Doing the right thing is a way of life. You live by a code, and that code is something you attend to every day. Whenever you slip, you reproach yourself for your weakness and then get right back on track. Your code probably includes moderation, respect for others, cleanliness, and other characteristics that most people would agree are virtues, while you eschew their opposites: sloth, greed, gluttony, and so on.

You gain the following characteristics:

Dauntless: +2 to your Might Pool.

Skill: You are trained in discerning people's true motives or seeing through lies.

Skill: Your adherence to a strict moral code has hardened your mind against fear, doubt, and outside influence. You are trained in Intellect defense tasks.

Initial Link to the Starting Adventure: From the following list of options, choose how you became involved in the first adventure.

1. The PCs are doing something virtuous, and you're all about that.
2. The PCs are on the road to perdition, and you see it as your task to set them on the proper moral route.
3. One of the other PCs invited you, hearing of your virtuous ways.
4. You put virtue before sense and defended someone's honor in the face of an organization or power far greater than you. You joined the PCs because they offered aid and friendship when, out of fear of reprisals, no one else would.

WEALTHY

You can't remember a time when you wanted for anything. You have always had money and have largely lived a life of comfort and plenty. You might be stingy with your wealth, hiding your abundance lest others try to steal it from you. Or you might be magnanimous, spreading it around to any and all who need it.

The source of your funds is up to you. Maybe you inherited your vast fortune from a relative. A sudden windfall could have made you flush with funds and given you a life you never dreamed of. You might be a successful merchant or entrepreneur, making your fortune through hard work and determination.

You gain the following characteristics:

Connected: You have connections, resources, and a head for business. Whenever you spend at least an hour in a community with a population of 1,000 or more, you can find comfortable accommodations for you and your companions for as long as you stay there. The accommodations also provide you with food and whatever inexpensive or moderately priced items you need.

Additional Starting Equipment: You start with an additional expensive item, and all your starting possessions are of very fine quality.

Money Is No Object: You can buy whatever inexpensive items you need wherever they are available.

Initial Link to the Starting Adventure: From the following list of options, choose how you became involved in the first adventure.

1. You crave a life of adventure. You hired all the other PCs for your expedition.
2. Having wealth only creates an appetite for more. You join the other PCs to grow your fortunes.
3. You want to do good works with your wealth, and you see the PCs' mission as an opportunity to help people.
4. The source of your wealth—a relative, a business, or your position in the community—controls your life, and you have begun to feel stifled. You disguise your true identity and accompany the PCs for a chance at the freedom your fortune denies you.

WEIRD

You aren't like anyone else, and that's fine with you. People don't seem to understand you—they even seem put off by you—but who cares? You understand the world better than they do because you're weird, and so is the world you live in. The concept of "the weird" is well known to you. Strange devices, ancient locales, bizarre creatures, storms that can transform you, living energy fields, conspiracies, aliens, and things most people can't even name populate the world, and you thrive on them. You have a special attachment to it all, and the more you discover about the weirdness in the world, the more you might discover about yourself.

Weird characters might be mutants or people born with strange qualities, but sometimes they started out "normal" and adopted the weird by choice.

You gain the following characteristics:

Inner Light: +2 to your Intellect Pool.

Distinctive Physical Quirk: You have a unique physical aspect that is, well, bizarre. Depending on the setting, this can vary greatly. You might have purple hair or metal spikes on your head. Maybe you have nothing but a massive scar where your nose used to be, or you were born without a nose. Perhaps your hands don't connect to your arms, although they move as if they do. Maybe a third eye stares out from the side of your head, or superfluous tendrils grow from your back. Whatever it is, your quirk might be a mutation, a supernatural trait (a blessing or curse), or a feature with no explanation.

A Sense for the Weird: Sometimes—at the GM's discretion—weird things relating to the supernatural or its effects on the world seem to call out to you. You can sense them from afar, and if you get within long range of such a thing, you can sense whether it is overtly dangerous or not.

Skill: You are trained in supernatural knowledge.

Inability: People find you unnerving. The difficulty of all tasks relating to pleasant social interaction is increased by one step.

Initial Link to the Starting Adventure: From the following list of options, choose how you became involved in the first adventure.

1. It seemed weird, so why not?
2. Whether the other PCs realize it or not, their mission has to do with something weird that you know about, so you got involved.
3. As an expert in the weird, you were specifically recruited by the other PCs.
4. You felt drawn to join the other PCs, but you don't know why.

RACE AS DESCRIPTOR

Sometimes, in settings that have alien races or fantasy races, players want to play a member of that race rather than the default (which is usually "human"). Most of the time, this choice is one of flavor rather than game mechanics. If you're a 7-foot-tall furry Rigellian with three eyes, that's great, but it doesn't change your stats or skills (though it may have roleplaying challenges). However, sometimes being a nonhuman results in more substantive changes. A PC ogre in a fantasy setting might have the Strong or Tough descriptor, or perhaps it has a descriptor simply called Ogre, which is similar but more pronounced (with greater Might but even greater drawbacks). This would mean that instead of being a Tough warrior who Controls Beasts, the character is an Ogre warrior who Controls Beasts.

The genre chapters in part 3 offer a few racial descriptors, but many GMs will want to create their own as suits their setting. It can't be stressed enough, however, that nine times out of ten, in most genres, racial differences aren't significant enough to warrant this treatment. The differences between a Mysterious character and a Vengeful one are probably greater than those between an Alpha Centauran and an Earthling.

Chapter 7

CHARACTER FOCUS

Focus is what makes your character unique. No two PCs in a group should have the same focus. Your focus gives you benefits when you create your character and each time you ascend to the next tier. It's the verb of the sentence "I am an *adjective noun* who *verbs*."

When you choose a character focus, you get a special connection to one or more of your fellow PCs, a first-tier ability, and perhaps additional starting equipment. A few foci offer slight alterations of other special abilities the character wields, so that the character overall meshes together into a thematic whole. Each focus also offers suggestions to the GM and the player for possible effects or consequences of really good or really bad die rolls.

As you progress to a new tier, your focus grants you more abilities. Each tier's benefit is usually labeled Action or Enabler. If an ability is labeled Action, you must take an action to use it. If an ability is labeled Enabler, it makes other actions better or gives some other benefit, but it's not an action. An ability that allows you to blast foes with lasers is an action. An ability that grants you additional damage when you make attacks is an enabler. You can use an enabler in the same turn as you perform another action.

Each tier's benefits are independent of and cumulative with benefits from other tiers (unless indicated otherwise). So if your first-tier ability grants you +1 to Armor and your fourth-tier ability also grants you +1 to Armor, when you reach fourth tier, you have a total of +2 to Armor.

Not all foci are appropriate for every genre. Obviously, the GM can include whatever foci seem most appropriate for her setting.

CHOOSING FOCI

Not all foci are appropriate for every genre. The genre chapters in part 3 provide guidance, but this section offers some broad generalizations. Obviously, the GM can include whatever foci are available in her setting. Foci end up being an important distinction in this case, because Commands Mental Powers, for example, makes it clear that psychic abilities exist in the setting, just as Howls at the Moon implies the existence of lycanthropes like werewolves, and Pilots Starcraft, of course, requires starships available to pilot.

See the lists on pages 92-93 for suggestions.

CUSTOMIZING FOCI

Sometimes, not everything about a focus is right for your character concept, or perhaps you need some guidelines for creating a brand new focus. Either way, the solution lies in looking at foci abilities at their most basic, default levels.

At any tier, a player can select one of the following abilities in place of the ability granted by the tier. Many of these replacement abilities, particularly at the higher tiers, might involve body modification, integration with high-tech devices, learning powerful magic spells, uncovering forbidden secrets, or something similar (appropriate to the genre).

TIER 1

Self-Improvement: You gain 6 new points to divide among your stat Pools however you wish. Enabler.

Bringing the Pain: You deal 1 additional point of damage with every attack you make. Enabler.

More Training: You gain an additional skill of your choice (not attacks or defense) in which you are not already trained. Enabler.

TIER 2

Lower-Tier Ability: Choose any tier 1 ability, above.

Part 3: Genres, page 235

Commands Mental Powers, page 107

Howls at the Moon, page 134

Pilots Starcraft, page 156

FOCI IN DIFFERENT GENRES

FANTASY

Abides in Stone
Awakens Dreams
Bears a Halo of Fire
Blazes With Radiance
Builds Robots
Carries a Quiver
Casts Spells
Channels Divine Blessings
Commands Mental Powers
Consorts With the Dead
Controls Beasts
Crafts Illusions
Crafts Unique Objects
Defends the Weak
Entertains
Exists in Two Places at Once
Exists Partially Out of Phase
Explores Dark Places
Fights Dirty
Fights With Panache
Focuses Mind Over Matter
Howls at the Moon
Hunts Nonhumans
Hunts Outcasts
Hunts With Great Skill
Infiltrates
Leads
Lives in the Wilderness
Looks for Trouble
Masters Defense
Masters the Swarm
Masters Weaponry
Metes Out Justice
Moves Like a Cat
Murders
Needs No Weapon
Never Says Die
Performs Feats of Strength
Rides the Lightning
Sees Beyond
Separates Mind From Body
Shepherds Spirits
Siphons Power
Slays Monsters
Speaks for the Land
Stands Like a Bastion
Throws With Deadly Accuracy
Travels Through Time
Wears a Sheen of Ice
Wields Two Weapons at Once
Works Miracles
Works the Back Alleys

MODERN/HORROR

Calculates the Incalculable
Commands Mental Powers*
Conducts Weird Science
Consorts With the Dead*
Crafts Unique Objects
Doesn't Do Much
Entertains
Explores Dark Places
Fights Dirty
Focuses Mind Over Matter*
Howls at the Moon*
Hunts Outcasts*
Hunts With Great Skill
Infiltrates
Interprets the Law
Is Idolized by Millions
Is Licensed to Carry
Leads
Lives in the Wilderness
Looks for Trouble
Masters the Swarm*
Masters Weaponry
Moves Like a Cat
Murders
Needs No Weapon
Never Says Die
Operates Undercover
Sees Beyond*
Separates Mind From Body*
Slays Monsters*
Solves Mysteries
Throws With Deadly Accuracy
Wields Two Weapons at Once
Works the Back Alleys
Works the System
Would Rather Be Reading

** Only if the setting has a supernatural element*

SCIENCE FICTION

Battles Robots
Builds Robots
Calculates the Incalculable
Commands Mental Powers
Conducts Weird Science
Doesn't Do Much
Entertains
Fights Dirty
Fights With Panache
Focuses Mind Over Matter
Fuses Flesh and Steel
Fuses Mind and Machine
Hunts Nonhumans
Infiltrates
Interprets the Law
Is Idolized by Millions
Looks for Trouble
Masters Defense
Masters Weaponry
Moves Like a Cat
Murders
Needs No Weapon
Never Says Die
Operates Undercover
Pilots Starcraft
Siphons Power
Solves Mysteries
Talks to Machines
Travels Through Time
Works the Back Alleys
Works the System
Would Rather Be Reading

Offensive Combat Training: Choose one type of attack in which you are not already trained: light bashing, light bladed, light ranged, medium bashing, medium bladed, medium ranged, heavy bashing, heavy bladed, or heavy ranged. You are trained in attacks using that type of weapon. Enabler.

Defensive Combat Training: Choose one type of defense task in which you are not already trained: Might, Speed, or Intellect. You are trained in defense tasks of that type. Enabler.

TIER 3

Lower-Tier Ability: Choose any tier 1 or 2 ability, above.

Incredible Health: Thanks to a dip in a magical pool, an injection of artificial antibodies and immune defense nanobots into your bloodstream, exposure to strange radiation, or something else, you are now immune to diseases, viruses, and mutations of any kind. Enabler.

Fusion Armor: A procedure gives you biometal implants in major portions of your body, you grow metal-hard skin, the blessings of an angel protect you, or something similar happens. These changes give you +1 to Armor even when you're not wearing physical armor. Enabler.

TIER 4

Lower-Tier Ability: Choose any tier 1, 2, or 3 ability, above.

Poison Resistance: Thanks to an injection of biological agents, a quaff of a magical elixir, a ring from a dying alien, or something just as extreme, you are now immune to poisons, toxins, or any kind of particulate threat. You are not immune to viruses, bacteria, or radiation. Enabler.

Built-in Weaponry: Biomechanical implants, a magical jewel fused to your forehead, or something just as wild now provides you with inherent weaponry. This allows you to fire a blast of energy that inflicts 5 points of damage with a range of 200 feet (61 m). There is no cost for you to use this ability. Action.

TIER 5

Lower-Tier Ability: Choose any tier 1, 2, 3, or 4 ability, above.

Adaptation: Thanks to a latent mutation, a device implanted in your spine, a ritual performed with dragon's blood, or some other gift, you now remain at a comfortable temperature; never need to worry about dangerous radiation, diseases, or gases; and always can breathe in any environment (even the vacuum of space). Enabler.

Defensive Field: Thanks to subdermal implants, a permanent spell, alien modifications, or something similar, you now have a force field that radiates 1 inch (3 cm) from your body and provides you with +2 to Armor. Enabler.

SUPERHEROES

Abides in Stone
Bears a Halo of Fire
Blazes With Radiance
Carries a Quiver
Commands Mental Powers
Controls Gravity
Crafts Illusions
Defends the Weak
Employs Magnetism
Exists in Two Places at Once
Exists Partially Out of Phase
Explores Deep Waters
Fights With Panache
Focuses Mind Over Matter
Fuses Flesh and Steel
Fuses Mind and Machine
Grows to Towering Heights
Howls at the Moon
Infiltrates
Leads
Looks for Trouble
Masters Defense
Masters Weaponry
Metes Out Justice
Moves Like a Cat
Moves Like the Wind
Needs No Weapon
Never Says Die
Operates Undercover
Performs Feats of Strength
Rages
Rides the Lightning
Siphons Power
Solves Mysteries
Stands Like a Bastion
Talks to Machines
Throws With Deadly Accuracy
Travels Through Time
Wears a Sheen of Ice

TIER 6

Lower-Tier Ability: Choose any tier 1, 2, 3, 4, or 5 ability, above.

Reactive Field: Thanks to a remarkable enhancement of science, magic, psionics, or something even stranger, you now have a force field that radiates 1 inch (3 cm) from your body and provides you with +2 to Armor. In addition, if struck by a melee attack, the field creates a backlash that inflicts 4 points of electricity damage to the attacker. Enabler.

FOCI

ABIDES IN STONE

Abides in Stone GM Intrusions: *Creatures of stone sometimes forget their own strength or weight. A walking statue can terrify common folk.*

You are a golem: a being of stone rather than flesh. Your stone body resembles that of a hulking humanoid, and you can move, speak, and feel pain. Your rock body means that it takes a lot to damage you, but once damaged, your wounds are not quite as easy to recover from.

As someone made of animate stone, you typically do not wear clothing, although your stone skin is usually carved to appear as if you're wearing it. Such carved clothing could be elaborate armor, robes, or stylistic ridges and ripples.

Connection: Choose one of the following.

1. Pick one other PC. She roused you from a long period of inactivity, and you feel indebted to her for returning you (perhaps accidentally) to mobility.
2. Pick one other PC. You were once convinced that he wanted to reduce you to rubble, but you have since grown to think that what you believed wasn't true, or at least no longer is so.
3. Pick one other PC. She knows the secret of your origin, but whenever she speaks of it, you forget it. Perhaps you suffer from a curse?
4. Pick one other PC. If you go berserk, you'll never attack that character.

Minor Effect Suggestion: You step on the target, and your immense weight prevents it from moving on its next turn.

Major Effect Suggestion: You break a weapon, shield, or piece of armor the target is using.

Tier 1: Golem Body. You gain +1 to Armor, +1 to your Might Edge, and 5 additional points to your Might Pool. You do not need to eat, drink, or breathe (though you do need rest and sleep). You move more stiffly than a creature of flesh, which means you can never be trained or specialized in Speed defense rolls.

Furthermore, you are practiced in using your stone fists as a medium weapon. Enabler.

Golem Healing. Your stone form is more difficult to repair than flesh, which means you are unable to use the first, single-action recovery roll of the day that other PCs have access to. Thus, your first recovery roll on any given day requires ten minutes of rest, the second requires an hour of rest, and the third requires ten hours. Enabler.

Tier 2: Golem Grip (3 Might points). Your attack with your stone fists is modified by one step in your favor. If you hit, you can grab the target, preventing it from moving on its next turn. While you hold the target, its attacks or attempts to break free are modified by one step to its detriment. If the target attempts to break free instead of attacking, you must make a Might-based roll to maintain your grip. If the target fails to break free, you can continue to hold it each round as your subsequent actions, automatically inflicting 4 points of damage each round by squeezing. Enabler.

Tier 3: Trained Basher. You are trained in using your stone fists as medium weapons. Enabler.

Golem Stomp (4 Might points). You stomp on the ground with all of your strength, creating a shock wave that attacks all creatures in immediate range. Affected creatures take 3 points of damage and are either pushed out of immediate range or fall down (your choice). Action.

Tier 4: Deep Reserves. Once each day, you can transfer up to 5 points among your Pools in any combination, at a rate of 1 point per round. For example, you could transfer 3 points of Might to Speed and 2 points of Intellect to Speed, which would take a total of five rounds. Action.

Tier 5. Specialized Basher. You are specialized in using your stone fists as medium weapons. Enabler.

Still As a Statue (5 Might points). You freeze in place, drawing your essence deep into your stone core. During this time, you lose all mobility as well as the ability to take physical actions. You cannot sense what's happening around you, and no time seems to pass for you. While Still As a Statue, you gain +10 to Armor against damage of all sorts. Under normal circumstances, you automatically rouse to normal wakefulness and mobility a day later. If an ally you trust shakes you hard enough (with a minimum cost of 2 Might points), you rouse earlier. Action to initiate.

Tier 6: Ultra Enhancement. You gain +1 to Armor and 5 additional points to each of your three stat Pools. Enabler.

AWAKENS DREAMS

Your dreams are more vivid than other people's. When you dream, those dreams linger on, and when the time is right, you can loose them into reality to impress, confuse, or scare other creatures. You've learned the oneiromancer's craft, which means that you know the secrets of lucid dreaming, gauging the dream state in others, and mixing herbal elixirs that bring about a restful, dream-filled sleep.

Your clothing probably reflects the eclectic dreamland where you spend so much of your time, including several layers, bright silk ribbons, and odd symbols that made sense when you were dreaming them.

Connection: Choose one of the following.

1. Pick one other PC. That character always recognizes your dreams as illusions free of substance and is not fooled or affected by them.
2. Pick one other PC. You accidentally sent that character into a sleep so deep she didn't wake for three days. Whether she forgives you or not is up to her.
3. Pick one other PC. You are certain that you created him from one of your dreams, even if he doesn't believe it.
4. Pick one other PC. You accidentally glimpsed that character's dreams and learned something that she was trying to keep a secret.

Minor Effect Suggestion: The target gets turned around, and its next attack is modified by one step to its detriment.

Major Effect Suggestion: You are refreshed by your dream and recover 4 points to one of your Pools.

Tier 1: Dreamcraft (1 Intellect point). You pull an image from a dream into the waking world and place it somewhere within long range. The dream lasts for up to one minute, and it can be tiny or fill an area an immediate distance in diameter. Though it appears solid, the dream is intangible. The dream (a scene, a creature, or an object) is static unless you spend your action each round animating it. As part of that animation, you could move the dream up to a short distance each round, as long as it remains within long range. If you animate the dream, it can make sound but does not produce odor. Direct

Awakens Dreams GM Intrusions: *A stray dream breaks free and comes after you. You begin sleepwalking. Your dream double tries to replace you. Allies have bad dreams after you use certain abilities.*

physical interaction or sustained interaction with the dream shatters it into dispersing mist. For example, attacking the dream shatters it, as does the strain of keeping up appearances when an NPC moves through a dream scene or engages a dream creature in conversation for more than a couple of rounds. Action to initiate; action to animate.

Oneirochemy. You are trained in tasks related to sleep and mixing natural elixirs to help creatures fall asleep. Enabler.

Tier 2: Dream Thief (2 Intellect points). You steal a previous dream from a living creature within short range. The creature loses 2 points of Intellect (ignores Armor), and you learn something the GM chooses to reveal about the creature—its nature, a portion of its plans, a memory, and so on. Action.

Nightmare: *level 5; health 15; inflicts 5 points of damage*

Tier 3: Dream Becomes Reality (4 Intellect points). You create a dream object of any shape you can imagine that is your size or smaller, which takes on apparent substance and heft. The object is crude and can have no moving parts, so you can make a sword, a shield, a short ladder, and so on. The dream object has the approximate mass of the real object, if you choose. Your dream objects are as strong as iron, but if you do not remain within long range of them, they function for only one minute before fading away. Action.

Consummate Dreamer. You add 2 points to your Intellect Pool. Enabler.

Tier 4: Daydream (4 Intellect points). You pull someone into a daydream, substituting a dream of your own creation for the target's reality for up to one minute. You can affect a target within long range that you can see, or a target within 10 miles (16 km) that you have hair or skin clippings from. To all outward appearances, an affected target stands (or lies) unmoving. But inside, the substituted reality (or dream within a dream, if the target was sleeping) is what the target experiences. If the target is under duress, it can attempt another Intellect defense roll each round to break free, though the target may not realize its state. Either the dream unfolds according to a script you prepared when you used this ability, or if you spend your own actions (forcing you into a similar state as the target), you can direct the unfolding dream from round to round. Using this ability on a sleeping target decreases the difficulty of your initial attack by one step. Action to initiate; if you direct the dream, action to direct per round.

Tier 5: Nightmare (5 Intellect points). You pull a horrifying creature from your worst nightmare into the waking world and sic it on your foes. The nightmare persists each round while you spend your action concentrating on it (or until you disperse it or it is destroyed). It has one of the following abilities, which you choose when you call it.

Horrify. Instead of making a normal attack, the nightmare's attack horrifies the target, dropping the target to its knees (or similar appendages). The target takes 3 points of damage that ignore Armor and is dazed for one round, during which time the difficulty of all its tasks is modified by one step to its detriment.

Confusion. Instead of making a normal attack, the nightmare's attack confuses the target for one round. On its next action, the target attacks an ally.

Pustule Eruption. Instead of making a normal attack, the nightmare's attack causes rancid, painful pustules to rise all over the target's skin for one minute. If the target takes a forceful action (such as attacking another creature or moving farther than an immediate distance), the pustules burst, dealing 5 points of damage that ignore Armor.

Tier 6. Chamber of Dreams (8+ Intellect points). You and your allies can step into a chamber of dreams, decorated as you wish, that contains a number of doors. The doors correspond with other locations that you have visited or know reasonably well. Stepping through one of the doors delivers you to the desired location. This is a difficulty 2 Intellect-based task (which could be modified upward by the GM if the location is warded). Action to step into chamber of dreams; action to move through a door in the chamber.

BATTLES ROBOTS

Life is for the living—the biological. Automatons, robots, animate machines, thinking machines, and anything similar are abominations. You excel at battling these anathemas, cleansing the world of their contaminating presence.

Maybe your desire to battle automatons comes from religious zealotry. Maybe it's steeped in revenge for some past crime committed by a machine. Maybe you don't know why you're driven to destroy animate machines. Maybe you're just good at it.

You probably bear the trophies of former "kills" on you, wearing bits of circuitry or servos on your belt or around your neck. You also likely use heavy weaponry, ideal for penetrating armor. While sometimes a big, heavy weapon is useful against these foes, those who are quick and nimble, able to leap in and cut a few vital wires here or slice through a component panel there, also excel as robot hunters.

Connection: Choose one of the following.

1. Pick one other PC. You suspect that this character is put off by your hatred of animate machines. You can choose whether or not she knows of your suspicions.
2. Pick one other PC. You know that this character has suffered at the hands of automatons in the past, and perhaps you can convince him to help you in your calling. Regardless, you feel protective of him.
3. Pick one other PC. This character does not appear to share your feelings about automatons. In fact, you believe that she might secretly have machine parts herself.
4. Pick one other PC. This character comes from the same place you do, and you knew each other as children.

Additional Equipment: You have bits and pieces that you tore from the husks of automatons you have destroyed in the past.

Anti-Machine Abilities: If you wield special abilities (like spells, psionics, and so on) that inflict damage, they inflict 1 additional point of damage to robots and similar beings, and 1 less point of damage to biological, living targets. If you have abilities that normally would not work against robots (like mind control), they will now.

Minor Effect Suggestion: Your robot foe experiences an error for one round, during which time the difficulty of all its tasks is modified by one step to its detriment.

Major Effect Suggestion: Your robot foe experiences a major error and loses its next turn.

Tier 1: Machine Vulnerabilities. You inflict 3 additional points of damage against robots and animate machines of all kinds. Enabler.

Machine Knowledge. You are trained in robotics and computers. Enabler.

Tier 2: Defense Against Robots. You have studied your enemy and can anticipate the actions that an automaton or machine is likely to take in a fight. The difficulty of all defense tasks against such foes is decreased by one step. Enabler.

Machine Hunting. The difficulty of tracking, spotting, or otherwise finding automatons and animate machines is decreased by one step. You are also trained in all stealth tasks. Enabler.

Tier 3: Disable Mechanisms (3 Speed points). With a keen eye and quick moves, you disrupt some of an automaton's functions and inflict upon it one of the following maladies:

- The difficulty of all tasks is increased by one step for one minute.
- The robot's speed is halved.
- The robot can take no action for one round.
- The robot deals 2 fewer points of damage (minimum 1 point) for one minute.

You must touch the robot to disrupt it (if you are making an attack, it inflicts no normal damage). Action.

Tier 4: Machine Fighter. You are trained in all attacks against robots or similar animate machines. Enabler.

Pierce Metal Hides. You ignore 2 points of Armor on a robot. Enabler.

Tier 5: Drain Power (5 Speed points). You affect the main power source of the robot, inflicting upon it all four conditions listed for Disable Mechanisms at once. You must touch the robot to do this (if you are making an attack, it inflicts no normal damage). Action.

Battles Robots GM Intrusions: *Not all robots should be destroyed. Some might explode when defeated. Eventually, organized thinking machines will seek out and try to kill someone who seeks to destroy them.*

Tier 6: Blind Machine (6 Speed points). You deactivate the sensory apparatus of the robot, making it effectively blind. You must either touch the target or strike it with a ranged attack (inflicting no normal damage). Action.

BEARS A HALO OF FIRE

Bears a Halo of Fire GM Intrusions: *Fire burns flammable material. Fire spreads, perhaps beyond the control of the one who started it. Primitive creatures fear fire and often attack what they fear.*

You can create a sheath of flames around your body. You leave scorch marks wherever you go, and you can't handle combustible objects without first dousing your inherent flames. If you have other extraordinary abilities, all your effects are tainted with flame. Fiery visuals accompany your powers, and in some cases, your predilection for flame actually reshapes your abilities to take on a fiery nature where none existed before.

You probably wear red and yellow, or perhaps black.

Connection: Choose one of the following.

1. Pick one other PC. Through a quirk of fate, your fire cannot harm that character.
2. Pick one other PC. You recently discovered that if she stands near you when you use your Shroud of Flame ability, she too becomes covered in flames. This doesn't harm her, and anyone who tries to touch her or strike her with a melee attack suffers 1 point of damage. She must remain within short range of you.
3. Pick one other PC. He had a devastating experience with fire in his past and must decide how to react to your constant use of flame around him.
4. Pick one other PC. For some reason, one of his limbs is especially vulnerable to your flames. Occasionally when you use Hurl Flame to harm a foe, his vulnerable body part bursts into flame. The flame doesn't harm him or his equipment, but it can be an impediment during combat due to surprise.

Additional Equipment: You have an artifact—a device that sprays inanimate objects to make them fire-resistant. All your starting gear has already been treated unless you don't want it to be.

Fire Abilities: If you perform special abilities, those that would normally use force or other energy (such as electricity) instead use fire. For example, force blasts are blasts of flame. These alterations change nothing except the type of damage and the fact that it might start fires. As another example, a wall of energy instead creates a wall of roaring flames. In this case, the alteration changes the ability so that the barrier is not solid but instead inflicts 1 point of damage to anything that touches it and 4 points of damage to anyone who passes through it.

Bears a Halo of Fire is perfect for a superhero setting, but in a fantasy one, the same focus could just as easily represent a fire mage.

Minor Effect Suggestion: The target or something near the target catches fire.

Major Effect Suggestion: An important item on the target's person is destroyed.

Tier 1: Shroud of Flame (1 Intellect point). At your command, your entire body becomes shrouded in flames that last up to ten minutes. The fire doesn't burn you, but it automatically inflicts 2 points of damage to anyone who tries to touch you or strike you with a melee attack. Flames from another source can still hurt you. While the shroud is active, you gain +2 to Armor only against damage from fire from another source. Enabler.

Tier 2: Hurl Flame (2 Intellect points). While your Shroud of Flame is active, you can reach into your halo and hurl a handful of fire at a target. This is a short-range attack that deals 4 points of fire damage. Action.

Tier 3: Fiery Hand of Doom (3 Intellect points). While your Shroud of Flame is active, you can reach into your halo and produce a hand made of animate flame that is twice the size of a human hand. The hand acts as you direct, floating in the air. Directing the hand is an action. Without a command, the hand does nothing. It can move a long distance in a round, but it never moves farther away from you than long range. The hand can grab, move, and carry things, but anything it touches takes 1 point of damage per round from the heat. The hand can also attack. It's a level 3 creature and deals 1 extra point of damage from fire when it attacks. Once created, the hand lasts for ten minutes. Action to create; action to direct.

Tier 4: Flameblade (4 Intellect points). When you wish it, you extend your halo of fire to cover a weapon you wield in flame for one hour. The flame ends if you stop holding or carrying the weapon. While the flame lasts, the weapon inflicts 2 additional points of damage. Enabler.

Tier 5: Fire Tendrils (5 Intellect points). When you wish it, your halo sprouts three tendrils of flame that last for up to ten minutes. As an action, you can use the tendrils to attack, making a separate attack roll for each. Each tendril inflicts 4 points of damage. Otherwise, the attacks function as standard attacks. If you don't use the tendrils to attack, they remain but do nothing. Enabler.

Tier 6: Fire Servant (6 Intellect points). You reach into your halo and produce an automaton of fire that is your general shape and size. It acts as you direct each round. Directing the servant is an action, and you can command it only when you are within long range of it. Without a command, the servant continues to follow your previous command. You can also give it a simple programmed action, such as "Wait here, and attack anyone who comes within short range until they're dead." The servant lasts for ten minutes, is a level 5 creature, and deals 1 extra point of damage from fire when it attacks. Action to create; action to direct.

BLAZES WITH RADIANCE

You have the ability to create and sculpt light, to bend it away from you or gather it to use as a weapon. You might gain your powers from the sun, or you might wield a mysterious artifact that produces light that you can manipulate. Regardless, you love the light and curse the darkness. People are often drawn to those wielding the light, either because they are heartened by it (as opposed to someone lurking in darkness) or because it is dramatic and impressive. Of course, those who enjoy the darkness or fear the light despise you.

Most people able to command light favor bright colors in their clothing since those colors reflect light rather than absorb it.

Connection: Choose one of the following.

1. Pick one other PC. You have a strong emotional connection to this character, and when in his presence, you can change the color of the light you create.

2. Pick one other PC. She is especially sensitive to your light, and occasionally your flashes leave her dazzled, increasing the difficulty of her defense actions by one step.

3. Pick one other PC. Something about his nature dampens the light. When he stands immediately next to you, your light-based powers cost 1 additional Intellect point.

4. Pick one other PC. This character appears to have a treasured item that was once yours, but that you lost in a game of chance years ago.

Additional Equipment: You have a crystal lens. When you shine light through it, the light extends for double the normal distance.

Radiant Abilities: If you possess powers that would normally use force or other energy, they instead use light and heat. For example, if you use Ward, light dapples your body and flares when you would be attacked, preventing your enemies from landing a solid blow.

Ward, page 32

Minor Effect Suggestion: A flash of light leaves the creature dazzled. The difficulty of defense actions to resist the creature's attacks decreases by one step.

Major Effect Suggestion: An intense flash of light leaves the creature blinded for one minute.

Blazes With Radiance GM Intrusion: *Sudden bright light can leave others dazzled or even blinded when you don't intend them to be.*

Tier 1: Enlightened. You are trained in any perception task that involves sight. Enabler.

Illuminating Touch (1 Intellect point). You touch an object, and that object sheds light to illuminate everything in short range. The light remains until you use an action to touch the object again. Action.

Tier 2: Dazzling Radiance (2 Intellect points). As an Intellect action, you send a barrage of dazzling colors at a creature within short range, dealing 2 points of damage. In addition, until the end of the next round, the difficulty of all defense actions to resist the creature's attacks is reduced by one step. The difficulty is not reduced if the creature relies on senses other than sight to "see." Action.

Tier 3: Burning Light (3 Intellect points). As an Intellect action, you send a beam of light at a creature within long range and tighten the beam until it burns, dealing 5 points of damage. Action.

Tier 4: Sunlight (3 Intellect points). A mote of light travels from you to a spot you choose within 100 feet (30 m). When the mote reaches that spot, it flares and casts bright light in a 200-foot (61 m) radius, and darkness within 1,000 feet (305 m) of the mote becomes dim light. The light lasts for one hour or until you use an action to dismiss it. Action.

Tier 5: Disappear (4 Intellect points). You bend light that falls on you so you seem to disappear. You are invisible to other creatures for ten minutes. While invisible, you are specialized in stealth and Speed defense tasks. This effect ends if you do something to reveal your presence or position—attacking, using an ability, moving a large object, and so on. If this occurs, you can regain the remaining invisibility effect by taking an action to focus on hiding your position. Action to initiate or reinitiate.

Tier 6: Living Light (5 Intellect points). Your body dissolves into a cloud of photons that instantly travels to a location you choose and then reforms. You can choose any open space big enough to contain you that you can see within long range. When you reform, it takes until the end of the round for your body to become fully solid, so until the start of the next round, you take half damage (minimum 1 point) from all physical sources. Action.

Builds Robots GM Intrusions: *A robot can be hacked. A robot gains a mind of its own. A robot struck in combat unexpectedly detonates. A robot becomes jealous of your living allies.*

The word "robot" is used globally in this focus, though the robot you create might look very different from one created by someone else, depending on the genre. Steampunk robots, organic robots, or even magical golems are all feasible "robots."

Robot assistant: *level 2; health 6; inflicts 2 points of damage*

BUILDS ROBOTS

Your brilliance is mechanically focused, and it allows you to create artificial entities who accept you for who you are. As an added bonus, they do what you command without complaint. You're not entirely sure you've arrived at nirvana by surrounding yourself with artificial beings, but it'll do for now.

Because your robots don't have an opinion, you're not too concerned with your appearance. You tend to throw the same shop coat over whatever you happen to be wearing beneath.

Connection: Choose one of the following.

1. Pick one other PC. Your robotic artificial assistant will take commands from that character as well as from you.
2. Pick one other PC. You created a robot companion for that character, but it promptly tried to kill her, so it had to be destroyed. You're not sure what went wrong.
3. Pick one other PC. You are certain that character is secretly an artificial entity, even if he denies it.
4. Pick one other PC. You created a robotic catlike entity (a level 1 creature) for that character that sometimes shows up but is usually absent pursuing vermin.

Additional Equipment: Robot spare parts, robot tool kit.

Minor Effect Suggestion: The robot jolts your foe, which modifies any action taken by the foe on its next turn by one step to its detriment.

Major Effect Suggestion: Your robot takes an immediate extra action that you choose.

Tier 1: Robot Assistant. A level 2 robot of your size or smaller (built by you) accompanies you and follows your instructions. You and the GM must work out the details of your robot. You'll probably make rolls for your robot when it takes actions. An assistant robot in combat usually doesn't make separate attacks but helps with yours. On your action, if the artificial assistant is next to you, it serves as an asset for one attack you make on your turn. If the robot is destroyed, you can repair the original with a few days' worth of tinkering, or build a new one with a week's worth of half-time labor. Enabler.

Robot Builder. You are trained in tasks related to building and repairing robots. For the purposes of repair, you can use this skill to heal robots that use similar technology. Enabler.

Tier 2: Robot Control (2+ Intellect points). You use your knowledge of robot command and control (and possibly devices that transmit on the proper frequency) to affect any mechanized system or robot of level 2 or lower within short range. You can render several targets inactive for as long as you focus all your attention on them. If you focus on just one target, you can attempt to take active control of it for one minute, commanding it to do simple tasks on your behalf while you concentrate. Instead of applying Effort to decrease the difficulty, you can apply Effort to increase the maximum level of the mechanized system or robot. Thus, to affect a level 4 target (two levels above the normal limit), you must apply two levels of Effort. Action to initiate.

Tier 3: Robot Improvement. Your artificial assistant increases to level 4. Enabler.

Tier 4: Robot Upgrade. You modify your artificial assistant with one new capability. Standard options include the following. Work with your GM if you prefer a different capability.

Flight. The robot can fly a long distance each round. It can carry you, but only for up to an hour between each of your ten-hour recovery rolls. Enabler.

Cypher Pod. The robot can carry one extra cypher for you. Enabler.

Force Shield. The robot can erect an opaque level 5 force field around itself and anyone within 10 feet (3 m) of it for one minute (or until it is destroyed). It cannot do so again until after your next recovery roll. Action.

Mounted Laser Configuration. The robot can reconfigure itself and become an immobile laser weapon on a gimbal mount. In this configuration, the robot is a heavy weapon that deals 7 points of damage. If the robot acts as an autonomous turret, treat it as a level 3 creature instead of level 4. However, if the laser is fired by you or someone else who has your permission, the difficulty of the laser attacks is decreased by one step. Action to reconfigure; action to return to normal robot configuration.

Tier 5: Robot Fleet. You can choose another upgrade from tier 4, or you can take Robot Fleet. If you take Robot Fleet, you build up to four level 2 robot assistants, each no larger than yourself. (They are in addition to the assistant you built at first tier, which has seen a few upgrades since then.) You and the GM must work out the details of these additional robots. If a robot is destroyed, you can build a new one (or repair the old one from its parts) after a week of half-time labor. Enabler.

Tier 6: Robot Evolution. You can choose another upgrade from tier 4, or you can take Robot Evolution. If you take Robot Evolution, your first artificial assistant increases to level 5, and each of your level 2 robots increases to level 3. Enabler.

CALCULATES THE INCALCULABLE

Other people are a little in awe of your mind, though you feel normal enough. Admittedly, you are sometimes surprised when others fail to grasp easy concepts, or how they don't share your appreciation of the beauty in dynamical systems theory, elliptic curve geometry, Riemann meromorphic functions, and all the other wondrous things.

You live a little too much in your head to concern yourself with how you look. Your hair is probably slightly too long and tousled, your clothing is casual and stained with coffee, and your socks don't match.

Connection: Choose one of the following.

1. Pick one other PC. If it wasn't for you, this character never would have passed his college math requirements.

2. Pick one other PC. She seems strangely interested in your mathematical skills. It's up to her whether she is fascinated or disturbed by them.

Healing, page 210

Evolved robot assistant: *level 5; health 15; inflicts 5 points of damage*

Improved robot assistant: *level 4; health 12; inflicts 4 points of damage*

Calculates the Incalculable GM Intrusions: *Your calculation fails to include pertinent data. Predictive Model reveals how to avoid an attack, but it requires that an adjacent ally be affected instead. You get lost in the beauty of the equations for a round and take no actions.*

3. Pick one other PC. Based on a couple of comments you've overheard, you suspect that this character doesn't hold math in the highest regard.

4. Pick one other PC. The character seems to be a variable that never quite solves the same way twice when you include him in an equation, but you haven't the slightest idea why.

Minor Effect Suggestion: You don't have to spend an action observing to make your next predictive equation or predictive model.

Major Effect Suggestion: Intuition flares, and you can ask the GM one question about what you're looking at.

Tier 1: Predictive Equation (2 Intellect points). You observe or study a creature, object, or location for at least one round. The next time you interact with it (possibly in the following round), the difficulty of a related task (such as persuading the creature, attacking it, or defending from its attack) is reduced by one step. Action.

Higher Mathematics. You are trained in standard and higher mathematics.

Carries a Quiver GM Intrusions: *Arrows that miss their target strike unwanted targets. Bowstrings break.*

Tier 2: Predictive Model (2+ Intellect points). If you've used Predictive Equation on a creature, object, or location within the last few days, you can learn one random fact about the subject that is pertinent to a topic you designate. If you also have the magic flavor ability Premonition, one use of either ability grants you two random but related facts about the subject. In addition, you can use Predictive Model on the same subject multiple times (even if you've learned a creature's level), but each time you do, you must apply one additional level of Effort than on your previous use. Action.

Premonition, page 57

Tier 3: Subconscious Defense. Your subconscious constantly runs predictive models for avoiding danger. The difficulty of your Speed defense tasks is reduced by one step. Enabler.

Tier 4: Cognizant Offense. During combat, your brain shifts into a sort of battle mode where all potential attacks you could make are plotted on vector graphs in your mind's eye, which always provides the best option. The difficulty of your attacks is reduced by one step. Enabler.

Tier 5: Genius. The more you use your brain, the better it gets. You add 5 points to your Intellect Pool. Enabler.

Further Mathematics. You are specialized in higher mathematics. If you are already specialized, choose some other sphere of knowledge to become trained in. Enabler.

Tier 6: One Step Ahead of Everyone (6 Intellect points). Few things elude your intellectual grasp. Ask the GM one question and get a general answer. The GM assigns a level to the question, so the more obscure the answer, the more difficult the task. Generally, knowledge that you could find by looking somewhere other than your current location is level 1, and obscure knowledge of the past is level 7. Gaining knowledge of the future is impossible, unless you have the ability to see into the future through other means. Action.

CARRIES A QUIVER

The archer is a skilled combatant, deadly in any fight. With a keen eye and quick reflexes, you can eliminate foes at range before they reach you. A good archer also learns to make his own arrows and bows.

You probably wear no more than light armor so you can move quickly when needed.

You can use this focus with crossbows instead of bows if you wish.

Connection: Choose one of the following.

1. Pick one other PC to be the true friend who gave you the excellent bow that you currently use. Secretly pick a second PC (preferably one who is likely to get in the way of your attacks). When you miss with a bow and the GM rules that you struck someone other than your target, you hit the second character, if possible.

2. Pick one other PC that you've known for a while. The two of you used to do an act where you shot an apple out of her mouth, either for money or just the enjoyment of friends. One time you missed and hit her in the cheek. She may or may not still bear a physical or mental scar from this experience. Either way, you never did your act again.

3. Pick one other PC who is interested in studying archery. He is a quick learner, and if you spend one hour teaching him a few of your secrets, you both gain +1 to any die rolls when you fight the same foe using your bows.

4. Pick one other PC. That person brings up strong emotions in you, whether of anger, desire, or something else. If she is within short range while you're using your bow, you find it difficult to concentrate and shoot straight.

Additional Equipment: You start with a well-made bow and two dozen arrows.

Minor Effect Suggestion: Hit in a tendon or muscle, the target takes 2 points of Speed damage as well as normal damage.

Major Effect Suggestion: The target is pinned in place with an arrow.

Tier 1: Archer. To be truly deadly with a bow, you must know where to aim. You can spend points from either your Speed Pool or your Intellect Pool to apply levels of Effort to increase your bow damage. As usual, each level of Effort adds 3 points of damage to a successful attack. Enabler.

Fletcher. You are trained in making arrows. Enabler.

Tier 2: Covering Fire (1 Speed point). In a round where you attack with your bow, if you fire an additional arrow, the difficulty of attacks and special abilities used by the target is increased by one step. Enabler.

Bowyer. You are trained in making bows. Enabler.

Tier 3: Trained Archer. You are trained in using bows. Enabler.

Master Fletcher. You are specialized in making arrows. Enabler.

Tier 4: Quick Shot. If you roll a natural 17 or higher with a bow attack, instead of adding damage or having a minor or major effect, you can make another attack with your bow. This attack reuses the same Effort and bonuses (if any) from the first attack. Enabler.

Master Bowyer. You are specialized in making bows. Enabler.

Tier 5: Phenomenal Archer. You are specialized in using bows. Enabler.

Tier 6: Powerful Shot (2 Might points). You inflict 3 additional points of damage with a bow. The Might points spent to use this ability are in addition to any Speed points spent on the attack. Enabler.

CASTS SPELLS

You can cast spells of arcing lightning, rolling fire, creeping shadow, and summoning. As a spellcaster, you understand that the world is a construct built on hidden formulas, flows of energy, and encrypted arcane secrets. Spells are specific flaws in reality that have been identified, studied, and codified into a

Casts Spells GM Intrusions: *A spell in your spellbook is defaced and ruined. A summoned creature turns on you regardless of precautions. A rival spellcaster tries to steal your spellbook. A Fire Bloom spell goes awry and catches one or more allies in its area.*

Given how Casts Spells functions, a spellcaster might discover other spells exist for each tier. Of course, the character would first have to track them down and enter them into her spellbook.

Some spellcasters carry pouches filled with a variety of odd dusts, scales of strange beasts, oils of suspicious origin, and related materials that are useful aids for casting spells. Others get by without these trappings.

spellbook for ease of reference and use. Though you likely apprenticed under a more accomplished spellcaster, sorcerer, or wizard, you quickly learned that the most powerful spells—those that can alter a creature's form, open pathways to other worlds, or kill with a single word—are jealously guarded secrets even among friendly spellcasters, including between master and apprentice.

You probably wear sturdy robes stitched with esoteric symbols, carry a staff etched with indecipherable glyphs, and, last but certainly not least, carry a tome of magic spells wherever you go.

Connection: Choose one of the following.

1. Pick one other PC. You worry that she is trying to get a look at your spellbook, but you don't know why.

2. Pick one other PC. You once accidentally turned him into a tiny, insignificant creature. Though you were unable to revert him, he eventually returned to his normal form.

3. Pick one other PC. That character is related to the spellcaster you apprenticed under.

4. Pick one other PC. Every so often when you cast a spell, that character later reacts as if she had an allergic reaction. She doesn't yet know the cause of her affliction, but you do. You're still debating whether to tell her or let her suffer in ignorance while you work on a spell to assuage her condition.

Additional Equipment: Spellbook, notes taken from another caster's spellbook you've yet to decipher.

Spellcasting Special Abilities: If you have other dramatic abilities, they are spells you cast, which involve an arcane gesture or two, a few mystical words, and possibly a pinch of dust or other material to invoke the effect. (These abilities appear as spells codified in your spellbook.) This alteration changes nothing other than how you trigger the effects. For example, when a character who Casts Spells uses Enthrall, she does so by first making a particular hand gesture and uttering the syllables of the spell, after which her eyes glow with a captivating, enthralling light.

Enthrall, page 45

Minor Effect Suggestion: Your spell hazes the target's vision with a magical glow so that the difficulty of all tasks it attempts on its next action is modified by one step to its detriment.

Major Effect Suggestion: A pulse of arcane energy removes the target from reality for a brief period. When the target reappears a couple of rounds later, no time has passed for it.

Tier 1: Spellbook. You've compiled a tome of spells, formulas, and notes that grants you flexibility that other sorcerers don't possess. With your spellbook, you can replace one of your readied spells (such as Arcane Flare, Magic Shield, Ray of Confusion, and so on) with a different one of the same tier that is also in your spellbook. You can have only one readied spell of a given tier at a time. To make the switch, spend ten minutes studying your spellbook, after which time your readied spell is changed out. A spellcaster can choose to vary her readied spells up to twice per day, immediately after a one-hour or ten-hour recovery roll. (Changing out the spell requires only about a minute.)

Choose one of the following spells as your readied spell for tier 1.

Arcane Flare (1 Intellect point). You enhance the damage of another attack spell with an extra charge of energy so that it deals 1 additional point of damage. Alternatively, you attack a target within long range by projecting a flare of raw magic that inflicts 4 points of damage. Enabler for enhancement; action for long-range attack.

Magic Shield (1 Intellect point). You gain +1 to Armor for an hour. Action to initiate.

Tier 2: Spellbook. You add the following spells to your spellbook. Choose one of them as your readied spell for tier 2.

Ray of Confusion (2 Intellect points). You project a grey beam of confusion at a creature within short range, inflicting 1 point of damage that ignores Armor. In addition, until the end of the next round, the difficulty of all tasks, attacks, and defenses the target attempts is modified by one step to its detriment. Action.

Lock (2+ Intellect points). A door, gate, chest, drawer, locket, or other object that can be closed within long range snaps shut and is magically locked (level 3 effect) for one hour. If an object or creature is physically holding the target object open, you must also succeed on an Intellect-based attack. For each level of Effort you apply, the quality of the magical lock increases by one level. Action to initiate.

Tier 3: Spellbook. You add the following spells to your spellbook. Choose one of them as your readied spell for tier 3.

Fire Bloom (4+ Intellect points). Fire blooms within long range, filling an area 10 feet (3 m) in radius and inflicting 3 points of damage on all affected targets. Effort applied to one attack counts for all attacks against targets in the area of the bloom. Even on an unsuccessful attack, a target in the area still takes 1 point of damage. Flammable objects in the area may catch fire. Action.

Summon Giant Spider (4+ Intellect points). A giant spider appears within immediate range. If you applied a level of Effort as part of the summoning, the spider is amenable to your instructions; otherwise, it acts according to its nature. Regardless, the creature persists for up to one minute before it fades away. Action to initiate.

Tier 4: Spellbook. You add the following spells to your spellbook. Choose one of them as your readied spell for tier 4.

Soul Interrogation (5 Intellect points). You determine the weaknesses, vulnerabilities, qualities, and mannerisms of a single creature within long range. The GM should reveal the creature's level, basic abilities, and obvious weaknesses (if any). The difficulty of all actions you attempt that affect that creature—attack, defense, interaction, and so on—is reduced by one step for a few months afterward. Action.

Elemental Protection (4+ Intellect points). You and every target you designate within immediate range gains +5 to Armor against direct damage from one type of elemental damage (such as fire, lightning, shadow, or thorn) for one hour, or until you cast this spell again. Each level of Effort applied increases the elemental protection by +2. Action to initiate.

Tier 5: Spellbook. You add the following spells to your spellbook. Choose one of them as your readied spell for tier 5.

Dragon's Maw (6 Intellect points). You fashion and control a "hovering" phantasmal construct of magic within long range that resembles a dragon's head. The construct lasts for up to an hour, until it is destroyed, or until you cast another spell. It is a level 4 construct that inflicts 6 points of damage with its bite when directed. While the construct persists, you can use it to manipulate large objects, carry heavy items in its mouth, or attack foes. If you use it to attack foes, you must spend your action directly controlling the phantom maw for each attack. Action to initiate.

Granite Wall (7+ Intellect points). You create a level 6 granite wall within short range. The wall is 1 foot (30 cm) thick and up to 20 feet by 20 feet (6 m by 6 m) in size. It appears resting on a solid foundation and lasts for about ten hours. If you apply three levels of Effort, the wall is permanent until destroyed naturally. Action to initiate.

Tier 6: Spellbook. You add the following spells to your spellbook. Choose one of them as your readied spell for tier 6.

Summon Demon (7+ Intellect points). A demon appears within immediate range. If you applied a level of Effort as part of the summoning, the demon is amenable to your instructions; otherwise, it acts according to its nature. Regardless, the demon persists for up to one minute before it fades away—you hope. Action to initiate.

Demon, page 284

Word of Death (5+ Intellect points). Your attack is the utterance of a magic word so terrible that it snuffs the life from a living target within short range. The target must be level 1. Instead of applying Effort to decrease the difficulty, you can apply Effort to increase the maximum level of the target. Thus, to kill a level 5 target (four levels above the normal limit), you must apply four levels of Effort. Action.

CHANNELS DIVINE BLESSINGS

You are a devout follower of a divine being and serve as its representative among mortals. In other words, you are a priest. The power of your god or gods flows through you and allows you to perform miracles on their behalf.

Channels Divine Blessings GM Intrusions: *A spirit, demon, or similar creature's faith overcomes your blessing. An NPC is possessed by a demon. An NPC ally in the faith proves to be corrupt. Your symbol of faith cracks for no apparent reason.*

You wear simple clothes, though you also display the symbols and insignia of your deity. Normally humble, you are strident when speaking with the authority of the divine.

Connection: Choose one of the following.

1. Pick one other PC. You were a drunk or otherwise lost to questionable practices until this character plucked you out of the gutter and cleaned you up. You found your calling after that.
2. Pick one other PC. You're concerned that her spirit is bound for darkness.
3. Pick one or more other PCs. You say a prayer for each of them, each day. They may or may not know or care that you are doing so.
4. Pick one other PC. That character has confided in you that he doesn't think the gods are real. You're not sure how to deal with that.

Additional Equipment: A symbol of your faith carved in iron.

Minor Effect Suggestion: The power of faith knocks the target back several paces.

Major Effect Suggestion: The power of faith knocks the target prone.

Tier 1: Divine Knowledge. You are trained in all tasks related to knowledge of godly beings. Enabler.

Other types of blessings are possible with different kinds of gods.

Blessing of the Gods. As a servant of the gods, you can call up blessings in their name. This blessing depends on the god's general demeanor and area of influence. Choose two of the abilities described below.

Authority/Law/Peace (3 Intellect points). You prevent a foe that can hear and understand you from attacking anyone or anything for one round. Action.

Benevolence/Righteousness/Spirit (2+ Intellect points). One level 1 demon, spirit, or similar creature within short range is destroyed or banished. Instead of applying Effort to decrease the difficulty, you can apply Effort to increase the maximum level of the target. Thus, to destroy or banish a level 5 target (four levels above the normal limit), you must apply four levels of Effort. Action.

Death/Darkness (2 Intellect points). A target you choose within short range withers, suffering 3 points of damage. Action.

Desire/Love/Health (3 Intellect points). With a touch, you restore 1d6 points to one stat Pool of any creature, including yourself. This ability is a difficulty 2 Intellect task. Each time you attempt to heal the same creature, the task difficulty increases by one step. The difficulty returns to 2 after that creature rests for ten hours. Action.

Earth/Stone. You are trained in climbing, stonecraft, and spelunking. Enabler.

Knowledge/Wisdom (3 Intellect points). Choose up to three creatures (potentially including yourself). For one minute, the difficulty of a particular type of task (but not an attack roll or defense roll) is reduced by one step for those creatures, but only while they remain within immediate range of you. Action.

Nature/Animals/Plants. You are trained in botany and handling natural animals. Enabler.

Protection/Silence (3 Intellect points). You create a quiet bubble of protection around you to an immediate radius for one minute. The bubble moves with you. The difficulty of all defense rolls for you and all creatures you designate within the bubble is decreased by one step, and no noise, regardless of its origin, sounds louder than a normal speaking voice. Action to initiate.

Sky/Air (2 Intellect points). A creature you touch is immune to airborne toxins or contaminants for ten minutes. Action.

Sun/Light/Fire (2 Intellect points). You cause one creature or object within short range to catch fire, inflicting 1 point of ambient damage each round until the fire is extinguished (requiring an action). Action.

Trickery/Greed/Commerce. You are trained in detecting the deceptions of other creatures. Enabler.

War (1 Intellect point). A target you choose within short range (potentially yourself) deals 2 additional points of damage with its next successful weapon attack. Action.

Water/The Sea (2 Intellect points). A target you touch can breathe water for ten minutes. Action.

Tier 2: Divine Fortitude. Your faith gives you additional reserves. Add 4 points to your Intellect Pool.

Tier 3: Divine Radiance (2 Intellect points). Your prayer calls divine radiance from the heavens to punish an unworthy target within long range, inflicting 4 points of damage. If the target is a demon, spirit, or something similar, it also stands in unwilling awe of the divine energy coursing through it and is unable to act on its next turn. Once exposed to this blessing, the target can't be awed by this attack again for several hours. Action.

Tier 4: Overawe (5 Intellect points). A blast of divine radiance from the heavens spotlights a target you select within long range, pushing the target to its knees (or similar appendages, if any) and rendering it helpless in the light for up to ten minutes, or until it breaks free. The overawed target cannot defend itself, make attacks, or attempt anything other than to shake free of the divine awe each round. If the target is a demon, spirit, or something similar, it also takes 1 point of damage that ignores Armor each round it remains affected. Action to initiate.

Tier 5: Divine Intervention (2 Intellect points, or 2 Intellect Points + 4 XP). You ask the divine to intervene on your behalf, usually against a creature within long range, changing the course of its life in a small way by introducing a major special effect upon it. The major special effect is akin to what occurs when you roll a natural 20 on an attack. If you want to try for a larger effect, and if the GM allows it, you can attempt a divine intervention with a more far-reaching effect, which is more like the kind of GM intrusion initiated by the GM on her players. In this case, Divine Intervention costs 4 XP, the effect may not work out exactly like you hope, and you may not make another plea for divine intervention for a week. Action.

Tier 6: Divine Symbol (5+ Intellect points). You invoke divine power by scribing a glowing symbol in the air with your fingers. Writhing pillars of divine radiance spear up to five targets within long range. A successful attack on a target inflicts 5 points of damage. If you apply Effort to increase the damage, you deal 2 additional points of damage per level of Effort (instead of 3 points); however, targets take 1 point of damage even if you fail the attack roll. Action.

COMMANDS MENTAL POWERS

You have always had special abilities that others didn't seem to share. Through practice and devotion, you have honed this unique talent so that you can harness the power of your mind to perform deeds.

No one can tell that you have this ability just by looking at you, although you wear a crystal or jewel somewhere on your head to help focus your power. Either this focusing object was given to you by someone who recognized your ability, or you came upon it by accident and it triggered your abilities. Some people with mental powers—often called psychics or psionics by ordinary folks—are secretive and a little paranoid.

Connection: Choose one of the following.

1. Pick one other PC. You have found that this character is particularly tuned into your mental powers. While you're within short range of him, the two of you are always in telepathic contact, and he is never harmed by your Psychic Burst.
2. Pick one other PC. She is what you might call a "loud thinker," and her thoughts sometimes come through to you when you are within short range, even when you're not using your Mind Reading ability. You can't seem to turn this off. Whether you tell her or not is up to you.
3. Pick one other PC. For some reason, he seems to act as an antenna for your mental powers. If the two of you are touching, your Telepathic and Mind Reading abilities sometimes extend to long range.
4. Pick one other PC. Your close mentor or teacher once used Mind Control on her and forced her to do something against her will. To this day, you haven't talked about it, but you are both intensely aware of the connection.

Additional Equipment: You have a crystal or jewel artifact that, when worn against your forehead or temple, adds 1 point to your Intellect Pool. If you're ever without the artifact, subtract 5 points from your Intellect Pool; the points are restored if you regain the item.

Mental Abilities: If you have abilities like Mind Control or Mind Reading from your

Commands Mental Powers GM Intrusions: *Other beings that have mental or psychic powers often seek to destroy those like themselves out of jealousy and fear. Some beings feed on the mental energies of others, and psychics are the most desired meal of all.*

type (or elsewhere), you're automatically trained in them. Enabler.

Minor Effect Suggestion: The range or duration of the mental power is doubled.

Major Effect Suggestion: You can take another action on that same turn.

Tier 1: Telepathic (1+ Intellect point). You can speak telepathically with others who are within short range. Communication is two-way, but the other party must be willing and able to communicate. You don't have to see the target, but you must know that it's within range. You can have more than one active contact at once, but you must establish contact with each target individually. Each contact lasts up to ten minutes. If you apply a level of Effort to increase the duration rather than affect the difficulty, the contact lasts for twenty-four hours. Action to establish contact.

Tier 2: Mind Reading (2 Intellect points). You can read the surface thoughts of a creature within short range, even if the target doesn't want you to. You must be able to see your target. Once you have established contact, you can read the target's thoughts for up to one minute. If you also have the Mind Reading ability from your type or another source, you can use this ability at long range, and you don't need to be able to see the target (but you do have to know that the target is within range). Action to initiate.

Tier 3: Psychic Burst (3+ Intellect points). You blast waves of mental force into the minds of up to three targets within short range (make an Intellect roll against each target). This burst inflicts 3 points of Intellect damage (ignores Armor). For each 2 additional Intellect points you spend, you can make an Intellect attack roll against an additional target. Action.

Tier 4: Use Senses of Others (4 Intellect points). You can see, hear, smell, touch, and taste through the senses of anyone with whom you have telepathic contact. You can attempt to use this ability on a willing or unwilling target within long range; an unwilling target can try to resist. You don't need to see the target, but you must know that it's within range. Your shared senses last ten minutes. Action to establish.

Tier 5: Mind Control (6+ Intellect points). You control the actions of another creature you touch. This effect lasts for ten minutes. The target must be level 2 or lower. Once you have established control, you maintain mental contact with the target and sense what it senses. You can allow it to act freely or override its control on a case-by-case basis. Instead of applying Effort to decrease the difficulty, you can apply Effort to increase the maximum level of the target. Thus, to control the mind of a level 5 target (three levels above the normal limit), you must apply three levels of Effort. When the effect ends, the creature doesn't remember being controlled or anything it did while under your command. Action to initiate.

Tier 6: Telepathic Network (0+ Intellect points). When you wish it, you can contact up to ten creatures known to you, no matter where they are. All targets must be willing and able to communicate. You automatically succeed at establishing a telepathic network; no roll is required. All creatures in the network are linked and can communicate telepathically with one another. They can also "overhear" anything said in the network, if they wish. Activating this ability doesn't require an action and doesn't cost Intellect points; to you, it's as easy as speaking out loud. The network lasts until you choose to end it. If you spend 5 Intellect points, you can contact twenty creatures at once, and for every 1 Intellect point you spend above that, you can add ten more creatures to the network. These larger networks last for ten minutes. Creating a network of twenty or more creatures does require an action to establish contact. Enabler.

CONDUCTS WEIRD SCIENCE

You could be a respected scientist, having been published in several peer-reviewed journals. Or you might be considered a crank by your contemporaries, pursuing fringe theories on what others consider to be scant evidence. Truth is, you have a particular gift for sifting the edges of what's possible. You can find new insights and unlock odd phenomena with your experiments. Where others see a crackpot cornucopia, you sift the conspiracy theories for revelation. Whether you conduct your enquiries as a government contractor, a university researcher, a corporate scientist, or an indulger of curiosity in your own garage lab following your muse, you push the boundaries of what's possible.

You probably care more about your work than trivialities such as your appearance, polite or proper behavior, or social norms, but then again, an eccentric like you might turn the tables on that stereotype too.

Connection: Choose one of the following.

1. Pick one other PC. The character believes your experiments once cured someone close to her of a fatal condition. You're not sure if they did, or if the condition just went into remission.

2. Pick one other PC. You created a scientific instrument designed to give this character a restful night's sleep, but you now fear unanticipated long-term side effects.

3. Pick one other PC. You're pretty sure that one of your experiments from when you were younger and brasher is responsible for giving him some special gifts or drawbacks. The PC might know this, or he might just vaguely remember you from long ago.

4. Pick one other PC. She asked you to design a gun that could shoot through walls. You took the cash, but you are still working on the prototype.

Minor Effect Suggestion: You learn one additional piece of information in your analysis.

Major Effect Suggestion: Foes within sight are dazed for one round upon seeing your strange creation or its results. During this time, the difficulty of all tasks they perform is modified by one step to their detriment.

Tier 1: Lab Analysis (3 Intellect points). You analyze the scene of a crime, the site of a mysterious incident, or a series of unexplained phenomena, and maybe learn a surprising amount of information about the perpetrators, the participants, or force(s) responsible. To do so, you must collect samples from the scene. Samples are paint or wood scrapings, dirt, photographs of the area, hair, an entire corpse, and so on. With samples in hand, you can discover up to three pertinent pieces of information about the scene, possibly clearing up a lesser mystery and pointing the way to solving a greater one. The GM will decide what you learn and what level of difficulty is needed to learn it. (For comparison, discovering that a victim was killed not by a fall, as seems immediately obvious, but rather by electrocution, is a difficulty 3 task for you.) The difficulty of the task is modified by one step in your favor if you take the time to transport the samples to a permanent lab (if you have access to one), as opposed to conducting the analysis with your field science kit. Action to initiate, 2d20 minutes to complete.

Scientist: You are trained in one area of scientific knowledge of your choice.

Conducts Weird Science GM Intrusions: *Creations get out of control. Side effects cannot always be predicted. Weird science terrifies people and can draw the media. When a device created or modified by weird science is depleted, it detonates.*

As someone who Conducts Weird Science, a PC in a modern-day setting could be given the "mad scientist" label by the media if news of her exploits becomes public. Whether she conducts her science ethically or with disregard for the safety of others (or whether she really is insane) is the only true measure of how "mad" she is.

Tier 2: Modify Device (4 Intellect points). You jury-rig a piece of mechanical or electrical equipment to make it function above its rated specs for a very limited time. To do so, you must use spare parts equal to an expensive item, have a field science kit (or a permanent lab, if you have access to one), and succeed at a difficulty 3 Intellect-based task. When complete, using the device modifies all tasks performed in conjunction with the device by one step in the user's favor, until the device inevitably breaks. For example, you could overclock a computer so research tasks using it are easier, modify an espresso maker so that each cup of coffee made with it is better, modify a car's engine so that it goes faster (or its steering, so it handles better), and so on. Each use of the modified device requires a depletion roll of 1–5 on a d20. Action to initiate, one hour to complete.

Depletion, page 186

Tier 3: Better Living Through Chemistry (4 Intellect points). You've developed drug cocktails specifically designed to work with your own biochemistry. Depending on which one you inject, it makes you smarter, faster, or tougher, but when it wears off, the crash is a doozy, so you use it only in desperate situations. You gain 2 to your Might Edge, Speed Edge, or Intellect Edge for one minute, after which you can't gain the benefit again for one hour. During this follow-up hour, every time you spend points from a Pool, increase the cost by 1. Action.

Consorts With the Dead GM Intrusions: *People who interact with the dead have frightening reputations. They might be outlawed in some places and hailed as saviors in others. Communicating with the spirits of dead aliens or other inhuman creatures can lead to madness.*

Tier 4: Extensive Training. You are specialized in one area of knowledge of your choice. Enabler.

Just a Bit Mad. You are trained in Intellect defense tasks. Enabler.

Tier 5: Weird Science Breakthrough (5 Intellect points). Your research leads to a breakthrough, and you imbue an object with a truly amazing property, though you can use the item only once. To do so, you must buy spare parts equivalent to an expensive item, have a field science kit (or a permanent lab, if you have access to one), and succeed at a difficulty 4 Intellect-based roll to create a random cypher of up to level 2. The GM decides the nature of the cypher you create. Attempting to create a specified cypher increases the difficulty by two steps. Creating a cypher does not allow you to surpass your normal cypher limit. Action to initiate, one hour to complete.

Tier 6: Incredible Feat of Science (12 Intellect points). You do something amazing in the lab. This takes a full day of work (or longer, depending on the circumstances) and parts and materials equivalent to three expensive items. Possible incredible feats include:

- Reanimate and command a dead body for one hour.
- Create an engine that runs on perpetual motion.
- Create a teleportation gate that remains open for one minute.
- Transmute one substance into another substance.
- Cure one person with an incurable disease or condition.
- Create a weapon designed to hurt something that can't otherwise be hurt.
- Create a defense designed to protect against something that can't otherwise be stopped.

Improved Weird Science Breakthrough. When you successfully use Weird Science Breakthrough, you can create a cypher of up to level 6. Enabler.

CONSORTS WITH THE DEAD

Through the study of science or magic to which most people give a wide berth, you have mastered the ability to speak with and reanimate the dead. Necromancy, however, is shunned as a taboo. It is gruesome, morbid, and in the eyes of most, forbidden.

You probably wear black clothing, which might be adorned with skulls, bones, teeth, or other symbols of death. Some who consort with the dead paint their skin and dye their hair black, red, and white to bring them visually closer to the bodies they interact with.

Connection: Choose one of the following.

1. Pick one other PC. You suspect that this character finds your predilections abhorrent. You can choose whether or not she knows of your suspicions.

2. Pick one other PC. This character recently lost a loved one and wants you to contact that person in the afterlife. Whether

you try to explain that this isn't how it works is up to you.

3. Pick one other PC. This character looks upon you as some kind of religious figure (whether you encourage this behavior is up to you).

4. Pick one other PC. This character comes from the same place you do, and you knew each other as children.

Additional Equipment: You carry an innocuous memento of someone close to you who died. It might be a locket, a ring, a letter, a coin, or something similar.

Necromantic Abilities: If you perform abilities that would normally use force or other energy (such as electricity), they instead use deathly energies. For example, a force blast is a blast of cold, life-draining energy. This alteration changes nothing except that the type of damage is different, and it harms only living creatures.

Minor Effect Suggestion: The animated creature adds 1 to all rolls, or the target is dazed for one round, during which time the difficulty of all its tasks is modified by one step to its detriment.

Major Effect Suggestion: The animated creature adds 2 to all rolls, or the target is stunned and loses his next turn.

Tier 1: Speaker for the Dead (2+ Intellect points). You can ask a question of a dead being whose corpse you are touching. Because the answer comes through the filter of the being's understanding and personality, it can't answer questions that it wouldn't have understood in life, and it can't provide answers that it wouldn't have known in life. In fact, the being is not compelled to answer at all, so you might need to interact with it in a way that would have convinced it to answer while it was alive. For each additional Intellect point you spend when you activate the ability, you can ask the being an additional question. Action.

Tier 2: Necromancy (3+ Intellect points). You animate the body of a dead creature of approximately your size or smaller, creating a level 1 creature. It has none of the intelligence, memories, or special abilities that it had in life. The creature follows your verbal commands for one hour, after which it becomes an inert corpse. Unless the creature is killed by damage, you can reanimate it again when its time expires, but any damage it had when it became inert applies to its newly reanimated state. If you have access to multiple bodies, you can create an additional undead creature for each additional Intellect point you spend when you activate the ability. Action to animate.

Tier 3: Reading the Room (3 Intellect points). You gain knowledge about an area by speaking with dead spirits or reading residual energies from the past. You can ask the GM a single, matter-of-fact question about the location and get an answer if you succeed on the Intellect roll. "What killed the cattle in this barn?" is a good example of a simple question. "Why were these cattle killed?" is not an appropriate question because it has more to do with the mindset of the killer than the barn. Simple questions usually have a difficulty of 2, but extremely technical questions or those that involve facts meant to be kept secret can have a much higher difficulty. Action.

Tier 4: Greater Necromancy (5+ Intellect points). This ability works like the second-tier Necromancy ability except that it creates a level 3 creature. Action to animate.

Tier 5: Death Gaze (6 Intellect points). You project a chilling gaze at all living creatures within short range who can see you. Make a separate Intellect attack roll for each target. Success means that the creature is frozen in fear, not moving or taking actions for one minute or until it is attacked. Some creatures without minds (such as robots) might be immune to Death Gaze. Action.

Tier 6: True Necromancy (8+ Intellect points). This ability works like the second-tier Necromancy ability except that it creates a level 5 creature. Action to animate.

CONTROLS BEASTS

To say that you have a way with animals and nonhuman creatures doesn't begin to cover it. Your mastery and communication with beasts is positively uncanny. They come to you fearlessly, and it's not uncommon for

Controls Beasts GM Intrusions: *Most civilized communities are reluctant to welcome dangerous animals and look warily on those who consort with such creatures. Out-of-control beasts can be a real hazard.*

birds to alight on your shoulder or for small animals to climb up your arms or legs.

You probably wear tough clothing and have a disheveled or grizzled appearance that suggests a rugged, outdoor life. Perhaps you even smell like an animal.

Connection: Choose one of the following.

1. Pick one other PC. That character seems to disturb your creatures in a way that you can't explain. You know that you must keep your animals away from him if possible, or you might lose control of them.

2. Pick one other PC. The creature that you're bonded with seems to have a special bond with this other person as well. You must decide whether it brings up feelings of jealousy or camaraderie within you and whether to thwart the connection or help it blossom.

3. Pick one other PC. Recently, he accidentally (or perhaps intentionally) put your beast companion in a position of danger. Your companion is now nervous around him, and you are struggling with your own emotional response to the incident.

4. Pick one other PC. She dislikes beasts of all kinds, seeing them as little more than food or prey. You hope that exposing her to your beast companion will change her mind. It's up to that player how her character responds to the experience.

Additional Equipment: You have three days' worth of food for your beast companion, plus a harness, collar, or similar accoutrements.

Minor Effect Suggestion: The duration of calmness or control is doubled.

Major Effect Suggestion: The duration of calmness or control extends to twenty-four hours.

A creature's level determines its target number, health, and damage, unless otherwise stated. So a level 2 beast companion has a target number of 6 and a health of 6, and it inflicts 2 points of damage. A level 4 beast companion has a target number of 12 and a health of 12, and it inflicts 4 points of damage. And so on.

Tier 1: Beast Companion. A level 2 creature of your size or smaller accompanies you and follows your instructions. You and the GM must work out the details of your creature, and you'll probably make rolls for it in combat or when it takes actions. The beast companion acts on your turn. Its movement is based on its creature type (avian, swimmer, and so on). If your beast companion dies, you can hunt in the wild for 1d6 days to find a new companion. Enabler.

Tier 2: Soothe the Savage (2 Intellect points). You calm a nonhuman beast within 30 feet (9 m). You must speak to it (although it doesn't need to understand your words), and it must see you. It remains calm for one minute or for as long as you focus all your attention on it. The GM has final say over what counts as a nonhuman beast, but unless some kind of deception is at work, you should know whether you can affect a creature before you attempt to use this ability on it. Aliens, extradimensional entities, very intelligent creatures, and automatons never count. Action.

Communication (2 Intellect points). You can convey a basic concept to a creature that normally can't speak or understand speech. The creature can also give you a very basic answer to a simple question. Action.

Tier 3: Mount. A level 3 creature serves you as a mount and follows your instructions. While you're mounted on it, the creature can move and you can attack on your turn, or it can attack foes when you do. You and the GM must work out the details of the creature, and you'll probably make rolls for it in combat or when it takes actions. The mount acts on your turn. If your mount dies, you can hunt in the wild for 3d6 days to find a new one. Enabler.

Tier 4: Beast Eyes (3 Intellect points). You can sense through your beast companion's senses if it is within 1 mile (2 km) of you. This effect lasts up to ten minutes. Action to establish.

Improved Companion. Your beast companion increases to level 4. Enabler.

Tier 5: Beast Call (5 Intellect points). You summon a horde of small animals or a single level 4 beast to help you temporarily. These creatures do your bidding for as long as you focus your attention, but you must use your action each turn to direct them. Creatures are native to the area and arrive under their own power, so if you're in an unreachable place, this ability won't work. Action.

Tier 6: Control the Savage (6 Intellect points). You can control a calm nonhuman beast within 30 feet (9 m). You control it for as long as you focus all your attention on it, using your turn each round. The GM has final say over what counts as a nonhuman beast, but unless some kind of deception is at work, you should know whether you can affect a creature before you attempt to use this ability on it. Aliens, extradimensional entities, very intelligent creatures, and robots never count. Action.

Improved Companion. Your beast companion increases to level 5. Enabler.

CONTROLS GRAVITY

Gravity is a force so basic and primal that we take it for granted. Through a quirk of fate, some unique device(s), or supreme devotion (or a combination of all three), you have learned to tap into the power of gravity.

You might prefer billowy garments that display your mastery of gravity's pull and conceal your identity and intentions.

Controls Gravity GM Intrusions: *Many people are frightened to be around someone who controls gravity. Losing command of such powers could inadvertently send objects careening off into the sky, perhaps even into orbit.*

Connection: Choose one of the following.

1. Pick one other PC. In the recent past, while using your gravitational powers, you accidentally sent that character hurtling into the air or plummeting toward the ground. Either way, she barely survived. It is up to the player of that character to decide whether she resents, fears, or forgives you.

2. Pick one other PC whose focus intertwines with yours. This odd connection affects her in some way. For example, if the character Carries a Quiver, your ability to manipulate gravity sometimes extends the range of her arrows. If she Entertains, her jumps, dances, and juggling balls seem less bound by the laws of gravity. If she Masters Weaponry, her weapons sometimes feel lighter.

Carries a Quiver, page 102

Entertains, page 120

Masters Weaponry, page 148

3. Pick one other PC. He is deathly afraid of heights. Through your ability to control gravity, you would like to teach him how to be more comfortable with his feet off the ground. He must decide whether or not to take you up on your offer.

4. Pick one other PC. She is skeptical of your ability to control gravity and thinks it's just one big illusion. She might even attempt to discredit you or discover the "secret" behind your so-called skills.

Additional Equipment: You have a pen-sized device that tells the weight of whatever you point it at (within short range). The weight is displayed on a small glass plate in letters that only you can decipher.

Minor Effect Suggestion: The duration of the effect is doubled.

Major Effect Suggestion: An important item on the target's person is destroyed.

Tier 1: Hover (1 Intellect point). You float slowly into the air. As your action, you can concentrate to remain motionless in the air or float up to a short distance; otherwise, you drift with the wind or with any momentum you have gained. This effect lasts for up to ten minutes. If you also have this ability from another source, you can hover for twenty minutes and move your normal speed. Action to initiate.

Crafts Illusions GM Intrusions: *Obviously, illusions of things that someone has never seen before are not likely to be believable. An NPC might realize that an illusion is false at just the wrong moment.*

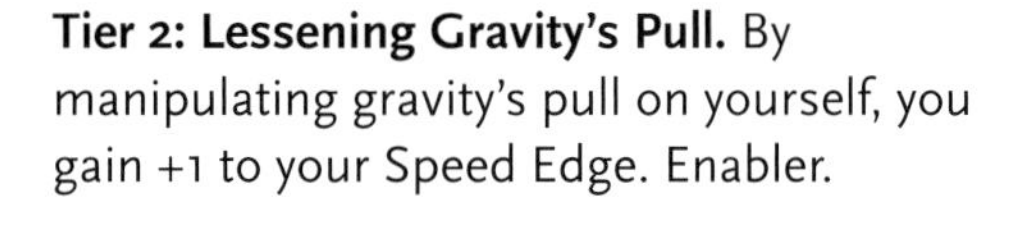

Tier 2: Lessening Gravity's Pull. By manipulating gravity's pull on yourself, you gain +1 to your Speed Edge. Enabler.

Tier 3: Gravity Cleave (3 Intellect points). You can harm a target within short range by rapidly increasing gravity's pull on one portion of the target and decreasing it on another, inflicting 6 points of damage. Action.

Tier 4: Field of Gravity (4 Intellect points). When you wish it, a field of manipulated gravity around you pulls incoming ranged projectile attacks to the ground. You are immune to such attacks until your turn in the next round. You must be aware of an attack to foil it. This ability does not work on energy attacks. Enabler.

Tier 5: Flight (4+ Intellect points). You can float and fly through the air for one hour. For each level of Effort applied, you can affect one additional creature of your size or smaller. You must touch the creature to bestow the power of flight. You direct the other creature's movement, and while flying, it must remain within sight of you or fall. In terms of overland movement, a flying creature moves about 20 miles (32 km) per hour and is not affected by terrain. Action to initiate.

Tier 6: Weight of the World (6+ Intellect points). You can increase a target's weight dramatically. The target is pulled to the ground and can't move physically under its own power for one minute. The target must be within short range. For each level of Effort applied, you can affect one additional creature. Action.

CRAFTS ILLUSIONS

You create holographic images that appear real. You are, in effect, an artist—a crafter of light and sound. Holographic images can never inflict direct harm or exert real force, but they can fool creatures, changing opinions and even behaviors if you craft them cleverly.

You likely dress with flair and color. The appearance of things is important to you, both their beauty and their ugliness. You are a visual performer who can entertain, terrify, or fool everyone you encounter.

Connection: Choose one of the following.

1. Pick one other PC. This character is never fooled by your illusions and is never affected by the trickery of your special abilities. You can choose whether or not you know this fact.
2. Pick one other PC. He has a special angle on your illusions and can sometimes point out potential places of weakness.
3. Pick two other PCs who are willing to be trained as your assistants. When you use your Minor Illusion ability, if both of these characters are in immediate range, they can assist you, together decreasing the difficulty of your action by one step.
4. Pick one other PC. That character's face is so intriguing to you in a way you don't understand that your minor illusions sometimes look like him, even when you don't intend them to.

Psychedelic Abilities: If you have other overt abilities, they take on flamboyant visual and auditory qualities of your choosing. This alteration changes nothing other than the appearance of the effects. For example, your attack might look like a monster made of energy that assails your foes. If you have the Stasis ability, it might look like a tentacled beast holds the victim in place. If you have Teleportation, it might seem like a hole in space opens up and swallows you.

Minor Effect Suggestion: Your illusion has a special quality to it—perhaps an observer sees an image of something from his past.

Major Effect Suggestion: The illusion lasts for one hour, or if it already lasts that long, it lasts for twenty-four hours.

Tier 1: Minor Illusion (1 Intellect point). You create a single image of a creature or object within immediate range. The image must fit within a 10-foot (3 m) cube. The image can move (for example, you could make the illusion of a person walk or attack), but it can't leave the area defined by the cube. The illusion includes sound but not smell. It lasts for ten minutes, but if you want to change the original illusion significantly—such as making a creature appear to be wounded—you must concentrate on it again (though doing so doesn't cost additional Intellect points). If you move beyond immediate range of the cube, the illusion vanishes. Action to create; action to modify.

Tier 2: Disguise (2+ Intellect points). You appear to be someone or something else, roughly of your size and shape, for up to one hour. Once created, the disguise requires no concentration. For each additional Intellect point you spend, you can disguise one other creature. All disguised creatures must stay within sight of you or lose their disguise. Action to create.

Tier 3: Major Illusion (3 Intellect points). You create a complex scene of images within immediate range. The entire scene must fit within a 100-foot (30 m) cube. The images can move, but they can't leave the area defined by the cube. The illusion includes sound and smell. It lasts for ten minutes and changes as you direct (no concentration is needed). If you move beyond immediate range of the cube, the illusion vanishes. Action to create.

Tier 4: Illusory Selves (4 Intellect points). You create four holographic duplicates of yourself within short range. The duplicates last for one minute. You mentally direct their actions, and the duplicates aren't mirror images—each one can do different things. If struck violently, they either disappear permanently or freeze motionless (your choice). Action to create.

Stasis, page 33

Teleportation, page 36

Tier 5: Terrifying Image (6 Intellect points). You use a bit of subtle telepathy to learn which images would appear terrifying to creatures that you choose within long range. Those images appear within that area and menace the appropriate creatures. Make an Intellect attack roll against each creature you want to affect. Success means the creature flees in terror for one minute, pursued by its nightmares. Failure means the creature ignores the images, which do not hamper it in any way. Action.

Tier 6: Grandiose Illusion (8 Intellect points). You create a fantastically complex scene of images that fit within a 1-mile (2 km) cube that you are also within. You must be able to see the images when you create them. The images can move in the cube and act in accordance with your desires. They can also act logically (such as reacting appropriately to fire or attacks) when you aren't directly observing them. The illusion includes sound and smell. For example, armies can clash in battle, with air support from machines or flying creatures, on and above terrain of your creation. The illusion lasts for one hour (or longer, if you concentrate on it after that time). Action.

CRAFTS UNIQUE OBJECTS

Crafts Unique Objects GM Intrusions: *Although created devices can break, tinkering with an artifact can lead to catastrophic failure, causing explosions, mutation, rifts between dimensions, or anything in between.*

The raw materials for a crafter offer themselves to those who know where to look. You are a maker, a crafter, an inventor, and a builder. You might start out working with wood or metal, but eventually you will master far greater creations. Whether magic or technology is your field, you know that you can master it and use it for your own designs.

You likely carry a wide array of tools and spare parts wherever you go. Your work apron is probably a mainstay of your wardrobe, its pockets and loops brimming with the instruments of your trade. Your calloused fingers might be stained with grease that will never come completely clean, but these marks are badges of honor.

Cyphersmith works only in a setting where the cyphers are physical objects. If this isn't the case, this ability should probably be replaced with something akin to Weird Science Breakthrough from the Conducts Weird Science focus, page 110.

Connection: Choose one of the following.

1. Pick one other PC. The character has an extra item of regular equipment that you fashioned for her. (She chooses the item.)
2. Pick one other PC. She seems to have in her possession an object that you made for someone else a long time ago.
3. Pick one other PC. He has commissioned you to create something for him. You've already been paid but haven't yet completed the item.
4. Pick one other PC. You've seen that character admiring your crafting skills many times. Perhaps he would like a lesson. (You won't know until you ask.)

Additional Equipment: You begin the game with a bag of light tools, the tools needed to make your first-tier crafts, and any normal item (of level 1 or 2) that you can make with your skills.

Minor Effect Suggestion: Any rolls you make regarding that artifact gain a +1 bonus for twenty-four hours.

Major Effect Suggestion: Any rolls you make regarding that artifact gain a +2 bonus for twenty-four hours.

Tier 1: Crafter. You are trained in the crafting of two kinds of items. Enabler.

Master Identifier. You are trained in identifying the function of any kind of device. Enabler.

Tier 2: Tinkerer. If you spend at least one day tinkering with an artifact in your possession, it functions at one level higher than normal. This applies to all artifacts in your possession, but they retain this bonus only for you. Enabler.

Quick Work (3+ Intellect points). One use of any artifact (or one minute of its continuous function) is increased by one level if you use it within the next minute. If you spend 4 additional Intellect points, the use is increased by two levels if you use it within the next minute. Action.

Tier 3: Master Crafter. You are trained in the crafting of two more kinds of items, or you are specialized in two kinds of items that you are already trained in. Enabler.

Tier 4: Cyphersmith. All cyphers you use function at one level higher than normal. If given a week and the right tools, chemicals, and parts, you can tinker with one of your cyphers, transforming it into another cypher of the same type that you had in the past. The GM and player should collaborate to ensure that the transformation is logical—for example, you probably can't transform a pill into a helmet. Enabler.

Tier 5: Innovator. You can modify any artifact to give it different or better abilities as if that artifact were one level lower than normal, and the modification takes half the normal time. Enabler.

Tier 6: Inventor. You can create new artifacts in half the time, as if they were two levels lower, by spending half the normal XP. Enabler.

DEFENDS THE WEAK

Defends the Weak GM Intrusions: *A character focused on protecting others may periodically leave himself vulnerable to attacks.*

Someone has to stand up for the helpless, the weak, and the unprotected. You believe this duty, this obligation, falls to you, and thus you have spent much of your life watching out for the people around you. When you see them in trouble, you are the

first to come to their aid. You might give up your last dime to help the hungry, take a beating to save a person from the same, or rally your friends to take on injustice wherever you find it.

You probably bear many scars from previous conflicts, but for each scar, you likely also have a token of gratitude. You may have a dried flower given to you by a lady you saved from brigands, or a bit of metal given to you by a starving man you fed.

Connection: Choose one of the following.

1. Pick one other PC. You failed to protect this character at some point in the past, and you feel compelled to make up for it.
2. Pick one other PC. That character claimed innocence during a long-ago event, and you protected him. Now that time has passed, you're not entirely convinced that he was blameless.
3. Pick two other PCs. They seem to think that you are more of an arbitrator than you really are, and they keep asking you to choose which one of them is correct.
4. Pick one other PC. She believes that one of the tokens of gratitude you carry came from her father.

Additional Equipment: You have a shield.

Minor Effect Suggestion: You can draw an attack without having to use an action at any point before the end of the next round.

Major Effect Suggestion: You can take an extra action. You can use this action only to guard.

Draw the attack, page 211

Tier 1: Courageous. You are trained in Intellect defense tasks and initiative tasks. Enabler.

Warding Shield. You have +1 to Armor while you are wielding a shield. Enabler.

Tier 2: Devoted Defender (2 Intellect points). Choose one character you can see. That character becomes your ward. You are trained in all tasks involving finding, healing, interacting with, and protecting your ward. You can have only one ward at a time. Action to initiate.

Astute. You are trained in tasks to discern others' motives and to ascertain their general nature. You have a knack for sensing whether or not someone is truly innocent. Enabler.

Tier 3: True Guardian (2 Might points). When you stand guard as your action, you decrease the difficulty of all defense tasks by one step for characters you choose that are adjacent to you. This lasts until the end of your next turn. Enabler.

Tier 4: Combat Challenge. You are trained in intimidation tasks and in Intellect tasks made to draw an attack. Enabler.

Draw the attack, page 211

Take the attack, page 211

Willing Sacrifice. When you take an attack for another character, the attack does not deal 1 additional point of damage. Enabler.

Tier 5: Drive Back (4 Might points). When you deal damage with an attack, you can drive the creature away from your companions. Until the end of the next round, all characters other than you have an asset on Speed defense rolls made to resist attacks from this creature. Enabler.

Tier 6: True Defender (6 Intellect points). This ability functions as your Devoted Defender ability, except the benefit applies to up to three characters you choose. If you choose just one character, you become specialized in the tasks described under the Devoted Defender ability. Action to initiate.

DOESN'T DO MUCH

Doesn't Do Much GM Intrusions: *New situations are confounding and stressful. Past actions (or inactions) come back to haunt you.*

You're a slacker. You've had a number of jobs in your life, but nothing's really stuck. No one thing consumes you, compels you, or drives you. You float from event to event. That doesn't mean you're unhappy, necessarily. It's not a bad life. You like to take it easy. Appreciate the little things. Partake in a few relaxing substances now and again. Enjoy the rug that ties the whole room together. Not a lot of stress, and you know a little about a lot of different things.

You dress casually. You might be in decent physical shape—if, you know, that's your thing—or maybe you're more cerebral (a pseudo-intellectual). It's all good.

Connection: Choose one of the following.

1. Pick one other PC. She's always been there for you. Got you out of jams from time to time. She's cool.
2. Pick one other PC. This character is too uptight for your tastes. He's got to learn to chill.
3. Pick one other PC. You're a little jealous of this character because she's better than you at your favorite hobby (bowling, karaoke, or whatever it is).
4. Pick one other PC. You owe him money, but you're hoping he'll forget that.

Minor Effect Suggestion: You draw on your experiences and reduce the difficulty of your next action by one step.

Major Effect Suggestion: You get a free, no-action recovery roll.

Tier 1: Life Lessons. Choose any two noncombat skills. You are trained in those skills. Enabler.

Tier 2: Totally Chill. Your ten-minute recovery roll takes you only one round. Enabler.

Tier 3: Taking Care of Yourself. Choose one type of attack in which you are not already trained: light bashing, light bladed, light ranged, medium bashing, medium bladed, medium ranged, heavy bashing, heavy bladed, or heavy ranged. You are trained in attacks using that type of weapon. Enabler.

Tier 4: Life Lessons. Choose any two noncombat skills. You are trained in those skills. Enabler.

The Best Offense. You are trained in Might defense, Speed defense, or Intellect defense (your choice). If you are already trained in that type of defense, you are specialized. Enabler.

Tier 5: Abiding. Either you keep fit (giving you 5 points to divide between your Might Pool and your Speed Pool however you wish) or you have street smarts (giving you 5 points to add to your Intellect Pool)—your choice. Enabler.

Tier 6: Drawing on Life's Experiences (6 Intellect points). You've seen a lot and done a lot, and that experience comes in handy. Ask the GM one question, and you'll receive a general answer. The GM assigns a level to the question, so the more obscure the answer, the more difficult the task. Generally, knowledge that you could find by looking somewhere other than your current location is level 1, and obscure knowledge of the past is level 7. Action.

EMPLOYS MAGNETISM

Electromagnetism is a fundamental force in the universe, and it is yours to command. You are a master of metal.

You probably wear a lot of metal, perhaps as part of your clothing or armor, as part of your accessories (such as jewelry or piercings), embedded into your body surgically, or in some combination of these options.

Connection: Choose one of the following.

1. Pick one other PC. Whenever you use your powers, the metallic items on that character's body shudder, rattle, clink, and shake if he is within short range.
2. Pick one other PC. You worked together in the past, and the job ended badly.
3. Pick two other PCs. While practicing your Diamagnetism ability, you once accidentally sent them careening into each other. You've never been able to repeat it. Whether you tell them that you've been trying to replicate the strange effect is up to you.
4. Pick one other PC who has metallic elements in his body. You're afraid to use your magnetism abilities near him because you once had a bad experience involving Move Metal and a (probably former) friend's mechanical eyes.

Minor Effect Suggestion: The duration of the effect is doubled.

Major Effect Suggestion: An important item on the target's person is destroyed.

Tier 1: Move Metal (1 Intellect point). You can exert force on metal objects within short range for one round. Once activated, your power has an effective Might Pool of 10, a Might Edge of 1, and an Effort of 2 (approximately equal to the strength of a fit, capable adult human), and you can use it to move metal objects, push against metal objects, and so on. For example, in your round, you could lift and pull a light metal object anywhere within range to yourself or move a heavy object (like a piece of furniture) about 10 feet (3 m). This power lacks the fine control to wield a weapon or move objects with much speed, so in most situations, it's not a means of attack. You can't use this ability on your own body. Action.

Tier 2: Repel Metal. By manipulating magnetism, you are trained in Speed defense tasks against any incoming attack that uses metal. Enabler.

Tier 3: Destroy Metal (3 Intellect points). You instantly tear, rip, or burst a metal object that is within sight, within short range, and no bigger than half your size. Make an Intellect roll to destroy the object; the difficulty of this task is decreased by three steps (compared to breaking it with brute strength). Action.

Tier 4: Magnetic Field (4 Intellect points). When you wish it, a field of magnetism around you pulls incoming ranged, metallic projectile attacks (such as arrows, bullets, a thrown metal knife, and so on) to the ground. You are immune to such attacks for one round. You must be aware of an attack to foil it. Enabler.

Tier 5: Command Metal (5 Intellect points). You reshape a metallic item as you desire. The item must be within sight and within short range, and its mass can be no greater than your own. You can affect multiple items at once as long as their combined mass falls within these limits. You can fuse multiple items together. You can use this power to destroy a metal object (as the Destroy Metal ability), or you can craft it into another desired shape (crudely, unless you have the proper crafting skills). You can then move the new object anywhere within range. For example, you could take a few metal shields, fuse them together, and use the resulting shape to block a doorway. You can use this ability to make an attack—causing a foe's armor to constrict, rendering a metal item into shards that you fling across the battlefield, and so on—against one target within short range. Regardless of the form of the attack, it is an Intellect action that deals 7 points of damage. Action.

Tier 6: Diamagnetism. You magnetize any nonmetallic object within short range so that it can be affected by your other powers. Thus, with Move Metal, you can move any object. With Repel Metal, you are trained in all Speed defense tasks, regardless of

Employs Magnetism GM Intrusions: *Metal can twist and bend in unexpected ways. A lapse in concentration might cause something to slip or drop at just the wrong time.*

Crafting, page 217

whether the incoming attack uses metal. And so on. Enabler.

ENTERTAINS

Entertains GM Intrusions: *Failing to entertain can be worse than not having tried, as you often end up annoying or offending your audience. Musical instruments break, paints dry in their pots, and the words to a poem or song, once forgotten, never return.*

You are an entertainer: a singer, dancer, poet, storyteller, or something similar. You perform for the benefit of others. Naturally charismatic and talented, you have also studied to master your art. You know all the old poems, songs, jokes, and stories, and you're skilled at creating new ones, too.

You probably wear flamboyant or at least fashionable clothes and use cosmetics, tattoos, or hair stylings for dramatic effect.

Connection: Choose one of the following.

1. Pick one other PC. This character is your worst critic. Your abilities to help or inspire others don't function for her.

2. Pick one other PC. He seems to really enjoy your attempts to entertain, and this brings out the performer in you. It's up to that character whether his appreciation is real or if he is just being polite.

3. Pick one other PC. She is so inspired and put at ease by your stories or other forms of entertainment when you use Levity that she gains +2 to her recovery rolls (instead of +1).

4. Pick one other PC. This person knows the secret to one of your favorite forms of entertainment. You worry constantly that he will steal it or reveal it.

Additional Equipment: You start with a musical instrument or other tools needed to perform.

Minor Effect Suggestion: You enchant the target, who remains enchanted as long as you focus all your attention on keeping her that way.

Major Effect Suggestion: The target is forever favorably disposed toward you.

Tier 1: Levity. Through wit, charm, humor, and grace, you are trained in all social interactions other than those involving coercion or intimidation. During rests, you put friends and comrades at ease so much that they gain +1 to their recovery rolls. Enabler.

Tier 2: Inspiration. Through stories, songs, art, or other forms of entertainment, you inspire your friends. After spending twenty-four hours with you, once per day each of your friends can decrease the difficulty of a task by one step. This benefit is ongoing while you remain in the friend's company. It ends if you leave, but it resumes if you return to the friend's company within twenty-four hours. If you leave the friend's company for longer than that, you must spend another twenty-four hours together to reactivate the benefit. Enabler.

Tier 3: Knowledge. Your stories and songs contain truth. You are trained in two areas of knowledge of your choosing. Enabler.

Tier 4: Calm (3 Intellect points). Through jokes, song, or other art, you prevent a living foe from attacking anyone or anything for one round. Action.

Tier 5: Able Assistance. When you help someone with a task, you always reduce the difficulty of the task by one step regardless of your own skill at that task. Enabler.

Tier 6: Master Entertainer. Your Inspiration ability works more effectively, allowing your friends to decrease the difficulty of a task by two steps rather than one step. Enabler.

EXISTS IN TWO PLACES AT ONCE

Exists in Two Places at Once GM Intrusions: *Perceiving the world from two different places can be disorienting and cause momentary vertigo, nausea, or confusion.*

One day, you looked into a mirror or another reflective surface and noticed that the reflection didn't quite match your movements. After some time, the image stepped free from the surface and where there was one, there were now two.

You have a doppelganger, a duplicate you can call into existence when you wish. This duplicate may be a quirk of your nature, brought on by exposure to weird energy or a piece of scarcely understood technology. Then again, this other might hail from another reality, a branching timeline that may be similar to or quite different from your own. Of course, the copy could simply be a manifestation of your will on a cloud of nanites that assume your shape when you command them. Whatever the reason for your ability, you can call forth the copy and be in two places at once.

Your duplicate is your twin. It shares more than your appearance. It duplicates your mannerisms, manner of speech, expressions, and habits. In effect, you have another you.

Connection: Choose one of the following.

1. Pick one other PC. This character finds your talent unnerving and unsettling. For her, the difficulty of any task made to help your duplicate is increased by one step.
2. Pick one other PC. This character seems convinced that you are really a pair of identical twins with no actual powers.
3. Pick one other PC with a companion. This PC's companion seems to have an unusual relationship with your duplicate.
4. Pick one other PC. You used to move in the same social circles and knew of each other, but you had never been introduced.

Four Hands Are Better Than Two: When you and your duplicate work together to complete a task, the difficulty of that task is decreased by one step (if cooperation would be helpful).

Minor Effect Suggestion: For your target, the difficulty of the next task it attempts involving you or your duplicate before the end of the next round is increased by one step.

Major Effect Suggestion: You have an asset on the next roll you make within the next hour.

Tier 1: Duplicate (2 Might points). You cause a duplicate of yourself to appear at any point you can see within short range. The duplicate has no clothing or possessions when it appears. The duplicate is a level 2 NPC with 6 health. The duplicate obeys your commands and does as you direct it. The duplicate remains until you dismiss it using an action or until it is killed. When the duplicate disappears, it leaves behind anything it was wearing or carrying. If the duplicate disappears because it was killed, you take 4 points of damage that ignore Armor, and you lose your next action. Action to initiate.

Tier 2: Share Senses. While your duplicate is in existence and within 1 mile (2 km), you know everything it experiences and can communicate with it telepathically. Enabler.

Tier 3: Superior Duplicate (2 Might points). When you use your Duplicate ability, you can create a superior duplicate instead of a normal duplicate. A superior duplicate is a level 3 NPC with 15 health. Enabler.

Tier 4: Damage Transference. When you or your duplicate would take damage, you can transfer 1 point of damage from one to the other provided that you and your duplicate are within 1 mile (2 km) of each other. Enabler.

Tier 5: Coordinated Effort (3 Intellect points). When you and your duplicate would attack the same creature, you can choose to make one attack roll with an asset. If you hit, you inflict damage with both attacks and treat the attacks as if they were one attack for the purpose of subtracting Armor from the damage. Action.

Resilient Duplicate. Increase the health of any duplicate you create by 5.

Tier 6: Multiplicity (6 Might points). This ability functions as Duplicate, except you can create two duplicates. Action to initiate.

EXISTS PARTIALLY OUT OF PHASE

Exists Partially Out of Phase GM Intrusions: *Losing your grip on your phase state could send you into another dimension or even out of existence for a time. People are likely to panic if they see someone who looks ghostly.*

You have the ability to change your phase state. In fact, you're always slightly out of phase, giving you a ghostly translucence. With concentration, you can pass your hand through a solid object, allow a solid object to pass harmlessly through you, or literally walk through walls. However, moving in and out of different phase states requires extreme force of will and can be mentally taxing.

You might do whatever you can to play up your translucent appearance by wearing diaphanous, billowy clothing, or, depending on your personality, you might do just the opposite.

Connection: Choose one of the following.

1. Pick one other PC. You have known that character for a while, and he helped you gain control of your phase states.

2. Pick one other PC. Sometime in his past, he had a devastating experience with going out of phase. Whether he chooses to tell you about it is up to him.

3. Pick one other PC. You once accidentally moved your hand right through her. It was clearly an unnerving experience for you both.

4. Pick two other PCs. They both really want to go out of phase and have been pestering you about it. But you're not convinced they even know what that phrase means.

Minor Effect Suggestion: While out of phase, you also gain +1 to all Speed defense rolls.

Major Effect Suggestion: While out of phase, you are also invisible.

Tier 1: Walk Through Walls (2 Intellect points). You can slowly pass through physical barriers at a rate of 1 inch (3 cm) per round (minimum of one round to pass through any barrier). You can't act (other than moving) or perceive anything until you pass entirely through the barrier. You can't pass through energy barriers. Action.

Tier 2: Defensive Phasing (2 Intellect points). You can change your phase so that some attacks pass through you harmlessly. For the next ten minutes, the difficulty of all your Speed defense tasks is reduced by one step, but during this time you lose any benefit from armor you wear. Action to initiate.

Tier 3: Phased Attack (3 Intellect points). The attack you make on this turn ignores your foe's Armor. The ability works for whatever kind of attack you use (melee, ranged, energy, and so on). Enabler.

Tier 4: Ghost (4 Intellect points). For the next ten minutes, you are trained in sneaking tasks. During this time, you can move through solid barriers (but not energy barriers) at a rate of 1 foot (30 cm) per round, and you can perceive while phased within a barrier or object, which allows you to peek through walls. Action to initiate.

Tier 5: Untouchable (6 Intellect points). You change your phase state for the next minute so that you can't affect or be affected by normal matter or energy. Only mental attacks and special transdimensional energies, devices, or abilities can affect you, but likewise you can't attack, touch, or otherwise affect anything. Action to initiate.

Tier 6: Enhanced Phased Attack (5 Intellect points). This ability works like the third-tier Phased Attack ability except that your attack also disrupts the foe's vitals, dealing 5 additional points of damage. Enabler.

EXPLORES DARK PLACES

You explore foreboding ruins, mysterious locales of ancient times, dungeons deep, dark caverns, and similar places, trained in such activities by those who have gone before you. You're the archetypal treasure hunter, scavenger, and finder of lost things. You spend so much of your time in the dark that you slowly adapt to it, almost becoming a creature of the gloom yourself. Even in civilized areas, you prefer to keep to the shadows.

Most likely, you wear dark clothing to help you blend into the blackness. On the other hand, you might wear sensible garments and gear because you have serious and dangerous business to attend to in the dark.

Connection: Choose one of the following.

1. Pick one other PC. This character has been your adventuring partner in previous expeditions, and the two of you work so well together that you both gain +1 to any die rolls when you collaborate on the same task, fight the same foe, and so on.
2. Pick two other PCs. You think you once saw them through a keyhole doing something illegal. You can choose whether or not to share that information. The characters can choose whether it was really them (it could have been neither, one, or both), and they may or may not share that information in return.
3. Pick one other PC. This person always seems to hear you, no matter how stealthy you try to be.
4. Pick one other PC. She is so loud in everything she does that you feel obligated to try to help her learn to move more quietly through the world. Whether or not she's interested is up to her.

Explores Dark Places GM Intrusions: *Sometimes items fall out of pockets or bags in the dark, never to be found again—or, at least, not by the one who lost them.*

Additional Equipment: You carry an explorer's pack with rope, two days' rations, a bedroll, and other tools needed for outdoor survival.

Shadow Abilities: If you have other overt abilities (spells, psionic powers, or the like), they make almost no sound, and whatever visual displays they produce are dark and shadowy. These alterations change nothing other than the appearance of the effects. A Flash is a silent burst of shadows, a Barrier is a mass of shadowy wisps, and so on.

Flash, page 33

Barrier, page 33

Minor Effect Suggestion: The target is also dazed for one round, during which time the difficulty of all tasks it performs is modified by one step to its detriment.

Major Effect Suggestion: The target is also stunned and loses its next turn.

Tier 1: Trained Explorer. You are trained in searching, listening, climbing, balancing, and jumping tasks. Enabler.

Tier 2: Trained Infiltrator. You are trained in lockpicking and tinkering with devices. Enabler.

Eyes Adjusted. You can see in very dim light as though it were bright light. You can see in total darkness as if it were very dim. Enabler.

Tier 3: Slippery Customer. You are trained in escaping from bonds, fitting in tight spaces, and other contortionist tasks. Thanks to your experience, you also are trained in Speed defense tasks while wearing light armor or no armor. Enabler.

Tier 4: Resilient. In your explorations of dark places, you've been exposed to all sorts of terrible things and are developing a general resistance. You gain +1 to Armor and are trained in Might defense tasks. Enabler.

Tier 5: Dark Explorer. You ignore penalties for any action (including fighting) in very dim light or in cramped spaces. Combined with your Eyes Adjusted ability, you can act without penalty even in total darkness. You are also trained in sneaking tasks while in dim or no light. Enabler.

Tier 6: Blinding Attack (3 Speed points). If you have a source of light, you can use it to make a melee attack against a target. If successful, the attack deals no damage, but the target is blinded for one minute. Action.

EXPLORES DEEP WATERS

You have nothing to fear from the depths. You have always been a good swimmer, able to hold your breath longer than anyone else, tread water for as long as you wanted, and delve deeper into the swirling darkness than your friends, all without stretching your resources. The depths you so freely explore harbor many secrets, and the waters that shelter you become part of who you are, an extension of your identity.

Explores Deep Waters GM Intrusions: *Spending a lot of time underwater might make you more susceptible to dehydration and exhaustion when exploring arid environments.*

When you bother to wear clothes, you favor snug, tight-fitting garments that stay close to your skin and do not hamper your mobility.

The abilities granted by this focus might result from special equipment you make along the way, weird transformations that began when you first swam into the deepest, darkest places, or simply an expression of an unusual gift or heritage.

Connection: Choose one of the following.

1. Pick one other PC. That character nearly drowned while following you on one of your expeditions underwater. It's up to him whether he trusts you in such an environment again.

2. Pick one other PC. She knows something about your past that you wish she didn't.

3. Pick one other PC. You think he suspects that you were involved with pirates or other criminals. Whether you were or not is up to you.

4. Pick one other PC. She can't swim very well and fears open water. You believe that you can help her overcome these issues, if she is willing to let you.

Additional Equipment: You have a special device that, when fitted in your mouth, allows you to breathe underwater. The device functions for up to four hours at a time, after which you must wait four hours before you can use it again.

Water Abilities: If you wield powers that would normally use force or other energy, they instead use water or ice. For example, a blast of energy might create a wave of water that crashes down on your target.

In addition, if you wish, you can swap an ability gained from your type for the following.

Create Water (2 Intellect points). You cause water to bubble up from a spot on the ground you can see. The water flows from that spot for one minute, creating about 1 gallon (4 liters) by the time it stops.

Minor Effect Suggestion: You can take an extra action. You may use this action only to move or perform a movement-related activity.

Major Effect Suggestion: The difficulty of any Speed defense actions you take before the end of the next round is reduced by one step.

Tier 1: Diver. You can safely dive into water from heights of up to 100 feet (30 m), and you can withstand pressure when in water as deep as 100 feet (30 m). Enabler.

Hold Breath. You can hold your breath for up to five minutes. Enabler.

Trained Swimmer. While underwater, you are trained in escaping, perception, sneaking, and swimming tasks, as well as in tasks to identify aquatic creatures and geography. Enabler.

Tier 2: Eyes Adjusted. You can see in very dim light as though it were bright light. You can see in total darkness as if it were very dim light. Enabler.

Resist Underwater Hazards. Whether you're resisting the crushing waters from exploring the depths or a sting from a poisonous fish, the difficulty of all defense actions while submerged in water is reduced by one step. Enabler.

Tier 3: Aquatic Combatant. You ignore penalties for any action (including fighting) in underwater environments. Enabler.

Athletic Conditioning. You add 1 point to your Might Pool and your Speed Pool. Enabler.

Tier 4: Nimble Swimmer. You are trained in all defense actions while underwater. Enabler.

Swim (1+ Intellect points). You can swim like a fish through water and similar liquid for one hour. For each level of Effort applied, you can extend the duration by one hour. You swim about 10 miles (16 km) per hour, and you are not affected by currents in the water. Action to initiate.

Tier 5: Communication (2 Intellect points). You can convey a basic concept or ask a simple question to a creature that lives underwater and cannot speak or understand speech, and the creature can provide you with a basic answer. Action.

Elusive (2 Speed points). When you succeed on a Speed defense action, you immediately gain an action. You can use this action only to move. Enabler.

Tier 6: Deep Water Guide. While underwater, any creature you choose that can see you has an asset on swimming tasks. Enabler.

Master of the Deep Waters. While underwater, your Might Edge, Speed Edge, and Intellect Edge each increase by 1. Enabler.

Water Adaptation. You can breathe water as easily as you breathe air. Enabler.

FIGHTS DIRTY

You know one thing for certain: the only important element of a fight is who wins. How? Why? These questions are inconsequential. Thus, you'll do anything to win a fight. Some might say you have no honor, no class, or some other foolish statement, but they're missing the point. You come out on top in a battle—and that's all that matters.

You bite, scratch, kick, and trip. You tangle foes in draperies, push them down stairs, and throw dirt in their eyes. You trick them into looking the wrong way, call them names, and say terrible things about their mothers.

Maybe you learned your methods while living on the streets, or maybe you barely survived a particularly horrific battle in a military campaign. Perhaps you simply have never bought into the idea of rules or honor when your life is on the line.

You're likely to carry a few hidden tricks, sometimes literally up your sleeve. You might have a knife in your boot, a poisoned needle in your ring, a razor in the hem of your cloak, or a handful of stinging and

Fights Dirty GM Intrusions: *People look poorly upon those who "cheat" or fight without honor. Sometimes a dirty trick backfires, and you end up with a handful of dirt in your eyes instead.*

itching powder in a hidden pocket. Your clothing probably has a lot of pockets, actually—more than a few of them well hidden.

Connection: Choose one of the following.

1. Pick one other PC. He's a good fighter, but if you could teach him a few of your tricks, he'd really excel.
2. Pick one other PC. In the past, she taught you a few tricks to use in a fight.
3. Pick one other PC. This character doesn't seem to approve of your methods.
4. Pick one other PC. Long ago, the two of you were on opposite sides of a fight. You won, using your particular tactics. Now she's interested in a (friendly) rematch at some point and claims to be ready for you.

Additional Equipment: You have a weapon that is easily hidden and a dose of level 3 poison that inflicts 6 points of damage.

Minor Effect Suggestion: You manage to make your foe trip and fall prone.

Major Effect Suggestion: You tangle something around your foe's legs, and he not only falls down but also loses his next turn.

Tier 1: Taking Advantage. When your foe is weakened, dazed, stunned, moved down the damage track, or disadvantaged in some other way, the difficulty of your attacks against that foe is decreased by one step beyond any other modifications due to the disadvantage. Enabler.

Liar. You are trained in all forms of deception. Enabler.

Tier 2: Eye Gouge (2 Speed points). You make an attack against a creature with an eye. The difficulty of the attack is increased by one step, but if you hit, the creature has trouble seeing for the next hour. During this time, the difficulty of the creature's tasks that rely on sight (which is most tasks) is increased by one step. Action.

Fights With Panache GM Intrusions: *Looking silly, clumsy, or unattractive can be the swashbuckler's greatest fear.*

Tier 3: Spot Weakness. If a creature that you can see has a special weakness, such as a vulnerability to fire, a negative modification to perception, or so on, you know what it is. (Ask and the GM will tell you.) Enabler.

Betrayal. Any time you convince a foe that you are not a threat and then suddenly attack it (without provocation), the attack deals 4 additional points of damage. Enabler.

Tier 4: Mind Games (3 Intellect points). You use lies and trickery against a foe that can understand you. If successful, the foe is stunned for one round and cannot act, and it is dazed in the following round, during which time the difficulty of its tasks is increased by one step.

Tooth and Nail. If, during a melee combat, you are willing to literally bite and claw at a foe in addition to attacking with your normal weapon, you inflict 1 additional point of damage each time you strike with your standard attack. Some creatures (such as automatons or incorporeal creatures) might not be subject to this, and attempting to bite some creatures might be dangerous. Enabler.

Tier 5: Using the Environment (4 Intellect points). You find some way to use the environment to your advantage in a fight. For the next ten minutes, the difficulty of attack rolls and Speed defense rolls is decreased by one step. Action to initiate.

Tier 6: Twisting the Knife (4 Speed points). In a round after successfully striking a foe with a melee weapon, you can opt to automatically deal standard damage to the foe with that same weapon without any modifiers (2 points for a light weapon, 4 points for a medium weapon, or 6 points for a heavy weapon). Action.

FIGHTS WITH PANACHE

You know that style is at least as important as substance. Defeating foes is secondary to looking good while doing it. Some might call you a swashbuckler or daredevil. You leap through the air, make a flourish with your weapon, and attack, usually with a clever, biting show of wit. Your enemies hate you, but your allies adore you. Just watching you fight is entertaining.

You very likely wear no armor, instead preferring stylish clothing—perhaps even a hat with a feather.

Connection: Choose one of the following.

1. Pick one other PC. You're always trying to impress this character with your skill,

wit, appearance, or bravado. Perhaps she is a rival, perhaps you need her respect, or perhaps you're romantically interested in her.

2. Pick one other PC. This character seems to anticipate your next move almost before you even begin it. When he collaborates with you on the same task or fights the same foe, you gain +1 to any die rolls.

3. Pick one other PC. You fear that she is jealous of your abilities and worry that it might lead to problems.

4. Pick one other PC. This character is so enamored of your swashbuckling, entertaining ways during combat that he sometimes forgets to take action himself.

Additional Equipment: You begin with a set of extremely stylish clothes and a jeweled weapon.

Minor Effect Suggestion: The target is so dazzled by your style that it is dazed for one round, during which time the difficulty of its tasks is modified by one step to its detriment.

Major Effect Suggestion: Make an additional attack with your weapon on your turn.

Tier 1: Attack Flourish. With your attack, you add stylish moves, entertaining quips, or a certain something that entertains or impresses others. Choose any number of creatures within short range who can see you; each of them gains a +1 bonus to its next die roll. Enabler.

Tier 2: Quick Block. If you use a light or medium weapon, the difficulty of your Speed defense actions is decreased by one step. Enabler.

Tier 3: Acrobatic Attack (3 Speed points). You leap into the attack, twisting or flipping through the air. This motion decreases the difficulty of your attack by one step. If you roll a natural 17 or 18, you can choose to have a minor effect rather than deal extra damage. You can't use this ability if your Speed is modified from wearing armor. Enabler.

Tier 4: Mobile Fighter (3 Speed points). As part of your attack, you can leap on or over obstacles, swing from ropes, run along narrow surfaces, or otherwise move around the battlefield at your normal speed as if such tasks were routine (difficulty 0). You can't use this ability if your Speed is modified from wearing armor. Enabler.

Tier 5: Block for Another. If you use a light or medium weapon, you can block attacks made against an ally near you. Choose one creature within immediate range. You decrease the difficulty of that creature's Speed defense actions by one step. You can't use Quick Block while using Block for Another. Enabler.

Tier 6: Agile Wit. When attempting a Speed task, you instead can roll (and spend points) as if it were an Intellect action. If you apply Effort to this task, you can spend points from your Intellect Pool instead of your Speed Pool (in which case you also use your Intellect Edge instead of your Speed Edge). Enabler.

Focuses Mind Over Matter GM Intrusions: *One mental slip, and moving objects drop or fragile objects break. Sometimes the wrong item moves, falls, or breaks.*

FOCUSES MIND OVER MATTER

Telekinesis. Psychokinesis. Mind over matter. The power has many names, but in the end, it all boils down to one thing—the molecules that make up all matter are yours to command. You likely call yourself a telekinetic or just a TK.

Many telekinetics prefer to wear tight clothing without many accoutrements so there is little another TK could grab hold of psychically. On the other hand, you have the power to create very minor telekinetic effects at will, so your hair might always be in motion, you could have a few tiny objects floating around you, or you might wear a long cape that's always billowing.

Connection: Choose one of the following.

1. Pick one other PC. This character can cause your telekinetic powers to act oddly. Every once in a while, if he stands directly next to you, your powers are canceled, but at other times, they seem improved when used near him.
2. Pick one other PC. This person thinks that your powers are completely hypothetical.
3. Pick one other PC. You once joked that you could read her mind. Whether she found that exciting or utterly terrifying is up to her.
4. Pick one other PC. You feel strangely protective of that character and plan to do your best to keep him from harm.

Mental Abilities: If you wield other overt abilities, those that would normally use force or other energy instead use telekinetic force. For example, a force blast is a telekinetic blast from your mind. This alteration changes nothing except that you don't need a free hand to perform abilities that otherwise require it.

Minor Effect Suggestion: An object moves faster or more efficiently.

Major Effect Suggestion: You can move or affect twice as much as normal.

Tier 1: Deflect Attacks (1 Intellect point). Using your mind, you protect yourself from incoming attacks. For the next ten minutes, you are trained in Speed defense tasks. Action to initiate.

Tier 2: Telekinesis (2 Intellect points). You can exert force on objects within short range. Once activated, your power has an effective Might Pool of 10, a Might Edge of 1, and an Effort of 2 (approximately equal to the strength of a fit, capable adult human), and you can use it to move objects, push against objects, and so on. For example, you could lift and pull a light object anywhere within range to yourself or move a heavy object (like a piece of furniture) about 10 feet (3 m). This power lacks the fine control to wield a weapon or move objects with much speed, so in most situations, it's not a means of attack. You can't use this ability on your own body. The power lasts for one hour or until its Might Pool is depleted—whichever comes first. Action.

Tier 3: Enhance Strength (3 Intellect points). For the next ten minutes, tasks that depend on brute force—such as moving a heavy object, smashing down a door, or hitting someone with a melee weapon—are easier for you. The difficulty of all such tasks is decreased by one step. Action to initiate.

Tier 4: Apportation (4 Intellect points). You call a physical object to you. You can choose any piece of normal standard equipment, or (no more than once per day) you can allow the GM to determine the object randomly. If you call a random object, it has a 20 percent chance of being a cypher or an artifact, a 40 percent chance of being a piece of standard equipment, and a 40 percent chance of being a bit of worthless junk. You can't use this ability to take an item held by another creature. Action.

Tier 5: Psychokinetic Attack (5 Intellect points). You can use this attack in one of two ways. The first is to pick up a heavy object and hurl it at someone within short range, an Intellect action that deals 6 points of damage to the target and to the hurled object (which could be another foe, although that would require two rolls—one to grab the first foe and another to hit the second foe with the first). The second way to use Psychokinetic Attack is to unleash a shattering burst of power that works only against an inanimate object no larger than half your size. Make an Intellect roll to instantly destroy the object; the difficulty of this task is decreased by three steps (compared to breaking it with brute strength). Action.

Tier 6: Reshape Matter (6 Intellect points). Your mastery of telekinesis is so great that you can reshape objects on a molecular level. You can affect a single object no larger than you, which must be visible and close enough to touch. You can use this ability to damage the object (as if using Psychokinetic Attack, except the difficulty of the task is decreased by four steps instead of three), or you can attempt a crafting task to reshape the object into another form. Reshaping an object usually has a difficulty equal to 1 plus the level of the finished object.

Crafting, page 217

FUSES FLESH AND STEEL

At some point in your past, some of your organic parts were replaced with artificial components. You are a cyborg. Bionic. Alternatively, you belong to a secret race of biomechanical hybrids. Your artificial components might be subdermal, or they might resemble overt metal or synth plating on your skin. They can also take the form of threadlike tendrils of circuitry winding across your flesh. Whatever their appearance, these components give you special abilities. As you advance, you can add to, modify, or discover new functions for them. Unfortunately, your artificial body also has special requirements when it takes damage.

You probably wear a cloak with a hood or something similar to hide your artificial parts from those who would persecute you. Because your components are tricky to repair, as time goes on, it might become more difficult to conceal your true nature, with exposed circuitry, metal plates, and more in a state of partial disassembly.

Connection: Choose one of the following.

1. Pick one other PC. This character knows your true nature, even if no one else does. If your components are not particularly hidden, she knows a different secret of yours, such as a preprogrammed word that will shut you down for ten minutes.
2. Pick one other PC. Being close to this person sometimes makes your mechanical parts vibrate slightly. You can decide whether this sensation is unnerving or pleasant.
3. Pick one other PC. You're pretty sure that he is just here to mine you for parts. He chooses whether or not this is true.

Fuses Flesh and Steel GM Intrusion: *People in most societies are afraid of someone who is revealed to have mechanical parts.*

Psychokinesis doesn't necessarily mean "mental powers." Someone who uses it might actually be accessing a mechanical or bioengineered portion of their brain to direct nanites that move or change matter.

4. Pick one other PC who also has mechanical parts. The two of you have bonded over conversations about this element you share, and you feel a special connection.

Additional Equipment: You have a bag of light tools and a variety of parts to repair yourself.

Minor Effect Suggestion: Your servos learn from your successful actions. You gain a +1 bonus to similar actions involving the same task (such as making attacks against the same foe or operating the same device).

Major Effect Suggestion: You discharge a small pulse of power into your foe. Make an immediate attack against that foe (using the same stat as the action that caused the major effect). If the attack succeeds, it deals 4 points of electrical damage.

Tier 1: Enhanced Body. You gain +1 to Armor, 3 additional points to your Might Pool, and 3 additional points to your Speed Pool. Enabler.

Special Healing. Traditional healing skills, medicines, and techniques work only half as well for you. Each time you start at full health, the first 5 points of damage you take can never be healed in these ways or recovered normally. Instead, you must use repairing skills and abilities to restore those points. For example, if you start with a full Might Pool of 10 and take 8 points of damage, you can use recovery rolls to restore 3 points, but the remaining 5 points must be restored using repairing methods. The difficulty of the task is equal to the number of points of damage sustained.

Tier 2: Interface. By directly plugging into a device, you can identify and learn to operate it as though the task were one level lower. Enabler.

Tier 3: Weaponization. One light or medium melee weapon of your choice is built into your body, and you are trained in this weapon (even if you are not trained in other weapons of that type). The weapon is concealed until you wish to use it. Enabler.

Tier 4: Fusion. You can fuse your cyphers and artifacts with your body. These fused devices function as if they were one level higher. Enabler.

Tier 5: Deep Reserves. Once each day, you can transfer up to 5 points between your Pools in any combination, at a rate of 1 point per round. For example, you could transfer 3 points of Might to Speed and 2 points of Intellect to Speed, which would take a total of five rounds. Action.

Tier 6: Ultra Enhancement. You gain +1 to Armor and 5 additional points to each of your three stat Pools. Enabler.

FUSES MIND AND MACHINE

You believe that the finest machine ever created is the human brain (although some scientists would disagree). Experience and training have taught you that any machine can be improved. Through the use of implants and mechanical enhancements, your brain processes input faster, stores more information, and eventually can tap right into the Internet (or similar data network). Mentally, you function on an entirely different level than your fellows.

Did you make these improvements yourself? Did someone else? Was it with your blessing or against your will? Regardless, you are now more than just a person. You are both living creature and machine. But unlike what others might assume, all of your refinements and upgrades are on the inside. You don't need mech eyes or metal arms to be enhanced. It's all about what's inside your skull.

Connection: Choose one of the following.

1. Pick one other PC. This character knows a few things that can help when your implants and enhancements malfunction.
2. Pick one other PC. He seems to find you off-putting. You wonder if it's because you're clearly smarter than he is or if it's for some other reason.
3. Pick one other PC. This character has a small device that can shut down your brain with a single switch. However, you don't think he has any idea of what it is or what it can do.
4. Pick one other PC. Within your memory circuits, you have data of someone who looks just like that character committing terrible crimes—hundreds of years ago. You have no explanation.

Additional Equipment: You have an artifact that protects your implants and enhancements from disruption or intrusion. The difficulty of resisting such attacks is decreased by one step.

Minor Effect Suggestion: You foresee your foes' moves so well that the difficulty of your Speed defense rolls for the next round is decreased by one step.

Major Effect Suggestion: Processing surge! On your next action, you can use points from your Intellect Pool rather than your Might or Speed Pools.

Tier 1: Mechanical Assistance. You gain 4 additional points to your Intellect Pool through the use of implants and tiny processing devices. Enabler.

Stored Memories: You are trained in one area of knowledge (history, geography, astronomy, and so on) of your choice. Enabler.

Tier 2: Network Tap (4 Intellect points). You can ask the GM one question and get a very short answer. Action.

Tier 3: Action Processor (4 Intellect points). Drawing upon stored information and the ability to process incoming data at amazing speeds, you are trained in one physical task of your choice for ten minutes. For example, you can choose running, climbing, swimming, Speed defense, or attacks with a specific weapon. Action to initiate.

Tier 4: Processing Power. You gain 2 additional points to your Intellect Pool and +1 to your Intellect Edge. Enabler.

More Stored Memories: You are trained in one area of knowledge (history, geography, astronomy, and so on) of your choice. Enabler.

Tier 5: See the Future (6 Intellect points). Based on all the variables you perceive, you can predict the next few minutes. This has the following effects:

- For the next ten minutes, the difficulty of your defense rolls is reduced by one step.
- You have a sort of "danger sense." For the next ten minutes, you can predict the actions of those around you. You are trained in seeing through deceptions and attempts to betray you as well as avoiding traps and ambushes.
- You know what people are probably thinking and what they will say before they say it. You are trained in all skills involving interaction and deception.

Enabler.

Tier 6: Reboot. In addition to your normal recovery rolls each day, you can—at any time between ten-hour rests—recover 1d6 + 6 points to your Intellect Pool. Action.

Fuses Mind and Machine GM Intrusions: *Machines malfunction and shut down. Powerful machine intelligences can take control of lesser thinking machines. Some people don't trust a person who isn't fully organic.*

Enhancement. Any time you use Effort on an Intellect action, add one of the following enhancements to the action (your choice):

- +2 to the roll
- +2 to damage
- Automatic minor effect

Enabler.

GROWS TO TOWERING HEIGHTS

Grows to Towering Heights GM Intrusions: *Rapid growth knocks over furnishings or smashes through ceilings or hanging lights. While enlarged, you break through the floor. People scream and run. An unexpected side effect from an energy attack causes you to shrink.*

You have the ability to become a towering giant for short periods. When you do, everything and everyone seems to shrink around you, until it's like you're walking through a children's play area, where everything is sized for toddlers. As you grow ever larger, your sense of scale shifts further. At your maximum height, most other creatures are as insects, and unless you take care, you easily crush them beneath your colossal feet.

When you're not growing, you look normal. Only the clothing in direct contact with your skin grows with you, so you wear expensive outerwear only when you're fairly certain you won't have to trigger your Enlarge ability.

Connection: Choose one of the following.

1. Pick one other PC. When you grow, if that character is next to you, she also grows, but only about a foot in height.
2. Pick one other PC. That character helped you find a way to mentally control your ability to grow; at first, it triggered only when you were emotionally distressed.
3. Pick two other PCs. At great risk to themselves, they pulled your oversized, unconscious body from a bad situation and saved your life.
4. Pick one other PC. This character inadvertently hinders your actions. If he is within immediate range, the difficulty of any action that you take related to this focus is increased by one step.

Minor Effect Suggestion: Your opponent is so startled by your size that it is dazed, during which time the difficulty of all tasks it performs is modified by one step to its detriment.

Major Effect Suggestion: All opponents within short range are so startled by your sudden growth that they are dazed, during which time the difficulty of all tasks they perform is modified by one step to their detriment.

Tier 1: Enlarge (1+ Might point). You trigger the enzymatic reaction that draws additional mass from another dimension, and you (and your clothing or suit) grow larger. You achieve a height of 9 feet (3 m) and stay that way for about a minute. During that time, you add 4 points to your Might Pool, add +1 to Armor, and add +2 to your Might Edge. While you are larger than normal, the difficulty of your Speed defense rolls is increased by one step, and you are practiced in using your fists as heavy weapons.

When the effects of Enlarge end, your Armor and Might Edge return to normal, and you subtract a number of points from your Might Pool equal to the number you gained (if this brings the Pool to 0, subtract the overflow first from your Speed Pool and then, if necessary, from your Intellect Pool). Each additional time you use Enlarge before your next ten-hour recovery roll, you must apply an additional level of Effort. Thus, the second time you use Enlarge, you must apply one level of Effort; the third time you use Enlarge, two levels of Effort; and so on. Action to initiate.

Freakishly Large. Your increased size intimidates most people. While you enjoy the effects of Enlarge, the difficulty of all intimidation tasks you attempt is decreased by one step. Enabler.

Tier 2: Bigger. When you use Enlarge, you can choose to grow up to 12 feet (4 m) in height, and you add a total of 7 temporary points to your Might Pool. Enabler.

Advantages of Being Big. You're so big that you can move massive objects more easily, climb buildings by using hand- and footholds unavailable to regular-sized people, and jump much farther. While you enjoy the effects of Enlarge, the difficulty of all climbing, lifting, and jumping tasks is decreased by one step. Enabler.

Tier 3: Huge. When you use Enlarge, you can choose to grow up to 16 feet (5 m) in height. When you do, you add +1 to Armor (a total of +2 to Armor) and deal 2 additional points of damage with melee attacks. Enabler.

Tier 4: Grab. While you are Enlarged, you can attack by attempting to wrap your massive hands around a target the size of a normal human or smaller. While you maintain your hold as your action, you keep the target from moving or taking physical actions (other than attempts to escape). The target's escape attempt is modified by two steps to its detriment due to your size. If you wish, you can automatically inflict 3 points of damage each round on the target while you hold it, but you can also keep it protected (by taking all attacks otherwise meant for the target). Action.

Tier 5: Gargantuan. When you use Enlarge, you can choose to grow up to 30 feet (9 m) in height, and you add a total of 10 temporary points to your Might Pool. Enabler.

Tier 6: Colossal. When you use Enlarge, you can choose to grow up to a base height of 60 feet (18 m). When you do, you add a total of 15 temporary points to your Might Pool, and you deal a total of 4 additional points of damage with melee attacks. For each level of Effort you apply to increase your height further, your total height increases by 10 feet (3 m), and you add 1 point to your Might Pool. Thus, the first time you use Enlarge after a ten-hour recovery roll, if you apply two levels of Effort, your base height is 80 feet (24 m), and you add a total of 17 temporary points to your Might Pool. Enabler.

GROWING TO TOWERING HEIGHTS

Once a character becomes so large that she towers over buildings, she can accomplish a variety of tasks that a GM can adjudicate. For instance, a character who is 120 feet (37 m) tall covers a short distance (up to 50 feet [15 m]) with her average stride, and if she spent her action moving, she'd cover about 500 feet (152 m) instead. She could attempt to use her Grab ability on targets much larger than a regular-sized human, make melee attacks against airplanes, leave behind enormous footprints that might serve as pits, and so on.

HOWLS AT THE MOON

Howls at the Moon GM Intrusions: *People are terrified of monsters, and savage beasts that can take the form of ordinary folks are even more frightening.*

You are a lycanthrope—a werewolf, werebear, wererat, weretiger, or something similar. You are cursed and blessed to be able to transform into a powerful creature, drawing additional mass from a transdimensional source. You and the GM should work out the exact nature of the creature, including its appearance, but it's a wild beast of rage and blood—at least until you learn to control it.

Style and appearance are probably low on your list of concerns. Your clothes might be ragged because your transformation is hard on them (or they're cheap because you know they'll be destroyed the next time you transform).

Connection: Choose one of the following.

1. Pick one other PC. That character is able to soothe you when you're in beast form. You'll never attack him while transformed, and if he spends three consecutive turns using his action to calm you down, you can revert to your normal form without having to make a roll.

2. Pick one other PC. You believe that he intends to convince you (or capture you) to join the circus or some other entertainment venue. He chooses whether or not this is true.

3. Pick two other PCs. They know that it's beneficial for you to kill and eat a creature while you're in beast form, and they often work together to make sure that happens.

4. Pick one other PC. Since she saw you in beast form, she has clearly been terrified of you. You are determined to show her that you're not as dangerous as she thinks.

Additional Equipment: You have an accurate timepiece that always lets you know when the next transformation is coming.

Minor Effect Suggestion: The target is so intimidated by your bestial attack that it is dazed for one round, during which time the difficulty of all tasks it performs is modified by one step to its detriment.

Major Effect Suggestion: Your attack conveys a small bit of your lycanthropy. If your foe survives, one month later, he transforms into an uncontrolled beast. The GM decides what happens from there.

Tier 1: Beast Form. On five consecutive nights each month, you change into a

monstrous beast for up to one hour each night. In this new form, you gain +8 to your Might Pool, +1 to your Might Edge, +2 to your Speed Pool, and +1 to your Speed Edge. While in beast form, you can't spend Intellect points for any reason other than to try to change to your normal form before the one-hour duration is over (a difficulty 2 task). In addition, you attack any and every living creature within short range. After you revert to your normal form, you take a –1 penalty to all rolls for one hour. If you did not kill and eat at least one substantial creature while in beast form, the penalty increases to –2 and affects all your rolls for the next twenty-four hours. Action to change back.

Tier 2: Controlled Change. You can try to change into your beast form on any night you wish (a difficulty 3 Intellect task). Any transformations you make using this power are in addition to the five nights per month that you change involuntarily. Action to change.

Tier 3: Greater Beast Form. Your beast form gains the following additional bonuses: +1 to your Might Edge, +2 to your Speed Pool, and +1 to your Speed Edge. Enabler.

Tier 4: Greater Controlled Change. You no longer change into your beast form unless you want to. Transforming into your beast form or back to your normal form is now a difficulty 1 Intellect task. Enabler.

Tier 5: Enhanced Beast Form. Your beast form gains the following additional bonuses: +3 to your Might Pool, +2 to your Speed Pool, and +2 to Armor. Enabler.

Tier 6: Perfect Control. You no longer need to make a roll to change into your beast form or your normal form. You can change back and forth as your action. When you return to your normal form, you no longer take a penalty to your rolls. Enabler.

HUNTS NONHUMANS

You see orcs, lizard people, aliens from Rigel, elves, undead, or some other sort of inhuman group as a threat to humanity. The threat is obvious to you—they attack, abduct, enslave, prey upon, or murder humans. But the threat can also be far more subtle. They infiltrate, control, subvert, undermine, and terrorize. These threats must be eradicated for the good of all.

Nonhuman hunters choose their dedicated foe and focus all their attention on that one opponent whenever possible. In this context, a nonhuman is something that isn't human and often comes in great numbers. In a fantasy setting, it might be goblins. In a science fiction setting, it might be insectlike alien hordes. Zombies and in some cases mutants might also fit the bill, but keep in mind the similar focus Hunts Outcasts for those who specialize in fighting foes with supernatural abilities.

Whatever the foe, hunters of nonhumans know their enemy's tactics, methods, weapons, defenses, and abilities.

Connection: Choose one of the following.

1. Pick one other PC. This character has had experiences with the foe in the past, and you'd like to know more about them.
2. Pick one other PC. You are friends, and you'd hate to see this character harmed.
3. Pick one other PC. This character doesn't understand just how dangerous and horrible the foe can be.
4. Pick one other PC. The inhuman foes are sometimes drawn to certain people. They always seem to attack those people first and with more fervor. This character appears to be one such person.

Minor Effect Suggestion: Your foe is so intimidated by your prowess that it backs away, unwilling to attack. It can still defend itself.

Major Effect Suggestion: Your foe is terrified by your skill and flees.

Tier 1: Tracker and Hunter. When tracking, looking for, interacting with, or hiding from your chosen foe, the difficulty of the task is decreased by one step. Enabler.

Nonhuman Fighter. You inflict 2 additional points of damage when fighting nonhumans. Enabler.

Hunts Nonhumans GM Intrusions: *Nonhumans are often smart enough to take out the biggest threat first. They sometimes make surprising use of poison, traps, and ambushes.*

Hunts Outcasts, page 136

Tier 2: Nonhuman Sense (2 Intellect points). Through scent, specific signs, and past experience, you know when your foe is within long range for one hour. Enabler.

Expert Combatant. Choose one type of attack in which you are not already trained: light bashing, light bladed, light ranged, medium bashing, medium bladed, medium ranged, heavy bashing, heavy bladed, or heavy ranged. You are trained in attacks using that type of weapon. Enabler.

Tier 3: Horde Fighting. When two or more foes attack you at once in melee, you can use them against each other. The difficulty of Speed defense rolls or attack rolls (your choice) against them is reduced by one step. Enabler.

Tier 4: Improved Nonhuman Fighter. You inflict 3 additional points of damage when fighting nonhumans. Enabler.

Tier 5: Nonhuman Slayer. When fighting nonhumans, the difficulty of all attack rolls and defense rolls is decreased by one step. Enabler.

Tier 6: Master Combatant. Choose one type of attack in which you are already trained: light bashing, light bladed, light ranged, medium bashing, medium bladed, medium ranged, heavy bashing, heavy bladed, or heavy ranged. You are specialized in attacks using that type of weapon. Enabler.

Hunts Nonhumans and Hunts Outcasts require a bit of specific adjustment to fit the setting. The GM should provide nonhuman or outcast groups of NPCs for the character to hunt.

HUNTS OUTCASTS

Mutants. Witches. Aliens. They've got weird powers, and they're a threat to everything you hold dear. They represent everything that is wrong with your world. They are a scourge upon humanity—a disease that must be put down. You don't necessarily take pleasure in their eradication, but it must be done for the good of the human race. If this cancer is not destroyed now, it will only spread.

You must choose a type of forbidden outcast or a hated supernatural person or being appropriate to the setting at hand. In this context, an outcast is something or someone that has powers or abilities beyond those of normal humans; examples include wizards or fey in a magical setting, mutants in a science fiction setting, weird psionic aliens, ghosts, vampires, and so on. You hunt them.

You very likely have had experiences with the outcasts in your past. You know that they're all not hideous monstrosities—that's the problem. Outcasts who are not obvious typically pose the greatest threat because they can hide in plain sight.

As an outcast hunter, you know that it takes special tools to fight creatures with crazy powers and abilities. You have learned to adapt devices to aid in finding outcasts and defending yourself against them. This might mean imbibing or injecting potions, nanites, or other strange treatments to even the odds.

Hunts Outcasts GM Intrusions: *Outcasts might begin hunting the hunter. Outcasts sometimes manifest powers that they didn't know they had. Sometimes you just can't tell if a person is an outcast.*

Connection: Choose one of the following.

1. Pick one other PC. You believe that this character might hate and fear outcasts as much as you do (although it's up to him as to whether this is true).
2. Pick one other PC. In the past, when you were with this character, she was harmed by an outcast, which helped inspire you to hunt them in the first place.
3. Pick one other PC. This character seems to believe that outcasts should be left in peace.
4. Pick one other PC. You worry that this character might be a latent outcast.

Additional Equipment: You have a small collection of items, such as charms, chemicals, or nanites, that you believe help you hunt and destroy outcasts.

Minor Effect Suggestion: Your foe is so intimidated by your prowess that it backs away, unwilling to attack. It can still defend itself.

Major Effect Suggestion: Your foe is disrupted and off balance and can't use any special powers that require an action for two rounds.

Tier 1: Outcast Fighter. You inflict 3 additional points of damage when fighting outcasts. Enabler.

Tier 2: Outcast Tracker (2+ Intellect points). You can sense the presence of an outcast within long range. Once you have found a specific outcast, if you then use a level of Effort, you can attempt to "lock on" to it. If you succeed, you always know the distance and direction to it. Enabler.

Tier 3: Defense Against Outcast Powers. Outcast powers can come in many forms. You are trained in all types of defense. Enabler.

Tier 4: Outcast Disruption (4 Intellect points). One outcast you touch cannot access any of the benefits of its powers for ten minutes. Action.

Tier 5: Fire With Fire. Through the use of magic, nanites, drugs, or biomechanical alterations, you give yourself abilities. You gain two abilities of tier 2 or lower from any character type in chapter 5. You're always quick to point out that these modifications are not truly mutations or anything else that would make you an outcast. Enabler.

Tier 6: True Defense Against Outcast Powers. Outcast powers can come in many forms. You are specialized in all types of defense.

HUNTS WITH GREAT SKILL

You are a tracker. Perhaps you hunt animals or more deadly creatures. Perhaps you go after people as a bounty hunter, law enforcer, or killer for hire. Whatever form your hunting takes, you are trained in stalking your quarry and bringing it down. You are a dangerous individual.

If you hunt animals or creatures, you might carry the trophies of past kills, such as teeth or skins. If you're a bounty hunter, you probably wear whatever your quarry would find most intimidating so it feels as though it has no chance of getting away from you.

Connection: Choose one of the following.

1. Pick one other PC. That person once saw you show surprising mercy toward your prey, and now you hope she keeps that information quiet—it might harm your reputation.
2. Pick one other PC. You accidentally caught her in one of your traps and she had to free herself.
3. Pick one other PC. Back in your bounty hunter days (which may or may not be over), you were hired to track down someone close to him.
4. Pick one other PC. You've noticed that it's almost impossible to track him, but you're determined to figure out a way.

Minor Effect Suggestion: You can attempt an intimidating task to cause your foe to immediately surrender.

Major Effect Suggestion: Your foe pauses, terrified by your prowess, and takes no action on his turn.

Tier 1: Tracker. You are trained in following and identifying tracks. Enabler.

Hunts With Great Skill GM Intrusions: *Even the slightest noise or movement can alert the quarry that it's being hunted.*

Stalker. You are trained in all types of movement tasks (including climbing, swimming, jumping, and balancing). Enabler.

Tier 2: Sneak. You are trained in stealth and initiative tasks. Enabler.

Sprint and Grab (2 Speed points). You can run a short distance and make a melee attack to grab a foe of your size or smaller. A successful attack means you grab the foe and bring it to a halt if it was moving (this can be treated as a tackle, if appropriate). Action.

Tier 3: Quarry (2 Intellect points). Choose a quarry (a single individual creature that you can see). You are trained in all tasks involving following, understanding, interacting with, or fighting that creature. You can have only one quarry at a time. Action to initiate.

Tier 4: Surprise Attack. If you attack from a hidden vantage, with surprise, or before your opponent has acted, the difficulty of your attack is decreased by one step. On a successful hit, you inflict 2 additional points of damage. Enabler.

Tier 5: Hunter's Drive (5 Intellect points). Through force of will, when you wish it, you grant yourself greater prowess in the hunt for ten minutes. During this time, the difficulty of all tasks involving your quarry, including attacks, is decreased by one step. Your quarry is the creature you selected with your third-tier ability. Enabler.

Tier 6: Multiple Quarry (6 Intellect points). This ability functions like the third-tier Quarry ability except that you can select up to three creatures as quarry. You must be able to see all three creatures when you initiate this ability. Your Hunter's Drive ability applies to all three creatures. Action to initiate.

Infiltrates GM Intrusions: *Spies are treated harshly when caught. Their allies disavow them to protect secrets. Some secrets are better left unknown.*

INFILTRATES

You focus on subtlety, guile, and stealth. Your body has been trained (or perhaps even genetically or magically altered) to make you the perfect infiltrator. You use a wide variety of disguises and tools to perform your duties, but your greatest tools are your own skills and training.

Infiltrators are spies, agents, thieves, assassins, or information gatherers. They often wear slick bodysuits and face-concealing masks when not wearing a disguise.

Connection: Choose one of the following.

1. Pick one other PC. This character inadvertently foils your actions, or at least makes them more difficult. If this PC is within immediate range, the difficulty of any action that you take related to this focus is increased by one step.
2. Pick one other PC. No matter how hard you try, you cannot seem to hide from him.
3. Pick two other PCs. The three of you worked as a team on a mission long ago, but you had a falling out.
4. Pick one other PC. That character is your sibling, and thus you look very much alike.

Minor Effect Suggestion: Your opponent is so startled by your moves that it is dazed, during which time the difficulty of all tasks it performs is increased by one step.

Major Effect Suggestion: All opponents within short range are so startled by your moves that they are dazed, during which time the difficulty of all tasks they perform is increased by one step.

Tier 1: Stealth. You are lithe and quiet. You know how to alter your position, your stance, and your clothing to best suit your surroundings. All this combines to give you an asset for stealth-related tasks. Enabler.

Sense Attitudes: You are trained in sensing lies and whether a person is likely to (or already does) believe your lies.

Tier 2: Impersonation. You can subtly change your features and alter your voice dramatically. This is an asset for any attempts at disguising your identity. Enabler.

Flight Not Fight. If you use your action only to move, the difficulty of all Speed defense tasks is reduced by one step. Enabler.

Tier 3: Awareness (3 Intellect points). You become hyperaware of your surroundings. For ten minutes, you are aware of all living things within long range, and by concentrating (an action) you can learn the general emotional state of any one of them.

Tier 4: Invisibility (4 Intellect points). Thanks to tiny magical or technological devices secreted about your person, you become invisible for ten minutes. While invisible, you are specialized in stealth and Speed defense tasks. This effect ends if you do something to reveal your presence or position—attacking, using an ability, moving a large object, and so on. If this occurs, you can regain the remaining invisibility effect by taking an action to focus on hiding your position. Action to initiate or reinitiate.

Tier 5: Evasion. You can't be good at getting in if you don't survive getting out. You are trained in all defense tasks.

Tier 6: Control. You use trickery, well-spoken lies, and mind-affecting chemicals (or other means, like magic or high technology) to make others temporarily do what you want them to do. You control the actions of another creature you touch. This effect lasts for one minute. The target must be level 3 or lower. You can allow it to act freely or override its control on a case-by-case basis as long as you can see it. Instead of applying Effort to decrease the difficulty, you can apply Effort to increase the maximum level of the target. Thus, to control the mind of a level 6 target (three levels above the normal limit), you must apply three levels of Effort. When the duration ends, the creature doesn't remember being controlled or anything it did while under your influence. Action to initiate.

INTERPRETS THE LAW

You know the law as well as the back of your hand. Broad mandates, narrow rulings, well-meaning overreaches, regulatory considerations, and outright loopholes in the law are all the tools you need to twist outcomes to suit your desire. Knowledge is power, which is why many people who have crossed you now fear you. It's your decision whether you put your prowess toward noble causes or use it for your own aggrandizement.

You wear nice suits and designer sunglasses, carry a briefcase, and walk around in shoes that cost more than many people earn in a month.

Connection: Choose one of the following.

1. Pick one other PC. That character seriously hurt someone in an altercation, but you got her off with no charges. She may feel grateful or ashamed.
2. Pick one other PC. He borrowed your copy of *The Prince* by Niccolò Machiavelli and still hasn't returned it.
3. Pick one other PC. You once defended him in a court of law but suffered one of your very few defeats because of the case or perhaps your own failing—you're not sure which.
4. Pick one other PC. That character has confided in you that she hates "bloodsucking lawyers" and is glad you're not one. You haven't decided yet if you're going to reveal your profession to her.

Additional Equipment: Suit and briefcase.

Minor Effect Suggestion: The target is confused, causing it to stumble and drop whatever it's holding.

Major Effect Suggestion: The target can't believe what you just said and is dazed and unable to take actions for a round as it tries to reconcile your statement with reality.

Interprets the Law GM Intrusions: *The law has changed since you last researched it. You have a coughing fit during an important speech. You left a briefcase of files in the car.*

Is Idolized by Millions GM Intrusions: *Fans are endangered or hurt on your behalf. Someone in your entourage betrays you. Your show, tour, contract, or other event is canceled. The media posts photos of you in an embarrassing situation.*

Tier 1: Opening Statement. You're trained in tasks related to persuasion, deception, and detecting the falsehoods of others. Enabler.

Knowledge of the Law. You're trained in the law of the land. If you don't know the answer to a question of law, you know where and how to research it (a university's law library is a good place to start, but you've also got online sources). Enabler.

Tier 2: Debate (3 Intellect points). In any gathering of two or more people trying to establish the truth or come to a decision, you can sway the verdict with masterful rhetoric. If you are given one minute or more to argue your point, either the decision goes your way or, if someone else effectively argues a competing point, the difficulty of any associated persuasion or deception task is decreased by two steps. One minute to initiate.

Tier 3: Able Assistance. When you help someone with a task related to research or codified knowledge, you always reduce the difficulty of the task by one step regardless of your own skill at that task. Enabler.

Keen Mind. You gain +1 to your Intellect Edge.

Tier 4: Objection (3 Intellect points). Your vociferous, booming objection to a target's intended action prevents it from taking any action (including attacking or defending itself from an attack) for one round. Each additional time you attempt this ability against the same target, you must apply one more level of Effort than you applied on the previous attempt. Action.

Tier 5: No One Knows Better. You are trained in two of the following skills: persuasion, deception, intimidation, research, knowledge in one area, or seeing through deception. If you choose a skill in which you're already trained, you become specialized in that skill instead. Enabler.

Tier 6: Master Barrister. You add 5 points to your Intellect Pool.

Legal Intern. You gain a level 4 follower who is mostly interested in helping with your law-related tasks, but who might also help you in other areas. Enabler.

IS IDOLIZED BY MILLIONS

Some celebrities are known for their talent, while others are simply known for being known. However the spotlight found you, you're a celebrity now, and people love you—often a little too much. You can't go anywhere publicly without people recognizing you, approaching you for a shared selfie, or pointing at you from afar. Whenever you do anything, whether it's going to the beach, adopting a new pet, or going out clubbing, the event becomes pablum for celebrity TV shows and websites, which often twist the facts into a caricature of reality. But hey, like your publicists say, no PR is bad PR.

You wear oversized sunglasses, designer clothing, and expensive shoes that are also comfortable.

Connection: Choose one of the following.

1. Pick one other PC. You were childhood friends. As you got famous, she continued to live a normal life, and you worry that she resents you.
2. Pick one other PC. That character knows that though you're quick with a smile, as if having the time of your life, on the inside you feel empty and alone.
3. Pick one other PC. That character once called you a "narcissistic douchecopter" on social media. You're not sure if it was a joke.
4. Pick one other PC. The media thinks that you and that character have a secret relationship and uses any pretext to revisit the story and give it new life.

Additional Equipment: Designer clothing and sunglasses.

Minor Effect Suggestion: Your foe realizes who you are and leaves himself open; the difficulty of your next attack is reduced by one step.

Major Effect Suggestion: Nearby strangers recognize you, scream your name, and run to get your autograph, shielding you from enemy attacks for a couple of rounds.

Tier 1: Entourage. Your entourage (five level 1 twenty-somethings) accompanies you wherever you go unless you purposefully disband it for a particular outing. You can ask them to deliver things for you, run messages, pick up your dry cleaning—pretty much whatever you want, within reason. They can also run interference if you're trying to avoid someone, help hide you from media attention, help you muscle through a crowd, and so on. On the other hand, if a situation becomes physically violent, they retreat to safety. Enabler.

Talent. You are trained in one of the following areas: writing, journalism, a particular style of art, a particular sport, chess, science communication, acting, news presentation, or some related area that led to your celebrity. Enabler.

Tier 2: Perks of Stardom. You are adept at claiming the rewards that fame can generate. When you are recognized, you can be seated at any restaurant, be let into any government building, be invited to any show or sports event (even if they're sold out), get a seat at a private function of any sort, or get into any club, no matter how exclusive. When dealing with someone who can't or won't immediately give in to your desire, you gain an asset on all tasks related to persuasion if that person recognizes you or is convinced that you're a celebrity even if he doesn't recognize you. Enabler.

Tier 3: Devoted Groupie. You gain a level 3 groupie who is completely devoted to you and follows you wherever you go (probably someone in your entourage makes this transition). You and the GM must work out the details. You'll probably make rolls for your groupie when he takes actions. A groupie in combat usually doesn't make separate attacks but instead helps you with yours. On your action, if the groupie is next to you, he serves as an asset for one attack you make on your turn. If you lose your groupie for any reason, you gain a new one after at least two weeks pass. Enabler.

Devoted groupie: *level 3; health 9; inflicts 3 points of damage*

Tier 4: Captivate With Starshine. For as long as you speak, you keep the attention of all level 2 or lower NPCs who can hear you. If you also have the Enthrall ability, you can similarly captivate all level 3 NPCs. Action to initiate.

Enthrall, page 45

Capable Groupie. Your groupie increases to level 4. Enabler.

Capable groupie: *level 4; health 12; inflicts 4 points of damage*

Tier 5: Do You Know Who I Am (3 Intellect points)? Acting only as someone who is famous and used to privilege can, you verbally harangue a living foe who can hear you so forcefully that it is unable to take any action, including making attacks, for one round. Whether you succeed or fail, the difficulty of the next action the target takes after your attempt is modified by one step to its detriment. Action.

Tier 6: Transcend the Script (5 Intellect points). Whether they are lines you wrote, acted, reported on, or otherwise incorporated into your talent, you compose an oratory on the fly that is so wonderful that even you believe it. For each ally who hears it (and you, too), the difficulty of a task attempted within the next hour is decreased by two steps.

Zealous Groupie. Your groupie increases to level 5. Enabler.

Zealous groupie: *level 5; health 15; inflicts 5 points of damage*

IS LICENSED TO CARRY

Is Licensed to Carry GM Intrusions: *Misfire or jam! The attack fails and the action is lost, plus an additional action is needed to fix the problem.*

You're a proficient adversary when armed. Hundreds of hours of training mean that you don't crack when under fire; you take care of business before the bad guys even know you're there. Those who are Licensed to Carry might be cops, crooks, hunters, or citizens interested in protecting themselves.

You dress in clothing that allows you either to conceal your weapon or to quickly access it, and preferably both, which is why you're probably known for your trench coat.

Connection: Choose one of the following.

1. Pick one other PC. In the recent past, while doing a little target practice, you accidentally winged him, leaving him badly wounded. It is up to that PC to decide whether he resents, fears, or forgives you.

2. Pick two PCs (preferably ones who are likely to get in the way of your attacks). When you miss with a gun and the GM rules that you struck someone other than your target, you hit one of these two characters.

3. Pick one other PC. You can see that the character needs some advice on how to handle a firearm.

4. Pick one other PC. You're not sure how or from where, but this character has a line on guns and ammunition and can get them for you for half price.

Additional Equipment: A firearm and three magazines of ammo.

Minor Effect Suggestion: After being hit on the side of the head, the target is deafened for a few minutes.

Major Effect Suggestion: An artery hit causes the target to bleed for 1 point of damage each round until he succeeds at a difficulty 3 Intellect or Speed task to bind the wound.

Tier 1: Gunner. You inflict 1 additional point of damage with guns. Enabler.

Practiced With Guns: You are practiced with using guns and suffer no penalty when using one. Enabler.

Tier 2: Careful Shot. You can spend points from either your Speed Pool or your Intellect Pool to apply levels of Effort to increase your gun damage. Each level of Effort adds 3 points of damage to a successful attack, and if you spend a turn lining up your shot, each level of Effort adds 5 points of damage to a successful attack instead. Enabler.

Tier 3: Trained Gunner. You can choose from one of two benefits. Either you are trained in using guns, or you have the Spray ability (which costs 2 Speed points): If a weapon has the ability to fire rapid shots without reloading (usually called a rapid-fire weapon, such as the automatic pistol), you can spray multiple shots around your target to increase the chance of hitting. This move uses 1d6 + 1 rounds of ammo (or all the ammo in the weapon, if it has less than the number rolled). The difficulty of the attack roll is decreased by one step. If the attack is successful, it deals 1 less point of damage than normal. Enabler (being trained in using guns) or action (Spray).

Tier 4: Snapshot. You can make two gun attacks as a single action, but the second attack is modified by two steps to your detriment. Enabler.

Tier 5: Legendary Gunner. You can choose from one of two benefits. Either you are trained in using guns (or specialized if you are already trained), or you have the Arc Spray ability, which costs 3 Speed points: If a weapon has the ability to fire rapid shots without reloading (usually called a rapid-fire weapon, such as the automatic pistol), you can fire your weapon at up to three targets (all next to one another) as a single action. Make a separate attack roll against each target. The difficulty of each attack is increased by one step. Enabler (being trained in using guns) or action (Arc Spray).

Tier 6: Special Shot. When you hit a target with your gun attack, you can choose to reduce the damage by 1 point but hit the target in a precise spot. Some of the possible effects include (but are not limited to) the following:

- You can shoot an object out of someone's hand.
- You can shoot the leg, wing, or other limb it uses to move, reducing its maximum movement speed to immediate for a few days or until it receives expert medical care.
- You can shoot a strap holding a backpack, armor, or a similarly strapped-on item so that it falls off.

Enabler.

LEADS

Using charisma, natural leadership, and perhaps some training, you command the actions of others, who follow you willingly. You are a politician, a captain, a leader, or a manager. Your skills allow you to make people do what you want, but you also have the wisdom to know what actions would be best for your followers and allies.

Since you need the respect of others, you probably dress and carry yourself in such a way that inspires, endears, or intimidates. You have a voice suited to barking orders that can be heard even on a noisy battlefield.

Connection: Choose one of the following.

1. Pick one other PC. That character was once a follower of yours, but you have since grown to think of her as a peer.
2. Pick one other PC. Independent and stubborn, he is not affected by your abilities.
3. Pick one other PC. She introduces you to the follower you gain at tier 2.
4. Pick one other PC. You were once very close with that character in the distant past.

Minor Effect Suggestion: The next time you attempt to command, captivate, or otherwise influence the same foe, the difficulty of the task is decreased by one step.

Major Effect Suggestion: The foe is influenced, captivated, or otherwise affected by your ability for twice as long as normal.

Tier 1: Natural Charisma. You are trained in all social interactions, whether they involve charm, learning a person's secrets, or intimidating others. Enabler.

Good Advice (1 Intellect point). You have a clear mind for determining the best way to proceed. When you give another character a suggestion involving his next action, the character is trained in that action for one round. Action.

Tier 2: Follower. You gain a level 2 NPC follower who is completely devoted to you. You and the GM must work out the details of the follower.

You'll probably make rolls for your follower when he takes actions. A follower in combat usually doesn't make separate attacks, but helps you with yours. On your action, if the follower is next to you, he serves as an asset for one attack you make on your turn.

If the follower dies, you gain a new one after at least two weeks and proper recruitment. Enabler.

Tier 3: Command (3 Intellect points). Through sheer force of will and charisma, you issue a simple command to a single living creature, which attempts to carry out your command as its next action. The

Although Is Licensed to Carry is designed with modern firearms in mind, it could apply to flintlock weapons, futuristic laser blasters, or other ranged weapons.

A creature's level determines its target number, health, and damage, unless otherwise stated. So a level 2 follower has a target number of 6 and a health of 6, and it inflicts 2 points of damage. A level 3 follower has a target number of 9 and a health of 9, and it inflicts 3 points of damage. And so on.

Leads GM Intrusions: *Followers fail, betray, lie, become corrupted, get kidnapped, or die.*

creature must be within short range and be able to understand you. The command can't inflict direct harm on the creature or its allies, so "Commit suicide" won't work, but "Flee" might. In addition, the command can require the creature to take only one action, so "Unlock the door" might work, but "Unlock the door and run through it" won't. Action.

Capable Follower. Your first follower increases to level 3. Enabler.

Tier 4: Captivate or Inspire. You can use this ability in one of two ways. Either your words keep the attention of all NPCs that hear them for as long as you speak, or your words inspire all NPCs (of your choosing) that hear them to function as if they were one level higher for the next hour. Action.

Capable Follower. Your first follower increases to level 4. Enabler.

Tier 5: Band of Followers. You gain six level 2 NPC followers who are completely devoted to you. (They are in addition to the follower you gained at second tier.) You and the GM must work out the details of these followers. If a follower dies, you gain a new one after at least two weeks and proper recruitment. Enabler.

Tier 6: Mind of a Leader (6 Intellect points). When you develop a plan that involves your followers, you can ask the GM one very general question about what is likely to happen if you carry out the plan, and you will get a simple, brief answer. Action.

Capable Followers. Your first follower increases to level 5. Each of your level 2 followers increases to level 3. Enabler.

LIVES IN THE WILDERNESS

Lives in the Wilderness GM Intrusions: *People in cities and towns sometimes disparage those who look (and smell) like they live in the wilds, as if they were ignorant or barbaric.*

You dwell in the wilds. You probably have done so most, if not all, of your life, coming to understand the mysteries of nature, weather, and survival. The ways of flora and fauna are your ways.

Your rough, rugged clothing shows little concern for style. Most of the time, covering yourself in natural smells to keep your scent from arousing suspicion in the wilderness is more important than bathing to keep yourself presentable to other humans.

Connection: Choose one of the following.

1. Pick one other PC who isn't from the wilderness. You can't help but feel a little contempt for that character and her "civilized" ways, which show disdain for all things natural and (to your mind) true.
2. Pick one other PC. He is one of the few people that you are completely comfortable being around, and you are often surprised at how easily you let down your guard near him.
3. Pick one other PC. She once saved you from an uncomfortable social situation, and you still feel grateful.
4. Pick one other PC. This person seems to understand civilization in the same way that you understand the wilderness. You could choose to help each other or despise each other for this different way of seeing the world.

Additional Equipment: You have an extremely reliable compass.

Minor Effect Suggestion: A foe that is a natural creature flees rather than continue to fight you.

Major Effect Suggestion: A foe that is a natural creature becomes warily passive.

Tier 1: Wilderness Life. You are trained in climbing and swimming tasks. Enabler.

Wilderness Lore. You are trained in wilderness navigation and in identifying plants and creatures. Enabler.

Tier 2: Living off the Land. Given an hour or so, you can always find edible food and potable water in the wilderness. You can even find enough for a small group of people, if need be. Further, since you're so hardy and have gained resistance over time, the difficulty of resisting the effects of natural poisons (such as those from plants or living creatures) is decreased by one step. You're also immune to natural diseases. Enabler.

Tier 3: Animal Senses and Sensibilities. You are trained in listening and spotting things. In addition, most of the time, the GM should alert you if you're about to walk into an ambush or a trap that is lower than level 3. Enabler.

Wilderness Explorer. While taking any action (including fighting) in the wild, you ignore any penalties due to natural causes such as tall grass, thick brush, rugged terrain, weather, and so on. Enabler.

Tier 4: Wilderness Awareness (4 Intellect points). Your connection to the natural world extends to a degree that some would call supernatural. While in the wilderness, you can extend your senses up to a mile in any direction and ask the GM a very simple, general question about that area, such as "Where is the orc camp?" or "Is my friend Deithan still alive?" If the answer you seek is not in the area, you receive no information. Action.

Tier 5: The Wild Is on Your Side (5 Intellect points). While you're in the wilderness, foes within short range are tripped by rocks, tangled in vines, bitten by insects, and distracted or confused by small animals. The difficulty of any tasks performed by those foes is increased by one step. This effect lasts for ten minutes. Action to initiate.

Tier 6: One With the Wild (6 Intellect points). For the next ten minutes, natural animals and plants within long range will not knowingly harm you or those you designate. Action.

Master of the Wild. While you're in the wilderness, your Might Edge, Speed Edge, and Intellect Edge increase by 1. When you make a recovery roll in the wilderness, you recover twice as many points. Enabler.

LOOKS FOR TROUBLE

You are a fighter. A scrapper. You like nothing more than to take off the kid gloves and confront your opposition in the most direct way possible. You don't hide, and you don't shirk. You take things head-on in a physical way. Your friends all likely feel better about going into danger with you at their side or their back.

You probably wear bright colors—yellow, pink, or red—to help you stand out. You might even wear a T-shirt with a printed obscenity for added style.

Connection: Choose one of the following.

1. Pick one other PC. Due to past experiences, you watch over her. That PC is your default charge regarding your tier 2 ability, if you have not named someone else.
2. Pick one or two other PCs. They seem pretty tough, and you're secretly hoping that at some point you'll see who's tougher—you or them.
3. Pick one other PC. If this character is within immediate range when you're in a fight, sometimes she helps, and sometimes she accidentally hinders (50% chance either way, determined per fight). When this character helps, you gain a +1 bonus to all attack rolls. When she hinders, you suffer a –1 penalty to attack rolls.
4. Pick one other PC. You used to be in a relationship with him, but it's long since over.

Looks for Trouble GM Intrusions: *Weapons break or fly from even the strongest grip. Brawlers trip and fall. Even the battlefield can work against you with things falling or collapsing.*

Masters Defense GM Intrusions: *Shields break when hit, as do weapons used to parry. Armor straps break.*

Additional Equipment: A melee weapon of your choice.

Minor Effect Suggestion: The target is also dazed for one round, during which time the difficulty of all tasks it performs is modified by one step to its detriment.

Major Effect Suggestion: You destroy a piece of equipment worn or held by your opponent.

Tier 1: Brawler. You inflict 1 additional point of damage in melee (including with your bare fists).

Wound Tender. You are trained in healing.

Tier 2: Protector. You designate a single character to be your charge. You can change this freely every round, but you can have only one charge at a time. As long as that charge is within immediate range, he gains an asset for Speed defense tasks because you have his back. Enabler.

Straightforward. You are trained in one of the following tasks (choose one): breaking things, climbing, jumping, or running.

Tier 3: Lethal Battler. Choose one type of attack in which you are not already trained: light bashing, light bladed, medium bashing, medium bladed, heavy bashing, or heavy bladed. You are trained in attacks using that type of weapon. Enabler.

Tier 4: Knock Out (5 Might points). You make a melee attack that inflicts no damage. Instead, if the attack hits, make a second Might-based roll. If successful, a foe of level 3 or lower is knocked unconscious for one minute. For each level of Effort used, you can affect one higher level of foe, or you can extend the duration for an additional minute. Action.

Tier 5: Epic Fighter. Choose one type of attack in which you are already trained: light bashing, light bladed, medium bashing, medium bladed, heavy bashing, or heavy bladed. You are specialized in attacks using that type of weapon. Enabler.

Tier 6: Juggernaut. You add 5 points to your Might Pool, and you inflict 1 additional point of damage with melee attacks. Enabler.

True Healer. You are specialized in healing.

MASTERS DEFENSE

Protecting yourself is obviously important in dangerous situations, and you are particularly good at it. Cautious and prudent, you learn techniques to defend against all kinds of attacks, both physical and mental. The winner is often the last person standing, and you've done all you can to ensure that person will be you.

You carry a shield and probably wear the best armor you can find.

Connection: Choose one of the following.

1. Pick one other PC. This character protected you from harm recently, and you feel indebted to him for saving your life.
2. Pick one other PC. She thinks you are an incredibly selfish person, perhaps based on her belief that you always save yourself first.
3. Pick one other PC. You once fought on opposite sides of a combat.
4. Pick one other PC. This character seems to be a jinx for you. Whenever she is next to you, the difficulty of your defense tasks is increased by one step. However, you're the opposite for her—when you're next to her, the difficulty of her defense tasks is decreased by one step.

Additional Equipment: You have a shield.

Minor Effect Suggestion: You gain a +1 bonus to Speed defense rolls for one round.

Major Effect Suggestion: You gain a +2 bonus to Speed defense rolls for one round.

Tier 1: Shield Master. When you use a shield, in addition to the asset it gives you (lowering the difficulty of Speed defense tasks by one step), you can act as if you are trained in Speed defense tasks. However, in any round in which you use this benefit, the difficulty of your attacks is increased by one step. Enabler.

Tier 2: Sturdy. You are trained in Might defense tasks. Enabler.

Armor Expert. When you wear any armor, you reduce the Speed cost for wearing armor by 1. Enabler.

Tier 3: Dodge and Resist (3 Speed points). You can reroll any of your Might, Speed, or Intellect defense rolls and take the better of the two results. Enabler.

Tier 4: Tower of Will. You are trained in Intellect defense tasks. Enabler.

Armor Master. When you wear any armor, you reduce the Speed cost for wearing armor by 1. Enabler.

Tier 5: Nothing but Defend. If you do nothing on your turn but defend, you are specialized in all defense tasks for that one round. Action.

Tier 6: Defense Master. Every time you succeed at a Speed defense task, you can make an immediate attack against your foe. Your attack must be the same type (melee weapon, ranged weapon, or unarmed) as the attack you defend against. If you don't have an appropriate type of weapon ready, you can't use this ability. Enabler.

MASTERS THE SWARM

Insects. Rats. Bats. Even birds. You master one type of small creature, and they respond to you in number. It's a weird skill—as you've been told far too many times—but you've seen the benefits both in and out of battle, and you've fully embraced it.

Your dress likely bears some mark of your predilections. Random creatures of your chosen kind sometimes alight on your person even when you don't purposefully call them.

Connection: Choose one of the following.

1. Pick one other PC. This person seems deathly afraid of your creatures and has a watchful eye on you.
2. Pick one other PC. Your creatures are attracted to this person for reasons you cannot understand.
3. Pick one other PC. You are indebted to this character for an act of kindness in the past.
4. Pick one other PC. This character has an oddly shaped birthmark, mole, or other feature that reminds you of your creatures. Does it mean something?

Minor Effect Suggestion: The swarm is particularly thick and angry, and everyone within it suffers 1 point of damage this round.

Major Effect Suggestion: Everyone within the swarm suffers 3 points of damage this round.

Tier 1: Influence Swarm (1 Intellect point). Your creatures within short range will not harm you or those you designate as allies for one hour. Action to initiate.

Tier 2: Control Swarm (2 Intellect points). Your creatures within short range do as you telepathically command for ten minutes. Even common insects (level 0) in large enough numbers can swarm about a single creature and modify its task difficulty by one step to its detriment. Action to initiate.

Tier 3: Living Armor (4 Intellect points). If you're in a location where it's possible for your creatures to come, you call a swarm around you for one hour. They crawl over your body or fly around you in a cloud. During this time, the difficulty of Speed defense tasks is decreased by one step, and you gain +1 to Armor. Action to initiate.

Tier 4: Call Swarm (4 Intellect points). If you're in a location where it's possible for your creatures to come, you call a swarm of them for one hour. During this hour, they do as you telepathically command as long as they are within long range. They can swarm about and modify any or all opponents' task difficulties by one step to their detriment. While the creatures are in long range, you can speak to them telepathically and perceive through their senses. Action to initiate.

Tier 5: Companion. You gain a special specimen as a constant companion. It is level 4, probably the size of a small dog, and follows your telepathic commands. You and the GM must work out the details of your creature, and you'll probably make rolls for it in combat or when it takes actions. The companion acts on your turn. If your companion dies, you can hunt in the wild for 1d6 days to find a new companion. Enabler.

Tier 6: Deadly Swarm (6 Intellect points). If you're in a location where it's possible for

Masters the Swarm GM Intrusions: *You might think you have perfect control of your creatures' minds, but that's not always how it works. Telepathic connections break. A swarm receives an incorrect signal. Accidental stings or bites occur.*

A creature's level determines its target number, health, and damage, unless otherwise stated. So a level 4 companion has a target number of 12 and a health of 12, and it inflicts 4 points of damage. And so on.

Swarms don't usually have game stats, but if needed, a typical swarm is level 2. Only attacks that affect a large area affect the swarm.

your creatures to come, you call a swarm of them for ten minutes. During this time, they do as you telepathically command as long as they are within long range. They can swarm about and modify any or all opponents' task difficulties by one step to their detriment, or they can focus the swarm and attack all opponents within immediate range of each other (all within long range of you). The attacking swarm inflicts 4 points of damage. While the creatures are in long range, you can speak to them telepathically and perceive through their senses. Action to initiate.

MASTERS WEAPONRY

Masters Weaponry GM Intrusions: *Weapons break. Weapons can be stolen. Weapons can be dropped or forced out of your hand.*

You have worked long and hard with one particular type of weapon: swords, axes, daggers, whips, or whatever you choose. Thus, you are a swordsman, an axemaster, a mistress of knives, or whatever is appropriate to your chosen weapon. A master of the rapier is different from a master of the warhammer.

You might wear a symbol—a badge, a pin, a tattoo, an amulet, certain colors, and so on—that indicates the school in which you trained, the style of fighting you have mastered, or the name of your mentor. Your weapon is almost certainly your finest possession. Not only is it well cared for and of high quality, but you probably keep it in a beautiful scabbard, harness, belt, case, or something similar.

Connection: Choose one of the following.

1. Pick one other PC. That character shows potential in the use of your weapon. You would like to train her, but you're not necessarily qualified to teach (that's up to you), and she might not be interested (that's up to her).

2. Pick one other PC. If she is within immediate range when you're in a fight, sometimes she helps, and sometimes she accidentally hinders (50% chance either way, determined per fight). When she helps, you gain +1 to all attack rolls. When she hinders, you suffer a –1 penalty to attack rolls.

3. Pick one other PC. You once saved his life, and he clearly feels indebted to you. You wish he didn't; it's all just part of the job.

4. Pick one other PC. This person recently mocked your combat stance. How you deal with this (if at all) is up to you.

Additional Equipment: You have a high-quality weapon of your choosing.

Weaponry Abilities: If you cast spells or have similarly overt abilities, your attacks always look like your chosen weapon. So a force blast appears to be a large weapon made of force. These alterations change nothing other than the appearance of the effects. As another example, Barrier becomes a wall of swirling blades of energy. This alteration changes the ability such that it is not a solid barrier but rather inflicts 1 point of damage to anyone who touches it and 4 points of damage to anyone who passes through it.

Minor Effect Suggestion: The target is so dazzled by your expertise that it is dazed for one round, during which time the difficulty of all tasks it performs is modified by one step to its detriment.

Major Effect Suggestion: Make an immediate additional attack with the weapon as part of your turn.

Tier 1: Weapon Master. You deal 1 additional point of damage with your chosen weapon. Enabler.

Tier 2: Weapon Defense. While your chosen weapon is in your hand or hands, you are trained in Speed defense tasks. Enabler.

Tier 3: Rapid Attack (3 Speed points). Once per round, you can make an additional attack with your chosen weapon. Enabler.

Tier 4: Never Fumble. If you roll a natural 1 when attacking with your chosen weapon, you can ignore or countermand the GM's intrusion for that roll. You can never be disarmed of your chosen weapon, nor will you ever drop it accidentally. Enabler.

Tier 5: Extreme Mastery (4 Might points). When using your chosen weapon, you can reroll any attack roll you wish and take the better of the two results. Enabler.

Tier 6: Damage Dealer. You deal 2 additional points of damage with your chosen weapon. This is on top of the damage from the Weapon Master ability, giving you a total of 3 additional points of damage. Enabler.

Death Dealer (5 Might points). If you strike a foe of level 3 or lower with your chosen weapon, you kill the target instantly. Action.

METES OUT JUSTICE

So much injustice in the world. It takes a special person to take it upon himself to right wrongs, protect the innocent, and punish the guilty. You are such a person.

Justicars, as they are sometimes called, are often knights errant who wear armor, bear swords and shields, and travel the land looking for tyranny, corruption, or oppression. But some operate a little less ostentatiously. Sometimes justice comes from more subtle tactics. In a more modern setting, a justicar might be a masked vigilante or just a badass who rights wrongs.

The importance of justice in your life might come from religion, your upbringing, or your highly developed sense of principles. Regardless, you not only adhere to your values, but you also believe it is your calling to act on them and help make the world more just, more fair, and more ethical. You want to see wrongdoing punished.

Connection: Choose one of the following.

1. Pick one other PC. You strongly suspect that this person has a past that might involve serious crimes or wrongdoing. You have no proof, however, and you've never witnessed him do anything seriously wrong.
2. Pick one other PC. This character seems to share your value systems and sees right and wrong the same way you do, which is refreshing.
3. Pick one other PC. This character, while ethical, defines right and wrong in different ways than you do.
4. Pick one other PC. In the past, you and this character witnessed an event that helped shape your moral code. She may or may not have come away with a similar outlook.

Additional Equipment: You have a shield to help you protect yourself and the innocents you find (if appropriate to the setting).

Minor Effect Suggestion: You shame or intimidate your foe so much that he is shaken and uses his next turn to flee.

Major Effect Suggestion: You mark your foe permanently with a distinctive scar so that her guilt will be known by all.

Metes Out Justice GM Intrusions: *Guilt or innocence can be complicated. Some people resent the presumption of a self-appointed judge. Passing judgment makes enemies.*

Barrier, page 33

GM intrusion, page 193

Tier 1: Make Judgment. You are skilled in discerning the truth of a situation, seeing through lies, or otherwise overcoming deception. Enabler.

Designation. You assign an "innocent" or "guilty" label to one creature within immediate range, based on your general assessment of a given situation or a predominant feeling. In other words, someone who is labeled "innocent" can be innocent in a certain circumstance, or he can be generally innocent of terrible crimes (such as murder, major theft, and so on). Likewise, you can declare that a creature is "guilty" of a particular crime or of terrible deeds in general. The accuracy of your assessment isn't important as long as you believe it to be the truth; the GM may require you to give a rationale. Henceforth, the difficulty of tasks to socially interact with someone you designate as innocent is decreased by one step, and the difficulty of attacks against those you designate as guilty is decreased by one step. You can change your assessment, but it requires another designation action. The benefits of the designation last until you change it or until you are shown proof that it is wrong. Action.

Moves Like a Cat GM Intrusions: *Even a cat can be clumsy sometimes, especially when overconfident. A well-calculated jump isn't quite as easy as it looks. An escape move is so overzealous that it sends the character right into harm's way.*

Tier 2: Defend the Innocent (2 Speed points). For the next ten minutes, if someone you have designated as an innocent stands next to you, that creature shares any defensive advantages that you might have, other than mundane armor. These advantages include the Speed defense from your shield, the Armor offered from a force field, and so on. In addition, the difficulty of Speed defense rolls made by the innocent creature is decreased by one step. You can protect only one innocent creature at a time. Action to initiate.

Tier 3: Punish the Guilty (2 Might points). For the next ten minutes, if you attack someone you have designated as guilty, you inflict 2 additional points of damage. Action to initiate.

Tier 4: Find the Guilty. If you have designated someone as guilty, you are trained in tracking him, spotting him when he is hidden, or otherwise finding him. Enabler.

Greater Designation. You can assign an "innocent" or "guilty" label (as described above) to all creatures within immediate range. Action.

Tier 5: Punish All the Guilty (3 Speed points). You can attack all foes within immediate range that you have designated as guilty. Make separate attack rolls for each foe, but all attacks count as a single action in a single round. You remain limited by the amount of Effort you can apply on one action. Anything that modifies your attack or damage applies to all attacks. Action.

Tier 6: Defend All the Innocent. You protect everyone within immediate range who you have designated as innocent. The difficulty of Speed defense rolls made by such creatures is decreased by one step. Enabler.

MOVES LIKE A CAT

You are extremely dexterous. Your speed and agility make you almost a thing of wonder. Your body is lithe, flexible, and graceful. Your training—or perhaps a bit of magic or technology—allows you to move quickly and smoothly, land safely when you fall, and avoid danger.

You likely wear tight clothing that doesn't hinder you as you move. Likewise, you probably don't allow yourself to be overburdened by a lot of equipment. You'll wear armor only if it doesn't slow you down.

Connection: Choose one of the following.

1. Pick one other PC. His occasional clumsiness and loud behavior irritates you.
2. Pick one other PC. This character comes from the same place you do, and you knew each other as children.
3. Pick one other PC. You aid her with advice and a helping hand when she needs it. Anytime the two of you are next to each other, the difficulty of balancing, climbing, and jumping tasks is decreased by one step for her.
4. Pick one other PC. He owes you a significant amount of money.

Minor Effect Suggestion: You restore 2 points to your Speed Pool.

Major Effect Suggestion: You can take a second action this round.

Tier 1: Reflexes. You gain 3 additional points to your Speed Pool. Enabler.

Balance. You are trained in balancing. Enabler.

Tier 2: Movement. You are trained in climbing and jumping. Enabler.

Safe Fall. You reduce the damage from a fall by 5 points. Enabler.

Tier 3: Greater Reflexes. You gain 1 to your Speed Edge. Enabler.

Hard to Touch. You are trained in Speed defense tasks. Enabler.

Tier 4: Quick Strike (4 Speed points). You make a melee attack with such speed that it is hard for your foe to defend against, and it knocks him off balance. The difficulty of making the attack is decreased by two steps, and the foe, if struck, is dazed so that for the next round, the difficulty of his tasks is increased by one step. Action.

Tier 5: Phenomenal Reflexes. You gain 5 additional points to your Speed Pool.

Slippery: You are trained in escaping any kind of bond or grasp.

Tier 6: Burst of Action (6 Speed points). You can take two separate actions this round. Enabler.

MOVES LIKE THE WIND

You are extraordinarily fast. Through some agency beyond human limits (such as magic, technology, mutant powers, or the like), you are a blur of movement. You can outrun anyone, and as your abilities increase, you can eventually run rings around flying birds or speeding cars.

You likely wear tight clothing that doesn't hinder you as you move. Likewise, you probably don't allow yourself to be overburdened by a lot of equipment.

Connection: Choose one of the following.

1. Pick one other PC. He moves so slowly! It irritates you.
2. Pick one other PC. This character is attractive and alluring to you.
3. Pick one other PC. She inspires you. When she is within immediate distance, the difficulty of all physical actions (other than defense) is decreased by one step.
4. Pick one other PC. He owes you a significant amount of money.

Minor Effect Suggestion: You restore 2 points to your Speed Pool.

Major Effect Suggestion: You can take a second action this round.

Moves Like the Wind GM Intrusions: *Surfaces can be slick or offer hidden obstacles. The movement of other creatures can be unpredictable, and the character might run into them. Leg injuries can slow a runner down.*

Murders GM Intrusions: *Most people do not react well to a professional killer.*

Tier 1: Speed. You gain 5 additional points to your Speed Pool. Enabler.

Running Speed. You move much farther than normal in a round. This means that as a part of another action, you can move up to a short distance. As an action, you can move a long distance, or up to 200 feet (61 m) as a Speed-based task with a difficulty of 4. Enabler.

Tier 2: More Speed. You gain 5 additional points to your Speed Pool. Enabler.

Hard to Hit. You are trained in Speed defense tasks. Enabler.

Tier 3: Speed Burst (4 Speed points). You can take two separate actions in this round. In the following round, the difficulty of all actions is increased by one step. You cannot use this ability two rounds in a row. Enabler.

Tier 4: Blink of an Eye (4 Speed points). You move up to 1,000 feet (305 m) in one round. Action.

Up to Speed. If you do nothing but move for three actions in a row, you accelerate greatly and can move up to 200 mph (about 2,000 feet each round) for up to ten minutes (about 35 miles), after which you must stop and make a recovery roll. (Move up to 322 kph [about 610 m each round] for up to ten minutes [about 56 km].) Enabler.

Tier 5: Even More Speed. You gain 5 additional points to your Speed Pool. Enabler.

Hard to See. When you move, you are a blur. It is impossible to make out your identity as you run past, and in a round where you do nothing but move, the difficulty of stealth tasks and Speed defense tasks is decreased by one step. Enabler.

Tier 6: Perfect Speed Burst (6 Speed points). You can take two separate actions this round. Enabler.

Incredible Running Speed. You move much farther than normal in a round. This means as a part of another action, you can move up to a long distance. As an action, you can move up to 200 feet (61 m), or up to 500 feet (152 m) as a Speed-based task with a difficulty of 4. Enabler.

MURDERS

The murderous assassin is a master of dealing death. No one is better at sneaking into a location, eliminating a target, and slipping out again. Obviously, a professional killer is not likely to have a lot of friends.

You probably wear dark colors—black, charcoal grey, or midnight blue—to help blend into the shadows. But since you're also a master of disguise, in truth you could look like anyone.

Connection: Choose one of the following.

1. Pick one other PC. That character knows your real identity, profession, and background. To all others, the truth about you is a closely guarded secret.

2. Pick one other PC. You were recently approached by someone who wanted to hire you to take that character out. You haven't yet decided whether to take the job or warn her that her life's in danger.

3. Pick two other PCs. One night after perhaps too much celebrating, you loudly claimed responsibility for a murder you didn't commit. These two characters were the only ones who heard. Whether they believe you or not is up to them.

4. Pick one other PC. That character is the one who got you started down the path of taking lives, whether he knows it or not.

Additional Equipment: You start with a disguise kit and three doses of a level 2 blade poison that inflicts 5 points of damage.

Disguise kit, page 254

Minor Effect Suggestion: No one but the foe notices that you make the attack.

Major Effect Suggestion: If you have poison amid your belongings, you were able to apply it just before the strike, adding the poison's effects to the normal attack damage.

Tier 1: Surprise Attack. If you attack from a hidden vantage, with surprise, or before an opponent has acted, the difficulty of your attack is reduced by one step. On a successful hit with this surprise attack, you inflict 2 additional points of damage. Enabler.

Trained Assassin. You are trained in stealth and disguise tasks. Enabler.

Tier 2: Quick Death (2 Speed points). You know how to kill quickly. When you hit with a melee or ranged attack, you deal

4 additional points of damage. You can't make this attack in two consecutive rounds. Action.

Tier 3: Poison Crafter. You are trained in crafting, sensing, identifying, and resisting poisons. Enabler.

Trained Infiltrator. You are trained in all interactions involving lies or trickery. Enabler.

Tier 4: Better Surprise Attack. When you use Surprise Attack, the difficulty of your attack is reduced by two steps instead of one, and you deal 4 additional points of damage instead of 2. Enabler.

Tier 5: Slayer (5 Speed points). With a swift and sudden attack, you strike a foe in a vital spot. If the target is level 3 or lower, it is killed outright. Action.

Tier 6: Escape Plan. When you kill a foe, you can attempt a sneaking action to immediately hide from anyone around, assuming that a suitable hiding place is nearby. Enabler.

NEEDS NO WEAPON

You don't use weapons—you *are* a weapon. With powerful punches, kicks, and full-body moves, you inflict incredible damage on your foes. By focusing your energy, the combined power of your body and mind means you can do incredible amounts of damage without depleting your energy reserves. You might have gained your skills through intense training, various implants and enhancements, genetic mutations, or any combination of these things. Whatever the origin of your feats, you likely take good care of your body, ensuring that it remains the sharpest, most dependable weapon at your disposal.

Weaponless martial artists are both feared and revered. They wear loose, comfortable clothing that allows them a full range of movement, and they rarely use weapons other than their body's own implements (although some carry items designed to enhance their body movements for greater effect, such as knuckle weapons, knee spikes, or boot blades).

Connection: Choose one of the following.

1. Pick one other PC. He seems to believe that the only true weapons are those that you can hold in your hand, and he might look at you with disdain.
2. Pick one other PC. This person seems incredibly unaware of her body and always happens to get in your way. If you miss your foe and accidentally hit someone else in close range, it's likely to be her.
3. Pick one other PC. You once trained with a close friend of his, and you owe that mutual friend much.
4. Pick two other PCs. Once these two heard about your skills, they expressed interest in being your students. However, only one seems to have any aptitude.

Minor Effect Suggestion: You trip your target and knock him prone.

Needs No Weapon GM Intrusions: *Striking certain foes hurts you as much as it hurts them. Opponents with weapons have greater reach. Complicated martial arts moves can knock you off balance.*

Major Effect Suggestion: You strike your target in a limb, making that limb useless for the next minute.

Tier 1: Fists of Fury. You inflict 2 additional points of damage with unarmed attacks. Enabler.

Flesh of Stone: You have +1 to Armor if you do not wear physical armor. Enabler.

Tier 2: Advantage to Disadvantage (2 Speed points). With a number of quick moves, you make an attack against a foe wielding a weapon, inflicting damage and disarming him so that his weapon is now 10 feet (3 m) away on the ground, or in your hands—your choice. The difficulty of the attack is increased by one step. Action.

Fighting Style: You are trained in unarmed attacks. Enabler.

Tier 3: Moving Like Water (3 Speed points). You spin and move so that your defense and attacks are aided by your fluid motion. For one minute, the difficulty of your attacks and Speed defense rolls is decreased by one step. Enabler.

Tier 4: Deflect Attacks (4 Speed points). For one minute, you automatically deflect or dodge any ranged projectile attacks. However, during this time, the difficulty of all other actions is increased by one step in any round in which you are attacked by ranged projectiles. Action to initiate.

Tier 5: Stunning Attack (4 Might points). You hit your foe in just the right spot, stunning him so that he loses his next action. This attack inflicts no damage. Action.

Damage track, page 202

Tier 6: Master of Style. You are specialized in unarmed attacks. If you are already specialized in unarmed attacks, you instead deal 2 additional points of damage with unarmed attacks. Enabler.

NEVER SAYS DIE

Never Says Die GM Intrusions: *Even if you never give out, sometimes your equipment or weapons do.*

You are as stalwart, hardy, and driven as can be imagined. When others are ready to quit, you're just getting started.

You probably don't spend a lot of time on your appearance—it is far less important than actions. For that matter, so are words. You're likely not much of a talker. You're a doer.

Characters with this focus are sometimes called stalwarts or diehards. They often are soldiers, mercenaries, or other tough-as-nails individuals, but sometimes they take a more heroic stance. A character who is hard to kill is around longer to help others, after all.

Connection: Choose one of the following.

1. Pick one other PC. You feel the overwhelming need to impress this character, although you're not sure why.
2. Pick one other PC. This character seems quite capable, but in your mind, his spirit needs motivating. You're constantly trying to convince him to keep trying, go the distance, and fight the good fight.
3. Pick one other PC. You feel very protective of this character and don't want to see her harmed.
4. Pick one other PC. This character comes from the same place you do, and you knew each other as children.

Minor Effect Suggestion: You restore 2 points to your Might Pool.

Major Effect Suggestion: The difficulty of your next action is decreased by two steps.

Tier 1: Rapid Recovery. Your ten-minute recovery roll takes one action instead, so that your first two recovery rolls take one action, the third takes one hour, and the fourth takes ten hours. Enabler.

Push on Through (2 Might points). You ignore the effects of terrain while moving for one hour. Enabler.

Tier 2: Ignore the Pain. You ignore the impaired condition of the damage track and treat the debilitated condition as impaired. Enabler.

Tier 3: Hidden Reserves. When you make a one-action recovery roll, you also gain 1 to your Might Edge and Speed Edge for ten minutes thereafter. Enabler.

Tier 4: Increasing Determination. If you fail at a noncombat physical task (pushing open a door or climbing a cliff, for example) and then retry the task, the difficulty is reduced by one step. If you fail again, you gain no special benefits. Enabler.

Outlast the Foe. If you have been in combat for five full rounds, the difficulty of all tasks in the remainder of that combat is decreased by one step, and you deal 1 additional point of damage per attack. Enabler.

Tier 5: Throw off Affliction (5 Might points). If you are affected by an unwanted condition or affliction (such as disease, paralysis, mind control, broken limb, and so on, but not damage), you can ignore it and act as if it does not affect you for one hour. If the condition would normally last less than an hour, it is entirely negated. Action.

Tier 6: Not Dead Yet. When you would normally die, you instead fall unconscious for one round and then awaken. You immediately gain 1d6 + 6 points to restore your stat Pools and are treated as if debilitated (which for you is like being impaired, thanks to your Ignore the Pain ability) until you rest for ten hours. If you die again before you take your ten-hour recovery roll, you are truly dead. Enabler.

OPERATES UNDERCOVER

Espionage is not something you know anything about. At least, that's what you want everyone to believe, because in truth, you've been trained as a spy or covert agent. You might work for a government or for yourself. You might be a police detective or a criminal. You could even be an investigative reporter.

Regardless, you learn information that others attempt to keep secret. You collect rumors and whispers, stories and hard-won evidence, and you use that knowledge to aid your own endeavors and, if appropriate, provide your employers with the information they desire. Alternatively, you might sell what you have learned to those willing to pay a premium.

You probably wear dark colors—black, charcoal grey, or midnight blue—to help blend into the shadows, unless the cover you've chosen requires you to look like someone else.

Connection: Choose one of the following.

1. Pick one other PC. The character knows your real identity (if that's a secret) or that you work undercover (if that's a secret), and has kept that information private until now.
2. Pick one other PC. You know an important secret about her, but she is unaware that you know.
3. Pick two other PCs. You know about an important connection between these two that even they don't know about.
4. Pick one other PC. No matter how you hide or disguise yourself, this character always seems to know where and who you really are.

Additional Equipment: A disguise kit.

Disguise kit, page 254

Minor Effect Suggestion: You can immediately attempt to hide after this action.

Major Effect Suggestion: You get a +2 bonus to Speed defense rolls for one round.

Tier 1: Investigate. You are trained in perception, cryptography, deceiving, and breaking into computers. Enabler.

Tier 2: Disguise. You are trained in disguise. You can alter your posture, voice, mannerisms, and hair to look like someone else for as long as you keep up the disguise. However, it is extremely difficult to adopt the appearance of a specific individual without a disguise kit at your disposal. Enabler.

Operates Undercover GM Intrusions: *People don't like to be manipulated and resent those who try. Even the best disguise can have a fatal flaw. When you are not what you seem, sometimes other people aren't either.*

Tier 3: Agent Provocateur. Choose one of the following to be trained in: attacking with a weapon of your choice, demolitions, or sneaking and lockpicking (if you choose this last option, you are trained in both). Enabler.

Tier 4: Pull a Fast One (3 Intellect points). When you're running a con, picking a pocket, fooling or tricking a dupe, sneaking something by a guard, and so on, you treat the task as if it were one level lower. Enabler.

Tier 5: Using What's Available (4 Intellect points). If you have the time and the freedom to scrounge for everyday materials in your environment, you can fashion a temporary asset that will aid you once to accomplish a specific task. For example, if you need to climb a wall, you could create some sort of climbing assistance device; if you need to break out of a cell, you can find something to use as a lockpick; if you need to create a small distraction, you could put together something to make a loud bang and flash; and so on. The asset lasts for a maximum of one minute, or until used for the intended purpose. One minute to assemble materials; action to create asset.

Tier 6: Trust to Luck (3 Intellect points). Sometimes, you've just got to roll the dice and hope things add up in your favor. When you use Trust to Luck, roll a d6. On any even result, the task you're attempting is modified by two steps in your favor. On a roll of 1, the task is modified by one step to your detriment. Enabler.

Assassin (5 Might points). If you strike a foe of level 3 or lower with a weapon you're practiced or trained with, you kill the target instantly. Action.

PERFORMS FEATS OF STRENGTH

Performs Feats of Strength GM Intrusions: *A strong character might not realize her own strength and accidentally damage or destroy a delicate object she handles.*

A lifetime of physical training rewards you with incredible power. Your muscles ripple beneath your skin, evident in your extraordinary build and frame, and you can do things others would not dream possible. You can haul incredible weight, hurl your body through the air, and punch through doors.

Superior strength can manifest in many ways. You could have the physique of a bodybuilder, almost godlike in its perfection, or you might be a lumbering, hulking monster of a person, as heavy with fat as you are with muscle. Then again, you could be short and wiry, your strength belied by your slight frame.

Connection: Choose one of the following.

1. Pick one other PC. You have been friends with this character for as long as you remember and often heed her advice and guidance.

2. Pick one other PC. For some reason—nerves, perhaps, or attraction—he makes you feel weak in the knees. You prefer if he stays out of immediate range when you're in combat.

3. Pick one other PC. You once carried him from combat after he was wounded. Whether he feels embarrassment, gratitude, or something else is up to him.

4. Pick two other PCs. They have a game where they ask you to perform harder and harder feats of strength. Whether you play along is up to you.

Additional Equipment: You have a heavy weapon.

Minor Effect Suggestion: You knock the creature to the ground.

Major Effect Suggestion: You send the creature flying through the air so that it lands on the ground in a heap 1d20 feet away from you.

Tier 1: Athlete. You are trained in carrying, climbing, jumping, and smashing. Enabler.

Strong. Your Might Edge increases by 1. Enabler.

Tier 2: Feat of Strength (1 Might point). The difficulty of any task that depends on brute force is decreased by one step. Examples include smashing down a barred door, tearing open a locked container, lifting or moving a heavy object, or striking someone with a melee weapon. Enabler.

Tier 3: Iron Fist. Your unarmed attacks deal 4 points of damage. Enabler.

Throw (2 Might points). When you deal damage to a creature of your size or smaller with an unarmed attack, you can choose to throw that creature up to 1d20 feet away from you. The creature lands prone. Enabler.

Tier 4: Powerful. Your Might Pool increases by 5 points. Enabler.

Tier 5: Brute Strike (4 Might points). You deal 4 additional points of damage with all melee attacks until the end of the next round. Enabler.

Tier 6: Juggernaut (5 Might points). Until the end of the next round, you can move through solid objects such as doors and walls. Only 2 feet (60 cm) of wood, 1 foot (30 cm) of stone, or 6 inches (15 cm) of metal can stop your movement. Enabler.

PILOTS STARCRAFT

Pilots Starcraft GM Intrusions: *The starcraft gets lost in space. The vessel breaks down in the middle of nowhere. Enemy starcraft suddenly appear at the edge of sensor range. You find an alien stowaway.*

Before you choose this focus, work with your GM to be sure that you'll have the opportunity to access a starcraft.

You're a crack starship pilot. You feel most alive when the engines are running hot, the floor plates are thrumming beneath your feet, and the stars stream past the viewports in a continuous accelerating streak. Whether you pilot starcraft along a dangerous trade route, explore places no one has gone before, or work as a courier, you are the master of your own domain: your starship.

Piloting is a glamorous job that requires glamorous attire, so you wear striking clothing, possibly including holo-tattoos, data jewelry, and other elaborate accessories.

Connection: Choose one of the following.

1. Pick one other PC. You promised that character a trip anywhere she wanted to go in a starship. She hasn't yet taken you up on your offer.
2. Pick one other PC. You smuggled goods in your starcraft for him in the past, and it ended up entangling you in legal trouble. You've mostly forgotten the incident. Mostly.
3. Pick one other PC. That character confided in you that she suspects you are an agent of an enemy organization. You deny it.
4. Pick one or more other PCs. You accidentally crashed your starcraft when those characters were aboard. Everyone was hurt, and one other former comrade was killed in the incident.

Additional Equipment: With your GM's approval, access to a small starcraft.

Minor Effect Suggestion: The difficulty of the next task attempted by an ally (either personally or in operating one of the starcraft's systems, such as communication, sensors, weapons, and so on) is reduced by one step.

Major Effect Suggestion: You can take an immediate extra action, either personally or in operating one of the starcraft's systems, such as communication, sensors, weapons, and so on.

Tier 1: Pilot. You are trained in all tasks related to piloting a starcraft. Generally speaking, piloting tasks are Speed-based tasks, though using sensors and communication instruments are Intellect-based tasks. Enabler.

Flex Lore. After each ten-hour recovery roll when you have access to the starcraft's digital library, choose one field of knowledge related to a specific planet or some other location. The field might be habitations, customs, governments, characteristics of the main race or races, important figures, and so on. You're trained in that field until you use this ability again. You could use this ability with an area of knowledge you're already trained in to become specialized. Enabler.

Tier 2: Salvage and Comfort (2 Intellect points). You're familiar with open space. If you spend an hour using your craft's sensors and make a difficulty 3 Intellect roll, you can find salvage in the form of

Sample starships, page 255

abandoned spacecraft, drifting motes of matter that were once inhabited, or a place to hide from pursuit in what most people would otherwise assume to be empty space (such as in a nebula, an asteroid field, or the shadow of a moon). Salvage you turn up includes enough food and water for you and several others, as well as the possibility of weapons, clothing, technological artifacts, survivors, or other usable items. In other contexts, this ability counts as training in tasks related to perception. One hour.

Mentally Tough. Staring into the naked weave of hyperspace, warped space, or a similar effect related to faster-than-light travel is hard on the mind, but you've developed resistance. You're trained in Intellect defense tasks. Enabler.

Tier 3: Expert Pilot. You are specialized in all tasks related to piloting a starcraft. Enabler.

Passing Mechanic. You are trained in tasks related to the repair and maintenance of a starcraft. Enabler.

Tier 4: Sensor Array (3 Intellect points). You are trained in using starcraft sensory instruments. These instruments allow users to answer general questions about a location, such as "How many people are in the mining colony?" or "Where did the other spacecraft crash?" Action.

Pilot Expertise. You add 3 points to your Speed Pool. Enabler.

Tier 5: Like the Back of Your Hand. The difficulty of all tasks directly related to a starcraft that you own or have a direct connection with is decreased by one step. Tasks include repair, refueling, finding a breach in the hull, finding a stowaway, and so on. The same goes for any attack or defense rolls you make within the starcraft against enemy boarders, as well as any attack or defense rolls you make with the ship against enemy ships. Enabler.

Tier 6: Remote Control (5 Intellect points). You can use a starcraft's communication and sensor arrays to launch an attack that briefly renders an enemy starcraft within 20 miles (32 km) inoperative for up to a minute. Action.

Incomparable Pilot. While on a starcraft you own or have a direct connection with, your Might Edge, Speed Edge, and Intellect Edge increase by 1. When you make a recovery roll on a starcraft you're familiar with, you recover 5 additional points. Enabler.

RAGES

Rages GM Intrusions: *It's easy for a berserker to lose control and attack friend as well as foe.*

The berserker is a feared fighter who cannot be stopped. You put yourself into a howling battle frenzy that can make you a terror on the battlefield. You might hail from a less civilized society, perhaps even a tribal one.

You likely wear little or no armor so as not to restrict your speed or maneuverability. Your clothing is probably simple and utilitarian.

Connection: Choose one of the following.

1. Choose one other PC. You feel strangely protective of that character and don't want to see her come to harm.
2. Pick one other PC. That character knows a secret about your past that is tied to your Frenzy ability.
3. Pick one other PC. The first time you went into a frenzy was in an attempt to save her loved one from an attack. You failed, partly because of your inexperience.
4. Choose one other PC. He is terrified by your rage and sometimes can't help but flee at inopportune times.

Minor Effect Suggestion: When fighting multiple foes, you knock one into another, putting both off balance. As a result, treat both foes as one level lower for one round.

Major Effect Suggestion: Your foe is terrified of your rage and uses his next two actions to flee.

Tier 1: Frenzy (1 Intellect point). When you wish, while in combat, you can enter a state of frenzy. While in this state, you can't use points from your Intellect Pool, but you gain +1 to your Might Edge and your Speed Edge. This effect lasts for as long as you wish, but it ends if no combat is taking place within range of your senses. Enabler.

Tier 2: Hardy. You gain 5 additional points to your Might Pool. These additional points can be used only to absorb damage. You can't spend them to apply Effort to rolls. Enabler.

Mobile Fighter. You are trained in climbing and jumping tasks. Enabler.

Tier 3: Power Strike (3+ Might points). If you successfully attack a target, you knock it prone in addition to inflicting damage. The target must be your size or smaller. You can knock down a target larger than you if you apply a level of Effort to do so (rather than to decrease the difficulty of the attack). Enabler.

Unarmored Fighter. While unarmored, you are trained in Speed defense tasks. Enabler.

Tier 4: Greater Frenzy (4 Intellect points). When you wish, while in combat, you can enter a state of greater frenzy. While in this state, you can't use points from your Intellect Pool, but you gain +2 to your Might Edge and your Speed Edge. This effect lasts for as long as you wish, but it ends if no combat is taking place within range of your senses. You can use this ability or your first-tier Frenzy ability, but you can't use both at the same time. Enabler.

Tier 5: Attack and Attack Again. Rather than granting additional damage or a minor or major effect, a natural 17 or higher on your attack roll allows you the option of immediately making another attack. Enabler.

Tier 6: Tough and Fast. You gain 6 additional points to your Might Pool and 6 additional points to your Speed Pool. Enabler.

RIDES THE LIGHTNING

Through practice and inherent ability (or the subtle use of hidden or implanted devices), you control electricity. Not only can you create and discharge electrical power, but you can eventually learn to use it to transport yourself.

You probably wear tight-fitting clothing that allows you to move quickly. Your garments might be blue and black, perhaps with a lightning-bolt motif.

Connection: Choose one of the following.

1. Pick one other PC. This character has been your friend for a long time, and you have learned to bring her along when you ride the lightning. If the character is standing right next to you, you can take her with you when you use Bolt Rider or Electrical Flight. (Normally, neither ability allows you to transport other creatures.)
2. Pick two other PCs. You know about an important connection between them that even they don't know about.
3. Pick one other PC. This character has interesting ideas about electricity and how it can be harnessed. If you are trained with machines, after you talk to this character for an hour, you gain an asset on any task involving identifying, crafting, or repairing a machine that uses electricity.
4. Pick one other PC. He has the worst luck with electrical devices of anyone you've ever met. You want to help him, but you aren't sure how or even whether he will be open to your assistance.

Additional Equipment: You have a bag of miscellaneous batteries and power cells (if appropriate to the setting). Whenever you find a new device that operates on batteries or cells (GM discretion), there is a 75% chance that the bag contains one that will power the device if it depletes.

Electrical Abilities: If you use special abilities that would normally use force or other energy, they instead use electricity. For example, a force blast is a blast of lightning. This alteration changes nothing other than the type of damage and the fact that it might start fires.

Minor Effect Suggestion: The target is dazed by electricity for one round, during which time the difficulty of all tasks it performs is modified by one step to its detriment. Electricity can also shut down an android, robot, or other automaton for one round.

Major Effect Suggestion: Devices filled with electrical power explode. You can target and destroy an artifact that a foe is holding or wearing.

Tier 1: Shock (1 Intellect point). Your hands crackle with electricity, and the next time you touch a creature, you inflict 3 points of damage. Alternatively, if you wield a weapon, for ten minutes it crackles with electricity and inflicts 1 additional point of damage per attack. Action for touch; enabler for weapon.

Charge (1+ Intellect points). You can charge an artifact or other device (except a cypher) so that it can be used once. The cost is 1 Intellect point plus 1 point per level of the device. Action.

Rides the Lightning GM Intrusions: *Overcharged batteries explode.*

Tier 2: Bolt Rider (4 Intellect points). You can move a long distance from one location to another almost instantaneously, carried by a bolt of lightning. You must be able to see the new location, and there must be no intervening barriers. Action.

Tier 3: Lightning Swift. You gain 3 additional points to your Speed Pool and +1 to your Speed Edge. Enabler.

Drain Charge. You can drain the power from an artifact or device, allowing you to regain 1 Intellect point per level of the device. You regain points at the rate of 1 point per round and must give your full concentration to the process each round. The GM determines whether the device is fully drained (likely true of most handheld or smaller devices) or retains some power (likely true of large machines). Action to initiate; action each round to drain.

Tier 4: Bolts of Power (5+ Intellect points). You blast a fan of lightning out to short range in an arc that is approximately 50 feet (15 m) wide at the end. This discharge inflicts 4 points of damage. If you apply Effort to increase the damage rather than to decrease the difficulty, you deal 2 additional points of damage per level of Effort (instead of 3 points), and targets in the area take 1 point of damage even if you fail the attack roll. Action.

Tier 5: Electrical Flight (5 Intellect points). You exude an aura of crackling electricity that lets you fly for ten minutes. You can't carry other creatures with you. Action to activate.

Tier 6: Wall of Lightning (6 Intellect points). You create a barrier of crackling electricity up to 2,500 square feet (230 sq. m) in size, shaped as you wish. The wall is a level 7 barrier. Anyone within immediate distance of the wall automatically takes 10 points of damage. The wall lasts for one hour. Action to create.

Sees Beyond GM Intrusions: *Not everything that can be seen should be seen. Sometimes seeing too much can be overwhelming.*

SEES BEYOND

Unlike most people, you know there are far more than three dimensions. More colors than can be found in the rainbow. More things in the world than most can see, sense, or even understand. With practice and help (through drugs, lenses, manipulated energy fields, magic, special heritage, or a combination of some or all of these), you can perceive things that others cannot.

What you see in other dimensions has changed your understanding of even the most basic things like weapon and dress. Where others might see your drab outfit and plain weapons, you see something entirely different—myriad colors and patterns that showcase your unique vision of the world. Your weapons likely bear marks of other dimensions as well.

Connection: Choose one of the following.

1. Pick one other PC. You are fairly certain that this character doesn't believe that your abilities are real.
2. Pick one other PC. You see a gathering of energy and colors on this character that seem to imply that she too can see beyond. Whether you ask her about it is up to you.
3. Pick one other PC. Whenever this character is near, your abilities seem to take longer and become more difficult.
4. Pick one other PC. Wherever this character goes, you are aware of the general distance and direction of his location.

Minor Effect Suggestion: The period of concentration needed is cut in half.

Major Effect Suggestion: You see even more than you normally do and can ask the GM one question about what you're looking at.

Tier 1: See the Unseen. You can perceive creatures and objects that are normally invisible, out of phase, or only partially in this universe. When looking for things more conventionally hidden, the difficulty of the task is also reduced by one step. Enabler.

Tier 2: See Through Matter (3 Intellect points). You can see through matter as if it were transparent (or you had "x-ray vision"). You can see through up to 6 inches (15 cm) of material for one round, although some materials might be harder to see through than others. Action.

Tier 3: Find the Hidden (4+ Intellect points). You see the traceries of objects as they move through space and time. You can sense the distance and direction of any specific inanimate object that you once touched. This takes anywhere from one action to hours of concentration, depending on what the GM feels is appropriate due to time, distance, or other mitigating circumstances. However, you don't know in advance how long it will take. If you use at least two levels of Effort, once you have established the distance and direction, you remain in contact with the object for one hour per level of Effort used. Thus, if it moves, you are aware of its new position. Action to initiate; action each round to concentrate.

Tier 4: Remote Viewing (6 Intellect points). Distance is an illusion, as all space is one space. With great concentration, you can see another place. This ability can be used in one of two ways:

- Pick a spot a specific distance away and in a specific direction. For one minute, you see from that vantage point, as if that was where you stood.
- Think of a place that you have seen before, either conventionally or using the other application of this power. For one minute, you see from that vantage point, as if that was where you stood.

Either application takes anywhere from one action to hours of concentration, depending on what the GM feels is appropriate due to time, distance, or other mitigating circumstances. However, you don't know in advance how long it will take. Action to initiate; action each round to concentrate.

Tier 5: See Through Time (7 Intellect points). Time is an illusion, as all time is one time. With great concentration, you can see into another time. You specify a time period regarding the place where you now stand. Interestingly, the easiest time to view is about one hundred years in the past or future (difficulty 5). Viewing other times is more difficult—seeing a million years in the past or future, or moments behind or ahead of the present, are both difficulty 10.

This takes anywhere from one action to hours of concentration, depending on what the GM feels is appropriate due to time, distance, or other mitigating circumstances.

Characters who See Beyond or Separate Mind From Body know that there's far more to the world than the obvious material universe around them. Either or both could be seen as visionaries. Perhaps coincidentally, they would make extremely good spies.

However, you don't know in advance how long it will take. Action to initiate; action each round to concentrate.

Tier 6: Total Awareness. You possess such a high level of awareness that it's very difficult to surprise, hide, or sneak up on you. The difficulty of any initiative or perception task that you attempt is reduced by three steps. Enabler.

SEPARATES MIND FROM BODY

Separates Mind From Body GM Intrusions: *Reuniting mind and body can sometimes be disorienting and require a character to spend a few moments to get her bearings.*

Your mind is to your body as a captain is to her ship. Your body obeys your commands, moving and behaving as you direct it, but at any time you choose, your mind can wriggle free from its container and explore the world freely. When you project your mind, there are few places you cannot go, few secrets that can remain hidden from you.

You probably regard your body as merely a vessel. As a result, you're not likely to put a lot of effort into style or keeping yourself especially clean. Your clothing is likely tattered and dirty.

Connection: Choose one of the following.

1. Pick one other PC. Through a quirk of fate or careful cultivation (your choice), you always know where that character is in relation to you. You are always aware of the direction and distance you must travel to reach him.
2. Pick two other PCs. You believe that while using your Third Eye power, you once saw them engaged in something covert and possibly illegal. It's up to those characters whether one, both, or neither were actually involved.
3. Pick one other PC. For reasons beyond understanding, your focus abilities do not function when she is next to you and in your field of vision.
4. Pick one other PC. He is fascinated by your skills and wants to study you more closely. It's up to you whether or not you let him.

Additional Equipment: You possess a silvery ball about 3 inches (8 cm) in diameter. The ball's highly polished surface looks as if it reflects your surroundings, but examining its surface reveals that it reflects the surroundings of another location, one you have not yet found. In the images shown on the ball, you have seen many strange and unsettling things.

Minor Effect Suggestion: You have an asset on any action that involves using your senses, such as perceiving or attacking, until the end of the next round.

Major Effect Suggestion: Your Intellect Edge increases by 1 until the end of the next round.

Tier 1: Third Eye (1 Intellect point). You visualize a place within short range and cast your mind to that place, creating an immobile, invisible sensor for one minute or until you choose to end this ability. While using your third eye, you see through your sensor instead of your eyes using your normal visual abilities. You may perceive the area around your body using your other senses as normal. Action.

Tier 2: Open Mind (3 Intellect points). You open your mind to increase your awareness. The difficulty of any task involving perception is decreased by one step. While you have this asset and you are conscious and able to take actions, other characters gain no benefit for surprising you. The effect lasts for one hour. Action.

Sharp Senses. You are trained in all tasks involving perception. Enabler.

Tier 3: Roaming Third Eye (3 Intellect points). When you use your Third Eye ability, you can place the sensor anywhere within long range. In addition, until that ability ends, you can use an action to move the sensor anywhere within short range of its starting position. Enabler.

Tier 4: Sensor (4 Intellect points). You create an immobile, invisible sensor within immediate range that lasts for twenty-four hours. At any time during that duration, you can concentrate to see, hear, and smell through the sensor, no matter how far you move from it. The Sensor doesn't grant you sensory capabilities beyond the norm. If you already have the sensor ability from another source, it lasts for 48 hours when you create it. Action to create; action to check.

Improved Sensor (2 Intellect points). When you use Sensor, you can place the sensor anywhere you choose within long range. Enabler.

Tier 5: Psychic Passenger (6 Intellect points). You place your mind into the body of a willing creature you choose within short range and remain in that body for up to one hour. Your own body falls down and becomes insensate until this ability ends.

You see, hear, smell, touch, and taste using the senses of the character whose body you inhabit. When you speak, the words come from your defenseless body, and the character you inhabit hears those words in his mind.

The character you inhabit can use your Intellect Edge in place of his own. In addition, you and the character have an asset on any task that involves perception.

When you take an action, you use the character's body to perform that action if he allows it. Action to initiate.

Tier 6: Mental Projection (6+ Intellect points). Your mind fully leaves your body and manifests anywhere you choose within immediate range. Your projected mind can remain apart from your body for up to twenty-four hours. This effect ends early if your Intellect Pool is reduced to 0 or if your projection touches your resting body.

Your disembodied mind has a form that looks just like you. It has little physical substance, however, and its frayed edges trail off into nothingness. You control this body as if it were your normal body and can act and move as you normally would with a few exceptions.

You can move through solid objects as if they weren't there, and you ignore any terrain feature that would impede your movement.

Your attacks deal half damage, and you take half damage from physical sources. Regardless of the source, however, you take all damage as Intellect damage.

Your mind can travel up to 1 mile (2 km) from your body. Instead of applying Effort to decrease the difficulty, you can extend the range that you can travel by 1 mile for each level of Effort you apply.

Your physical body is helpless until this effect ends. You cannot use your senses to perceive anything. For example, your body could sustain a significant injury, and you wouldn't know it. Your body cannot take Intellect damage, so if your body takes enough damage to reduce both your Might Pool and your Speed Pool to 0, your mind snaps back to your body, and you are stunned until the end of the next round as you try to reorient yourself to your predicament. Action to initiate.

SHEPHERDS SPIRITS

You see things that others do not: wandering souls of the dead, nature spirits, ephemeral figures leaping amid the flames of a fire, and all the other unseen folk. You can speak to these otherworldly entities and interact with them. They are drawn to you, for they recognize that you walk in two worlds.

Shepherds usually wear distinctive robes and a variety of symbols, often with macabre imagery. Runes stitched across your cloak help you concentrate on your abilities.

Connection: Choose one of the following.

1. Pick one other PC. When spirits whisper to you, as they often do (you've learned to ignore it), that character can sometimes hear what they say.
2. Pick one other PC. She came to you with questions for a departed friend, family member, or enemy.
3. Pick one other PC. You may or may not have told him this, but the spirits whisper to you that he is destined to die soon.
4. Pick one other PC. You owe that character a significant amount of money.

Spirit Abilities: When you perform abilities that would normally use force or other energy, they instead use spirit energy. For example, a force blast appears as if delivered by a ghostly revenant whose touch drains life energy. This alteration changes nothing other than the type of damage.

Minor Effect Suggestion: You can ask an additional question of a spirit you petition.

Major Effect Suggestion: The spirit you are questioning knows a surprising amount of information about the topic.

Tier 1: Question the Spirits (2 Intellect points). You can call a spirit to you and petition it to answer a few questions (usually no more than three before the spirit fades).

First, you must summon a spirit. If it is a spirit of the dead, you must have personally known the person, have an object that was

Shepherds Spirits GM Intrusions: *Some people don't trust those who deal with spirits. The dead sometimes don't want shepherding.*

An insubstantial creature can't affect or be affected by anything unless indicated otherwise, such as when an attack is made with a special weapon. An insubstantial creature can pass through solid matter without hindrance, but solid energy barriers, such as magical fields of force, keep it at bay.

In some settings, the Shepherds Spirits focus applies to only one kind of spirit, such as spirits of the deceased, nature spirits, and so on.

owned by the person, or touch the physical remains of the creature. For other spirits, you must know the spirit's full name or have a great deal of an element (such as fire or earth) that the spirit is associated with.

If the spirit responds, it can manifest as an insubstantial shade that answers for itself, it can inhabit an object or any remains you provide, or it can manifest as an invisible presence that you speak for.

The spirit may not wish to answer your questions, in which case you must persuade it to help. You can attempt to psychically wrestle the spirit into submission (an Intellect task), or you can try diplomacy, deception, or blackmail ("Answer me, or I'll tell your children that you were a philanderer," or, "I'll destroy this relic that belonged to you").

The GM determines what the spirit might know, based on the knowledge it possessed in life. Action to initiate.

Tier 2: Spirit Accomplice. A level 3 spirit accompanies you and follows your instructions. The spirit must remain within immediate range—if it moves farther away, it fades at the end of your following turn and cannot return for a day. You and the GM must work out the details of your spirit accomplice, and you'll probably make rolls for it when it takes actions. The spirit accomplice acts on your turn, can move a short distance each round, and exists partially out of phase (allowing it to move through walls, though it makes a poor porter). The spirit takes up residence in an object you designate, and it manifests as either an invisible presence or a ghostly shade. Your spirit accomplice is specialized in one knowledge skill the GM determines.

The spirit is normally insubstantial, but if you spend an action and 3 Intellect points, it accretes enough substance to affect the world around it. As a level 3 creature with substance, it has a target number of 9 and a health of 9. It doesn't attack creatures, but while substantial, it can spend its action to serve as an asset for any one attack you make on your turn.

While corporeal, the spirit can't move through objects or fly. A spirit remains corporeal for up to ten minutes at a time, but fades back to being insubstantial if not

actively engaged. If your spirit accomplice is destroyed, it reforms in 1d6 days, or you can attract a new spirit in 2d6 days. Enabler.

Tier 3: Command Spirit (3 Intellect points). You can command a spirit or animated dead creature of up to level 5 within short range. If you are successful, the target cannot attack you for one minute, during which time it follows your verbal commands if it can hear and understand you. Action to initiate.

Tier 4: Wraith Cloak. At your command, your spirit accomplice wraps itself around you for up to ten minutes. The spirit automatically inflicts 4 points of damage to anyone who tries to touch you or strike you with a melee attack. While the wraith cloak is active, the difficulty of all tasks to evade the perceptions of others is decreased by one step. Enabler.

Tier 5: Call Dead Spirit (6 Intellect points). At your touch, the remains of a creature dead no longer than seven days appears as a manifest (and apparently physical) spirit. The raised spirit persists for up to a day (or less, if it accomplishes something important to it before then), after which the spirit fades away and cannot return again.

The raised spirit remembers everything it knew in life and possesses most of its previous abilities (though not necessarily its equipment). In addition, it gains the ability to become insubstantial as an action for up to a minute at a time. The raised spirit is not beholden to you, and it does not need to stay near you to remain manifest. Action to initiate.

Call Otherworldly Spirit (6 Intellect points). You summon a spirit creature that manifests for up to a day (or less, if it accomplishes something important to it before then), after which the spirit fades away and cannot be summoned again. The spirit is a creature of level 6 or lower, and it can be substantial or insubstantial as it wishes (using an action to change). The spirit is not beholden to you, and it does not need to stay near you to remain manifest. Action to initiate.

Tier 6: Infuse Spirit. When you kill a creature or destroy a spirit with an attack, if you choose, its spirit (if unprotected) immediately infuses you, and you regain 1d6 points to one of your Pools (your choice). The spirit is stored within you, which means it cannot be questioned, raised, or restored to life by any means unless you allow it.

Improved Command Spirit. When you use your Command Spirit ability, you can command a spirit or animate undead creature of up to level 7.

SIPHONS POWER

You are an energy vampire, draining power from machines or living creatures. You use this power to restore your own physical energy reserves. Perhaps you take great joy in this ability, or perhaps you grudgingly accept it as a boon to yourself and your companions and use it only when you must. Either way, you are likely feared and unwelcome in many communities for your dangerous powers. You might try to conceal your true nature, dressing so that you don't attract attention and give yourself away, or perhaps you flaunt it, using the rumors to your advantage, wearing black clothing and embodying a sinister countenance.

Connection: Choose one of the following.

1. Pick one other PC. This character is immune to your powers for some inexplicable reason.
2. Pick one other PC. This character appears to think of you as some kind of monster.
3. Pick one other PC with a living or machine companion. This character seems convinced that you're going to use his companion for your own ill-gotten purposes.
4. Pick one other PC. You believe she can help you control and understand your abilities, if you can get her to talk about it.

Minor Effect Suggestion: When draining, you gain 2 additional points to divide between your Speed Pool and Might Pool.

Major Effect Suggestion: When draining, you gain 5 additional points to divide between your Speed Pool and Might Pool.

Tier 1: Drain Machine (2 Intellect points). You can drain the power from an artifact or device you touch, allowing you to regain 1 point per level of the device. You can use these points to restore your Might Pool or

Siphons Power GM Intrusions: *Sometimes power drained from another source carries with it something unwanted—compulsions, afflictions, or alien thoughts. Siphoned power can overload the character, causing feedback.*

Automatons and other living machines should be treated as creatures, not machines, for the purposes of siphoning power from them.

Speed Pool. You regain points at the rate of 1 point per minute and must give your full concentration to the process during this time. The GM determines whether the device is fully drained (likely true of most handheld or smaller devices) or retains some power (likely true of large machines). Action to initiate.

Tier 2: Drain Creature (2 Intellect points). You can drain the power from a living creature you touch, allowing you to regain 1 point per level of the creature. You can use these points to restore your Might Pool or Speed Pool. You regain points at the rate of 1 point per minute and must give your full concentration to the process during this time, meaning that the creature probably has to be subdued in some fashion, because it loses 3 points of health for every point you gain. Creatures drained of all their health die. (PCs drained lose points from their Pools.) Action to initiate.

Slays Monsters GM Intrusions: *Monsters can be craftier and tougher than you think. They sometimes possess abilities you don't know about. Monsters sometimes hunt you instead of the other way around.*

Tier 3: Quick Drain (3 Intellect points). You can drain the power from a machine or a living creature you touch, allowing you to regain up to 3 points to restore your Might Pool or Speed Pool. You regain the points immediately. If the device is level 3 or lower, it is fully drained. Otherwise, the GM decides what happens to it. Creatures drained suffer 5 points of damage. After using Quick Drain on a device or creature, you can't drain it again using any of your abilities. Action.

Tier 4: Drain at a Distance. You can use your Drain Machine, Drain Creature, or Quick Drain abilities on any target within short range. Enabler.

Tier 5: Share the Power. You can take points that you have gained through draining and give them to another creature that you touch. PC recipients can distribute the points to any of their stat Pools, while NPC recipients restore lost health. Action.

Although wielding a sword—particularly an ancient sword from your monster-slaying secret society, handed down through the generations—in a setting where people usually do not carry such weapons is really cool, you can change the Slays Monsters sword-related abilities to use a different weapon, such as a gun with silver bullets.

Tier 6: Consume (6 Intellect points). You can drain the power from a machine or a living creature you touch, allowing you to regain up to 7 points to restore your Might Pool or Speed Pool. You regain the points immediately. If the device is level 5 or lower, it is entirely consumed and disappears. Otherwise, the GM decides what happens to it. Creatures drained suffer 10 points of damage. If that is enough to kill them, they are entirely consumed and disappear. After using Consume on a device or creature, you can't drain it again using any of your abilities. Action.

SLAYS MONSTERS

You live in a world populated not just by normal folk, but by creatures that should belong only to tall tales or nightmares. Dragons. Gorgons. Many-headed hydras. Werewolves. Worse.

You decided to stand up to this menace, even though it means putting yourself in more peril. And if you give your life, others will tell stories of your bravery. Usually heavily armed and armored knights, monster slayers are often afforded great respect.

Connection: Choose one of the following.

1. Pick one other PC. You saved him from a monster (though not by defeating the creature, which is still out there).

2. Pick one other PC. You tried but failed to save her loved one from a monster. You still bear the scars.

3. Pick one other PC. He knows the name and lair of a monster, but for some reason he won't share that information with you.

4. Pick one other PC. That character shows potential in the art and philosophy of monster slaying. You would like to train her but aren't sure she's interested.

Minor Effect Suggestion: You can immediately move up to a short distance after this action.

Major Effect Suggestion: You can immediately take a second action during this turn.

Tier 1: Sword Wielder. You are practiced with swords. Enabler.

Monster Bane. You inflict 1 additional point of damage with weapons. When you inflict damage to creatures more than twice as large or massive as you, you inflict 3 additional points of damage. Enabler.

Monster Lore. You are trained in the names, habits, suspected lairs, and related topics regarding the monsters of your

world. You can make yourself understood in their languages (if they have one). Enabler.

Tier 2: Will of Legend. You are immune to attacks that would captivate, mesmerize, charm, or otherwise influence your mind. Enabler.

Tier 3: Trained Slayer. You are trained in using swords. Enabler.

Improved Monster Bane. When you inflict damage to creatures more than twice as large or massive as you, you inflict 3 additional points of damage. Enabler.

Rider. You are trained in riding any kind of creature that serves as a mount, such as a noble warhorse. Enabler.

Tier 4: Fight On. You do not suffer the normal penalties for being impaired on the damage track. If debilitated, instead of suffering the normal penalty of being unable to take most actions, you can continue to act; however, the difficulty of all tasks increases by one step. Enabler.

Tier 5: Specialized Slayer. You are specialized in using swords. Enabler.

Heroic Monster Bane. When you inflict damage to creatures more than twice as large or massive as you, you inflict 3 additional points of damage. Enabler.

Tier 6: Slayer (2 Might points). You inflict 3 additional points of damage with a sword, regardless of your target. This ability means that against creatures more than twice as large or massive as you, you inflict a total of 12 additional points of damage. Enabler.

SOLVES MYSTERIES

You are a master of deduction. With a keen eye for detail and a quick wit, you can use a selection of clues to figure out what really happened when others are left scratching their heads. While a character that solves mysteries might be thought of as a detective or an investigator, a professor or even a scientist might also be a mystery solver.

You wear sensible clothing and comfortable shoes, walking that fine line between practical and stylish. You might carry a briefcase for all the tools you require to solve mysteries.

Solves Mysteries GM Intrusions: *Evidence disappears, red herrings confuse, and witnesses lie. Initial research can be faulty.*

Damage track, page 202

Connection: Choose one of the following.

1. Pick one other PC. She is the true friend who got you started reading mysteries and detective fiction, which led to your current obsession.
2. Pick one other PC. That character does not seem to trust or like you, but you feel compelled to win him over.
3. Pick one other PC. This character is a good sounding board. After you talk to her for an hour, you gain an asset on any knowledge-based task you are trained in.
4. Pick one other PC. You were rivals with him in some endeavor in the past.

Minor Effect Suggestion: You discover an additional clue about the mystery you are attempting to solve.

Major Effect Suggestion: When you solve a mystery, the target of your revelation is stunned by your dazzling wit, unable to move or act for a round.

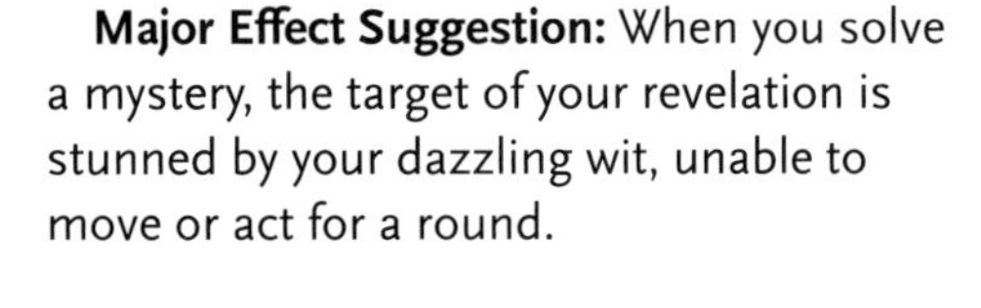

Tier 1: Investigator. To really shine as an investigator, you must engage your mind and body in your deductions. You can spend points from your Might Pool, Speed Pool, or Intellect Pool to apply levels of Effort to any Intellect-based task. Enabler.

Sleuth. Finding the clues is the first step in solving a mystery. You are trained in perception. Enabler.

Tier 2: Out of Harm's Way. No matter how careful, an investigator sometimes ends up in a scrap. Knowing how to survive is more than half the battle. You are trained in Speed defense tasks. Enabler.

Tier 3: You Studied. To be able to put two and two together to reach a deduction, you have to know a few things. You are trained in two areas of knowledge of your choosing (as long as they are not physical actions or combat related) or specialized in one area. Enabler.

Tier 4: Draw Conclusion (3 Intellect points). After careful observation and investigation (questioning one or more NPCs on a topic, searching an area or a file, and so on) lasting a few minutes, you can learn a pertinent fact. This ability is a difficulty 3 Intellect task. Each additional time you use this ability, the task difficulty increases by one step. The difficulty returns to 3 after you rest for ten hours. Action.

Tier 5: Diffuse Situation. During the course of an investigation, your questions sometimes elicit an angry or even violent response. Through dissembling, verbal distraction, or similar evasion, you prevent a living foe from attacking anyone or anything for one round. Action.

Tier 6: Seize the Initiative (5 Intellect points). Within one minute of successfully using your Draw Conclusion ability, you can take one additional, immediate action, which you can take out of turn. After using this ability, you can't use it again until after your next ten-hour recovery roll. Enabler.

SPEAKS FOR THE LAND

You not only speak for the land, you also protect it and the natural creatures and forests that it supports. In that sense, you are the land's champion. You might be part of an ancient priesthood of a select few who are able to commune with the spirits of nature and who call upon the magic of the forest, moon, storm, and beast. In particular, you know how certain long-lived trees are conduits of worldly magic. When lightning falls from the sky, fires rage, or the earth shakes, these elder trees channel that elemental fury into themselves. An event may burn away a limb or blow off bark, but the energy contained within the tree becomes part of the magic of the land—magic that you, in turn, draw upon.

As a speaker for the land, you probably wear rough, rugged clothing that shows little concern for style. Most of the time, covering yourself in natural smells to keep your scent from spooking wildlife is more important than bathing to be presentable to other humans.

Connection: Choose one of the following.

1. Pick one other PC. You found that character lying unconscious in the woods with no memory of how she got there. Without your help, she likely would have died of exposure.

2. Pick one or more other PCs not from the wilderness. You've decided that you will mentor them to become more appreciative of the land and its natural beauty.

3. Pick one other PC. More often than not, that character is accidentally singed, snagged, bitten, or otherwise caught when you use one of your special abilities.

4. Pick one other PC. That character's sibling is responsible for felling a sacred elder tree that was important to you.

Additional Equipment: A talisman of petrified oak.

Minor Effect Suggestion: A hawk or raven attacks your foe's head for one round, during which time the difficulty of all tasks the foe performs is modified by one step to its detriment.

Major Effect Suggestion: A large ferret, eagle, or similar natural creature snags and makes off with a piece of equipment worn or held by your foe.

Tier 1: Seeds of Fury (1 Intellect point). You throw a handful of seeds in the air that ignite and speed toward a target within long range, scratching the air with twisting smoke trails. The attack deals 3 points of damage and catches the target on fire, which inflicts 1 additional point of damage per round for up to a minute or until the target spends an action dousing the flame. Action.

Wilderness Lore. You are trained in wilderness navigation and in identifying plants and creatures. Enabler.

Tier 2: Grasping Foliage (3+ Intellect points). Roots, branches, grass, or other natural foliage in the area snags and holds a foe you designate within short range for up to one minute. A foe caught in the grasping foliage can't move from its position, and all physical tasks, attacks, and defenses are modified by one step to the victim's detriment, including attempts to free itself. Instead of applying Effort to reduce the difficulty of your attack, you can apply Effort to deal damage with the initial attack. Each level applied inflicts 2 additional points of damage when Grasping Foliage first snags and holds your foe.

You can also use this ability to clear an area of entangling growth in the immediate radius, such as an area of tall grass, thick brush, impenetrable vines, and so on. Action.

Tier 3: Soothe the Savage (3 Intellect points). You calm a nonhuman beast within 30 feet (9 m). You must speak to it (although it doesn't need to understand your words), and it must see you. It remains calm for one minute or for as long as you focus all your attention on it. The GM has final say over what counts as a nonhuman beast, but unless some kind of deception is at work, you should know whether you can affect a creature before you attempt to use this ability on it. Demons, dragons, very intelligent creatures, robots, and golems are never affected. Action.

Communication (2 Intellect points). You convey a basic concept to a creature that normally can't speak or understand speech. The creature can also give you a very basic answer to a simple question. Action.

Speaks for the Land GM Intrusions: *An injured natural (but dangerous) creature is discovered. Someone's been poaching the wildlife for their skins, leaving the carcasses to rot. A tree falls in the forest, one of the last surviving elder trees.*

Stands Like a Bastion GM Intrusions: *Armor that you rely on falls apart. A weakness in your body causes ripple effects. Small foes conspire against you in ways you don't expect.*

GM intrusion, page 193

Tier 4: Moon Shape (4+ Intellect points). You change into a monstrous natural beast, such as a wolf, bear, or other terrestrial creature, for up to one hour. If you try to change during daylight hours when you are not deep underground (or otherwise away from the daylight), you must apply a level of Effort. In your new form, you add 8 points to your Might Pool, gain +2 to your Might Edge, add 2 points to your Speed Pool, and gain +2 to your Speed Edge. Reverting to your normal form is a difficulty 2 task. While in beast form, you are prone to fits of rage (triggered by GM intrusion), during which you attack every living creature within short range, and the only way to end the rage is to revert to your normal form. Either way, after you revert to your normal form, you take a –1 penalty to all rolls for one hour. If you did not kill and eat at least one substantial creature while in beast form, the penalty increases to –2 and affects all your rolls for the next twenty-four hours. Action to change; action to revert.

Tier 5: Insect Eruption (6 Intellect points). You call a swarm of insects in a place where it is possible for insects to appear. They remain for one minute, and during this time, they do as you command while they are within long range. They can swarm about and modify any or all creatures' task difficulties by one step to their detriment, or you can focus the swarm and attack all targets within immediate range of each other (all within long range of you). The attacking swarm inflicts 2 points of damage per round. You can also command the swarm to move heavy objects through collective effort, eat through wooden walls, and perform other actions suitable for a supernatural swarm. Action to initiate.

Some characters who Stand Like a Bastion might already have Practiced in Armor. They can choose an additional tier 1 ability instead.

Tier 6: Call the Storm (7+ Intellect points). If you are outside or in a location that has a ceiling at least 300 feet (91 m) above the floor, you summon a boiling layer of lightning-lit, rumbling clouds up to 1,500 feet (457 m) in diameter for ten minutes. During daylight hours, natural illumination beneath the storm is reduced to dim light. While the storm rages, you can spend an action to send a lightning bolt from the cloud to attack a target you can see directly, inflicting 4 points of damage (you can spend Effort normally on each individual lightning bolt attack). Three actions to initiate; action to call down a lightning strike.

STANDS LIKE A BASTION

You are a wall. A stone. An island against a storm of weapons and words. Nothing moves you. Nothing even really dents you. Perhaps it's your physical size that lends you such stopping power, perhaps you've enhanced your physique with mechanisms and machinery, or perhaps it's merely your incredible strength of will that forces foes to stay their swings.

Your armor is probably just like you: solid, strong, and utterly impenetrable. Every flourish and bit of flair—if you have any—does double duty as protection.

Connection: Choose one of the following.

1. Pick one other PC. You feel indebted to this character and go out of your way to protect her from harm.
2. Pick one other PC. You once saved this character from a dangerous situation.
3. Pick one other PC. This character once ran full bore into you while running away from . . . something. You stopped him just by being in the wrong place at the wrong time, but he seems to hold it against you.
4. Pick two other PCs. You would like to ask them to help you train by attacking you at the same time, but you're uncertain how to approach them with this request.

Additional Equipment: You have armor of your choice and a shield.

Minor Effect Suggestion: You add +2 to Armor.

Major Effect Suggestion: You regain 2 points to your Might Pool.

Tier 1: Experienced Defender. When wearing armor, you gain +1 to Armor.

Practiced in Armor. You can wear armor for long periods of time without tiring and can compensate for slowed reactions from wearing armor. You can wear any kind of armor. You reduce the Speed cost for wearing armor by 1. You start the game with a type of armor of your choice. Enabler.

Tier 2: Resist the Elements. You resist heat, cold, and similar extremes. You have a

special +2 bonus to Armor against ambient damage or other damage that would normally ignore Armor.

Tier 3: Unmovable (3 Might points). You avoid being knocked down, pushed back, or moved against your will as long as you are upright and able to take actions. Enabler.

Mighty. You gain 5 additional points to your Might Pool. Enabler.

Tier 4: Living Wall (3 Might points). You specify a confined area—such as an open doorway, a hallway, or a space between two trees—where you stand. For the next ten minutes, if anyone attempts to enter or pass through that area and you don't wish it, you make an automatic attack against them. If you hit, not only do you inflict damage, but they must also stop their movement. Enabler.

Tier 5: Hardiness. You are trained in Might defense tasks.

Mastery With Armor. When you wear any armor, you reduce the armor's penalties to 0. Enabler.

Tier 6: Shield Training. If you use a shield, the difficulty of Speed defense tasks is decreased by two steps instead of one. Enabler.

Wall With Teeth. You inflict 2 additional points of damage with all attacks when using your Living Wall ability.

TALKS TO MACHINES

Since you were young, you had an affinity for machines. It seemed almost like you were speaking to them.

You were. You have the ability to use your organic brain like a computer, interfacing "wirelessly" with any electronic device. You can control and influence them in ways that others can't. Computers are your friends and companions. You have also learned to repair machines of all kinds because the better they work, the better off you are as well.

You likely wear a tool belt full of various implements, and machine oils stain your clothes and fingertips.

Connection: Choose one of the following.

1. Pick one other PC. That character seems to have a terrible relationship with

Talks to Machines GM Intrusions: *Sometimes machines malfunction or act unpredictably. In addition, many people look upon someone who interfaces so well with machines as a witch—or at least as a dangerous individual.*

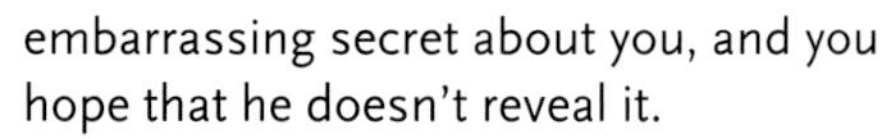

machines—or at least the machines that you communicate with. If she is next to a machine that you interact with in a friendly manner, that machine is treated in all ways as being one level lower than normal (unless doing so benefits you or her, in which case the level does not change).

2. Pick one other PC. He seems especially leery of you, though this could just be your perception.

3. Pick one other PC. She has a small machine among her equipment but won't tell you any details about it or let you see it.

4. Pick one other PC. You know that this character knows an incriminating or embarrassing secret about you, and you hope that he doesn't reveal it.

Additional Equipment: A bag of small tools.

Minor Effect Suggestion: The duration of influence or control is doubled.

Major Effect Suggestion: The duration of influence or control becomes twenty-four hours.

Tier 1: Machine Affinity. You are trained in all tasks involving electrical machines. Enabler.

Distant Activation (1 Intellect point). You can activate or deactivate any machine you can see within short range, even if normally you would have to touch or manually operate the device. To use this ability, you must understand the function of the machine, it must be your size or smaller, and it can't be connected to another intelligence (or be intelligent itself). Action.

Tier 2: Coaxing Power (2 Intellect points). You boost the power or function of a machine so that it operates at one level higher than normal for one hour. Action to initiate.

Charm Machine (2 Intellect points). You convince an unintelligent machine to "like" you. A machine that likes you is 50 percent less likely to function if said function would cause you harm. Thus, if a foe attempts to detonate a bomb near you controlled by a detonator that likes you, there is a 50 percent chance that it won't explode. Action to initiate.

Tier 3: Intelligent Interface (3 Intellect points). You can speak telepathically with any intelligent machine within long range. Further, you are trained in all interactions with intelligent machines. Such machines and automatons that normally would never communicate with a human might talk to you. Enabler.

Tier 4: Machine Companion. You create a level 3 animate, intelligent machine that accompanies you and acts as you direct. If the machine is destroyed, it takes you one month to create a new one. Enabler.

Robot Fighter. When fighting an automaton or intelligent machine, you are trained in attacks and defense. Enabler.

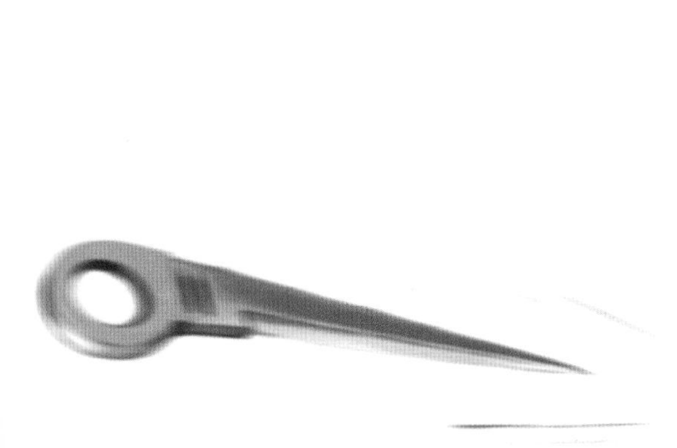

Tier 5: Information Gathering (5 Intellect points). You speak telepathically with any or all machines within 1 mile (2 km). You can ask one basic question about themselves or anything happening near them and receive a simple answer. For example, while in an area with many machines, you could ask "Where is the ravage bear?" and if the creature is within a mile of you, one or more machines will probably provide the answer. Action.

Tier 6: Control Machine (6 Intellect points). You can control the functions of any machine, intelligent or otherwise, within short range. This effect lasts for ten minutes. Action.

THROWS WITH DEADLY ACCURACY

Sometimes you wonder if your hand and your mind's eye are connected in an intricate perfection of timing and aim. Everything that leaves your hand goes exactly where you'd like it to and at the range and speed to make the perfect impact. Your expertise might be in carefully crafted throwing daggers and shuriken, or perhaps you use whatever's nearby.

What you wear doesn't matter, as long as it doesn't come between you and your throwing implements. Lots of pockets, equipment belts, and pouches make it easy to keep your preferred weapons close at hand. You might even have a hat with a variety of throwing items tucked into its brim, ready to meet their target with your perfect aim.

Connection: Choose one of the following.

1. Pick one other PC. You believe that this character shows potential for being an excellent ranged attacker, but you don't know if she would be interested in the rigorous training and practice required.
2. Pick one other PC. This character once saved you from a dangerous situation.
3. Pick one other PC. You owe this character a significant amount of money.
4. Pick one other PC. He is always getting in the way. If the GM determines that your attack strikes the wrong target, it almost always hits this character.

Additional Equipment: You have three throwing weapons of your choice.

Minor Effect Suggestion: You hit your target in the eye and blind him for one round.

Major Effect Suggestion: You strike your target in a limb, making that limb useless for the next minute.

Tier 1: Precision. You deal 2 additional points of damage with attacks using weapons that you throw. Enabler.

Throws With Deadly Accuracy GM Intrusions: *Missed attacks strike the wrong target. Ricochets can be dangerous. Improvised weapons break.*

Tier 2: Careful Aim. You are trained in attacks with all weapons that you throw. Enabler.

Tier 3: Rapid Fire (2 Speed points). When you make an attack by throwing a light weapon, you can draw another light weapon and make another thrown attack against the same target or a different target as part of the same action. Action.

Tier 4: Everything Is a Weapon. You can take any small object—a coin, a pen, a bottle, a stone, and so on—and throw it with such force and precision that it inflicts damage as a light weapon. Enabler.

Killer Accuracy. You are specialized in attacks with all weapons that you throw. Enabler.

Tier 5: Spray Attack (5 Speed points). With a large handful of small objects—tiny knives, shuriken, stones, jagged bits of metal, coins, or whatever is on hand—you attack every creature in an immediate area within short range. You must make attack rolls against each target. The difficulty of each attack is increased by one step. You inflict 3 points of damage on targets you hit. Action.

Tier 6: Force and Accuracy. You inflict 3 additional points of damage with attacks using weapons that you throw. Enabler.

TRAVELS THROUGH TIME

Travels Through Time GM Intrusions: *Moving through time creates countless possibilities for paradoxes, both small and large. As reality flows in to correct these snarls in time, certain events the character experienced may become rewritten. Other people might remember events differently than the time traveler does.*

You have the unusual ability to travel through time in a way others can never dream of. You have likely experienced jumps where time seems to have passed but you have no memory of what happened. You probably also suffer from déjà vu, sensing that you have been in a situation or witnessed an event before and are now experiencing it all over again. You have begun to realize the extent of your powers and work to master them so that perhaps one day you can travel farther into the future or deeper into the past.

Time travel poses many risks. Often, you have no clear sense about what the future might hold or what might have been happening in the spot where you appear when you travel to the past. Death waits for the bold and the incautious.

Worse than mishap, you must guard against paradox. When you change an event in the past, you could inadvertently cause the future to be rewritten. On the other hand, cosmic forces may move in to correct paradoxes by changing circumstances to accommodate the ability, causing your memories to become false ones when the world you know changes to adapt to your meddling. Of course, if you attempt anything too radical, the universe might write you out of existence so that your efforts to change the past never occur.

You likely wear clothing and have personal effects in a range of styles, choosing items from many different periods. This eclectic approach to your possessions may give you a shabby appearance or make you look strange and alien to others in the present.

Any type of character can have this focus, though its power is extraordinarily rare.

Connection: Choose one of the following.

1. Pick one other PC. You are either a distant ancestor or a descendant of that character. He served as a focal point for your travel and anchors you to the present.
2. Pick one other PC. For some reason, when you use your Anticipation power to look ahead, you specifically see how her future might unfold. You can choose whether or not to tell her what you see.
3. Pick one other PC. You secretly believe that he can also travel through time, since you once fought a person who looked exactly like him.
4. Pick one other PC. You once stepped forward in time to save her from death, but she doesn't know it. You may choose whether or not to tell her.

Temporal Abilities: If you have other overt powers, time appears to slow down when you use them. You and everything around you moves in slow motion for a moment, and then time snaps back into place. The temporal distortion changes nothing about the effects of your abilities except for the appearance of the world around you.

Minor Effect Suggestion: One creature you choose within short range either acts first or acts last during the next round.

Major Effect Suggestion: You step a few moments into the future. To other characters, it looks as if you disappear. At the start of the next round, you reappear and you have an asset for any task you perform during that round.

Tier 1: Anticipation (1 Intellect point). You look ahead to see how your actions might unfold. You have an asset for the first task you perform before the end of the next round. Enabler.

Tier 2: See History (4 Intellect points). You touch an object and immediately visualize up to three significant past events that involved the object or happened near it, starting with the most recent. The events are those that involved intense emotion or sensation, or that had an impact on the way history unfolded afterward. The GM decides whether you see the event, gain some understanding of what happened, or receive impressions of what was experienced. Afterward, you have an asset on any task to identify the object. Action.

Tier 3: Temporal Acceleration (5 Intellect points). You or one willing character you touch moves more quickly through time. The effect lasts for one minute. Everything moves more slowly for the affected character, while to all others, the character seems to move at preternatural speed. The character has an asset on all tasks until the effect ends. After the effect ends, the difficulty of all tasks is increased by one step for one hour because the character is exhausted and disoriented by the experience. Action to initiate.

Tier 4: Temporal Dislocation (7 Intellect points). You disappear and travel up to one hour into the future or the past. You remain there until you catch up to the present or the present catches up to you. While dislocated in time, you perceive events as they transpire from your position using your normal senses. No other character can see you or interact with you. Similarly, you cannot interact with your environment. Action to initiate.

Tier 5: Time Loop (7 Intellect points). You call yourself from a few moments in the future to help in the present. Your future self appears anywhere you choose within immediate range and remains until the end of the next round, at which point both you and your future self disappear. At the end of the next round, you reappear in the space your future self left when he disappeared.

Your future self shares your stats, so any damage that either of you takes applies to the same stat Pools. When you appear from the future, you may immediately use an action. During the next round, your present self and your future self both act.

If an attack against your future self deals

FOR THE GM: MANAGING TIME TRAVEL

Although time travel offers plenty of grist for the storytelling mill, it also brings plenty of complications. If you allow a player to choose this focus, you need to decide whether the character can change history by traveling through time.

The easiest way to manage time travel is to simply say that the characters jump to a different timeline when they move forward or backward through time. Anything they do while displaced in time affects only events on that line. The point the PCs left becomes a nexus of many timelines. Characters returning to that point might find themselves in their original time, in which case nothing they altered in the past affects their present or future, or they might be in a different timeline, where their past actions have had a great effect on the current world.

The biggest benefit of the multiple timelines approach is that it sidesteps the problems of paradoxes. Whenever a paradox would occur, the characters create another timeline instead. So if a PC goes back in time to a point before he is born and kills his grandfather, he erases himself from that timeline, but not from his own. Thus, the character continues to exist.

You can use other methods for managing time travel, allowing characters to change past events to create a new future, paradoxes be damned. Or you might have the PCs merely observe, unable to interact with anything outside of the point you decide is the present.

Although all character choices are subject to GM approval, Travels Through Time is a focus that the GM and player should probably have a long conversation about ahead of time, so the player knows the rules of time travel (if any) that exist in the GM's setting. A character with this focus can drastically alter a setting, if the rules of time travel allow it.

Wears a Sheen of Ice GM Intrusions: *Ice makes surfaces slippery. Extreme cold causes objects to crack and break.*

damage sufficient to kill you, your future self dies, but you don't die until after the effect causes you to disappear. Action to initiate.

Tier 6: Time Travel (10+ Intellect points). You and up to three willing characters you choose within immediate range travel to a point in time that you specify when you use this ability. The point in time must be within ten years of the present. For each level of Effort applied, you can travel ten more years. When you appear in the new moment in time, you do so in the same position you were in when you used this ability. Upon arriving at your temporal destination, you and each character that traveled with you are stunned for one minute. In order to return to the original time, you must use the power again. Action.

Barrier, page 33

WEARS A SHEEN OF ICE

Through your studies, you have learned to focus your natural talents to command the powers of ice and cold. People might refer to you as an ice mage. Sometimes ice mages are thought to come into conflict with those known as fire mages, but this is a fallacy believed by ordinary folks more than anything based in truth.

You likely wear white or blue garments that are heavier than they need to be—unless you live in a cold region or wintry clime, in which case you probably wear less clothing than other people do because the cold doesn't bother you.

Connection: Choose one of the following.

1. Pick one other PC. Due to a quirk of fate, if that character is standing next to you when you use your Ice Armor ability, he is also protected by a sheen of ice. (He does not get the added protection of your Resilient Ice Armor ability.)
2. Pick one other PC. For a reason unknown to you, her very presence seems to heat the air around you, making it more difficult to command the powers of ice and cold. If she is within immediate range, her presence occasionally makes it one step more difficult to hit a target with a focus ability.
3. Pick one other PC. That person is especially susceptible to the cold that radiates from you. How he handles that vulnerability is up to him.
4. Pick one other PC. The two of you have a long history and almost always disagree about the best way to handle situations.

Ice Abilities: If you possess abilities that would normally use force or other energy, they instead use cold and ice. For example, a force blast is a ray of frost. This alteration changes nothing other than the type of damage. As another example, Barrier creates a wall of ice. This alteration changes nothing except the wall's appearance and the fact that it takes 2 additional points of damage from fire.

Minor Effect Suggestion: The surface around the target becomes slick and difficult to stand on.

Major Effect Suggestion: The target is covered in ice that hinders its movement for one minute, during which time the difficulty of all tasks it performs is modified by one step to its detriment.

Tier 1: Ice Armor (1 Intellect point). When you wish it, your body is covered in a sheen of ice for ten minutes that gives you +1 to Armor. While the sheen is active, you feel no discomfort from normal cold temperatures and have an additional +2 to Armor against cold damage specifically. Enabler.

Tier 2: Frost Touch (1 Intellect point). Your hands become so cold that the next time you touch a creature, you inflict 3 points of damage. Alternatively, you can touch a weapon, and for the next ten minutes, the weapon inflicts 1 additional point of damage from the cold. Action for touch; enabler for weapon.

Tier 3: Freezing Touch (4 Intellect points). Your hands become so cold that, in addition to inflicting damage as described under Frost Touch, your touch freezes solid a living target of your size or smaller, rendering it immobile for one round. Action.

Tier 4: Resilient Ice Armor. The sheen of ice you generate using your Ice Armor ability gives you an additional +1 to Armor. Enabler.

Tier 5: Cold Burst (5+ Intellect points). You emit a blast of cold in all directions, up to short range. All within the burst take 5 points of damage. If you apply Effort to increase the damage rather than to decrease the difficulty, you deal 2 additional points of damage per level of Effort (instead of 3 points), and targets in the area take 1 point of damage even if you fail the attack roll. Action.

Tier 6: Ice Creation (6 Intellect points). You create a solid object of ice that is your size or smaller. The object is crude and can have no moving parts, so you can make a sword, a shield, a short ladder, and so on. Your ice objects are as strong as iron, but if you're not in constant contact with them, they function for only 1d6 + 6 rounds before breaking or melting. For example, you can make and wield an ice sword, but if you give it to another PC, the sword won't last as long for that character. Action.

WIELDS TWO WEAPONS AT ONCE

You bear steel with both hands, ready to take on any foe. You fight with two weapons in melee, sometimes called dual wielding. A fearsome warrior, quick and strong, you believe that the best defense is a strong offense.

You probably sheathe one weapon on each side or both crossed behind your back. They are likely your most prized possessions, and you might have names for them.

Connection: Choose one of the following.

1. Pick one other PC. You have trained with this character so much that if the two of you stand back to back in a fight, you both gain a +1 bonus to Speed defense rolls.
2. Pick one other PC. This character always seems to inadvertently foil your actions, or at least make them more difficult. If she is within immediate range, the difficulty of any action related to this focus is increased by one step.
3. Pick one other PC. You recently had a weapon go missing, and you're becoming convinced that he took it. Whether or not he did is up to him.
4. Pick one other PC. You used to dislike him immensely, but as you get to know him, you're growing fond of him against your better judgment.

Additional Equipment: You start with an additional light melee weapon.

Minor Effect Suggestion: The target is intimidated and flees as its next action.

Major Effect Suggestion: You can make an immediate additional attack with one of your weapons.

Tier 1: Dual Light Wield. You can use two light weapons at the same time, making two separate attacks on your turn as a single action. You remain limited by the amount of Effort you can apply on one action, but because you make separate attacks, your opponent's Armor applies to both. Anything that modifies your attack or damage applies to both attacks, unless it's specifically tied to one of the weapons. Enabler.

Tier 2: Double Strike (3 Might points). When you wield two weapons, you can choose to make one attack roll against a foe. If you hit, you inflict damage with both weapons plus 2 additional points of damage, and because

Wields Two Weapons at Once GM Intrusions: *With so many strikes and slices, it's easy to imagine a blade snapping in two or a weapon flying loose from its bearer's grip.*

you made a single attack, the target's Armor is subtracted only once. Action.

Tier 3: Dual Medium Wield. You can use two light weapons or medium weapons at the same time (or one light weapon and one medium weapon), making two separate attacks on your turn as a single action. This ability otherwise works like the Dual Light Wield ability. Enabler.

Tier 4: Dual Defense. When you wield two weapons, you are trained in Speed defense tasks. Enabler.

Tier 5: Dual Distraction (4 Speed points). When you wield two weapons, your opponent's next attack is hindered. As a result, the difficulty of your defense roll against that attack is reduced by one step, and the difficulty of your next attack is reduced by one step. Enabler.

Tier 6: Whirling Dervish. When you wield two weapons, you can attack up to six times in one round as a single action, but you must make each attack against a different foe. Make a separate attack roll for each attack. You remain limited by the amount of Effort you can apply on one action, and because you make separate attacks, Armor applies to each of them. Anything that modifies your attack or damage applies to all attacks (positively or negatively), unless it's specifically tied to one of the weapons, in which case it applies to only half of the attacks. Enabler.

Works Miracles GM Intrusions: *Attempts to heal might cause harm instead. Sometimes, a community or individual needs a healer so desperately that they hold one against his will.*

WORKS MIRACLES

You manipulate matter and time to help others and are beloved by everyone you encounter. Some people consider you a representative of the gods or a power from beyond this world. Perhaps they're right. Your abilities might be a gift of the angels or a powerful and benevolent god.

You probably wear simple clothes—nothing too flashy or stylish. There's no need to call more attention to yourself.

Connection: Choose one of the following.

1. Pick one other PC. This character quietly suspects that you're a messiah or supernatural being. You can choose whether or not you're aware of his suspicion.

2. Pick one other PC. He knows a secret of yours, and you desperately hope that he doesn't tell anyone.

3. Pick one other PC. She believes that you cured someone close to her of a deadly disease, and she is grateful. You aren't sure whether you actually helped or if that person wasn't as sick as she thought.

4. Pick one other PC. You secretly believe that she might be a hypochondriac, and you're never sure whether she actually needs your help.

Minor Effect Suggestion: The target is healed for 1 additional point.

Major Effect Suggestion: The target is healed for 2 additional points.

Tier 1: Healing Touch (1 Intellect point). With a touch, you restore 1d6 points to one stat Pool of any creature. This ability is a difficulty 2 Intellect task. Each time you attempt to heal the same creature, the task difficulty increases by one step. The difficulty returns to 2 after that creature rests for ten hours. Action.

Tier 2: Alleviate (3 Intellect points). You attempt to cancel or cure one malady (such as disease or poison) in one creature. Action.

Tier 3: Font of Healing. With your approval, other creatures can touch you and regain 1d6 points to either their Might Pool or their Speed Pool. This healing costs them 2 Intellect points. A single creature can benefit from this ability only once each day. Enabler.

Tier 4: Inspiration (4 Intellect points). Through mental inspiration and the manipulation of time, one creature you choose within short range is granted an additional, immediate action, which it can take out of turn. Action.

Tier 5: Undo (5 Intellect points). You turn back time a few seconds, effectively undoing a single creature's most recent action. That creature can then immediately repeat the same action or try something different. Action.

Tier 6: Greater Healing Touch (4 Intellect points). You touch a creature and restore its Might Pool, Speed Pool, and Intellect Pool to their maximum values, as if it were fully rested. A creature can benefit from this ability only once each day. Action.

WORKS THE BACK ALLEYS

The thief, the burglar, the pickpocket: these are the dangerous individuals who haunt the back alleys of every community. You are a thief in a city or town, making your livelihood at the expense of the wealthy. Your talents, however, prepare you for all kinds of pursuits, even when you're not crouching in an alley or climbing into a window.

Usually, you dress to blend in with the crowd. When you're on a mission, black, form-fitting clothing allows you to swim in the shadows.

Connection: Choose one of the following.

1. Pick one other PC. The character knew you beforehand and convinced you to leave your life of crime for other pursuits—at least temporarily.

2. Pick one other PC. A while back, you attempted to "borrow" something from her, but she busted you in the process. You managed to convince her that it was a simple misunderstanding, but she may not entirely trust you.

3. Pick one other PC. You never seem to be able to hide so that he can't see you.

4. Pick one other PC. She knows your real identity (if it's a secret) or that you work undercover (if it's a secret) and has kept the knowledge to herself so far. It's up to her whether she continues to do so.

Additional Equipment: You start with a bag of light tools.

Minor Effect Suggestion: You can immediately attempt to hide after this action.

Major Effect Suggestion: You can immediately take a second action during this turn.

Tier 1: Thief. You are trained in stealth, pickpocketing, and lockpicking tasks. Enabler.

Tier 2: Underworld Contacts. You know many people in a variety of communities who engage in illegal activities. These people are not necessarily your friends and might not be trustworthy, but they recognize you as a peer. You and the GM should work out the details of your underworld contacts. Enabler.

Works the Back Alleys GM Intrusions: *When things go wrong for thieves, they end up in jail. Even when things go right, thieves can earn the enmity of powerful people, including criminals.*

A character in a setting without magic or gods who Works Miracles might—knowingly or unknowingly—be using nanites to help repair wounds or improve the physiology of themselves or another creature. Alternatively, it might be that a part of the character's brain can speak to individual cells in a creature's body, directing and speeding up the cells' mitotic phase or even the migration of cells in the system, reorganizing entire biological structures.

Tier 3: Pull a Fast One (3 Intellect points). When you're running a con, picking a pocket, fooling or tricking a dupe, sneaking something by a guard, and so on, you treat the task as if it were one level lower. Enabler.

Tier 4: Master Thief. You are trained in climbing, escaping from bonds, slipping through narrow places, and other contortionist moves. Enabler.

Tier 5: Dirty Fighter (2 Speed points). You distract, blind, annoy, hamper, or otherwise interfere with a foe, hindering his attack and defense rolls for one minute. As a result, the difficulty of your defense rolls and attack rolls against the foe is reduced by one step. Action.

Tier 6: Alley Rat (4 Intellect points). While in a city, you find or create a significant shortcut, secret entrance, or emergency escape route where it looked like none existed. You and the GM should work out the details. Action.

When you're hacking the impossible, the GM will decide if your hack is reasonable and determine its level of difficulty. For comparison, discovering a normal password when you have direct access to the system is a difficulty 2 task for you.

Works the System GM Intrusions: *Contacts sometimes have ulterior motives. Devices sometimes have failsafes or even traps.*

WORKS THE SYSTEM

You've knocked around a lot and run afoul of the law a few times, but you've evaded authorities on a variety of fronts more often than not. That's because you are adept at noticing flaws and exploits in systems, whether those systems are civil laws, investment regulations, computer codes, games of all sorts, or similar artificial constructions. Once you notice and fully comprehend a system, you can manipulate it to your own ends.

You are a manipulator, but you likely keep a term like that to yourself. Tell people you're an entrepreneur—that always sounds good.

Connection: Choose one of the following connections.

1. Pick one other PC. You turned her failing grade into a passing one, fixed an immigration issue, made a driving offense disappear from computer records, or managed some similar aid for that character.

2. Pick one other PC. You're aware that he knows an incriminating or embarrassing secret about you.

3. Pick one other PC. Whenever he is next to you, the difficulty of tasks involving interactions with people or attempts to use machines is increased by one step.

4. Pick one other PC. Whenever you charm or persuade others, this character always gains the same benefits of your actions as you do.

Additional Equipment: A laptop computer and a smartphone.

Minor Effect Suggestion: You learn something completely unexpected but useful.

Major Effect Suggestion: You can immediately take a second action during this turn.

Tier 1: Hack the Impossible (3 Intellect points). You can persuade automatons, machines, and computers to do your bidding. You can discover an encrypted password, break through security on a website, briefly turn off a machine such as a surveillance camera, or disable a robot with a moment's worth of fiddling. Action.

Computer Programming. You are trained in using (and exploiting) computer software, you know one or more computer languages well enough to write basic programs, and you are fluent in Internet protocol. Enabler.

Tier 2: Connected. You know people who get things done—not just respected people in positions of authority, but also a variety of online hackers and regular street criminals. These people are not necessarily your friends and might not be trustworthy, but they owe you a favor. You and the GM should work out the details of your contacts. Enabler.

Tier 3: Confidence Artist. When you're hacking into a computer system, running a con, picking a pocket, fooling or tricking a dupe, sneaking something by a guard, and so on, you treat the task as if it were one level lower. Enabler.

Tier 4: Confuse Enemy (4 Intellect points). Through a clever bit of misdirection involving a flourish of your coat, ducking at just the right moment, or a similar stratagem, you can attempt to redirect a physical melee attack that would otherwise hit you. When you do, the misdirected attack hits another creature you choose within immediate range of both you and the attacking foe. This ability is a difficulty 2 Intellect task. Enabler.

Tier 5: Work the Friendship (4 Intellect points). You know just what to say to draw a little extra effort from an ally. This grants one creature you choose within short range an additional, immediate action, which it can take out of turn. The creature uses the action you give it however it wishes. Action.

Tier 6: Call in Favor (4 Intellect points). A guard, doctor, technician, or hired thug in the employ of or allied with a foe is secretly your ally or owes you a favor. When you call in the favor, the target does what he can to help you out of a specific fix (unties you, slips you a knife, leaves a cell door unlocked) in a way that minimizes his risk of revealing his divided loyalties to his employer or other allies. This ability is a difficulty 3 Intellect task. Each additional time you use this ability, the difficulty increases by one step. The difficulty returns to 3 after you rest for ten hours. Action.

WOULD RATHER BE READING

Your whole life, people have been asking you why you read so much. Would you rather read about life than live it, they ask? *Yes*, you answer, probably inwardly. Books are your friends. You love fiction that gives you escape and nonfiction that enriches your mind. You're always learning new things. What's more important than knowledge? Nothing.

You probably carry a bag of books (or a tablet with ebooks on it, or both) with you at all times.

Connection: Choose one of the following.

1. Pick one other PC. She seems to understand you and knows that you need your space and time alone to read now and again.

2. Pick one other PC. This character is ignorant and uneducated, in your opinion.

3. Pick one other PC. He reminds you a lot of the main character of one of your favorite books. You can't help but like him.

4. Pick one other PC. This character owes you a fair bit of money.

Minor Effect Suggestion: You draw on your experiences and reduce the difficulty of your next action by one step.

Major Effect Suggestion: You can make a free, no-action recovery roll.

Tier 1: Knowledge Is Power. Choose two noncombat skills in which you are not trained. You are trained in those skills. Enabler.

Tier 2: Enriched Mind. You add 5 points to your Intellect Pool. Enabler.

Tier 3: Applying Your Knowledge. You can assist in any action undertaken by another character and reduce the difficulty by one step. Action.

Tier 4: Knowledge Is Power. Choose two noncombat skills. You are trained in those skills. If you are already trained, you are specialized in those skills instead. Enabler.

Trivia (5 Intellect points). If you have ten minutes to consult some of your books, you can ask the GM one question and get a general answer. The GM assigns a level to the question, so the more obscure the answer, the more difficult the task. Generally, knowledge that you could find by looking somewhere other than your current location is level 1, and obscure knowledge of the past is level 7. Action.

Tier 5: Smarter Every Day. You add 5 points to your Intellect Pool. Enabler.

Tier 6: Tower of Intellect. You are trained in Intellect defense tasks. If you are already trained, you are specialized in those tasks instead. Enabler.

Knowledge Is Power. Choose two noncombat skills. You are trained in those skills. If you are already trained, you are specialized in those skills instead. Enabler.

Would Rather Be Reading GM Intrusions: *Books burn, get wet, or get lost. Computers break or lose power. Glasses break.*

CHAPTER 8

EQUIPMENT

Equipment in the Cypher System plays only a small role. It's far more important to focus on what you can do than on what you have. Still, sometimes it's important to know if you've got enough rope, or what kind of gun your space pilot has at her hip.

For any game set in the present day, catalogs or shopping websites can provide prices for any kind of item that you might need.

CURRENCY AND PRICES

Dollars, pounds, euros, credits, gold pieces, Martian solval beads, bottle caps—a lot of different currencies might be used in your game, depending on the setting and the genre. You should use whatever you like. In the Cypher System rules, we talk in generalities rather than specifics. Not unlike saying immediate or short distance rather than giving precise numbers, we talk about goods and services in terms of inexpensive, moderately priced, expensive, very expensive, or exorbitant.

The GM can figure out what those things mean in her setting. In a fantasy setting, an inexpensive item might be 1 or 2 copper pennies, while an expensive item might require gold on the table. The exact amount can vary, and in many campaigns, the exact amount will matter. The GM will develop a detailed price list for her setting, and players will track their money on their character sheets to determine what they can afford, often ignoring the terms inexpensive, moderately priced, and so on.

Of course, some GMs might want to keep things simple and use only the general terms, indicating currency just as flavor now and then. In a space opera game, where the PCs are the crew of a starship blazing about the galaxy in search of adventure and profit, fuel and upkeep for the ship might be expensive. Hauling a few passengers from Epsilon Eridani back to Earth might earn enough to purchase six expensive items but cost the equivalent of two expensive items, leaving the crew with the means to refuel and maintain the ship for two further voyages. In such a game, where money only means keeping the ship flying, no one has to talk in specific amounts. Characters might refer

to "galactic credits" or something similar, but amounts might not be tracked on the character sheets.

PRICE CATEGORIES

There are five price categories for goods and services.

An **inexpensive item** is something that common people buy. A simple meal or a drink in the bar. A pen and some paper. A book or magazine.

A **moderately priced item** is something that common people buy, but not too often and not in great quantities. A small piece of furniture. A major entertainment. An expensive meal. A new outfit.

An **expensive item** is something that would strain a common person's finances. Rent on a simple apartment. A major piece of furniture. A very nice outfit. The cost to travel a long distance (if appropriate to the setting).

A **very expensive item** is probably out of the reach of most people except in very special circumstances. Jewelry. Luxury furnishings.

An **exorbitant item** is something only the very rich can afford. A very nice house. A ship. Extremely expensive jewelry or art.

Think of the categories as powers of 10. That is to say, a moderately priced item is ten times more costly than an inexpensive item. An expensive item is 10 times more costly than a moderately priced item, and thus 100 times the cost of something inexpensive. A very expensive item is 10 times the cost of an expensive one, 100 times the cost of a moderate one, and 1,000 times the cost of an inexpensive one. An exorbitant item is priced 10 times beyond that.

USING THE PRICE CATEGORIES

Regardless of how precise you want to be with prices and currency, you can use the price categories in a variety of ways.

It's easy for a GM to say to a player, "You can afford two extra moderately priced things at the start of the game." She can look on the list and pick two moderately priced items without worrying about their cost. Plus, this approach makes it clear that

In some settings, even the generalization offered by the pricing categories might be too specific or cumbersome. In many superhero games, for example, prices are relatively moot. After saving the city, typical superheroes don't worry about paying rent or how much dinner will cost. (On the other hand, in a grittier superhero game, maybe that's exactly what they worry about.)

she gets two items, not twenty inexpensive items or one more expensive item that perhaps would not be appropriate for a starting character. The categories make it easy to lump similar items together.

The GM can also say, "You can have whatever inexpensive items you want, and don't worry about the cost." At higher tiers, when the PCs have more wealth, followers, and so on, the GM can do this with moderate or even expensive items. This allows the group to skip over playing through a shopping trip to get supplies, and players don't have to track prices down to the last penny.

Finally, the categories can be shorthand when evaluating loot, dividing up the spoils among the PCs, and resolving other story-based occurrences that crop up in the game without dealing in the minutiae of exact prices. This is of particular use in high-powered games where the PCs are rich and powerful.

ARMOR

Characters expecting danger frequently wear armor. Even the simplest protective covering helps against stabs and cuts, and more sophisticated or heavier armor protects against graver threats.

You can wear only one type of armor at a time—you cannot wear chainmail hauberk and scale armor together, for example. However, Armor bonuses from multiple sources combine to provide a total Armor rating. For example, if you have subdermal implants that give you +1 to Armor, a force field that offers another +1 to Armor, and beastskin that grants +2 to Armor, you have a total of +4 to Armor.

In general, light armor is a moderately priced item, medium armor is expensive, and heavy armor is very expensive. The genre chapters offer more specific details on the kinds of armor available in a given setting. Keep in mind that in many genres, it's quite odd, at best, to run around in armor tougher than a leather jacket.

USING ARMOR

Anyone can wear any armor, but it can be taxing. Wearing armor increases the cost of using a level of Effort when attempting a Speed-based action. So if you're wearing light armor and want to use two levels of Effort on a Speed-based roll to run across difficult terrain, it costs 7 points from your Speed Pool rather than 5 (3 for the first level of Effort, plus 2 for the second level of Effort, plus 1 per level for wearing light armor). Edge reduces the overall cost as normal. If you are not experienced with a certain type of armor but wear it anyway, this cost is further increased by 1. Having experience with a type of armor is called being practiced with the armor.

Some characters have abilities that reduce or even negate the costs of wearing armor.

Armor	Speed Effort Additional Cost
Light	+1
Medium	+2
Heavy	+3

WEAPONS

Not all characters are familiar with all weapons. Warriors know their way around most types, but explorers prefer light or medium weapons, and adepts and speakers usually stick to light weapons. If you wield a weapon that you have no experience with, the difficulty of making an attack with that weapon is increased by one step. Having experience with a weapon is called being practiced with the weapon.

Light weapons inflict only 2 points of damage, but they reduce the difficulty of the attack roll by one step because they are fast and easy to use. Light weapons are punches, kicks, knives, handaxes, darts, very small pistols, and so on. Weapons that are particularly small are light weapons.

Medium weapons inflict 4 points of damage. Medium weapons include broadswords, battleaxes, maces, crossbows, spears, typical handguns, light rifles, sawed-off shotguns, and so on. Most weapons are medium. Anything that could be used in one hand (even if it's often used in two hands, such as a quarterstaff or spear) is a medium weapon.

Heavy weapons inflict 6 points of damage, and you must use two hands to attack with them. Heavy weapons are huge swords, great hammers, massive axes, halberds, heavy crossbows, rifles, regular shotguns, assault rifles, and so on. Anything that must be used in two hands is a heavy weapon.

Weapon	Damage
Light	2 points (attack difficulty reduced by one step)
Medium	4 points
Heavy	6 points

In general, light weapons are moderately priced items, medium weapons are expensive, and heavy weapons are very expensive. Ammunition for a ranged weapon is inexpensive. The genre chapters offer more specific details on weapons available in a given setting. Keep in mind that in many genres, it's not acceptable to run around carrying dangerous weapons.

EXPLOSIVE WEAPONS

Bombs, grenades, missiles, and other explosives operate differently than other weapons. They affect all targets within an area (usually an immediate area) and inflict damage to all of them. A separate attack roll is required for each (or a Speed defense roll if the PCs are the targets of such an attack), although to simplify, the player can make one attack roll and compare it to the difficulty to attack each target. Usually, even if the attack roll fails (or the Speed defense roll succeeds), the targets still suffer a smaller amount of damage, often 1 point.

Explosives like grenades can be thrown a short distance. Otherwise, another launcher weapon is needed to project them a long distance (or farther).

CONTEXT

Context in pricing is important. A match is almost worthless in a modern setting (many establishments give away books of them), but consider how valuable it would be in 1000 BC. Likewise, a sword might be expensive in a fantasy setting, but mostly worthless in the far future other than as a collector's item (although it hurts just the same if you're hit with it), making it either inexpensive or very expensive. A motorcycle would be expensive in a modern setting, moderate at best in a future setting—again, unless it's a collector's item—and utterly priceless if it somehow found its way to 1000 BC (where it would be an artifact). Maybe in a fantasy setting, assuming a fair bit of magic, the same motorcycle would merely be exorbitant compared to the flying carpets and whatnot that are available.

This is why you can't have a standardized price list that applies to every setting, genre, and time period. It's all about context.

MISCELLANEOUS ITEMS AND SERVICES

Although the types of items for sale vary greatly based on the setting, a few things are always present, like food, lodging, and clothing. However, these goods and services can span the price categories. For example, you can get an inexpensive meal, a moderately priced meal, an expensive meal, and so on. An inexpensive meal is light and probably not very nutritious. An expensive meal is available only in nice restaurants in certain locations. An exorbitant meal is probably a feast for a crowd, with the finest foods and drink available.

Nightly lodging is similar, although the bottom end starts out worse. An inexpensive night's lodging is probably a flea-ridden mat on the floor of a room filled with other lodgers. Typical lodging (a private room with a decent bed) is probably in the moderately priced range. Very expensive lodging might be a suite of rooms with delicious meals and personal services (such as massages and grooming) included.

Inexpensive clothing is just a step up from rags, but moderately priced clothing is decent enough. For a formal party, you'd want expensive clothing. The very rich likely wear very expensive clothing most of the time, and exorbitant clothing (and jewelry) when they go to their elite galas.

Other sorts of miscellaneous items can be found in the genre chapters.

CYPHERS

Cyphers can sometimes be physical items, like equipment, but they work very differently. To be entirely accurate, cyphers might have the veneer of equipment, but

In general, mundane equipment is about level 4—less if of inferior quality or materials, more if of superior quality or materials. This means that in a setting based on the distant past, the default level might be 3, while in the future it might be 5 or 6. So an average serf's tool in the Dark Ages is level 3, easily broken, while an average tool on a space station is level 6, made of advanced polymers.

Some explosives create smoke, poison gas, flame, or other effects.

don't fall into the trap of confusing the two. Cyphers are far more akin to PC special abilities than to gear. In a fantasy game, they might be potions, scrolls, or charms. In a science fiction game, cyphers might be interesting throwaway devices or alien crystals of unknown providence. In other games, they might just represent good fortune or sudden inspiration.

ARTIFACTS

Artifacts are more powerful than equipment and can't simply be purchased. The genre chapters offer a few sample artifacts appropriate for various settings.

Each artifact has a level and a rate of power depletion. When an artifact is used or activated, the player rolls the designated die (1d6, 1d10, 1d20, or 1d100). If the die shows the depletion number(s), the item works, but that is its last use. A depletion entry of "—" means that the artifact never depletes, and an entry of "automatic" means that it can be used only once.

Depowered artifacts can sometimes be recharged using the repair rules, depending on the item's nature. Other special abilities can also repower an expended item, but probably for only one use.

Repair, page 217

FINDING, IDENTIFYING, AND USING ARTIFACTS

Characters can sometimes find artifacts while on adventures. They might be in ancient ruins, either intact or in need of manipulation to get them working. They could have been stolen from well-guarded military installations. They might be granted as rewards or taken from fallen foes. Sometimes they can even be purchased from a specialized source, but this occurs more rarely than most PCs would probably like.

After the characters find an artifact, identifying it is a separate Intellect task. The GM sets the difficulty of the task, but it is usually equal to the artifact's level. Identifying it takes fifteen minutes to three hours. If the PCs can't identify an artifact, they can bring it to an expert to be identified or, if desired, traded or sold.

Characters can attempt to use an artifact that has not been identified, which is usually an Intellect task equal to the artifact's level + 2. Failure might mean that the PCs can't figure out how to use the artifact or they use it incorrectly (GM's discretion). Of course, even if characters use an unidentified artifact correctly the first time, they have no idea what the effect might be.

Once characters identify an artifact, using it for the first time requires an additional Intellect action; this process is far more complex than pushing a button. It can involve manipulating touchscreens, reciting the proper arcane words, or anything else that fits the setting. The GM sets the difficulty, but it is usually equal to the artifact's level.

Part 2

RULES

CHAPTER 9

RULES OF THE GAME

Cypher System games are played in the joint imagination of all the players, including the GM. The GM sets the scene, the players state what their characters attempt to do, and the GM determines what happens next. The rules and the dice help make the game run smoothly, but it's the people, not the rules or the dice, that direct the action and determine the story—and the fun. If a rule gets in the way or detracts from the game, the players and the GM should work together to change it.

Training, page 7

Equipment, page 182

Special abilities, page 21

This is how you play the Cypher System:

1. The player tells the GM what she wants to do. This is a *character action*.

2. The GM determines if that action is routine (and therefore works without needing a roll) or if there's a chance of failure.

3. If there is a chance of failure, the GM determines which stat the task uses (Might, Speed, or Intellect) and the task's difficulty—how hard it will be on a scale from 1 (really easy) to 10 (basically impossible).

Might, page 14

Speed, page 14

Intellect, page 15

4. The player and the GM determine if anything about her character—such as training, equipment, special abilities, or various actions—can modify the difficulty up or down by one or more steps. If these modifications reduce the difficulty to less than 1, the action is routine (and therefore works with no roll needed).

5. If the action still isn't routine, the GM uses its difficulty to determine the target number—how high the player must roll to succeed at the action (see the Task Difficulty Chart on page 191). The GM doesn't have to tell the player what the target number is, but he can give her a hint, especially if her character would reasonably know if the action was easy, average, difficult, or impossible.

6. The player rolls a d20. If she rolls equal to or higher than the target number, her character succeeds.

That's it. That's how to do anything, whether it's identifying an unknown device, calming a raging drunk, climbing a treacherous cliff, or battling a demigod. Even if you ignored all the other rules, you could still play the Cypher System with just this information. The key features here are: character actions, determining task difficulty, and determining modifications.

TAKING ACTION

Each character gets one turn each round. On a character's turn, she can do one thing—an action. All actions fall into one of three categories: Might, Speed, or Intellect (just like the three stats). Many actions require die rolls—rolling a d20.

Every action performs a task, and every task has a difficulty that determines what number a character must reach or surpass with a die roll to succeed.

Most tasks have a difficulty of 0, which means the character succeeds automatically. For example, walking across a room, opening a door, and throwing a stone into a nearby bucket are all actions, but none of them requires a roll. Actions that are usually difficult or that become difficult due to the situation (such as shooting at a target in a blizzard) have a higher difficulty. These actions usually require a roll.

Some actions require a minimum expenditure of Might, Speed, or Intellect points. If a character cannot spend the minimum number of points needed to complete the action, she automatically fails at the task.

DETERMINING TASK STAT

Every task relates to one of a character's three stats: Might, Speed, or Intellect. Physical activities that require strength, power, or endurance relate to Might. Physical activities that require agility, flexibility, or fast reflexes relate to Speed. Mental activities that require force of will,

Demigod, page 283

KEY CONCEPTS

ACTION: Anything a character does that is significant—punch a foe, leap a chasm, activate a device, use a special power, and so on. Each character can take one action in a round.

CHARACTER: Any creature in the game capable of acting, whether it is a player character (PC) run by a player or a nonplayer character (NPC) run by the game master (GM). In the Cypher System, even bizarre creatures, sentient machines, and living energy beings can be "characters."

DIFFICULTY: A measure of how easy it is to accomplish a task. Difficulty is rated on a scale from 1 (lowest) to 10 (highest). Altering the difficulty to make a task harder is referred to as increasing the difficulty. Altering it to make a task easier is referred to as reducing or decreasing the difficulty. All changes in difficulty are measured in steps. Difficulty often equates directly with level, so opening a level 3 locked door probably has a difficulty of 3.

EFFORT: Spending points from a stat Pool to reduce the difficulty of a task. A PC decides whether or not to apply Effort on his turn before the roll is made. NPCs never apply Effort.

LEVEL: A way to measure the strength, difficulty, power, or challenge of something in the game. Everything in the game has a level. NPCs and objects have levels that determine the difficulty of any task related to them. For example, an opponent's level determines how hard she is to hit or avoid in combat. A door's level indicates how hard it is to break down. A lock's level determines how hard it is to pick. Levels are rated on a scale from 1 (lowest) to 10 (highest). PC tiers are a little like levels, but they go only from 1 to 6 and mechanically work very differently than levels—for example, a PC's tier does not determine a task's difficulty.

ROLL: A d20 roll made by a PC to determine whether an action is successful. Although the game occasionally uses other dice, when the text simply refers to "a roll," it always means a d20 roll.

ROUND: A length of time about five to ten seconds long. There are about ten rounds in a minute. When it's really important to track precise time, use rounds. Basically, it's the length of time to take an action in the game, but since everyone more or less acts simultaneously, all characters get to take an action each round.

STAT: One of the three defining characteristics for PCs: Might, Speed, or Intellect. Each stat has two values: Pool and Edge. Your Pool represents your raw, innate ability, and your Edge represents knowing how to use what you have. Each stat Pool can increase or decrease over the course of play—for example, you can lose points from your Might Pool when struck by an opponent, spend points from your Intellect Pool to activate a special ability, or rest to recover points in your Speed Pool after a long day of marching. Anything that damages a stat, restores a stat, or boosts or penalizes a stat affects the stat's Pool.

TASK: Any action that a PC attempts. The GM determines the difficulty of the task. In general, a task is something that you do and an action is you performing that task, but in most cases they mean the same thing.

TURN: The part of the round when a creature takes its actions. For example, if a warrior and an adept are fighting an orc, each round the warrior takes an action on his turn, the adept takes an action on her turn, and the orc takes an action on its turn. Some abilities or effects last only while a creature takes its turn or end when a creature starts its next turn.

memory, or mental power relate to Intellect. This means you can generalize tasks into three categories: Might tasks, Speed tasks, and Intellect tasks. You can also generalize rolls into three categories: Might rolls, Speed rolls, and Intellect rolls.

The category of the task or roll determines what kind of Effort you can apply to the roll and may determine how a character's other abilities affect the roll. For example, an adept may have an ability that makes him better at Intellect rolls, and a warrior may have an ability that makes her better at Speed rolls.

DETERMINING TASK DIFFICULTY

The most frequent thing a GM does during the game—and probably the most important thing—is setting a task's difficulty. To make the job easier, use the Task Difficulty table, which associates difficulty rating with a descriptive name, a target number, and general guidance about the difficulty.

Every difficulty from 1 to 10 has a target number associated with it. The target number is easy to remember: it's always three times the difficulty. The target number is the minimum number a player needs to roll on a d20 to succeed at the task. Moving up or down on the table is called increasing or decreasing the difficulty, which is measured in steps.

For example, reducing a difficulty 5 task to a difficulty 4 task is "reducing the difficulty by one step." Most modifiers affect the difficulty rather than the player's roll. This has two consequences:

1. Low target numbers such as 3 or 6, which would be boring in most games that use a d20, are not boring in the Cypher System. For example, if you need to roll a 6 or higher, you still have a 25% chance to fail.

2. The upper levels of difficulty (7, 8, 9, and 10) are all but impossible because the target numbers are 21 or higher, which you can't roll on a d20. However, it's common for PCs to have abilities or equipment that reduce the difficulty of a task and thus lower the target number to something they *can* roll on a d20.

A character's tier does not determine a task's level. Things don't get more difficult just because a character's tier increases—the world doesn't instantly become a more difficult place. Fourth-tier characters don't deal only with level 4 creatures or difficulty 4 tasks (although a fourth-tier character probably has a better shot at success than a first-tier character does). Just because something is level 4 doesn't necessarily mean it's meant only for fourth-tier characters. Similarly, depending on the situation, a fifth-tier character could find a difficulty 2 task just as challenging as a second-tier character does.

Therefore, when setting the difficulty of a task, the GM should rate the task on its own merits, not on the power of the characters.

Unless for some reason you're telling the players directly, they'll never know if you change an NPC's stats or a task's difficulty on the fly. If you're doing it to make a better story, that's your purview.

TASK DIFFICULTY

Task Difficulty	Description	Target No.	Guidance
0	Routine	0	Anyone can do this basically every time.
1	Simple	3	Most people can do this most of the time.
2	Standard	6	Typical task requiring focus, but most people can usually do this.
3	Demanding	9	Requires full attention; most people have a 50/50 chance to succeed.
4	Difficult	12	Trained people have a 50/50 chance to succeed.
5	Challenging	15	Even trained people often fail.
6	Intimidating	18	Normal people almost never succeed.
7	Formidable	21	Impossible without skills or great effort.
8	Heroic	24	A task worthy of tales told for years afterward.
9	Immortal	27	A task worthy of legends that last lifetimes.
10	Impossible	30	A task that normal humans couldn't consider (but one that doesn't break the laws of physics).

MODIFYING THE DIFFICULTY

After the GM sets the difficulty for a task, the player can try to modify it for her character. Any such modification applies only to this particular attempt at the task. In other words, rewiring an electronic door lock normally might be difficulty 6, but since the character doing the work is skilled in such tasks, has the right tools, and has another character assisting her, the difficulty in this instance might be much lower. That's why it's important for the GM to set a task's difficulty without taking the character into account. The character comes in at this step.

The important thing to remember is that a skill can reduce the difficulty by no more than two steps, and assets can reduce the difficulty by no more than two steps, regardless of the situation. Thus, no task's difficulty will ever be reduced by more than four steps without using Effort.

By using skills and assets, working together, and—perhaps most important—applying Effort, a character can decrease a task's difficulty by multiple steps to make it easier. Rather than adding bonuses to the player's roll, reducing the difficulty lowers the target number. If she can reduce the difficulty of a task to 0, no roll is needed; success is automatic. (An exception is if the GM decides to use a GM intrusion on the task, in which case the player would have to make a roll at the original difficulty.)

GM intrusion, page 193

There are three basic ways in which a character can decrease the difficulty of a task: skills, assets, and Effort. Each of them decreases the difficulty by at least one step—never in smaller increments.

SKILLS

Characters may be skilled at performing a specific task. A skill can vary from character to character. For example, one character might be skilled at lying, another might be skilled at trickery, and a third might be skilled in all interpersonal interactions. The first level of being skilled is called being *trained*, and it decreases the difficulty of that task by one step. More rarely, a character can be incredibly skilled at performing a task. This is called being *specialized*, and it decreases the difficulty of a task by two steps instead of one. Skills can never decrease a task by more than two steps; being trained and specialized in a skill decreases the difficulty by only two steps, not three.

Special roll, page 193

ASSETS

An asset is anything that helps a character with a task, such as having a really good crowbar when trying to force open a door or being in a rainstorm when trying to put out a fire. Appropriate assets vary from task to task. The perfect awl might help when woodworking, but it won't make a dance performance much better. An asset usually reduces a task's difficulty by one step. Assets can never decrease the difficulty by more than two steps.

EFFORT

A player can apply Effort to decrease the difficulty of a task. To do this, the player spends points from the stat Pool that's most appropriate to the task. For example, applying Effort to push a heavy rock off a cliff requires a player to spend points from her character's Might Pool; applying Effort to activate an unusual machine interface requires her to spend points from her character's Intellect Pool. For every level of Effort spent on a task, the task's difficulty decreases by one step. It costs 3 points from a stat Pool to apply one level of Effort, and it costs 2 additional points for every level thereafter (so it costs 5 points for two levels of Effort, 7 points for three levels of Effort, and so on). A character must spend points from the same stat Pool as the type of task or roll—Might points for a Might roll, Speed points for a Speed roll, or Intellect points for an Intellect roll.

Every character has a maximum level of Effort she can apply to a single task.

ROLLING THE DIE

To determine success or failure, a player rolls a die (always a d20). If she rolls the target number or higher, she succeeds. Most of the time, that's the end of it—nothing else needs to be done. Occasionally, a character might apply a small modifier to the roll. If she has a +2 bonus when attempting specific actions, she adds 2 to the number rolled. However, the original roll matters if it's a special roll.

If a character applies a modifier to her die roll, it's possible to get a result of 21 or higher, in which case she can attempt a task with a target number above 20. But if there is no possibility for success—if not even rolling a natural 20 (meaning the d20 shows that number) is sufficient to accomplish the task—then no roll is made. Otherwise, characters would have a chance to succeed at everything, even impossible or ridiculous tasks such as climbing moonbeams, throwing elephants, or hitting a target on the opposite side of a mountain with an arrow.

If a character's modifiers add up to +3, treat them as an asset instead. In other words, instead of adding a +3 bonus to the roll, reduce the difficulty by one step. For example, if a warrior has a +1 bonus to attack rolls from a minor effect, a +1 bonus to attack rolls from a special weapon quality, and a +1 bonus to attack rolls from a special ability, she does not add 3 to her attack roll—instead, she reduces the difficulty of the attack by one step. So if she attacks a level 3 foe, she would normally roll against difficulty 3 and try to reach a target number of 9, but thanks to her asset, she rolls against difficulty 2 and tries to reach a target number of 6.

This distinction is important when stacking skills and assets to decrease the difficulty of an action, especially since reducing the difficulty to 0 or lower means no roll is needed.

THE PLAYER ALWAYS ROLLS

In the Cypher System, players always drive the action. That means they make all the die rolls. If a PC leaps out of a moving vehicle, the player rolls to see if she succeeds. If a PC searches for a hidden panel, the player rolls to determine whether she finds it. If a rockslide falls on a PC, the player rolls to try to get out of the way. If a PC and an NPC arm wrestle, the player rolls, and the NPC's level determines the target number. If a PC attacks a foe, the player rolls to see if she hits. If a foe attacks the PC, the player rolls to see if she dodges the blow.

As shown by the last two examples, the PC rolls whether she is attacking or defending. Thus, something that improves defenses might help or hinder her rolls. For example, if a PC uses a low wall to gain cover from attacks, the wall decreases the difficulty of the player's defense rolls. If a foe uses the wall to gain cover from the PC's attacks, it increases the difficulty of the player's attack rolls.

SPECIAL ROLLS

If a character rolls a natural 1, 17, 18, 19, or 20 (meaning the d20 shows that number), special rules come into play. These are explained in more detail in the following sections.

1: Intrusion. The GM makes a free intrusion (see below) and doesn't award experience points (XP) for it.

17: Damage Bonus. If the roll was a damage-dealing attack, it deals 1 additional point of damage.

18: Damage Bonus. If the roll was a damage-dealing attack, it deals 2 additional points of damage.

19: Minor Effect. If the roll was a damage-dealing attack, it deals 3 additional points of damage. If the roll was something other than an attack, the PC gets a minor effect in addition to the normal results of the task.

20: Major Effect. If the roll was a damage-dealing attack, it deals 4 additional points of damage. If the roll was something other than an attack, the PC gets a major effect in addition to the normal results of the task. If the PC spent points from a stat Pool on the action, the point cost for the action decreases to 0, meaning the character regains those points as if she had not spent them at all.

GM INTRUSION

GM intrusion is explained in more detail in chapter 19, but essentially it means that something occurs to complicate the character's life. The character hasn't necessarily fumbled or done anything wrong (although perhaps she did). It could just be that the task presents an unexpected difficulty or something unrelated affects the current situation.

For GM intrusion on a defense roll, a roll of 1 might mean that the PC takes

For complete details about GM intrusion and how to use it to best effect in the game, see page 372.

2 additional points of damage from the attack, indicating that the opponent got in a lucky blow.

MINOR EFFECT

A minor effect happens when a player rolls a natural 19. Most of the time, a minor effect is slightly beneficial to the PC, but not overwhelming.

A climber gets up the steep slope a bit faster. A repaired machine works a bit better. A character jumping down into a pit lands on her feet. Either the GM or the player can come up with a possible minor effect that fits the situation, but both must agree on what it should be.

Don't waste a lot of time thinking of a minor effect if nothing appropriate suggests itself. Sometimes, in cases where only success or failure matters, it's okay to have no minor effect. Keep the game moving at an exciting pace.

In combat, the easiest and most straightforward minor effect is dealing 3 additional points of damage with an attack. The following are other common minor effects for combat:

Strike a specific body part: The attacker strikes a specific spot on the defender's body. The GM rules what special effect, if any, results. For example, hitting a creature's tentacle that is wrapped around an ally might make it easier for the ally to escape. Hitting a foe in the eye might blind it for one round. Hitting a creature in its one vulnerable spot might ignore Armor.

Knock back: The foe is knocked or forced back a few feet. Most of the time, this doesn't matter much, but if the fight takes place on a ledge or next to a pit of lava, the effect can be significant.

Move past: The character can move a short distance at the end of the attack. This effect is useful to get past a foe guarding a door, for example.

Distract: For one round, the difficulty of all tasks the foe attempts is modified by one step to its detriment.

Usually, the GM just has the desired minor effect occur. For example, rolling a 19 against a relatively weak foe means it is knocked off the cliff. The effect makes the round more exciting, but the defeat of a minor creature has no significant impact on

the story. Other times, the GM might rule that an additional roll is needed to achieve the effect—the special roll only gives the PC the opportunity for a minor effect. This mostly happens when the desired effect is very unlikely, such as pushing a 50-ton battle automaton off a cliff. If the player just wants to deal 3 additional points of damage as the minor effect, no extra roll is needed.

MAJOR EFFECT

A major effect happens when a player rolls a natural 20. Most of the time, a major effect is quite beneficial to the character. A climber gets up the steep slope in half the time. A jumper lands with such panache that those nearby are impressed and possibly intimidated. A defender makes a free attack on his foe.

Either the GM or the player can come up with a possible major effect that fits the situation, but both must agree on what it should be. As with minor effects, don't spend a lot of time agonizing over the details of a major effect. In cases where only success or failure matters, a major effect might offer the character a one-time asset (a modification of one step) to use the next time she attempts a similar action. When nothing else seems appropriate, the GM can simply grant the PC an additional action on her turn that same round.

In combat, the easiest and most straightforward major effect is dealing 4 additional points of damage with an attack. The following are other common major effects for combat.

Knock down: The foe is knocked prone. It can get up on its turn if it wishes.

Disarm: The foe drops one object that it is holding.

Stun: The foe loses its next action.

Impair: For the rest of the combat, the difficulty of all tasks the foe attempts is modified by one step to its detriment.

As with minor effects, usually the GM just has the desired major effect occur, but sometimes he might require an extra roll if the major effect is unusual or unlikely.

RETRYING A TASK AFTER FAILURE

If a character fails a task (whether it's climbing a wall, picking a lock, trying to figure out a mysterious device, or something else) she can attempt it again, but she must apply at least one level of Effort when retrying that task. A retry is a new action, not part of the same action that failed, and it takes the same amount of time as the first attempt did.

Sometimes the GM might rule that retries are impossible. Perhaps a character has one chance to convince the leader of a group of thugs not to attack, and after that, no amount of talking will stop them.

This rule doesn't apply to something like attacking a foe in combat because combat is always changing and fluid. Each round's situation is new, not a repeat of a previous situation, so a missed attack can't be retried.

INITIAL COST

The GM can assign a point cost to a task just for trying it. Called an *initial cost*, it's simply an indication that the task is particularly taxing. For example, let's say a character wants to try a Might action to open a heavy cellar door that is partially rusted shut. The GM says that forcing the door open is a difficulty 5 task, and there's an initial cost of 3 Might points simply to try. This initial cost is in addition to any points the character chooses to spend on the roll (such as when applying Effort), and the initial cost points do not affect the difficulty of the task. In other words, the character must spend 3 Might points to attempt the task at all, but that doesn't help her open the door. If she wanted to apply Effort to lower the difficulty, she'd have to spend more points from her Might Pool.

Edge helps with the initial cost of a task, just as it does with any expenditure from a character's Pool. In the previous example, if the character had a Might Edge of 2, she would have to spend only 1 point (3 points minus 2 from her Might Edge) for the initial cost to attempt the task. If she also applied a level of Effort to open the door, she couldn't use her Edge again—Edge applies only once per action—so using the Effort would cost the full 3 points. Thus, she'd spend a total of 4 points (1 for the initial cost plus 3 for the Effort) from her Might Pool.

Star troopers are guards; *see page 337*

The rationale of the initial cost rule is that even in the Cypher System, where things like Effort can help a character succeed on an action, logic still suggests that some actions are very difficult and taxing, particularly for some PCs more than others.

DISTANCE

Distance is simplified into three basic categories: immediate, short, and long.

The words "immediate" and "close" can be used interchangeably to talk about distance. If a creature or object is within arm's reach of the character, it can be considered both immediate and close.

Immediate distance from a character is within reach or within a few steps; if a character stands in a small room, everything in the room is within immediate distance. At most, immediate distance is 10 feet (3 m). Immediate distance is sometimes referred to as close, or even point-blank, particularly when referring to ranges.

Short distance is anything greater than immediate distance but less than 50 feet (15 m) or so.

Long distance is anything greater than short distance but less than 100 feet (30 m) or so. Beyond that range, distances are always specified—500 feet (152 m), 1 mile (2 km), and so on.

All weapons and special abilities use these terms for ranges. For example, all melee weapons have immediate range—they are close-combat weapons, and you can use them to attack anyone within immediate distance. A thrown knife (and most other thrown weapons) has short range. A small handgun also has short range. A rifle has long range.

A character can move an immediate distance as a part of another action. In other words, she can take a few steps to the light switch and flip it on. She can lunge across a small room to attack a foe. She can open a door and step through.

A character can move a short distance as her entire action for a turn. She can also try to move a long distance as her entire action, but the player might have to roll to see if the character slips, trips, or stumbles for moving so far so quickly.

GMs and players don't need to determine exact distances. For example, if the PCs are fighting a group of star troopers, any character can likely attack any foe in the general melee—they're all within immediate range. However, if one trooper stays back to fire his blaster, a character might have to use her entire action to move the short distance required to attack that foe. It doesn't matter if the trooper is 20 feet (6 m) or 40 feet (12 m) away—it's simply considered short distance. It does matter if he's more than 50 feet (15 m) away because that distance would require a long move.

OTHER DISTANCES

In rare cases where distances beyond long are needed, real-world distances are best (1 mile, 100 kilometers, and so on). However, the following shorthand distances can be useful in some settings:

Planetary: On the same planet.

Interplanetary: Within a single solar system.

Interstellar: Within a single galaxy.

Intergalactic: Anywhere in the same universe.

Interdimensional: Anywhere.

TIMEKEEPING

Generally, keep time the same way that you normally would, using minutes, hours, days, and weeks. Thus, if the characters walk overland for 15 miles (24 km), about eight hours pass, even though the journey can be described in only a few seconds at the game table. Precision timekeeping is rarely important. Most of the time, saying things like "That takes about an hour" works fine.

This is true even when a special ability has a specific duration. In an encounter, a duration of "one minute" is mostly the same as saying "the rest of the encounter." You don't have to track each round that ticks by if you don't want to. Likewise, an ability that lasts for ten minutes can safely be considered the length of an in-depth conversation, the time it takes to quickly explore a small area, or the time it takes to rest after a strenuous activity.

TIMEKEEPING

Action	Time Usually Required
Walking a mile over easy terrain	About fifteen minutes
Walking a mile over rough terrain (forest, snow, hills)	About half an hour
Walking a mile over difficult terrain (mountains, thick jungle)	About forty-five minutes
Moving from one significant location in a city to another	About fifteen minutes
Sneaking into a guarded location	About fifteen minutes
Observing a new location to get salient details	About fifteen minutes
Having an in-depth discussion	About ten minutes
Resting after a fight or other strenuous activity	About ten minutes
Resting and having a quick meal	About half an hour
Making or breaking camp	About half an hour
Shopping for supplies in a market or store	About an hour
Meeting with an important contact	About half an hour
Referencing a book or website	About half an hour
Searching a room for hidden things	At least half an hour, perhaps one hour
Searching for cyphers or other valuables amid a lot of stuff	About an hour
Identifying and understanding a cypher	Fifteen minutes to half an hour
Identifying and understanding an artifact	At least fifteen minutes, perhaps three hours
Repairing a device (assuming parts and tools available)	At least an hour, perhaps a day
Building a device (assuming parts and tools available)	At least a day, perhaps a week

ENCOUNTERS, ROUNDS, AND INITIATIVE

Sometimes in the course of the game, the GM or players will refer to an *encounter*. Encounters are not so much measurements of time as they are events or instances in which something happens, like a scene of a movie or a chapter in a book. An encounter might be a fight with a foe, a dramatic crossing of a raging river, or a stressful negotiation with an important official. It's useful to use the word when referring to a specific scene, as in "My Might Pool is low after that encounter with the soul sorcerer yesterday."

A *round* is about five to ten seconds. The length of time is variable because sometimes one round might be a bit longer than another. You don't need to measure time more precisely than that. You can estimate that on average there are about ten rounds in a minute. In a round, everyone—each character and NPC—gets to take one action.

To determine who goes first, second, and so on in a round, each player makes a Speed roll called an *initiative roll*. Most of the time, it's only important to know which characters act before the NPCs and which act after the NPCs. On an initiative roll, a character who rolls higher than an NPC's target number takes her action before the NPC does. As with all target numbers, an NPC's initiative roll target number is three times the NPC's level. Many times, the GM will have all NPCs take their actions at the same time, using the highest target number from among all the NPCs. Using this method, any characters who rolled higher than the target number act first, then all the

NPCs act, and finally any characters who rolled lower than the target number act.

The order in which the characters act usually isn't important. If the players want to go in a precise order, they can act in initiative order (highest to lowest), by going around the table, by going oldest to youngest, and so on.

For example, Charles, Tammie, and Shanna's characters are in combat with two level 2 security guards. The GM has the players make Speed rolls to determine initiative. Charles rolls an 8, Shanna rolls a 15, and Tammie rolls a 4. The target number for a level 2 creature is 6, so each round Charles and Shanna act before the guards, then the guards act, and finally Tammie acts. It doesn't matter whether Charles acts before or after Shanna, as long as they think it's fair.

After everyone—all PCs and NPCs—in the combat has had a turn, the round ends and a new round begins. In all rounds after the first, everyone acts in the same order as they did in the first round. The characters cycle through this order until the logical end of the encounter (the end of the fight or the completion of the event) or until the GM asks them to make new initiative rolls. The GM can call for new initiative rolls at the beginning of any new round when conditions drastically change. For example, if the NPCs gain reinforcements, the environment changes (perhaps the lights go out), the terrain changes (maybe part of the balcony collapses under the PCs), or something similar occurs, the GM can call for new initiative rolls.

An initiative roll is a d20 roll. Since your initiative depends on how fast you are, if you spend Effort on the roll, the points come from your Speed Pool.

Since the action moves as a cycle, anything that lasts for a round ends where it started in the cycle. If Umberto uses an ability on an opponent that hinders its defenses for one round, the effect lasts until Umberto acts on his next turn.

Faster Initiative (Optional Rule): To make an encounter move faster, if at least one character rolls high enough to beat the target number of the NPC(s), all the characters act before the NPC(s). If nobody rolls high enough to beat the target number of the NPCs, all the characters act after the NPC(s). On the characters' turn, go clockwise around the table. If you're playing using an online video chat or virtual table, start with the leftmost player and move right; repeat.

ACTIONS

Anything that your character does in a round is an action. It's easiest to think of an action as a single thing that you can do in five to ten seconds. For example, if you use your dart thrower to shoot a strange floating orb, that's one action. So is running for cover behind a stack of barrels, prying open a stuck door, using a rope to pull your friend up from a pit, or activating a cypher (even if it's stored in your pack).

Opening a door and attacking a security guard on the other side are two actions. It's more a matter of focus than time. Drawing your sword and attacking a foe is all one action. Putting away your bow and pushing a heavy bookcase to block a door are two actions because each requires a different train of thought.

If the action you want to accomplish is not within reach, you can move a little bit. Essentially, you can move up to an

A CLOSER LOOK AT SITUATIONS THAT DON'T INVOLVE PCs

Ultimately, the GM is the arbiter of conflicts that do not involve the PCs. They should be adjudicated in the most interesting, logical, and story-based way possible. When in doubt, match the level of the NPCs (characters or creatures) or their respective effects to determine the results. Thus, if a level 4 NPC fights a level 3 NPC, he'll win, but if he faces a level 7 NPC, he'll lose. Likewise, a level 4 creature resists poisons or devices of level 3 or lower but not those of level 5 and above.

The essence is this: in the Cypher System, it doesn't matter if something is a monster, a poison, or a gravity-dispelling ray. If it's a higher level, it wins; if it's a lower level, it loses. If two things of equal level oppose each other, there might be a long, drawn-out battle that could go either way.

immediate distance to perform your action. For example, you can move an immediate distance and attack a foe, open a door and move an immediate distance into the hallway beyond, or grab your hurt friend lying on the ground and pull him back a few steps. This movement can occur before or after your action, so you can move to a door and open it, or you can open a door and move through it.

The most common actions are:
Attack
Activate a special ability
(one that isn't an attack)
Move
Wait
Defend
Do something else

ACTION: ATTACK

An attack is anything that you do to someone that he doesn't want you to do. Slashing a foe with a curved dagger is an attack, blasting a foe with a lightning artifact is an attack, wrapping a foe in magnetically controlled metal cables is an attack, and controlling someone's mind is an attack. An attack almost always requires a roll to see if you hit or otherwise affect your target.

In the simplest kind of attack, such as a PC trying to stab a thug with a knife, the player rolls and compares his result against the opponent's target number. If his roll is equal to or greater than the target number, the attack hits. Just as with any kind of task, the GM might modify the difficulty based on the situation, and the player might have a bonus to the roll or might try to lower the difficulty using skills, assets, or Effort.

A less straightforward attack might be a special ability that stuns a foe with a mental blast. However, it's handled the same way: the player makes a roll against the opponent's target number. Similarly, an attempt to tackle a foe and wrestle it to the ground is still just a roll against the foe's target number.

Attacks are sometimes categorized as "melee" attacks, meaning that you hurt or affect something within immediate reach, or "ranged" attacks, meaning that you hurt or affect something at a distance.

Melee attacks can be Might or Speed actions—player choice. Physical ranged attacks (such as bows and thrown weapons) are almost always Speed actions, but those that come from special abilities are probably Intellect actions. Effects that require touching the target require a melee attack.

If the attack misses, the power is not wasted, and you can try again each round as your action until you hit the target, use another ability, or take a different action that requires you to use your hands. These attempts in later rounds count as different actions, so you don't have to keep track of how much Effort you used when you activated the ability or how you used Edge. For example, let's say that in the first round of combat, you activate a special ability that requires you to touch your foe, use Effort to reduce the difficulty of the attack roll, and miss your foe. In the second round of combat, you can try attacking again and use Effort to reduce the difficulty of the attack roll.

The GM and players are encouraged to describe every attack with flavor and flair. One attack roll might be a stab to the foe's arm. A miss might be the PC's sword slamming into the wall. Combatants lunge, block, duck, spin, leap, and make all kinds of movements that should keep combat visually interesting and compelling. Chapter 19 has much more guidance in this regard.

Common elements that affect the difficulty of a combat task are cover, range, and darkness. The rules for these and other modifiers are explained in the Attack Modifiers and Special Situations section (page 204).

DAMAGE

When an attack strikes a character, it usually means the character takes damage.

An attack against a PC subtracts points from one of the character's stat Pools—usually the Might Pool. Whenever an attack simply says it deals "damage" without specifying the type, it means Might damage, which is by far the most common type. Intellect damage, which is usually the result of a mental attack, is always labeled as Intellect damage. Speed damage is often a physical attack, but attacks that deal Speed damage are fairly rare.

NPCs don't have stat Pools. Instead, they have a characteristic called *health*. When an NPC takes damage of any kind, the amount is subtracted from its health. Unless described otherwise, an NPC's health is always equal to its target number. Some NPCs might have special reactions to or defenses against attacks that would normally deal Speed damage or Intellect damage, but unless the NPC's description specifically explains this, assume that all damage is subtracted from the NPC's health.

Objects are like NPCs: they have health instead of stat Pools.

Damage is always a specific amount determined by the attack. For example, a slash with a broadsword or a blast with a spike thrower deals 4 points of damage. An adept's Onslaught deals 4 points of damage. Often, there are ways for the attacker to increase the damage. For example, a PC can apply Effort to deal 3 additional points of damage, and rolling a natural 17 on the attack roll deals 1 additional point of damage.

Onslaught, page 31

ARMOR

Pieces of equipment and special abilities protect a character from damage by giving him Armor. Each time a character takes damage, subtract his Armor value from the damage before reducing his stat Pool or health. For example, if a warrior with 2 Armor is hit by a gunshot that deals 4 points of damage, he takes only 2 points of damage (4 minus 2 from his Armor). If Armor reduces the incoming damage to 0 or lower, the character takes no damage from the attack. For example, the warrior's 2 Armor protects him from all physical attacks that deal 1 or 2 points of damage.

The most common way to get Armor is to wear physical armor, such as a leather jacket, a bulletproof vest, a chainmail hauberk, or bioengineered carapace grafts, depending on the setting. All physical armor comes in one of three categories: light, medium, or heavy. Light armor gives the wearer 1 point of Armor, medium gives 2 points of Armor, and heavy gives 3 points of Armor.

When you see the word "Armor" capitalized in the game rules (other than in the name of a special ability), it refers to your Armor characteristic—the number you subtract from incoming damage. When you see the word "armor" in lowercase, it refers to any physical armor you might wear.

Other effects can add to a character's Armor. If a character is wearing chainmail (+2 to Armor) and has an ability that covers him in a protective force field that grants +1 to Armor, his total is 3 Armor. If he also has a cypher that hardens his flesh temporarily for +1 to Armor, his total is 4 Armor.

Some types of damage ignore physical armor. Attacks that specifically deal Speed damage or Intellect damage ignore Armor; the creature takes the listed amount of damage without any reduction from Armor. Ambient damage (see below) usually ignores Armor as well.

A creature may have a special bonus to Armor against certain kinds of attacks. For example, a protective suit made of a sturdy, fire-resistant material might normally give its wearer +1 to Armor but count as +3 to Armor against fire attacks. An artifact worn as a helmet might grant +2 to Armor only against mental attacks.

AMBIENT DAMAGE

Some kinds of damage aren't direct attacks against a creature, but they indirectly affect everything in the area. Most of these are environmental effects such as winter cold, high temperatures, or background radiation. Damage from these kinds of sources is called ambient damage. Physical armor usually doesn't protect against ambient damage, though a well-insulated suit of armor can protect against cold weather.

DAMAGE FROM HAZARDS

Attacks aren't the only way to inflict damage on a character. Experiences such as falling from a great height, being burned in a fire, and spending time in severe weather also deal damage. Although no list of potential hazards could be comprehensive, the Damage From Hazards table includes common examples.

DAMAGE FROM HAZARDS

Source	Damage	Notes
Falling	1 point per 10 feet (3 m) fallen (ambient damage)	—
Minor fire	3 points per round (ambient damage)	Torch
Major fire	6 points per round (ambient damage)	Engulfed in flames; lava
Acid splash	2 points per round (ambient damage)	—
Acid bath	6 points per round (ambient damage)	Immersed in acid
Cold	1 point per round (ambient damage)	Below freezing temperatures
Severe cold	3 points per round (ambient damage)	Liquid nitrogen
Shock	1 point per round (ambient damage)	Often involves losing next action
Electrocution	6 points per round (ambient damage)	Often involves losing next action
Crush	3 points	Object or creature falls on character
Huge crush	6 points	Roof collapse; cave-in
Collision	6 points	Large, fast object strikes character

THE EFFECTS OF TAKING DAMAGE

When an NPC reaches 0 health, it is either dead or (if the attacker wishes it) incapacitated, meaning unconscious or beaten into submission.

When an object reaches 0 health, it is broken or otherwise destroyed.

As previously mentioned, damage from most sources is applied to a character's Might Pool. Otherwise, stat damage always reduces the Pool of the stat it affects.

If damage reduces a character's stat Pool to 0, any further damage to that stat (including excess damage from the attack that reduced the stat to 0) is applied to another stat Pool. Damage is applied to Pools in this order:

1. Might (unless the Pool is 0)
2. Speed (unless the Pool is 0)
3. Intellect

Even if the damage is applied to another stat Pool, it still counts as its original type for the purpose of Armor and special abilities that affect damage. For example, if a character with 2 Armor is reduced to 0 Might and then is hit by a creature's claw for 3 points of damage, it still counts as Might damage, so his Armor reduces the damage to 1 point, which then is applied to his Speed Pool. In other words, even though he takes the damage from his Speed Pool, it doesn't ignore Armor like Speed damage normally would.

In addition to taking damage from their Might Pool, Speed Pool, or Intellect Pool, PCs also have a damage track. The damage track has four states (from best to worst): hale, impaired, debilitated, and dead. When one of a PC's stat Pools reaches 0, he moves one step down the damage track. Thus, if he is hale, he becomes impaired. If he is already impaired, he becomes debilitated. If he is already debilitated, he becomes dead.

Some effects can immediately shift a PC one or more steps on the damage track. These include rare poisons, cellular disruption attacks, and massive traumas (such as falls from very great heights, being

When NPCs (who have only health) suffer Speed or Intellect damage, normally this is treated the same as Might damage. However, the GM or the player has the option to suggest an appropriate alternate effect—the NPC suffers a penalty, moves more slowly, is stunned, and so on.

Enthrall, page 45

The damage track allows you to know how far from death you are. If you're hale, you're three steps from death. If you're impaired, you're two steps from death. If you're debilitated, you are only one small step from death's door.

run over by a speeding vehicle, and so on, as determined by the GM).

Some attacks, like a serpent's poisonous bite or a speaker's Enthrall, have effects other than damage to a stat Pool or shifting the PC on the damage track. These attacks can cause unconsciousness, paralysis, and so on.

THE DAMAGE TRACK

Hale is the normal state for a character: all three stat Pools are at 1 or higher, and the PC has no penalties from harmful conditions. When a hale PC takes enough damage to reduce one of his stat Pools to 0, he becomes impaired. Note that a character whose stat Pools are much lower than normal can still be hale.

Impaired is a wounded or injured state. When an impaired character applies Effort, it costs 1 extra point per level applied. For example, applying one level of Effort costs 4 points instead of 3, and applying two levels of Effort costs 7 points instead of 5.

An impaired character ignores minor and major effect results on his rolls, and he doesn't deal as much extra damage in combat with a special roll. In combat, a roll of 17 or higher deals only 1 additional point of damage.

When an impaired PC takes enough damage to reduce one of his stat Pools to 0, he becomes debilitated.

Debilitated is a critically injured state. A debilitated character may not take any actions other than to move (probably crawl) no more than an immediate distance. If a debilitated character's Speed Pool is 0, he can't move at all.

When a debilitated PC takes enough damage to reduce a stat Pool to 0, he is dead.

Dead is dead.

RECOVERING POINTS IN A POOL

After losing or spending points in a Pool, you recover those points by resting. You can't increase a Pool past its maximum by resting—just back to its normal level. Any extra points gained go away with no effect. The amount of points you recover from a rest, and how long each rest takes, depends on how many times you have rested so far that day.

When you rest, make a recovery roll. To do this, roll a d6 and add your tier. You recover that many points, and you can divide them among your stat Pools however you wish. For example, if your recovery roll is 4 and you've lost 4 points of Might and 2 points of Speed, you can recover 4 points of Might, or 2 points of Might and 2 points of Speed, or any other combination adding up to 4 points.

The first time you rest each day, it takes only a few seconds to catch your breath. If you rest this way in the middle of an encounter, it takes one action on your turn.

The second time you rest each day, you must rest for ten minutes to make a recovery roll. The third time you rest each day, you must rest for one hour to make a recovery roll. The fourth time you rest each day, you must rest for ten hours to make a recovery roll (usually, this occurs when you stop for the day to eat and sleep).

After that much rest, it's assumed to be a new day, so the next time you rest, it takes only a few seconds. The next rest takes ten minutes, then one hour, and so on, in a cycle.

If you haven't rested yet that day and you take a lot of damage in a fight, you could rest a few seconds (regaining 1d6 points + 1 point per tier) and then immediately rest for ten minutes (regaining another 1d6 points + 1 point per tier). Thus, in one full day of doing nothing but resting, you could recover 4d6 points + 4 points per tier.

Each character chooses when to make recovery rolls. If a party of five explorers rests for ten minutes because two members want to make recovery rolls, the other characters don't have to make rolls at that time. Later in the day, those three can decide to rest for ten minutes and make recovery rolls.

Recovery Roll	Rest Time Needed
First recovery roll	One action
Second recovery roll	Ten minutes
Third recovery roll	One hour
Fourth recovery roll	Ten hours

RESTORING THE DAMAGE TRACK

Using points from a recovery roll to raise a stat Pool from 0 to 1 or higher also automatically moves the character up one step on the damage track.

If all of a PC's stat Pools are above 0 and the character has taken special damage that moved him down the damage track, he can use a recovery roll to move up one step on the damage track instead of recovering points. For example, a character who is debilitated from a hit with a cell-disrupting biotech device can rest and move up to impaired rather than recover points in a Pool.

SPECIAL DAMAGE

In the course of playing the game, characters face all manner of threats and dangers that can harm them in a variety of ways, only some of which are easily represented by points of damage.

Dazed and Stunned: Characters can be dazed when struck hard on the head, exposed to extremely loud sounds, or affected by a mental attack. When this happens, for the duration of the daze effect (usually one round), the difficulty of all tasks attempted by the character increases by one step. Similar but more severe attacks can stun characters. Stunned characters lose their turn (but can still defend against attacks normally).

Poison and Disease: When characters encounter poison—whether the venom of a serpent, rat poison slipped into a burrito, cyanide dissolved in wine, or an overdose of acetaminophen—they make a Might defense roll to resist it. Failure to resist can result in points of damage, moving down the damage track, or a specific effect such as paralysis, unconsciousness, disability, or something stranger. For example, some poisons affect the brain, making it impossible to say certain words, take certain actions, resist certain effects, or recover points to a stat Pool.

Diseases work like poisons, but their effect occurs every day, so the victim must make a Might defense roll each day or suffer the effects. Disease effects are as varied as poisons: points of damage, moving down

GMs should always remember that above all else, describing the action and how it fits into the situation at hand is more important than the mechanics of it.

the damage track, disability, and so on. Many diseases inflict damage that cannot be restored through conventional means.

Paralysis: Paralytic effects cause a character to drop to the ground, unable to move. Unless otherwise specified, the character can still take actions that require no physical movement.

Other Effects: Other special effects can render a character blind or deaf, unable to stand without falling over, or unable to breathe. Stranger effects might negate gravity for the character (or increase it a hundredfold), transport him to another place, render him out of phase, mutate his physical form, implant false memories or senses, alter the way his brain processes information, or inflame his nerves so he is in constant, excruciating pain. Each special effect must be handled on a case-by-case basis. The GM adjudicates how the character is affected and how the condition can be alleviated (if possible).

NPCs AND SPECIAL DAMAGE

The GM always has final say over what special damage will affect an NPC. Human NPCs usually react like characters, but nonhuman creatures might react very differently. For example, a tiny bit of venom is unlikely to hurt a gigantic dragon, and it won't affect an android or a demon at all.

If an NPC is susceptible to an attack that would shift a character down the damage track, using that attack on the NPC usually renders it unconscious or dead. Alternatively, the GM could apply the debilitated condition to the NPC, with the same effect as it would have on a PC.

ATTACK MODIFIERS AND SPECIAL SITUATIONS

In combat situations, many modifiers might come into play. Although the GM is at liberty to assess whatever modifiers he thinks are appropriate to the situation (that's his role in the game), the following suggestions and guidelines might make that easier. Often the modifier is applied as a step in difficulty. So if a situation hinders attacks, that means if a PC attacks an NPC, the difficulty of the attack roll is increased by one step, and if an NPC attacks a PC, the difficulty of the defense roll is decreased by one step. This is because players make all rolls, whether they are attacking or defending—NPCs never make attack or defense rolls.

When in doubt, if it seems like it should be harder to attack in a situation, the difficulty of the attack rolls increase by one step. If it seems like attacks should gain an advantage or be easier in some way, the difficulty of the defense rolls increase by one step.

COVER

If a character is behind cover so that a significant portion of his body is behind something sturdy, attacks are modified by one step in the defender's favor.

If a character is entirely behind cover (his entire body is behind something sturdy), he can't be attacked unless the attack can go through the cover. For example, if a character hides behind a thin wooden screen and his opponent shoots the screen with a rifle that can penetrate the wood, the character can be attacked. However, because the attacker can't see the character clearly, this still counts as cover (attacks are modified by one step in the defender's favor).

POSITION

Sometimes where a character stands gives him an advantage or a disadvantage.

Prone Target: In melee, a prone target is easier to hit (modified by one step in the attacker's favor). In ranged combat, a prone target is harder to hit (modified by one step in the defender's favor).

Higher Ground: In either ranged or melee combat, an opponent on higher ground gets the advantage (modified by one step in her favor).

SURPRISE

When a target isn't aware of an incoming attack, the attacker has an advantage. A ranged sniper in a hidden position, an invisible assailant, or the first salvo in a successful ambush are all modified by two steps in the attacker's favor. For the attacker to gain this advantage, however, the defender truly must have no idea that the attack is coming.

If the defender isn't sure of the attacker's location but is still on guard, the attacker's modifier is only one step in his favor.

RANGE

In melee, you can attack a foe who is adjacent to you (next to you) or within reach (immediate range). If you enter into melee with one or more foes, usually you can attack most or all of the combatants, meaning they are next to you, within reach, or within reach if you move slightly or have a long weapon that extends your reach.

The majority of ranged attacks have only two ranges: short range and long range. Short range is generally less than 50 feet (15 m) or so. Long range is generally from 50 feet (15 m) to about 100 feet (30 m). Greater precision than that isn't important in the Cypher System. If anything is longer than long range, the exact range is usually spelled out, such as with an item that can fire a beam 500 feet (152 m) or teleport you up to 1 mile (2 km) away.

Thus, the game has three measurements of distance: immediate, short, and long. These apply to movement as well (see page 208). A few special cases—point-blank range and extreme range— modify an attack's chance to successfully hit.

Point-Blank Range: If a character uses a ranged weapon against a target within immediate range, the attack is modified by one step in the attacker's favor.

Extreme Range: Targets just at the limit of a weapon's range are at extreme range. Attacks against such targets are modified by one step in the defender's favor.

ILLUMINATION

What characters can see (and how well they can see) plays a huge factor in combat.

Dim Light: Dim light is approximately the amount of light on a night with a bright full moon or the illumination provided by a torch, flashlight, or desk lamp. Dim light allows you to see out to short range. Targets in dim light are harder to hit. Attacks against such targets are modified by one step in the defender's favor. Attackers trained in low-light spotting negate this modifier.

Very Dim Light: Very dim light is approximately the amount of light on a starry night with no visible moon, or the glow provided by a candle or an illuminated control panel. Very dim light allows you to see clearly only within immediate range and perceive vague shapes to short range. Targets in very dim light are harder to hit. Attacks against targets within immediate range are modified by one step in the defender's favor, and attacks against those in short range are modified by two steps in the defender's favor. Attackers trained in low-light spotting modify these difficulties by one step in their favor. Attackers specialized in low-light spotting modify these difficulties by two steps in their favor.

Darkness: Darkness is an area with no illumination at all, such as a moonless night with cloud cover or a room with no lights. Targets in complete darkness are nearly impossible to hit. If an attacker can use other senses (such as hearing) to get an idea of where the opponent might be, attacks against such targets are modified by four steps in the defender's favor. Otherwise, attacks in complete darkness fail without the need for a roll unless the player spends 1 XP to "make a lucky shot" or the GM uses GM intrusion. Attackers trained in low-light spotting modify this difficulty by one step in their favor. Attackers specialized in low-light spotting modify this difficulty by two steps in their favor.

VISIBILITY

Similar to illumination, factors that obscure vision affect combat.

Mist: A target in mist is similar to one in dim light. Ranged attacks against such targets are modified by one step in the defender's favor. Particularly dense mist makes ranged attacks nearly impossible (treat as darkness), and even melee attacks become difficult (modify by one step in the defender's favor).

Hiding Target: A target in dense foliage, behind a screen, or crawling amid the rubble in a ruin is hard to hit because she's hard to see. Ranged attacks against such

Precise ranges are not important in the Cypher System. The broadly defined "immediate," "short," and "long" ranges let the GM quickly make a judgment call and keep things moving. Basically, the idea is: your target is right there, your target is close, or your target is pretty far away.

In certain situations, such as a PC on top of a building looking across an open field, the GM should allow long-range attacks to go farther than 100 feet (30 m)—often much farther. In perfect conditions, a good archer can hit a large target with an arrow at 500 feet (152 m).

targets are modified by one step in the defender's favor.

Invisible Target: If an attacker can use other senses (such as hearing) to get an idea of where the opponent might be, attacks against such targets are modified by four steps in the defender's favor. Otherwise, attacks against an invisible creature fail without the need for a roll unless the player spends 1 XP to "make a lucky shot" or the GM uses GM intrusion.

WATER

Being in shallow water can make it hard to move, but it doesn't affect combat. Being in deep water can make things difficult, and being underwater entirely can seem as different as being on another world.

Deep Water: Being in water up to your chest (or the equivalent thereof) hinders your ability to attack. Attacks made in such conditions are modified by one step in the defender's favor. Aquatic creatures ignore this modifier.

Underwater Melee Combat: For nonaquatic creatures, being completely underwater makes attacking very difficult. Melee attacks with slashing or bashing weapons are modified by two steps in the defender's favor. Attacks with stabbing weapons are modified by one step in the defender's favor. Aquatic creatures ignore the penalties for underwater melee combat.

Underwater Ranged Combat: As with melee combat, nonaquatic creatures have difficulty fighting underwater. Some ranged attacks are impossible underwater—you can't throw things, fire a bow or crossbow, or use a blowgun. Many firearms also do not work underwater. Attacks with weapons that do work underwater are modified by one step in the defender's favor. Ranges underwater are reduced by one category; long-range weapons work only to short range, and short-range weapons work only to immediate range.

Cooperative actions, page 211

MOVING TARGETS

Moving targets are harder to hit, and moving attackers have a difficult time as well.

Target Is Moving: Attackers trying to hit a foe who is moving very fast are penalized. (A foe moving very fast is one who is doing nothing but running, mounted on a moving creature, riding on a vehicle or moving conveyance, and so on.) Attacks are modified by one step in the defender's favor.

Attacker Is Moving: An attacker trying to make an attack while moving under its own power (walking, running, swimming, and so on) takes no penalties. An attacker mounted on a moving creature or vehicle has some difficulty; its attacks are modified by one step in the defender's favor. An attacker trained in riding ignores this penalty.

Attacker Is Jostled: Being jostled, such as while standing on a listing ship or a vibrating platform, makes attacking difficult. Such attacks are modified by one step in the defender's favor. Conceivably, training could offset this disadvantage. For example, characters trained in sailing would ignore penalties for being on a ship.

SPECIAL SITUATION: COMBAT BETWEEN NPCs

When an NPC ally of the PCs attacks another NPC, the GM can designate a player to roll and handle it like a PC attacking. Often, the choice is obvious. For example, a character who has a trained attack animal should roll when her pet attacks enemies. If an NPC ally accompanying the party leaps into the fray, that ally's favorite PC rolls for him. NPCs cannot apply Effort. Of course, it's perfectly fitting (and easier) to have the NPC ally use the cooperative action rules to aid a PC instead of making direct attacks, or to compare the levels of the two NPCs (higher wins).

SPECIAL SITUATION: COMBAT BETWEEN PCs

When one PC attacks another PC, the attacking character makes an attack roll, and the other character makes a defense roll, adding any appropriate modifiers. If the attacking PC has a skill, ability, asset, or other effect that would decrease the attack's difficulty if it were made against an NPC, the character adds 3 to the roll for each step reduction (+3 for one step, +6 for two steps, and so on). If the attacker's final result is higher, the attack hits. If the defender's result is higher, the attack misses. Damage is resolved normally. The GM mediates all special effects.

SPECIAL SITUATION: AREA ATTACKS

Sometimes, an attack or effect affects an area rather than a single target. For example, a grenade or a landslide can potentially harm or affect everyone in the area.

In an area attack, all PCs in the area make appropriate defense rolls against the attack to determine its effect on them. If there are any NPCs in the area, the attacker makes a single attack roll against all of them (one roll, not one roll per NPC) and compares it to the target number of each NPC. If the roll is equal to or greater than the target number of a particular NPC, the attack hits that NPC.

Some area attacks always deal at least a minimum amount of damage, even if the attacks miss or if a PC makes a successful defense roll.

For example, consider a character who uses Shatter to attack six cultists (level 2; target number 6) and their leader (level 4; target number 12). The PC applies Effort to increase the damage and rolls an 11 for the attack roll. This hits the six cultists, but not the leader, so the ability deals 3 points of damage to each of the cultists. The description of Shatter says that applying Effort to increase the damage also means that targets take 1 point of damage if the PC fails the attack roll, so the leader takes 1 point of damage. In terms of what happens in the story, the cultists are caught flat-footed by the sudden detonation of one of their knives, but the leader ducks and shields herself from the blast. Despite the leader's quick moves, the blast is so intense that a few bits of metal slice her.

SPECIAL SITUATION: ATTACKING OBJECTS

Attacking an object is rarely a matter of hitting it. Sure, you can hit the broad side of a barn, but can you damage it? Attacking inanimate objects with a melee weapon is a Might action. Objects have levels and thus target numbers. An object's target number also serves as its health to determine whether it is destroyed. You track the object's health just as you would with an NPC.

Hard objects, like those made of stone, have 1 Armor. Very hard objects, like those made of metal, have 2 Armor. Extremely hard objects, like those made of diamond or an advanced metal alloy, have 3 Armor. Armor subtracts from every attack's damage.

Shatter, page 32

ACTION: ACTIVATE A SPECIAL ABILITY

Special abilities are granted by foci or provided by cyphers or other devices. If a special ability affects another character in any kind of unwanted manner, it's handled as an attack. This is true even if the ability is normally not considered an attack. For example, if a character has a healing touch, but her friend doesn't want to be healed for some reason, an attempt to heal her unwilling friend is handled as an attack.

Plenty of special abilities do not affect another character in an unwanted manner. For example, a PC might use Hover on herself to float into the air. A character with a matter-reorganizing device might change a stone wall into glass. A character who activates a phase changer cypher might walk through a wall. None of these requires an attack roll (although when turning a stone wall to glass, the character must still make a roll to successfully affect the wall).

Hover, page 33

Phase changer, page 357

If the character spends points to apply Effort on her attempt, she might want to roll anyway to see if she gets a major effect, which would reduce the cost for her action.

ACTION: MOVE

As a part of another action, a character can adjust his position—stepping back a few feet while using an ability, sliding over in combat to take on a different opponent to help his friend, pushing through a door he just opened, and so on. This is considered an immediate distance, and a character can move this far as part of another action.

In a combat situation, if a character is in a large melee, he's usually considered to be next to most other combatants, unless the GM rules that he's farther away because the melee is especially large or the situation dictates it.

If he's not in melee but still nearby, he is considered to be a short distance away—usually less than 50 feet (15 m). If he's farther away than that but still involved in the combat, he is considered to be a long distance away, usually 50 to 100 feet (15 to 30 m).

Beyond that distance, only special circumstances, actions, or abilities will allow a character to be involved in an encounter.

In a round, as an action, a character can make a short move. In this case, he is doing nothing but moving up to about 50 feet (15 m). Some terrain or situations will change the distance a character can move, but generally, making a short move is considered to be a difficulty 0 action. No roll is needed; he just gets where he's going as his action.

A character can try to make a long move—up to 100 feet (30 m) or so—in one round. This is a Speed task with a difficulty of 4. As with any action, he can use skills, assets, or Effort to decrease the difficulty. Terrain, obstacles, or other circumstances can increase the difficulty. A successful roll means the character moved the distance safely. Failure means that at some point during the move, he stops or stumbles (the GM determines where this happens).

A character can also try to make a short move and take another (relatively simple) physical action, like make an attack. As with the attempt to make a long move, this is a Speed task with a difficulty of 4, and failure means that the character stops at some point, slipping or stumbling or otherwise getting held up.

LONG-TERM MOVEMENT

When talking about movement in terms of traveling rather than round-by-round action, typical characters can travel on a road about 20 miles (32 km) per day, averaging about 3 miles (5 km) per hour, including a few stops. When traveling overland, they can move about 12 miles (19 km) per day, averaging 2 miles (3 km) per hour, again with some stops. Mounted characters, such as those on horseback, can go twice as far. Other modes of travel (cars, airplanes, hovercraft, sailing ships, and so on) have their own rates of movement.

MOVEMENT MODIFIERS

Different environments affect movement in different ways.

Rough Terrain: A surface that's considered rough terrain is covered in loose stones or other material, uneven or with unsure footing, unsteady, or a surface that requires movement across a narrow space, such as a cramped corridor or a slender ledge. Stairs are also considered rough terrain. Rough terrain does not slow normal movement on a round-by-round basis, but it increases the difficulty of a move roll by one step. Rough terrain cuts long-term movement rates in half.

Difficult Terrain: Difficult terrain is an area filled with challenging obstacles—water up to waist height, a very steep slope, an especially narrow ledge, slippery ice, a foot or more of snow, a space so small that one must crawl through it, and so on. Difficult terrain is just like rough terrain, but it also halves movement on a round-by-round basis. This means that a short move is about 25 feet (8 m), and a long move is about 50 feet (15 m). Difficult terrain reduces long-term movement to a third of its normal rate.

Water: Deep water, in which a character is mostly or entirely submerged, is just like rough terrain except that it also quarters movement. This means that a short move is about 12 feet (4 m), and a long move is about 25 feet (8 m). Characters trained in swimming halve their movement while in deep water.

SPECIAL SITUATION: CHASE

When a PC is chasing an NPC or vice versa, the player should attempt a Speed action, with the difficulty based on the NPC's level. If he succeeds at the roll, he catches the NPC, or he gets away if he is the one being chased. In terms of the story, this one-roll mechanic can be the result of a long chase over many rounds.

Alternatively, if the GM wants to play out a long chase, the character can make many rolls (perhaps one per level of the NPC) to finish the pursuit successfully. For every failure, the PC must make another success, and if he ever has more failures than successes, he doesn't catch the NPC, or he doesn't get away if he is the one being chased. For example, if the PC is being chased through a crowded marketplace by a level 3 enemy, he must succeed at three chase rolls. If he succeeds at one but fails the second, he must succeed at the third one, or he will have more failures than successes, and the foe will catch him. The GM is encouraged to describe the results of these rolls with flavor. A success might mean the PC has rounded a corner and gained some distance. A failure might mean that a basket of fruit topples over in front of him, slowing him down. Vehicle chases are handled similarly.

Vehicle chases, page 214

ACTION: WAIT

You can wait to react to another character's action.

You decide what action will trigger your action, and if the triggering action happens, you get to take your action first (unless going first wouldn't make sense, like attacking a foe before she comes into view). For example, if an orc threatens you with a halberd, on your turn you can decide to wait, stating, "If she stabs at me, I'm going to slash her with my sword." On the orc's turn, she stabs, so you make your sword attack before that happens.

Orc, page 308

Waiting is also a useful tool for cooperative actions (page 211).

ACTION: DEFEND

Defending is a special action that only PCs can do, and only in response to being attacked. In other words, an NPC uses its action to attack, which forces a PC to make a defense roll. This is handled like any other kind of action, with circumstances, skill, assets, and Effort all potentially coming into play. Defending is a special kind of action in that it does not happen on the PC's turn. It's never an action that a player decides to take; it's always a reaction to an attack. A PC can take a defense action when attacked (on the attacking NPC's turn) and still take another action on his own turn.

The type of defense roll depends on the type of attack. If a foe attacks a character with an axe, she can use Speed to duck or block it with what she's holding. If she's struck by a poisoned dart, she can use a Might action to resist its effects. If a psi-worm attempts to control her mind, she can use Intellect to fend off the intrusion.

Sometimes an attack provokes two defense actions. For example, a poisonous reptile tries to bite a PC. She tries to dodge the bite with a Speed action. If she fails, she takes damage from the bite, and she must

Difficult terrain, page 209

also attempt a Might action to resist the poison's effects.

If a character does not know an attack is coming, usually she can still make a defense roll, but she can't add modifiers (including the modifier from a shield), and she can't use any skill or Effort to decrease the roll's difficulty. If circumstances warrant—such as if the attacker is right next to the character—the GM might rule that the surprise attack simply hits her.

A character can always choose to forgo a defense action, in which case the attack automatically hits her.

Some abilities may allow you to do something special as a defense action.

ACTION: DO SOMETHING ELSE

Players can try anything they can think of, although that doesn't mean anything is possible. The GM sets the difficulty—that's her primary role in the game. Still, guided by the bounds of logic, players and GMs will find all manner of actions and options that aren't covered by a rule. That's a good thing.

In the Cypher System, players are not rewarded for killing foes in combat, so using a smart idea to avoid combat and still succeed is just good play. Likewise, coming up with an idea to defeat a foe without hammering on it with weapons is encouraged—creativity is not cheating!

Players should not feel constrained by the game mechanics when taking actions. Skills are not required to attempt an action. Someone who's never picked a lock can still try. The GM might assign a negative step modifier to the difficulty, but the character can still attempt the action.

Thus, players and GMs can return to the beginning of this chapter and look at the most basic expression of the rules. A player wants to take an action. The GM decides, on a scale of 1 to 10, how difficult that task is and what stat it uses. The player determines whether he has anything that might modify the difficulty and considers whether to apply Effort. Once the final determination is made, he rolls to see if his character succeeds. It's as easy as that.

As further guidance, the following are some of the more common actions a player might take.

CLIMBING

When a character climbs, the GM sets a difficulty based on the surface being climbed. If the character succeeds at the roll, she uses the movement rules as though she were moving normally, although climbing is like moving through difficult terrain: it raises the difficulty of a move roll by one step and halves movement. Unusual circumstances, such as climbing while under fire (or while *on* fire!) pose additional step penalties. Being skilled in climbing reduces the difficulty of this task.

CLIMBING DIFFICULTY

Difficulty	Surface
2	Surface with lots of handholds
3	Stone wall or similar surface (a few handholds)
4	Crumbling or slippery surface
5	Smooth stone wall or similar surface
6	Metal wall or similar surface
8	Smooth, horizontal surface (climber is upside down)
10	Glass wall or similar surface

GUARDING

In a combat situation, a character can stand guard as her action. She does not make attacks, but the difficulty of her defense tasks is decreased by one step. Further, if an NPC tries to get by her or take an action that she is guarding against, she can attempt a Speed action (based on the level of the NPC) with the difficulty decreased by one step. Success means the NPC is prevented from taking the action on his turn. This is useful for blocking a doorway, guarding a friend, and so forth.

If an NPC is standing guard, use the same procedure, but to get past the guard, the PC attempts a Speed action with the difficulty increased by one step. For example, Diana is an NPC human with a level 3 bodyguard. The bodyguard uses his action to guard Diana. If a PC wants to attack Diana, she first must succeed at a difficulty 4 Speed task to get past the guard. If she succeeds, she can make her attack normally.

HEALING

You can administer aid through bandaging and other succor, attempting to heal each patient once per day. This healing restores points to a stat Pool of your choice. Decide how many points you want to heal, and then make an Intellect action with a difficulty

COOPERATIVE ACTIONS

There are many ways multiple characters can work together. None of these options, however, can be used at the same time by the same characters.

Helping: If a character attempts a task and gets help from another character who is trained or specialized in that task, the acting PC gets the benefit of the helping PC. The helping character uses his action to provide this help. If the helper does not have training or specialization in that task, or if the acting character already is as trained or specialized as the helper, the acting character instead gets a +1 bonus to the roll. For example, if Scott is trying to climb a steep incline but has no skill at climbing, and Sarah (who is trained in climbing) spends her turn helping him, the difficulty of Scott's climb is decreased by one step. If Scott were also trained in climbing, or if neither character were, he would gain a +1 bonus to the roll instead. A character with an inability in a task cannot help another PC with that task—the character with the inability provides no benefit in that situation.

Complementary Actions: If a character attempts an action, and a second character skilled in that type of action attempts a complementary action, both actions gain a +2 bonus to the roll. For example, if Scott tries to convince a ship captain to allow him on board, and Sarah is trained in persuasion, she can use a complementary—but different—action in the situation to gain the +2 bonus. She might try to supplement Scott's words with a flattering lie about the captain (a deception action), a display of knowledge about the region where the ship is headed (a geography action), or a direct threat to the captain (an intimidation action).

Complementary actions work in combat as well. If Scott attacks an enemy using Pierce (a warrior ability) and Sarah also has the ability to make Pierce attacks, she can attack the same enemy using any other kind of attack, such as Bash, and get a +2 bonus. And she gives Scott a +2 bonus as well.

The players involved should work out complementary actions together and describe them to the GM.

Distraction: When a character uses his turn to distract a foe, the difficulty of that foe's attacks is modified by one step to its detriment for one round. Multiple characters distracting a foe have no greater effect than a single character doing so—a foe is either distracted or not.

Draw the Attack: When an NPC attacks a character, another PC can prominently present herself, shout taunts, and move to try to get the foe to attack her instead.

In most cases, this action succeeds without a roll—the opponent attacks the prominent PC instead of her companions. In other cases, such as with intelligent or determined foes, the prominent character must use an Intellect action to draw the attack. If she succeeds, the difficulty of her defense tasks is modified by one step to her detriment.

Two characters attempting to draw an attack at the same time cancel each other out.

Take the Attack: A character can use her action to throw herself in front of an attack to save a nearby comrade. The attack automatically succeeds against her, and it deals 1 additional point of damage. A character cannot willingly take more than one attack each round in this way.

The Old One-Two-Three: If three or more characters attack the same foe, each character gains a +1 bonus to the attack.

High and Low: If one character makes a melee attack against a foe and another character makes a ranged attack against that same foe, they can coordinate their actions. As a result, if both attacks damage the foe, the difficulty of the foe's next task is modified by one step to its detriment.

Covering Fire: A character using a ranged attack or ability can aim near a foe but narrowly miss on purpose, making an attack that inflicts no damage but harasses and frightens the foe. If the attack is successful, it deals no damage, but the difficulty of the foe's next attack is modified by one step to its detriment.

Inability, page 63

Players are encouraged to come up with their own ideas for what their characters do rather than looking at a list of possible actions. That's why there is a "do something else" action. PCs are not pieces on a game board—they are people in a story. And like real people, they can try anything they can think of. (Succeeding is another matter entirely.) The task difficulty system provides GMs with the tools they need to adjudicate anything the players come up with.

equal to that number. For example, if you want to heal someone for 3 points, that's a difficulty 3 task with a target number of 9. Being skilled in healing reduces the difficulty. A PC can use the rules for retrying a task if she attempts to heal a character using bandages and similar aids, but she can achieve only one success per day.

Retrying a task after failure, page 195

INTERACTING WITH CREATURES

The level of the creature determines the target number, just as with combat. Thus, bribing a guard works much like punching him or affecting him with an ability. This is true of persuading someone, intimidating someone, calming a wild beast, or anything of the kind. Interaction is an Intellect task. Being skilled in persuasion, intimidation, bribery, deception, animal handling, or something of that nature can decrease the difficulty of the task, if appropriate. Interacting usually requires a common language or some other way to communicate. Learning new languages is the same as learning a new skill.

JUMPING

Decide how far you want to jump, and that sets the difficulty of your Might roll. For a standing jump, subtract 4 from the distance (in feet) to determine the difficulty of the jump. For example, jumping 10 feet (3 m) has a difficulty of 6.

If you run an immediate distance before jumping, it counts as an asset, reducing the difficulty of the jump by one step.

If you run a short distance before jumping, divide the jump distance (in feet) by 2 and then subtract 4 to determine the difficulty of the jump. Because you're running an immediate distance (and then some), you also count your running as an asset. For example, jumping a distance of 20 feet (6 m) with a short running start has a difficulty of 5 (20 feet divided by 2 is 10, minus 4 is 6, minus 1 for running an immediate distance). Being skilled in jumping reduces the difficulty.

For a vertical jump, the distance you clear (in feet) is equal to the difficulty of the jumping task. If you run an immediate distance, it counts as an asset, reducing the difficulty of the jump by one step.

LOOKING OR LISTENING

Generally, the GM will describe any sight or sound that's not purposefully difficult to detect. But if you want to look for a hidden enemy, search for a secret panel, or listen for someone sneaking up on you, make an Intellect roll. If it's a creature, its level determines the difficulty of your roll. If it's something else, the GM determines the difficulty of your roll. Being skilled in perception reduces the difficulty of this task.

JUMP DISTANCE

	Type of Jump			
Difficulty	Standing	Immediate Run*	Short Run*	Vertical*
0	4 ft. (1.2 m)	5 ft. (1.5 m)	10 ft. (3 m)	0 ft.
1	5 ft. (1.5 m)	6 ft. (1.8 m)	12 ft. (3.7 m)	1 ft. (30 cm)
2	6 ft. (1.8 m)	7 ft. (2.1 m)	14 ft. (4.3 m)	2 ft. (60 cm)
3	7 ft. (2.1 m)	8 ft. (2.4 m)	16 ft. (4.9 m)	3 ft. (90 cm)
4	8 ft. (2.4 m)	9 ft. (2.7 m)	18 ft. (5.5 m)	4 ft. (1.2 m)
5	9 ft. (2.7 m)	10 ft. (3 m)	20 ft. (6.1 m)	5 ft. (1.5 m)
6	10 ft. (3 m)	11 ft. (3.4 m)	22 ft. (6.7 m)	6 ft. (1.8 m)
7	11 ft. (3.4 m)	12 ft. (3.7 m)	24 ft. (7.3 m)	7 ft. (2.1 m)
8	12 ft. (3.7 m)	13 ft. (4 m)	26 ft. (7.9 m)	8 ft. (2.4 m)
9	13 ft. (4 m)	14 ft. (4.3 m)	28 ft. (8.5 m)	9 ft. (2.7 m)
10	14 ft. (4.3 m)	15 ft. (4.6 m)	30 ft. (9.1 m)	10 ft. (3 m)

* *If you are skilled in jumping, move one row down to determine your distance. If you are specialized in jumping, move two rows down to determine your distance.*

There's nothing wrong with the GM simply assigning a difficulty level to a jump without worrying about the precise distance. The rules here are just so everyone has some guidelines.

MOVING A HEAVY OBJECT

You can push or pull something very heavy and move it an immediate distance as your action.

The weight of the object determines the difficulty of the Might roll to move it; every 50 pounds (23 kg) increases the difficulty by one step. So moving something that weighs 150 pounds (68 kg) is difficulty 3, and moving something that weighs 400 pounds (181 kg) is difficulty 8. If you can reduce the difficulty of the task to 0, you can move a heavy object up to a short distance as your action. Being skilled in carrying or pushing reduces the difficulty of this task.

OPERATING OR DISABLING A DEVICE, OR PICKING A LOCK

As with figuring out a device, the level of the device usually determines the difficulty of the Intellect roll. Unless a device is very complex, the GM will often rule that once you figure it out, no roll is needed to operate it except under special circumstances. So if the PCs figure out how to use a hovercraft, they can operate it. If they are attacked, they might need to roll to ensure that they don't crash the platform into a wall while trying to avoid being hit.

Disabling a device or picking a lock usually require rolls. These actions often involve special tools and assume that the character is not trying to destroy the device or lock. (A PC who *is* attempting to destroy it probably should make a Might roll to smash it rather than a Speed or Intellect roll requiring patience and know-how.) Being skilled in operating devices or picking locks reduces the difficulty.

RIDING OR PILOTING

If you're riding an animal that's trained to be a mount, or driving or piloting a vehicle, you don't need to make a roll to do something routine such as going from point A to point B. However, staying mounted during a fight or doing something tricky with a vehicle requires a Speed roll to succeed. A saddle or other appropriate gear is an asset and reduces the difficulty by one step. Being skilled in riding, driving, or piloting reduces the difficulty.

RIDING OR PILOTING DIFFICULTY

Difficulty	Maneuver
0	Riding
1	Staying on the mount (including a motorcycle or similar vehicle) in a battle or other difficult situation
3	Staying on a mount (including a motorcycle or similar vehicle) when you take damage
4	Mounting a moving steed
4	Making an abrupt turn with a vehicle while moving fast
4	Getting a vehicle to move twice as fast as normal for one round
5	Coaxing a mount to move or jump twice as fast or far as normal for one round
5	Making a long jump with a vehicle not intended to go airborne (like a car) and remaining in control

SNEAKING

The difficulty of sneaking by a creature is determined by its level. Sneaking is a Speed roll. Moving at half speed reduces the difficulty by one step. Appropriate camouflage or other gear may count as an asset and decrease the difficulty, as will dim lighting conditions and having plenty of things to hide behind. Being skilled in sneaking reduces the difficulty of this task.

SWIMMING

If you're simply swimming from one place to another, such as across a calm river or lake, use the standard movement rules, noting the fact that your character is in deep water. Being skilled in swimming decreases the difficulty. However, sometimes, special circumstances require a Might roll to make progress while swimming, such as when trying to avoid a current or being dragged into a whirlpool.

UNDERSTANDING, IDENTIFYING, OR REMEMBERING

When characters try to identify or figure out how to use a device, the level of the device determines the difficulty. For a bit of knowledge, the GM determines the difficulty. Being skilled in the appropriate area (geography, history, geology, local knowledge, and so on) reduces the difficulty of this task.

UNDERSTANDING, IDENTIFYING, OR REMEMBERING DIFFICULTY

Difficulty	Knowledge
0	Common knowledge
1	Simple knowledge
3	Something a scholar probably knows
5	Something even a scholar might not know
7	Knowledge very few people possess
10	Completely lost knowledge

VEHICULAR MOVEMENT

Vehicles move just like creatures. Each has a movement rate, which indicates how far it can move in a round. Most vehicles require a driver, and when moving, they usually require that the driver spends every action controlling the movement. This is a routine task that rarely requires a roll. Any round not spent driving the vehicle increases the difficulty of the task in the next round by one step and precludes any change in speed or direction. In other words, driving down the road normally is difficulty 0. Spending an action to retrieve a backpack from the back seat means that in the following round, the driver must attempt a difficulty 1 task. If he instead uses his action to pull a handgun from the backpack, in the next round the difficulty to drive will be 2, and so on. Failure results are based on the situation but might involve a collision or something similar.

In a vehicular chase, drivers attempt Speed actions just like in a regular chase, but the difficulty may be based either on the level of the driver (modified by the level and movement rate of the vehicle) or on the level of the vehicle (modified by the level of the driver). So if a PC driving a typical car is chasing a level 3 NPC driving a level 5 sports car, he would make three chase rolls with a difficulty of 5. If the PC's car is a souped-up custom vehicle, it might grant him an asset in the chase. If he's not in a car at all, but riding a bicycle, it might increase the difficulty by two or three steps, or the GM might simply rule that it's impossible.

VEHICULAR COMBAT

Much of the time, a fight between foes in cars, boats, or other vehicles is just like any other combat situation. The combatants probably have cover and are moving fast. Attacks to disable a vehicle or a portion of it are based on the level of the vehicle. If the vehicle is an armored car or a tank, all attacks are likely aimed at the vehicle, which has a level and probably an appropriate Armor rating, not unlike a creature. The only time this isn't true is with battles where only vehicles and not characters are involved. Thus, if the PCs are in a shootout with bank robbers and both groups are in cars, use the standard rules. If the PCs are in a submarine, a tank, or a starship and they are fighting opponents who are likewise in a vehicle, special rules are needed.

Battles between starships of various kinds—from gigantic capital ships to single-pilot fighters—are a frequent occurrence in far-future science fiction settings. A submarine battle between two deep sea craft could be quite exciting. Characters in a modern-day game might find themselves in a tank fight. If PCs are involved in combat in which they are entirely enclosed in vehicles (so that it's not really the characters fighting, but the vehicles), use the following quick and easy guidelines.

On this scale, combat between vehicles isn't like traditional combat. Don't worry about health, Armor, or anything like that. Instead, just compare the levels of the vehicles involved. If the PCs' vehicle has the higher level, the difference in levels becomes a reduction in the difficulty of attack and defense rolls involved. If the PCs' vehicle has the lower level, the difference is an increase in difficulty. If the levels are the same, there is no modification.

These attack and defense rolls are modified by skill and Effort, as usual. Some vehicles also have superior weapons, which reduce the difficulty of the attack (since there is no "damage" amount to worry about), but this circumstance is probably uncommon in this abstract system and should not affect the difficulty by more than one or maybe two steps. Further, if two vehicles coordinate their attack against one vehicle, the difficulty of the attack is reduced by one step. If three or more vehicles coordinate, the difficulty is reduced by two steps.

Cover, page 204

The attacker must try to target a specific system on or portion of an enemy vehicle. This modifies the attack in the defender's favor based on the system or portion targeted:

Movement combat modifiers, page 206

Targeting Task	Modification	Effect
Disable weapons	Two steps	One or more of the vehicle's weapons no longer function
Disable defenses (if applicable)	Two steps	Difficulty of attacks against the vehicle are reduced by one step
Disable engine/drive	Three steps	Vehicle cannot move, or movement is hampered
Disable maneuverability	Two steps	Vehicle cannot alter its present course
Strike power core or vital spot	Five steps	Vehicle is completely destroyed

That's a lot of modifications. But it's not really that hard. Let's look at an example. A PC in a small level 2 fighter attacks a level 4 frigate. Since the frigate is level 4, the difficulty of the attack starts at 4. But the attacking craft is weaker than the defender, so the difference in their levels (2) is added to the difficulty. The fighter pilot must make a difficulty 6 attack on the frigate. However, the fighter is trying to swoop in and damage the frigate's drive, which modifies the attack by another three steps, for a total difficulty of 9. If the fighter pilot is trained in space combat, she reduces the difficulty to 8, but it's still impossible without help. So let's say that two other PCs—also in level 2 fighters—join in and coordinate their attack. Three ships coordinating an attack on one target reduces the difficulty by two steps, resulting in a final difficulty of 6. Still, the attacking PC would be wise to use Effort.

In some cases, the GM may wish to use the level of an NPC pilot or driver rather than the level of the vehicle, but this is only for special circumstances, such as a very skilled or very inept pilot.

Then the frigate retaliates and the PC needs to make a defense roll. The level difference between the ships is a two-step modification in the frigate's favor, so the difficulty of the defense roll starts out at 6. But the frigate tries to take out the fighter's weapons, reducing the difficulty of the defense roll by two steps. Thus, the PC needs to succeed at a difficulty 4 task or lose his main weapons systems.

It's important to remember that a failed attack doesn't always mean a miss. The target ship might rock and reel from the hit, but the bulk of the damage was absorbed by the shields, so there's no significant damage.

This bare-bones system should allow the GM and players to flesh out exciting encounters involving the whole group. For example, perhaps while one PC pilots a ship, another mans the guns, and another frantically attempts to repair damage to the maneuvering thrusters before they crash into the space station they're trying to defend.

During a vehicular battle, particularly a space battle, there's a lot of chatter about shields failing, hull integrity, being outmaneuvered, coming in too fast, and whatnot. These sorts of details are great, but they're all flavor, so they're represented in the rules generally, rather than specifically.

For more details about vehicles, refer to the appropriate genre chapter.

SPECIAL: GAINING INSIGHT

Sometimes GMs like to keep lots of mystery in their games and present the players with many unknowns. This can be fun, and it's realistic—there's always some unknown factor in any situation that can creep up and cause trouble. And trouble is good because it makes things more interesting. These unknown factors are usually best portrayed as GM intrusions.

However, when a master thief plans to break into a vault and steal the jewels, she doesn't go in unless she is sure. She might know exactly what sorts of alarms are rigged to the door, or what schedule the security guards follow when they patrol. This isn't guesswork. The thief knows these things for certain. That's how she came up with her break-in plan in the first place. It's what separates her from bumbling criminals.

Similarly, the PCs are competent individuals—sometimes even experts—and such people can make decisions and devise plans with confidence. Yet players often find this difficult for two reasons. First, while their characters might be world-class con artists, infiltration specialists, or demolition experts, the players are not. And second, they're hindered by all the previously mentioned unknowns.

This is why PCs can gain Insights to help them. If a character is thinking about a plan, doing research, gathering information, casing a job, or scouting ahead, she can

If there are no Insights to be gained in a particular situation (or no more Insights to be gained), the PC looking for one still loses the Intellect points.

SAMPLE INSIGHTS

The mob boss's bodyguard always falls asleep after a big lunch.
The mayor won't press charges if he thinks his daughter is involved.
There must be a secret room at the center of the level because the walls don't match up.
The guard at the gate can't be bribed.
The starship captain won't believe anything a Narvelian says.
The shopkeeper knows he has to sell the stolen goods by the end of the day and will do anything to do so.
The queen is having an affair with the noblewoman.
The magic amulet sank to the bottom of the Garvanas Trench in the Talvar Sea when the ship went down.
The kidnappers are holding the boy as far away from the cathedral as possible.
Orcs hate the taste of anise.
The castle's defenses include counterspells that negate invisibility effects.
The bridge will collapse if more than one person walks across it.
The judge knows who the murderer is.
The two magic rings will cancel each other out.
The alarm system is wired to every door, but not to the windows on the second floor.
The fugitives couldn't be more than one hour's drive away.
The ambassador shows the telltale signs of being a shapeshifter.
The dwarves of the ancient fortress always put exactly three traps on their doors.
The general's assistant is fiercely loyal and will never betray her.

spend 3 Intellect points and one action to gain a single bit of special knowledge from the GM that she can count on with certainty. Insights are always presented as absolutes, and once established, they should never be changed, unless it is through the direct and deliberate intervention of the PCs. For example, if the PCs gain an Insight that giving the guard at the gate a bottle of booze by 10 p.m. ensures that he's drunk by midnight, and they kill that guard and a new one is stationed there, the Insight is invalidated and all bets are off. Likewise if they use a psychic power to make the guard hate alcohol. Either way, it changes only because the PCs changed it deliberately. Thus, they know for certain, ahead of time, that the Insight has become invalid.

Insights are never an end in themselves—they are a means to an end. If the whole point of an adventure is to identify a murderer, the characters can't get an Insight to learn the killer's identity. They could, however, use Insights to help them along. For example, they might learn that the murderer is left-handed, or that the accountant is definitely *not* the murderer.

Ultimately, the GM decides each Insight's revelation, so there's no chance that the PCs will gain too much information (if such a thing is even possible). But GMs are highly, highly encouraged to give a valuable Insight if the characters look for one (by spending Intellect points and an action), even if it must be made up on the spot. Doing so allows the players to make intelligent plans and feel confident and—more important—competent.

GM-INSTIGATED INSIGHTS

Sometimes, the GM can flag a potential Insight to a player in a given area. Usually, this is something the GM has specifically designed ahead of time for this purpose. After the PCs have explored an area and are ready to leave, the GM might say, "There's an Insight to be had here." This kind of Insight can't be gained by spending Intellect points. Instead, if the character wants to follow up on the GM's comment, she spends 2 XP as if she were buying a short-term benefit. No player is required to make this expenditure.

SPECIAL: CRAFTING, BUILDING, AND REPAIRING

Crafting is tricky in the Cypher System because the same rules that govern building a spear also cover repairing a machine that can take you into hyperspace. Normally, the level of the item determines the difficulty of creating or repairing it as well as the time required. For items unique to a world or race other than your own, such as a Martian tripod walker, add 5 to the item's level to determine the difficulty of building or repairing it. If the item is artistic in nature, the GM might add to the difficulty and time required. A crude wooden stool could be hammered together in an hour, but a beautiful finished piece might take a week or longer and would require more skill on the part of the crafter.

A level 0 object requires no skill to make and is easily found in most locations. Sling stones and firewood are level 0 items—producing them is routine. Making a torch from spare wood and oil-soaked cloth is simple, so it's a level 1 object. Making an arrow or a spear is fairly standard, so it's a level 2 object.

If a character wants to create a permanent nonstandard object, she must spend XP. If she fails her roll, no XP are spent.

MATERIALS

Generally speaking, a device to be crafted requires materials equal to its level and all the levels below it. So a level 5 device requires level 5 material, level 4 material, level 3 material, level 2 material, and level 1 material (and, technically, level 0 material).

The GM and players can gloss over much of the crafting details, if desired. Gathering all the materials to make a mundane item might not be worth playing out—but then again, it might be. Making a wooden spear in a forest isn't very interesting, but what if the PCs have to make a spear in a treeless desert? Finding the wreckage of something made of wood or forcing a PC to fashion a spear out of the bones of a large beast could be interesting.

The cost of gaining Insight is not reduced by any Edge you may have.

Circumstances really matter. For example, sewing a dress by hand might take five times as long, or more, as using a sewing machine.

Short-term benefit, page 222

CRAFTING DIFFICULTY AND TIME

Difficulty	Craft	General Time to Build
0	Something extremely simple like tying a rope or finding an appropriately sized rock	A few minutes at most
1	A torch	Five minutes
2	A spear, a simple shelter or piece of furniture	One hour
3	A bow, a door, a basic article of clothing	One day
4	A sword, a chainmail vest	One to two days
5	Common technological item (electric light), a nice piece of jewelry or art object	One week
6	Technological item (a watch, a transmitter), a really nice piece of jewelry, art object, or elegant craftwork	One month
7	Technological item (a computer), a major work of art	One year
8	Technological item (something from beyond Earth)	Many years
9	Technological item (something from beyond Earth)	Many years
10	Technological item (something from beyond Earth)	Many years

The GM is free to overrule some attempts at creation, building, or repair, requiring that the character have a certain level of skill, proper tools and materials, and so forth.

TIME

The time required to create an item is up to the GM, but the guidelines in the crafting table are a good starting point. Generally, repairing an item takes somewhere between half the creation time and the full creation time, depending on the item, the aspect that needs repairing, and the circumstances. For example, if creating an item takes one hour, repairing it takes between thirty minutes and one hour.

Sometimes a GM will allow a rush job if the circumstances warrant it. This is different than using skill to reduce the time required. In this case, the quality of the item is affected. Let's say that a character needs to create a tool with a powerful laser that will cut through solid steel (a level 7 item), but she has to do it in one day. The GM might allow it, but the device might be extremely volatile, inflicting damage on the user, or it might work only once.

SKILLS

The skill level of the crafter reduces the difficulty as normal in all ways except materials and time. If a PC trained in graphic design wants to create a cover for a novel and the GM decides it's a level 3 "item," it's only a standard (difficulty 2) task, but it still takes a full day and requires proper tools. A particularly great piece of image manipulation software could serve as an asset, with GM approval.

A character can reduce the time or materials needed instead of the difficulty (again, with GM approval, and if it makes sense to do so). A trained fletcher making arrows (level 2 items) could attempt a difficulty 2 task rather than a difficulty 1 task to create an arrow in fifteen minutes instead of an hour, or to create it in an hour but with substandard (level 1) materials. However, sometimes the GM will rule that reducing the time is not possible. For example, a single human can't make a chainmail vest in one hour without some kind of machine to help.

Possible areas for character training include:

- Armoring
- Bowyering/Fletching
- Chemistry
- Computer science
- Electronics
- Engines
- Genetic engineering
- Glassblowing
- Gunsmithing
- Leatherworking
- Metalworking
- Neural engineering
- Weaponsmithing
- Woodcrafting

FAILURE

Failing the roll means that the device is not completed or repaired. To continue to work on it, the character must gather more materials (generally, the highest-level material needed) and take the required amount of time again.

TINKERING WITH REALLY WEIRD STUFF

Characters might try to make a cypher, an artifact, or an alien psionic starship do something other than its intended function. Sometimes, the GM will simply declare the task impossible. You can't turn a vial of healing elixir into a two-way communicator. But most of the time, there is a chance of success.

That said, tinkering with weird stuff is not easy. Obviously, the difficulty varies from situation to situation, but difficulties starting at 7 are not unreasonable. The time, tools, and training required would be similar to the time, tools, and training needed to repair a device. If the tinkering results in a long-term benefit for the character—such as creating an artifact that she can use—the GM should require her to spend XP to make it.

EXPERIENCE POINTS

Experience points (XP) are the currency by which players gain benefits for their characters. The most common ways to earn XP are through GM intrusions and by discovering new and amazing things. Sometimes experience points are earned during a game session, and sometimes they're earned between sessions. In a typical session, a player might earn 2 to 4 XP, and between sessions, perhaps another 2 XP (on average). The exact amounts depend on the events of the session and the discoveries made.

GM INTRUSION

At any time, the GM can introduce an unexpected complication for a character. When he intrudes in this way, he must give that character 2 XP. That player, in turn, must immediately give one of those XP to another player and justify the gift (perhaps the other player had a good idea, told a joke, or performed an action that saved a life).

Often, the GM intrudes when a player attempts an action that should be an automatic success. However, the GM is free to intrude at other times. As a general rule, the GM should intrude at least once each session, but no more than once or twice each session per character.

Anytime the GM intrudes, the player can spend 1 XP to refuse the intrusion, though that also means she doesn't get the 2 XP. If the player has no XP to spend, she can't refuse.

If a player rolls a 1 on a die, the GM can intrude without giving her any XP.

Example 1: Through skill and the aid of another character, a fourth-tier PC reduces a wall-climbing task from difficulty 2 to difficulty 0. Normally, she would succeed at the task automatically, but the GM intrudes and says, "No, a bit of the crumbling wall gives way, so you still have to make a roll." As with any difficulty 2 task, the target number is 6. The PC attempts the roll as normal and gains 2 XP because the GM intruded. She immediately gives one of those XP to another player.

Example 2: During a fight, a PC swings his axe and damages a foe with a slice across the shoulder. The GM intrudes by saying that the foe turned just as the axe struck, wrenching the weapon from the character's grip and sending it clattering across the floor. The axe comes to a stop 10 feet (3 m) away. Because the GM intruded, the PC gains 2 XP, and he immediately gives one of those XP to another player. Now the character must deal with the dropped weapon, perhaps drawing a different weapon or using his next turn to scramble after the axe.

DISCOVERING NEW THINGS

The core of gameplay in the Cypher System—the answer to the question "What do characters do in this game?"—is "Discover new things." Discovery makes characters more powerful because it almost certainly grants new capabilities or options,

Obviously, weird stuff will vary from setting to setting, and sometimes the concept might not apply at all. But many times, there will be something in the setting that is too strange, too alien, too powerful, or too dangerous for PCs to mess around with (or at least mess around with easily). Einstein may have been extraordinary, but that doesn't mean he could reverse-engineer a teleporter made in another dimension.

For much more on GM intrusion, see page 372.

Typically, PCs will earn about half their total experience points by making discoveries.

It's a fine line, but ultimately the GM decides what constitutes a discovery as opposed to just something weird in the course of an adventure. Usually, the difference is, did the PCs successfully interact with it and learn something about it? If so, it's probably a discovery.

Experience point awards for artifacts should usually apply even if the artifact was given to the PCs rather than found, because often such gifts are the rewards for success.

DISCOVERY

While GM intrusion is interesting, the game also has a more conventional method of awarding XP between sessions. But it has nothing to do with killing monsters.

That's weird for a lot of players. Defeating opponents in battle is the core way you earn XP in many games. But not in the Cypher System. The game is based on the premise of awarding players experience points for the thing you expect them to do in the game.

Experience points are the reward pellets they get for pushing the button—oh, wait, no, that's for rats in a lab. Well, same principle: give the players XP for doing a thing, and that thing is what they'll do.

In the Cypher System, that thing is discovery.

but it's also a reward unto itself and results in a gain of XP.

Discovery can include finding a significant new location, such as a hidden chamber, a secret fortress, a lost land, a new planet, or an unexplored dimension. In this fashion, PCs are explorers. It can also include a new significant aspect of a setting, such as a secret organization, a new religion, and so on.

Discovery can also mean finding a new procedure or device (something too big to be considered a piece of equipment) or even previously unknown information. This could include a source of magical power, a unique teleportation device, or the cure for a plague. These are all discoveries. The common thread is that the PCs discover something that they can understand and put to use.

Last, depending on the GM's outlook and the kind of campaign the group wants to play, a discovery could be a secret, an ethical idea, an adage, or even a truth.

Artifacts: When the group gains an artifact, award XP equal to the artifact's level and divide it among the PCs (minimum 1 XP for each character). Round down if necessary. For example, if four PCs discover a level 5 artifact, they each get 1 XP. Money, standard equipment, and cyphers are not worth XP.

Miscellaneous Discoveries: Various other discoveries might grant 1 XP to each PC involved.

GM AWARDS

Sometimes, a group will have an adventure that doesn't deal primarily with discovery or finding things. In this case, it's a good idea for the GM to award XP for accomplishing other tasks. A goal or a mission is worth 1 to 4 XP for each PC involved, depending on the difficulty and length of the work. As a general rule, a mission should be worth at least 1 XP per game session involved in accomplishing it. For example, saving a family on an isolated farm beset by raiding cultists might be worth 1 XP for each character. Of course, saving the family doesn't always mean killing the bad guys; it might mean relocating them, parlaying with the cultists, or chasing off the raiders.

Delivering a message to a hermit in a tiny cave isolated in the mountains—one that requires the PCs to face dangerous conditions and risk possible attacks by predators—is probably a mission worth 2 XP per character. On the other hand, if the PCs can teleport directly to the cave, the mission is probably worth 1 XP per character. Thus, GM awards are based not only on the task, but on the PCs and their capabilities as well.

However, that doesn't mean the characters should earn fewer XP if they make a lot of lucky rolls or devise a clever plan to overcome obstacles. Being lucky or smart doesn't make a difficult challenge less difficult—it just means the PCs succeed more easily.

PLAYER-DRIVEN AWARDS

Players can create their own missions by setting goals for their characters. If they succeed, they earn XP just as if they were sent on the mission by an NPC. For example, if the characters decide on their own to help find a lost caravan in the mountains, that's a goal and a mission.

Sometimes character goals are more personal. If a PC vows to avenge the death of her brother, that's still a mission. These kinds of goals that are important to a character's background should be set at or near the outset of the game. When completed, a character goal should be worth at least 1 XP (and perhaps as much as 4 XP). This encourages players to develop their characters' backgrounds and to build in opportunities for action in the future. Doing so makes the background more than just backstory or flavor—it becomes something that can propel the campaign forward.

SPENDING EXPERIENCE POINTS

Experience points are meant to be used. Hoarding them is not a good idea; if a player accumulates more than 10 XP, the GM can require her to spend some of them.

Generally, experience points can be spent in four ways: immediate benefits, short- and medium-term benefits, long-term benefits, and character advancement.

PROGRESSING TO A NEW TIER

Tiers in the Cypher System aren't entirely like levels in other roleplaying games. In the Cypher System, gaining tiers is not the players' only goal or the only measure of achievement. Starting (first-tier) characters are already competent, and there are only six tiers. Character advancement has a power curve, but it's only steep enough to keep things interesting. In other words, gaining levels is cool and fun, but it's not the only path to success or power. If you spend all your XP on immediate, short- and medium-term benefits, you would be different from someone who spends her points on long-term benefits, but you would not be "behind" that character.

The general idea is that most characters will spend half their XP on tier advancement and long-term benefits, and the rest on immediate and short-term benefits (which are used during gameplay). Some groups might decide that XP earned during a game is to be spent on immediate and short-term benefits (gameplay uses), and XP awarded between sessions for discoveries is to be spent on character advancement (long-term uses).

Ultimately, the idea is to make experience points into tools that the players and the GM can use to shape the story and the characters, not just a bookkeeping hassle.

IMMEDIATE BENEFITS

The most straightforward way for a player to use XP is to reroll any roll in the game—even one that she didn't make. This costs 1 XP per reroll, and the player chooses the best result. She can continue to spend XP on rerolls, but this can quickly become an expensive proposition. It's a fine way to try to prevent disaster, but it's not a good idea to use a lot of XP to reroll a single action over and over.

A player can also spend 1 XP to refuse a GM intrusion.

This optional system would work well for groups that are used to a more traditional level-dependent game and might undervalue spending XP for other things. The expectations of a Cypher System game aren't quite so rigid, but you can run it that way if it better suits your style. For more information, see Chapter 10: Optional Rules.

Often the best scenarios are the ones in which the players take the initiative and are proactive about attaining a goal that they set for themselves. Whether they want to case and rob a noble's estate, start their own business, clear out an area of the wilderness to make their home, or anything else, players should make their own adventures sometimes.

Experience points should not be a goal unto themselves. Instead, they are a game mechanic to simulate how—through experience, time, toil, travail, and so on—characters become more skilled, more able, and more powerful. Spending XP to explain a change in a character's capabilities that occurred in the course of the story, such as if the PC made a new device or learned a new skill, isn't a waste of XP—it's what XP are for.

The skill you choose for character advancement can be anything you wish, such as climbing, jumping, persuading, or sneaking. You can also choose to be knowledgeable in a certain area of study, such as history or geology. You can even choose a skill based on your character's special abilities. For example, if your character can make an Intellect roll to blast an enemy with mental force, you can become trained in using that ability, treating its difficulty as one step lower than normal.

SHORT- AND MEDIUM-TERM BENEFITS

By spending 2 XP, a character can gain a skill—or, more rarely, an ability—that provides a short-term benefit. Let's say a character notices that the computer terminals in the facility she's infiltrating are similar to those used by the company she once worked for. She spends 2 XP and says that she has a great deal of experience in using these. As a result, she is trained in operating (and breaking into) these computers. This is just like being trained in computer use or hacking, but it applies only to computers found in that particular location. The skill is extremely useful in the facility, but nowhere else.

Medium-term benefits are usually story based. For example, a character can spend 2 XP while climbing through mountains and say that she has experience with climbing in regions like these, or perhaps she spends the XP after she's been in the mountains for a while and says that she's picked up the feel for climbing there. Either way, from now on, she is trained in climbing in those mountains. This helps her now and any time she returns to the area, but she's not trained in climbing everywhere.

This method allows a character to get immediate training in a skill for half the normal cost. (Normally, it costs 4 XP to become trained in a skill.) It's also a way to gain a new skill even if the PC has already gained a new skill as a step toward attaining the next tier.

In rare cases, a GM might allow a character to spend 2 XP to gain an entirely new ability—such as a device, a special ability, or a special mental power—for a short time, usually no longer than the course of one scenario. The player and the GM should agree on a story-based explanation for the benefit. Perhaps the ability has a specific, rare requirement, such as a tool, a battery, a drug, or some kind of treatment. For example, a character who wants to explore a submerged location has several biotech enhancements, and he spends 2 XP to cobble together a device that lets him breathe underwater. This gives him the ability for a considerable length of time, but not permanently—the device might work for only eight hours. Again, the story and the logic of the situation dictate the parameters.

LONG-TERM BENEFITS

In many ways, the long-term benefits a PC can gain by spending XP are a means of integrating the mechanics of the game with the story. Players can codify things that happen to their characters by talking to the GM and spending 3 XP. For example, a character named Jessica spends a long time working in a kitchen in a restaurant that she believes is owned by a man who works for shapechanging spies from another planet. During that time, she becomes familiar with cooking. Jessica's player talks with the GM and says that she would like the experience to have a lasting effect on her character. She spends 3 XP and gains familiarity with cooking.

Some things that a PC can acquire as a long-term benefit are story based. In the course of play, the character might gain a friend (a contact) or build a log cabin (a home). These benefits are probably not the result of spending XP. The new contact comes to the PC and starts the relationship. The new home is granted to him as a reward for service to a powerful or wealthy patron, or maybe the character inherits the home from a relative.

Things that affect character abilities, like a familiarity or an artifact, are different. They likely require XP and time, money, and so on.

Long-term benefits can include the following.

Familiarity: The character gains a +1 bonus to rolls involving one kind of task.

Contact: The character gains a long-term NPC contact of importance—someone who will help him with information, equipment, or physical tasks. The player and GM should work out the details of the relationship.

Home: The PC acquires a full-time residence. This can be an apartment in a city, a cabin in the wilderness, a base in an ancient complex, or whatever fits the situation. It should be a secure place where the PC can leave his belongings and sleep soundly. Several characters could combine their XP and buy a home together.

Title or job: The PC is granted a position of importance or authority. It might come with responsibilities, prestige, and rewards, or it might be an honorary title.

Wealth: The PC comes into a considerable amount of wealth, whether it's a windfall, an inheritance, or a gift. It might be enough to buy a home or a title, but that's not really the point. The main benefit is that the PC no longer needs to worry about the cost of simple equipment, lodging, food, and so on. This wealth could mean a set amount—perhaps 50,000 dollars (or whatever is appropriate in the setting)—or it could bestow the ability to ignore minor costs, as decided by the player and GM.

Artifact: The PC creates an artifact that has a power of his choosing. If the item is fairly simple, the GM can skip the crafting details and just say that after a period of time, the PC creates it. For an item that significantly alters gameplay—granting the character vast telepathic powers or giving him the ability to teleport at will—the GM might require difficult rolls, a considerable amount of time, and rare, hard-to-find components and materials.

CHARACTER ADVANCEMENT

Progressing to the next tier involves four stages. When a PC has spent 4 XP on each of the stages, he advances to the next tier and gains all the type and focus benefits of that tier. The four stages can be purchased in any order, but each can be purchased only once per tier. In other words, a PC must buy all four stages and advance to the next tier before he can buy the same stage again.

Increasing Capabilities: You gain 4 new points to add to your stat Pools. You can allocate the points among your Pools however you wish.

Moving Toward Perfection: You add 1 to your Might Edge, your Speed Edge, or your Intellect Edge (your choice).

Extra Effort: Your Effort score increases by 1.

Skills: You become trained in one skill of your choice, other than attacks or defense. If you choose a skill that you are already trained in, you become specialized in that skill.

Other Options: Players can also spend 4 XP to purchase other special options. Selecting one of these options counts as purchasing one of the four stages necessary to advance to the next tier. The other three need to be from the other categories. The special options are as follows:

- Reduce the cost for wearing armor. This option lowers the Speed penalty for wearing armor by 1.
- Add 2 to your recovery rolls.

GMs and players should work together to make XP awards and expenditures fit the ongoing story. If a PC stays in a location for two months to learn the inhabitants' unique language, the GM might award her a few XP, which are then immediately spent to grant the character the ability to understand and speak that language.

CHAPTER 10

OPTIONAL RULES

In an attempt to keep the game relatively simple, the rules in the previous chapter are designed to be streamlined, straightforward, and easy to use. However, some players and GMs might desire a bit more complexity, especially as the game goes on, in order to remain engaged and challenged. If you find yourself wanting more robust rules or more options to tailor the game, use some or all of the optional rules in this chapter.

The GM is the final arbiter of which optional rules are available in the game.

TRADING DAMAGE FOR EFFECT

You can decrease the amount of damage you inflict in combat in exchange for a special effect that is usually attained only on a roll of 19 or 20. To determine the amount of damage you must sacrifice from a single attack, consult the following table, and add the amount for the desired effect to the foe's level. For example, if you want to impair a level 5 creature, you'd have to sacrifice 12 points of damage from an attack (7 plus 5). The player can wait to determine if he hits before deciding whether to trade damage for an effect.

Damage Reduction	Effect
1	Hinder/Distract
2	Specific body part
3	Knock back
3	Move past
3	Strike held object
4	Knock down
7	Disarm
7	Impair
8	Stun

Hinder/Distract: For one round, the difficulty of the opponent's actions is modified by one step to his detriment.

Specific Body Part: The attacker strikes a specific spot on the defender's body. The GM decides what special effect, if any, results. For example, hitting a creature's tentacle that is wrapped around your ally

might make it easier for the ally to escape. Hitting a foe in the eye might blind it for one round. Hitting a creature in its one vulnerable spot might ignore Armor.

Knock Back: The foe is knocked or forced back a few feet. Most of the time, this effect doesn't matter much, but if the fight takes place on a ledge or next to a pit of lava, the effect can be significant.

Move Past: The character can make a short move at the end of the attack. This effect is useful to get past a foe guarding a door, for example.

Strike Held Object: Instead of striking the foe, you strike what the foe is holding. To determine results, refer to the rules for attacking objects.

Knock Down: The foe is knocked prone. It can get up on its turn if it wishes.

Disarm: The opponent drops one object that it is holding.

Impair: For the rest of the combat, the difficulty of all tasks attempted by the foe is modified by one step to its detriment.

Stun: The opponent loses its next turn.

LASTING DAMAGE

For a more realistic simulation of damage, the GM can use a GM intrusion to indicate that damage suffered by a player character is "lasting." Most of the time, this damage is described as being a concussion, a broken bone, a torn ligament, or severe muscle or tissue damage. This damage does not heal normally, so the points lost cannot be regained by making recovery rolls. Instead, they return at a rate of 1 point per day of complete rest (or 1 point per three days of regular activity). Until the points are restored, the damage has a secondary effect.

Using lasting damage is particularly appropriate in cases where it would be an obvious consequence, such as when a character falls a long distance. It is also appropriate for characters who are already impaired or debilitated.

Attacking objects, page 207

Lasting and permanent damage could also be caused by a particularly vicious disease, the effect of an especially hellish curse, a brush with a psychic or cybernetic entity with godlike intelligence, standing at ground zero when the bomb goes off, and so on.

PERMANENT DAMAGE

Similar to lasting damage, permanent damage is a special situation adjudicated by the GM. Permanent damage never heals normally, although extraordinary technologies and magic can potentially repair damage or replace lost body parts. This kind of damage should be used sparingly and only in special situations.

LASTING OR PERMANENT DAMAGE INSTEAD OF DEATH

The GM can use lasting or permanent damage as a substitute for death. In other words, if a PC reaches 0 in all of her stat Pools, she would normally be dead, but instead you could say that she is knocked unconscious and wakes up with some kind of lasting or permanent damage.

MODIFYING ABILITIES ON THE FLY

Sometimes, a player can use a special ability in a way that goes beyond its normal bounds. Such changes can be done on the fly. In some cases, it simply costs more points to use the ability in a new way. In other cases, more challenges are involved.

For any Intellect ability with a specific range, you can increase the range by using more mental energy. If you spend 1 additional Intellect point, you can change the range by one step—either from short to long, or from long to 500 feet (152 m). You can't increase a range beyond 500 feet by spending more points. Any Intellect ability that has a duration (anything more than a single action in a single round) usually lasts one minute, ten minutes, or one hour. By spending 1 additional point of Intellect, you

LASTING DAMAGE

Damage Type	Description	Other Effect
Might	Broken arm	Useless arm
Might	Muscle damage	Difficulty of physical tasks increased by one step
Might	Tissue damage	Difficulty of all tasks increased by two steps
Might	Torn ligament	Move at half speed; short move is no more than 25 feet (8 m); long move is no more than 50 feet (15 m)
Speed	Broken leg	Cannot move without assistance
Intellect	Concussion	Difficulty of Intellect actions increased by one step

PERMANENT DAMAGE

Damage Type	Description	Other Effect
Might	Severed hand or arm	Self-explanatory
Speed	Permanent limp	Move at half speed; short move is no more than 25 feet (8 m); long move is no more than 50 feet (15 m)
Speed	Severed leg	Cannot move without assistance
Intellect	Missing eye	Difficulty of most or all physical actions increased by one step
Intellect	Brain damage	Difficulty of Intellect actions increased by one step
Intellect	Blindness	Character acts as if always in complete darkness
Intellect	Deafness	Character cannot hear

can increase the duration by one step, so an ability that lasts one minute can be made to last ten minutes. Durations cannot be increased more than one step.

A player can make a special roll to modify the range, area, or other aspects of an ability. The roll is always modified by the stat it's normally based on. The GM sets the difficulty for the roll based on the degree of modification. Like any roll, the player can use Effort, skill, and assets to reduce the difficulty. Generally, the difficulty falls into one of three categories:

- **Impossible** (modifying an ability to accomplish an effect that has nothing to do with its description or intent)
- **Formidable** (modifying an ability to do something similar to the description or intent, but changing its nature)
- **Difficult** (modifying an ability to do something within the spirit and general idea of the ability)

For example, say an adept has the Hover ability and wants to modify its use in the middle of an encounter. If he wanted to use it to blast someone with fire, that's an impossible task (difficulty 10) because fire has nothing to do with the ability.

If he wanted to use it offensively within the general description of the ability, he might try to make a foe fly up and hit its head on the ceiling. However, turning an ability that is not offensive into an attack changes its nature, making the task formidable (difficulty 7).

If he wanted to use it to make a friend hover rather than himself, that's within the spirit and general idea of the ability. That's difficult (difficulty 4) but not unreasonable.

CHOOSING TO ROLL

Sometimes, if a player spends points on an action (for example, to apply Effort or to activate an ability), she might want to toss a die even if there is no chance for failure because a roll of 20 reduces the number of points that need to be spent. In addition, in some situations, particularly in combat, a roll of 17 or higher indicates more damage or a special effect.

In these cases, players are allowed to roll not to determine success but to determine whether they achieve an above-and-beyond success. However, there is risk involved because if they roll a 1, that results in a GM intrusion. It does not necessarily mean failure, although that's an obvious GM intrusion to use.

GM intrusion, page 219

ACTING WHILE UNDER ATTACK

When a character is engaged in melee combat, doing anything other than fighting makes him more vulnerable. This is true for PCs and NPCs. If a character engaged in melee takes an action other than fighting, each of his opponents can make an immediate extra attack. The only exception to this rule is moving. If the character's only action is to move, he is assumed to be moving slowly and carefully out of the fight, safely withdrawing from combat.

For example, Tom has his back against a security door while fighting two guards. If he tries to open the door using its control terminal, he is taking an action other than fighting, and both guards get to make an attack against him.

Hover, page 33

MODIFYING THE RANGE OF WEAPONS

If a character with a ranged weapon wants to attack a foe outside the weapon's range, he can do so, but the difficulty of the attack is increased by two steps. Generally, the increase in range does not extend infinitely. A character using a weapon that has a short range can try to hit a target that is a long distance away. A character using a weapon that has a long range can try to hit a target up to 200 feet (61 m) away with a difficulty modification of two steps, a target up to 500 feet (152 m) away with a difficulty modification of four steps, and a target up to 1,000 feet (300 m) away with a difficulty modification of six steps. Modifications of weapons with ranges that start out greater than long range must be adjudicated by the GM.

Attacks with hard limits, such as the blast radius of an explosive, can't be modified.

OPTIONAL MAJOR EFFECT

When a player's roll would grant him a major effect, instead of taking the effect, he can choose to roll a d6 and add the result to the initial roll. This option makes it possible to succeed at tasks with target numbers greater than 20 without decreasing the difficulty.

WEAPON DISTINCTIONS

Weapons have only a few distinctions—they are light, medium, or heavy, and they are melee or ranged. However, you can also add the following distinctions.

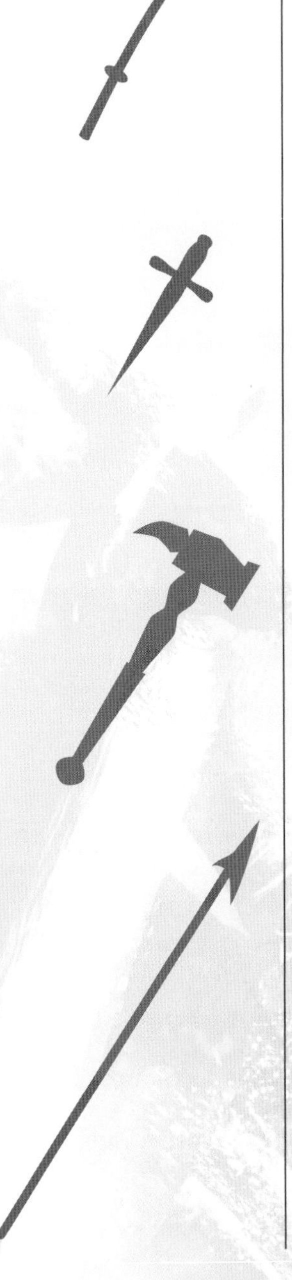

Slashing: Weapons with sharp edges, like swords and axes, are slashing weapons. On a successful hit, they inflict 1 additional point of damage against an unarmored foe but 1 less point against an armored opponent. The claws of a creature might be considered slashing weapons.

Stabbing: Weapons with a point, like daggers, spears, and arrows, are stabbing weapons. When an attacker using one rolls a 17 or higher on a successful attack, he inflicts 1 additional point of damage beyond any bonus damage normally granted by his roll. However, if he rolls a 5 or less on a successful attack, he inflicts 1 less point of damage as the weapon glances or grazes off the foe. A creature's pointed teeth might be considered stabbing weapons.

Crushing: Blunt weapons like clubs and hammers are crushing weapons, effective against even well-armored foes. Crushing weapons ignore 1 point of Armor, but they inflict 1 less point of damage against unarmored foes. The powerful bashes of a creature's flailing tendrils might be considered crushing weapons.

Reaching: A reaching weapon is a long melee weapon, like a long spear, a pike, or a whip, that can attack foes at a bit of a distance. Someone with a reaching weapon can hold attackers at bay (unless they also have reaching weapons). Attacks against someone with a reaching weapon are modified by one step in the defender's favor. In certain situations, such as close-quarters fighting, a reaching weapon might be hindered (the wielder's attack difficulty is increased by one step), or using such a weapon might be impossible. The attacks of a very large creature or one with long arms might be considered reaching weapons.

USING MINIATURES

Some players like to use miniatures, counters, or other tokens to represent their characters, particularly in a battlefield situation. Miniatures showing the location of the PCs, NPCs, and terrain features can be useful visual aids. They help people see who is closest to the door, which foe stands where, and who will be crushed if the dangerously weak part of the ceiling caves in.

DISTANCE

Often, players who use miniatures also use a grid to represent distance. If you do this, it's probably best to say that each 1-inch (2.5 cm) square represents about 5 feet (1.5 m). Simply move your figure the right number of squares; for example, a short distance would be ten squares.

However, a grid isn't necessary in the Cypher System. Since most things have one of three possible distances—immediate, short, and long—that's all you need to worry about. Thus, you could cut three lengths of string: one 2 inches (5 cm) long, one 10 inches (25 cm) long, and one 20 inches (51 cm) long. If something has immediate range, stretch the 2-inch (5 cm) string from the origin point to see how far it goes. Any character whose figure is within 2 inches (5 cm) of another figure can make a melee attack against that figure. (The attacker is assumed to move closer to the target, so slide the figures together.) If a character wants to move a short distance, use the 10-inch (25 cm) string to measure from her starting point to her intended destination. If the string can reach that far, so can she. For long range, anything you can reach with the 20-inch (51 cm) string is in range. Soon, you'll find that you can eyeball the distances—precision isn't that important.

SIZE

In some games that use miniatures, the size of the miniature's base is important. In the Cypher System, such precision isn't necessary. However, it certainly helps if larger creatures have larger bases, representing that they take up more room.

Speaking of which, GMs are free to consider any appropriate creature "big." An appropriate creature would likely be one that is more than 10 feet (3 m) tall or 10 feet (3 m) long. Big creatures don't have to move their miniature when making a melee attack within immediate distance. They can just reach that far.

GMs can also designate some creatures "huge." Huge creatures are 20 feet (6 m) tall or 20 feet (6 m) long. For them, immediate distance is a string 4 inches (10 cm) long—or four squares on a grid—and they don't have to move to make melee attacks.

As a rule of thumb, the maximum number of attackers that can attack a single creature is the same as the number of figures whose bases can fit around the creature. In general, this means that larger creatures can be attacked by more assailants.

TACTICAL PLAY

When you use miniatures, some aspects of the game become more important, including range, movement, and special effects that move characters. If a character is knocked back, move his miniature back 1 or 2 inches (or squares), as appropriate.

That means terrain becomes important, too. If a deep chasm is nearby, the players need to know exactly where it is in relation to their figures in case they have the opportunity to knock a foe into that chasm (or face that same risk themselves). Likewise, things to hide behind, the layout of interior chambers, and so on become important and must be depicted along with the miniatures. Many people enjoy playing this kind of game on a dry-erase or wet-erase surface so they can draw the features and place the figures right in the action. Sketching them on paper works fine, too, as does using books, pencils, or other things to represent ledges, walls, and so forth. And, of course, terrain pieces can be used for extra flavor. Some pieces are made of paper to keep them inexpensive.

Line of sight also becomes more important, and if you already cut a string to handle distance, it works for this purpose as well. Place the string anywhere on the base of the character taking the action, and stretch the string toward the target. If the string can be stretched to any part of the base of the target, the attacker has line of sight.

POSSIBLE DRAWBACKS

The downside to using miniatures is that the exacting detail they offer sometimes gets in the way of the GM's narrative control. For example, without miniatures, she can use GM intrusion to say, "You are standing on the trapdoor when it opens." With miniatures, a player usually knows exactly where he is standing at any given moment.

Also, psychologically, miniatures seem to encourage combat. If you place a miniature on the game table representing a new creature that the PCs encounter, some players assume that they need to engage with it in tactical combat rather than talk to it, sneak past it, or try some other course of action.

OPTIONAL XP RULES

Usually, players earn experience points by making discoveries or through GM awards. As an alternative to that system, players can suggest that other players earn XP. The GM calls for nominations at the end of an adventure, and the players discuss who did what, who came up with the best ideas, who handled a particular situation well, and so forth. Every character still receives XP, but the players decide who gets how much.

Another option is for a GM to offer XP to the group between sessions and let them split it up however they feel is fair. This method can be used with XP earned for discovery or through GM awards.

Last, the group can decide that experience points earned in different ways are spent differently. One method is to declare that XP earned through GM intrusion is available only for immediate, short- and medium-term, and long-term uses, while XP awarded between sessions is used for advancing in levels. The advantage to this option is that all characters advance through the six tiers at about the same rate—an important issue for some players. Of course, a good GM can achieve this result on his own by carefully handing out rewards, and many groups will discover while playing that equal advancement isn't an important issue in the Cypher System, but people should get to play the game they want to play.

GETTING AN XP ADVANCE

By introducing a story complication based on her character's background, a player can start the game with a significant amount of XP (and can spend them immediately if desired, even to purchase enough benefits to advance to the next tier). The GM has final approval over this option, and it should be used only in groups that don't insist on all characters having precisely the same power levels. This story-based concept allows a player to create exactly the character she wants at the outset at the cost of building in a narrative complication for herself.

For example, a player might want to start the game with a robotic companion or a beam weapon. Under the normal rules, these options aren't available to a beginning player, but she could find or build them given time (and perhaps after spending XP). With the optional rule, the character gets an advance XP amount that can be used to "buy" the automaton or weapon, but in exchange, she has an inability with all NPC interactions.

As another example, let's say a player doesn't want to start by playing a new, young character—he wants to play someone who is older and more experienced. Although the Cypher System does not assume that all starting characters are fresh young recruits, the player's vision doesn't quite sound like a first-tier character. So he comes up with a significant drawback, such as a severe addiction to a costly drug, in exchange for an advance of XP that allows him to start at the second tier, with all the benefits of a second-tier character.

These story complications are worth an advance of 4 to 6 XP:

- People find the character extremely unlikable. No matter what he says or does, intelligent creatures and animals find him unpleasant. Any attempt to interact with creatures is treated as if it were one step more difficult than normal. Further, the GM should make a default assumption that all people treat the character with distaste and contempt as a baseline.
- The character has a bum leg. It acts up every now and then (at least once per adventure, and usually once per session), and when it does, the difficulty of all Speed tasks is increased by one step for him.
- The character has an inability with a significant task, such as attacks, defense, movement, or something of that nature. As a result, the difficulty of such tasks is increased by one step for him.
- The character has an occasionally debilitating condition, such as a bad back, alcoholism, eating issues, and so on. This problem results in a significant penalty once per session.
- The character is wanted by the law and must keep a low profile. This can cause story-based complications rather than mechanical ones, but it can make life difficult for him at times.
- The character has a defenseless relative or friend who is often at risk. Again, this is not a mechanical issue, but one that will affect how the character is played. At times, he will have to stop what he is doing to help the person out of a jam. At other times, the person's life might be truly in jeopardy, compelling the PC to action.
- The character must perform a regular action to retain his abilities. For example, each morning, he must "commune" with an ultrapowerful, artificially intelligent "god" who grants his powers. If this communion is disturbed or prevented, or if the transmission is broken or blocked, the PC does not have access to his powers that day.
- The character must have a particular item to be able to use his abilities. For example, he needs a power cell, a focusing crystal, or another object that can be lost, stolen, or destroyed. Perhaps, like a power cell, it needs to be replaced or recharged from time to time.

These story complications are worth an advance of 12 to 20 XP:

- The character is wanted by the law and is actively pursued by multiple NPCs. This isn't just a matter of lying low when she is in town. Instead, NPCs will show up at the worst possible times and attempt to abduct or kill her.
- The character has a condition such that the difficulty of all tasks involving combat or NPC interaction is increased by one step.
- The character has a truly debilitating condition, such as blindness, deafness, being crippled, severe drug addiction, and so on.
- The character has a defenseless relative or friend who (for some vital reason) must accompany her at least 75 percent of the time. She will spend many actions protecting this person instead of doing what she'd rather be doing.
- The character's abilities rely on a rare drug that is difficult to obtain. Without a regular dose of this substance, she is virtually powerless.
- The character was experimented on as a young child, which gave her powers and abilities. Now, to gain any new abilities, she must find the original experimenter and replicate the process. This is a major mission and could result in a long delay in character advancement (effectively giving her a boost in power at the beginning of the game but no boosts for a long time afterward).

FURTHER CUSTOMIZING CHARACTERS

Character creation in the Cypher System is meant to be simple and fast. However, it's also meant to provide players with the character they want to play. Options for modifying types with flavors, choosing new tier abilities for foci, and designing new descriptors can be found in their respective chapters. But sometimes, players want more than the options provided. For them, some tweaking and modifying is required.

SKILLS FROM BACKGROUNDS

A warrior's background says that he worked in a smithy as a young lad. But there's no way a warrior can begin with weaponsmithing as a skill (he can get this skill as he progresses). Should he start with that skill? This question has four potential answers.

Getting an XP advance, page 230

1. *No.* He might know the basics of the task. However, a skill doesn't represent a simple familiarity, but extensive training, experience, or talent. Not everyone who works in a restaurant is a chef.

2. *Sure.* In the scope of things, will weaponsmithing wreck the game or make the character unplayable? Is it unfair to the other players? Probably not. For that matter, give all the characters a background skill. Require that it ties into the character's background and doesn't have a lot of direct adventuring applications. For example, a PC can have cooking, animal care, philosophy, or woodworking, but not climbing, sneaking, or anything similar, and certainly not a skill with attack or defense.

3. *Yes.* Use the optional rules for giving experience point advances, where the character takes on a story complication in exchange for receiving 4 XP to buy the new skill.

4. *Yes.* Allow the player to have an XP deficit. The character starts with the desired skill, but before he can gain any of the four benefits required to advance to the next tier, he must pay off this deficit. It's probably unwise to allow a character to start with a deficit of greater than 4 XP.

TRADING ABILITIES

Sometimes a player wants to be an adept but also wants to wear armor without a penalty. Combat flavor for the type would offer this, but maybe the player just wants the one ability. To make armor easier to wear, you can use the rule that allows a character to purchase an ability other than one of the four benefits (usually a new skill).

But there are other options as well. On a case-by-case basis, you can take an ability from one type (or focus) and make it available to another type at the same tier (or perhaps a higher tier).

If you want a slightly more "balanced" alternative, require that the character sacrifice something to gain something. If an adept wants an explorer ability, she has to give up some aspect of being an adept. Perhaps she can wear armor with the Practiced in Armor ability, but she has to give up her magic knowledge, or she can use cyphers only like an explorer, and so on.

This works best for nonvariable abilities. But what about other tier abilities? Sometimes, a player might want just one ability from another type. For example, a warrior wants to use a particular speaker ability as his special ability for that tier. That's probably okay, but again, it should be done on a case-by-case basis and very rarely. And it's still viable to ask that player to give something up. For example, if a warrior wants a speaker ability at second tier, he should give up one of his own second-tier ability options permanently. Or even better, he should have to wait and take the speaker ability at third tier instead.

MODIFYING ABILITIES

Characters can spend additional points or make a special roll to make an ability work beyond the bounds of its normal parameters. This is called modifying an ability, and it works on the fly.

But what if a player wants to modify an ability permanently? What if a character who Moves Like a Cat wants her fourth-tier Quick Strike ability to stun foes rather than daze them? Consider the following questions.

Is the modified ability more powerful?
In our example, it is, because stunned foes lose their next action, while dazed foes simply take a penalty to actions. If the answer is yes, a permanent price must be paid for the modification. First of all, increase the point cost (if any) by at least 50 percent.

Alternatively, require that a level of Effort be used with the ability. If there is no cost—if the ability is always active, for example—give it a duration (perhaps an hour) and a point cost. Usually the point cost would be the tier + 1.

Is the modified ability less powerful?
If so, reduce the point cost by at least 50 percent. If the ability has no cost to reduce, consider giving the character an extra skill.

Is the modified ability about the same?
Then call it even.

Sometimes a player wants to have an entirely new ability—not one from another type or focus, and not just a modification of an existing ability. In this case, the player and the GM should work out the details together, basing the power level of the new ability on the one that it is replacing. This is tricky, of course, but the broad strokes—damage inflicted, point cost, and so on—can be transferred if applicable, and minor aspects like range and duration should simply fit the new ability rather than be a "balance" consideration.

SWITCHING DESCRIPTORS AND FOCI AFTER CHARACTER CREATION

As the campaign goes along, it's possible that a player might want to switch the descriptor or focus that she chose when creating her character.

Moves Like a Cat, page 150

It's best if these changes occur organically rather than being forced. In other words, a character's descriptor changes because something happened in the game to change her, or her focus changes because a new opportunity arose in the course of play. (Don't do it if a player wants to change just for the sake of variety or to become more powerful in the current situation. In those cases, she should make a new character instead.)

Changing a descriptor is both easy and appropriate. For example, in the course of play, a Strong warrior's father is killed by a terrible villain. The warrior is fueled now by revenge. This story event could easily justify the warrior changing his descriptor to Vengeful or Driven. If he became a terrible person because of it, he might take the Dishonorable descriptor. Likewise, a Learned adept who falls into a vat of acid might become Hideous or Mad.

As with everything, switching descriptors and foci should be worked out between the player and the GM. The best play experiences come from good communication.

Of course, these characters lose their old descriptor and any benefits it conveyed, but that can be a part of the story, too. The Strong warrior who is now a Vengeful warrior stopped exercising and physically pushing his body. He might still be strong, but it's not his defining characteristic—he's not as strong as he was. He's vengeful instead. Likewise, the Learned adept forgets some of her schooling and loses her focus on such pursuits due to the accident that made her Hideous.

There's no limitation on the number of times a character can change his descriptor. For example, if the aforementioned warrior achieves his vengeance, maybe he goes back to being strong—as long as it fits the story.

Switching a focus is a bit trickier, and the story reason is probably more awkward. How does an explorer who Carries a Quiver become an explorer who Bears a Halo of Fire? The change likely involves time to train and a story reason. Perhaps the explorer trained at a monastery she found in the hills where they specialize in "fire magic," or maybe she discovered some fire-related device. Perhaps she was kidnapped by strange forces and bathed in weird energies. Almost anything is possible. You just have to work at it a bit.

Focus changes should occur only when a character attains a new tier, and it probably shouldn't be allowed more than once per character.

Mechanically, the new focus does not "overwrite" the old focus the way a new descriptor replaces an old descriptor. Instead, the old focus abilities remain, and at the new tier, the character gains an ability from the new focus, but the ability must come from a tier lower than the one just attained. For example, if our explorer who Carries a Quiver begins to Bear a Halo of Fire at third tier, she keeps her first-tier and second-tier abilities from carrying a quiver, and for her third-tier ability, she chooses either the first-tier or the second-tier ability from Bears a Halo of Fire (probably the first-tier ability, because that makes more sense). When she reaches fourth tier, she chooses from the first three tier abilities of Bears a Halo of Fire (although obviously she can't choose the one she already selected). The character always chooses new abilities from tiers lower than the one she attains in her new focus. This means that the only way to get the sixth-tier ability of a focus is to start with that focus.

Customizing foci, page 91

A character can't choose abilities from her former focus. Once the change is made, it's made.

TIERS ABOVE SIXTH

It will take a good long campaign to get a character up to the sixth tier. But what if you want to keep playing the character after that point? There is no seventh tier. Neither character types nor foci go beyond sixth.

However, you can simulate continued advancement quite easily. Allow characters to continue to pay for character benefits (4 XP each) as normal, with the following caveats:

- Do not allow characters to increase their Effort beyond 6. Instead, let them choose another skill or an alternative ability, such as adding 2 to their recovery rolls, reducing the cost of wearing armor, or selecting a new type ability.
- Do not allow a character to have an Edge higher than 6 in any one stat.
- When a character gains four benefits, he normally gains a new tier. Instead, allow him to choose another ability suited to his character type. Further, allow him to choose any ability (of any tier) from the options for customizing foci abilities.

It's likely that gameplay will become less satisfying after a while spent at tiers above sixth. Sixth-tier characters are already legendary in their prowess. Those who become even more powerful won't find most situations very challenging.

Part 3
GENRES

CHAPTER 11

FANTASY

For our purposes here, fantasy is any genre that has magic, or something so inexplicable it might as well be magic. The sort of core default of this type is Tolkienesque fantasy, also known as second-world fantasy because it includes a completely new world not our own. Big fantasy epics like those penned by J. R. R. Tolkien (hence the name), C. S. Lewis, George R. R. Martin, Stephen R. Donaldson, David Eddings, Ursula K. LeGuin, and others are indicative of this genre. It usually involves swords, sorcery, nonhuman races (such as elves, dwarves, and orcs), and epic struggles.

Elf, page 243

Dwarf, page 243

Orc, page 308

Of course, fantasy might also involve the modern world, with creatures of myth and sorcerers dwelling among us. It might involve mythic traditions of any number of cultures (elves, dwarves, and the like, usually being decidedly European) or bear little resemblance to anything on Earth, past or present. It might even involve some of the trappings of science fiction, with spaceships and laser guns amid the wizardry and swords (this is often called science fantasy).

Fantasy can also be defined by the amount of fantasy elements within it. A second-world fantasy filled with wizards, ghosts, dragons, curses, and gods is referred to as high fantasy. Fantasy with a firmer grounding in reality as we know it in our world is low fantasy. (In fact, low fantasy often takes place in our world, or in our world's distant past, like the stories of Conan.) No single element indicates concretely that a given fantasy is high or low. It's the prevalence of those elements.

The point is, there are many, many types of fantasy.

CREATING A FANTASY SETTING

There are so many fantasy settings—so many fantasy roleplaying game settings—out there that we don't need to dwell on this

topic much. If you're reading this, you've probably played a fantasy RPG. That said, here are a few things to keep in mind.

Default high fantasy needs bad guys in great numbers. That doesn't mean the stories always need to be about fighting, but rather that there is always a threat to cope with, and the threat is always of some dire evil.

Players need to understand the rules of the setting, at least a bit—not the Cypher System rules, but the rules of magic and the fantastical elements of the setting. Are faeries real or superstition? Can dead people be brought back to life? Are the gods real? Is there any limit to what a powerful wizard can do? These are the kinds of questions players need answers to so they can understand the world in which their characters live.

Spend at least a bit of time outlining the parameters of the fantasy elements of the world. Who's the most powerful wizard? Where does one go to find the mightiest artifact? Where does the most fearsome dragon dwell?

How do the normal people fit in? Who lives in the little villages the PCs will come upon, and how do they look at their world?

RUNNING A FANTASY GAME

Running a fantasy game means managing a lot of magic, including magic items and mystical creatures. In a default high fantasy, you might want the PCs to discover magic artifacts, like swords (which usually give an increase in damage or an asset to attacks), wands (which usually contain a dramatic power with a small number of uses), or rings (which usually have an always-on power that works like a free skill or asset). Also, keep the following in mind:

The default high fantasy setting is heroic. That is to say, brave heroes face overwhelming odds and win in the end. Good and evil are usually clearly defined. Orcs and demons are evil, and heroes are good.

Low fantasy tends to deal with protagonists struggling against a dark world. Rather than fighting to defeat the evil lord on an epic quest, low-fantasy characters might simply be trying to earn enough coins to pay for their supper. Low fantasy is often about survival. People frequently use words like "grim" and "gritty" to describe such stories.

Default high fantasy, probably more than any other genre, embraces the concept of lowly nobodies rising to great stature and power. "Zero to hero" is the phrase sometimes used. In the Cypher System, that likely means either slightly decreasing the power of the PCs at the lower tiers, or increasing them at higher tiers. The former is tricky, but the latter could come from an increase in opportunities to learn new skills (including attack and defense skills) starting at tier 4.

Type, page 22

Flavor, page 50

SUGGESTED TYPES FOR A FANTASY GAME

Role	Character Type
Warrior	Warrior
Knight	Warrior
Ranger	Explorer
Barbarian	Explorer flavored with combat
Thief	Explorer flavored with stealth
Wizard	Adept
Cleric	Speaker flavored with magic
Druid	Explorer flavored with magic
Warrior mage	Warrior flavored with magic
Bard	Speaker

SUGGESTED FOCI FOR A FANTASY GAME

Focus, page 90

Abides in Stone
Awakens Dreams
Bears a Halo of Fire
Blazes With Radiance
Builds Robots
Carries a Quiver
Casts Spells
Channels Divine Blessings
Commands Mental Powers
Consorts With the Dead
Controls Beasts
Crafts Illusions
Crafts Unique Objects
Defends the Weak
Entertains
Exists in Two Places at Once
Exists Partially Out of Phase
Explores Dark Places
Fights Dirty
Fights With Panache
Focuses Mind Over Matter
Howls at the Moon
Hunts Nonhumans
Hunts Outcasts
Hunts With Great Skill
Infiltrates
Leads
Lives in the Wilderness
Looks for Trouble
Masters Defense
Masters the Swarm
Masters Weaponry
Metes Out Justice
Moves Like a Cat
Murders
Needs No Weapon
Never Says Die
Performs Feats of Strength
Rides the Lightning
Sees Beyond
Separates Mind From Body
Shepherds Spirits
Siphons Power
Slays Monsters
Speaks for the Land
Stands Like a Bastion
Throws With Deadly Accuracy
Travels Through Time
Wears a Sheen of Ice
Wields Two Weapons at Once
Works Miracles
Works the Back Alleys

SUGGESTED CREATURES AND NPCs FOR A FANTASY GAME

Creatures, page 274

NPCs, page 334

Assassin
Chimera
Demigod
Demon
Devil
Djinni
Dragon
Dream sallow
Elemental
Fallen angel
Ghost
Ghoul
Giant
Giant rat
Giant snake
Giant spider
Goblin
Golem
Guard
Mechanical soldier
Occultist
Ogre
Orc
Shadow elf
Skeleton
Statue, animate
Thug/bandit
Vampire
Wendigo
Werewolf
Witch
Wizard, mighty
Zombie

OTHER CREATURES AND NPCs FOR A FANTASY GAME

Bat: level 1
Hawk: level 2; flies a long distance each round
Dog: level 2, perception as level 3
Dog, guard: level 3, attacks and perception as level 4
Horse: level 3; moves a long distance each round
Rat: level 1
Viper: level 2; bite inflicts 3 points of Speed damage (ignores Armor)
Warhorse: level 4; moves a long distance each round
Wolf: level 3, perception as level 4
Blacksmith: level 2, metalworking as level 4; health 8
Farmer: level 2, animal handling as level 3; health 8
Merchant: level 2, haggling and assessment tasks as level 3
Villager: level 1

ADDITIONAL FANTASY EQUIPMENT

In the default Medieval Europe-style fantasy setting, the following items (and anything else appropriate to that time period) are usually available.

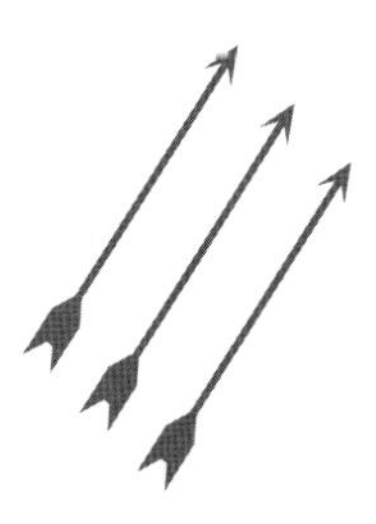

INEXPENSIVE ITEMS

Weapons	Notes
Arrows (12)	
Crossbow bolts (12)	
Knife (rusty and worn)	Light weapon (won't last long)
Wooden club	Light weapon

Other Items	Notes
Burlap sack	
Candle	
Iron rations (1 day)	
Torch (3)	

MODERATELY PRICED ITEMS

Weapons	Notes
Blowgun	Light weapon, immediate range
Dagger	Light weapon
Handaxe	Light weapon
Sword (substandard)	Medium weapon (won't last long)
Throwing knife	Light weapon, short range

Armor	Notes
Hides and furs	Light armor
Leather jerkin	Light armor

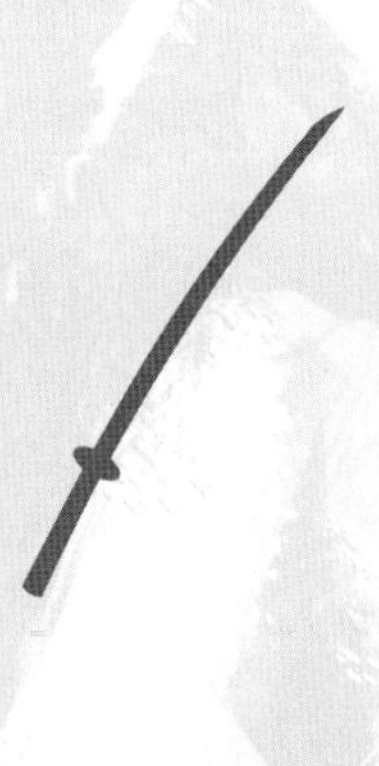

Other Items	Notes
Backpack	
Bedroll	
Crowbar	
Hourglass	
Lantern	
Rope	Hemp, 50 feet
Signal horn	
Spikes and hammer	10 spikes
Tent	

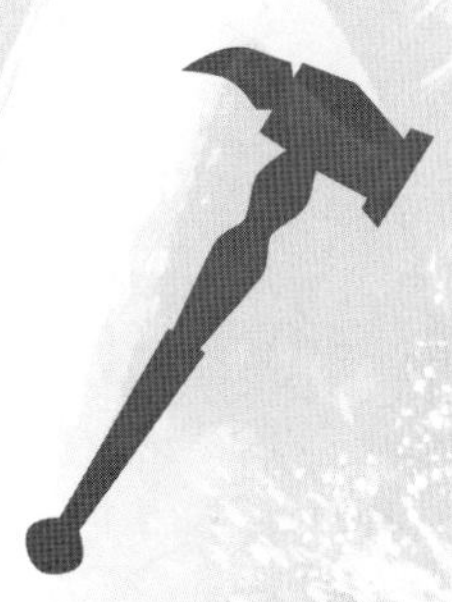

EXPENSIVE ITEMS

Weapons	Notes
Battleaxe	Medium weapon
Bow	Medium weapon, long range
Cutlass	Medium weapon
Light crossbow	Medium weapon, long range
Quarterstaff	Medium weapon (requires 2 hands)
Sword	Medium weapon

Armor	Notes
Breastplate	Medium armor
Brigandine	Medium armor
Chainmail	Medium armor

Other Items	Notes
Bag of heavy tools	
Bag of light tools	

VERY EXPENSIVE ITEMS

Weapons	Notes
Greatsword	Heavy weapon
Heavy crossbow	Heavy weapon, long range
Sword (jeweled)	Medium weapon

Armor	Notes
Dwarven breastplate	Medium armor, encumbers as light armor
Full plate armor	Heavy armor

Other Items	Notes
Disguise kit	Asset for disguise tasks
Healing kit	Asset for healing tasks
Spyglass	Asset for perception tasks at range

EXORBITANT ITEMS

Armor	Notes
Elven chainmail	Medium armor, encumbers as no armor

Other Items	Notes
Sailing ship (small)	

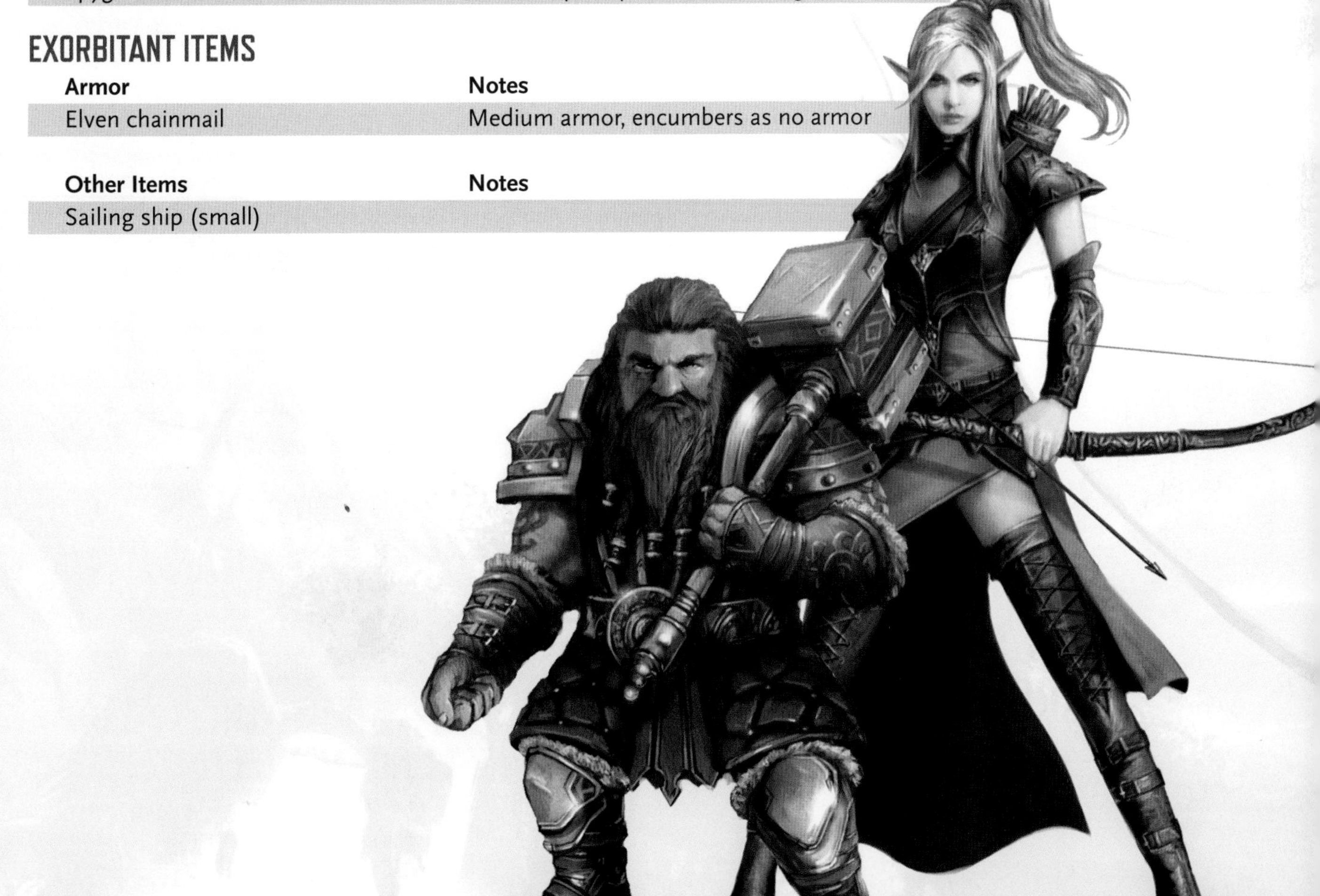

FANTASY ARTIFACTS

In many ways, fantasy is the genre for artifacts. All magic items—wands that shoot lightning, magic carpets, singing swords, rings that make the wearer invisible, and so on—are artifacts. Below are a few sample artifacts to give a template for GMs to follow. Those running a fantasy campaign will likely want to create many magic artifacts.

ANGELIC WARD

Level: 1d6 + 2

Form: A tiny figurine of a winged angel

Effect: Once activated, the figurine's spirit emerges and becomes semisolid as a glowing, human-sized winged angel. It follows within 3 feet (1 m) of the figurine owner. Anything within long range that attacks the owner is attacked by the spirit ward, which sends out a bolt of flesh-rotting energy, doing damage equal to the artifact's level. Once activated, it functions for a day.

Depletion: 1 in 1d10

RING OF DRAGON'S FLIGHT

Level: 1d6 + 2

Form: A green iron ring that appears like a dragon wound around the finger

Effect: When the wearer activates the ring, dragon wings unfurl from his back, and for one minute he can fly up to long range. The ring does not confer the ability to hover or make fine adjustments while in flight.

Depletion: 1 in 1d10

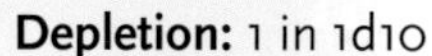

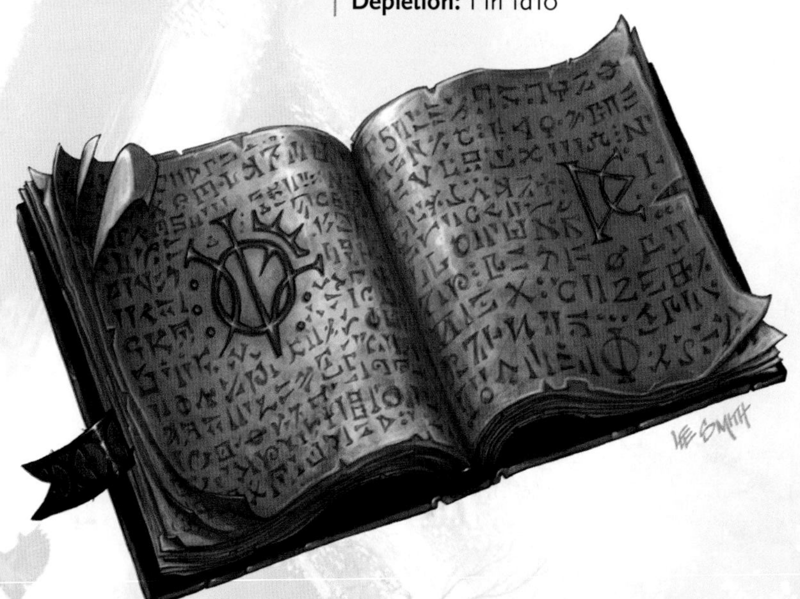

SOULFLAYING WEAPON

Level: 1d6 + 1

Form: A weapon of any type, with engraved glowing runes denoting soulflaying

Effect: This weapon functions as a normal weapon of its kind. The wielder can use an action to activate its soulflaying magic for one minute. During that time, if the weapon scores a hit, it inflicts normal damage, plus 3 additional points of Intellect damage on all creatures that have souls (not automatons, mindless undead, or the like).

Depletion: 1 in 1d100

SPELLBOOK OF THE AMBER MAGE

Level: 1d6

Form: A weighty tome bound in amber filled with pages of spell runes

Effect: When the user incants from the spellbook and succeeds at a level 3 Intellect-based task, she can attempt to trap a creature within long range inside a block of amber. Only creatures whose level is equal to or lower than the artifact's level can be targeted. A creature successfully caught is preserved in perfect stasis until the encasing amber is broken away (the amber has 10 points of health per level of the artifact).

Depletion: 1 in 1d20

WAND OF FIREBOLTS

Level: 1d6 + 2

Form: A wand of red wood 8 inches (20 cm) long, carved with intricate flamelike images

Effect: When activated, the wand looses a blast of fire at a chosen target within short range, inflicting damage equal to the artifact's level.

Depletion: 1 in 1d20

MIXING IT UP: FANTASY AND SCIENCE FICTION

Sword and planet. Science fantasy. There are many ways to mix fantasy and science fiction. If the base is fantasy, the science fiction elements usually are exceptions, with out-of-place high technology seeming almost like another kind of magic. Maybe a starship from another planet crashed in the fantasy world, or perhaps the occasional relic surfaces from a highly advanced civilization that flourished in ancient history. Perhaps a wizard opened a gate to the future or to a technological world and brought back wonders of science. The sudden appearance of a robot as the defender of a fantasy castle, or an evil knight producing a blaster rifle after being unhorsed in a joust, can be a fun and surprising twist on the genre.

RACIAL DESCRIPTORS

In a high fantasy setting, some GMs may want dwarves and elves to be mechanically different from humans. Below are some possibilities for how this might work.

DWARF

You're a stocky, broad-shouldered, bearded native of the mountains and hills. You're also as stubborn as the stone in which the dwarves carve their homes under the mountains. Tradition, honor, pride in smithcraft and warcraft, and a keen appreciation of the wealth buried under the roots of the world are all part of your heritage. Those who wish you ill should be wary of your temper. When a dwarf is wronged, he never forgets.

You gain the following characteristics:

Stalwart: +2 to your Might Pool.

Skill: You are trained in Might defense rolls.

Skill: You are trained in tasks related to stone, including sensing stonework traps, knowing the history of a particular piece of stonecraft, and knowing your distance beneath the surface.

Skill: You are practiced in using axes.

Skill: You are trained in using the tools required to shape and mine stone.

Inability: When you fail an Intellect defense roll to avoid damage, you take 1 extra point of damage.

Additional Equipment: You have an axe.

Initial Link to the Starting Adventure: From the following list of options, choose how you became involved in the first adventure.

1. You found the PCs wandering a maze of tunnels and led them to safety.
2. The PCs hired you to dig out the entrance to a buried ruin.
3. You tracked down the thieves of your ancestor's tomb and found they were the PCs. Instead of killing them, you joined them.
4. Before a dwarf settles down, he needs to see the world.

ELF

You haunt the woodlands and deep, natural realms, as your people have for millennia. You are the arrow in the night, the shadow in the glade, and the laughter on the wind. As an elf, you are slender, quick, graceful, and long lived. You manage the sorrows of living well past many mortal lifetimes with song, wine, and an appreciation for the deep beauties of growing things, especially trees, which can live even longer than you do.

You gain the following characteristics:

Agile: +2 to your Speed Pool.

Long-Lived: Your natural lifespan (unless tragically cut short) is thousands of years.

Skill: You are specialized in tasks related to perception.

Skill: You are practiced in using one bow variety of your choice.

Skill: You are trained in stealth tasks. In areas of natural woodland, you are specialized in stealth tasks.

Fragile: When you fail a Might defense roll to avoid damage, you take 1 extra point of damage.

Additional Equipment: You have a bow and a quiver of arrows to go with it.

Initial Link to the Starting Adventure: From the following list of options, choose how you became involved in the first adventure.

1. Before putting an arrow in the forest intruders, you confronted them and met the PCs, who were on an important quest.
2. Your heart yearned for farther shores, and the PCs offered to take you along to new places.
3. Your home was burned by strangers from another place, and you gathered the PCs along the way as you tracked down the villains.
4. An adventure was in the offing, and you didn't want to be left behind.

CHAPTER 12

MODERN

The modern setting is easy because it's just the real world, right? Well, yes and no. It's easy for players to understand the context of a modern setting. They know the default assumptions—cities, cars, cell phones, the Internet, and so on. It's also easier for some players to get into character, because their character could be someone they might very well pass on the street. It can be easier to wrap your mind around a history professor than a thousand-year-old elf wizard. These things make it easier on the GM as well.

But for the same reason, it's not easy. The setting is the real world we all know, so it's easy to get facts wrong or let them bog you down. What happens when you pull the fire alarm on the thirty-fifth floor of a major hotel in a large city? How fast do the authorities arrive? In truth, the facts aren't as important as the story you're creating, but some verisimilitude is nice.

CREATING A MODERN SETTING

You don't have to create a setting if the whole game takes place in London, Dallas, or the Outback, because those places really exist. The only time you need to do any worldbuilding is if you're creating original places (an amusement park that you made up) or organizations (a secret spy organization that the PCs belong to). Still, that doesn't mean you have no work to do. The modern world has implications to consider.

In a world with GPS, mobile phones, and the Internet, it's very difficult to imagine getting seriously lost, not being in communication, or not knowing the answer to a question. Rather than constantly thwart these truths (no cell phone reception here!), think of ways to use them.

You need to figure out what happens if the PCs just call the police rather than deal with a situation themselves.

You need to go the extra mile to make NPCs realistic and believable, because the players have real people to compare them to.

You need to decide if your campaign setting will remain in the real world or deviate from it. In other words, can campaign events break from the believable world we see around us? If aliens land in Nebraska in your game, and everyone knows it, the setting is no longer the world we see outside our window. (There is no wrong choice, but you still need to decide.)

RUNNING A MODERN GAME

Preparation is important in a modern game, and most of that entails being ready with realistic ramifications of potential PC actions. How quickly will the authorities arrive if the characters start a shootout with gangsters? What happens if the PCs are arrested? In a fantasy game, you can make things up as you go along—who's to say that the queen's guards wouldn't show up that quickly, or that faeries can't see in the dark? When the world is fictional, you have freedom. But when it's real, you need to know what you're talking about. Consider the following tips.

Use a phone book or an online directory to generate names for your NPCs.

Use real-world resources to get maps, photo references, forms, and similar items to enhance the game. You'll be surprised what you can find online for free.

Incorporate the PCs' real-world lives into the game. If the characters have jobs, work with the players to generate some details about those occupations. Real-world people have families, homes, friends, hobbies, and so on. Not only is that great for character development, but you can also work it into the story. If a PC always goes to the gym on Tuesday, have a significant plot encounter happen there.

MOLDING CHARACTERS FOR A MODERN GAME

If you're trying to portray a psychic with a few basic powers, you might not want to use the adept character type. Instead, choose a different type (perhaps a speaker) and encourage foci such as Commands Mental Powers or Focuses Mind Over Matter. Some of the adept's powers might be too over the top for the genre.

Similarly, the technology flavor is probably too high-tech for a modern game. For someone with technical skills, use the skills and knowledge flavor instead.

Sometimes, the types might be more physical than is always desirable for a modern game, but that's because the least physical type, the adept, is often inappropriate for other reasons. The Calm descriptor is very good for such characters, not only granting them a great deal of skill and knowledge, but also reducing their physical capabilities.

Last, don't forget foci such as Doesn't Do Much or Would Rather Be Reading for "normal" characters who have useful skills but not much in the way of flashy abilities.

Commands Mental Powers, page 107

Focuses Mind Over Matter, page 128

Calm, page 66

Flavor, page 50

Doesn't Do Much, page 118

Would Rather be Reading, page 181

Type, page 22

SUGGESTED TYPES FOR A MODERN GAME

Role	Type
Police officer	Explorer with combat flavor
Detective	Explorer with stealth flavor
Soldier	Warrior
Criminal	Explorer with stealth flavor
Teacher	Speaker
Professional (accountant, writer, etc.)	Speaker with skills and knowledge flavor
Technical profession	Explorer with skills and knowledge flavor
Dilettante	Speaker with skills and knowledge flavor
Doctor/Nurse	Explorer with skills and knowledge flavor
Politician	Speaker
Lawyer	Speaker
Scholar	Explorer with skills and knowledge flavor
Occultist	Adept
Mystic/Psychic	Adept

SUGGESTED FOCI FOR A MODERN GAME

Calculates the Incalculable
Commands Mental Powers*
Conducts Weird Science
Consorts With the Dead*
Crafts Unique Objects
Doesn't Do Much
Entertains
Explores Dark Places
Fights Dirty
Focuses Mind Over Matter
Howls at the Moon*
Hunts Outcasts*
Hunts With Great Skill
Infiltrates
Interprets the Law
Is Idolized by Millions
Is Licensed to Carry
Leads
Lives in the Wilderness
Looks for Trouble
Masters the Swarm*
Masters Weaponry
Moves Like a Cat
Murders
Needs No Weapon
Never Says Die
Operates Undercover
Sees Beyond*
Separates Mind From Body*
Slays Monsters*
Solves Mysteries
Throws With Deadly Accuracy
Wields Two Weapons at Once
Works the Back Alleys
Works the System
Would Rather Be Reading

** Only if the setting has a supernatural element*

SUGGESTED CREATURES AND NPCs FOR A MODERN GAME

Assassin
Crime boss
Detective
Ghost
Giant rat
Giant snake
Giant spider
Guard (works for police officers and soldiers as well)
Occultist
Secret agent
Thug/bandit

OTHER CREATURES AND NPCs FOR A MODERN GAME

Cat: level 1, Speed defense as level 3
Dog: level 2, perception as level 3
Dog, guard: level 3, attacks and perception as level 4
Horse: level 3; moves a long distance each round
Rat: level 1
Businessperson: level 1
Clerk: level 1
Worker: level 2; health 8

ADDITIONAL MODERN EQUIPMENT

In a modern setting, the following items (and anything else appropriate to the real world) are usually available.

INEXPENSIVE ITEMS

Weapons	Notes
Ammo (box of 50 rounds)	
Knife (simple)	Light weapon (won't last long)

Other Items	Notes
Duct tape roll	
Flashlight	
Padlock with keys	
Trail rations (1 day)	

MODERATELY PRICED ITEMS

Weapons	Notes
Hand grenade	Explosive weapon, inflicts 4 points of damage in immediate radius
Hunting knife	Light weapon
Machete	Medium weapon
Nightstick	Light weapon

Armor	Notes
Leather jacket	Light armor

Other Items	Notes
Backpack	
Bag of heavy tools	
Bag of light tools	
Binoculars	Asset for perception tasks at range
Bolt cutters	
Cell phone	
Climbing gear	
Crowbar	
Electric lantern	
First aid kit	Asset for healing tasks
Handcuffs	
Rope	Nylon, 50 feet
Sleeping bag	
Tent	

EXPENSIVE ITEMS

Weapons	Notes
Light handgun	Light weapon, short range
Medium handgun	Medium weapon, long range
Bow	Medium weapon, long range
Rifle	Medium weapon, long range
Shotgun	Heavy weapon, immediate range

Armor	Notes
Kevlar vest	Medium armor

Other Items	Notes
Camera designed to be concealed	Transmits at long range
Microphone designed to be concealed	Transmits at long range
Cold weather camping gear	
Nightvision goggles	
Scuba gear	
Smartphone	
Straightjacket	

VERY EXPENSIVE ITEMS

Heavy handgun	Heavy weapon, long range
Assault rifle	Heavy weapon, rapid-fire weapon, long range
Heavy rifle	Heavy weapon, 300-foot (91 m) range
Submachine gun	Medium weapon, rapid-fire weapon, short range

Armor	Notes
Lightweight body armor	Medium armor, encumbers as light armor
Military body armor	Heavy armor

Other Items	Notes
Disguise kit	Asset for disguise tasks
Used car	Level 3
Small boat	Level 3

EXORBITANT ITEMS

Other Items	Notes
Large boat	Level 5
Luxury car	Level 5
Sports car	Level 6

MODERN ARTIFACTS

The concept of artifacts is probably inappropriate for a modern setting without some kind of supernatural, fantastical, or science fiction element. The exception to this would be in an espionage-focused game, where characters are given special high-tech items that have limited uses, such as a jacket with buttons that can be used as grenades, or a watch that conceals a laser. If your modern setting has supernatural elements, look to one of the other appropriate genre chapters for artifact ideas.

MIXING IT UP: MODERN AND FANTASY

Often labeled "urban fantasy," stories of wizards and fantastic creatures living among us in the modern world (usually covertly, but not always) can make for a fun campaign. It mixes the crazy weirdness of fantasy with the comfortable familiarity of the real world. The PCs could be lurkers in the shadows, combating evil spellcasters, vampires, werewolves, and other creatures to safeguard the world we know. Alternatively, the characters could be young wizards just discovering their powers, perhaps gathering at a school to master their abilities.

HISTORICAL GAMING

A subset of "modern" is "historical." Setting your campaign in World War 2, the Renaissance, or the 1930s can be fun and interesting. However, setting it in ancient Greece or feudal Japan, for example, probably makes it more like fantasy without all the orcs and magic (although a game set in feudal Japan with orcs and magic could be fascinating).

The big challenge with historical gaming is often the tech (or lack thereof) that the PCs have access to. For example, foci such as Infiltrates and Works the System assume some level of technology or magic. That might mean such foci must be altered or even disallowed in a game set in the Old West or Napoleonic France.

To prepare for that sort of game, all you need is a good history book on the time period in question. For even more flavorful ideas, look for a book that specifically details what life was like in the time period. This will go beyond battles and dates and give you a good feel for what it was like to live in ancient Egypt or in a Mayan city-state.

Of course, you can mix other genres into a historical game. A horror Old West game, for example, would be cool. Fantasy games set in Medieval Europe or the ancient Middle East are obvious choices. More interesting and innovative might be a fantasy game set in Africa a thousand years ago. And a Victorian science fiction game would simply be steampunk.

CHAPTER 13

SCIENCE FICTION

Science fiction is an incredibly broad category. It covers UFOs, space opera, near-future dystopias, otherworldly epics, and everything in between. Even when compared to fantasy, science fiction is so wide that it almost isn't a single genre at all. Truthfully, there's not all that much to tie, say, *The Time Machine* by H. G. Wells with a dark cyberpunk story except for the technology involved, which is at a higher level than we possess or understand today. But even that part of science fiction is contentious. Should the science be purely that which obeys the laws of physics as we understand them today (often called hard science fiction), or is it more of an "anything goes" proposition? Is science we can't explain really just magic?

A careful definition of each genre isn't important here. Whether your setting is fantasy or science fiction is up to you. The difference is just nomenclature.

For our purposes here, we'll think of futuristic space opera as the default: aliens, spaceships that allow travel to other stars, energy weapons and shields, and so on. It's a familiar setting to almost everyone interested in science fiction. But your science fiction setting can be anything you can imagine.

CREATING A SCIENCE FICTION SETTING

Crafting a futuristic science fiction setting is a lot of work. You've got to think about technology levels, the history that led up to the setting, future society, future government, communications, alien races, and more. Consider these suggestions.

Don't reinvent the wheel. If there's a science fiction setting that does a lot of what you like, steal liberally from it. If it's useful to your players, be upfront about the setting you're borrowing from to give them context.

Don't explain more than you need to. Your setting has faster-than-light travel? Great. Unless it's integral to the story (or fun for you), don't worry about explaining it.

Don't create more than you need to. Be ready to tell the PCs what they see and who they encounter when they set down on a new planet, but don't design a lot of alien races, cultures, and worlds that they will probably never see.

Use broad strokes. Give each alien species and planet one or maybe two unique aspects. Don't worry about creating a fully conceived culture or environment. More than likely, your PCs will hang around for only a session at most before they rocket off to someplace new.

RUNNING A SCIENCE FICTION GAME

The main reason that science fiction roleplaying games become problematic is that the players don't fully understand their options. If the PCs are the crew of a starship, the players don't know all the things the ship can and can't do. To make matters worse, they don't know where they can and can't travel in the ship, and what the ramifications of their travel will be. Modern settings and even fantasy settings have an inherent context that players grab hold of almost instinctively.

Similarly, GMs of science fiction settings sometimes flounder wondering what PCs should do. Fantasy is easier because there are very manageable genre tropes (go into the dungeon and fight the dark lord) and explanations for whatever the GM wants to have happen (it's magic). But science fiction involves, well, science, and we don't all have a mastery of advanced biology or quantum mechanics. The trick is not to worry about it too much. As Arthur C. Clarke said, "Any sufficiently advanced technology is indistinguishable from magic," so you can often toss off super high-tech explanations for almost anything without having an advanced degree. On the other hand, it's okay to have people in a science fiction

Want a science fiction dungeon? How about a derelict alien spacecraft drifting in space? "Dungeon" exploration in environment suits gives the experience a whole new wrinkle.

setting act like people in the modern world (commute to work, go to restaurants, live in apartments, enjoy a variety of entertainment, and so on). Just change the trappings a bit to seem more futuristic. You're not trying to predict the future of culture and society as it is shaped by technology and events. You're trying to run an entertaining game session.

Here are a few other tips to consider.

Be generous with players who want to extrapolate the science elements of the game. If someone wants to reconfigure the ship's sensor array to do something odd but useful, let her try.

Don't be afraid of a little exposition. Explain the normal procedures for docking with another spaceship, and then let the PCs decide if they should do that or something else. Don't forget that the characters have a lot of knowledge that the players do not.

When trying to figure out what the PCs should do, steal plots from science fiction stories you like. Science fiction rarely has dungeons to explore or evil wizards to defeat (although versions of both are possible), so coming up with the story can be more challenging.

Science fiction has room for small stories as well as those in which the heroes save the whole galaxy. In such a large setting, in fact, small, character-driven stories are probably best.

Type, page 22

Flavor, page 50

SUGGESTED TYPES FOR A SCIENCE FICTION GAME

Role	Type
Soldier	Warrior
Technician	Explorer with technology flavor
Pilot	Explorer with technology flavor
Diplomat	Speaker
Doctor	Speaker with skills and knowledge flavor
Spy	Explorer with stealth flavor
Scientist	Explorer
Psion	Adept
Psychic knight	Warrior with magic flavor

Focus, page 90

SUGGESTED FOCI FOR A SCIENCE FICTION GAME

Battles Robots
Builds Robots
Calculates the Incalculable
Commands Mental Powers
Conducts Weird Science
Doesn't Do Much
Entertains
Fights Dirty
Fights With Panache
Focuses Mind Over Matter
Fuses Flesh and Steel
Fuses Mind and Machine
Hunts Nonhumans
Infiltrates
Interprets the Law
Is Idolized by Millions
Looks for Trouble
Masters Defense
Masters Weaponry
Moves Like a Cat
Murders
Needs No Weapon
Never Says Die
Operates Undercover
Pilots Starcraft
Siphons Power
Solves Mysteries
Talks to Machines
Travels Through Time
Works the Back Alleys
Works the System
Would Rather Be Reading

Creatures, page 274

NPCs, page 334

SUGGESTED CREATURES AND NPCs FOR A SCIENCE FICTION GAME

Assassin
Blitzer
Chronophage
CRAZR
Deinonychus
Enthraller
Ghoul
Giant spider
Grey
Guard
Kaiju
Mechanical soldier
Mi-go
Mokuren
Neveri
Philethis
Ravage bear
Replicant
Scrap drone
Secret agent
Thug/bandit
Tyrannosaurus rex
Vat reject
Wardroid
Xenoparasite
Zhev
Zombie

OTHER CREATURES AND NPCs FOR A SCIENCE FICTION GAME

Innocuous rodent: level 1
Guard beast: level 3, perception as level 4
Corporate drone: level 1
Physical laborer: level 2; health 8

ADDITIONAL SCIENCE FICTION EQUIPMENT

In a science fiction setting, the following items (and anything else appropriate to the setting) are usually available.

INEXPENSIVE ITEMS

Weapons	Notes
Energy pack (50 shots)	
Knife (simple)	Light weapon

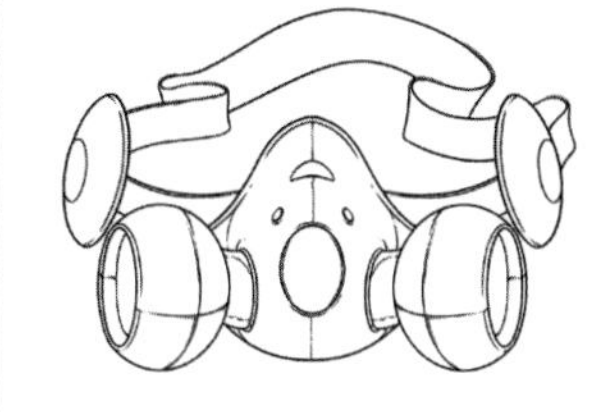

Other Items	Notes
Flashlight	
Survival rations (1 day)	

MODERATELY PRICED ITEMS

Weapons	Notes
Hunting knife	Light weapon
Machete	Medium weapon
Grenade (sonic)	Explosive weapon, inflicts 2 points of damage in immediate radius, plus Might defense roll or lose next turn
Grenade (thermite)	Explosive weapon, inflicts 5 points of damage in immediate radius

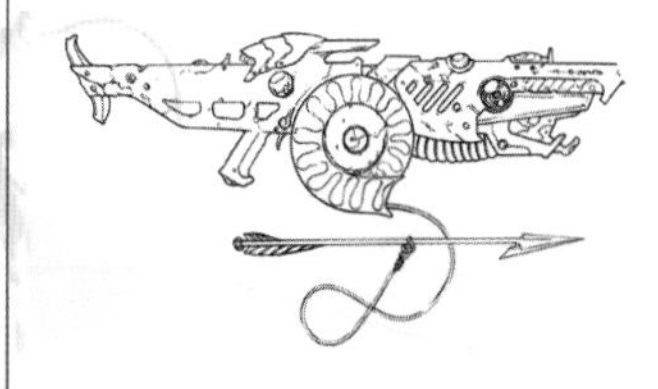

Armor	Notes
Leather jacket	Light armor

Other Items	Notes
Backpack	
Bag of heavy tools	
Bag of light tools	
Binoculars	Asset for perception tasks at range
Breather	8 hours of breathable air
Climbing gear	Asset for climbing tasks
Communicator	Planetary range
Crowbar	
Environment tent	
First aid kit	Asset for healing tasks
Handcuffs	
Nightvision goggles	
Portable lamp	
Rope	Nylon, 50 feet
Sleeping bag	

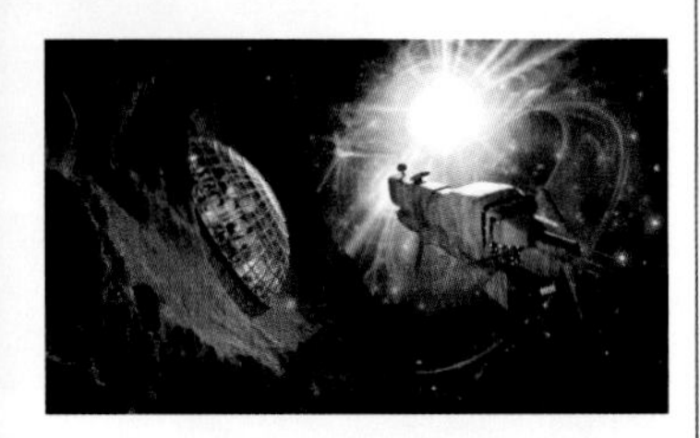

Remember, armor (lowercase a) is something you wear. Armor (capital A) is the bonus you get. You can have only one type of armor at a time, but you can have many sources of Armor, theoretically.

EXPENSIVE ITEMS

Weapons	Notes
Light blaster	Light weapon, short range
Medium blaster	Medium weapon, long range
Needler	Light weapon, long range
Shotgun	Heavy weapon, immediate range
Stunstick	Medium weapon, inflicts no damage but human-sized or smaller target loses next action

Armor	Notes
Armored bodysuit	Medium armor
Lightweight body armor	Medium armor

Other Items	Notes
Camera designed to be concealed	Transmits at long range
Microphone designed to be concealed	Transmits at long range
Environment suit	Provides 24 hours of atmosphere and +10 to Armor against extreme temperatures
Wrist computer	Asset for most knowledge-based tasks

VERY EXPENSIVE ITEMS

Weapons	Notes
Heavy blaster	Heavy weapon, long range
Heavy blaster rifle	Heavy weapon, 300-foot (91 m) range
Pulse laser gun	Medium weapon, rapid-fire weapon, long range

Armor	Notes
Battlesuit	Heavy armor, also works as environment suit

Other Items	Notes
Disguise kit	Asset for disguise tasks
Gravity regulator	Belt-mounted device that regulates gravity to 1 G for wearer if within 0 G to 3 G conditions
Handheld scanner	Asset for identifying tasks
Hovercraft	Level 4
Infiltrator	Asset for lockpicking tasks when used with electronic locks
Jetpack	Level 4
Stealthsuit	Asset for stealth tasks

EXORBITANT ITEMS

Weapons	Notes
Blast cannon	10 points of damage, 500-foot (152 m) range, requires a tripod and two people to operate

Armor	Notes
Force field	Not armor, offers +1 to Armor

Other Items	Notes
Luxury hovercar	Level 5
Robot servant	Level 3
Small spaceship	Level 4

SCIENCE FICTION ARTIFACTS

Artifacts in a science fiction game can be strange relics from an unknown alien source or tech items that aren't yet widely available. In a galactic setting, for example, it's easy to imagine that innovations or specialized items might not have spread everywhere.

AMBER CASEMENT

Level: 1d6 + 4

Form: A series of short, rounded tubes and hoses about 12 inches (30 cm) long

Effect: The device solidifies the air in a 10-foot (3 m) cube of space, the center of which must be within short range. The air is turned into an amberlike substance, and those trapped in it will likely suffocate or starve.

Depletion: 1–4 in 1d6

METABOLISM BUD

Level: 1d6

Form: An organic pod, almost like a small, hemispherical bit of brain; once grafted to a host, the host's flesh grows over the pod until it is only a lump

Effect: The pod grafts onto any living host (usually near the brain or spine) and injects chemicals that boost the creature's metabolism. This permanently raises the host's Speed Pool maximum by 5 points.

Depletion: —

MIND IMAGER

Level: 1d6 + 2

Form: A handheld device with a plastic panel screen and wires that must be affixed to the head of a creature

Effect: This device shows a visual image of what a creature is thinking. The affected creature need not be conscious.

Depletion: 1 in 1d20

PSYCHIC CRYSTAL

Level: 1d6 + 4

Form: A violet crystal the size of a fist

Effect: The crystal allows the user to transmit his thoughts telepathically at an interstellar distance. Even at that range, communication is instantaneous. Each use allows about a minute's worth of communication, and the communication is entirely one way (so having two crystals would be handy).

Depletion: 1 in 1d10

REPAIR SPHERE

Level: 1d6 + 2

Form: A small spherical automaton about 8 inches (20 cm) in diameter

Effect: This device comes with a small module that can be affixed to a machine. Floating along, the sphere attempts to follow within immediate range of the module (though it can be directed to remain where it is). It moves a short

STARSHIPS

Here are a few sample starship types:

Starship	Level	Crew	Weapon Systems
Fighter	1	1	1
Interceptor	2	1	1
Freighter	3 (4 for defense)	4	1
Frigate	4	20	4
Cruiser	4	25	5
Battleship	10	1,000	36

"Crew" indicates the minimum number of people needed to operate the ship. Many ships can carry more passengers. "Weapon Systems" indicates the maximum number of different enemies the ship can target at once (but only one attack per ship in any circumstance).

Since it's frighteningly easy to die in a space battle if your ship is destroyed, most ships have escape pods. Even fighter craft have ejection systems that put the pilot out into space in an environment suit. In other words, GMs should try to give PCs a way out of immediately dying if they get on the wrong end of a space battle.

distance each round. It can come to the module from a range of up to 10 miles (16 km) away. If the module is attached to a machine and that machine takes damage, the sphere moves to repair the damage with sophisticated tools that restore 1d6 – 2 points per round (meaning that if a 1 or 2 is rolled, no damage is repaired that round). This requires no action on the part of the machine being repaired. The sphere can attempt to repair a machine a number of times per day equal to its level. The sphere must be newly activated each day.
Depletion: 1 in 1d100

MIXING IT UP: SCIENCE FICTION AND MODERN

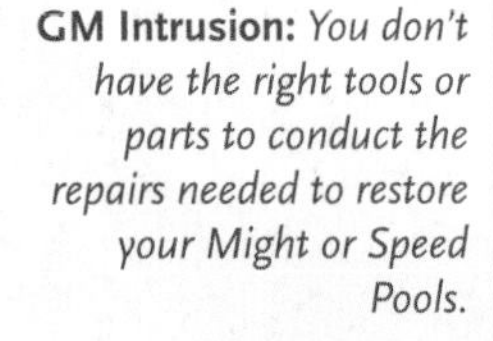

GM Intrusion: *You don't have the right tools or parts to conduct the repairs needed to restore your Might or Speed Pools.*

The truth is out there. What if there are aliens among us? What if scientists and secret cabals are using fringe science to create weapons and devices that modern society can't even comprehend? The theme here is that science—alien or otherwise—with all its wonders and horrors is intruding upon our normal lives. Lurking in the shadows, PCs in such a campaign would know glimpses of the truth but would always be questing for more. Perhaps they work for a secret society or a covert government agency assigned to deal with the growing alien menace. Conspiracies, intrigue, and secrets are the hallmarks of this kind of campaign, which could easily incorporate elements of horror as well.

RACIAL DESCRIPTORS

In a science fiction setting, some GMs may want to offer alien races or androids, who are mechanically different from humans, as options for player characters. This can be accomplished by using descriptors. Two examples are below.

ARTIFICIALLY INTELLIGENT

You are a machine—not just a sentient machine, but a sapient one. Your awareness might make you an exception, or there may be many like you, depending on the setting.

Artificially intelligent characters have machine minds of one type or another. This can involve an advanced computer brain, but it could also be a liquid computer,

a quantum computer, or a network of smart dust particles creating an ambient intelligence. You might even have been an organic creature whose mind was uploaded into a machine.

Your body, of course, is also a machine. Most people refer to you as a robot or an android, although you know neither term describes you very well, as you are as free-willed and free-thinking as they are.

You gain the following characteristics:

Superintelligent: +4 to your Intellect Pool.

Artificial Body: +3 to your Might Pool and your Speed Pool.

Shell: +1 to Armor.

Limited Recovery: Resting restores points only to your Intellect Pool, not to your Might Pool or your Speed Pool.

Mechanics, Not Medicines: Conventional healing methods, including the vast majority of restorative devices and medicines, do not restore points to any of your Pools. You can recover points to your Intellect Pool only by resting, and you can recover points to your Speed and Might Pools only through repair. The difficulty of the repair task is equal to the number of points of damage sustained, to a maximum of 10. Repairing your Might and Speed Pools are always two different tasks.

Machine Vulnerabilities and Invulnerabilities: Damaging effects and other threats that rely on an organic system—poison, disease, cell disruption, and so on—have no effect on you. Neither do beneficial drugs or other effects. Conversely, things that normally affect only inorganic or inanimate objects can affect you, as can effects that disrupt machines.

Uncanny Valley: You have a hard time relating to organic beings, and they don't react well to you. The difficulty of all positive interaction tasks with such beings is increased by two steps.

QUINTAR

You are a quintar from the planet Quint. You are basically humanoid but taller, thinner, and blue skinned. Your hands end in three very long fingers. Quintar have five genders, but all quintar prefer to be addressed as a female when speaking to more binary species. Human emotions and sexuality fascinate them, but not because they don't have such concepts—quintar emotions and sexuality are just very different from those of humans. In general, quintar are more cerebral than other races, valuing knowledge over all else.

Quint is relatively Earthlike, with slightly less gravity but a slightly denser atmosphere.

You gain the following characteristics:

Cerebral: +4 to your Intellect Pool.

Skill: You are trained in one type of knowledge task of your choice.

Skill: Quintar fascination with human behavior decreases the difficulty of all interaction rolls (pleasant or not) with humans by one step.

Difficult Rest: Quintar subtract 2 from all recovery rolls (minimum 1).

The varjellen and the lattimor in Numenera would make good alien races for a science fiction game. See the Numenera *corebook, pages 121–122.*

CHAPTER 14

HORROR

Although it's very likely a subset of the modern genre, horror as a genre gets special treatment. Unlike the other genres, horror doesn't necessarily suggest a setting. Any setting can be horrific. Horror is more of a style. An approach. A mood.

You could easily have horror in other times and settings, but for our purposes, we'll deal with a default setting in the modern day. The PCs are probably normal people, not secret agents or special investigators (although being a part of a secret agency that deals with monsters in the shadows could make for a fine horror game).

Suggested foci, types, and additional equipment for a horror setting are the same as in a modern setting, so refer to Chapter 12: Modern for that information.

Chapter 12: Modern, page 244

CREATING A HORROR SETTING

Whatever the setting, the main thing to remember when preparing to run a horror-themed game is that if everything is terrifying, nothing is. Think about every good horror movie you've seen or story you've read, in which scenes of horror are paced nicely with scenes of normal life. The key is the contrast. People need rising and falling tension, or they will break from the story. So you need a setting that has ordinary scenes, encounters, and events as well as horrific ones. Even a world overcome by hordes of zombies needs to offer moments of respite for the characters.

RUNNING A HORROR GAME

Running a good horror game is difficult. You've got to maintain mood and atmosphere at almost all times. Consider these tips.

Give the players time to develop their characters before going to the haunted house, spooky cemetery, or mysterious ruin. Let them get attached to the characters, at least a little, so that when those PCs are in jeopardy, the players will be frightened.

Use music, lighting, and the environment to help create a mood. Don't hesitate to use candles or flashlights in a dark room rather than conventional lighting. Shake things up—if you normally play in the dining room when you run sessions in other genres, play in the basement for your horror game.

Unnerve your players as well as the characters. As you describe a scene in the game, occasionally glance out the window or toward the door, particularly if it's behind one or more players, as though you hear something strange. Make it seem like creepy things are going on, but be subtle. Make the players sense it without being fully aware of it.

Startle the players as well as the characters. When the monster finally appears, shout at the top of your lungs! Turn out the lights suddenly. Do something shocking.

Horror games are often one-shot sessions or a short arc of a few sessions. They are very difficult to run as long-term campaigns, but it's possible. If that's what you want, remember that you need rising and falling tension. There must be respites and calm moments between the horror.

Horror needs to be brutal and ruthless, even if—or rather, especially if—other games you run are relatively safe for PCs. Kill characters. Maim characters.

Focus on the startling and unexpected when possible. Blood and gore can be shocking sometimes, but only in a context in which they are unexpected. In other words, they might be expected on a battlefield, but not in the middle of a happy religious ceremony or family gathering.

Fear of the unknown is the greatest, most primal fear. It's the thing the PCs don't see that scares them the most. Take your time and allow them to hear the horrific creature approach before the encounter begins. Let them see its shadow before they see the rest of it. Let them react to the unknown threat before they can identify it.

Creatures, page 274

NPCs, page 334

SUGGESTED CREATURES AND NPCs FOR A HORROR GAME

Assassin
Chronophage
Crime boss
Deep one
Demigod
Demon
Devil
Dream sallow
Enthraller
Ghost
Ghoul
Giant rat
Giant spider
Guard
Killing white light
Mi-go
Neveri
Nuppeppo
Occultist
Ravage bear
Replicant
Secret agent
Skeleton
Slidikin
Statue, animate
Thug/bandit
Vampire
Wendigo
Werewolf
Witch
Xenoparasite
Zombie

OTHER CREATURES AND NPCs FOR A HORROR GAME

Cat: level 1, Speed defense as level 3
Dog: level 2, perception as level 3
Dog, vicious: level 3, attacks and perception as level 4
Rat: level 1
Tarantula: level 1
Businessperson: level 1
Clerk: level 1
Groundskeeper/caretaker: level 2; health 8
Man in Black: level 4; carries weird weapons, including those with long range

HORROR ARTIFACTS

Most of the time, a horror artifact will be something really weird—an ancient tome of forbidden necromancy, an alien device that humans can barely understand, and so forth. They are often unique items rather than one of a type. Horror artifacts should probably come with a risk, such as a built-in cost, a drawback, or something else that makes using them another way to heighten the tension of the game. A couple of examples are below.

BOOK OF INVERSION

Level: 8
Form: A very large book of ancient providence, the cover bound in iron and wrapped in chains with a level 6 padlock
Effect: When opened, the Book of Inversion shows a pair of pages that detail a magic spell in the reader's language, complete with disturbing diagrams. The spell's effect varies, but it is always some kind of horrible attack—a target is driven mad, a target is turned inside out, a target seeks to murder her best friend, several targets are cursed with a rotting disease, and so forth. The reader can automatically cast the spell as an action, one time only. More insidiously, if successful, the spell confers pleasure to the caster and fully restores all of his Pools. The caster must make an immediate Intellect defense roll or be compelled to use the book (and thus a new spell) again in the next twenty-four hours. This compulsion is so strong that the caster will kill his dearest loved one to complete the task. If he is unable to use the book again, he is driven permanently mad. Woe to the caster who uses the book on the last time before it is depleted (at which point it crumbles to dust).
Depletion: 1 in 1d10

SHADOW BOX

Level: 7
Form: A wooden and black metal box, about 12 inches by 7 inches by 3 inches (30 by 18 by 8 cm), with a hinged lid and a clasp
Effect: When the box opens, shadows seethe out. These shadows coalesce into a form that best represents a deep fear in the subconscious of the person

who opened the box. The opener must make an Intellect defense roll to master the shadow thing, which then acts as a level 7 creature under her control for five rounds before fading away. If the roll fails, the creature attacks the opener and anyone else around. To make matters worse, the opener spends the first round frozen in terror, doing nothing.

Depletion: 1–2 in 1d6

SPHERE 23

Level: 1d6 + 4

Form: A 7-inch (18 cm) sphere of what appears to be fluid metal, tinted red

Effect: Possibly one of a number of identical alien artifacts recovered in remote locales across the earth, the so-called sphere 23 will grant a wish to anyone who holds it and uses an action to concentrate on it. The wish can be anything, including something that bends reality: raising the dead, altering time, and so forth. However, the wisher must immediately make a Might defense roll or be consumed by the sphere. If the roll succeeds, he must then make an Intellect defense roll or be driven permanently and irrevocably mad.

Depletion: 1–3 in 1d6

OPTIONAL RULE: SHOCK

When the PCs encounter something shocking, many times the most realistic response is to scream, stand in abject horror, or run. That might not be the smartest thing to do in the situation, but it's genuine. What would your accountant do if he saw an axe-wielding maniac coming at him? Let's face it, unless he truly steeled himself with all his will, he'd probably scream and run.

When a PC encounters something horrific, utterly disgusting, dreadful, impossible, or otherwise shocking, call for an Intellect defense roll based on the level of the creature involved, or simply an appropriate level as decided by the GM (see below). Failure might mean that for one round, the player loses control of the character, and the GM decides what the PC does next. This usually means that the

SHOCK LEVELS

Event	Level
Something unexpected darts or jumps out	1
Something suddenly moves just out of the corner of the eye	2
A sudden loud noise (like a scream)	2
Unexpectedly seeing a corpse	2
Watching someone die	3
Seeing something impossible (like an inanimate object sliding across the floor)	4
Watching a friend die	5
Seeing a monstrous creature	Creature level
Witnessing something supernatural (like a spell)	5
Seeing something mind-bending (like an impossible, multidimensional demigod coalescing out of thin air)	8

A GM intrusion is often appropriate in sanity-blasting moments that make a PC faint, run away screaming, or stand and gibber, unable to form a coherent thought. This lives outside the mechanics of the shock optional rule.

character runs, screams, gibbers, stares slack-jawed, or just does nothing. However, GMs should welcome player input into this situation. The point is to portray that when we're shocked, we don't always react in the best way, the smartest way, or even the way we want to. Fear is a powerful thing.

Alternatively, failure on the Intellect defense roll might mean that the character suffers Intellect damage equal to the level of the defense task. This indicates an overall toll that numerous shocks and horrors can have on a person. You might have a situation where a character literally dies of fright.

OPTIONAL RULE: HORROR MODE

Horror Mode is a very "meta" rule. It gives players knowledge that their characters don't have. This is similar to how the viewers of a horror movie or readers of a horror story often know more than the characters on the screen or page. It heightens the tension. Players can express the start of Horror Mode by having their characters talk about goosebumps or a feeling of being watched, but this is not necessary.

For horror games, GMs can implement a rule called Horror Mode. The idea is to create a feeling of escalating dread and menace by changing one die roll mechanic. In the game, things begin as normal. The PCs interact with each other and the NPCs, investigate, research, travel, and so on. But when they enter the haunted house, the serial killer gets close, the elder things beneath the earth awaken, or whatever horrific situation planned by the GM begins, things change. At this time, the GM announces that the game has gone into Horror Mode.

This is a key for the players (not the characters) to recognize that things are getting bad. It's the RPG equivalent of spooky music beginning to play in a horror film. While in Horror Mode, the rules for GM intrusions governed by die rolls change. Normally this happens only on a roll of 1, but when Horror Mode starts, it becomes a roll of 1 or 2. And then it escalates. As time passes, GM intrusions happen on a roll of 1 to 3, then a roll of 1 to 4, and so on. This potentially means that a die roll in Horror Mode can indicate success in a task and still trigger a GM intrusion.

As the intrusion range changes with each escalation, the GM should announce this to the players. The feeling of rising tension should be dramatic and overt.

ESCALATION RATE

Activity	Intrusion range increases by 1
Exploring a large area	Every time a new intrusion is indicated by a die roll
Exploring	Every ten minutes or every time a new intrusion is indicated by a die roll
Combat	Each round

For example, while the PCs are exploring a dark swamp (a large area), the game goes into Horror Mode and intrusions are indicated on a 1 or 2. During this exploration, one of the players rolls a 2. Not only is there an intrusion, but now the range escalates to 1, 2, or 3. The character is almost dragged into a spot of quicksand-like muck. Then the PCs find an old abandoned house in the middle of the swamp. They enter, and now the escalation rate goes up if they roll a 1, 2, or 3, or every ten minutes that passes in the game. They explore the house for twenty minutes (escalating intrusions to 1 to 5), and during the investigation of the kitchen, someone rolls a 3, triggering an intrusion. A cabinet opens mysteriously and a strangely carved clay pot falls, striking the character. This also escalates the intrusion rate, so they now occur on a roll of 1 to 6. When the PCs reach the attic, they encounter the dreaded swamp slayer, a half man, half beast that thrives on blood. It attacks, and now the range goes up during each round of combat. After four rounds of fighting, intrusions happen on a roll of 1 to 10—half the time. Things are getting dicey, and they're only going to get worse.

When the GM announces that Horror Mode has ended, the GM intrusion rate goes back to normal, happening only on a roll of 1 or when the GM awards XP.

USING GM INTRUSIONS IN HORROR MODE

With the GM intrusions coming fast and furious toward the end of Horror Mode, it's easy to run out of ideas. In combat, intrusions might just mean that the monster or villain gets a surprise extra attack or inflicts more damage. Perhaps a PC is thrown to the ground or nearer to the edge of a cliff. If the characters are running away, one might trip and fall. If the PCs are exploring, a bookcase topples, potentially hitting someone. Think of all the similar moments you've seen in horror films.

Sometimes, if the GM prefers, the GM intrusion can simply be something frightening, like a moan or a whisper. These aren't dangerous to the PCs, but they escalate the tension and indicate that something bad is getting closer.

GMs may want to limit the number of intrusions to no more than one per round, no matter what the dice indicate, but that should be based on the situation.

In fact, while in Horror Mode, GMs should mostly refrain from doing anything bad, ominous, or dangerous unless it's an intrusion (either from a die roll or through the awarding of XP). In a horror game, GM intrusions are an indication that things are bad and getting worse, and whenever possible, the GM should allow the Horror Mode escalation to drive the action. This makes the GM more of a slave to the dice than in other Cypher System situations, but that's okay.

Consider this example. The PCs have tracked something that is probably committing a series of horrific murders to an old factory. They enter the building to explore. The GM knows where the creature is hiding in the factory, but she decides that it doesn't become aware of the characters until an intrusion is indicated. The only clue the PCs have is a mysterious noise off in the darkness. The creature doesn't move toward them until another GM intrusion occurs. Now they hear something dragging across the factory floor, coming closer. But it's not until a third intrusion occurs that the creature lunges out from behind an old machine at the PC who rolled the die.

In some ways, the status quo doesn't change until an intrusion happens. This could be seen as limiting the GM and the need for pacing, but remember that she can still have an intrusion occur anytime she wishes it, in addition to waiting for the low die rolls.

OPTIONAL RULE: MADNESS

Having characters descend into madness is an interesting facet of some kinds of horror and can make long-term horror campaigns more interesting. The easiest way to portray blows to a character's sanity is through Intellect damage. When a PC encounters something shocking, as described above, she always takes Intellect damage. If she would normally move one step down the damage track due to the damage, she instead immediately regains points (equal to 1d6 + her tier) in her Intellect Pool but loses 1 point from her maximum in that Pool. A character whose Intellect Pool reaches 0 permanently is insane. She loses her current descriptor and adopts the Mad descriptor, regains 1d6 + tier points to her Intellect Pool, and gains +1 to her Intellect Edge. If she ever reaches a permanent Intellect Pool maximum of 0 again, she goes stark raving mad and is no longer playable.

Intellect Edge offers an interesting means to portray a character who is knowledgeable (and perhaps even powerful in terms of mental abilities) yet mentally fragile. A character with a low Intellect Pool but a high Intellect Edge can perform Intellect actions well (since Edge is very helpful) but is still vulnerable to Intellect damage (where Edge is of no help).

Since Cypher System games are meant to be story based, players should recognize that the degrading sanity of their character is part of the story. A player who feels that her character is going mad can talk to the GM, and the two of them can work out the means to portray that—perhaps by using the Mad descriptor, permanently trading up to 4 points from her Intellect Pool to gain +1 to her Intellect Edge, or anything else that seems appropriate. Mental disorders, manias, psychopathy, schizophrenia, or simple phobias can be added to a character's traits, but they don't need to be quantified in game statistics or die rolls. They're simply a part of the character.

Inabilities in personal interaction or any area requiring focus might be appropriate, perhaps allowing the PC to gain training in weird lore or forbidden knowledge. Or maybe the opposite is true—as the character's mind slowly slips away, he becomes oddly compelled or can obsessively focus on a single task for indefinite periods, and thus gains training in that topic or skill. These kinds of changes could be balanced with inabilities, such as being unable to remember important details.

As another way to represent madness, the GM could increase the difficulty of Intellect-based tasks that would be considered routine, such as "remembering your friends and family" or "caring what happens to your best friend" or "stopping yourself from injecting a mysterious substance into your veins." These routine tasks normally have a difficulty of 0, but for a PC who has lost his mind, they might have a difficulty of 1, 2, or even higher. Now the character must make rolls to do even those simple things.

Mad, page 79

MIXING IT UP: HORROR AND SCIENCE FICTION

Sometimes, it's fun to spring horror on a group that's not expecting it. If the players in a science fiction game set in the not-so-far future are prepared to explore a mysteriously abandoned asteroid-mining facility, how wild would it be to have the facility be haunted by ghosts? The PCs probably expect aliens or some other science fiction threat. How will they deal with spectral beings that ignore their high-tech weaponry and show up on their scanners as odd energy fluctuations?

You can also make a horror game out of standard science fiction tropes. A murderous, nigh-unstoppable alien that is stalking the PCs on their own starship can make for a particularly frightening scenario. Using Horror Mode the entire time the alien is on board heightens the tension and forces the PCs to act quickly to get that thing off their ship. (Bonus points if they do it without resorting to the old out-the-airlock trick.)

Inability, page 63

CHAPTER 15

SUPERHEROES

Brash, page 65

Adept, page 29

Bears a Halo of Fire, page 98

Tough, page 87

Warrior, page 22

Performs Feats of Strength, page 156

Mystical, page 81

Exists Partially Out of Phase, page 122

Mysterious, page 80

Explorer, page 38

Solves Mysteries, page 167

Fast, page 73

Moves Like the Wind, page 151

Like horror, the superhero genre is really a subset of the modern genre with extensive special considerations. In many ways, it might appear that the Cypher System is a strange fit for superheroes. But if you think about it, with foci like Bears a Halo of Fire and Wears a Sheen of Ice, the Cypher System makes all genres a little bit "superhero-ish." Character sentences might look like the following:

Firebrand is a Brash energy projector (adept) who Bears a Halo of Fire.

King Brick is a Tough warrior who Performs Feats of Strength.

Dimensionar is a Mystical warlock (adept) who Exists Partially Out of Phase.

Dark Ronin is a Mysterious crimefighter (explorer) who Solves Mysteries.

Speedburst is a Fast crimefighter (explorer) who Moves Like the Wind.

And so on.

CREATING A SUPERHERO SETTING

Even by roleplaying game standards, superhero games are all about the PCs. Think of the PCs as the main characters of their own comic book. They are the stars of the show. Rather than create a world and have the players make superhero PCs to fit into it, have the players create characters first and build the world around them. They are the superhero team that the setting should revolve around, whether they are a new group or the heroes who have been defending the city for years.

Before you dig in, consider the following topics.

How prevalent are superpowered beings in the world? If they're common, how has the world adapted to this idea? Police or military units particularly suited for superpowered threats, special prisons for holding powered criminals, and special laws for superpowers (is it a crime to rob a bank

while under the effects of mind control?) are all obvious issues that will come up. If superbeings are not common, how will ordinary people react when they learn of the PCs? With shock and awe? Fear? Respect?

Are aliens, magic, mutants, and impossible technologies at play in the setting? (The answer is almost certainly yes.) If so, does the majority of the world know about these things, understand them, and accept them?

Superhero games are usually confined to one major city, but occasionally the heroes have adventures that take them around the globe or even into space.

Do the PCs already have arch-foes? If so, developing a bit of history of their previous battles and adventures can add a lot of flavor.

RUNNING A SUPERHERO GAME

Superhero stories, unlike others, rarely have a definitive end. Doctor Vengeance may have been defeated this time, but he'll be back with a whole new plan of conquest sooner than anyone expects. Think of your superhero game as a comic book series. Each session is an issue, often ending in an exciting cliffhanger. Stories are told in arcs over multiple issues, but sometimes those arcs overlap. In other words, a new story arc starts while the previous arc is still going on. You can play with this concept further and have special "double-sized" issues for epic confrontations with a lot of "splash pages." If you really want to do something different, have each PC have his or her own series, playing sessions with just one player, and then have crossover issues where all the characters come together to defeat a powerful threat.

Here are some other tips to consider.

There's a danger that superhero PCs become entirely reactive. They wait for the villains to do something and then try to stop them. If you can occasionally find ways

Want to run a superhero game? Read a comic or two (or a few dozen). That's all the inspiration and instruction you'll really need.

for the heroes to take actions that are more proactive, that's a nice change of pace.

Death for PCs and NPCs should probably be a fluid concept unless you want to go against type. Seemingly impossible events save characters at the last minute or bring them back from the brink. Players probably should not have to fear death much in this genre, which encourages heroic actions.

Similarly, heroes in this genre don't kill. That dictates PC actions somewhat, but it also means that the GM should not create a lot of situations that encourage or force killing. Fights with incredible destruction and serious consequences are fine—you can't have superheroes without them—but in the end, the villains should be knocked out, surrender, or make a frustrating last-minute escape.

Type, page 22

Flavor, page 50

SUGGESTED TYPES FOR A SUPERHERO GAME

Role	Type
Strong hero	Warrior
Brawler hero	Warrior with stealth flavor
Gadget hero	Explorer with technology flavor
Pilot	Explorer with technology flavor
Charmer	Speaker
Leader	Speaker with combat flavor
Shadowy vigilante	Explorer with stealth flavor
Scientist hero	Explorer with skills and knowledge flavor
Energy-wielding hero	Adept with combat flavor
Wizard	Adept
Mentalist	Adept
Psychic ninja	Warrior with magic flavor

In a superhero game, a character's focus is almost certainly more important than her type or descriptor. It's probably the primary manifestation of her superpower.

Focus, page 90

SUGGESTED FOCI FOR A SUPERHERO GAME

Abides in Stone
Bears a Halo of Fire
Blazes With Radiance
Carries a Quiver
Commands Mental Powers
Controls Gravity
Crafts Illusions
Defends the Weak
Employs Magnetism
Exists in Two Places at Once
Exists Partially Out of Phase
Explores Deep Waters
Fights With Panache
Focuses Mind Over Matter
Fuses Flesh and Steel
Fuses Mind and Machine
Grows to Towering Heights
Howls at the Moon
Infiltrates
Leads
Looks for Trouble
Masters Defense
Masters Weaponry
Metes Out Justice
Moves Like a Cat
Moves Like the Wind
Needs No Weapon
Never Says Die
Operates Undercover
Performs Feats of Strength
Rages
Rides the Lightning
Siphons Power
Solves Mysteries
Stands Like a Bastion
Talks to Machines
Throws With Deadly Accuracy
Travels Through Time
Wears a Sheen of Ice

Creatures, page 274

NPCs, page 334

SUGGESTED CREATURES AND NPCs FOR A SUPERHERO GAME

Anathema (supervillain)
Assassin
Blitzer
Chronophage
CRAZR
Crime boss
Djinni
Doctor Dread (supervillain)
Dragon
Enthraller
Grey
Guard
Kaiju
Magnetar (supervillain)
Mechanical soldier
Mister Genocide (supervillain)
Mokuren
Replicant
Scrap drone
Secret agent
Thug/bandit
Vampire
Vat reject
Wardroid
Wendigo
Wrath (supervillain)
Zhev

OTHER CREATURES AND NPCs FOR A SUPERHERO GAME

Dog, guard: level 3, attacks and perception as level 4
Genetically enhanced bruiser: level 3, attacks as level 4; health 15; 5 points of melee damage
Ninja: level 3, stealth as level 6
Robot minion: level 4; Armor 2
Bystander: level 1
Scientist: level 1, science-related tasks as level 4
Worker: level 2; health 8

TAILORING THE CYPHER SYSTEM FOR SUPERHEROES

In a superhero game, the GM should be generous when allowing players to choose powers, even from outside the ones they normally have access to, so they can create the character they want (as discussed in the Further Customizing Characters section in chapter 10). For example, no existing combination of type and focus might easily allow a character to fight well, shoot blasts, and fly, but that's not an unreasonable concept for a hero.

Sometimes an ability a character gets from, say, his focus might not be entirely true to the character concept. For example, our hero who can fight, blast, and fly might be a Tough adept (with combat flavor) who Controls Gravity. This isn't perfect, however, because Controls Gravity gives him the ability to hover and eventually fly, but the tier 3, 4, and 6 abilities aren't quite right. Rather than not giving him what he wants, those tiers give him more than he wants. Refer to the Customizing Foci section in chapter 7 for suggestions of what the character might want at those tiers instead.

Last, keep in mind that an optional rule called modifying abilities on the fly is particularly useful for the superhero genre since it lets PCs use their existing abilities in new and original ways.

Customizing Foci, page 91

Modifying Abilities on the Fly, page 226

Further Customizing Characters, page 231

ADDITIONAL SUPERHERO EQUIPMENT

Suggested additional equipment is the same as in a modern setting, so refer to Chapter 12: Modern for that information. Keep in mind, however, that for many heroes, "equipment" can be superfluous. Where do you stash the flashlight and rope when all you're wearing is spandex tights?

Superhero games are perfect for using power boost cyphers. See page 365.

Chapter 12: Modern, page 244

SUPERHEROES AND EQUIPMENT

Most superheroes don't worry about equipment like backpacks and flashlights. If a character has devices that he regularly uses as weapons or that are the source of his power—such as an advanced suit of armor or a utility belt filled with gimmicks—these should be represented by abilities as if they were inherent powers. Thus, a gadget-using hero might be an adept who has various devices that grant his abilities (to give him more options, he might have the Casts Spells focus, with each spell expressed as a gadget). An armored hero might be a Strong warrior with the magic flavor and the Abides in Stone focus. The boost in Might from his descriptor and focus, as well as the Armor from the focus, actually come from the suit of armor he wears. At tier 2, he chooses Concussive Blast as his ability from the magic flavor to represent blasters in his gauntlets.

In other words, from a story point of view, the PCs are all about equipment, while from a game mechanic point of view, it's not equipment at all—it's part of their character. If an armored hero is ever caught without his suit of armor, he has no special powers other than his skills, but that's entirely true to the genre, so it works.

Abides in Stone, page 94

Concussive Blast, page 58

Casts Spells, page 103

OPTIONAL RULE: POWER SHIFTS

Superheroes can do things that other people cannot. They throw cars, blast through brick walls, leap onto speeding trains, and cobble together interdimensional gateways in a few hours. It's tempting to say that such characters are stronger, faster, or smarter, so they should have higher Might, Speed, or Intellect Pools. However, simply bumping up stat Pools or Edge doesn't fully represent this dramatic increase in power. Instead, consider using an optional rule called power shifts.

Under this rule, all superhero characters get five power shifts. Power shifts are like permanent levels of Effort that are always active. They don't count toward a character's maximum Effort use (nor do they count as skills or assets). They simply reduce the difficulty of tasks that fall into specific categories, which include (but are not necessarily limited to) the following.

Accuracy: All attack rolls

Dexterity: Movement, acrobatics, initiative, and Speed defense

Healing: One extra recovery roll per shift (each one action, all coming before other normal recovery rolls)

Intelligence: Intellect defense rolls and all knowledge, science, and crafting tasks

Power: Use of a specific power, including damage (3 additional points per shift) but not attack rolls

Resilience: Might defense rolls and Armor (+1 per shift)

Single Attack: Attack rolls and damage (3 additional points per shift)

Strength: All tasks involving strength, including jumping and dealing damage in melee or thrown attacks (3 additional points of damage per shift) but not attack rolls

Each shift reduces the difficulty of the task by one step (except for shifts that affect damage or Armor, as specified in the list above).

A character assigns her five power shifts as desired, but most characters should not be allowed to assign more than three to any one category. Once the shifts are assigned, they should not change.

For example, a superstrong character might put three of his shifts into strength and the other two into resilience. Whenever he lifts something heavy, smashes through a wall, or throws an object, he reduces the task's difficulty by three steps before applying Effort, skill, or assets. Thus, all difficulties from 0 to 3 are routine for him. He smashes through level 3 doors as if they don't exist. As another example, a masked vigilante character with a utility belt full of gadgets and great acrobatic skills might put two shifts in dexterity, one in accuracy, one in intelligence, and one in healing. She's not actually superpowered, just tough and well trained.

Some GMs will want to allow PCs to increase their power shifts. Having a character spend 10 XP to do so would probably be appropriate. Other GMs will want to run superhero games with PCs of greater or lesser power (cosmic-level heroes or street-level heroes, perhaps). In such cases, more or fewer power shifts should be granted to the PCs at the game's start.

SUPERPOWERED NPCs AND POWER SHIFTS

NPC superheroes and villains get power shifts, too. Most of the time, this adds to their level. For example, Blast Star is a level 5 fiery villain who has three power shifts. When he blasts through a level 7 iron security door, he does so easily because in this circumstance, he's actually level 8.

Sometimes, NPC power shifts make things harder for the PCs. For example, Fleetfoot the level 4 speedster puts all three of her shifts in dexterity. When she runs past a character who tries to grab her, the difficulty to do so is increased by three steps to 7.

REALLY IMPOSSIBLE TASKS

In superhero games, due to conventions of the genre, difficulty caps at 15 instead of 10. Difficulty 10 is labeled "impossible," but that label is for regular folks. For superpowered characters, "impossible" means something different, thanks to power shifts.

Think of each difficulty above 10 as being one more step beyond impossible. Although a GM in another genre would say there's no chance that a character could leap 100 feet (30 m) from one rooftop to another, in a superhero game, that might just be difficulty 11. Picking up a city bus isn't something normal characters could do, but for a strong superhero, it might be difficulty 12.

In theory, NPCs in such a game can go up to level 15 as well. Levels above 10 represent opponents that only a superhero would consider taking on: a robot that's 1,000 feet (305 m) tall (level 11); Galashal, Empress of Twelve Dimensions (level 14); or a space monster the size of the moon (level 15).

SUPERHERO ARTIFACTS

Supervillains build doomsday devices. Ancient artifacts present a threat to all humanity if in the wrong hands. Weird machines from alien dimensions offer solutions to unsolvable problems. Artifacts are an important part of superhero stories. A few examples are below.

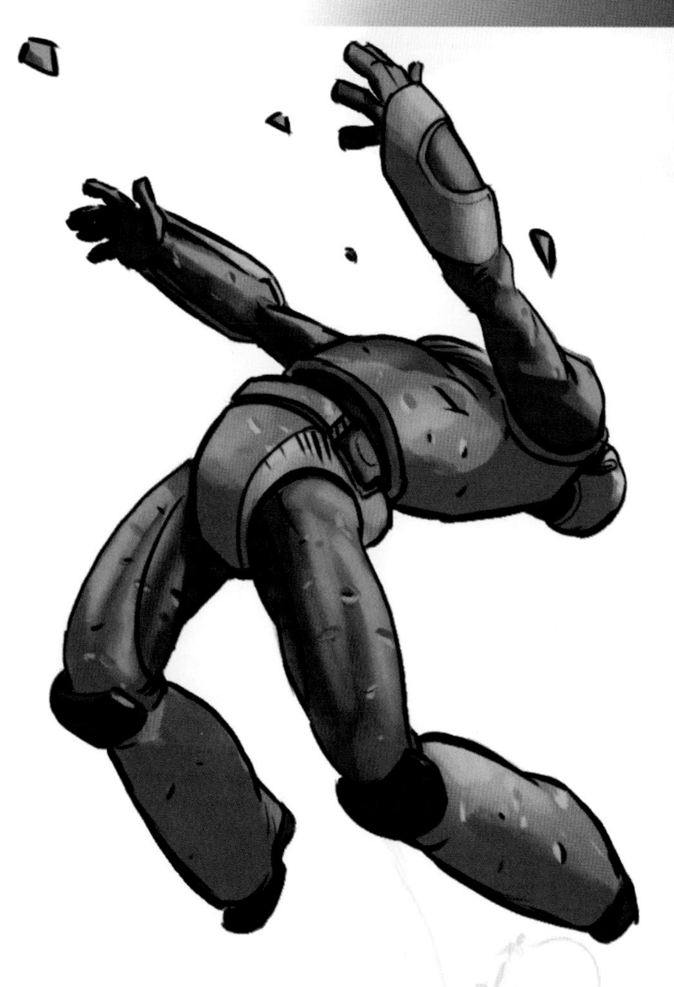

DOCTOR DREAD'S TIME PORTAL

Level: 9

Form: An arch of metal big enough to walk through

Effect: Anyone who steps through it goes to a predetermined point in the past or future (a minimum of fifty years in either direction), which can be anywhere on the planet.

Depletion: 1 in 1d20

STELLAREX CRYSTAL

Level: 1d6 + 4

Form: A multifaceted purple stone the size of a fist

Effect: Created in the dawning of the universe, this artifact grants the wielder the ability to not only fully restore all her stat Pools, but also increase each Pool temporarily by 10 points. These extra points fade after twenty-four hours if not used.

Depletion: 1–3 in 1d10

SYRUM X

Level: 1d6 + 2

Form: A vial or syringe of red fluid

Effect: Strips someone of all superpowers (including abilities granted by magic, psionics, mutation, or science) for twenty-four hours. The target retains only skills and abilities that are mundane, as agreed by the GM and player.

Depletion: Automatic

MIXING IT UP: SUPERHEROES AND SCIENCE FICTION

Sure, superheroes usually safeguard a city on Earth from criminals, but what if they guard the solar system from alien threats instead? Flying around in spaceships, dealing with foes wielding blasters rather than revolvers, and traveling to new planets every session might be the trappings of a space opera game, but they could easily work for a space-focused superhero game as well. In fact, with the characters' powers and abilities, a space opera science fiction setting might fit superhero PCs even better than a modern setting.

EVENING THE ODDS

With power shifts and other mechanics at play, situations will arise where it will be impossible for low-level foes like street thugs to hurt a PC hero. That's okay. There are different ways you can handle it. Allow the hero to wade through them easily—it happens in comic books all the time. Perhaps such a battle need not even be played out using mechanics. Alternatively, use a GM intrusion now and again to represent that the thugs topple a huge stack of crates or produce a bomb that can hurt the hero. And of course, the thugs might not be able to hurt the hero, but what about nearby bystanders who quickly become hostages?

Conversely, the PCs might find themselves in a situation where they can't hurt a powerful villain. Again, this is right out of the pages of comic books. However, many villains aren't overcome by punches, but by heroes who come up with a desperate plan to take them out—or at least put the kibosh on their scheme.

PART 4

GAMEMASTER SECTION

CHAPTER 16

CREATURES

This chapter describes many common and uncommon creatures that the characters might meet—and fight—in a Cypher System game and gives their stats. The variety of creatures that populate the possible settings and genres is so great that this chapter only scratches the surface. It does, however, provide examples of kinds of inhabitants—bestial and civilized, living and undead, organic and inorganic—so that you can easily extrapolate and create your own.

The creatures in this chapter are examples to showcase the various kinds of approaches. Still, it does its best to cover some of the obvious bases that you might need, particularly those that can be used in multiple genres, like vampires, zombies, killer robots, dinosaurs, and so on.

UNDERSTANDING THE LISTINGS

Level: Like the difficulty of a task, each creature and NPC has a level attached to it. You use the level to determine the target number a PC must reach to attack or defend against the opponent. In each entry, the difficulty number for the creature or NPC is listed in parentheses after its level. As shown on the following table, the target number is three times the level.

Level	Target Number
1	3
2	6
3	9
4	12
5	15
6	18
7	21
8	24
9	27
10	30

Description: Following the name of the creature or NPC is a general description of its appearance, nature, intelligence, or background.

Motive: This entry is a way to help the GM understand what a creature or NPC wants. Every creature or person wants something, even if it's just to be left alone.

Environment: This entry describes whether the creature tends to be solitary or travel in groups and what kind of terrain it inhabits (such as "They travel in packs through dry wastes and temperate lowlands").

Health: A creature's target number is usually also its health, which is the amount of damage it can sustain before it is dead or incapacitated. For easy reference, the entries always list a creature's health, even when it's the normal amount for a creature of its level.

Damage Inflicted: Generally, when creatures hit in combat, they inflict their level in damage regardless of the form of attack. Some inflict more or less or have a special modifier to damage. Intelligent NPCs often use weapons, but this is more a flavor issue than a mechanical one. In other words, it doesn't matter if a level 3 foe uses a sword or claws—it deals the same damage if it hits. The entries always specify the amount of damage inflicted, even if it's the normal amount for a creature of its level.

Armor: This is the creature's Armor value. Sometimes the number represents physical armor, and other times it represents natural protection. This entry doesn't appear in the game stats if a creature has no Armor.

Movement: Movement determines how far the creature can move in a single turn. Creatures have movements of immediate, short, or long, which equate to the ranges of the same name. Most PCs have an effective movement of short, so if they are chasing (or being chased by) a creature with immediate movement, their Speed tasks are one step easier; if the creature's movement is long, the PCs' Speed tasks are one step harder.

Modifications: Use these default numbers when a creature's information says to use a different target number. For example, a level 4 creature might say "defends as level 5," which means PCs attacking it must reach a target number of 15 (for difficulty 5) instead of 12 (for difficulty 4). In special circumstances, some creatures have other modifications, but these are almost always specific to their level.

Combat: This entry gives advice on using the creature in combat, such as "This monster uses ambushes and hit-and-run tactics." At the end of the combat listing, you'll also find any special abilities, such as immunities, poisons, and healing skills. GMs should be logical about a creature's reaction to a particular action or attack by a PC. For example, a mechanical creation is immune to normal diseases, a character can't poison a being of energy (at least, not with a conventional poison), and so on.

Interaction: This entry gives advice on using the creature in interactions, such as "These creatures are willing to talk but respond poorly to threats," or "This creature is an animal and acts like an animal."

Use: This entry gives the GM suggestions for how to use the creature in a game session. It might provide general notes or specific adventure ideas.

Loot: This entry indicates what the PCs might gain if they take items from their fallen foes (or trade with or trick them). It doesn't appear in the game stats if the creature has no loot.

GM Intrusion: This optional entry in the stats suggests a way to use GM intrusion in an encounter with the creature. It's just one possible idea of many, and the GM is encouraged to come up with her own uses of the game mechanic.

CREATURES BY LEVEL

Creature	Level
Goblin	1
Nuppeppo	2
Orc	2
Skeleton	2
Deinonychus	3
Giant rat	3
Giant spider	3
Mokuren	3
Scrap drone	3
Vampire, transitional	3
Vat reject	3
Zombie	3
Chronophage	4
Deep one	4
Devil	4
Elemental, fire	4
Ghost	4
Ghoul	4
Giant snake	4
Grey	4
Ogre	4
Mechanical soldier	4
Ravage bear	4
Shadow elf	4
Werewolf	4
Blitzer	5
CRAZR	5
Demon	5
Dream sallow	5
Elemental, earth	5
Fallen angel	5
Killing white light	5
Mi-go	5
Mister Genocide (supervillain)	5
Philethis	5
Replicant	5
Slidikin	5
Wendigo	5
Witch	5
Zhev	5
Chimera	6
Enthraller	6
Golem	6
Vampire	6
Wardroid	6
Xenoparasite	6
Wrath (supervillain)	6
Anathema (supervillain)	7
Djinni	7
Doctor Dread (supervillain)	7
Dragon	7
Giant	7
Neveri	7
Statue, animate	7
Tyrannosaurus rex	7
Magnetar (supervillain)	8
Demigod	9
Vampire lord	9
Kaiju	10

NORMAL ANIMALS

Rat: level 1

Hawk: level 2; flies a long distance each round

Dog: level 2, perception as level 3

Dog, guard: level 3, attacks and perception as level 4

Rattlesnake: level 2; bite inflicts 3 points of Speed damage (ignores Armor)

Horse: level 3; moves a long distance each round

Bear, black: level 3, attacks as level 4

Bear, grizzly: level 5; health 20; Armor 1

BLITZER 5 (15)

A cybernetics experiment gone wrong, a blitzer can become a menace at any moment. Thick cables of arteries feed pulsing muscles so hot that they glow like embers beneath this monstrosity's translucent skin. Metallic shunts coil and beep, visibly nestled side by side with muscle and organs. Every few seconds, a fresh wave of heat pours from the blitzer as it conspicuously swells in size and muscle mass, and its capacity for destruction almost doubles. Once a blitzer begins to grow (or "blitz" as it's commonly referred to), it ceases its rampage only when it destroys whatever set it off or when it overheats and drops dead, a smoking husk of overcooked meat and metallic parts.

Motive: Destruction

Environment: Almost anywhere, usually alone

Health: 20

Damage Inflicted: 6 to 15 points (see Combat)

Armor: 4

Movement: Short; long when blitzing

Modifications: See Combat for escalating attack level modification.

Combat: The creature is either passive or blitzing. A "blitz" is an episode of rampage that increases the creature's mass, damage, and attack level each round while it continues, according to the following schedule:

Round 1: Damage 6 points; attacks as level 5

Round 2: Damage 9 points; attacks as level 6

Round 3: Damage 12 points; attacks as level 7

Round 4: Damage 15 points; attacks as level 8

Round 5: Blitzer overheats, falls dead, and begins to smolder

A blitzer bludgeons and slightly scorches foes with its massive fists. A blitzer stops blitzing if it's killed (by a greater force or by its own deadly biochemistry) or if every creature within immediate range of it is debilitated or dead on the blitzer's turn. When a blitzer stops rampaging, it shrinks back to its original mass and wanders off, apparently dazed, seeking someplace cool to sleep, preferably in running water with its head just above the waterline. The creature can blitz no more than once per hour.

Interaction: A blitzer can be interacted with before or after (but not during) its cycle of rampage. Before a blitz, the creature is prickly and takes offense easily. Afterward, it is dazed and sleepy and wants nothing more than to cool off, though a few have their own interests as well.

Use: While the PCs make their way through a crowded market, a youth caught stealing falls writhing and spitting, seized by a fit of apoplexy. When he rises, it's as a blitzer.

Loot: A burnt-out blitzer doesn't yield anything salvageable, but one killed before it burns out might yield a couple of cyphers.

Blitzers are believed to be the result of massive surgical intervention on unsuspecting victims. Prior to their transformation, some blitzers complained of a daylong gap in their memory. It's not known who or what might be modifying people, giving them the capacity to blitz.

GM Intrusion: *The blitzer brings its hands together so violently that it creates a thunderclap. Every creature in immediate range must succeed on a Might defense roll. Those who fail are unable to do anything but move on their next turn and are deafened for one minute (and thus unable to communicate with allies vocally during that time).*

CHIMERA 6 (18)

Chimeras are unsettling hybrids that combine the features of many different animals, often arranged in odd formations. The fusion of animal forms is the only thing that unifies these creatures—otherwise, different chimeras often look very different from each other. They include combinations of goat and lion, lizard and bat, dragon and spider, dinosaur and giant insect. A few even display human features, such as an improbably located face or hands instead of claws. Some chimeras can fly. Others slither across the ground.

A chimera typically has a dominant form to which other animal parts are grafted. The base form must be large enough to support the weight of the extra heads, so lions, bears, and horses are popular as the base form.

Chimeras kill even when not hungry and throw their victims' remains around a wide area in a wild rage. When not feeding or tormenting prey, a chimera that can fly takes to the air, beating its enormous leather wings to scour the landscape for new prey.

Motive: Hungers for human flesh

Environment: Anywhere, usually alone

Health: 21

Damage Inflicted: 4 points

Movement: Short while on the ground; long while flying (if it can fly)

Modifications: Speed defense rolls as level 5 due to size.

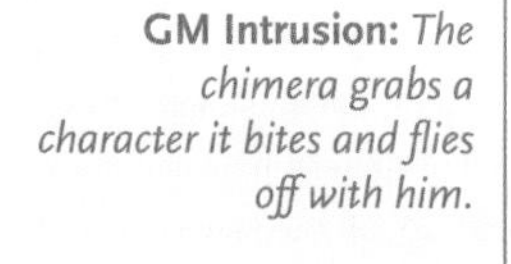
GM Intrusion: *The chimera grabs a character it bites and flies off with him.*

Combat: All chimeras have a number of ways to kill. The exact methods vary, but most can bite, sting, and gore (three attacks) as a single action, either attacking the same opponent or attacking different foes within immediate range of each other. A chimera's sting carries a powerful toxin, and a stung target must succeed on a Might defense roll or take 4 additional points of damage. Chimeras with spikes can project them at up to three targets within long range as a single action.

Interaction: Chimeras are a lot like wild animals with rabies. They're confused and violent, and they behave erratically. Savage, ferocious beasts, they hate all other creatures and seize any opportunity to kill.

Use: While exploring an island, the PCs find carcasses that have been torn apart, the pieces scattered in all directions. A chimera lairs nearby, and if the characters draw attention to themselves, it hunts them down, too.

CHRONOPHAGE 4 (12)

These segmented, 6-foot (2 m) long creatures look partly like larvae that have grown gargantuan and vicious. They appear in places where time moves more slowly or more quickly than normal, where balls and liquids flow upslope, or where a time traveler has visited.

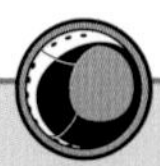

Chronophages are creatures that seem drawn to time paradoxes and disruptions in space-time. They tend to eat those responsible (and those affected), potentially alleviating the disturbance in the fabric of things, though that outcome might just be a side effect. First and foremost, chronophages are parasites that phase into existence near a spatial anomaly and feed to sate their own hunger. However, there are hints that the larvae may represent the first stage of life of a far more powerful and enigmatic entity.

Motive: Hungers for the flesh of those who create, or were created by, time anomalies

Environment: Clutches of four to eight fade into existence within long range of space-time fractures in almost any location.

Health: 18

Damage Inflicted: 5 points

Armor: 1

Movement: Short; can phase into the dimension of time (and disappear) as a move. On its next action, it can phase back into the world up to 300 feet (91 m) from where it disappeared as an action.

Modifications: Perception as level 5.

Combat: A chronophage attacks with its crushing mandibles.

A chronophage can phase back and forth between its home dimension, and it uses this ability to great effect when hunting prey. For instance, it can close on prey otherwise protected by barriers or features of the landscape. It can also use the ability to draw a victim's attention and then launch a surprise attack from behind after it has effectively teleported. However, it is an action for the feeder to shift its phase between the dimension of time and normal reality.

Interaction: Chronophages are unswerving in their drive to find prey. Once one marks its target, only killing the creature can sway it from the prey.

Use: When the PCs happen upon a location where the rules of space-time are loose and malleable, or if the PCs trigger a cypher or other device that interferes with time's regular flow, a clutch of chronophages may soon come calling.

Loot: The skin of a chronophage can be salvaged to create a silvery cloak that reflects its surroundings, but the reflection is one hour behind the present.

GM Intrusion: *If a chronophage's prey fails its Speed defense roll, the attack ignores Armor, and the prey must make an Intellect defense roll (difficulty 4) or be phased into the chronophage's home dimension of time. He automatically phases back into reality on his next turn but is displaced by 100 feet (30 m) straight up or to the closest open space. This usually results in a fall that potentially deals 10 points of damage, knocks the character prone, and dazes him for a round.*

CRAZR 5 (15)

Machines built for destruction, CRAZRs are designed to run down and destroy targets as quickly and efficiently as possible. CRAZR stands for Canid Robotic Zealous Reapers (the "A" doesn't stand for anything, except to let the acronym evoke the word "crazy," which these machines are). They attack without fear and, despite not being particularly tactical or tough, inflict so much harm in so little time that they can bring down much more powerful targets.

CRAZRs preferentially go after other machines, not creatures of flesh, following programming that assesses a higher chance that another entity like itself is the most dangerous foe, all else being equal. That said, a human with a computer and hacking knowledge is likely able to bring down a CRAZR more quickly than anything else.

Motive: Destroy preprogrammed targets

Environment: Anywhere guards, trackers, or soldiers are deployed

Health: 15

Damage Inflicted: 5 points

Movement: Long

Modification: Resist hacking attempts as level 7 (see Interaction).

Combat: A CRAZR makes attacks with spinning saw blades designed to chew through the metal hides of other machine creatures. Thus, CRAZR attacks ignore up to 1 point of a target's Armor.

A CRAZR is quick; as a single action, it can move a long distance each round, or move a short distance and attack with all four spinning blades. This quickness comes with a cost: its metallic covering is light, thinner than skin, and just as delicate (which is why CRAZRs have no Armor). It also makes a CRAZR more susceptible to radio-enabled hacking attempts (see Interaction).

A CRAZR can emit a brilliant spotlight to see in the dark, and it's able to track prey by noting small clues in the environment like scratches, footprints, doors left ajar, and so on.

Interaction: CRAZRs constantly operate in berserker mode. Short of destroying one, hacking one is the only way to interact. Someone with a direct connection or a radio-enabled probe can hack a CRAZR and order it to switch off as a level 7 hacking task. Gaining control of a CRAZR or reprogramming it using this method isn't nearly as easy because of built-in failsafes; treat the attempt as a level 8 hacking task.

Use: PCs who enter a sealed area disturb a CRAZR that at first seemed like an inert piece of machinery.

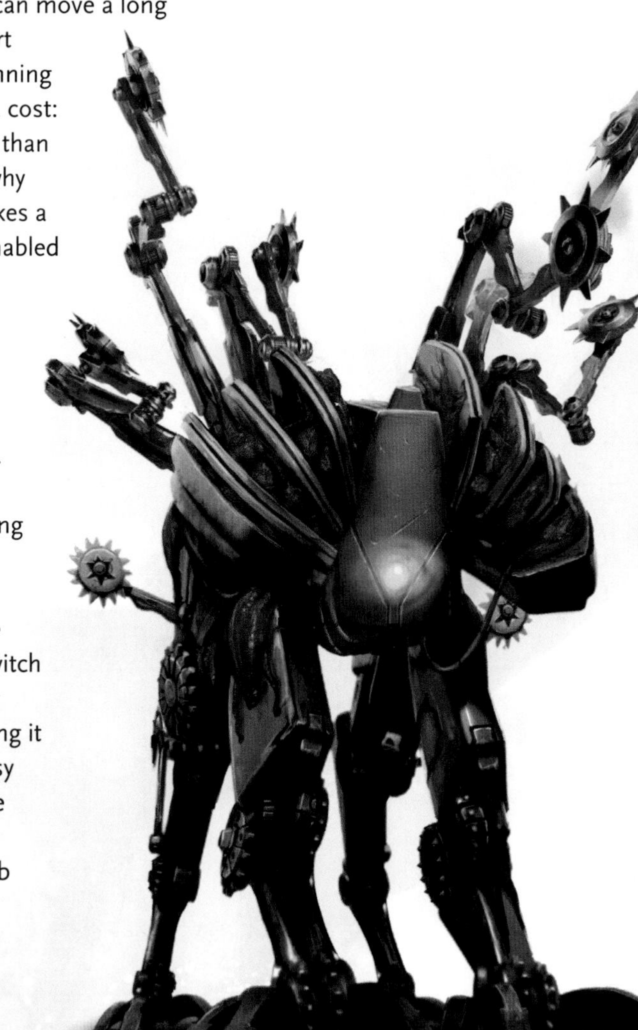

GM Intrusion: *A CRAZR's spinning blade risks destroying an important piece of the character's equipment.*

DEEP ONE 4 (12)

"Their forms vaguely suggested the anthropoid, while their heads were the heads of fish, with prodigious bulging eyes that never closed. At the sides of their necks were palpitating gills, and their long paws were webbed. They hopped irregularly, sometimes on two legs and sometimes on four. I was somehow glad that they had no more than four limbs. Their croaking, baying voices, clearly used for articulate speech, held all the dark shades of expression which their staring faces lacked ... They were the blasphemous fish-frogs of the nameless design—living and horrible."

—The Shadow Over Innsmouth

Some deep ones dwell in coastal regions on land, usually in isolated villages where they might attempt to pass for human. They are able to breathe both air and water. Most, however, thrive in the ocean depths, in ancient underwater cities like "Cyclopean and many-columned Y'ha-nthlei." Deep ones sometimes breed with insane humans to produce squamous offspring that eventually develop fully into deep ones well after maturity (or even middle age).

Motive: Hungers for flesh

Environment: Anywhere near a large body of salt water

Health: 15

Damage Inflicted: 5 points

Armor: 2

Movement: Short on land; long in the water

Modifications: Swims as level 6; perception as level 3.

Combat: Deep ones attack with tooth and claw most often, although occasionally one might use a weapon. They usually give no quarter, nor ask for it. Their skin is subject to drying, and they take 1 extra point of damage (ignores Armor) from any attack that deals fire or heat damage. Because of this weakness, deep ones sometimes retreat from fire and fire attacks.

Interaction: Deep ones are a strange mix of utter alienness and the vestiges of lost humanity. They are foul and degenerate creatures by human standards, however. Many still retain the ability to speak human languages, but all speak their own slurred, unearthly tongue.

Deep ones spend a great deal of time in the sincere adoration of their gods, Mother Hydra, Father Dagon, and Cthulhu. Their religion demands frequent blood sacrifices.

Use: The PCs wander into a small coastal village where everyone seems standoffish and oddly distant. A few people appear to be sickly and malformed, perhaps from mutation or birth defects. Some of the villagers have squamous skin because they are transforming into deep ones. And, of course, true deep ones hide within the community as well.

Loot: A few deep ones will have a cypher.

Two deep ones that have grown colossal and powerful over time are called Mother Hydra and her consort, Father Dagon. Each stands 15 feet (5 m) tall, and they serve as deity-rulers among the deep ones.

Mother Hydra and Father Dagon: *level 8; health 38 each; Armor 4; each inflicts 10 points of damage*

GM Intrusion: *The deep one produces a net and throws it over the character. The only physical action the PC can take is to try to get free, as either a Might-based or a Speed-based action.*

DEINONYCHUS 3 (9)

Popularly known as the velociraptor, the dinosaur genus called *Deinonychus* doesn't care if its prey gets the proper terminology sorted. Meat tastes like meat. The "terrible claw" these carnivores are named after refers to their massive, sickle-shaped claws, which are unsheathed from their hind legs when attacking prey.

Deinonychus are pack hunters, which means they work together as a unit, each taking on different roles to scare, flush, and direct even intelligent prey into the claws of an ambush.

Motive: Hungers for flesh

Environment: Wherever they can hunt food, in packs of three to seven

Health: 15

Damage Inflicted: 4 points

Armor: 1

Movement: Short

Modifications: Perception as level 5; attacks and Speed defense as level 4 due to quickness; overcoming obstacles and figuring out tricks as level 4.

Combat: When a deinonychus bites its prey, the victim takes damage and must make a Might defense roll. On a failure, the deinonychus holds the victim in place with its jaws while it slices him to ribbons with its terrible claws, automatically inflicting 6 points of damage each round in which he fails a Might-based task to break free (not attempting to break free counts as a failed attempt). For a human-sized or smaller victim held in the jaws, the difficulty of all other tasks is increased by two steps.

Interaction: Vicious, cunning, and a little too smart to be classified as simple predators, these creatures are unlikely to negotiate, give quarter, or back off from a fight even if contact could be made.

Use: Some fool decided to build a Cretaceous-themed zoo. The only question is: How long before the dinosaurs get loose and take over the local mall?

GM Intrusion: *The fleeing deinonychus was actually leading the character over a cliff, into a deadfall trap, or into an ambush with more deinonychus.*

DEMIGOD 9 (27)

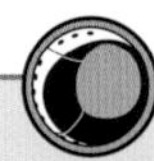

"With all his speed not yet the sun
Through half his race has run,
Since I, to execute thy dread command,
Have thrice encompass'd sea and land."
~Iris, messenger of the gods, in Handel's Semele

GM Intrusion: *The divine nature of the demigod allows it to act out of turn, take control of an object (such as an artifact or a cypher) that the PC is about to use against it, and either deactivate the object or turn it against the character.*

Lesser gods, divine children of gods and mortals, and other beings bequeathed with partly divine power are called demigods. Their capacities so radically exceed those of regular people that they have transcended humanity. Demigods are so physically and mentally powerful that it's difficult for them to hide their semi-divine appearance to mortal creatures—not that most would make the effort in the first place.

Motive: Ineffable

Environment: Anywhere other divine entities exist (or once existed)

Health: 99

Damage Inflicted: 12 points

Armor: 5

Movement: Short; long when flying

Combat: Demigods can attack foes up to half a mile (1 km) away with bolts of divine energy (usually in the form of lightning). A demigod can dial up the level of destruction if it wishes, so that instead of affecting only one target, a bolt deals 9 points of damage to all targets within short range of the primary target. Targets caught in the conflagration who succeed on a Speed defense roll still suffer 5 points of damage.

Demigods are just as scary in hand-to-hand combat and can attack all targets within immediate range as an action. They can also call on a variety of other abilities that seem like magic to lesser foes and mimic the effect of any cypher of level 5 or lower.

A demigod doesn't need to alter reality to heal itself, as it automatically regains 2 points of health per round.

Interaction: For all their power, demigods share most human traits and weaknesses. This means it's possible to negotiate with one, though the consequences for angering a demigod in the process are dire.

Use: A demigod was banned from the higher realm of her birth for unknown reasons. Now she seeks to show her worth by undertaking a great quest in the mortal world, and she is looking to assemble a group of mortal comrades (sycophants?) to aid her.

Loot: Demigods might carry an artifact related to some aspect of their domain (such as wind, messages, or death), if they have one, and 1d6 cyphers.

DEMON 5 (15)

A demon prefers to attempt possession before its potential host is aware of its presence, but it might choose to possess a victim in combat, too.

One way to exorcise a demon is to command it out in the name of an entity that has power over the demon. This can be attempted once per day. It grants the possessed character an additional Intellect defense roll to eject the demon.

GM Intrusion: *The PC who attempts an exorcism of a possessed target is successful, but the demon moves directly from the former victim into the PC. The PC can make an Intellect-based roll to eject the demon, but only after the first round of possession.*

Many demon varieties plague the world, but the most common are the formless spirits of the dead who have undergone horrifying transformations in tortuous nether realms, until all that was good or caring was burned away, forging a being of spite and hate.

A demon remembers only fragments of its former life—every good memory is cauterized, and every slight, misfortune, snub, and pain is amplified, motivating the creature to tempt others into the same state as itself.

Having no flesh to call its own, a demon is a shadowed, ephemeral horror able to possess others. A demon can cause great harm in a short time by forcing its possessed host to lie, steal, and deliver violence upon loved ones.

Motive: Hungers for others' pain and fear

Environment: Anywhere

Health: 25

Damage Inflicted: 6 points

Movement: Short; immediate while flying in immaterial form

Modifications: All stealth tasks as level 7 in immaterial form; deception tasks as level 6.

Combat: The immaterial touch of a demon can have two effects. Either it inflicts 5 points of damage as the target's form is decayed and eroded by necrosis, or it allows the demon to attempt to possess the target. The target of an attempted possession must make an Intellect defense roll or become possessed, whereupon the demon's immaterial form disappears into the target.

The first round in which a character is possessed, he can act normally. In the second and all subsequent rounds, the possessing demon can control the actions of the host, but the character can attempt an Intellect defense roll to resist each suggested action. Successful resistance means that the character does nothing for one round. In other rounds, the character can act as he chooses. A possessing demon's actions are limited to attempts to control its host and leaving the host.

A possessed target is allowed an Intellect defense roll to eject the demon once per day, barring any exorcism attempts. The difficulty of the defense roll increases by 1 for each day of possession after the first seven days. An ejected or cast-out demon is powerless for one or more days.

A demon not possessing another creature is immaterial and can pass through solid objects whose level is lower than its own. While the demon is immaterial, it takes only 1 point of damage from mundane attacks, but it takes full damage from magical, energy, and psychic attacks. While it possesses another creature, the demon is immune to most attacks (though not so the host; killing the host will eject the demon).

Interaction: A demon allows a possessed host to act normally, as long as it doesn't reveal the demon's presence. If its presence is known, the demon might negotiate, but only after a tirade of lies and obscenity, and the demon likely betrays any deal reached.

Use: An ally of the PCs has begun acting differently, and not for the good.

DEVIL 4 (12)

Devils are manifest evil. As "native fauna" of various tortuous nether realms, devils come in many forms, though most are iterations on a theme that includes a humanoid shape, large batwings, bestial faces, and twisting horns. Most stink of brimstone and sport tails that end in a fork. Devils fill the ranks of hellish armies, guard evil vaults, and appear at the magical summons of warlocks and sorcerers who are not afraid for the sanctity of their own souls.

Motive: Collect souls

Environment: Anywhere in various nether realms; sometimes called by mortal magic

Health: 12

Damage Inflicted: 5 points

Armor: 3

Movement: Short when walking or flying

Modifications: All tasks related to deception as level 7.

Combat: When possible, a devil attacks with surprise. If successful, it unfurls two great wings and claws at the ends of its fingers. It leaps into the air, flies up to a short distance toward the nearest foe, and attacks that creature as a single action.

Some devils carry tridents. The weapon inflicts 5 points of damage, and the target must either move to a position within an immediate distance chosen by the devil or take 2 additional points of damage from being impaled (a total of 7 points of damage). An impaled foe automatically takes 5 points of damage each round until she spends an action to pull herself free.

Interaction: Evil, cruel, and malevolent, devils are more than happy to talk, especially to those already caught and being readied for torture. Devils serve yet more powerful devils out of fear. If they find someone or something they fear more, they readily betray their master and become obsequious and cringing, though betrayal is always on the table.

Use: A spate of violent murders grips a city in fear—a devil has escaped into the world of mortals without a leash. It spends nights hunting anyone it spots from its perches atop the city's holy places.

GM Intrusion: *A devil anticipates the character's melee attack and brings its wing down "just so" on his weapon. If the PC fails a Speed defense roll, the weapon breaks. Either way, he fails to hit the devil.*

DJINNI 7 (21)

Some djinn inhabit pocket dimensions whose entry points are affixed within the mouths of urns, pots, or lamps.

GM Intrusion: *When the character is touched by a djinni, instead of taking damage, the PC is turned to smoke and fire and sent whirling off in a random direction. He loses his next turn and returns to normal almost 300 feet (91 m) from where he started.*

Islamic texts describe djinn as inhabiting unseen dimensions beyond the visible universe. Just like normal creatures, djinn are individuals, and they can be good, evil, or unconcerned about the fates and doings of others.

Motive: Unpredictable

Environment: Almost anywhere

Health: 35

Damage Inflicted: 9 points

Movement: Short; long when flying

Modifications: Knowledge of Arabian history as level 8.

Combat: With a touch, a djinni can warp a victim's flesh, inflicting damage. Djinn can also spend an action to send out a magitech "EMP pulse" that renders all artifacts, machines, and lesser magic devices within short range inoperable for one minute. (If the item is part of a character's equipment, she can prevent this outcome by succeeding on a Speed defense roll.) Instead of disabling all devices in range, a djinni can instead take control of one item within range for one minute, if applicable.

A djinni can transform into a being of smoke and flame as its action. While in this form, it has +10 to Armor but can't attack foes. It gains the ability to fly a long distance each round and retains the ability to communicate normally. The first time each day that a djinni returns to physical form after having become smoke, it regains 25 points of health.

Some djinn have the ability to grant wishes, and a few are beholden to do so thanks to an ancient, unexplained agreement with other djinn. Those who grant wishes twist them against the asker, especially if a wish is poorly worded or there are multiple ways to interpret the wish. The level of the effect granted is no greater than level 7, as determined by the GM, who can modify the effect of the wish accordingly. (The larger the wish, the more likely the GM will limit its effect.)

Finally, most djinn have a couple of cyphers and possibly an artifact useful in combat.

Interaction: When a djinni interacts with characters, it's narcissistic, certain in its own immense power, and unlikely to let slights pass. That said, low-tier characters could negotiate with one peacefully because even djinni have needs and desires.

Use: Agents of a foreign power retrieved a magic lamp from an ancient Arabian ruin. The PCs' job is to determine whether there is reason for alarm.

Loot: Most djinn carry a couple of cyphers, and some have a magic artifact.

DRAGON 7 (21)

Dragons are exceptionally territorial, vain, and greedy. Apex predators, dragons must eat large meals on a regular basis. They prefer virgins, though they will settle for normal people, horses, or even wild pigs in a pinch. They love games of all sorts, especially when they get to consume the loser. Drawn to wealth and magic, dragons accumulate hoards of golden treasure. A dragon's hoard is not only an end in itself, but part of a never-ending contest between dragons of a certain age to see which one can accumulate the largest trove.

Motive: Self-aggrandizement, hungers for flesh, treasure collection

Environment: Dragons thrive where wilderness meets the civilized frontier

Health: 45

Damage Inflicted: 10 points

Armor: 3

Movement: Short; long while flying

Modifications: Perception and riddles as level 8; Speed defense as level 6 due to size.

Combat: A dragon can bite one target or claw two opponents in immediate range as a single action. When bitten, the target is also immobilized until he succeeds on a Might defense roll to break free (or the dragon drops him).

Most dragons have one or more additional magical abilities they can bring to bear in combat, including the following.

Fiery Breath: A dragon can breathe a stream of fire up to long range, doing 7 points of damage to all targets within immediate range of each other. Targets who succeed on a Speed defense roll to avoid the full effect of the fire still take 3 points of damage. This ability cannot be used in consecutive rounds.

Change Shape: A dragon with this ability can take the form of a human or similar humanoid as its action, or return to its regular shape. When so changed, the dragon's disguise is nearly impenetrable without special knowledge. As a human, the dragon is a level 5 creature.

Captivate: A dragon with this ability can psychically mesmerize a nondragon target in immediate range who fails an Intellect defense roll. A captivated target does the dragon's verbal bidding for one or more hours. Each time the target is confronted by a third party about its mental condition, the target is allowed another Intellect defense roll to break the effect.

Interaction: Like the many hues of dragon scales, dragon personalities run the gamut from beastly thug to refined connoisseur. Some dragons lie with every smoky breath, others consider the least bit of dishonesty a personal failing, and most fall somewhere in between. All of them can be flattered and even charmed by someone with courtly manners and grace.

Use: A dragon confronts the PCs, challenging them to a riddle game. If the characters win, they get a cypher. If the dragon wins, the PCs owe it a favor to be specified later . . . unless the dragon is hungry now.

Loot: A dragon's hoard might contain 2d6 cyphers, hard currency equivalent to 1d6 exorbitant items, and possibly a few artifacts (but a hoard is usually well guarded).

GM Intrusion: *The dragon breathes fire while the PC is caught in its mouth, which automatically inflicts maximum fire damage on the character.*

DREAM SALLOW 5 (15)

Branches covered with broad, pale green leaves droop from the rounded crown of this great tree whose roots seem as strong and tough as tower foundations. A pleasant scent, soporific and flowery, drifts from the sallow.

A look beneath the drooping branches reveals the remains of previous visitors, all of whom died in their sleep, though that evidence is not always obvious. Dream sallows prey on the minds of thinking creatures, perhaps as a means of sustenance or for some far stranger cause.

Motive: Hungers for minds

Environment: Lone dream sallows sometimes grow in the yards of dilapidated houses or at the edges of ancient ruins.

Health: 15

Damage Inflicted: See Combat

Armor: 3

Movement: None

Modifications: Knowledge as level 10.

Combat: Minuscule spores fill the air within short range of a dream sallow. Someone who breathes them in must succeed on an Intellect defense roll or decide that a nap in the tree's shade would be perfect. Someone who succeeds on her initial defense roll must continue to make defense rolls while in the area, but the difficulty of the task drops to 1.

Rootlets emerge from the ground and bore through the skull of a living creature who falls asleep or is otherwise helpless beneath the tree, creating a neurological connection that inflicts 1 point of damage and puts the victim in a coma. On average, the bodies of new victims die after about a week, but perhaps consciousness survives in the tree.

Cutting a victim free before he dies or cutting down the tree causes a victim who fails a Might defense roll a brain hemorrhage and a messy death. Even on a success, the victim's Intellect Pool drops to 0 until after his next ten-hour recovery roll.

Interaction: For most people, dream sallows seem like inert trees. However, those who have a psychic gift or who willingly choose to nap by the tree can attempt to interact with it, though both risk the sallow not letting go afterward. A sallow's dream avatar appears as a towering humanoid woman of bark and leaves, stem and bough, with hands of knotted root. In return for dealing with another threat to the tree, environmental or otherwise, a sallow may agree to release a negotiator's ally without risk of brain hemorrhage.

Use: After a long day's travel in the hot sun, the PCs come upon a pleasant grove of trees that look like weeping willows and offer shade.

Loot: 1d6 + 1 cyphers can be found buried in the soil beneath the tree, usually the belongings of previous victims.

GM Intrusion: *A character fleeing the presence of a dream sallow is attacked by a root that seeks to hold him in place to allow the spores to do their work.*

ELEMENTAL

Various elemental beings exist, including those of fire and earth.

ELEMENTAL, FIRE 4 (12)

Searing flame in a vaguely humanoid shape, a fire elemental exists only to burn that which is not already ash. They sometimes spin into being where great conflagrations burn.

Motive: Burn

Environment: Anywhere fires can burn

Health: 24

Damage Inflicted: 4 to 7 points; see Combat

Movement: Short

Modifications: See Combat for escalating attack level modification.

Combat: A fire elemental attacks with a flaming limb. The more the elemental burns foes, the more powerful it grows. Its power increases according to the number of successful attacks (that dealt fire damage) it made on another creature during the previous minute.

0 successful attacks: Deals 4 points of damage; attacks as level 4

1 successful attack: Deals 5 points of damage; attacks as level 5

3 successful attacks: Deals 6 points of damage; attacks as level 6

4+ successful attacks: Deals 7 points of damage; attacks as level 7

If a fire elemental hasn't burned a foe within the last minute, its combat stats drop back to its level 4 baseline.

A fire elemental is immune to fire attacks but vulnerable to cold; every time it takes 1 point of cold damage, it takes 1 additional point of damage.

Interaction: Fire elementals are barely sapient and usually respond only to those who know spells able to command them. However, there's a chance (about 10%) that a fire elemental commanded to accomplish a particular task breaks free and instead burns whatever's around until it exhausts all possible fuel sources.

Use: A rash of fires leads some people to suspect that an arsonist is on the loose, but the truth is worse.

GM Intrusion: *A character hit by the fire elemental's attack catches on fire and takes 3 points of damage each round until she spends an action patting, rolling, or smothering the flames.*

ELEMENTAL, EARTH 5 (15)

An excavation, a meteor fall, a still-shuddering earthquake—all these events can summon an earth elemental to take shape and expand the destruction further.

Motive: Crumble and break, reduce things to earth

Environment: Anywhere solid or earthen

Health: 30

Damage Inflicted: 6 points

Armor: 3

Movement: Immediate; short if burrowing

Combat: Earth elementals batter foes with heavy fists. They can also create earthquakes (no more than once every other round) that affect the ground within short range. Creatures standing in the area fall to the ground and take 5 points of damage on a failed Might defense roll.

An earth elemental is vulnerable to water. Any damage it takes while standing in or being doused in water ignores its Armor.

Interaction: Although brooding and slow to respond if encountered as immobile stone, earth elementals are intelligent. The ones that are summoned with a spell have about a 5% chance of breaking the geas and turning on their summoner.

Use: Oddly articulated monoliths were discovered high in the mountains around a shrine containing an ancient treasure. A merchant wants someone to investigate the monoliths in case they represent a trap. In fact, the monoliths are inactive earth elementals.

Structures in the area of a fire elemental's attack might catch on fire; those caught in the area of an earth elemental's earthquake might collapse.

GM Intrusion: *A character within range of the earth elemental's earthquake attack must succeed on a Speed defense roll or be covered in an avalanche from a collapsing structure or cliff face.*

ENTHRALLER 6 (18)

Hundreds of thousands of years ago, enthraller ancestors psychically dominated a group of interstellar spacefarers who had the misfortune to land on the enthraller homeworld. Leapfrogging technological prowess by mentally commandeering the know-how of every new species they encountered using their stolen space travel, the aliens fashioned the Enthraller Dominion, which stretches across vast swaths of space and is cemented by the psychic control of its alien overlords.

Individual enthraller psychic ability is fierce, but the overlords maintain control over longer distances and larger populations with technological aids. These include cranial circlets that give a single enthraller governor the ability to dominate a small city, solar-system-sized ring relays that boost their control across interstellar distances, and more.

Recently, a newly contacted race of aliens developed the technological means to resist the mental influence of the enthrallers. Now war bubbles across the Enthraller Dominion. Sometimes individual enthrallers, stripped of their technological enhancements as a consequence of this war, flee into virgin space, looking for new soldiers to dominate.

Motive: Domination of other creatures

Environment: Almost anywhere, alone or in groups of three

Health: 18

Damage Inflicted: 4 points; see Combat

Armor: 1

Movement: Short

Modifications: Speed defense as level 4; perception and ability to detect falsehoods as level 8.

Combat: An enthraller usually relies on dominated minions to make physical attacks on its behalf. An enthraller can make a psychic attack on a creature within short range. On a failed Intellect defense roll, the target acts as the enthraller mentally commands on its next action. If the same target is affected by this dominating attack a second time within a minute, the enthraller's mental control lasts for one minute.

Alternatively, as its action, an enthraller can emit a psychic burst that can target up to three creatures in short range. On a failed Intellect defense roll, a victim suffers 4 points of Intellect damage (ignores Armor) and is unable to take actions on her subsequent turn. If she is attacked while so stunned, the difficulty of her defense rolls is increased by two steps.

The enthraller's attack is a form of mental feeding. If it moves a PC down the damage track, the creature regains 4 points of health.

Interaction: An enthraller can communicate telepathically with characters within short range. It tries to mentally dominate whoever it runs across and will negotiate only with characters who are strong enough to harm it. Even if an enthraller makes a deal, it eventually reneges if it senses any advantage for doing so because it implicitly believes that other creatures are cattle.

Use: A spacecraft (or perhaps an escape pod) crash lands. Inside, a hurt enthraller lies in suspended animation. Investigators are unlikely to realize the enthraller's nature beforehand, but they certainly learn if they wake the alien.

Loot: Enthrallers wear light armor suited for their forms. They might have one or two cyphers and, rarely, an artifact that boosts their already fearsome mental capabilities.

GM Intrusion: *The enthraller's intrusion into the character's mind stirs up forgotten memories. The PC must deal with the contents of these memories and perhaps why they were repressed.*

FALLEN ANGEL 5 (15)

Angels are normally associated with virtue and service to higher moral beings. But just like people, sometimes angels are tempted into impure acts. Those who stray too far over the line may fall from higher realms and be forced to walk the Earth in penance. This experience drives most fallen angels insane.

Fallen angel abilities wax and wane according to the position of the sun. During the day, a fallen angel seems almost sane (and is less dangerous), but at night, it is volatile and threatening to everyone.

Motive: Revenge (but on whom and for what isn't clear, even to the fallen angel)

Environment: Anywhere, sometimes living alone in the wilderness, other times walking the hard streets of large cities

Health: 25

Damage Inflicted: 6 points by day, 8 points at night

Armor: 2

Movement: Short; long when flying

Modifications: At night, perceptions and attacks as level 7.

Combat: At night, a fallen angel can attack other creatures by projecting a long-range beam of burning light. Against foes within immediate range, the fallen angel manifests burning wings. A fallen angel can choose to make its attacks ignore Armor, but for each attack so modified, it loses 4 points of health.

On the rare occasion that a fallen angel is within immediate range of another of its kind, both regain 1 point of health per round.

By day, a fallen angel cannot project long-range attacks and has no visible wings with which to make melee attacks, though it may carry a melee weapon.

Interaction: By day, fallen angels are not automatically hostile, and they can be negotiated and reasoned with. They can seem truly angelic, though they are often confused and forgetful of their origin. But when night descends, fallen angels lose control of their faculties as they swell with rage and power. Unless a character directs a fallen angel toward another creature on which it can vent its wrath, the character becomes the object of the fury.

Use: A star slips down from the sky and lands in the country. The next day, travelers come upon a farm in the area and find everyone dead and burned. A trail of scorched earth leads up into the hills.

Loot: Fallen angels collect cyphers and usually have a few.

A fallen angel ultimately seeks revenge against whoever threw it from the higher realms. Since that vengeance is hard to gain, fallen angels take out their frustration on whatever crosses their path.

GM Intrusion: *A fallen angel's successful attack causes the character's cypher to detonate (if a grenade) or otherwise activate in a less-than-ideal fashion.*

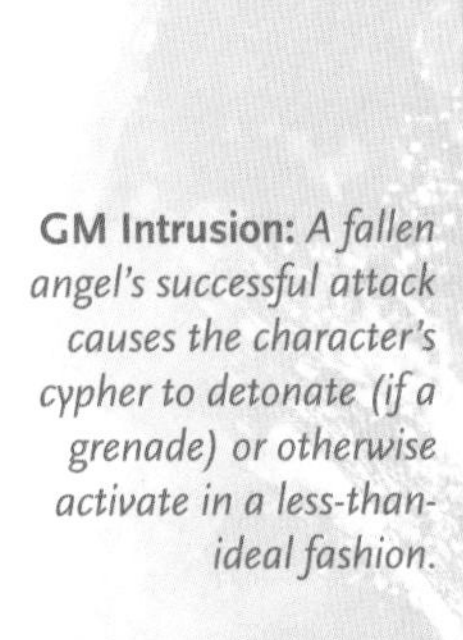

GHOST 4 (12)

Sounds with no apparent origin, such as the tap of footsteps on the stair, knocking behind the walls, crying from empty rooms, and haunting music might be signs of a ghost. If the sound is accompanied by a sudden temperature drop and the breath of living creatures begins to steam, it's a certainty.

Ghosts are the spectral remnants of humans, which persist either as fragments of memory or as full-fledged spirits. Though their appearance varies between individuals, many appear somewhat translucent, washed out, or physically warped from their time spent as a phantom.

The ghost of a high school girl named Emily supposedly haunts a covered bridge in Stowe, Vermont, though she appears only at midnight.

Motive: Unpredictable (but often seeking to complete unfinished business)
Environment: Almost anywhere
Health: 12
Damage Inflicted: 5 points
Movement: Short
Modifications: Stealth as level 7; tasks related to frightening others as level 6.
Combat: A ghost doesn't take damage from mundane physical sources, but it takes half damage from spells and attacks that direct energy, and full damage from weapons designed to affect spirits, psychic attacks, and similar attacks.

A ghost's touch inflicts freezing damage. Some ghosts can kill victims with fear. A ghost with this ability can attack all creatures within short range with a psychic display so horrible that targets who fail an Intellect defense roll take 4 points of Intellect damage (ignores Armor) and become terrified, freezing in place. In each subsequent round, a terrified victim can attempt an Intellect-based task to push away the fright. Each failed attempt moves the victim one step down the damage track. Not attempting to clear one's mind of fear counts as a failed attempt. Those killed by fear are marked by expressions of horror and hair that has turned white.

A ghost can move through solid objects of up to level 7 at will, although it can choose to pick up and manipulate objects if it focuses on them. Ghosts can also go into a state of apparent non-existence for hours or days at a time.

GM Intrusion: *The character must succeed on an Intellect defense roll or be possessed by the ghost until the PC succeeds on an Intellect-based task to push it out. While possessed, the character acts just like the ghost did when it was alive.*

Interaction: Some ghosts are talkative, some don't know they're dead, some want help for a task they failed to accomplish in life, and some only rage against the living and want to bring those who yet breathe into the same colorless existence they endure.

Use: A ghost (that at first appears fully human) wants help in eradicating a guild of ghost hunters that has targeted it and a few others haunting an abandoned structure. The ghost promises to tell secrets of the afterlife to any who accept its strange offer.

Loot: A ghost usually doesn't carry objects, though some might have a keepsake (like an amulet showing the face of a loved one) or an artifact.

GHOUL 4 (12)

Ghouls spend almost as much time beneath the ground as corpses do, but ghouls are very much alive. Their bodies are hairless and so porcelain-smooth that their faces are sometimes mistaken for masks, albeit gore-smeared masks. Ghouls come to the surface at night to gather humanoid remains or steal those recently interred from their graves, though many prefer to eat from still-living victims.

Most ghouls are orgiastic eaters of human flesh, but a rare few ghoul populations are more refined. These wear clothes, have language and sophisticated customs, live in grand subterranean cities of their own design, and fight with milk-white blades of bone. These civilized ghouls claim to hold dominion over the remains of all humans, according to ancient custom, even if they only sometimes assert that privilege. They eat the dead in order to absorb residual memories left in the corpses.

Civilized ghouls are rare and live in subterranean cities. The central purpose of each city is to maintain a massive central library filled with winding scrolls printed on vellum pressed from the skin of the dead.

Motive: Hunger for dead flesh; knowledge (in certain rare cases)

Environment: Anywhere above ground at night, usually in groups of three or more, or in subterranean lairs

Health: 12

Damage Inflicted: 5 points

Movement: Short

Modifications: Two areas of knowledge as level 5.

Combat: Ghoul saliva contains a paralytic agent. Ghoul bites (and weapons used by ghouls) inflict damage and, on a failed Might defense roll, render the target paralyzed for one minute. A paralyzed target can attempt a Might-based task each round to regain mobility, but for the next minute, the difficulty of attack, defense, and movement tasks is increased by one step.

Ghouls can see in the dark. They're blind in full daylight, but civilized ghouls who travel to the surface carry lenses that cover their eyes, allowing them to see without penalty in full sunlight.

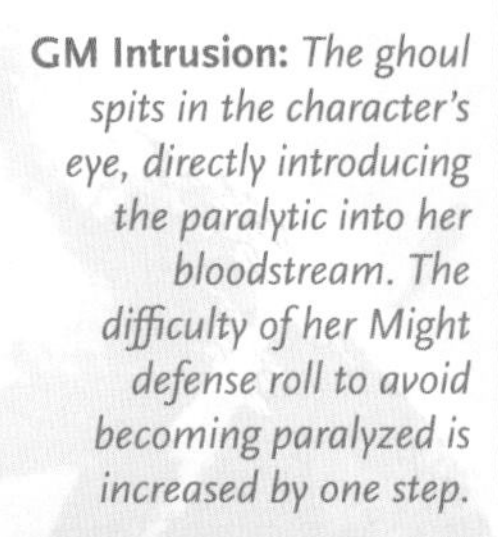

GM Intrusion: *The ghoul spits in the character's eye, directly introducing the paralytic into her bloodstream. The difficulty of her Might defense roll to avoid becoming paralyzed is increased by one step.*

Interaction: Common ghouls can't be negotiated with, though a rare civilized ghoul is an excellent linguist. These latter are willing to deal in return for the body of someone who was knowledgeable or who kept valuable secrets in life.

Use: If a PC needs a piece of information not otherwise obtainable, a trip down into a ghoul city might be worthwhile, for the creatures are rumored to keep lightless libraries below the earth that store knowledge once known by humans.

Loot: If the PCs defeat a group of civilized ghouls, they might find a cypher and a few sets of black goggles that allow the wearer to look directly at the sun and see it as a pale circle.

GIANT 7 (21)

Violent storms, earthquakes, typhoons, and other natural disasters draw giants. Standing 20 to 30 feet (6 to 9 m) tall, giants delight in rampaging through the middle of such calamities, creating even more destruction. Some giants grow so powerful that they can trigger natural disasters on their own.

Motive: Destruction

Environment: Underground, deserts, mountaintops, and similar desolate areas

Health: 40

Damage Inflicted: 9 points

Armor: 1

Movement: Short

Modifications: Speed defense as level 5 due to size; breaks and throws objects as level 8; sees through deceptions and tricks as level 3.

Combat: A giant smashes foes with her fists, possibly catching up to three human-sized targets with the same attack if all the targets are in immediate range of each other.

If a giant attacks a single target, she can choose to do regular damage or to grab hold of her victim, dealing 4 points of damage instead. On his turn, the victim can attempt a Might defense roll to struggle out of the grip, a Speed defense roll to slip out, or an Intellect-based task to distract the giant. If the victim fails, the giant throws him as high and as far as she can on her next turn. Damage on impact varies, depending on the environment, but a victim takes an average of 10 points of ambient damage.

A few giants can generate storms, tidal waves, earthquakes, and similar phenomena that can lash an area up to 1,000 feet (305 m) across for up to a minute, inflicting 3 points of damage each round to all creatures and objects not protected by shelter designed to withstand a storm (though few shelters protect against an earthquake).

Interaction: Most giants are not very bright. When a giant is rampaging, someone could attempt to distract her by singing, juggling, or doing some other trick, which some giants will pause to watch for at least one or two rounds.

Use: A giant came down out of the mountains and laid waste to half the nearby village. Survivors will pay someone to venture into the giant's mountain lair and destroy her.

Loot: Individual giants carry little, but giant lairs may contain currency equivalent to 1d6 expensive items, 1d6 cyphers, and a couple of artifacts.

GM Intrusion: *The giant's blow sprains one of the PC's limbs, making the limb useless for ten minutes.*

GIANT RAT 3 (9)

Giant rats are as large as big attack dogs, just as vicious, and more wily. Some giant rats are the lone matriarchs of a pack of ordinary level 1 rats, and others are just one of several making up a colony of oversized rodents. Like their smaller cousins, giant rats are known for harboring virulent disease

Motive: Defense, reproduction

Environment: Anywhere in ruins or sewers, in groups of one to seven

Health: 18

Damage Inflicted: 4 points

Movement: Short; long when jumping

Modifications: Perception as level 4; tasks related to overcoming obstacles and puzzles as level 5.

Combat: Victims damaged by a giant rat's diseased teeth and claws take 4 points of damage and, on a failed Might defense roll, are infected with a level 5 disease. Within twelve hours, the victim's lymph glands swell, creating visible buboes. Every twelve hours thereafter, the victim must succeed on a Might defense roll or take 5 points of ambient damage.

Interaction: Giant rats stubbornly pursue prey, but they flee if that prey proves to be too strong.

Use: A contact of the PCs dies of plague before she can deliver an important message. They'll have to backtrack her movements to discover what she wanted to tell them, which leads to a giant rat colony.

GM Intrusion: *A swarm of twelve ordinary rats—each level 1, but acting like a level 3 swarm—is summoned by the high-pitched squeaking of a giant rat.*

GIANT SNAKE 4 (12)

Those about to stumble into the presence of a giant snake at least 50 feet (15 m) long are warned by the skin it shed and discarded and by the cracked, slippery bones of digested victims.

Motive: Hungers for flesh

Environment: Anywhere a giant snake can lurk, including jungles, sewers, caves, and spacecraft access tubes

Health: 18

Damage Inflicted: 5 points

Armor: 2

Movement: Short

Modifications: Perception and stealth as level 6; Speed defense as level 3 due to size.

Combat: A giant snake bites foes, preferably from ambush. When it succeeds, the difficulty of the target's Speed defense roll increases by two steps, and the snake's bite deals 8 points of damage for that attack. On a failed Might defense roll, a bite also inflicts 3 points of Speed damage (ignores Armor). A giant snake may coil around a sleeping, stunned, or debilitated victim. Caught victims automatically take 5 points of crushing damage each round until they break free.

Giant snakes lose their perception and stealth modifications in cold climates and when attacked with abilities that reduce the temperature. Thus, the creatures retreat from cold.

Interaction: A giant snake is a predator that regards other creatures as food, though it ignores them when it is already busy digesting a meal.

Use: Characters note something amiss as they glimpse lambent eyes peering from the darkness, glaring as if seeking to pin victims in place with cold terror.

Loot: A giant snake's droppings or gullet might hold a few cyphers and possibly an artifact that the creature could not digest.

Once it kills a victim, a giant snake drags off the carcass and swallows it over the course of a minute. It takes the snake several hours to digest a human-sized creature.

GM Intrusion: *The snake's venom affects the character more strongly. Instead of merely inflicting Speed damage, it also paralyzes the PC for one minute, though after a couple of rounds, she can make another Might defense roll to throw off the effects of the poison early.*

GIANT SPIDER 3 (9)

Giant spiders result most commonly from radioactive accidents, magic, or genetic manipulation. Whatever their origin, they're terrifying hunters large enough to predate people. The creatures range from the size of a large dog to the size of a large horse.

Motive: Hungers for blood

Environment: Anywhere webs can be spun in the dark

Health: 12

Damage Inflicted: 3 points

Movement: Short; long when traveling on their webs

Modifications: Perception as level 5; Speed defense as level 4 due to quickness.

Combat: A giant spider's envenomed fangs inflict 3 points of damage, plus 3 points of Speed damage (ignores Armor) if a victim fails a Might defense roll. Debilitated victims are not killed but instead cocooned and hung for later dining. Giant spider webs (level 4) can hold victims immobile and unable to take actions until they manage to break free.

Giant spiders lose their perception and Speed defense modifications in bright light and thus often retreat from intense illumination.

Interaction: Most giant spiders are simple predators and react accordingly.

Use: Giant spider webs can infest unlit alleys, dungeon corridors, dark forests, and darkened hallways of decommissioned genetic labs.

Loot: Cocooned corpses of previous victims hanging in a giant spider's web sometimes contain all manner of valuables, including cyphers.

GM Intrusion: *Giant spider eggs hatch, and a level 3 swarm of tiny spiders attacks the character.*

GOBLIN 1 (3)

Goblins are wicked, grasping, and perversely resourceful. Usually no larger than children, they can seem like pesky rabble, but that illusion hides something altogether more cunning. Tribe members work together to accomplish their goals of murder, kidnapping, and theft.

Motive: Greed and theft

Environment: Tunnels and caves, usually in groups of ten or more

Health: 3

Damage Inflicted: 2 points

Movement: Short

Modifications: Tasks related to perception, stealth, and setting traps as level 5.

Combat: Goblins attack from the shadows with ambushes and hit-and-run tactics. When they have surprise, goblins attack as level 4 creatures and deal 2 additional points of damage, and they attempt to draw larger prey into level 5 traps they've previously set. They often flee in the face of real danger.

Interaction: Goblins are lying tricksters but can be cowed into cooperating for short periods.

Use: Thieves and murderers, goblins are foes to all, even rival goblin tribes.

Loot: Aside from weapons, each goblin carries a personal stash, including bones, shiny rocks, sticks, and other bits of worthless trash, plus currency equivalent to an inexpensive item.

GM Intrusion: *The goblin poisoned his knife. If struck, the PC must make a Might defense roll or immediately move one step down the damage track.*

GOLEM 6 (18)

Animate creatures of stone created by magic for a specific purpose, golems usually serve as guardians. However, they may also serve as soldiers, couriers, and banner-bearers. Golems that have accomplished their task may spend years without moving, like statuary posed in unexpected places stained, eroded, and forlorn. But if disturbed, a golem rumbles back to movement and attempts to restart the last task assigned to it by its maker.

Motive: Seeks to fulfill the commands of its creator

Environment: Anywhere that needs a sturdy magical guardian

Health: 30

Damage Inflicted: 8 points

Armor: 5

Movement: Short

Modifications: Intellect defense as level 2; Speed defense as level 4 due to slowness.

Combat: Skilled with large two-handed weapons, golems inflict 2 additional points of damage (total of 8 points) when using them. Golems cannot be stunned or dazed. They are immune to most poisons and disease, and 2 of their 5 points of Armor protect against ambient damage (environmental damage, heat, cold, falling, and so on).

On the other hand, golems are activated by light, even light as dim as a candle. In complete darkness, a golem is blind and suffers penalties to attack and defend normally. A golem subject to complete darkness may choose to freeze in place like a statue. When one does so, its Armor increases to 10 (and Armor against ambient damage increases to 5), but it can take no actions, including purely mental actions. Unless something can damage the golem through its Armor, it remains frozen indefinitely or until light returns.

Even if a golem is completely destroyed, the rubble of its form slowly reassembles over the course of three days, unless that rubble is ground to the finest gravel and spread widely.

Interaction: Most golems can't speak. Those that can are mournful, and a few have become cruel in their isolation, but at heart, all are lonely. Many are also tired of their stone existence, in which they can move but not really feel, and they wish for some sort of final end.

Use: Powerful sorcerers sometimes create golems and press them into service with yet more spells. These golems prove to be tough bodyguards, but sometimes the futility of such service overcomes a golem and it turns on the sorcerer, breaking free of the binding spells in its rage over being denied the peace of death.

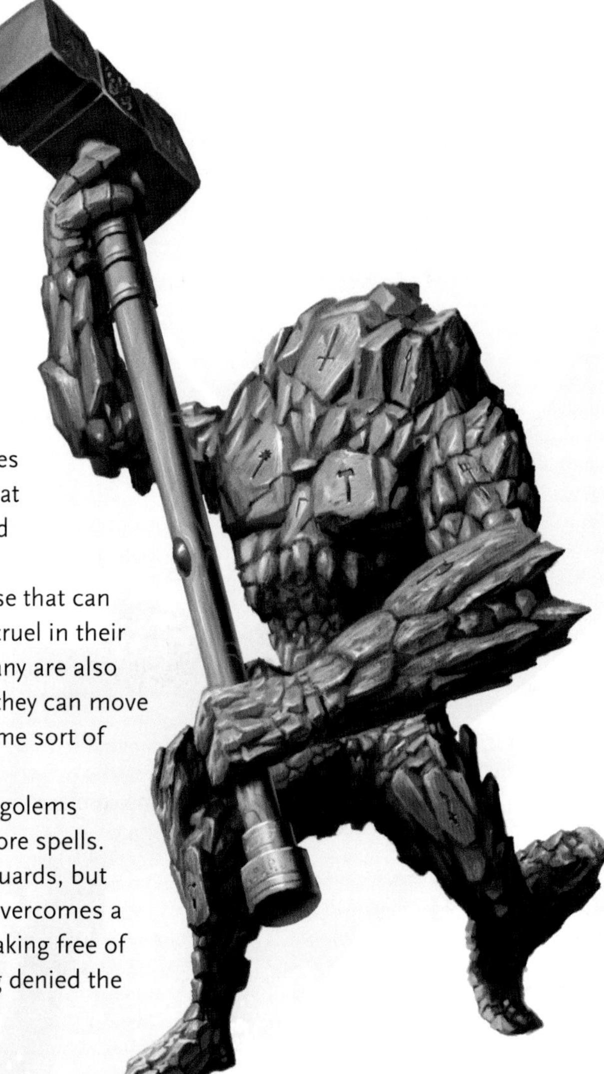

GM Intrusion: *The character hit by the golem is also grabbed and headbutted for 6 additional points of damage. The PC must break or slip free, or else she remains in the golem's grip.*

GREY 4 (12)

Greys are enigmatic creatures born of alien stars (or dimensions) who have learned to move across the vast distances that bridge neighboring star systems. The creatures descend through the atmosphere under the cover of night to abduct specimens for study and return the victims later after a thorough examination. Returned abductees are usually befuddled and confused, and they retain little memory of what happened to them. Victims of the greys' examination frequently sport strange marks on their flesh, oddly shaped wounds, gaps where teeth used to be, and strange or unknown metal lodged somewhere under the skin.

A grey stands 3 feet (1 m) tall. It has a narrow body with skinny limbs and a large, bulbous head. Two large black eyes, almond shaped, dominate a face that has only a suggestion of a nose and a narrow mouth. Greys wear skintight uniforms, carry numerous instruments to study their environments, and keep a weapon or two for protection.

Motive: Knowledge

Environment: Greys land their spacecraft in remote areas, where they have minimal risk of discovery.

Health: 12

Damage Inflicted: 6 points

Armor: 1

Movement: Short

Modifications: All tasks related to knowledge as level 6; Speed defense as level 5 due to size and quickness.

Combat: A grey carries a powerful ray emitter that can burn holes through solid steel. The grey can use the emitter to attack targets within long range. Against dangerous opponents, a grey can use an action to activate a personal shield that encapsulates it in a bubble of force. The shield gives it +3 to Armor, but while the shield is active, the grey can't fire its ray emitter.

Greys are scientists, but cautious ones. Leaving a trail of corpses as evidence of their existence isn't their preferred mode of operation. For this reason, one grey in every group has a memory eraser. When this grey activates the device, each target other than a grey within short range must succeed on an Intellect defense roll or become stunned for one minute, taking no action (unless attacked, which snaps the victim out of the condition). When the effect wears off naturally, the target has no recollection of encountering little grey creatures.

Interaction: Greys are curious about the places they visit but reluctant to move or act in the open. Secretive and mysterious, they prefer to observe creatures from afar and, on occasion, pick them up for closer inspection. Someone who offers a grey true knowledge might be treated as an equal rather than a lab animal.

Use: The PCs are called to investigate a series of disappearances of animals and people. One by one, the abductees return, usually in odd places, and always bearing physical markings that suggest they were subjected to invasive procedures. To protect others from a similar fate, the PCs must catch the abductors in the act.

Loot: A grey has one or two cyphers and might have a memory eraser that works as described under Combat (depletion roll of 1–2 on a 1d10).

Ray emitter, page 359

GM Intrusion: *A grey's ray emitter suffers a terrible mishap and explodes. The device kills the grey and destroys its body completely. For the next twenty-four hours, creatures that come within a short distance of where the grey died take 4 points of ambient damage from the psychic radiation each round they remain there.*

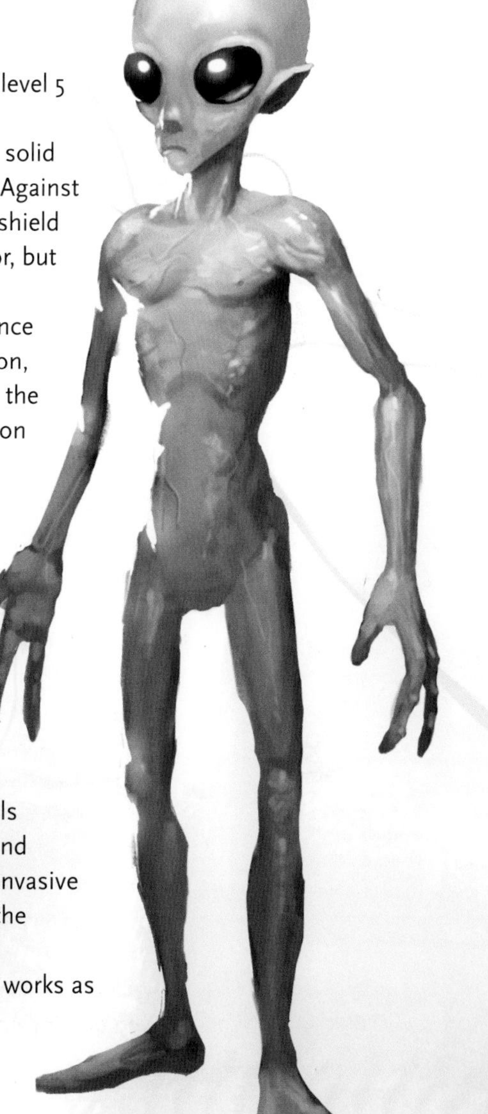

KAIJU 10 (30)

Kaiju come in a variety of shapes, but all share one difficult-to-ignore quality: mind-blowing size. Appearances of these colossal creatures are rare events that usually don't last for more than a few days. In that sense, they're akin to hundred-year storms and at least as destructive. When they emerge, they're attracted by artificial structures, the more densely situated and elaborate the better, which they set to smashing with a vengeance. It's hard to judge the size of things so far outside normal scale, but good estimates put most kaiju at over 300 feet (91 m) in height.

Kaiju rely primarily on their strength and mass, but many have some additional trick or ability that sets them apart from their kin, which usually translates into even more devastation.

The other quality all kaiju share is the talent of hiding after a rampage by diving into a nearby sea or burrowing deep into the earth. Sometimes the same kaiju will appear again days, months, years, or decades later, attacking the same location or someplace entirely new.

Other named kaiju include Kthama, a many-tentacled creature able to generate a tsunami of black fluid that sweeps away whole neighborhoods, and Tonboju, a massive, insectlike creature whose beating wings can generate windstorms, and whose missile stingers leave dozens of smoke trails in their wake and produce immense explosions when they reach their target.

Motive: Destruction

Environment: Usually near communities containing many high structures

Health: 140

Damage Inflicted: 18 points

Armor: 5

Movement: Short

Modifications: Speed defense as level 8 due to size.

Combat: A kaiju can punch, kick, or deliver a tail or tentacle lash at something within long range. Damage is inflicted on the target and everything within short range of the target, and even those that succeed on a Speed defense roll take 7 points of damage.

Kaiju heal quickly, usually at a rate of 2 points per round.

Kaiju are rare and devastating enough that most are dubbed with a unique identifier by survivors. The entry for each creature below notes only where it varies from the base creature described above.

Rampagion: This kaiju has been estimated to be almost 1,000 feet (305 m) high. Once per day, it can make a charging trample attack, dealing its damage in a line 300 feet (91 m) wide and 2 miles (3 km) long. Rampagion has 10 Armor and deals 20 points of damage with a physical attack (or 8 points if a victim makes a successful Speed defense roll).

Suneko: This kaiju's body, which resembles a cross between a lion and a lizard, is so hot that its skin glows like red coals, its mane like the sun's corona, and its eyes like beaming searchlights. Suneko automatically deals 10 points of damage to everyone within immediate range. The creature can emit twin rays of plasma from its eyes in a focused beam that can reach as far as the horizon, which from Suneko's height above the ground is about 22 miles (35 km). When it makes its eyebeam attack, it stops emitting killing heat in immediate range for about one minute.

GM Intrusion: *The character gains the direct attention of the kaiju. If the kaiju attacks the PC, she is awarded 5 XP, only 1 of which she has to give to a friend.*

Interaction: Most PCs can't directly interact with a kaiju unless they have some special device or association allowing them to get the attention of one of the massive creatures. Doing so could give the characters a chance to trick or lure the beast, or maybe even persuade one kaiju to fight another.

Use: After seeing the devastation caused by a kaiju, the PCs might decide (or be asked) to find a way to stop a projected future appearance by the same creature.

KILLING WHITE LIGHT 5 (12)

"The glow returned last night. It was as bright as a welder's torch! Everyone ran, our shadows leading the way. I escaped the killing white light, but my brother wasn't so lucky."

~Aida Chavez, refugee

A killing white light isn't a subtle hunter. At a distance, the creature is an eye-watering point of brilliance. When it closes in, it is nothing less than blinding, though its emanation isn't warm. Despite the blazing intensity, a killing white light is as cold as starlight on a December night, sapping heat and life from living things caught in its radiance.

By day, a killing white light is usually inactive. During this period, the creature hibernates in darkened areas, as if unwilling or unable to compete against the sun.

Motive: Eliminate organic life
Environment: Almost anywhere dark
Health: 15
Damage Inflicted: 5 points
Armor: 1
Movement: Short when flying
Combat: An active (glowing) killing white light can attack one target within immediate range each round with a pulse of its brilliant nimbus. A character who fails a Speed defense roll against the attack takes damage and experiences a cooling numbness. A victim killed by the creature is rendered into so much blowing ash, though her clothing and equipment are unharmed.

As it attacks, a killing white light emits a blinding nimbus of illumination that affects all creatures within short range. Targets in the area must succeed on a Might defense roll each round or be blinded for one round. A character in the area can avert her eyes when fighting a killing white light to avoid being blinded, but if she does so, the difficulty of her attacks and defenses against it is increased by one step.

A killing white light is vulnerable to strong sources of light other than its own. If exposed to daylight or caught in a high-intensity beam of light (such as a spotlight), the killing white light falters and takes no action for one round, after which it can act normally. However, if the competing light persists for more than three or four rounds, the creature usually retreats to a darkened place of safety.

Interaction: A killing white light is too alien for interaction and may not be intelligent in a way humans can understand.

Use: An inactive killing white light (which looks something like an albino lump of volcanic glass) is sometimes mistaken for a cypher whose properties can't quite be identified—until the creature becomes active, at which point its true nature is revealed.

Though normally hidden within the nimbus of its brilliant radiation, the core of a killing white light is a solid object about 1 foot (30 cm) in diameter. It looks like a bleached-white chunk of volcanic glass filled with tiny, bubblelike cavities, suggesting that the creature might be some kind of mineral-based life form.

GM Intrusion: *Normally resistant to interaction, a killing white light uses its blazing nimbus to burn an alien glyph of uncertain meaning in the character's flesh before the creature fades like a light bulb switched off.*

MECHANICAL SOLDIER 4 (12)

Clockwork automatons powered by steam, these mechanical men patrol about and guard locations of importance to their makers. Lanky and awkward in their movements, these quasihumanoid automatons stand almost 8 feet (2 m) tall. In their three-fingered hands, they wield a variety of weapons.

A few people have wondered if a gear-driven soldier could ever truly attain sentience. Most scoff at the suggestion, but is that a gleam in the glass lens of its eye?

Motive: Incomprehensible

Environment: Anywhere, usually in groups of three to eight

Health: 15

Damage Inflicted: 4 points

Armor: 3

Movement: Short

Modifications: Perception as level 5; leaps, runs, and balances as level 3.

GM Intrusion: *The destroyed soldier explodes in a gout of flame, black smoke, and steam, inflicting 6 points of damage to all within immediate range.*

Combat: Mechanical soldiers attack in groups using well-organized tactics. Although they can speak, they transmit information to one another silently and instantly within a 100-mile (161 km) range via wireless radio transmissions.

Soldiers armed with advanced weaponry typically carry rifle-like guns that can fire multiple rapid shots without reloading. The soldiers fire at up to three targets (all next to one another) at once. For each target after the first, the difficulty of defense rolls is decreased by one step.

In addition, one in four soldiers carries a back-mounted device that hurls bombs at long range with deadly accuracy. They explode in immediate range for 4 points of damage. Each device holds 1d6 such bombs.

A mechanical soldier that has lost its original weaponry scavenges whatever is available.

Certain frequencies of sound confuse these clockwork men, causing them to function at two levels lower than normal, and other frequencies prevent them from acting at all for 1d6 + 1 rounds.

Interaction: On their own, mechanical soldiers act on prior orders. Otherwise, they listen to and obey their creator—and only their creator.

Use: An enterprising bandit has captured and repurposed a number of mechanical soldiers, probably using sound. These soldiers remember nothing of their former duties and work for their new master as high-tech brigands and pirates. The bandit has no idea how to repair them if they are damaged, much less make new soldiers.

Loot: A determined scientist might scavenge the body of one of these automatons to find a cypher.

MI-GO 5 (15)

"[T]he creatures were a sort of huge, light-red crab with many pairs of legs and with two great batlike wings in the middle of the back. They sometimes walked on all their legs, and sometimes on the hindmost pair only, using the others to convey large objects of indeterminate nature. On one occasion they were spied in considerable numbers, a detachment of them wading along a shallow woodland watercourse three abreast in evidently disciplined formation. Once a specimen was seen flying—launching itself from the top of a bald, lonely hill at night and vanishing in the sky after its great flapping wings had been silhouetted an instant against the full moon."

~H. P. Lovecraft, "The Whisperer in Darkness"

These extraterrestrial creatures are known as the Fungi from Yuggoth or the Abominable Ones. They are a bizarre amalgam of insect and fungal entity, with many limbs and wings that can carry them aloft. They sometimes enslave humans to work for them in strange factories, mines, or other labor-intensive capacities.

Motive: Knowledge and power

Environment: Usually cold or temperate hills or mountains

Health: 19

Damage Inflicted: 5 points

Armor: 1

Movement: Short; long when flying

Modifications: All knowledge tasks as level 6.

Combat: Mi-go defend themselves with pincers and claws but are more likely to use technological devices as weapons. Assume that a mi-go has one of the following abilities from a device:

- Project a blast of electricity at long range that inflicts 6 points of damage
- Emit poison gas in a cloud that fills short range and inflicts 4 points of Intellect damage if the victim fails a Might defense roll (the mi-go is immune)
- Project a holographic image of itself to one side that increases the difficulty of attacks aimed at the real mi-go by two steps
- Project a sonic field that provides +2 to Armor

Mi-go have access to other devices as well, including translators, cylinders that can preserve a human's brain without its body, sophisticated tools, collars that control the actions of their wearers, and weird vehicles. Mi-go suffer no damage from cold and do not need to breathe.

Interaction: Although very few mi-go speak human languages, peaceful interaction with these creatures is not impossible. It's just very difficult (level 7), as they see most humans as little more than animals.

Use: The characters are attacked by mi-go intent on capturing and enslaving them. If caught, the PCs are sent to scavenge through primordial ruins for disturbing technological relics.

Loot: Mi-go always have 1d6 cyphers as well as many curious objects that have no obvious human function.

GM Intrusion: *Fungal spores from the mi-go's body overcome the character, who must succeed at a Might defense roll or lose her next turn. She faces this risk each round she is within immediate distance of the creature.*

MOKUREN 3 (9)

Mokuren are usually no larger than a cat, but they possess the ability to swell until they're the size of a bus (if only briefly). That ability, combined with their flashy pyrokinetic tails, make these creatures a particular favorite with children, at least in stories and picture books. Given that mokuren can "burrow" into paintings and other two-dimensional art, it's possible that some mokuren images are more than simple representations.

Motive: Play

Environment: Almost anywhere, usually as static images on walls or in storybooks

Health: 9

Damage Inflicted: 3 points, unless enlarged; see Combat

Movement: Short; long if flying

Modifications: Defends as level 5 due to size, unless enlarged; see Combat.

Combat: A mokuren exists in three states: as an image, as a cat-sized creature, and as a bus-sized behemoth.

As an image, a mokuren can't be harmed. Even if the image is defaced, the mokuren merely "burrows" away and reappears like graffiti on a new flat space within a few miles.

Alternatively, it could emerge from the image and become a physical cat-sized creature as a move. In this form, a mokuren can attack with its claws or bite. It can also direct a stream of fire from its glowing tail at a target within long range. (When a mokuren flies, it's by using its tail to create a jet that rockets it skyward.)

Finally, it can make an enlarged attack, in which it swells to the size of a bus and swipes at, bites, or lands on a target as part of the same action. When enlarged, the mokuren gains +5 to Armor and makes and defends against all attacks as a level 7 creature. On a hit, the enlarged mokuren deals 7 points of damage. However, a mokuren can remain enlarged for a total of only four rounds during any twenty-four-hour period, so it uses this ability sparingly or only when enraged.

Interaction: To see an active mokuren is considered good luck, unless you manage to get on the wrong side of one. Then an offering of sweets must be made to the offended creature. A mokuren can't talk, but it can understand the languages where it lives about as well as a trained courser or hound can.

Use: A mokuren can lead characters into unexplored areas, helping them find places they may have overlooked or skipped. It can also lead PCs into danger, but it usually does so only to bring aid (the characters) to someone else in trouble.

As images, mokuren can exist almost anywhere. They sometimes remain inactive without coming alive off a page for years or decades, until someone new comes along that the mokuren finds interesting.

GM Intrusion: *The character hit by the mokuren doesn't take damage. Instead, she must succeed on a Might defense roll or be pulled into the nearest wall, floor, or book with the creature, becoming a two-dimensional image. In this state, the PC is in stasis until the mokuren pulls her free, another creature "pries" her loose, or a day passes and she emerges naturally.*

NEVERI 7 (21)

In fiction, it's not uncommon to find incredibly powerful Evil Things, secured by Ancient Powers in a forgotten prison. But why? Why didn't those Ancient Powers simply destroy the Evil Thing? Many possibilities suggest themselves, but the plainest answer might be right: because the Evil Thing would not die.

A neveri is a floating blob of heaving, writhing flesh, 10 feet (3 m) in diameter, which always oozes pus, dark fluids, and the odor of a thousand graves. A neveri constantly extrudes new sections of skin, mouths, eyes, spines, clawed hands, and whipping tendrils, seemingly force-grown from the mass of dead matter that serves as the nucleus of its body.

Neveri are rare, apparently spending years at a time either inactive or imprisoned from some earlier epoch. When one becomes active (or escapes), it makes a lair in a hard-to-reach location within a day or two of a large population of living things and sets to work feeding its ravenous appetite.

Motive: Hungers for flesh
Environment: Anywhere
Health: 42
Damage Inflicted: 7 points
Armor: 2
Movement: Long when flying; immediate when burrowing
Modifications: Speed defense as level 5 due to size; knowledge tasks as level 8.
Combat: A neveri can create specialized organs that spray acid, spit enzymes, or generate bursts of radiation or plasma at long range against up to three targets at one time.

One character in immediate range of a neveri must succeed on a Might defense roll each round or be grasped by a mouth, tendril, or clawed hand. A grabbed character is pulled into contact with the neveri's writhing mass of rotting flesh. Each round, the victim sustains 10 points of damage. A character who dies from this damage is consumed, and his body becomes part of the neveri. A neveri can absorb only one victim at a time.

If a neveri has eaten in the last few days, it regains 3 points of health per round, even if its health drops to 0. If it hasn't eaten recently, a neveri still regains 1 point of health per year (or longer). Even if exploded and dispersed into seeming dust, eventually a neveri begins regaining health again.

Interaction: A neveri has a low-level telepathic ability that allows it to sense when living creatures come near and perhaps pick up bits of the thinking creature's language. It responds to attempts at communication by forming a mouth that issues horrifying threats. Then it attacks.

Use: An eroded metallic sculpture from an unidentified prehistoric people is discovered. It turns out that the sculpture was a prison, and the intense examination of the prison granted the neveri inside enough impetus to break free.

Loot: If sifted for valuables, the mass of regenerating flesh might contain 1d6 cyphers and an artifact or two.

A neveri is a horror, an entity so malign that its very existence challenges many people's sense of reality. Those who have survived a neveri interaction say that the creature is unkillable, and that the only way to stop one is by confining it or shunting it into an ultimate region of destruction, such as the sun.

GM Intrusion: *A neveri produces a head-sized "childlet" and flings it at a PC. If the character fails a Speed defense roll, the childlet adheres and sends mind-controlling rootlets into the victim. Each round the childlet remains attached, the PC must succeed on an Intellect defense roll or willingly come into contact with the neveri if no other victim is currently held in place. Detaching the childlet requires someone in their right mind to rip it free with a Might-based roll.*

NUPPEPPO 2 (6)

Nuppeppos are animated lumps of human flesh that walk on vaguely defined limbs. They smell of decay and death. They're spotted in graveyards, battlefields, coroner's offices, and other places where the dead are kept or interred. When witnessed in other places, nuppeppos seem to wander streets aimlessly, sometimes alone, sometimes in groups, and sometimes following a living person who'd rather be left alone.

Information about these creatures is scarce. They might be the unintended consequence of a reanimation attempt, one that's able to catalyze its animation in similarly dead tissue to form more nuppeppos. On the other hand, they could be particularly gruesome spirits of the dead.

A nuppeppo sometimes follows a living individual around like a silent, smelly pet that shows no affection. No one knows why.

If a nuppeppo begins to follow a character, the difficulty of all interaction tasks by that PC and her allies is increased by one or two steps. Most other creatures are put off by a lump of animate human flesh hanging around nearby.

Motive: Wander, graze on dead flesh

Environment: Near places of death at night, alone or in groups of up to eight

Health: 12

Damage Inflicted: 4 points

Armor: 1

Movement: Short

Combat: A nuppeppo can smash a foe with one of its lumpy limbs. If a nuppeppo is touched or struck in melee, the attacker's weapon (or hand) becomes stuck to the nuppeppo and can be pulled free only with a difficulty 5 Might roll.

A victim of a nuppeppo's attack (or someone who touched a nuppeppo) begins to decay at a rate of 1 point of Speed damage (ignores Armor) per round, starting in the round following contact. To stop the spread of the decay, the victim can cut off the layer of affected flesh, which deals 4 points of damage (ignores Armor).

Interaction: If approached, a nuppeppo turns to "face" its interlocutor, but it doesn't respond to questions or orders. However, it may begin to follow its interlocutor from that point forward unless physically prevented—at which point the nuppeppo becomes violent.

Use: The PCs open a grave, a coffin, or a sealed research lab, and several nuppeppos spill out. Unless stopped, the creatures attempt to "adopt" their discoverers.

GM Intrusion: *The character who allowed the nuppeppo to follow him around like a pet (or who has been unable to prevent it) wakes to find that the creature has settled upon him in the night and is using its touch-decay abilities to feed on him. In fact, the PC might already be incapacitated by the time he wakes.*

OGRE 4 (12)

A bestial brute, the ogre is a sadistic, 8-foot (2 m) tall, cannibalistic fiend that preys upon other creatures in the woods, mountains, or other wilderness areas. This often pits them against sylvan beings like elves and fey. Ogres dwelling in more civilized lands are also the enemy of humans, but these ogres usually come no closer to civilization than its very fringes.

Ogres speak whatever language is most common in the area in which they live, but their vocabulary is extremely limited. They typically dress in ragged, piecemeal clothing or nothing at all.

Motive: Hungers for flesh, sadistic

Environment: Anywhere, usually alone or (rarely) in a band of three or four

Health: 20

Damage Inflicted: 8 points

Armor: 1

Movement: Short

Modifications: Feats of raw strength as level 6; Intellect defense and seeing through deception as level 3; Speed defense as level 3 due to size.

Combat: Ogres usually use clubs or large, two-handed weapons with great power. Since they are accustomed to fighting smaller creatures, they are adept at using their size and strength to their advantage. If an ogre strikes a foe smaller than itself, either the victim is knocked back up to 5 feet (2 m), or it is dazed and the difficulty of its next action is increased by one step.

Ogres can also swing their huge weapons in wide arcs, attacking all foes within close range. The difficulty of defending against this attack is decreased by one step, and the attack inflicts 5 points of damage.

Ogres rarely flee from a fight, and only a foe of overwhelming power can force them to surrender.

Interaction: Ogres are stupid and cruel. They don't like conversation, even with their own kind. Reasoning with them is difficult at best, but sometimes they can be fooled.

Evil wizards and warlords like to enslave ogres and place them at the forefront of their armies. In these cases, the ogres are typically bribed, ensorcelled, or intimidated by great force, but the latter is the most difficult.

Use: A solitary ogre is an excellent encounter for a group of first-tier characters. A number of ogres, particularly well-equipped and well-trained warriors, make excellent troops or guards in the service of a powerful master.

Loot: Some ogres hoard gold or other valuables in their lairs, but they rarely have use for magic or cyphers.

GM Intrusion: *The ogre's mighty blow (whether it strikes a foe or not) hits the ground or the wall, causing major structural damage and a possible collapse, cave-in, or landslide. It might also expose a hidden underground cave or chamber.*

ORC 2 (6)

Born into squalor and fear, the orc race is composed of miserable, misbegotten humanoids that seem destined to serve as fodder for more powerful evil overlords. When left to their own devices, these loathsome creatures turn on each other, the strongest oppressing the next weakest (and so on down the line) with cruel barbs, gruesome jokes, and physical beatings. When these creatures have no masters to hate, they hate themselves.

No two orcs look exactly alike, but all have a mean, ugly, and shambolic facade. Never clean and often spattered with the remains of recent meals, orcs have a mouthful of sharp, broken teeth that can develop into true fangs. Adults range in height from no larger than a human child to massive specimens larger than a strapping man. Whether big or small, nearly all orcs have stooped backs and crooked legs. The hue of their skin is hard to ascertain, because they are covered by the sediment of years, not to mention the iron armor every orc constantly wears from the moment it's able to lift a weapon.

Motive: Make others more miserable than itself

Environment: Anywhere near, on, or under mountains, usually in groups of four to six, or in tribes dozens to hundreds strong

Health: 7

Damage Inflicted: 4 points

Armor: 2

Movement: Short

Modifications: Speed defense as level 3 when carrying a shield; pleasant interactions as level 1.

Powerful orc leader: *level 5; health 25; Armor 3; heavy sword that deals 8 points of damage*

Combat: Most orcs have bows able to target foes within long range. Some carry a shield and wield a medium axe, sword, or mace that inflicts 4 points of damage. Other orcs (usually those that are larger than their fellows) dispense with shields and wield heavy two-handed mauls and hammers that inflict 6 points of damage.

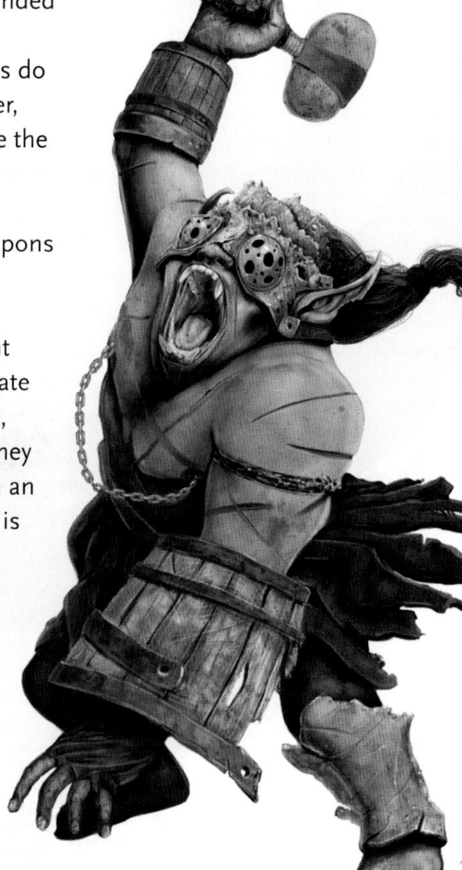

Orcs live short, brutish lives. The few that survive for years do so because of some special advantage; they're sneakier, stronger, tougher, or meaner than average. These have the following modifications, respectively:

- Stealth tasks as level 5
- Deal 2 additional points of damage with melee weapons
- +10 health
- Tasks related to trickery and deceit as level 5

Interaction: An orc would stab its own mother if it thought doing so would give it another hour of life in a desperate situation. That said, most orcs have been conditioned, through beatings and torture, to fear the evil master they serve (if any). Characters attempting to negotiate with an orc through intimidation find that short-term success is followed by medium-term betrayal.

Use: A band of orcs fires on the PCs from the edge of the forest. However, these orcs are crafty, and characters who rush directly into combat might fall victim to a hidden pit trap or other prepared ambush.

Loot: Orcs carry a lot of garbage. Amid this dross, a band of orcs might have currency equivalent to a moderately priced item among them.

GM Intrusion: *With a scream of savage glee, five more orcs rush to join the fight.*

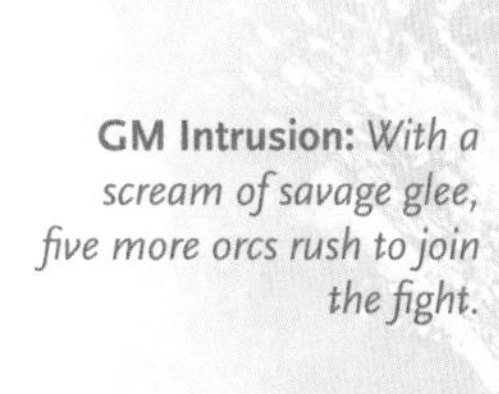

PHILETHIS 5 (15)

No one knows what the tall, mysterious philethis are. Some people think they might be advanced aliens, as they seem to have a far greater mastery of breakthrough technology than other creatures. Philethis bodies are completely cloaked, but the glimpses noted in what scant literature exists suggest a biomechanical hybrid form. Typically what is seen is a metal and glass "face" surrounded by voluminous cloaks.

Other speculation about the philethis includes claims that they are entirely robotic, they are extradimensional intruders, and their "face" is actually a viewport for a creature beyond space and time. Most theories about their nature don't even guess at what their goals or motivations might be. Philethis appear when and where they want to, and they usually seem to observe events from a distance (although another theory suggests that they influence the events somehow).

Motive: Unknown
Environment: Anywhere
Health: 30
Damage Inflicted: 5 points
Armor: 4
Movement: Short
Modifications: Defends as level 6; defends against mental attack as level 8.
Combat: Philethis seldom engage in combat. When they do, they are likely to produce a mysterious technological weapon—perhaps some kind of energy emitter, or maybe something of a more psychic nature that disrupts thought processes. However, because a philethis can teleport any distance, it usually just teleports away when threatened.
Although unlikely to do so in combat, a philethis can also modify probability in small ways, such as making a rope break, causing a gust of wind to close a door, and so forth. They do this to manipulate events in their favor. If the manipulation affects a PC, the GM can force the character to reroll a die at any time. (It also begs for frequent GM intrusions.)
Interaction: Philethis are not automatically hostile. If engaged in conversation, they might respond in their strange, machinelike voices, speaking in the native language of whomever they talk to. However, such interchanges usually make a philethis more enigmatic rather than less. Their explanations for things rarely make sense, and the questions they ask seem unrelated to anything going on around them.
A typical philethis interaction might go as follows.
Person: Who are you and what are you doing here?
Philethis: The moon is full, and the roses will bloom in just 437 hours.
Person: What are you talking about?
Philethis: When you were eleven years old and playing with that ball, why did you bounce it three times against the wall but four times against the ground?
Person: How do you know anything about when I was a child?
Philethis: The galaxies will collide soon. We must prepare.
Use: Philethis are meant to be an enigma. The characters should never fully understand the creatures, and if they believe that they do, something should happen to show that they are wrong. Moreover, the PCs should find out at odd times and in odd ways that the philethis are involved—or at least appear to be involved—in surprising situations. Are they just observing, or are they manipulating events somehow? And if so, why? The quest for this knowledge could be the basis for an entire campaign.
Loot: Philethis always have 1d6 cyphers and an artifact of some kind.

GM Intrusion:
Something unexpected and unpredictable happens when the philethis is near. The event is small, but it results in a significant change. For example, a PC slips and falls into a pit, suffering damage, but she finds something of great interest in the pit.

RAVAGE BEAR 4 (12)

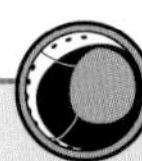

Ravage bears could be predators found on an alien planet, hunters from an alternate dimension, mutants, or even Kodiak bears in modern settings.

A ravage bear is a hideous predator that hunts entirely by the sense of smell. It is blind and nearly deaf, but it still tracks and senses prey easily. It is very protective of its young, and if hungry, it is extremely dangerous. Otherwise, it gives most creatures a wide berth.

Motive: Hungers for flesh

Environment: Ravage bears dwell alone or in pairs (usually with a few cubs) in wooded, rocky, or mountainous areas, typically in cold or temperate climes.

Health: 20

Damage Inflicted: 7 points

Armor: 1

Movement: Long

Modifications: Makes Might defense rolls as level 6; runs, climbs, and jumps as level 7.

Combat: A ravage bear grabs foes with its powerful arms, holds them fast, and then squeezes and tears at them until they are dead. It can hold only one creature at a time. While a ravage bear is holding a creature, it can attack only the held creature. In each round that a held creature does not escape, it suffers 4 points of damage in addition to damage from attacks made against it.

A ravage bear can move very quickly in short sprints. In combat, it can go into an insane fury and will fight to the death. If it takes 10 or more points of damage, its defense is reduced by one step, but its attacks are increased by one step.

Ravage bears are immune to visual effects, such as illusions. However, olfactory effects can confuse and "blind" them temporarily.

Interaction: Ravage bears are animals and act like animals.

Use: Ravage bears are likely chance encounters in the wilderness for unlucky travelers.

GM Intrusion: *In its rage, the ravage bear makes an extra attack that does 2 additional points of damage.*

REPLICANT 5 (15)

Virtually identical to an adult human, these biosculpted androids are stronger, faster, and potentially smarter. However, because they are manufactured beings with grafted memories, replicants rarely feel true human emotion, be that love, sadness, or empathy, though those who live long enough to lay down their own memories can develop the capacity to do so.

However, few gain the opportunity because replicants are created for a purpose, which could be to serve as police or guards, as soldiers in a distant war, or as impostors shaped to blend in with people so they can explore on behalf of an alien intelligence or a bootstrapped AI. In most of these cases, these purposes lead to a relatively short span of existence, which usually ends when the replicant chooses to detonate itself rather than be captured.

Motive: Exploration

Environment: Anywhere

Health: 18

Damage Inflicted: 6 points

Movement: Short

Modifications: Tasks related to pleasant social interaction, understanding human social norms, and deception as level 2.

Combat: Replicants blend in and prefer not to enter combat. Since destruction is not usually their principal goal, they avoid confrontation. If, however, something threatens their mission, they defend themselves to the best of their ability. Replicants might use weaponry but are adept in using their limbs to batter foes into submission.

A replicant poses the greatest danger when its physical form begins to fail through violence or natural degradation (many seem to have a natural "life" span of just a few years). When reduced to 0 points of health, the replicant explodes, inflicting 10 points of damage to everything in long range.

Interaction: Replicants are designed to look human and, at least during a casual interaction, pass as human. But extended conversation trips up a replicant more often than not. Eventually, a replicant gets something wrong and says inappropriate things or exhibits strange mannerisms.

Use: A contact of one of the characters is secretly a replicant. It has survived longer than expected, and its connection to whatever created it has weakened enough that it has gained some independence and made strong emotional connections to the PC. It knows its time is running out and may turn to the character for help.

Some replicants can interface with technological systems, such as computers, by extruding data tendrils for direct, high-speed transfer of information.

GM Intrusion: *The character struck by the replicant is smashed into the wall so hard that the surrounding structure begins to collapse on her.*

SCRAP DRONE 3 (9)

Scrap drones build themselves from the wreckage of other machines. Usually, that wreckage is caused by the scrap drones themselves, using weapons and defensive systems salvaged from previously defeated mechanisms in an endless cycle of destruction, salvage, and upgrade. Never satisfied with their current configuration, scrap drones are driven by some deep-seated code to continually improve themselves, regardless of the damage and mayhem they cause along the way.

Different scrap drones can have different forms, but to remain viable, they must have mobility, at least one functioning weapon system, and a reliable set of deployable salvage tools with which to rebuild themselves.

Scrap drones could be the result of military drones whose command and control code became corrupted, or instances of bootstrapped AI coming into existence.

Motive: Upgrade systems

Environment: Anywhere other machines are found

Health: 9

Damage Inflicted: 4 points

Armor: 2

Movement: Immediate; short when flying

Modifications: Speed defense as level 4 due to smaller size and quickness; tasks related to mechanical and electrical repair as level 7.

Combat: A scrap drone usually has at least one projectile weapon system it can fire at a foe within long range, and powerful cutting torches and waldos it can bring to bear on targets within immediate range. Most drones also have one of the following weapon systems, which they can call on once, or once every few minutes for rechargeable systems.

GM Intrusion: *The scrap drone deploys a single-use plasma cannon retrofitted from a much more powerful machine, and it targets the character at a range of up to 1 mile (2 km). On a failed Speed defense roll, the character takes 8 points of damage and descends one step on the damage track.*

Missile. The drone attacks a foe with a miniature missile at long range, which inflicts 6 points of damage on all targets within short range of the detonation.

EMP Pulse. All electronic machines or devices other than the drone within short range stop functioning for a minute. Independent or intelligent devices resist the power loss, as does any device in the possession of another creature. A creature can make a Speed defense roll to prevent its devices from losing power.

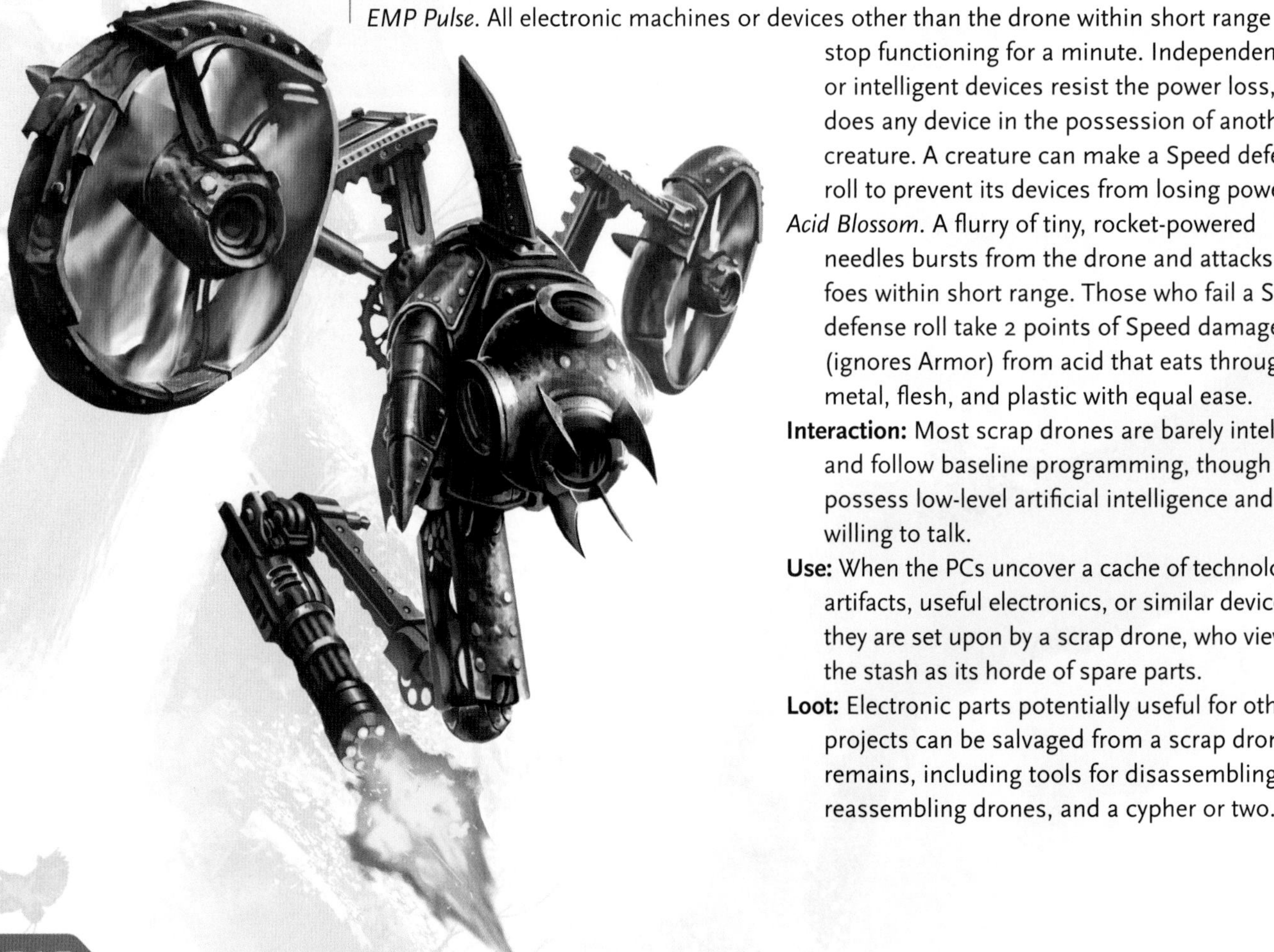

Acid Blossom. A flurry of tiny, rocket-powered needles bursts from the drone and attacks all foes within short range. Those who fail a Speed defense roll take 2 points of Speed damage (ignores Armor) from acid that eats through metal, flesh, and plastic with equal ease.

Interaction: Most scrap drones are barely intelligent and follow baseline programming, though a few possess low-level artificial intelligence and are willing to talk.

Use: When the PCs uncover a cache of technological artifacts, useful electronics, or similar devices, they are set upon by a scrap drone, who views the stash as its horde of spare parts.

Loot: Electronic parts potentially useful for other projects can be salvaged from a scrap drone's remains, including tools for disassembling and reassembling drones, and a cypher or two.

SHADOW ELF 4 (12)

Elves who faded from the surface to escape the justice of their fey cousins for crimes uncounted are sometimes called shadow elves, dark elves, or simply trow. It's widely assumed that shadow elves fled to new realms deep below the ground, and indeed, the routes that lead to their true abodes are mostly subterranean and include many grand underground keeps. However, the heart of the shadow elf kingdom lies in the colorless dimension of Shadow itself, where all things exist as a dim reflection of the real world.

Sometimes shadow elves appear on the surface, spilling from shadowed tunnels or, in some cases, from the shadows themselves. They raid for plunder, fresh slaves, and sacrifices. The sacrifices are made to their godqueen, a monstrously sized black widow spider that schemes in darkness.

When a shadow elf returns to the world of light, it can choose to appear as a silhouette only: a slender humanoid outline lurking as if at the nadir of a well.

Motive: Tortures for pleasure, serve the shadow elf godqueen

Environment: Almost anywhere dimly lit, singly or in groups of up to four

Health: 15

Damage Inflicted: 5 points

Armor: 1

Movement: Short

Modifications: Stealth and perception as level 6; Speed defense as level 6 due to shadowy nature.

Combat: Shadow elves attack with short blades, knives, and crossbow quarrels of steel-hard shadow. They can see in dim light and absolute darkness as if it were daylight.

Some shadow elves can cast spells, including the following. Each spell requires an action to cast.

d6	Spells
1	Enchant weapon to inflict 3 additional points of damage (8 total)
2	Enchant weapon to inflict 1 additional point of Speed damage (poison, ignores Armor), plus 2 points of Speed damage each additional round until victim succeeds on a Might defense roll
3	Fly a long range each round for ten minutes
4	Gain +2 to Armor (total of 3 Armor) for ten minutes
5	Long-range spell renders subject blind for ten minutes on failed Might defense roll
6	Long-range spell targets up to three creatures next to each other; holds them motionless in a shadow web for one minute on failed Speed defense rolls

If subject to full daylight, a shadow elf loses its modifications to stealth, perception, and Speed defense, and is likely to retreat.

Interaction: Shadow elves may negotiate and even ally with other creatures for a time. But they do so only until the best opportunity for a betrayal presents itself.

Use: Shadow elves have overrun an outlying keep, and even in broad daylight, the castle is shrouded in darkness and webs of shadow. The treasures said to lie in the keep's coffers may already be in the hands of the dark fey.

Loot: A shadow elf carries currency equivalent to an expensive item, in addition to weapons, light armor, and a cypher or two. Shadow elf leaders may carry an artifact.

GM Intrusion: *The shadow elf casts a spell that charms a PC on a failed Intellect defense roll. The character fights on the side of the shadow elf for up to one minute, though she can make another Intellect defense roll each round to try to break the influence.*

SKELETON 2 (6)

Some animate skeletons are created by spells, scrolls, or specific items. Others arise spontaneously after a great battle or if in the presence of strong death magic.

Skeletons are animated bones without much sense of self-preservation. They enjoy a crucial advantage over living creatures in one important and often exploited area: skeletons are dead shots with ranged weapons. Skeletons have no breath, no heartbeat, and no shaking hands to contend with as they release a shot, which means that skeletons armed with ranged weapons are something to be feared.

Motive: Defense or offense

Environment: Nearly anywhere, in formations of four to ten

Health: 6

Damage Inflicted: 3 points (claw) or 5 points (ranged weapon)

Armor: 1

Movement: Short

Modifications: Ranged attacks as level 5; Speed defense against most ranged attacks as level 5; resist trickery as level 1.

Combat: Skeletons can attack with a bony claw if they have no other weapon, but most attack (as level 5) with a long-range weapon. If a skeleton can see any portion of its target, the target loses any benefits of cover it might have otherwise enjoyed.

GM Intrusion: *A skeleton destroyed by a melee attack explodes like a grenade. The bone shrapnel inflicts 5 points of damage to every creature in immediate range.*

When in formation, a group of four or more skeletons with ranged weapons can focus their attacks on one target and make one attack roll as a single level 7 creature, dealing 7 points of damage.

Skeletons can see in the dark.

Reanimators: Some skeletons were created by a curse, and simply battering them into a pile of bones isn't enough to end their existence. Two rounds after reanimator skeletons are "killed," they regain full health in a flash of magical illumination. This regeneration can be prevented if the linchpin of the animating curse is separated from the skeleton after it falls. Such an item is usually obvious and might take the form of a lead spike through the skull, an ebony amulet, a dull sword through the ribs, a crown, and so on.

Interaction: A skeleton usually interacts only by attacking. Unless animated by a sapient spirit able to communicate via magic, skeletons lack the mechanisms for speech. However, they can hear and see the world around them just fine.

Use: Skeletons make ideal units in armies, especially when archery or artillery is required. A formation of four or more skeletons with ranged weapons atop a tower provides a surprisingly robust defense.

Loot: Sometimes the linchpin item required to create a reanimator skeleton is valuable.

SLIDIKIN 5 (15)

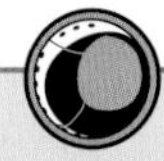

Slidikin might be the result of a magical curse, a demon possession by several entities at once, a transhuman experiment, a race of creatures driven insane after modifying themselves to speak with humans, or something else.

Skulking from shadow to shadow, the slidikin dwell on the fringes of society. They are bizarre creatures, their origins a complete mystery. While one might pass as a human from a distance, their chalk-white skin, lack of eyes or nose, and far-too-many mouths ensure that a close examination would prove them otherwise. In people's rare, brief, and frankly disturbing interactions with slidikin, they have made passing references to "the hideous game." This seems to be an incongruous competition among slidikin (and only slidikin) that involves dark deeds—theft, kidnapping, mutilation, and murder. (It likely involves other things as well, but no one knows what they are, focusing only on those activities that affect humanity.)

GM Intrusion: *The slidikin runs away and around a corner. If the character follows it, the creature is gone. Is there a secret door? Did it disappear into the shadows? Did it climb up to the roof? It's nowhere to be seen.*

Motive: The game
Environment: Edges of society
Health: 22
Damage Inflicted: 5 points
Movement: Long
Modifications: Speed defense and stealth as level 6.
Combat: Slidikin often use weapons in combat, although they never wear armor, preferring to remain agile rather than encumbered.
Interaction: Talking with a slidikin can be infuriating. No matter what the situation, the slidikin—with its multiple, grating, whispered voices—speaks with outlandish contempt for whomever it encounters, as if it knows a great many things that everyone else does not. It finds odd things (like physical threats) humorous, and many normal concepts (like justice or revenge) incomprehensible. It never tells anyone the nature of the game or anything of its own nature.
Use: A man stumbles out of a dark alleyway toward the PCs, blood running down his face. "The mouths," he whispers hoarsely. "The mouths." If the characters examine him, they see that his eyelids have been sliced off. He says that men—at least, he thought they were men at first—grabbed him the day before and held him in a dank cellar overnight, bound and gagged. They giggled and whispered among themselves the whole time. Then they mutilated him with knives and left him in the alley. He gives a frantic, fevered description of a slidikin.
Loot: A slidikin very likely carries currency equivalent to a moderately priced item and a cypher as well as a variety of knives and poisons, knockout drugs, lockpicks, and other tools.

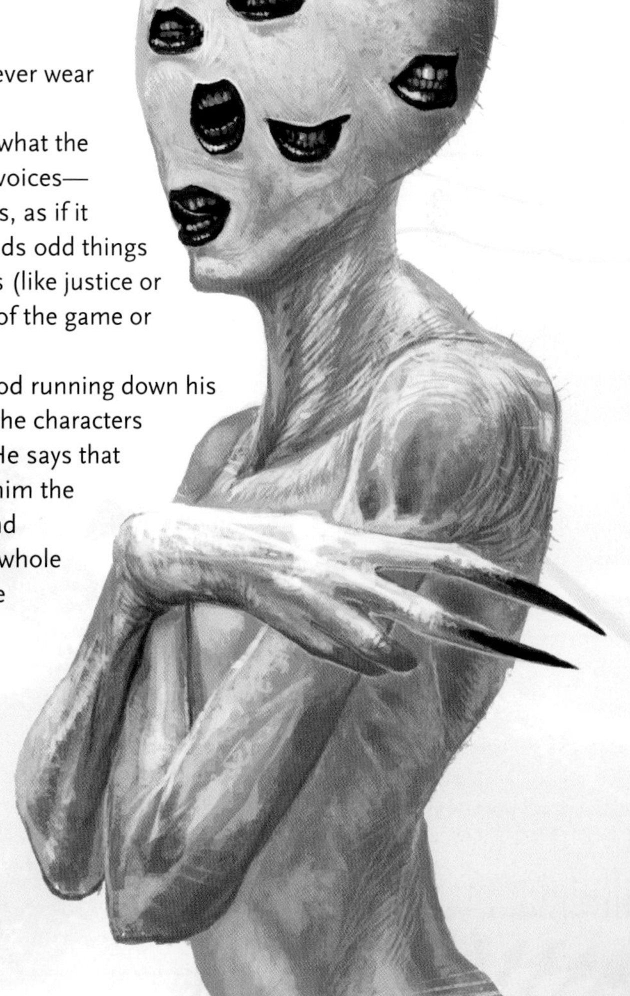

STATUE, ANIMATE 7 (21)

Towering statues carved from stone or cast in metal are sometimes more than humans rendered in moments of extreme agony and suffering. Sometimes a statue moves, usually in service to some ancient geas or command that animated it in the first place.

Most animate statues are vessels imprisoning the mind of a sentient creature. Such entrapment usually tumbles the spirits into the abyss of insanity, though most rest in a dormant state, their minds lost in whatever memories they retain. Disturbing animate statues can cause them to awaken, usually with disastrous results.

Motive: Release from imprisonment; guard an area

Environment: In out-of-the-way places, especially ancient ruins

Health: 33

Damage Inflicted: 9 points

Armor: 4

Movement: Short

Modifications: All tasks involving balance as level 2; Might defense as level 8; Speed defense as level 5 due to size.

Combat: An animate statue towers over most foes, and it can smash or stomp a target within short range as a melee attack. The statue's massive size and the material of its body means it can walk through nearly any obstacle, smashing through walls of solid rock, buildings, and trees. When walking, it pays no attention to what it steps on. Anything in its path is likely flattened. A character who is stepped on must make a Speed defense roll to dodge or be knocked down and take 9 points of damage.

Animate statues are strong and hard to hurt, but they are often top-heavy. If one falls or is knocked over, it takes a few rounds to rise and resume whatever it was doing.

Interaction: Statues spend years immobilized and insensate, their minds lost in half-remembered experiences and hallucinations. Rousing a statue has unpredictable results. Some might rampage. Others laugh, cry, or scream streams of nonsense. Regardless, if one has been commanded to guard an area or entrance, it also likely lashes out.

Use: An animate statue holds a treasure trove of knowledge. If the characters can keep it focused or knocked down long enough, they might coax from it the information they seek.

GM Intrusion: *The animate statue strikes a character so hard that she flies a long distance and lands in a heap, possibly dropping gear and weapons along the way.*

SUPERVILLAIN

People with amazing abilities who use them for evil earn the label of supervillain.

ANATHEMA 7 (21)

The supervillain called Anathema is big, bright red, and stronger than anyone on this planet or any other (or so he claims). Superheroes who go head to head with him learn that he can withstand almost any hit and always gives back twice as hard as he receives. He can bring down buildings with a punch and throw semi trucks across state lines.

Before he was Anathema, he was Sameer Stokes, a bitter and spiteful coder working for a large software company. Having failed in relationships, promotions, and retaining friends, Sameer retreated online and learned that he had power when he bullied people. He delighted in causing emotional distress in others in forums and social media. In effect, he was a troll. When the metamorphosis happened, he was turned into a troll for real. (Sameer doesn't recall the metamorphosis or the days before and immediately after his change, despite using therapy and drugs in an attempt to recover those memories.)

Assume that Anathema has three power shifts in strength and two in resilience; see page 270. These shifts are already figured into his modifications and other stats.

Motive: Accumulate wealth, live on the edge

Environment: Anywhere vast wealth can be stolen

Health: 70

Damage Inflicted: 12 points

Movement: Short; a few miles (5 km) per leap

Modifications: Strength tasks as level 10; Might defense as level 9; Speed defense as level 5 due to size.

Combat: Anathema hits foes with bone-shocking force. He can throw cars and large objects at targets within long range, dealing damage to all creatures within immediate range of his target.

Anathema has a healing factor that makes it hard to hurt him in any meaningful sense. He regains 10 points of health per round. In any round in which he regains health, his attacks deal 3 additional points of damage (15 total), and he seems to visibly swell with muscle.

Interaction: When Anathema is riled up during a fight, it's difficult to reason with him. However, he is willing to negotiate if someone offers him wealth or convinces him they have valuable secrets for breaking mental blocks. Anathema doesn't know how he became the way he is, and he wants to recover his missing memories.

Use: The rolling earthquake afflicting the city is actually Anathema fighting a group of newbie superheroes who haven't figured out that engaging the red mountain will likely cause more deaths than leaving him alone. (The first rule of fighting Anathema is to lead or move him somewhere with a low population density.)

Loot: Anathema doesn't normally carry wealth or other valuables.

"Clear out, or I'll smash you into paste. Red, screaming, bone-protruding paste. This is your only warning."

~Anathema

GM Intrusion: *Anathema's attack sends the character flying a long distance and potentially into dangerous terrain.*

Doctor Dread is usually accompanied by a handful of robot minions.

Dread's robot minion: *level 3; Armor 1; long-range laser attack inflicts 4 points of damage*

GM Intrusion: *Doctor Dread uses a function built into her robotic armor that is the perfect solution for her current predicament: healing herself, teleporting away, disintegrating a barrier, or whatever is needed.*

Assume that Doctor Dread has three power shifts in intelligence and two in resilience; see page 270. These shifts are already figured into her modifications and other stats.

DOCTOR DREAD 7 (21)

Doctor Dread is larger than life thanks to her brilliant mind, her media savvy, and the robotic armor she uses to enhance her otherwise normal abilities. Indeed, Doctor Dread has become the most feared terrorist on the planet. She uses her abilities to extort money, influence, and technology from the rich and powerful, whether her victims are individuals, governments, corporations, or superheroes.

Alicia Coleridge is Doctor Dread's secret identity. Born into relative obscurity, she received a full scholarship to the Russell Institute of Technology, where she studied the effects of radioactive substances on living tissue. In a freak lab accident, Alicia's fiancé was slain, and Alicia was disfigured and driven slightly insane, so much so that she built the Doctor Dread armor. She plows the vast wealth she accumulates through terrorism into research into the rejuvenation of dead flesh. She hopes to one day bring back her dead love, whose body she keeps in suspended animation.

Motive: Accumulate wealth; reanimate dead flesh

Environment: Wherever money can be extorted

Health: 40

Damage Inflicted: 7 points

Armor: 4

Movement: Short; long when flying

Modifications: Resists mental attacks and deception as level 8; understands, repairs, and crafts advanced technology as level 10.

Combat: Doctor Dread's armor allows her to exist without outside air (or air pressure), food, or water for up to ten days at a time. She can call on her robotic armor to accomplish a variety of tasks, including the following:

Plasma Blast: Long-range heat and electricity blast that inflicts 7 points of damage

Fade: Become invisible for one minute, or until she makes an attack

Barricade: Establish an immobile, two-dimensional field of transparent force 10 feet by 10 feet (3 m by 3 m) for ten minutes

Energy Cloak: Create an energy field that gives her +5 to Armor against heat, cold, or magnetism (one at a time, chosen when she uses the power) for ten minutes

Interaction: Doctor Dread is slightly mad, but that's normally disguised by her amazing brilliance. She is an egomaniac but will negotiate in return for a promise of wealth or biomedical lore she doesn't already know.

Use: The PCs are called to handle a hostage situation at a party in which many of the city's wealthy elite are being held captive by Doctor Dread. She promises to let them go once sufficient wealth is paid into her offshore accounts.

Loot: Most of Doctor Dread's considerable wealth is tied up in online accounts, two or three secret fortresses, and cutting-edge biological research equipment.

MAGNETAR 8 (24)

Not much is known about Magnetar other than its powerful ability to generate and control magnetic fields. Various research groups theorize that Magnetar is an alien, a sentient and self-improving robot, or even some kind of manifestation of a fundamental force. Given Magnetar's vaguely humanoid shape, a few people even suggest that the villain is actually a man with a mutant ability so powerful that it burned out all memories of his former self.

In truth, Magnetar is the animate, sentient, and self-regulating nucleus of a neutron star that is able to rein in its immense electromagnetic signature. One of two such beings an advanced alien race created from a single magnetar (a type of neutron star with an extremely powerful magnetic field), Magnetar was sent on a mission of exploration. After millennia, it crashed on Earth and was damaged. Having lost most of its memory data, Magnetar knows that something was taken from it (its twin), but it can't remember what. It has decided to blame the humans.

Motive: Revenge; regain memory

Environment: Almost anywhere, searching for what it has lost

Health: 50

Damage Inflicted: 10 points

Armor: 8

Movement: Short; long when magnetically levitating

Modifications: Speed defense as level 5 due to mass; tasks related to controlling and shaping metal through electromagnetic manipulation as level 11.

Combat: Magnetar's fist packs a wallop, since it can selectively add mass to the punch. However, its most potent ability is its level 11 control over all metal within 300 feet (91 m), which it uses to create anything it can imagine, including walls, attacks, pincers, and more. Magnetar can lift bridges, vehicles, and structures infused with rebar that it can see within its area of influence. When it throws such a large object as part of an attack, the target and everything within short range of the target takes 10 points of damage.

Magnetar's only weakness is psychic attacks, which is fortunate since reducing it to 0 health through an old-fashioned beating could release an uncontrolled neutron star chunk on the Earth's surface.

Interaction: Morose and gruff, Magnetar generally would rather be alone, but every so often, it goes on a rampage, hoping that a display will draw out whoever or whatever made it the way it is. Magnetar constantly feels the drag of emotional loss, but it doesn't know why (it doesn't realize that the feeling comes from the loss of its twin).

Use: Doctor Dread has put a bounty on Magnetar's head because she wants to study the advanced technology woven through its body. The bounty amount is outrageous, but then again, so is Magnetar.

GM Intrusion: *On a failed Might defense roll, all of the character's loose metallic items (including weapons) are stripped from him and become stuck to a nearby metallic buttress.*

Assume that Magnetar has three power shifts in its magnetic power and two in resilience; see page 270. These shifts are already figured into its modifications and other stats.

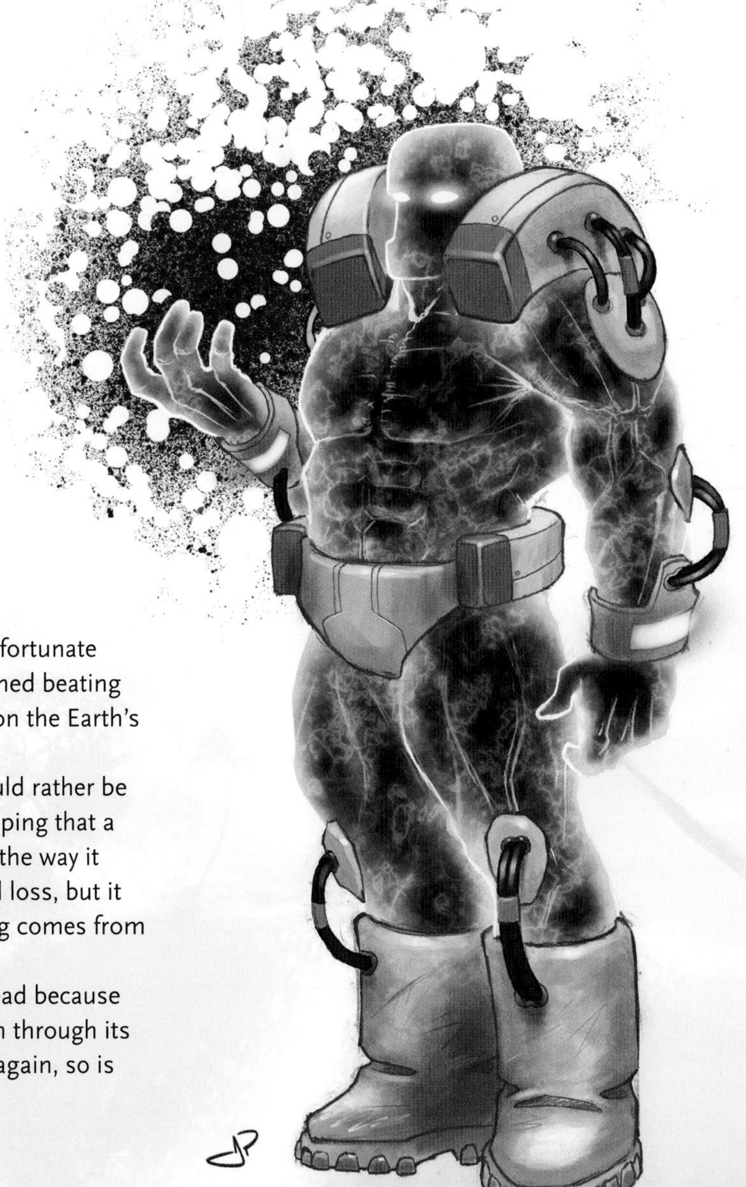

Mister Genocide sometimes teams up with Anathema, because the red mountain is the only villain who can withstand the poison that Genocide constantly emits.

GM Intrusion: *A character affected by the poison must make a second Might defense roll or fall unconscious from shock. Unconsciousness lasts for up to a minute, or until the victim is jostled awake.*

Assume that Mister Genocide has two power shifts in his poison power, one in intelligence, and two in resilience; see page 270. These shifts are already figured into his modifications and other stats.

MISTER GENOCIDE 5 (15)

Real name Alfred Webster, Mister Genocide has the unfortunate ability to synthesize deadly poison from his skin. His touch can kill, but if he wishes it, so can his spittle or even his breath.

Anyone who spends too much time in Mister Genocide's presence becomes ill, even if the villain isn't actively using his power. Thus, his cronies usually wear gas masks and protective clothing. Mister Genocide has promoted himself to the head of the mob in the city where he resides and is always looking to expand his operations, sometimes at the expense of other criminals.

When victims are killed by Mister Genocide's poison, their skin and the whites of their eyes take on a bright green hue, which increases the terror that normal people feel regarding him. Even superheroes have been brought down by his toxins.

Motive: Accumulate power

Environment: Anywhere crime lords congregate

Health: 15

Damage Inflicted: 5 points; see Combat

Armor: 1

Movement: Short

Modifications: Poison breath attack and Might defense as level 7; Intellect defense and evil genius as level 6.

Combat: Targets touched by Mister Genocide must make a difficulty 7 Might defense roll or take 5 points of Speed damage (ignores Armor) from the poison transmitted. Worse, the poison continues to inflict 2 points of Speed damage each round until the victim succeeds at a Might defense roll.

Every other round, Mister Genocide can make a level 7 poison attack that can affect up to ten victims within short range as a single action. Those who fail a Might defense roll take 7 points of Speed damage (ignores Armor) and spend a round helpless as they cough and gag. The inhalant poison does not continue to inflict damage each round.

Mister Genocide is immune to most venoms, toxins, and poisons.

Interaction: Certifiably insane, Mister Genocide likes to kill people. He may negotiate for a while, but if there is not enough gain to be had, he might kill everyone with a breath just for the fun of watching them suffocate and turn green.

Use: Gang warfare between two criminal organizations is shooting up downtown, and many innocent bystanders caught in the crossfire end up bullet-ridden or poisoned (with green skin). Someone needs to put a stop to Mister Genocide.

Loot: The supervillain carries currency equivalent to 1d6 expensive items, a cypher or two, and a variety of poisoned knives, needles, and vials.

WRATH 6 (18)

The head of an elite group of assassins, Wrath wants to save the world by killing everyone who impedes her vision of perfection—which turns out to be the better part of humanity. In addition to being one of the most accomplished martial artists to walk the earth (thanks to her connection with a mystical entity called the Demon), Wrath is also a criminal mastermind whose assassins are just one layer of the organization she controls.

Born over two hundred and fifty years ago in China to a name lost to history, Wrath was taken in by a monastery and trained in the ways of fist and sword. Everything changed when raiders attacked and killed everyone in her monastery, leaving her the sole survivor. Vowing revenge against the raiders and the world that allowed animals like them to exist, she acquired a magical amulet that contains the Demon. The Demon in turn bequeathed her with extraordinary speed, strength, and longevity.

Wrath is content to let her assassins (and mobsters, lawyers, and politicians) accomplish many of her goals, though she relishes being present when particularly important adversaries are brought down.

Motive: Save the world

Environment: Anywhere wrongs (to Wrath's way of thinking) must be righted

Health: 36

Damage Inflicted: 8 points

Armor: 1

Movement: Short

Modifications: Stealth, attacks, and Speed defense as level 8.

Combat: Wrath prefers a sword, though she is equally adept with a crossbow or, in rare cases, modern weapons. In melee she can attack two foes as a single action every round.

Thanks to the influence of the Demon, Wrath regains 3 points of health each round, even if reduced to 0 health. The only way to permanently kill her is to reduce her to 0 health and keep her that way long enough to burn away the tattoo of the Demon that is engraved across her back.

Interaction: Wrath is arrogant and confident, though not so much that she is easily fooled by flattery. She is usually amenable to negotiating, because she can anticipate the agenda of others and usually gain far more for herself in the end. However, she is not one to betray her word.

Use: Wrath is making a bid to form a group of supervillains—all of whom will answer to her, of course—and it seems that initial talks are going well. The only holdout is Mister Genocide, who feels threatened by Wrath's larger organization, and this tension has led to ongoing warfare in the streets as assassins battle mobsters.

Loot: In addition to weapons and armor, Wrath likely possesses the equivalent of five exorbitant items, 1d6 cyphers, and possibly one or two artifacts.

Assassin of Wrath: *level 4, stealth as level 7*

GM Intrusion: *Just as things seem bleakest for her, Wrath summons a group of assassins waiting in the wings to surround the PCs and demand their surrender.*

Assume that Wrath has two power shifts in dexterity, two in accuracy, and one in resilience; see page 270. These shifts are already figured into her modifications and other stats.

TYRANNOSAURUS REX 7 (21)

The short arms of a tyrannosaurus have been much parodied in Earth social media circles, but the arms aren't really important when a hunting tyrannosaurus is after you. It's more the soul-shivering roar, designed to freeze prey in place, and a skull and mouth so enormous that the entire creature is cantilevered by a massive tail that itself can be used as a powerful weapon.

As vicious as tyrannosauruses likely were 66 million years ago, the versions still hunting today could be even more dangerous. That's because the ones with a taste for humans have learned to adapt to human defenses and to use their roar to terrorize prey as they hunt.

Even though the tyrannosaurus rex was the largest carnivore in its environment, some paleontologists believe that the creature was more of a scavenger than an apex predator. However, many scientists think that it was both—it preyed upon things that ran, but it wasn't adverse to stripping a carcass from another predator's kill.

Motive: Hungers for flesh

Environment: Tyrannosauruses hunt solo or in pairs; they're drawn to loud, unfamiliar noises (like motor engines).

Health: 50

Damage Inflicted: 10 points

Movement: Short

Modifications: Perception as level 5; Speed defense as level 5 due to size.

Combat: A tyrannosaurus attacks with its massive bite. Not only does it deal damage, but the target must also make a Might defense roll to pull free or be shaken like a rat in the mouth of a pit bull for 3 additional points of Speed damage (ignores Armor). The shaking recurs each subsequent round in which the target fails a Might-based task to pull free.

A tyrannosaurus can also make a trampling attack if it can charge from just outside of short range. When it does, it moves 50 feet (15 m) in a round, and anything that comes within immediate range is attacked. Even those who make a successful Speed defense roll take 2 points of damage.

GM Intrusion: *The tyrannosaurus's tail swings around and knocks the PC tumbling out of short range and possibly into dangerous terrain.*

Finally, a tyrannosaurus can roar. The first time creatures within short range hear the roar on any given day, they must succeed on a difficulty 2 Intellect defense roll or stand frozen in fear for a round. Attacks against them are modified by two steps in the attacker's favor and deal 2 additional points of damage.

For all their power, tyrannosauruses are not above self-preservation. They never fight to the death if they are outclassed, and they usually break off if they take more than 30 points of damage in a conflict.

Interaction: Tyrannosauruses are animals, but they're clever hunters, too. When they hunt in pairs, they work to keep prey penned between them.

Use: Something is killing big game in a forest preserve. Poachers are suspected at first, but when they are also found dead, it's clear that something else is to blame.

VAMPIRE

Several varieties of vampires exist, including the three kinds detailed here.

VAMPIRE 6 (18)

Vampires are undead creatures, risen from the grave to drink blood. Their very nature and essence are evil and anti-life, even as they revel in their own endless existence. Most vampires are vain, arrogant, sadistic, lustful, and domineering. Their powers allow them to manipulate others, and they frequently toy with their prey before feeding. Vampires come out only at night, as the sun's rays will destroy them.

The bite of a vampire over three nights (in which it exchanges a bit of its own blood) ensures that the victim will rise as a vampire under the thrall of the one that killed it. While vampires are careful not to create too many of their kind (which amount to competition), each thrall conveys a bit more supernatural power to a vampire. Eventually, a vampire with a multitude under its command becomes the vampire lord.

Motive: Thirsts for blood

Environment: Usually solitary, on the edges of civilization

Health: 24

Damage Inflicted: 7 points

Movement: Long

Modifications: Climb, stealth, and perception as level 8; Speed defense as level 7 due to fast movement.

Combat: Vampires are strong and fast. They have impressive fangs, but these are usually used in feeding, not in battle. They typically fight with their fists or hands (which basically become claws) but sometimes use weapons.

A vampire can change into a bat or a wolf. This transformation does not change its stats or abilities except that, as a bat, it can fly. Vampires can also transform into shadow or mist, and in these forms they can't be harmed by anything (but also can't affect the physical world).

Vampires possess an unholy charisma and can mesmerize victims within immediate distance so that they stand motionless for one round. In subsequent rounds, the victim will not forcibly resist the vampire, and the vampire can suggest actions to the victim (even actions that will cause the victim to harm himself or others that he cares about). Each round, the victim can attempt a new Intellect defense roll to break free.

Vampires are notoriously difficult to hurt. Unless a weapon is very special (blessed by a saint, has specific magical enchantments against vampires, or the like), no physical attack harms a vampire. They simply don't take the damage. Exceptions include the following:

Fire: Vampires burn, though the damage doesn't kill them. It only causes pain, and a vampire regains all health lost to fire damage within twenty-four hours.

Running water: Complete immersion inflicts 10 points of damage per round. If not destroyed, the vampire can use a single action to regain all health lost in this way.

Holy water: This inflicts 4 points of damage and affects a vampire exactly like fire.

Sunlight: Exposure to sunlight inflicts 10 points of damage per round. If not destroyed, the vampire regains all health lost to exposure in twenty-four hours.

Wooden stake: This weapon inflicts 25 points of damage, effectively destroying the vampire in one blow. However, if the vampire is aware and able to move, the difficulty of this attack is increased by two steps.

Further, vampires have the following special weaknesses:

Garlic: Significant amounts of garlic within immediate distance increase the difficulty of a vampire's tasks by one step.

If desired, a vampire can bite for only one round and then stop, starting the process of creating a new vampire. The victim becomes a transitional vampire the next night.

To ensure that a defeated vampire can never come back to life, most vampire hunters decapitate it and stuff its mouth with holy wafers.

Vampires will not enter a home unless invited in.

Cross, holy symbol, or mirror: Presenting any of these objects forcefully stuns a vampire, causing it to lose its next action. While the object is brandished and the vampire is within immediate range, the difficulty of its tasks is increased by two steps.

Interaction: Most vampires look upon humans as cattle upon which to feed. They rarely have respect for anything but other vampires, and they often hate other supernatural creatures that they cannot enslave.

Use: Strange stories of shadows in the night, people disappearing from their beds, and graves missing their former occupants could portend the arrival of a vampire in the region.

TRANSITIONAL VAMPIRE 3 (9)

It's possible for a vampire to turn a fresh corpse into a transitional vampire. Unlike others of its kind, it is truly undead—like a vampire—and cannot take on a human nature during the day. But it will never become a full vampire and always remains in its lesser state.

When a human is "visited upon" (bitten) by a vampire, she might be killed, or she might be left alive to begin a slow transformation into a creature of the night. If a victim is bitten three times, she becomes a vampire forever under the control of the one that bit her. From the time of the first bite until her complete transformation after the third bite, she is a transitional vampire. The only ways to return a transitional vampire to normal are using special ancient rituals or destroying the vampire that bit her in the first place.

Transitional vampires usually serve as guardians, consorts, or spies for their masters.

Motive: Thirsts for blood

Environment: Anywhere, usually solitary but sometimes in groups of two or three

Health: 12

Damage Inflicted: 4 points

Movement: Short

Modifications: Climb and stealth as level 4.

Combat: Transitional vampires can maintain a human existence during the day without any of a vampire's powers or weaknesses. However, they have a disdain for garlic and the sun. At night they take on all the characteristics of a vampire, and if confronted by any of the traditional vampiric weaknesses (a wooden stake, a cross, and so on), they flee unless their master is present.

Interaction: Transitional vampires are utterly devoted to their master.

Use: Transitional vampires lie in the intersection of foe and victim. A loved one or trusted companion who has been turned into a transitional vampire will try to betray, defeat, and kill the PCs, but the characters are motivated to save him rather than destroy him.

GM Intrusion: *The character struck by the vampire is caught fast in its powerful grip. If she doesn't escape immediately, the vampire bites her automatically.*

VAMPIRE LORD 9 (27)

The vampire lord is the most powerful vampire in the world and is often (but not always) the most ancient of its kind. It has many vampires under its control, and even those that it did not create pay it respect and homage.

Motive: Thirsts for blood

Environment: Anywhere, usually solitary

Health: 40

Damage Inflicted: 10 points

Armor: 2

Movement: Long

Modifications: Climb, stealth, and perception as level 10; Speed defense as level 10 due to fast movement.

Combat: Vampire lords have all the powers and weaknesses of a regular vampire, plus one or two unique abilities. It's possible that the traditional methods of killing a vampire are only temporary setbacks for the vampire lord, and the only way to destroy it for good is mysterious and unique, such as an ancient ritual, a special weapon, or the like.

Interaction: As the apex predator among apex predators, the vampire lord is extremely arrogant. Interacting with it on any level other than supplication will likely arouse anger.

Use: The vampire lord is a villain for the end of a campaign—a deadly challenge for even the most powerful characters.

Loot: The vampire lord has at least one artifact and very likely 1d6 + 1 cyphers, as well as the wealth of kings.

Some vampire lords are also versed in sorcery and spells.

VAT REJECT 3 (9)

Vat rejects come into being when clone vats meant to produce clone soldiers or similar mass-produced entities are corrupted. How the carefully controlled process becomes compromised varies, but possibilities include yeast contamination, sunspot activity, nanovirus evolution, or even purposeful meddling with control parameters. Unskilled operators experimenting with derelict cloning equipment can also produce a vat of rejects.

Vat rejects fear nothing and welcome death, except that their existential rage requires an outlet other than immediate suicide. Their warped forms mean that most are in constant pain, and they somehow understand that this was artificially stamped into them by their creators. Revenge is their only possible redemption.

Motive: Self-destruction through endless aggression

Environment: Anywhere in lost and lonely places

Health: 9

Damage Inflicted: 3 points

Movement: Short

Modifications: Speed defense as level 4 due to frenzied alacrity.

Combat: Vat rejects charge into battle with berserk speed, which increases the difficulty of defending against their initial attack by one step. All vat rejects are able to inflict damage directly by cutting, bashing, or biting a victim, depending on their particular morphology. Some also have additional abilities; roll on the chart below for each reject.

d6	Ability
1	Reject deals +3 damage in melee (6 points total)
2	Reject has short-range acid spit attack that inflicts 2 points of damage, plus 2 points of damage each additional round until victim succeeds on a Might defense roll
3	Reject can fly a long distance as an action
4	Reject has 2 Armor
5	Reject has long-range destructive eye ray attack that inflicts 6 points of damage
6	When struck by an attack, reject detonates in an immediate radius, inflicting 6 points of damage in a radioactive explosion (and 1 point even on a successful Speed defense roll)

Interaction: Vat rejects are usually always enraged, making interaction nearly impossible. However, some may negotiate if offered a reasonable hope of salvation through extreme surgery or other transformation.

Use: A long-missing derelict ship, famous for carrying a load of planet-buster superweapons, is found. However, salvagers discover it to be overrun by vat rejects. No one knows if the rejects plan to use the superweapons, if they have been released by someone else as a distraction, or if they are part of a mutated ship defense system.

GM Intrusion: *The vat reject also has a radioactive sting. On a failed Might defense roll, the PC struck by the reject descends one step on the damage track.*

WARDROID 6 (18)

When star troopers need heavy support, they sometimes bring in wardroids. These fearsome robots, standing about 8 feet (2 m) tall, are ruthless even by trooper standards and are known to kill innocent bystanders as often as they kill foes. It is said that when wardroids are unleashed, wise troopers fall back and take cover.

Motive: Maintain control, crush, kill, destroy

Environment: Anywhere

Health: 30

Damage Inflicted: 8 points

Armor: 3

Movement: Short; some models can fly a short distance each round

Modifications: Attacks as level 7.

Combat: A wardroid's main weapon is a bank of laser blasters that it can use to attack up to three foes standing next to each other as one action. When damaged, a wardroid regains 1 point of health each round. Furthermore, each wardroid has one additional capability:

d6	Ability
1	Emit poison gas that inflicts 5 points of damage to organic beings in immediate range
2	Project grenades up to long distance that detonate in an immediate radius, inflicting 5 points of damage
3	Fire a beam that stuns an organic being for one round, during which it cannot take actions
4	Emit a field that disrupts machines; technological devices and machine creatures in immediate range cannot function for one round
5	Fire a piercing projectile up to long range that inflicts 6 points of damage that ignores physical armor (but not necessarily other Armor)
6	Spray a corrosive that inflicts 5 points of damage to everything in immediate range

GM Intrusion: *When defeated, the wardroid detonates, inflicting 8 points of damage on all creatures within immediate range.*

Interaction: Interaction is difficult for those not authorized to communicate with a wardroid.

Use: Wardroids are often deployed in groups of two or three to guard a vault or the entrance to a spacecraft, or to track down intruders aboard a space station.

Loot: The remains of a wardroid can yield one or two cyphers to someone adept at salvage.

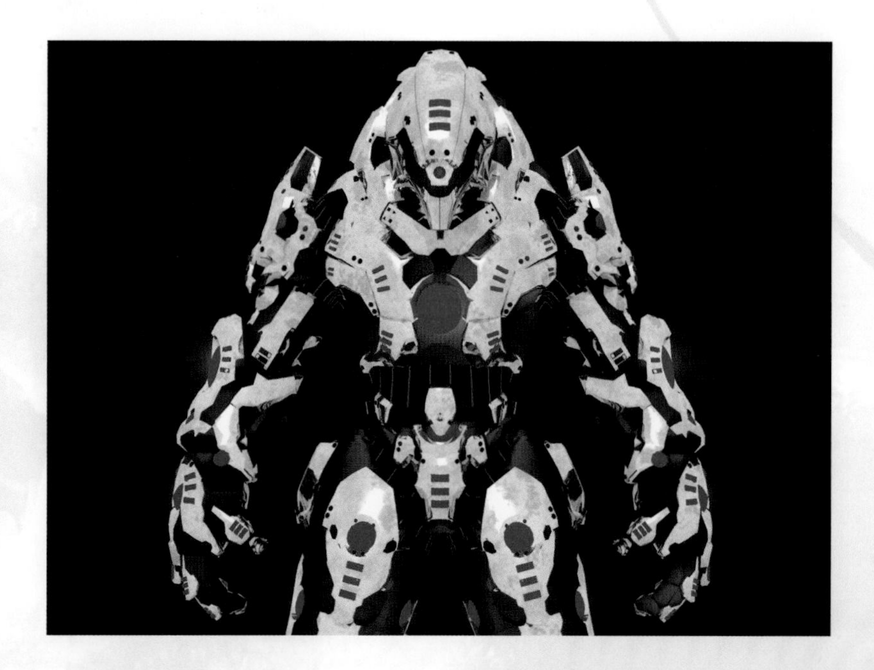

WENDIGO 5 (15)

Eating human flesh is taboo. Violators face a terrible curse, one that strips them of their humanity and turns them into terrifying monsters filled with an unnatural craving to eat their former kin. Driven to the hinterlands, they hibernate until winter begins to tighten its grip. With the first snows come the wendigos, and they prowl the darkest hours in search of people to snatch and devour.

The curse that transforms a person into a wendigo destroys much of his humanity, leaving behind a skeletal body, bones pressing against taut skin, and eyes sunken into skull-like visages, flicking back and forth for any signs of life. With gnarled fingers ending in long claws and mouths filled with sharp black teeth, wendigos have everything they need to pull apart their victims and stuff their greedy maws with raw flesh.

Motive: Hungers for flesh

Environment: Solitary hunters, wendigos drift like ghosts through the snow-covered plains.

Health: 20

Damage Inflicted: 5 points

Movement: Short

Modifications: All tasks related to intimidation and perception as level 7; Intellect defense as level 6 when hungry.

Combat: A reek of decay and death betrays a wendigo's approach. At first, the stench is nothing more than a malodorous presence, but as the wendigo draws nearer, the smell becomes overpowering. Any foe within a short distance of a wendigo must make a Might defense roll or become sickened. The difficulty of an affected victim's tasks is increased by one step. The victim can use an action to roll again and shake off the effects of the stench on a success.

A wendigo attacks foes with its teeth or claws. A foe who takes damage must make a Might defense roll or suffer as the wendigo tears free a gobbet of flesh. The bleeding wound inflicts 1 point of ambient damage each round until the target uses an action to stanch the wound.

Interaction: A wendigo gripped by unnatural hunger thinks about nothing else. After the creature feeds, it becomes lucid for a while—usually no more than a few hours—before the hunger pangs return. During its lucid period, it may regret what it's become, look for those it left behind, or take some other similarly motivated action.

Use: Locals make a regular offering of flesh to a wendigo to protect their people. They prefer to use outsiders as the offerings, and the PCs seem ideally suited to keep the creature at bay.

GM Intrusion: *A wendigo howl causes nearby animals to panic and flee, possibly trampling a character in their path, throwing her from her saddle, or otherwise discomfiting her.*

WEREWOLF 4 (12)

The curse of lycanthropy begins as nightmares about being chased or, somehow more terrifying, chasing someone else. As the dreams grow more fierce and each night's sleep provides less rest, the victim begins to wonder about the bloodstains on her clothing, the strange claw marks in her home, and eventually, the mutilated bodies she finds buried in her backyard.

When not transformed, many who suffer the curse seem like completely normal people, if emotionally traumatized by the fact that most of their friends and family have been brutally slaughtered over the preceding months. Some few, however, realize the truth of their condition, and depending on their natures, they either kill themselves before their next transformation or learn to revel in the butchery.

Favorite methods for curing a werewolf include medicine (wolfsbane), surgery, or exorcism. Many "cures" are effective only because they kill the werewolf in human form before she's able to transform again.

Motive: Slaughter when transformed; searching for answers when human

Environment: Anywhere dark, usually alone but sometimes as part of a small pack of two to five

Health: 24

Damage Inflicted: 5 points

Movement: Short; long when in wolf form

Modifications: Attacks as level 6 when half lupine; Speed defense as level 6 when full lupine; perception as level 7 when half or full lupine.

Combat: In normal human form, a werewolf has no natural attacks, though it may use a weapon. It also lacks the abilities described below; its only power is to transform into a half-lupine form or full lupine form, which takes 1d6 agonizing rounds. A handful of werewolves can control their transformation, but most change at night in response to moon-related cues.

Half Lupine: A half-lupine werewolf is part humanoid and part wolf, but completely terrifying. It attacks with its claws.

Full Lupine: A full lupine werewolf is a particularly large and vicious-looking wolf. It normally bites foes and deals 2 additional points of damage (7 points total) but can also use its claws.

GM Intrusion: *A PC who moves down one step on the damage track due to damage inflicted by a werewolf must succeed on a Might defense roll or be afflicted with the curse of lycanthropy.*

Half and Full Lupine: Half-lupine and full lupine werewolves both enjoy enhanced senses and regain 2 points of health per round. However, a werewolf that takes damage from a silver weapon or bullet stops regenerating for several minutes.

Interaction: In human form, werewolves have the goals and aspirations of normal people, and they often don't recall what they did while transformed or even realize that they suffer the curse of lycanthropy. In half- or full lupine form, there's no negotiating with one.

Use: When the moon is full, werewolves hunt.

WITCH 5 (15)

She studied the old ways at the dark of the moon. She heard the shuffle of unnamed things through the darkling forest, watched the convection of the bubbles rise in the cauldron, and attended to the mumbled instructions of withered crones and crumbling messages traced on dead leaves. Then one midnight, it all came together, and a witch was born.

Most witches are warped by the power they channel, both mentally and physically, but they can hide such transformations beneath layers of illusion.

Motive: Domination of others, knowledge

Environment: Almost anywhere, usually alone, but sometimes as part of a coven of three to seven witches

Health: 21

Damage Inflicted: 5 points

Movement: Short; long when flying (on a broomstick)

Modifications: Deception and disguise as level 7; Speed defense as level 6 due to familiar; knowledge of forests and dark secrets as level 6.

Combat: When attacked, a witch relies on the aid of her familiar to improve her Speed defense. The familiar could be a large black cat, an owl, a big snake, or some other creature. Killing a witch's familiar is so shocking to a witch that her Speed defense and attacks drop to level 4. It's also a way to ensure that she never forgives her foe or grants mercy.

Familiar: *level 3; health 9; Armor 1*

A witch can use her ritual blade to attack a creature in immediate range, but she'd much rather use curses, including the ones described below. A witch can't use the same curse more than once every other round.

Shrivel: A victim within long range and up to two creatures next to the victim must succeed on a Might defense roll or take 3 points of Speed damage (ignores Armor). In each subsequent round, a victim who failed the previous roll must make another Might defense roll with the same outcome on failure.

Charm: A victim within short range who fails an Intellect defense roll becomes the witch's slave. He turns on his allies or takes some other action described by his new master. The curse lasts for one minute, or until the victim succeeds on an Intellect defense roll; each time he fails a roll, the difficulty of the next roll increases by one step.

Witches are often female, but males take up the craft as well. A male witch is no less foreboding or dangerous, but given that the tradition was developed by women, most witches consider males to be lesser practitioners.

Hexbolt: A victim within long range is attacked with fire, cold, or psychic bolts, as the witch chooses. Psychic bolts deal 3 points of Intellect damage (ignores Armor).

Vitality: The witch regains 11 points of health and gains +3 to Armor for one minute. Multiple uses don't further improve her Armor.

Interaction: Most witches are deceptive and conniving, though a few work against the stereotype. All witches are willing to negotiate, though the devious ones usually do so in bad faith.

Use: The PCs need an old book to continue their investigation. Word is that the old woman who lives on the edge of the woods has the only copy.

Loot: A witch usually has an artifact or two on her person, possibly including a flying broom (which has a depletion roll of 1 in 1d10).

GM Intrusion: *After a PC succeeds on a defense roll against one of the witch's ongoing curse effects, she immediately tosses a hexbolt at him. If the PC is hit, the ongoing curse effect also continues.*

XENOPARASITE 6 (18)

This alien creature exists only to eat and reproduce. In doing so, it also destroys every form of life it encounters. Xenoparasites are not technological but were likely engineered by a species with advanced biological superscience. Xenoparasites don't travel between star systems on their own; they were presumably spread across an area of space by their creators to serve as a broad-spectrum bioweapon. What has become of the original maker species is unknown, but given the fecundity and ferocity of the xenoparasite, it's likely they were consumed by their own creation.

Xenoparasites use ovipositors to lay thousands of microscopic eggs in victims. The implanted eggs, like tiny biological labs, detect the particular biology of the new host, adapt accordingly, and use it to fertilize themselves. Within a day or two, victims who haven't already been consumed by adult xenoparasites (which are human sized) give explosive birth to multiple vicious juveniles (which are the size of cats). These juvenile xenoparasites have an edge in dealing with the particular species of creature they hatched from.

Motive: Eat and reproduce

Environment: Hunts alone or in small groups

Health: 28

Damage Inflicted: 6 points

Armor: 2

Movement: Short; long when flying

Modifications: All stealth actions as level 8.

Combat: A xenoparasite bites with its mandibles and stings one victim with its ovipositor as a single action. The bite inflicts 6 points of damage, and the ovipositor inflicts 3 points of damage and injects thousands of microscopic eggs if the victim fails a Might defense roll.

Once every other round, an adult can fly at least a short distance to build terrifying velocity and then make a flying attack with its mandibles, dealing 12 points of damage. The difficulty to defend against this attack is increased by one step.

An egg host requires the attention of someone skilled in medicine (and a successful difficulty 7 Intellect-based roll) to sterilize all the eggs in the victim's blood before they hatch twenty or more hours after being deposited, which kills the host and releases 1d6 juvenile xenoparasites. Juveniles are level 2 creatures, but they attack the species of the host they were hatched from as if level 4. After just a few days of feeding, they grow to full adult size.

Xenoparasites can survive at crushing ocean and gas giant pressures, as well as in the vacuum of space. They can encrust abandoned spacecraft and desolate moons for millennia in extended hibernation, only to become active again when vibrations alert them to potential new food sources.

Interaction: These creatures are built to consume, not negotiate.

Use: Xenoparasites are tough aliens. A colony of them would be a challenge even for PCs normally accustomed to stiff opposition. A single xenoparasite introduced into an inhabited area could turn the entire place into an infested hive within a week.

Adult xenoparasites build sprawling, wasplike nests in the areas they infest, using the nest as a base from which to slowly spread their influence. Whole space stations, moons, and planets have been covered in convoluted white nests crawling with death.

GM Intrusion: *An NPC shrieks, bursts, and births 1d6 juvenile xenoparasites.*

ZHEV 5 (15)

The Zhev are entities who often serve as the peacekeeping force in technologically advanced cities. They are cylinders 6 feet (2 m) high and 3 feet (1 m) in diameter, and they typically hover 3 feet (1 m) off the ground.

The Zhev have three triangular eyes that appear to be organic. The eyes usually stay together in a larger triangle formation, moving inside the cylinder, peering through a slit near the top that goes all the way around. The eyes can also separate, each looking in a different direction, but they do this rarely. Although the Zhev are essentially automatons, they have organic interior components as well as mechanical parts.

The Zhev patrol usually in pairs but sometimes alone, preventing infractions of the law and acting to keep order, keep the peace, and protect the lives of innocents. When forced to choose between options, they always make the choice that saves the most people from the greatest harm. Protecting innocents takes priority over enforcing laws. Some people assume they were manufactured for their role as a peacekeeping force, but their origins aren't clear.

Motive: Maintain order

Environment: Anywhere the Zhev have been retained to keep the peace

Health: 20

Damage Inflicted: 6 points

Armor: 4

Movement: Long

Modifications: Attacks as level 6; perception and knowledge of local law as level 7.

Combat: The Zhev usually begin a fight by firing stun gas canisters at long range that explode and impede actions for creatures within immediate range of the blast. Affected targets can take no actions for 1d6 rounds unless they make a Might defense roll to resist the gas. The Zhev also project nets within short range that immobilize a struck target unless he can break or wriggle free (a Might or Speed action). If the gas and nets fail, they attack with their metallic arms that are 10 feet (3 m) long and jointed like tentacles. The Zhev have three such arms and can attack three different foes as a single action if they are all within reach.

Unlike many automatons, the Zhev retreat if faced with a more powerful foe (unless they have been commanded to stay and fight). They usually try to get reinforcements and then return to engage the enemy.

GM Intrusion: *The Zhev grabs a character with its metallic arms and holds him fast, immobilizing him.*

Interaction: The Zhev obey the orders given to them by human superiors, if any. More important, they follow codified law in the area and may use a special interpretation of a law to supersede a command, especially if someone offers them such an interpretation. Otherwise, they are relentless and merciless, although they are ordered to capture criminals rather than use violent or lethal force if at all possible.

Use: The Zhev are dangerous, capable law enforcers and protectors. Where they are deployed, they are well respected but not always well liked. PCs who run afoul of them have likely done something very wrong.

Loot: The body of a Zhev can be scavenged for 1d6 + 1 cyphers, and perhaps an artifact.

ZOMBIE 3 (9)

Humans transformed into aggressive, hard-to-kill serial killers with no memory of their former existence are called zombies. Depending on a zombie's origin, the reason for its transformation varies. A zombie might arise from an undead curse, a psychic possession, an AI meatware overwrite, a viral infection, a drug overdose, or something else. Regardless of how the transformation happened, the result is much the same: a creature whose humanity has been burned out and replaced with unquenchable hunger.

Zombies aren't intelligent, but enough of them together sometimes exhibit emergent behavior, just as ants can coordinate activities across a colony. Thus, zombies alone or in small groups aren't an overwhelming threat for someone who has a baseball bat or can get away. But it's never wise to laugh off a zombie horde.

Motive: Hunger (for flesh, cerebrospinal fluid, certain human hormones, and so on)
Environment: Almost anywhere, in groups of five to seven, or in hordes of tens to hundreds
Health: 12
Damage Inflicted: 3 points
Movement: Immediate
Modifications: Speed defense as level 2.
Combat: Zombies never turn away from a conflict. They fight on, no matter the odds, usually attacking by biting, but sometimes by tearing with hands made into claws by the erosion of skin over their finger bones.

When zombies attack in groups of five to seven individuals, they can make a single attack roll against one target as one level 5 creature, inflicting 5 points of damage.

Zombies are hard to finish off. If an attack would reduce a zombie's health to 0, it does so only if the number rolled in the attack was an even number; otherwise, the zombie is reduced to 1 point of health instead. This might result in a dismembered, gruesomely damaged zombie that is still moving. Zombies can see in the dark at short range.

"Fresh" zombies are vulnerable to electricity. The first time a zombie takes 5 or more points of damage from an electrical attack, it falls limp and unmoving. Assuming nothing interferes with the process, the zombie arises minutes or hours later without the vulnerability.

Some zombies are infectious. Their bites spread a level 8 disease that moves a victim down one step on the damage track each day a Might defense roll is failed. Victims killed by the disease later animate as zombies.

Interaction: Zombies groan when they see something that looks tasty. They do not reason, cannot speak, and never stop pursuing something they've identified as a potential meal, unless something else edible comes closer.

Use: The characters are asked to clear out a space that once served as an old military depot. The appearance of zombies sealed in the area comes as an unpleasant surprise.

GM Intrusion: *When the character fails to kill a zombie by rolling an odd number on an attack that otherwise would have been successful, in addition to the normal effect, the zombie's arm comes free and animates as a separate level 2 zombie.*

CHAPTER 17

NPCs

The NPCs in this chapter are generic examples of character types that can be used in many genres. GMs will find that with a few tweaks, a guard can be a modern-day cop, a fantasy caravan guard, or a science fiction drone soldier.

Remember that NPCs don't have stat Pools. Instead, they have a characteristic called health. When an NPC takes damage of any kind, the amount is subtracted from its health. Unless described otherwise, an NPC's health is always equal to its target number. Some NPCs might have special reactions to or defenses against attacks that would normally deal Speed damage or Intellect damage, but unless the NPC's description specifically explains this, assume that all damage is subtracted from the NPC's health.

APPROPRIATE WEAPONS

NPCs use weapons appropriate to their situation, which might be swords and crossbows, knives and shotguns, malefic psychic weapons, blasters and grenades, and so on.

NPCs BY LEVEL

Guard	2
Crime boss	3
Detective	3
Thug	3
Occultist	5
Secret agent	5
Assassin	6
Wizard, mighty	8

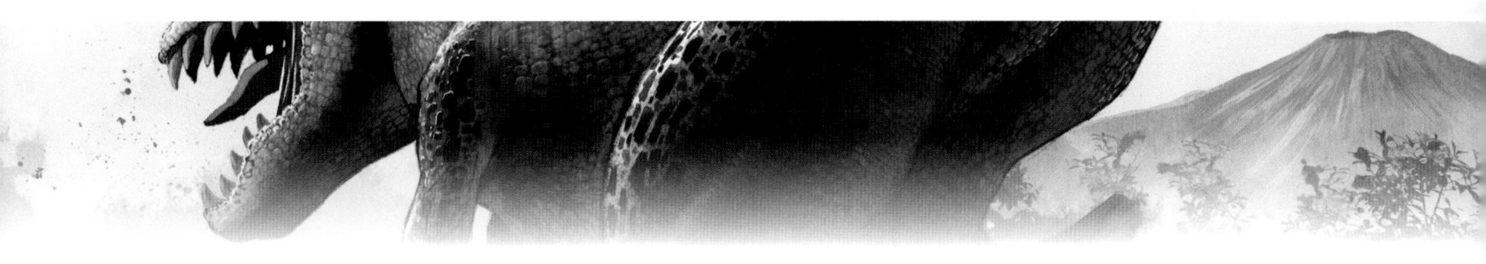

ASSASSIN 6 (18)

An assassin kills with poison, with high-velocity bullets from a distance, or by arranging for an unfortunate accident. Assassins accept contracts from governments, corporations, crime bosses, and aggrieved former spouses or partners, though some assassins pay themselves by tracking criminals into wilderness areas to collect on "dead or alive" bounties.

Motive: Murder (usually for hire)

Health: 18

Damage Inflicted: 6 points

Armor: 1

Movement: Short

Modifications: Stealth and deception tasks as level 8; when attacking from hiding, melee and ranged attacks as level 7.

Combat: An assortment of small weapons are hidden about an assassin's body. She can also coat her weapons or ammo with a level 6 poison that moves victims who fail a Might defense roll one step down the damage track.

Interaction: Some assassins have a sort of integrity about their work and can't be dissuaded from completing their contracts with bribes.

Use: An assassin is greatly feared by anyone with powerful, wealthy enemies.

Loot: Aside from their weapons and poisons, most assassins have currency equivalent to a very expensive item and maybe one or two cyphers.

GM Intrusion: *The character loses her next turn, stunned, as she recognizes the assassin to be the same murderer who killed someone important to her in her past.*

CRIME BOSS 3 (9)

A crime boss usually isn't physically powerful but wields power though lies, bribery, and control. Rarely encountered alone, a crime boss relies on guards, thugs, and other measures to provide physical security. A crime boss could be a petty noble, a mafia king, or the captain of a pirate ship that sails the seas or glides the space lanes.

Motive: Money and power

Health: 12

Damage Inflicted: 5 points

Armor: 1

Movement: Short

Modifications: Deception, persuasion, intimidation, and tasks related to friendly interaction as level 7.

Combat: Guards, thugs, and other followers deal 1 additional point of damage when the crime boss can see them and issue commands. If possible, crime bosses fight while mounted or in a vehicle, directing their followers from the rear of any conflict, concentrating first on issuing orders.

Interaction: Crime bosses are committed to their plans, whatever those might be. Most bosses rely on a lieutenant or trusted thug to interact with people in their place.

Use: A crime boss and her followers execute a heist on a secure location and take hostages when things go south. Someone must go in and talk to the crime boss to defuse the situation.

Loot: A crime boss has currency equivalent to a very expensive item in addition to weapons, medium armor, and miscellaneous gear.

GM Intrusion: *The crime boss blocks all incoming attacks in a given round of combat using a clever trick or cypher.*

DETECTIVE 3 (9)

Detectives are usually veterans of their organization (such as the police, city watch, marshals, space command, and so on) with extensive experience. Some detectives are freelance sleuths whose uncanny ability to see the truth comes from personal training combined with an underlying talent for noticing clues that others miss.

Motive: Solve the crime

Health: 12

Damage Inflicted: 4 points

Movement: Short

Modifications: Tasks relating to perception, intuition, initiative, and detecting falsehoods as level 6.

Combat: Detectives prefer to outwit their foes rather than engage in a straight-up fight. Even then, most conflicts occur in a place and a time of the detective's choosing, preferably in the presence of his allies. A detective can deduce weaknesses of his enemies (if any) and exploit them in combat.

Interaction: Some detectives are insufferable know-it-alls. Others have learned that humility is also a useful tool for getting answers from people.

Use: To the PCs, detectives can be obstacles (a detective is on their trail), allies (a detective helps them assemble clues), or both, but the sleuths are rarely a way for the characters to hand off responsibility for accomplishing a hard task.

Loot: Aside from their weapons, most detectives have currency equivalent to a very expensive item and a cypher.

GM Intrusion: *The detective intuits the character's next attack and moves perfectly so that an ally of the character takes the attack instead.*

GUARD 2 (6)

Guards keep the peace but don't usually show much initiative. Ultimately, they do as they're ordered by their superiors, regardless of legality. A guard might be a star trooper dressed in intimidating armor, a mall security guard, a beat police officer, or a mafia goon.

Motive: Keep the peace; follow orders

Health: 8

Damage Inflicted: 3 points

Armor: 1 or 2

Movement: Short

Modifications: Perception as level 3.

Combat: Guards are not often wily, but they understand strength in numbers. If two or more guards attack the same target with at least one melee attack in the same round, the difficulty of the target's Speed defense roll against those attacks is increased by one step.

Interaction: Interacting with a guard typically involves one issue: does the PC want to do something that the guard has been told to prevent? If so, the PC could have a difficult time.

Use: To the PCs, guards can be allies, obstacles, or both. Guards who serve the public good have their own duties and aren't interested in doing the characters' work for them.

Loot: A guard has currency equivalent to an inexpensive item in addition to weapons, armor, and basic gear.

When attacked, guards always call for the help of other guards, if possible.

GM Intrusion: *1d6 local citizens intervene on the guard's behalf, calling for more guards or even fighting the guard's foes.*

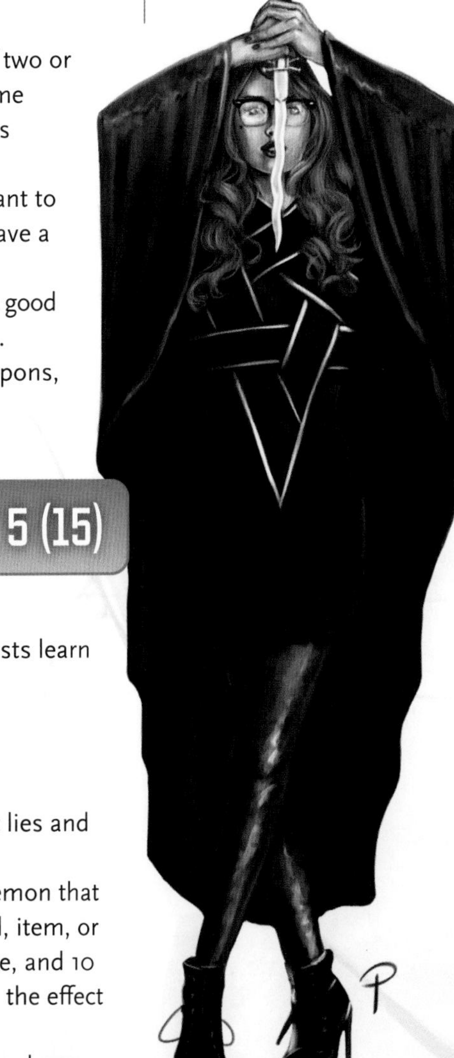

OCCULTIST 5 (15)

Paranormal researchers, cultists, secret practitioners of white magic, and coven members might be occultists. Thanks to their study of the metaphysical, occultists learn several magical tricks, including the ability to summon or banish the dead.

Health: 15

Damage Inflicted: 5 points

Movement: Short

Modifications: Knowledge of occult topics and rituals as level 8; ability to detect lies and tricks as level 2.

Combat: An occultist has a charm or device for summoning a level 5 spirit or demon that will do his bidding for ten minutes. Some also have (or instead have) a spell, item, or device that inflicts 5 points of damage on normal creatures within long range, and 10 points of damage on a demon or spirit (or, instead of dealing extra damage, the effect confines the demon or spirit in some way).

Interaction: Occultists are deeply concerned with spiritual or demonic matters and see those influences in all things, whether those influences exist or not. That makes them amenable to persuasion and deception, if couched in the language of spiritual influence.

Use: To find a needed answer, the spirit of a dead person must be questioned. Alternatively, a haunting presence must be excommunicated. Either way, the task requires an occultist.

Loot: In addition to their clothing and mundane weapons, occultists have currency equivalent to an inexpensive item, a cypher, and possibly an artifact related to their power over spirits or demons.

GM Intrusion: *A bony hand erupts from the ground at the character's feet. On a failed Speed defense roll, he is held in place until he succeeds on a Might-based task to escape. Each round the PC fails to escape, the hand squeezes him for 3 points of damage.*

SECRET AGENT 5 (15)

Secret agents are trained professionals who put their mission before their own well-being, regardless of which government agency, corporation, guild, or kingdom employs them. An agent operates under a fake cover, perhaps as an envoy, inspector, technician, actor, tourist, or bumbling fool.

Motive: Accomplish the goals of the employer while maintaining cover

Health: 15

Damage Inflicted: 5 points

Movement: Short

Modifications: Tasks related to disguise and deceiving as level 6.

Combat: A secret agent always has a covert, unexpected backup weapon that she can use to make a surprise attack, such as a ring or glove with a hidden poisoned needle (dealing 5 points of Speed damage that ignore Armor), a fake tooth filled with poison gas to blow in a victim's face (inducing sleep for ten minutes), or a ring with a miniature gun.

Interaction: Secret agents are confident, masterful, and always give the impression of being one step ahead of the game, even when caught off guard.

Use: As an ally, a secret agent can guide the PCs to their next mission, fill in gaps in their knowledge, and warn them of dangers. If the characters encounter an unfriendly agent, the NPC likely presents himself as their friend.

Loot: Agents typically have currency equivalent to an expensive item, a couple of cyphers, tools for spying and maintaining their cover, and possibly an artifact.

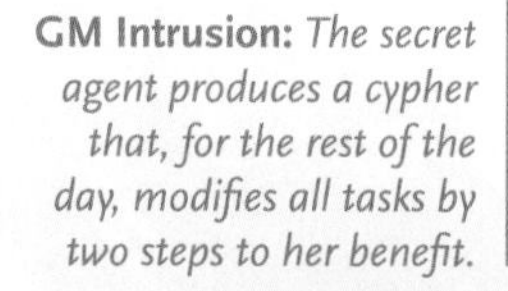
GM Intrusion: *The secret agent produces a cypher that, for the rest of the day, modifies all tasks by two steps to her benefit.*

THUG 3 (9)

Thugs are usually rough, crude, and harsh individuals who prey on those who follow the rules. A thug might be a streetwise drug dealer, a bandit who hunts lone travelers in the wilds, a savage warrior adroit with ranged weapons, or a cyberbully among pacifists. Most thugs work for themselves, but they may employ gangs of guards to help them conduct their business.

Motive: Take what they want

Health: 9

Damage Inflicted: 4 points

Armor: 1

Movement: Short

Combat: Thugs prefer ambushes, making ranged attacks from hiding if possible. Sometimes they spoil the ambush to issue an ultimatum before attacking: give us your valuables or you'll be sorry.

Interaction: Thugs are interested in money and power, which means they almost always accept bribes. If faced with a real threat, thugs usually retreat.

Use: Thugs are everywhere, sometimes accompanied by guards who are equally malicious but not quite as powerful.

Loot: A thug has currency equivalent to an inexpensive item in addition to weapons, shields, and light armor. One thug in a group might have a cypher.

GM Intrusion: *Another thug, hidden until just the right moment, appears and takes a shot with a ranged weapon before joining the fray.*

GM Intrusion: *The wizard casts two spells as a single action instead of just one.*

WIZARD, MIGHTY 8 (24)

Some wizards learn so many spells and accumulate so much lore that they become incredibly powerful. Some work for a higher purpose, whereas others are concerned only with themselves.

Motive: Seek powerful sources of magic (to collect or to keep safe)

Health: 40

Damage Inflicted: 8 points

Movement: Short

Modifications: All tasks related to knowledge of arcane lore as level 9.

Combat: When a wizard makes a long-range attack with his staff or strikes someone with it, arcane energy damages the target and, if desired, all creatures the wizard selects within short range of the target. Targets within immediate range of the wizard when they take damage are thrown out of immediate range.

A mighty wizard knows many spells, including spells that grant +5 to Armor for an hour, spells of teleportation, spells of finding, and so on. A wizard also likely carries several cyphers useful in combat.

Interaction: Care should be taken when negotiating with wizards because they are subtle and quick to anger. Even when negotiations succeed, a wizard's suggestions are usually cryptic and open to interpretation. A mighty wizard might be convinced to teach a character how to cast a spell.

Use: A wizard is putting together a team to challenge a great foe, and the PCs fit the bill.

Loot: A mighty wizard has 1d6 cyphers.

CHAPTER 18

CYPHERS

Cyphers are one-use abilities that characters gain over the course of play. In the majority of games, these come in the form of items, like magic potions or bits of alien technology. In others, they're more esoteric, like inspirations or divine blessings. Cyphers are designed for frequent discovery and use. PCs can have only a small number of cyphers at a given time, and since they're always finding more, they're encouraged to use them at a steady pace.

In theory, the cyphers discovered by the PCs are determined randomly. However, the GM can place them intentionally as well. They have cool powers that can heal, make attacks, or produce effects such as nullifying gravity or turning something invisible. Cyphers are single-use items and are always consumed when used.

Cyphers are found with such regularity that the PCs can use them freely. There will always be more, and they'll have different benefits. This means that in gameplay, cyphers are less like gear or treasure and more like character abilities that the players don't choose. This leads to fun game moments where a player can say, "Well, I've got an X that might help

Cyphers don't have to be used to make room for new ones. It's perfectly acceptable for the PCs to stash an extra cypher elsewhere for later use. Of course, that doesn't mean the cypher will still be there when they return.

WHY CYPHERS?

Cyphers are (not surprisingly, based on the name) the heart of the Cypher System. This is because characters in this game have abilities that rarely or never change and can always be counted on—pretty much like in all games—and they have abilities that are ever-changing and inject a great deal of variability in play. They are the major reason why no Cypher System game session should ever be dull or feel just like the last session. This week your character can solve the problem by walking through walls, but last time it was because you could create an explosion that would level a city block.

The Cypher System, then, is a game where PC abilities are fluid, with the GM and the players both having a role in their choice, their assignment, and their use. Although many things separate the game system from others, this aspect makes it unique, because cyphers recognize the importance and value of two things:

1. "Treasure" as character abilities makes the game fun and exciting. In the early days of roleplaying, in fact, treasure (usually in the form of magic items found in dungeons) was really the only customization of characters that existed. It means that the drive to go out and have adventures is that you can discover cool new things that help you when you go on the next adventures. This is true in many RPGs, but in the Cypher System, it's built right into the game's core.

2. Letting the GM have a hand in determining PC abilities makes the game move more smoothly. Some GMs prefer to generate cyphers randomly, but some do not. For example, giving the PCs a cypher that will allow them to teleport far away might be a secret adventure seed placed by a forward-thinking GM. Because the GM has an idea of where the story is going, she can use cyphers to help guide the path. Alternatively, if the GM is open to it, she can give out cyphers that enable the characters to take a more proactive role (such as teleporting anywhere they want). Perhaps most important, she can do these things without worrying about the long-term ramifications of the power. A device that lets you teleport multiple times might really mess up the game over the long term. But once? That's just fun.

in this situation," and X is always different. X might be an explosive device, a short-range teleporter, or a force field. It might be a powerful magnet or an injection that will cure disease. It could be anything. Cyphers keep the game fresh and interesting. Over time, characters can learn how to safely carry more and more cyphers, so the devices really do seem more like abilities and less like gear.

CYPHER LIMITS

All characters have a maximum number of cyphers they can have in their possession at any one time. If a character ever attempts to possess more, random cyphers disappear instantly until she has cyphers equal to her maximum. These cyphers are not recoverable.

FINDING AND IDENTIFYING CYPHERS

Cyphers are often found in groups of one to six (the GM can roll 1d6 to determine the number), usually because the PCs are looking for them. They might be among the possessions of a fallen foe, hidden in a secret room, or scattered amid the wreckage of a crashed starship. The GM can prepare a list ahead of time of what successful searchers find. Sometimes this list is random, and sometimes there is some logic behind it. For example, the PCs might find four different magic potions in the same location in a warlock's laboratory.

If the characters search for cyphers, the GM sets the difficulty of the task. It is usually 3 or 4, and scavenging can take fifteen minutes to an hour.

Scavenging is not the only way to obtain cyphers. They can also be given as gifts, traded with merchants, or sometimes purchased in a shop.

Once the PCs find a cypher, identifying it is a separate task, based on Intellect and modified by knowledge of the topic at hand. In a fantasy setting, that knowledge would probably be magic, but in a science fiction setting, it might be technology. The GM sets the difficulty of the task, but it is usually 1 or 2. Thus, even the smallest amount of knowledge means that cypher identification is automatic. The process takes one to ten minutes. If the PCs can't identify a

Cyphers are meant to be used regularly and often. If PCs are hoarding or saving their cyphers, feel free to give them a reason to pull the devices out and put them into play.

cypher, they can bring it to an expert for identification and perhaps trade, if desired.

A character can attempt to use a cypher that has not been identified; this is usually an Intellect task using the cypher's level. Failure might mean that the PC can't figure out how to use the cypher or that he uses it incorrectly (GM's discretion). Of course, even if the PC uses the unidentified cypher correctly, he has no idea what its effect will be.

Identified cyphers can be used automatically. Once a cypher is activated, if it has an ongoing effect, that effect applies only to the character who activated the cypher. A PC can't activate a cypher and then hand it to another character to reap the benefits.

USING CYPHERS

If a character uses a cypher, the action to use it is Intellect based unless described otherwise or logic suggests otherwise. For example, throwing a detonation might be Speed based because the device is physical and not really technical, but using a ray emitter is Intellect based.

Because cyphers are single-use items, cyphers used to make attacks can never be used with the Spray or Arc Spray abilities that some characters have. They are never treated as rapid-fire weapons.

Spray, page 26

Arc Spray, page 27

CYPHER FORMS

All cyphers have a level and an effect. The level sometimes determines an aspect of the cypher's power (how much damage it inflicts, for example) but otherwise only determines its general efficacy, the way level works with any object.

None of the cyphers in this book have a stated physical form. The entries don't tell you if something is a potion, a pill, or a device you hold in your hands because it varies greatly from genre to genre. Are they magic? Are they tech? That's up to the GM. It's flavor, not mechanics. It's as important or unimportant as the color of an NPC's hair or the color of the car the bad guys are driving. In other words, it's the kind of thing that is important in a roleplaying game, but at the same time doesn't actually change anything (and RPGs have a lot of things like that, if you think about it).

There is nothing to say that you can't use manifest cyphers and subtle cyphers in the same game. A horror game could begin with the PCs as normal people with subtle cyphers, but as time goes on, they find one-use spells in occult tomes, weird potions, and bone dust that has strange powers.

There are two types of cypher forms, manifest cyphers and subtle cyphers. It might be more accurate to say that all physical cypher forms are lumped together under the umbrella of manifest cyphers, and cyphers that have no form at all are called subtle cyphers.

MANIFEST CYPHERS

Manifest cyphers have physical form. They can be anything at all, but there are some obvious choices based on genre. The GM can design a setting that uses just one type, such as: all cyphers in this magical world are potions made by faeries. Or she can use many types, perhaps mixing them from different genres. Some suggestions include the following:

Fantasy
Potions
Scrolls
Runeplates
Tattoos
Charms
Powders
Crystals
Books with words of power

Modern
Drugs (injections, pills, inhalants)
Viruses
Smartphone apps

Science Fiction
Drugs (injections, pills, inhalants)
Computer programs
Crystals
Viruses
Biological implants
Mechanical implants
Nanotechnological injections

Horror
Burrowing worms or insects
Pages from forbidden books
Horrific images

Superhero
Gadgets
Crystals

SUBTLE CYPHERS

Subtle cyphers are a way to introduce cyphers into a game without overt "powered stuff"—no potions, alien crystals, or anything of that nature. They're most useful, perhaps, in a modern or horror setting without obvious fantasy elements. Subtle cyphers are more like the inherent abilities PCs have, adding boosts to Edge, recovering points from Pools, coming up with ideas, and so on. No laser beams or walking through walls with subtle cyphers. They don't break the fragile bubble of believability in genres where flashy powers and abilities don't make a lot of sense.

Subtle cyphers are particularly nice in a genre where the PCs are supposed to be normal people. The cyphers can simply be an expression of innate capabilities in characters that aren't always dependable. And in many ways, that's probably more realistic than an ability you can count on with certainty, because in real life, sometimes you can jump over a fence, and some days you just can't.

Some concepts for subtle cyphers include the following:

Good Fortune: Once in a while, things just go your way. You're in the right place at the right time.

Inspirations: Sometimes you get inspired to do something you've never done before and might not be able to do again. Call it adrenaline mixed with the right motivation, or just doing the right thing at the right place at the right time. Who can really define such things? Life's funny that way.

Alien Concepts: Complex and utterly inhuman memes have entered our world and worm their way into and out of human consciousnesses. When they do, it can cause mental distress and disorientation. It can also grant impossible abilities and advantages.

Blessings: In a fantasy world, there are nine gods. Each morning, all intelligent residents of the world pray to one of the gods, and some of the faithful gain a divine blessing. Some people believe that praying to different gods gives you different blessings.

Earworms: You know how some songs pop into your head and just won't leave? There's a power to those songs, and the right people know how to harness it. Make the songs disturbing, or reminiscent of evil chants, and you've got a perfect cypher concept for a horror campaign.

Mysterious Transmissions: What's that buzzing? That mechanical chittering? Those numbers repeating over and over? And why can only some people hear it? A few who are aware of the sounds have learned how to make use of them.

Supernatural Powers: Mental or mystical energies constantly shift and change, ebb and flow. But you've figured out how to attune your mind to them. There are no physical actions or paraphernalia required—just an inner conduit to the numinous.

DISCOVERING SUBTLE CYPHERS

Since subtle cyphers aren't physical objects, GMs will need to figure out when to give PCs new ones to replace those they might have used. The cyphers aren't items to be found. They probably shouldn't be tied to actions entirely under the characters' control—in other words, they shouldn't come as a result of meditation or anything of that nature. Instead, the GM should choose significant points in the course of the story when new subtle cyphers might simply come unbidden to the PCs. In the broader view, this is no different than placing physical cyphers in a creature's lair, a secret cache, or somewhere else for the characters to find. Either way, the GM is picking good spots to "refill" potentially used cypher-based abilities.

MANIFEST CYPHER TABLE

Roll 1d6: on 1-2, use column 1; on 3-4, use column 2; on 5-6, use column 3.

	COLUMN 1	COLUMN 2	COLUMN 3
01–02	Adhesion	Gas bomb	Ray emitter (paralysis)
03–04	Age taker	Gravity nullifier	Reality spike
05–06	Analeptic	Gravity-nullifying application	Reflex enhancer
07–08	Antivenom	Heat attack	Rejuvenator
09–10	Armor reinforcer	Hunter/seeker	Remembering
11–12	Attractor	Image projector	Remote viewer
13–14	Banishing	Inferno wall	Repair unit
15–16	Blackout	Infiltrator	Repeater
17–18	Blinking	Information sensor	Retaliation
19–20	Catholicon	Instant servant	Secret
21–22	Chemical factory	Instant shelter	Sheen
23–24	Comprehension	Intellect booster	Shock attack
25–26	Condition remover	Intelligence enhancement	Shocker
27–28	Contingent activator	Knowledge enhancement	Skill boost
29–30	Controlled blinking	Lightning wall	Slave maker
31–32	Curative	Machine control	Sleep inducer
33–34	Curse bringer	Magnetic attack drill	Sniper module
35–36	Darksight	Magnetic master	Solvent
37–38	Death bringer	Magnetic shield	Sonic hole
39–40	Density	Manipulation beam	Sound dampener
41–42	Detonation	Matter transference ray	Spatial warp
43–44	Detonation (creature)	Meditation aid	Speed boost
45–46	Detonation (desiccating)	Memory switch	Spy
47–48	Detonation (flash)	Mental scrambler	Stasis keeper
49–50	Detonation (gravity)	Metal death	Stim
51–52	Detonation (gravity inversion)	Mind meld	Strength boost
53–54	Detonation (massive)	Mind-restricting wall	Strength enhancer
55–56	Detonation (matter disruption)	Mind stabilizer	Subdual field
57–58	Detonation (pressure)	Monoblade	Telepathy
59–60	Detonation (singularity)	Monohorn	Teleporter (bounder)
61–62	Detonation (sonic)	Motion sensor	Teleporter (interstellar)
63–64	Detonation (spawn)	Null field	Teleporter (planetary)
65–66	Detonation (web)	Nullification ray	Teleporter (traveler)
67–68	Disguise module	Nutrition and hydration	Temporal viewer
69–70	Disrupting	Perfect memory	Time dilation (defensive)
71–72	Eagleseye	Personal environment field	Time dilation (offensive)
73–74	Effect resistance	Phase changer	Tissue regeneration
75–76	Effort enhancer	Phase disruptor	Tracer
77–78	Effort enhancer (combat)	Poison (emotion)	Trick embedder
79–80	Enduring shield	Poison (explosive)	Uninterruptible power source
81–82	Equipment cache	Poison (mind controlling)	Vanisher
83–84	Farsight	Poison (mind disrupting)	Visage changer
85–86	Fireproofing	Psychic communique	Visual displacement device
87–88	Flame-retardant wall	Radiation spike	Vocal translator
89–90	Force cube	Ray emitter	Warmth
91–92	Force field	Ray emitter (command)	Water adapter
93–94	Force screen projector	Ray emitter (fear)	Weapon enhancement
95–96	Force shield projector	Ray emitter (friend slaying)	Wings
97–98	Friction reducer	Ray emitter (mind disrupting)	X-ray viewer
99–00	Frigid wall	Ray emitter (numbing)	Zero point field

SUBTLE CYPHER TABLE

01–03	Analeptic	37–39	Intelligence enhancement	69–71	Secret
04–06	Condition remover	40–42	Knowledge enhancement	72–74	Skill boost
07–09	Contingent activator	43–45	Meditation aid	75–77	Sound dampener
10–15	Curative	46–48	Mind stabilizer	78–81	Speed boost
16–18	Darksight	49–51	Motion sensor	82–89	Stim
19–22	Eagleseye	52–54	Nutrition and hydration	90–93	Strength boost
23–26	Effort enhancer	55–57	Perfect memory	94–97	Strength enhancer
27–29	Effort enhancer (combat)	58–61	Reflex enhancer	98–00	Tissue regeneration
30–32	Enduring shield	62–65	Rejuvenator		
33–36	Intellect booster	66–68	Remembering		

A LISTING OF VARIOUS CYPHERS

All cyphers in this section may be manifest cyphers. Some could also be subtle cyphers, marked with an orange symbol.

ADHESION

Level: 1d6

Effect: Allows for automatic climbing of any surface, even horizontal ones. Lasts for twenty minutes.

AGE TAKER

Level: 1d6 + 4

Effect: Begins a process of rejuvenation that removes years from the wearer's physiological age. Over the course of the next seven days, the wearer sheds a number of years equal to three times the cypher's level. The cypher doesn't regress physiological age past the age of twenty-three.

ANALEPTIC

Level: 1d6 + 2

Effect: Restores a number of points equal to the cypher's level to the user's Speed Pool.

ANTIVENOM

Level: 1d6 + 2

Effect: Renders user immune to poisons of the same level or lower (and ends any such ongoing effects, if any, already in the user's system).

ARMOR REINFORCER

Level: 1d6 + 1

Effect: The user's Armor gains an enhancement for a day. Roll a d6 to determine the result.

1	+1 to Armor
2	+2 to Armor
3	+3 to Armor
4	+2 to Armor, +5 against damage from fire
5	+2 to Armor, +5 against damage from cold
6	+2 to Armor, +5 against damage from acid

ATTRACTOR

Level: 1d6 + 4

Effect: One unanchored item your size or smaller within long range is drawn immediately to you. This takes one round. The item has no momentum when it arrives.

BANISHING

Level: 1d6

Effect: For the next twenty-four hours, each time you strike a solid creature or object (with a weapon or your fist), a burst of energy teleports it an immediate distance in a random direction (not up or down). The difficulty of a teleported creature's actions (including defense) is modified by one step to its detriment on its next turn.

BLACKOUT

Level: 1d6 + 2

Effect: An area within immediate range of the user becomes secure against any effect outside the area that sees, hears, or otherwise senses what occurs inside. To outside observers, the area is a "blur" to any sense applied. Taps, scrying sensors, and other direct feed surveillance methods are also rendered inoperative within the area for twenty-four hours.

BLINKING

Level: 1d6

Effect: For the next twenty-four hours, each time you are struck hard enough to take damage (but not more than once per round), you teleport an immediate distance in a random direction (not up or down). Since you are prepared for this effect and your foe is not, the difficulty of your defense roll is modified by one step to your benefit for one round after you teleport.

CATHOLICON

Level: 1d6 + 2

Effect: Cures any disease of the same level or lower.

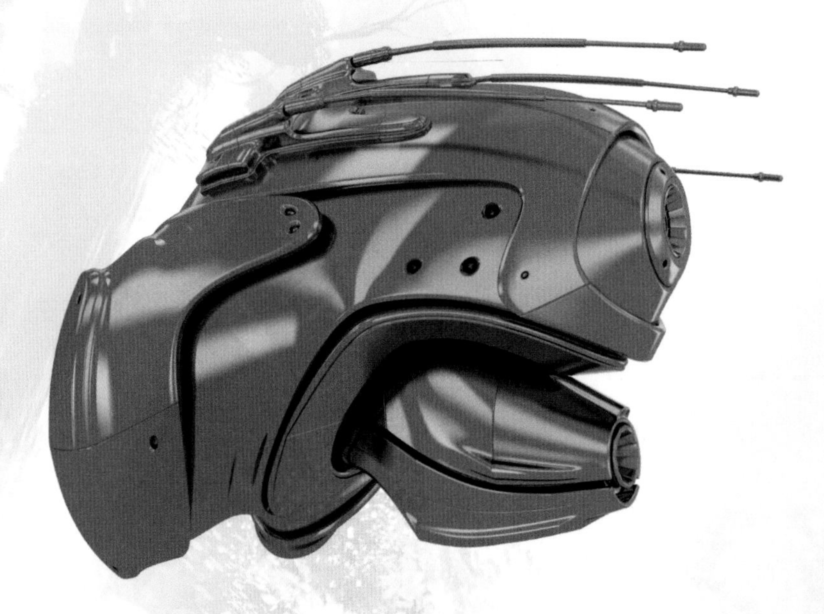

CHEMICAL FACTORY

Level: 1d6

Effect: After one hour, the sweat of the user produces 1d6 doses of a valuable liquid (these doses are not considered cyphers). They must be used within one week. Effects vary:

01–04	Euphoric for 1d6 hours
05–08	Hallucinogenic for 1d6 hours
09–12	Stimulant for 1d6 hours
13–16	Depressant for 1d6 hours
17–20	Nutrient supplement
21–25	Antivenom
26–30	Cures disease
31–35	See in the dark for one hour
36–45	Restores a number of Might Pool points equal to cypher level
46–55	Restores a number of Speed Pool points equal to cypher level
56–65	Restores a number of Intellect Pool points equal to cypher level
66–75	Increases Might Edge by 1 for one hour
76–85	Increases Speed Edge by 1 for one hour
86–95	Increases Intellect Edge by 1 for one hour
96–00	Restores all Pools to full

COMPREHENSION

Level: 1d6 + 1

Effect: Within five minutes, the user can understand the words of a specific language keyed to the cypher. This is true even of creatures that do not normally have a language. If the user could already understand the language, the cypher has no effect. Once the cypher is used, the effect is permanent, and this cypher no longer counts against the number of cyphers that a PC can bear.

SUBTLE CYPHERS ONLY

In a game that uses only subtle cyphers, attempting to portray them as luck or inspiration rather than something overt or supernatural, consider the following additional ideas:

BEST TOOL

Level: 1d6

Effect: Provides an additional asset for any one task using a tool, even if that means exceeding the normal limit of two assets.

BURST OF SPEED

Level: 1d6

Effect: For one minute, a user that normally moves a short distance as an action moves a long distance instead.

DISARM

Level: 1d6 + 1

Effect: One NPC of a level lower than the cypher within immediate range drops whatever he is holding.

PERFECTION

Level: 1d6 + 2

Effect: You get the result of having rolled a 20 on your next action.

REPEL

Level: 1d6 + 1

Effect: One NPC of a level lower than the cypher within immediate range decides to leave, using his next five rounds to move away quickly.

CONDITION REMOVER

Level: 1d6 + 3

Effect: Cures one occurrence of a specific health condition. It does not prevent the possibility of future occurrences of the same condition. Roll a d20 to determine what it cures.

d20	Cures
1	Addiction to one substance
2	Autoimmune disease
3	Bacterial infection
4	Bad breath
5	Blisters
6	Bloating
7	Cancer
8	Chapped lips
9	Flatus
10	Heartburn
11	Hiccups
12	Ingrown hairs
13	Insomnia
14	Joint problem
15	Muscle cramp
16	Pimples
17	Psychosis
18	Stiff neck
19	Viral infection
20	Hangover

CONTINGENT ACTIVATOR

Level: 1d6 + 2

Effect: If the device is activated in conjunction with another cypher, the user can specify a condition under which the linked cypher will activate. The linked cypher retains the contingent command until it is used (either normally or contingently). For example, when this cypher is linked to a cypher that provides a form of healing or protection, the user could specify that the linked cypher will activate if he becomes damaged to a certain degree or is subject to a particular dangerous circumstance. Until the linked cypher is used, this cypher continues to count toward the maximum number of cyphers a PC can carry.

CONTROLLED BLINKING

Level: 1d6 + 2

Effect: For the next twenty-four hours, each time you are struck hard enough to inflict damage (but no more than once per round), you teleport to a spot you desire within immediate range. Since you are prepared for this effect and your foe is not, the difficulty of your defense rolls is modified by one step to your benefit for one round after you teleport.

CURATIVE

Level: 1d6 + 2

Effect: Restores a number of points equal to the cypher's level to the user's Might Pool.

CURSE BRINGER

Level: 1d6 + 1

Effect: The curse bringer can be activated when given to an individual who doesn't realize its significance. The next time the victim attempts an important task when the cypher is in her possession, the difficulty of the task is modified by three steps to her detriment.

DARKSIGHT

Level: 1d6

Effect: Grants the ability to see in the dark for eight hours.

DEATH BRINGER

Level: 1d6

Effect: For the next minute, when the user strikes an NPC or creature whose level is equal to or less than the cypher's level, she can choose to make a second attack roll. If the second attack roll is a success, the target is killed. If the target is a PC, the character instead moves down one step on the damage track.

DENSITY

Level: 1d6

Effect: For the next twenty-four hours, each time you strike a solid creature or object with a weapon, the weapon suddenly increases dramatically in weight, causing the blow to inflict 2 additional points of damage.

DETONATION

Level: 1d6 + 2

Effect: Projects a small physical explosive up to a long distance away that explodes in an immediate radius, inflicting damage equal to the cypher's level. Roll for the type of damage:

01–10	Cell-disrupting (harms only flesh)
11–30	Corrosive
31–40	Electrical discharge
41–50	Heat drain (cold)
51–75	Fire
76–00	Shrapnel

DETONATION (CREATURE)

Level: 1d6 + 1

Effect: Projects a small physical explosive up to a long distance away that explodes and creates a momentary teleportation gate. A random creature whose level is equal to or less than the cypher's level appears through the gate and attacks the closest target.

DETONATION (DESICCATING)

Level: 1d6 + 2

Effect: Projects a small physical explosive up to a long distance away that bursts in an immediate radius, draining moisture from everything within it. Living creatures take damage equal to the cypher's level. Water in the area is vaporized.

DETONATION (FLASH)

Level: 1d6 + 2

Effect: Projects a small physical explosive up to a long distance away that bursts in an immediate radius, blinding all within it for one minute.

DETONATION (GRAVITY)

Level: 1d6 + 2

Effect: Projects a small physical explosive up to a long distance away that bursts in an immediate radius, inflicting damage equal to the cypher's level by increasing gravity tremendously for one second. All creatures in the area are crushed to the ground for one round and cannot take physical actions.

DETONATION (GRAVITY INVERSION)

Level: 1d6 + 1

Effect: Projects a small physical explosive up to a long distance away that explodes, and for one hour gravity reverses within long range of the explosion.

DETONATION (MASSIVE)

Level: 1d6 + 2

Effect: Projects a small physical explosive up to a long distance away that explodes in a short-range radius, inflicting damage equal to the cypher's level. Roll for the type of damage:

01–10	Cell-disrupting (harms only flesh)
11–30	Corrosive
31–40	Electrical discharge
41–50	Heat drain (cold)
51–75	Fire
76–00	Shrapnel

DETONATION (MATTER DISRUPTION)

Level: 1d6 + 4

Effect: Projects a small physical explosive up to a long distance away that explodes in an immediate radius, releasing nanites that rearrange matter in random ways. Inflicts damage equal to the cypher's level.

DETONATION (PRESSURE)

Level: 1d6 + 2

Effect: Projects a small physical explosive up to a long distance away that explodes in an immediate radius, inflicting impact damage equal to the cypher's level. Also moves unattended objects out of the area if they weigh less than 20 pounds (9 kg) per cypher level.

DETONATION (SINGULARITY)

Level: 10

Effect: Projects a small physical explosive up to a long distance away that explodes and creates a momentary singularity that tears at the fabric of the universe. Inflicts 20 points of damage to all within short range, drawing them (or their remains) together to immediate range (if possible). Player characters in the radius who fail a Might defense roll move down one step on the damage track.

DETONATION (SONIC)

Level: 1d6 + 2

Effect: Projects a small physical explosive up to a long distance away that explodes with terrifying sound, deafening all in an immediate radius.

DETONATION (SPAWN)

Level: 1d6 + 2

Effect: Projects a small physical explosive up to a long distance away that bursts in an immediate radius, blinding all within it for one minute and inflicting damage equal to the cypher's level. The burst spawns 1d6 additional detonations; in the next round, each additional detonation flies to a random spot within short range and explodes in an immediate radius. Roll for the type of damage dealt by all detonations:

01–10	Cell-disrupting (harms only flesh)
11–30	Corrosive
31–40	Electrical discharge
41–50	Heat drain (cold)
51–75	Fire
76–00	Shrapnel

DETONATION (WEB)

Level: 1d6 + 2

Effect: Projects a small physical explosive up to a long distance away that explodes in an immediate radius and creates sticky strands of goo. PCs caught in the area must use a Might-based action to get out, with the difficulty determined by the cypher level. NPCs break free if their level is higher than the cypher level.

The singularity detonation is a greatly feared device, sought by those interested in truly horrific destruction.

Rather than strands of sticky goo, some web detonations fill the area with a mass of quick-hardening foam that has the same result.

All damaging detonations inflict a minimum of 2 points of damage to those in the radius, regardless of attack or defense rolls.

DISGUISE MODULE

Level: 1d6 + 2

Effect: For the next hour, the user's features become almost identical to those of one designated person she has previously interacted with. This lowers the difficulty by two steps when the user attempts to disguise herself as the designated person. Once designated, the user cannot shift the effect to look like another person, though she can remove the module to look like herself again before the end of the hour.

DISRUPTING

Level: 1d6

Effect: For the next twenty-four hours, each time you strike a solid creature or object, you generate a burst of nanites that directly attack its organic cells. The target takes 1 additional point of damage and loses its next action.

EAGLESEYE

Level: 1d6

Effect: Grants the ability to see ten times as far as normal for one hour.

EFFECT RESISTANCE

Level: 1d6 + 1

Effect: Provides a chance for additional resistance to directly damaging effects of all kinds, such as fire, lightning, and the like for a day. (It does not provide resistance to blunt force, slashing, or piercing attacks.) If the level of the effect is less than or equal to the level of the cypher, the user gains an additional defense roll to avoid it. On a successful defense roll, treat the attack as if the user had succeeded on his regular defense roll.

EFFORT ENHANCER

Level: 1d6

Effect: The user can apply one level of Effort to a noncombat task without spending points from a Pool. The level of Effort provided by this cypher does not count toward the maximum amount of Effort a character can normally apply to one task.

EFFORT ENHANCER (COMBAT)

Level: 1d6 + 1

Effect: For the next hour, the user can apply one level of Effort to any task (including a combat task) without spending points from a Pool. The level of Effort provided by this cypher does not count toward the maximum amount of Effort a character can normally apply to one task.

ENDURING SHIELD

Level: 1d6 + 4

Effect: For the next day, the user has an asset to Speed defense rolls.

EQUIPMENT CACHE

Level: 1d6 + 1

Effect: The user can rummage around and produce from the cypher a desired piece of equipment (not an artifact) whose level does not exceed the cypher's level. The piece of equipment persists for up to twenty-four hours, unless its fundamental nature allows only a single use (such as with a grenade).

FARSIGHT

Level: 1d6 + 1

Effect: The user can observe a location he has visited previously, regardless of how far away it is (even across galaxies). This vision persists for up to ten minutes.

FIREPROOFING

Level: 1d6 + 4

Effect: A nonliving object treated by this cypher has Armor against fire damage equal to the cypher's level for twenty-four hours.

FLAME-RETARDANT WALL

Level: 1d6

Effect: Creates an immobile plane of permeable energy up to 20 feet by 20 feet (6 m by 6 m) for one hour. The plane conforms to the space available. Flames passing through the plane are extinguished.

FORCE CUBE

Level: 1d6 + 3

Effect: Creates an immobile cube composed of six planes of solid force, each 30 feet (9 m) to a side, for one hour. The planes conform to the space available.

FORCE FIELD

Level: 1d6

Effect: For the next twenty-four hours, the user is surrounded by a powerful force field, granting her +2 to Armor.

FORCE SCREEN PROJECTOR

Level: 1d6 + 3

Effect: Creates an immobile plane of solid force up to 20 feet by 20 feet (6 m by 6 m) for one hour. The plane conforms to the space available.

FORCE SHIELD PROJECTOR

Level: 1d6 + 3

Effect: Creates a shimmering energy shield around the user for one hour, during which time he gains +3 to Armor (or +4 to Armor if the cypher is level 5 or higher).

FRICTION REDUCER

Level: 1d6

Effect: Spread across an area up to 10 feet (3 m) square, this makes things extremely slippery. For one hour, the difficulty of movement tasks in the area is increased by three steps.

FRIGID WALL

Level: 1d6 + 2

Effect: Creates a wall of supercooled air up to 30 feet by 30 feet by 1 foot (9 m by 9 m by 30 cm) that inflicts damage equal to the cypher's level on anything that passes through it. The wall conforms to the space available. It lasts for ten minutes.

GAS BOMB

Level: 1d6 + 2

Effect: Thrown a short distance, this bursts in a poisonous cloud within an immediate area. The cloud lingers for 1d6 rounds unless conditions dictate otherwise. Effects vary:

01–10	Thick smoke: occludes sight while the cloud lasts.
11–20	Choking gas: living creatures that breathe lose their actions to choking and coughing for a number of rounds equal to the cypher's level.
21–50	Poison gas: living creatures that breathe suffer damage equal to the cypher's level.
51–60	Corrosive gas: everything suffers damage equal to the cypher's level.
61–65	Hallucinogenic gas: living creatures that breathe lose their actions to hallucinations and visions for a number of rounds equal to the cypher's level.
66–70	Nerve gas: living creatures that breathe suffer Speed damage equal to the cypher's level.
71–80	Mind-numbing gas: living creatures that breathe suffer Intellect damage equal to the cypher's level.
81–83	Fear gas: living creatures that breathe and think flee in a random direction in fear (or are paralyzed with fear) for a number of rounds equal to the cypher's level.
84–86	Amnesia gas: living creatures that breathe and think permanently lose all memory of the last minute.
87–96	Sleep gas: living creatures that breathe fall asleep for a number of rounds equal to the cypher's level or until awoken by a violent action or an extremely loud noise.
97–00	Rage gas: living creatures that breathe and think make a melee attack on the nearest creature and continue to do so for a number of rounds equal to the cypher's level.

Although a force cube's walls are not gaseous permeable, there is likely enough air within for trapped creatures to breathe for the hour it lasts.

Some force walls, shields, and cubes are transparent. Others are translucent. A few are opaque.

GRAVITY NULLIFIER

Level: 1d6 + 3

Effect: For one hour, the user can float into the air, moving vertically up to a short distance per round (but not horizontally without taking some other action, such as pushing along the ceiling). The user must weigh less than 50 pounds (23 kg) per level of the cypher.

GRAVITY-NULLIFYING APPLICATION

Level: 1d6 + 2

Effect: If a nonliving object no larger than a person is coated by this cypher, it floats 1d20 feet in the air permanently and no longer has weight if carried (though it needs to be strapped down).

HEAT ATTACK

Level: 1d6

Effect: For the next twenty-four hours, each time you strike a solid creature or object, you generate a burst of heat that inflicts 2 additional points of damage.

Stunned creatures lose their turn that round.

HUNTER/SEEKER

Level: 1d6

Effect: With long-range movement, this intelligent missile tracks and attacks a specified target, which must be within sight when selected. If it misses, it continues to attack one additional time per cypher level until it hits. For example, a level 4 hunter/seeker will attack a maximum of five times. Different hunter/seekers have different effects:

01–50	Inflicts 8 points of damage.
51–80	Bears a poisoned needle that inflicts 3 points of damage plus poison.
81–90	Explodes, inflicting 6 points of damage to all within immediate range.
91–95	Shocks for 4 points of electricity damage, and stuns for one round per cypher level.
96–00	Covers target in sticky goo that immediately hardens, holding him fast until he breaks free with a Might action (difficulty equal to the cypher's level + 2).

IMAGE PROJECTOR

Level: 1d6

Effect: Projects one of the following immobile images in the area described for one hour. The image appears 25 feet (8 m) away from the user. Scenes include movement, sound, and smell.

01–20	Terrifying creature of an unknown species, perhaps no longer alive in the world (10-foot [3 m] cube)
21–40	Huge machine that obscures sight (30-foot [9 m] cube)
41–50	Beautiful pastoral scene (50-foot [15 m] cube)
51–60	Food that looks delicious but may not be familiar (10-foot [3 m] cube)
61–80	Solid color that obscures sight (50-foot [15 m] cube)
81–00	Incomprehensible scene that is disorienting and strange (20-foot [6 m] cube)

INFERNO WALL

Level: 1d6 + 2

Effect: Creates a wall of extreme heat up to 30 feet by 30 feet by 1 foot (9 m by 9 m by 30 cm) that inflicts damage equal to the cypher's level on anything that passes through it. The wall conforms to the space available. It lasts for ten minutes.

INFILTRATOR

Level: 1d6

Effect: Tiny capsule launches and moves at great speed, mapping and scanning an unknown area. It moves 500 feet (152 m) per level, scanning an area up to 50 feet (15 m) per level away from it. It identifies basic layout, creatures, and major energy sources. Its movement is blocked by any physical or energy barrier.

INFORMATION SENSOR

Level: 1d6 + 2

Effect: Over the course of one day, the user can activate the cypher a total number of times equal to its level. Each time, she can select a living creature within long range and learn the following about it: level, origin, species, name, and possibly other facts (such as an individual's credit score, home address, phone number, and related information).

INSTANT SERVANT

Level: 1d6

Effect: Small device expands into a humanoid automaton that is roughly 2 feet (60 cm) tall. Its level is equal to the cypher's level, and it can understand the verbal commands of the character who activated it. Commanding the servant is not an action. It can make attacks or perform actions as ordered to the best of its abilities, but it cannot speak.

The automaton has short-range movement but never goes farther than long range away from the character who activated it. At the GM's discretion, the servant might have specialized knowledge, such as how to operate a particular device. Otherwise, it has no special knowledge.

It is easy to get addicted to the quick hit of training that comes from knowledge enhancement cyphers. Characters who rely on them too often may find themselves at a disadvantage when they run out, presenting a great opportunity for GM intrusion.

In any case, the servant is not artificially intelligent or capable of initiating action. It does only as commanded.

The servant operates for one hour per cypher level.

INSTANT SHELTER

Level: 1d6 + 3

Effect: With the addition of water and air, this expands into a simple one-room structure with a door and a transparent window. The structure is 10 feet by 10 feet by 20 feet (3 m by 3 m by 6 m). It is permanent and immobile once created.

INTELLECT BOOSTER

Level: 1d6 + 2

Effect: Adds 1 to the user's Intellect Edge for one hour.

INTELLIGENCE ENHANCEMENT

Level: 1d6

Effect: The difficulty of any task involving intelligent deduction—such as playing chess, inferring a connection between clues, solving a mathematical problem, finding a bug in computer code, and so on—is decreased by two steps for the user for one hour. In the subsequent hour, the strain increases the difficulty for the same tasks by two steps.

KNOWLEDGE ENHANCEMENT

Level: 1d6

Effect: For the next twenty-four hours, the character has training in a predetermined skill. Although the skill could be anything (including something specific to the operation of a particular device), common skills include:

01–10	Melee attacks
11–20	Ranged attacks
21–40	One type of academic or esoteric lore (biology, history, magic, and so on)
41–50	Repairing (sometimes specific to one device)
51–60	Crafting (usually specific to one thing)
61–70	Persuasion
71–75	Healing
76–80	Speed defense
81–85	Intellect defense
85–90	Swimming
91–95	Riding
96–00	Sneaking

LIGHTNING WALL

Level: 1d6 + 2

Effect: Creates a wall of electric bolts up to 30 feet by 30 feet by 1 foot (9 m by 9 m by 30 cm) that inflicts damage equal to the cypher's level on anything that passes through it. The wall conforms to the space available. It lasts for ten minutes.

MACHINE CONTROL

Level: 1d6 + 2

Effect: Splits into two pieces; one is affixed to a device and the other to a character. The character can then use his mind to control the device at long range, bidding it to do anything it could do normally. Thus, a device could be activated or deactivated, and a vehicle could be piloted. The control lasts for ten minutes, and once the device is chosen, it cannot be changed.

MAGNETIC ATTACK DRILL

Level: 1d6 + 2

Effect: The user throws this cypher at a target within short range, and it drills into the target for one round, inflicting damage equal to the cypher's level. If the target is made of metal or wearing metal (such as armor), the difficulty of the attack is decreased by one step.

MAGNETIC MASTER

Level: 1d6 + 2

Effect: Establishes a connection with one metal object within short range that a human could hold in one hand. The user can then move or manipulate the object anywhere within short range (each movement or manipulation is an action). For example, he could wield a weapon or drag a helm affixed to a foe's head to and fro. The connection lasts for ten rounds.

MAGNETIC SHIELD

Level: 1d6 + 2

Effect: For ten minutes, metal objects cannot come within immediate range of the user. Metal items already in the area when the device is activated are slowly pushed out.

MANIPULATION BEAM

Level: 1d6 + 2

Effect: Over the course of one day, the user can activate the cypher a total number of times equal to its level. Each time, she can affect an object she can see within long range that is not too heavy for her to affect physically. The effect must occur over the course of a round and could include closing or opening a door, keying in a number on a keypad, transferring an object a short distance, wresting an object from another creature's grasp (on a successful Might-based roll), or pushing a creature an immediate distance.

MATTER TRANSFERENCE RAY

Level: 1d6 + 3

Effect: The user can target one nonliving object within long range that is her size or smaller and whose level is less than or equal to the cypher's level. The object is transferred directly to a random location at least 100 miles (161 km) away. If the GM feels it appropriate to the circumstances, only a portion of an object is transferred (a portion whose volume is no more than the user's).

MEDITATION AID

Level: 1d6 + 2

Effect: Restores a number of points equal to the cypher's level to the user's Intellect Pool.

MEMORY SWITCH

Level: 1d6 + 2

Effect: The user selects a point within long range, and the minds of all thinking creatures within immediate range of that point are attacked. Victims are dazed and take no action for a round, and they have no memory of the preceding hour.

A manipulation beam could be used to operate a computer at a distance, which would make some infiltration and hacking jobs easier.

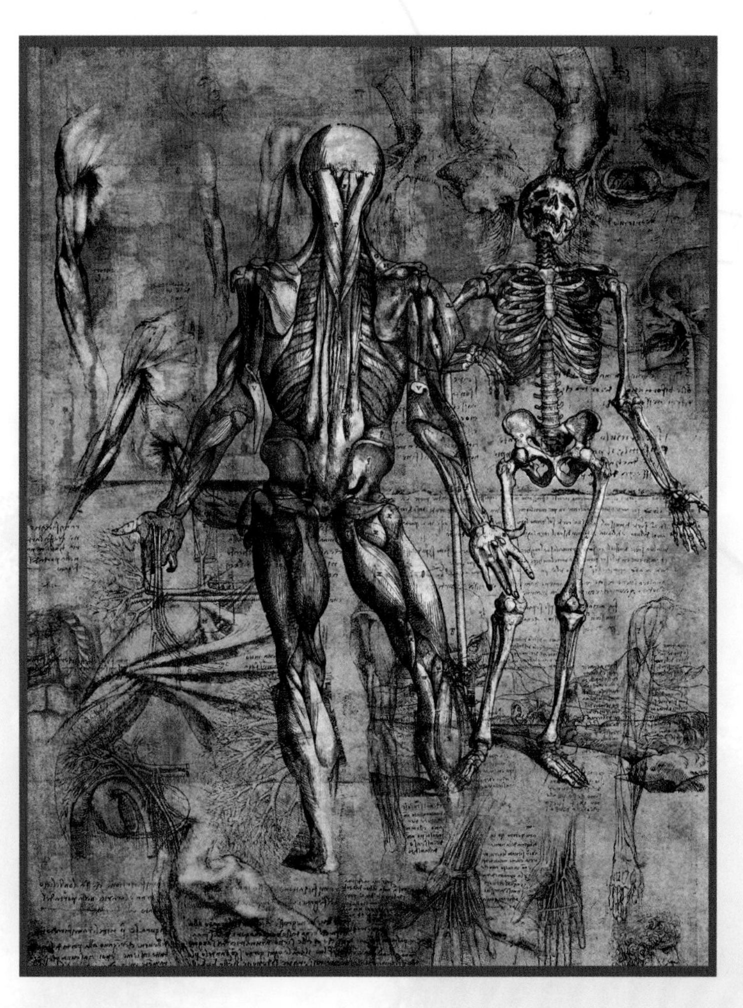

MENTAL SCRAMBLER

Level: 1d6 + 2

Effect: Two rounds after being activated, the device creates an invisible field that fills an area within short range and lasts for one minute. The field scrambles the mental processes of all thinking creatures. The effect lasts as long as they remain in the field and for 1d6 rounds after, although an Intellect defense roll is allowed each round to act normally (both in the field and after leaving it). Each mental scrambler is keyed to a specific effect. Roll a d100 for effect:

01–30	Victims cannot act.
31–40	Victims cannot speak.
41–50	Victims move slowly (immediate range) and clumsily.
51–60	Victims cannot see or hear.
61–70	Victims lose all sense of direction, depth, and proportion.
71–80	Victims do not recognize anyone they know.
81–88	Victims suffer partial amnesia.
89–94	Victims suffer total amnesia.
95–98	Victims lose all inhibitions, revealing secrets and performing surprising actions.
99–00	Victims' ethics are inverted.

Sometimes a monohorn cypher covers the user in a thin sheen of black hidelike material, which disguises the user's identity but doesn't interfere with his senses.

METAL DEATH

Level: 1d6 + 2

Effect: Produces a stream of foam that covers an area about 3 feet by 3 feet (1 m by 1 m), transforming any metal that it touches into a substance as brittle as thin glass. The foam affects metal to a depth of about 6 inches (15 cm).

MIND MELD

Level: 1d6 + 1

Effect: Lets the user speak telepathically with creatures he can see within short range for up to one hour. The user can't read a target's thoughts, except those that are specifically "transmitted." This effect transcends normal language barriers, but a target must have a mind that allows for such communication to be possible.

MIND-RESTRICTING WALL

Level: 1d6 + 2

Effect: Creates an immobile plane of permeable energy up to 20 feet by 20 feet (6 m by 6 m) for one hour. The plane conforms to the space available. Intelligent creatures passing through the plane fall unconscious for up to one hour, or until slapped awake or damaged.

MIND STABILIZER

Level: 1d6

Effect: The user gains +5 to Armor against Intellect damage.

MONOBLADE

Level: 1d6 + 2

Effect: Produces a 6-inch (15 cm) blade that's the same level as the cypher. The blade cuts through any material of a level lower than its own. If used as a weapon, it is a light weapon that ignores Armor of a level lower than its own. The blade lasts for ten minutes.

MONOHORN

Level: 1d6 + 3

Effect: The user gains a horn in the center of his forehead. The horn is deadly sharp and strong, and it spirals down to a solid base where it fuses with his flesh and bone. The user is specialized in making melee attacks with the horn, which is considered a medium weapon. The horn lasts for a number of hours equal to the cypher's level.

MOTION SENSOR

Level: 1d6 + 2

Effect: For one hour, this cypher indicates when any movement occurs within short range, and when large creatures or objects move within long range (the cypher distinguishes between the two). It also indicates the number and size of the creatures or objects in motion.

NULL FIELD

Level: 1d6 + 3

Effect: The user and all creatures within immediate range gain +5 to Armor against damage of a specified kind for one hour. Roll a d100 to determine the effect.

01–12	Fire
13–27	Cold
28–39	Acid
40–52	Psychic
53–65	Sonic
66–72	Electrical
73–84	Poison
85–95	Blunt force
96–00	Slashing and piercing

NULLIFICATION RAY

Level: 1d6 + 3

Effect: The user can immediately end one ongoing effect within long range that is produced by an artifact, cypher, or special ability.

NUTRITION AND HYDRATION

Level: 1d6 + 1

Effect: The user can go without food and water for a number of days equal to the cypher's level without ill effect.

PERFECT MEMORY

Level: 1d6

Effect: Allows the user to mentally record everything she sees for thirty seconds and store the recording permanently in her long-term memory. This cypher is useful for watching someone pick a specific lock, enter a complex code, or do something else that happens quickly.

PERSONAL ENVIRONMENT FIELD

Level: 1d6 + 2

Effect: Creates an aura of temperature and atmosphere that will sustain a human safely for twenty-four hours. The aura extends to 1 foot (30 cm) around the user. It does not protect against sudden flashes of temperature change (such as from a heat ray). A small number of these cyphers (1%) accommodate the preferred environment of a nonhuman, nonterrestrial creature.

PHASE CHANGER

Level: 1d6 + 1

Effect: Puts the user out of phase for one minute. During this time, she can pass through solid objects as though she were entirely insubstantial, like a ghost. She cannot make physical attacks or be physically attacked.

PHASE DISRUPTOR

Level: 1d6 + 2

Effect: Puts a portion of a physical structure (like a wall or floor) out of phase for one hour. It affects an area equal to a 10-foot (3 m) cube. While the area is out of phase, creatures and objects can pass through it as if it were not there, although one cannot see through it, and it blocks light.

POISON (EMOTION)

Level: 1d6 + 2

Effect: The victim feels a specific emotion for one hour. Roll a d100:

01–20	Anger. Likely to attack anyone who disagrees with him. Very hard to interact with; the difficulty of all such actions is increased by two steps.
21–40	Fear. Flees in terror for one minute when threatened.
41–60	Lust. Cannot focus on any nonsexual activity.
61–75	Sadness. The difficulty of all tasks is increased by one step.
76–85	Complacency. Has no motivation. The difficulty of all tasks is increased by two steps.
86–95	Joy. Easy to interact with in a pleasant manner; the difficulty of all such actions is decreased by one step.
96–00	Love. Much easier to interact with; the difficulty of all such actions is decreased by two steps, but temporary attachment is likely.

Most poisons are not considered cyphers, except for a very few that are unique.

POISON (EXPLOSIVE)

Level: 1d6 + 1

Effect: Once this substance enters the bloodstream, it travels to the brain and reorganizes into an explosive that detonates when activated, inflicting 10 points of damage (ignoring Armor). Roll a d100 to determine the means of detonation:

01–25	The detonator is activated (must be within long range).
26–40	A specified amount of time passes.
41–50	The victim takes a specific action.
51–55	A specific note is sung or played on an instrument within short range.
56–60	The victim smells a specific scent within immediate range.
61–80	The victim comes within long range of the detonator.
81–00	The victim is no longer within long range of the detonator.

POISON (MIND CONTROLLING)

Level: 1d6 + 2

Effect: The victim must carry out a specific action in response to a specific trigger. Roll a d100 to determine the effect:

01–20	Lies down for one minute with eyes closed when told to do so.
21–40	Flees in terror for one minute when threatened.
41–60	Answers questions truthfully for one minute.
61–75	Attacks close friend for one round when within immediate range.
76–85	Obeys next verbal command given (if it is understood).
86–95	For twenty-four hours, becomes sexually attracted to the next creature of its own species that it sees.
96–00	Moves toward the next red object seen in lieu of all other actions, ignoring self-preservation.

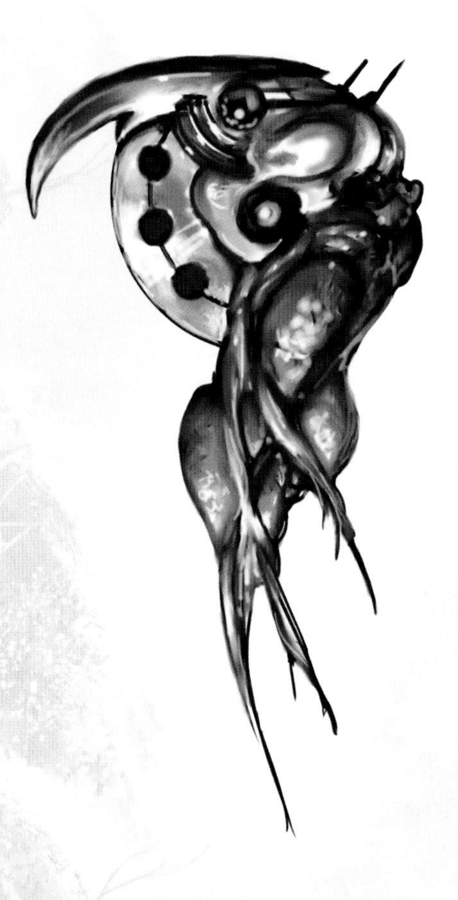

POISON (MIND DISRUPTING)

Level: 1d6 + 2

Effect: The victim suffers Intellect damage equal to the cypher's level and cannot take actions for a number of rounds equal to the cypher's level.

PSYCHIC COMMUNIQUE

Level: 1d6 + 2

Effect: Allows the user to project a one-time, one-way telepathic message of up to ten words, with an unlimited range, to anyone he knows.

RADIATION SPIKE

Level: 1d6 + 4

Effect: Delivers a powerful burst of radiation that disrupts the tissue of any creature touched, inflicting damage equal to the cypher's level.

RAY EMITTER

Level: 1d6 + 2

Effect: Allows the user to project a ray of destructive energy up to 200 feet (61 m) that inflicts damage equal to the cypher's level. Roll a d100 for the type of damage:

01–50	Heat/concentrated light
51–60	Cell-disrupting radiation
61–80	Force
81–87	Magnetic wave
88–93	Molecular bond disruption
94–00	Concentrated cold

RAY EMITTER (COMMAND)

Level: 1d6 + 2

Effect: Allows the user to project a ray up to 200 feet (61 m) that forces a target to obey the next verbal command given (if it is understood).

RAY EMITTER (FEAR)

Level: 1d6 + 2

Effect: Allows the user to project a ray up to 200 feet (61 m) that causes the target to flee in terror for one minute.

RAY EMITTER (FRIEND SLAYING)

Level: 1d6 + 2

Effect: Allows the user to project a ray up to 200 feet (61 m) that causes the target to attack its nearest ally for one round.

RAY EMITTER (MIND DISRUPTING)

Level: 1d6 + 2

Effect: Allows the user to project a ray of destructive energy up to 200 feet (61 m) that inflicts Intellect damage equal to the cypher's level. Also, the victim cannot take actions for a number of rounds equal to the cypher's level.

RAY EMITTER (NUMBING)

Level: 1d6 + 2

Effect: Allows the user to project a ray of energy up to 200 feet (61 m) that numbs one limb of the target, making it useless for one minute. A small number of these devices (5%) induce numbness that lasts for one hour.

RAY EMITTER (PARALYSIS)

Level: 1d6 + 2

Effect: Allows the user to project a ray of energy up to 200 feet (61 m) that paralyzes the target for one minute. A small number of these devices (5%) induce paralysis that lasts for one hour.

REALITY SPIKE

Level: 1d6 + 4

Effect: Once activated, the cypher does not move—ever—even if activated in midair. A Might action will dislodge it, but then it is ruined.

REFLEX ENHANCER

Level: 1d6

Effect: The difficulty of any task involving manual dexterity—such as pickpocketing, lockpicking, juggling, operating on a patient, defusing a bomb, and so on—is decreased by two steps for one hour.

REJUVENATOR

Level: 1d6 + 2

Effect: Restores a number of points equal to the cypher's level to one random stat Pool. Roll a d100:

01–50	Might Pool
51–75	Speed Pool
76–00	Intellect Pool

REMEMBERING

Level: 1d6

Effect: Allows the user to recall any one experience she's ever had. The experience can be no longer than one minute, but the recall is perfect, so (for example) if she saw someone dial a phone, she will remember the number.

REMOTE VIEWER

Level: 1d6

Effect: For one hour, the user can see everything going on in the vicinity of the cypher, regardless of the distance between them.

Even weirder ray emitters:

- *Turns target inside out*
- *Inflicts damage and turns flesh blue*
- *Renders target mute*
- *Damages only plants*
- *Damages only inorganic matter*
- *Turns flesh to dead, stonelike material*

REPAIR UNIT

Level: 1d10

Effect: The cypher becomes a multiarmed sphere that floats. It repairs one designated item (of a level equal to or less than its own) that has been damaged but not destroyed. The repair unit can also create spare parts, unless the GM rules that the parts are too specialized or rare (in which case, the unit repairs the device except for the specialized part). Repair time is 1d100 + 20 minutes.

REPEATER

Level: 1d6 + 1

Effect: For the next minute, the user's ranged weapon fires one additional time with ammo fabricated by the cypher. The weapon wielder can aim the free shot at the same target as the initiating shot, or at a target next to the first one.

RETALIATION

Level: 1d6

Effect: For the next twenty-four hours, anyone striking the user receives a small burst of electricity that inflicts 1 point of damage (no action or roll required).

SECRET

Level: 1d6

Effect: The user can ask the GM one question and get a general answer. The GM assigns a level to the question, so the more obscure the answer, the more difficult the task. Generally, knowledge that a PC could find by looking somewhere other than his current location is level 1, and obscure knowledge of the past is level 7. Gaining knowledge of the future is level 10, and such knowledge is always open to interpretation.

SHEEN

Level: 1d6

Effect: For one week, the user's cells are coated with a protective veneer that resists damage (+1 to Armor) and decreases the difficulty of Might defense rolls by two steps. However, healing is more difficult during this time; all recovery rolls suffer a –1 penalty.

SHOCK ATTACK

Level: 1d6

Effect: For the next twenty-four hours, each time the user strikes a solid creature or object, the user generates a burst of electricity, inflicting 1 additional point of damage.

SHOCKER

Level: 1d6 + 4

Effect: Delivers a powerful burst of electricity that shocks any creature touched, inflicting damage equal to the cypher's level.

SKILL BOOST

Level: 1d6

Effect: Dramatically but temporarily alters the user's mind and body so she can perform one specific physical action with the difficulty decreased by three steps. Once activated, this boost can be used a number of times equal to the cypher's level, but only within a twenty-four-hour period. The boost takes effect each time the action is performed. For example, a level 3 cypher boosts the first three times that action is attempted. The action can be one of many possibilities. Roll a d100:

d100	Action
01–15	Melee attack
16–30	Ranged attack
31–40	Speed defense
41–50	Might defense
51–60	Intellect defense
61–68	Jumping
69–76	Climbing
77–84	Running
85–92	Swimming
93–94	Sneaking
95–96	Balancing
97–98	Perceiving
99	Carrying
00	Escaping

SLAVE MAKER

Level: 1d6 + 2

Effect: To activate the cypher, the user must succeed on a melee attack against a creature about the size of the user and whose level does not exceed the cypher's level. The cypher bonds to the target, who immediately becomes calm. The target awaits the user's commands and carries out all orders to the best of its ability. The target remains so enslaved for a number of hours equal to the cypher's level minus the target's level. (If the result is 0, the target remains enslaved for one minute.)

SLEEP INDUCER

Level: 1d6

Effect: Touch puts the victim to sleep for ten minutes or until awoken by a violent action or an extremely loud noise.

SNIPER MODULE

Level: 1d6

Effect: For the next hour, the effective range of the user's ranged weapon increases to 2 miles (3 km).

SOLVENT

Level: 1d10

Effect: Dissolves 1 cubic foot of material each round. After one round per cypher level, the cypher becomes inert.

SONIC HOLE

Level: 1d6 + 2

Effect: Draws all sound within long range into the device for one round per cypher level. Within the affected area, no sound can be heard.

SOUND DAMPENER

Level: 1d6 + 2

Effect: Dampens all sound within immediate range, providing an asset for all creatures in the area to attempt stealth actions.

SPATIAL WARP

Level: 1d6 + 4

Effect: When affixed to a device that affects a single target at range, that range is increased to 1 mile (2 km) with no penalties. Space is temporarily warped in terms of seeing and reaching the target. If direct line of sight is important to the device's effect, it remains important.

SPEED BOOST

Level: 1d6 + 2

Effect: Adds 1 to Speed Edge for one hour.

SPY

Level: 1d6 + 2

Effect: Produces a tiny spying object that resists detection as a level 8 creature. The object moves at great speed, mapping and scanning an unknown area. It moves 500 feet (152 m) per level, scanning an area up to 50 feet (15 m) away from it. It identifies basic layout, creatures, and major energy sources. Its movement is blocked by any physical or energy barrier. At the end of its mapping run, it returns to the user and reports. If it discovers a predefined target during its run (such as "a creature of level 5 or higher," "a locked door," "a major energy source," and so on), it detonates instead, dealing electrical and shrapnel damage equal to the cypher's level to all creatures and objects in short range.

STASIS KEEPER

Level: 1d6

Effect: Puts a subject into stasis for a number of days equal to the cypher's level, or until it is violently disturbed. An object in stasis does not age and comes out of the stasis alive and in the same condition as it went in, with no memory of the period of inactivity.

STIM

Level: 1d6

Effect: Decreases the difficulty of the next action taken by three steps.

Sonic holes are much-loved by thieves everywhere but can also be used for less nefarious purposes, such as hunting prey and sneaking past enemies.

STRENGTH BOOST

Level: 1d6 + 2

Effect: Adds 1 to Might Edge for one hour.

STRENGTH ENHANCER

Level: 1d6

Effect: The difficulty of any noncombat task involving raw strength—such as breaking down a door, lifting a heavy boulder, forcing open elevator doors, competing in a weightlifting competition, and so on—is decreased by two steps for one hour.

SUBDUAL FIELD

Level: 1d6 + 3

Effect: Two rounds after being activated, the device creates an invisible field that fills a specified area (such as a cube of a certain size) within long range. The field lasts for one minute. It affects the minds of thinking beings within the field, preventing them from taking hostile actions. The effect lasts as long as they remain in the field and for 1d6 rounds after, although an Intellect defense roll is allowed each round to act normally (both in the field and after leaving it).

TELEPATHY

Level: 1d6 + 2

Effect: For one hour, the device enables long-range mental communication with anyone the user can see.

TELEPORTER (BOUNDER)

Level: 1d6 + 2

Effect: User teleports up to 100 × the cypher level in feet to a location he can see. He arrives safely with his possessions but cannot take anything else with him.

TELEPORTER (INTERSTELLAR)

Level: 1d6 + 4

Effect: User teleports anywhere in the galaxy to a location he has previously visited or seen. He arrives safely with his possessions but cannot take anything else with him.

TELEPORTER (PLANETARY)

Level: 1d6 + 4

Effect: User teleports anywhere on the planet to a location he has previously visited or seen. He arrives safely with his possessions but cannot take anything else with him.

TELEPORTER (TRAVELER)

Level: 1d6 + 4

Effect: User teleports up to 100 × the cypher level in miles to a location he has previously visited or seen. He arrives safely with his possessions but cannot take anything else with him.

TEMPORAL VIEWER

Level: 1d6 + 4

Effect: Displays moving images and sound, up to ten minutes in length, depicting events that occurred at the current location up to one year prior. The user specifies the time period shown by the viewer.

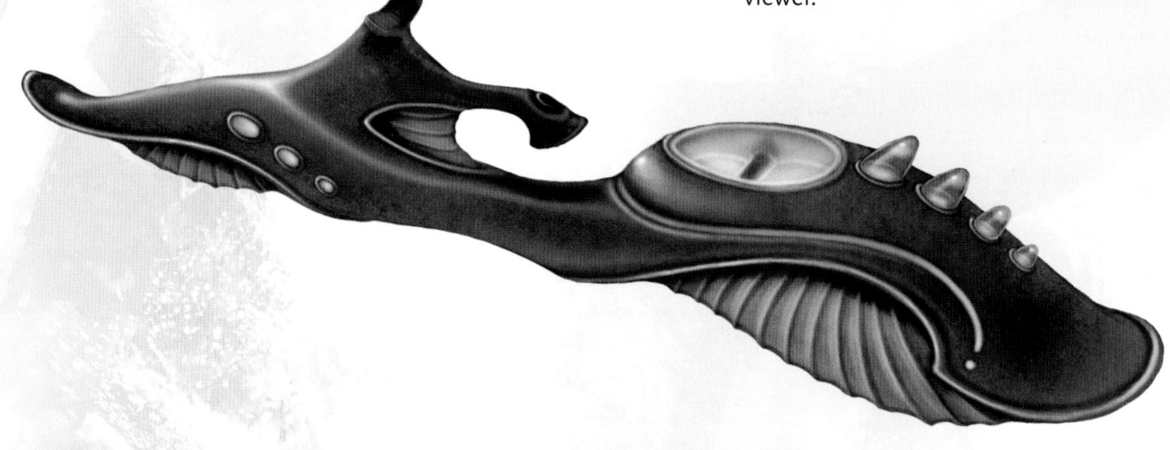

TIME DILATION (DEFENSIVE)

Level: 1d6

Effect: For the next twenty-four hours, when the user is attacked, she moves in rapid, seemingly random jumps, a few inches to one side or the other. This is an asset that modifies attacks by two steps in her favor.

TIME DILATION (OFFENSIVE)

Level: 1d6

Effect: For the next twenty-four hours, when the user makes a melee attack, she moves at almost instantaneous speed, modifying her attacks by two steps in her favor.

TISSUE REGENERATION

Level: 1d6 + 4

Effect: For the next hour, the user regains 1 point lost to damage per round, up to a total number of points equal to twice the cypher's level. As each point is regained, he chooses which Pool to add it to. If all his Pools are at maximum, the regeneration pauses until he takes more damage, at which point it begins again (if any time remains in the hour) until the duration expires.

TRACER

Level: 1d6

Effect: Fires a microscopic tracer that clings to any surface within short range. For the next twenty-four hours, the launcher shows the distance and direction to the tracer, as long as it is in the same dimension.

TRICK EMBEDDER

Level: 1d6

Effect: A nonintelligent animal immediately and perfectly learns one trick it is capable of physically performing (roll over, heel, spin, shake, go to an indicated place within long range, and so on). The trick must be designated when the cypher is activated.

UNINTERRUPTIBLE POWER SOURCE

Level: 1d6 + 4

Effect: Provides power appropriate to another device for up to a day. The device to be powered can be as simple as a light source or as complex as a small starcraft, assuming the cypher's level is equal to the item's power requirements. A desk lamp is a level 1 power requirement, a car engine is a level 5 power requirement, and a starship is a level 10 power requirement.

VANISHER

Level: 1d6 + 2

Effect: The user becomes invisible for ten minutes, during which time she is specialized in stealth and Speed defense tasks. This effect ends if she does something to reveal her presence or position—attacking, using an ability, moving a large object, and so on. If this occurs, she can regain the remaining invisibility effect by taking an action to focus on hiding her position.

VISAGE CHANGER

Level: 1d6

Effect: Changes the appearance of one human-sized creature. The change takes ten minutes to apply and lasts for twenty-four hours.

A tissue regeneration cypher can be used to regenerate a lost appendage (an arm, a foot, a leg, and so on) or to repair scar tissue from burns and other tissue-related disfigurements. If the cypher is used in this fashion, it restores only 1d6 points over the hour duration.

VISUAL DISPLACEMENT DEVICE

Level: 1d6

Effect: Projects holographic images of the user to confuse attackers. The images appear around the user, giving him an asset to Speed defense actions for ten minutes.

VOCAL TRANSLATOR

Level: 1d6

Effect: For twenty-four hours, translates everything said by the user into a language that anyone can understand.

WARMTH

Level: 1d6

Effect: Keeps the user warm and comfortable, even in the harshest cold temperatures, for twenty-four hours. During this time, the user has Armor equal to the cypher's level that protects against cold damage.

WATER ADAPTER

Level: 1d6

Effect: The user can breathe underwater and operate at any depth (without facing debilitating consequences of changing pressure) for eight hours.

A water adapter cypher can also be used in the regular atmosphere, allowing the user to ignore ill effects from very low or very high atmospheric pressure. The cypher does not protect against vacuum.

WEAPON ENHANCEMENT

Level: 1d6 + 2

Effect: Modifies a weapon's attack in a particular fashion for one hour. Roll a d100 for effect:

01–10	Decreases difficulty of attack by one step
11–20	Deals bonus electrical damage equal to cypher level
21–30	Deals bonus cold damage equal to cypher level
31–40	Deals bonus poison damage equal to cypher level
41–50	Deals bonus acid damage equal to cypher level
51–60	Deals bonus fire damage equal to cypher level
61–70	Deals bonus sonic damage equal to cypher level
71–80	Deals bonus psychic damage equal to cypher level
81–90	Knockback (on 18–20 on successful attack roll, target knocked back 30 feet [9 m])
91–95	Holding (on 18–20 on successful attack roll, target can't act on its next turn)
96–97	Decreases difficulty of attack by two steps
98	Banishing (on 18–20 on successful attack roll, target is sent to random location at least 100 miles [161 km] away)
99	Explodes, inflicting damage equal to cypher level to all within immediate range
00	Heart-seeking (on 18–20 on successful attack roll, target is killed)

WINGS

Level: 1d6 + 2

Effect: User can fly at her normal running speed for one hour.

X-RAY VIEWER

Level: 1d6 + 4

Effect: Allows the user to see through up to 2 feet (60 cm) of material, if the cypher's level is higher than the material's level. The effect lasts for one minute.

ZERO POINT FIELD

Level: 1d6 + 3

Effect: Renders an inanimate object outside the effects of most energy for one minute. This means the object cannot be harmed, moved, or manipulated in any way. It remains in place (even in midair).

Master thief Garthal North likes to use X-ray viewers in his work. "Never open a locked door if you don't already know what's on the other side," he says.

POWER BOOST CYPHERS

These cyphers increase, modify, or improve a character's existing powers. A burst boost cypher, for example, allows someone with the Bears a Halo of Fire focus to burst fire in all directions one time. Imagine this as being a fire-using superhero's ability to "go nova."

Power boost cyphers affect one use of a character's abilities but do not require an action. Their use is part of the action that they affect.

Power boost cyphers are a special type of cypher. In some Cypher System games, they may be inappropriate, and in others, they may be the main (or only) type of cypher available, as determined by the GM. They can be either subtle or manifest.

AREA BOOST

Level: 1d6 + 1

Effect: If you use an ability that affects a single target, this cypher expands the effect so it includes the immediate area around that target. If the power normally affects an immediate area, the area becomes short. Short areas are increased to long. Abilities with long-distance areas become 500-foot (152 m) areas. All other areas double in radius size.

BURST BOOST

Level: 1d6 + 2

Effect: If you use an ability that affects a single target at short range or farther, the range drops to immediate, but the ability affects all targets within immediate range.

DAMAGE BOOST

Level: 1d6 + 2

Effect: If you use an ability that inflicts damage, it inflicts additional damage equal to this cypher's level.

EFFICACY BOOST

Level: 1d6

Effect: The difficulty of using one of your abilities is reduced by one step.

ENERGY BOOST

Level: 1d6

Effect: If you use an ability that has a stat Pool cost, the cost is reduced to 0.

MAJOR EFFICACY BOOST

Level: 1d6 + 1

Effect: The difficulty of using one of your abilities is reduced by a number of steps equal to this cypher's level.

RANGE BOOST

Level: 1d6 + 1

Effect: The range of one of your abilities increases. Something that affects only you can now affect someone you touch. Abilities requiring touch can affect anyone within immediate range. An ability with immediate range becomes one with short range. Short-range powers become long range. Long-range powers increase to 500 feet (152 m). All other ranges double.

TARGET BOOST

Level: 1d6 + 2

Effect: If you use an ability that affects a target at range, you can affect an additional target within the same range.

Bears a Halo of Fire, page 98

Major efficacy boost cyphers might be appropriate only in superhero campaigns, at least with any regularity.

CHAPTER 19

RUNNING THE CYPHER SYSTEM

Unlike in the rest of this book, I'm going to write this chapter from me to you. I'm addressing you, the game master (or potential game master), directly because you are vital to turning a halfway-decent game into an amazing game. In uninformed hands, even the greatest rules and the greatest setting will make, at best, a mediocre game. You are the key in this process.

The game master (GM) is the architect of the game but not the sole builder. You're the facilitator as well as the arbiter. You're all of these things and more. It's a challenging role that's not quite like anything else. People try to equate the GM with a playwright, a referee, a judge, or a guide. And those are not terrible analogies, but none of them is quite right, either.

The Cypher System has been designed to make the challenging tasks of game mastering as simple as possible and allow you as the GM to focus on what's important. Rather than dealing with a lot of die rolls, modifiers, and rules minutiae, you can focus mainly on the flow of the story. This is not to say that you are the sole storyteller. The group is the storyteller. But it's the GM's job to pull together the actions, reactions, and desires of all the people sitting around the table, mesh them with the setting and background created before the session began, and turn it all into a cohesive story—on the fly. Sometimes this means using a heavy hand. Sometimes it means stepping back. Sometimes it means being open-minded. It always means giving the other players as much of the spotlight as you have as the GM, and attempting to give it to each of them in turn so that no one person dominates the narrative or the gameplay—not even you.

I will say this now, up front, and I will say it often: the rules are your tools to tell a story, to portray a character, and to simulate your world. The rules are not the final word—you are. You are not subservient to the rules. But you do have a master. That master is fun gameplay mixed with exciting story.

The Cypher System has also been designed to make game mastering work the way that many experienced GMs run games anyway. The GMs who recognize that they are not subservient to the rules are often forced to work against the rules, to work in spite of the rules, or to use the rules as smoke and mirrors to cover up what they're really doing (which is providing everyone with an exciting, compelling, and interesting narrative in which to participate). Hopefully, as a Cypher System GM, you will not find that to be the case. On the contrary, most of the rules were designed specifically to make it easier to run the game—or rather, to allow the GM to focus on helping to shepherd a great story.

In this chapter, we're going to talk about the rules and how to use them as your tools, as well as interacting with players, running games, and crafting great stories.

THE RULES VERSUS THE STORY

Upon first glance, it might seem that for a story-based game, there isn't a lot of "story" in the rules. A wall, a bear, a pit to leap, and a gun can be more or less summed up as a single number—their level. The thing is,

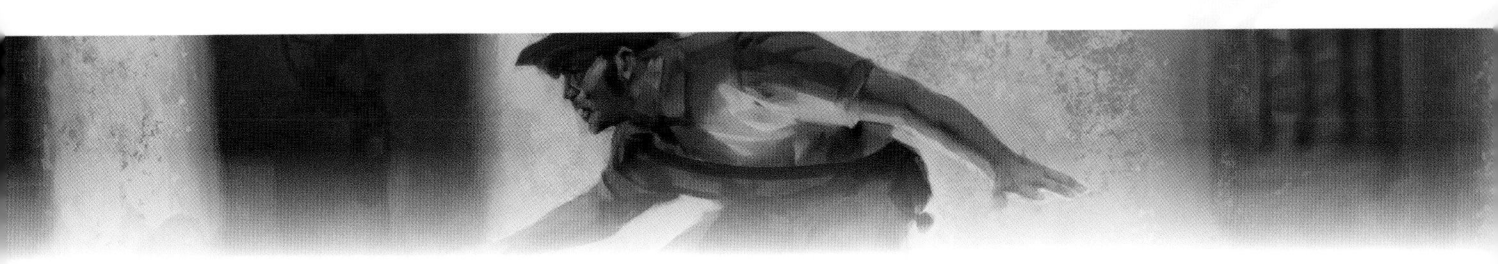

the Cypher System is a story-based game *because* the rules at their core are devoid of story. A wall, a bear, a pit to leap, and a gun can be summed up as levels because they're all just parts of the story. They're all just obstacles or tools.

There aren't a lot of specifics in the rules—no guidelines for particular judo moves or the differences between repairing an electrically powered force screen projector and a biomechanical aircraft. That's not because those kinds of things are to be ignored, but because those kinds of things are flavor—they are story, description, and elaboration for the GM and the players to provide. A player running a character in a fistfight can and should describe one attack as an uppercut and another as a roundhouse punch, even though there's no mechanical difference. In fact, *because* there's no mechanical difference. That's what a narrative game is all about. It's interesting and entertaining, and that's why you're all sitting at the table in the first place.

If different aspects of the game—walls, bears, pits, and so on—have distinctions, they come through as story elements, which are special exceptions to the rules. Having so few general rules makes adding special conditions and situations easier, because there is less rules tinkering to deal with. Fewer special circumstances to worry about. Less chance of contradictions and rules incompatibilities. For example, you can easily have a wall that can be destroyed only by mental attacks. A ravage bear has its unique grapple attack. A pit could have frictionless walls. A ray emitter could freeze foes solid. These are story elements that mechanically build on the very simple base mechanics, and they all make things more interesting.

SETTING DIFFICULTY RATINGS

The GM's most important overall tasks are setting the stage and guiding the story created by the group (not the one created by the GM ahead of time). But setting difficulty is the most important mechanical task the GM has in the game. Although there are suggestions throughout this chapter for various difficulty ratings for certain actions, there is no master list of the difficulty for every action a PC can take. Instead, the Cypher System is designed with the "teach a man to fish" style of good game mastering in mind. (If you don't know what that means, it comes from the old adage, "Give a man a fish and he'll eat for a day. Teach a man to fish and he'll eat for a lifetime." The idea is not to give GMs a ton of rules to memorize or reference, but to teach them how to make their own logical judgment calls.) Of course, most of the time, it's not a matter of exact precision. If you say the difficulty is 3 and it "should" have been 4, the world's not over.

For the most part, it really is as simple as rating something on a scale of 1 to 10, 1 being incredibly easy and 10 being basically impossible. The guidelines in the difficulty table, presented again on page 368 for reference, should help put you in the right frame of mind for assigning difficulty to a task.

For example, we make the distinction between something that most people can do and something that trained people can

Ravage bear, page 310

Ray emitter, page 359

do. In this case, "normal" means someone with absolutely no training, talent, or experience. Imagine your ne'er-do-well, slightly overweight uncle trying a task he's never tried before. "Trained" means the person has some level of instruction or experience but is not necessarily a professional.

With that in mind, think about the act of balance. With enough focus, most people can walk across a narrow bridge (like a fallen tree trunk). That suggests that it is difficulty 2. However, walking across a narrow plank that's only 3 inches (8 cm) wide? That's probably more like difficulty 3. Now consider walking across a tightrope. That's probably difficulty 5—a normal person can manage that only with a great deal of luck. Someone with some training can give it a go, but it's still hard. Of course, a professional acrobat can do it easily. Consider, however, that the professional acrobat is specialized in the task, making it difficulty 3 for her. She probably is using Effort as well during her performance.

Let's try another task. This time, consider how hard it might be to remember the name of the previous leader of the village where the character lives. The difficulty might be 0 or 1, depending on how long ago she was the leader and how well known she was. Let's say it was thirty years ago and she was only mildly memorable, so it's difficulty 1. Most people remember her, and with a little bit of effort, anyone can come up with her name. Now let's consider the name of the leader's daughter. That's much harder. Assuming the daughter wasn't famous in her own right, it's probably difficulty 4. Even people who know a little about local history (that is to say, people who are trained in the subject) might not be able to remember it. But what about the name of the pet dog owned by the daughter's husband? That's probably impossible. Who's going to remember the name of an obscure person's pet from thirty years ago? Basically no one. However, it's not forbidden knowledge or a well-guarded secret, so it sounds like difficulty 7. Difficulty 7 is the rating that means "No one can do this, yet some people still do." It's not the stuff of legend, but it's something you would assume people can't do. When you think there's no way you can get tickets for a sold-out concert, but somehow your friend manages to score a couple anyway, that's difficulty 7. (See the next section for more on difficulties 7, 8, 9, and 10.)

If you're talking about a task, ideally the difficulty shouldn't be based on the character performing the task. Things don't get inherently easier or harder depending on who is doing them. However, the truth is, the character does play into it as a judgment call. If the task is breaking down a wooden door, an 8-foot-tall (2 m) automaton made of metal with nuclear-driven motors

Unless for some reason you're telling the players directly, they'll never know if you change an NPC's stats or a task's difficulty on the fly. If you're doing it to make a better story, that's your purview.

TASK DIFFICULTY

Task Difficulty	Description	Target No.	Guidance
0	Routine	0	Anyone can do this basically every time.
1	Simple	3	Most people can do this most of the time.
2	Standard	6	Typical task requiring focus, but most people can usually do this.
3	Demanding	9	Requires full attention; most people have a 50/50 chance to succeed.
4	Difficult	12	Trained people have a 50/50 chance to succeed.
5	Challenging	15	Even trained people often fail.
6	Intimidating	18	Normal people almost never succeed.
7	Formidable	21	Impossible without skills or great effort.
8	Heroic	24	A task worthy of tales told for years afterward.
9	Immortal	27	A task worthy of legends that last lifetimes.
10	Impossible	30	A task that normal humans couldn't consider (but one that doesn't break the laws of physics).

should be better at breaking it down than an average human would be, but the task rating should be the same for both. Let's say that the automaton's nature effectively gives it two levels of training for such tasks. Thus, if the door has a difficulty rating of 4, but the automaton is specialized and reduces the difficulty to 2, it has a target number of 6. The human has no such specialization, so the difficulty remains 4, and he has to reach a target number of 12. However, when you set the difficulty of breaking down the door, don't try to take all those differences into account. The GM should consider only the human because the Task Difficulty table is based on the ideal of a "normal" person, a "trained" person, and so on. It's humanocentric.

Most characters probably are willing to expend one or two levels of Effort on a task, and they might have an appropriate skill or asset to decrease the difficulty by a step. That means that a difficulty 4 task will often be treated as difficulty 2 or even 1, and those are easy rolls to make. Don't hesitate, then, to pull out higher-level difficulties. The PCs can rise to the challenge, especially if they are experienced.

THE IMPOSSIBLE DIFFICULTIES

Difficulties 7, 8, 9, and 10 are all technically impossible. Their target numbers are 21, 24, 27, and 30, and you can't roll those numbers on a d20 no matter how many times you try. Consider, however, all the ways that a character can reduce difficulty. If someone spends a little Effort or has some skill or help, it brings difficulty 7 (target number 21) into the range of possibility—difficulty 6 (target number 18). Now consider that he has specialization, uses a lot of Effort, and has help. That might bring the difficulty down to 1 or even 0 (reducing it by two steps from training and specialization, three or four steps from Effort, and one step from the asset of assistance). That practically impossible task just became routine. A fourth-tier character can and will do this—not every time, due to the cost, but perhaps once per game session. You have to be ready for that. A well-prepared, motivated sixth-tier character can do that even with a difficulty 10 task. Again, she won't do it often (even with an Edge of 6, she'd have to spend 7 points from her Pool, and that's assuming she's specialized and has two levels of assets), but it can happen if she's really prepared for the task (being specialized and maxed out in asset opportunities reduces the difficulty by four more steps). That's why sixth-tier characters are at the top of their field, so to speak.

FALSE PRECISION

One way to look at difficulty is that each step of difficulty is worth 3 on the die. That is to say, increase the difficulty by one step, and the target number rises by 3. Decrease the difficulty by one step, and the target number is lowered by 3. Those kinds of changes are big, meaty chunks. Difficulty, as a game mechanic, is not terribly precise. It's measured in large portions. You never have a target number of 13 or 14, for example—it's always 3, 6, 9, 12, 15, and so on. (Technically, this is not true. If a character adds 1 to his roll for some reason, it changes a target number of 15 to 14. But this is not worth much discussion.)

Imprecision is good in this case. It would be false precision to say that one lock has a target number of 14 and another has a target number of 15. What false precision means in this context is that it would be a delusion to think we can be that exact. Can you really say that one lock is 5% easier to pick than another? And more important, even if you could, is the difference worth noting? It's better to interact with the world in larger, more meaningful chunks than to try to parse things so carefully. If we tried to rate everything on a scale of 1 to 30 (using target numbers and not difficulty), we'd start to get lost in the proverbial weeds coming up with a meaningful distinction between something rated as an 8 and something rating as a 9 on that scale.

Superhero games may want to take the task difficulty range up to 15. *See page 271.*

CONSISTENCY

Far more important than that level of precision is consistency. If the PCs need to activate a device that opens a spatial displacement portal, and the GM rules that it is a difficulty 6 task to get the antimatter rods spinning at the proper rates to achieve a specific harmonic frequency, then it needs to be a difficulty 6 task when they come back the next day to do it again (or there needs to be an understandable reason why it's not). The same is true for simpler tasks like walking across a narrow ledge or jumping up onto a platform. Consistency is key. The reason is that players need to be able to make informed decisions. If they remember how hard it was to open that portal yesterday, but it's inexplicably harder to open it today, they'll get frustrated because they tried to apply their experience to their decision-making process, and it failed them. If there's no way to make an informed decision, then all decisions are arbitrary.

Think about it in terms of real life. You need to cross the street, but a car is approaching. You've crossed the street thousands of times before, so you can look at the car and pretty easily judge whether you can cross safely or whether you have to wait for it to pass first. If the real world had no consistency, you couldn't make that decision. Every time you stepped into the street, you might get hit by a car. You'd never cross the street.

While I continually stress that the Cypher System is about story, not rules, it is still a game, which means that the PCs (and the players) can fail. That's why it's not accurate to think of the game as being identical to novels or movies. The system invites its own kind of storytelling. The players have to feel that there are real stakes. That if they screw up, there will be consequences—sometimes very harsh consequences. And they have to be right in that assumption.

Players need that kind of consistency, too. So when you assign a difficulty to a task, note that number and try to keep it consistent the next time the PCs try the same task. "Same" is the key word. Deciphering one code isn't necessarily like deciphering another. Climbing one wall isn't the same as climbing another.

You'll make mistakes while doing this, so just accept that fact now. Excuse any mistakes with quick explanations about "a quirk of fate" or something along the lines of a surprisingly strong wind that wasn't blowing the last time.

MISTAKES

Sometimes the PCs will break down a door, and you'll realize that you rated it too low. Or the PCs will try to paddle a raft down a fast-moving river, and you (and probably they) will quickly discover that the difficulty you gave the task was ridiculously high.

Don't fret.

That door was already weakened by an earthquake, a structural flaw, or the fact that other explorers pounded on it all day a while back. That river was actually moving far faster than the PCs thought at first, or their raft was faulty.

The point is, mistakes are easy to cover up. And sometimes, you can even tell your players it was just a mistake. They might even help provide an explanation if you do. It's not the end of the world.

More important, most of the time, no one will even know. Should have rated a task as difficulty 3 and instead you said it was 4? Oh well. Unless the player rolls a 9, 10, or 11—which would have succeeded for difficulty 3 but not difficulty 4—it won't matter. And even if he does roll one of those numbers, who cares? Maybe the rain was really coming down that day, and it increased the difficulty by a step.

The thing to take away is this: don't let the fear of making a mistake keep you from freely and quickly assessing the difficulty of a task and moving on with the game. Don't agonize over it. Give it a difficulty, call for a roll, and keep the game moving. Hesitating over a rating will be far more detrimental to the game than giving something the wrong rating.

ROUTINE ACTIONS

Don't hesitate to make actions routine. Don't call for die rolls when they're not really needed. Sometimes GMs fall into the trap illustrated by this dialogue:

GM: What do you do?
Player: I ________.
GM: Okay, give me a roll.

That's not a good instinct—at least, not for the Cypher System. Players should roll when it's interesting or exciting. Otherwise, they should just do what they do. If the PCs tie a rope around something and use it to climb down into a pit, you could ask for tying rolls, climbing rolls, and so on, but why? Just to see if they roll terribly? So the rope can come undone at the wrong time, or a character's hand can slip? Most of the time, that makes players feel inadequate

and isn't a lot of fun. A rope coming undone in the middle of an exciting chase scene or a battle can be a great complication (and that's what GM intrusions are for). A rope coming undone in the middle of a simple "getting from point A to point B" scene only slows down gameplay. The real fun—the real story—is down in the pit. So get the PCs down there.

There are a million exceptions to this guideline, of course. If creatures are throwing poisoned darts at the PCs while they climb, that might make things more interesting and require a roll. If the pit is filled with acid and the PCs must climb halfway down, pull a lever, and come back up, that's a situation where you should set difficulty and perhaps have a roll. If a PC is near death, carrying a fragile item of great importance, or something similar, climbing down the rope is tense, and a roll might add to the excitement. The important difference is that these kinds of complications have real consequences.

On the flip side, don't be afraid to use GM intrusion on routine actions if it makes things more interesting. Walking up to the king in his audience chamber in the middle of a ceremony only to trip on a rug? That could have huge ramifications for the character and the story.

GM intrusion, page 193

OTHER WAYS TO JUDGE DIFFICULTY

Rating things on a scale of 1 to 10 is something that most people are very familiar with. You can also look at it as rating an object or creature on a similar scale, if that's easier. In other words, if you don't know how hard it would be to climb a particular cliff face, think of it as a creature the PCs have to fight. What level would the creature be? You could look in the Creatures chapter and say, "I think this wall should be about as difficult to deal with as a demon. A demon is level 5, so the task of climbing the wall will be difficulty 5." That's a weird way to do it, perhaps, but it's fairly straightforward. And if you're the kind of GM who deals in terms of "How tough will this fight be?" then maybe rating tasks as NPCs to fight isn't so strange after all. It's just another way to relate to them. The important thing is that they're

Chapter 16: Creatures, page 274

on the same scale. Similarly, if the PCs have to tackle a knowledge task—say, trying to determine if they know where a caravan is headed based on its tracks—you could rate the task in terms of an object. If you're used to rating doors or other objects that the PCs have broken through recently, the knowledge task is just a different kind of barrier to bust through.

Everything in the Cypher System—characters, creatures, objects, tasks, and so on—has a level. It might be called a tier or a difficulty instead of a level, but ultimately it's a numerical rating system used to compare things. Although you have to be careful about drawing too many correlations—a first-tier character isn't easily compared to a difficulty 1 wall or a level 1 animal—the principle is the same. Everything can be rated and roughly compared to everything else in the world. (It works best to take PCs out of this equation. For example, you shouldn't try to compare a PC's tier to a wall's level. Character tiers are mentioned here only for completeness.)

Last, if your mind leans toward statistics, you can look at difficulty as a percentage chance. Every number on the d20 is a 5% increment. For example, you have a 5% chance of rolling a 1. You have a 10% chance of rolling a 1 or a 2. Thus, if you need to roll a 12 or higher, you have a 45% chance of success. (A d20 has nine numbers that are 12 or higher: 12, 13, 14, 15, 16, 17, 18, 19, and 20. And 9 × 5 equals 45.)

For some people, it's easier to think in terms of a percentage chance. A GM might think, "She has about a 30% chance to know that fact about geography." Each number on a d20 is a 5% increment, and it takes six increments to equal 30%, so there are six numbers that mean the PC succeeds: 15, 16, 17, 18, 19, and 20. Thus, since she has to roll 15 or higher, that means the target number is 15. (And that means the task is level 5, but if you've already determined the target number, you likely don't care about the level.)

GM INTRUSION

GM intrusion is the main mechanic that the GM uses to inject drama and additional excitement into the game. It's also a handy tool for resolving issues that affect the PCs but do not involve them. GM intrusion is a way to facilitate what goes on in the world outside the characters. Can the minotaur

ADVANTAGES TO THIS SYSTEM

1. The GM makes measured adjustments in large, uniform steps. That makes things faster than if players had to do arithmetic using a range of all numbers from 1 to 20.

2. You calculate a target number only once no matter how many times the PCs attempt the action. If you establish that the target number is 12, it's 12 every time a PC tries that action. (On the other hand, if you had to add numbers to your die roll, you'd have to do it for every attempt.) Consider this fact in light of combat. Once a player knows that she needs to roll a 12 or higher to hit her foe, combat moves very quickly.

3. If a PC can reduce the difficulty of an action to 0, no roll is needed. This means that an Olympic gymnast doesn't roll a die to walk across a balance beam, but the average person does. The task is initially rated the same for both, but the difficulty is reduced for the gymnast. There's no chance of failure.

4. This is how everything in the game works, whether it's climbing a wall, sweet-talking a guard, or fighting a bioengineered horror.

5. Perhaps most important, the system gives GMs the freedom to focus entirely on the flow of the game. The GM doesn't use dice to determine what happens (unless he wants to)—the players do. There aren't a lot of different rules for different actions, so there is little to remember and very little to reference. The difficulty can be used as a narrative tool, with the challenges always meeting the expected logic of the game. All the GM's mental space can be devoted to guiding the story.

Ultimately what you want is for the players to interact with the situations in the game, not with the rules and numbers that represent the situation. Don't let the players get too worked up over mechanics, dice percentages, and whatnot. That doesn't drive the story.

track the PCs' movements through the maze? Will the fraying rope hold?

Since the players roll all the dice, GM intrusion is used to determine if and when something happens. For example, if the PCs are fighting a noble's guards, and the GM knows that there are more guards nearby, the GM doesn't need to roll dice to determine if the other guards hear the scuffle and intervene (unless he wants to). He just decides when it would be best for the story—which is probably when it would be worst for the characters. In a way, GM intrusion replaces the GM's die rolling.

The mechanic is also one of the main ways that GMs award experience points to the PCs. This means that the GM uses experience points as a narrative tool. Whenever it seems appropriate, he can introduce complications into the game that affect a specific player, but when he does so, he gives that player 1 XP. The player can refuse the intrusion, but doing so costs her 1 XP. So by refusing an intrusion, the player does not get the experience point that the GM is offering, and she loses one that she already has. (This kind of refusal is likely to happen very rarely in your game, if ever. And, obviously, a player can't refuse an intrusion if she has no XP to spend.)

Here's how a GM intrusion might work in play. Say the PCs find a hidden console with some buttons. They learn the right order in which to press the buttons, and a section of the floor disappears. As the GM, you don't ask the players specifically where their characters are standing. Instead, you give a player 1 XP and say, "Unfortunately, you're standing directly over this new hole in the floor." If he wanted, the player could refuse the XP, spend one of his own, and say, "I leap aside to safety." Most likely, though, he'll make the defense roll that you call for and let it play out.

There are two ways for the GM to handle this kind of intrusion. You could say, "You're standing in the wrong place, so make a roll." (It's a Speed defense roll, of course.) Alternatively, you could say, "You're standing in the wrong place. The floor opens under your feet, and you fall down into the darkness." In the first example, the PC has a chance to save himself. In the second example, he doesn't. Both are viable options. The distinction is based on any number of factors, including the situation, the characters involved, and the needs of the story. This might seem arbitrary or even capricious, but you're the master of what the intrusion can and can't do. RPG mechanics need consistency so players can make intelligent decisions based on how they understand the world to work. But they'll never base their decisions on GM intrusions. They don't know when intrusions will happen or what form they will take. GM intrusions are the unpredictable and strange twists of fate that affect a person's life every day.

When player modifications (such as skill, Effort, and so on) determine that success is automatic, the GM can use GM intrusion to negate the automatic success. The player must roll for the action at its original difficulty level or target number 20, whichever is lower.

PLAYER-AWARDED EXPERIENCE POINTS

Players who gain 1 XP as the result of GM intrusion also get 1 XP to award to another player for whatever reason they wish—maybe the other player had a good idea, told a funny joke, lent a helping hand, or whatever seems appropriate. This means that whenever the GM uses GM intrusion, he's actually giving out 2 XP. The ability to award XP to your friends is empowering and interactive. It helps the players regulate the flow of XP so that no one is left out. It rewards good play that pleases the group as a whole, ensuring that everyone contributes to everyone else's enjoyment. It shouldn't just be the GM who decides which players have done well. Some groups will want to decide the criteria for player-awarded points ahead of time. Some will just want to play it by ear.

Variant: Alternatively, the group could combine the player-awarded points and vote at the end of a session to decide who gets how many XP. This might be the most egalitarian way to do it, but it's probably not as fun or empowering to the individual players.

Remember, any time you give a player 1 XP for a GM intrusion, you're actually giving her 2—one to keep and one to give to another player.

USING GM INTRUSION AS A NARRATIVE TOOL

A GM can use this narrative tool to steer things. That doesn't mean railroad the players or direct the action of the game with a heavy hand. GM intrusion doesn't enable you to say, "You're all captured, so here's your 1 XP." Instead, the GM can direct things more subtly—gently, almost imperceptibly influencing events rather than forcing them. GM intrusion represents things going wrong. The bad guys planning well. Fortune not favoring the characters.

Consider this scenario: the GM plants an interesting adventure seed in a small village, but the PCs don't stay there long enough to find it. Just outside the village, the PCs run afoul of a vicious viper that bites one of them. The GM uses intrusion to say that the poison from the snake will make the character debilitated unless he gets a large dose of a very specific antitoxin, which the group doesn't have. Of course, they aren't required to go back to the village where the GM's interesting adventure can start, but it's likely that they will, looking for the antitoxin.

Some players might find intrusion heavy handed, but the XP softens the blow. And remember, they can refuse these narrative nudges. Intrusion is not meant to be a railroading tool—just a bit of a rudder. Not an inescapable track, but a nudge here and there.

What's more, the GM doesn't need to have a deliberate goal in mind. The complication he introduces could simply make things more interesting. He might not know where it will take the story, just that it will make the story better.

This is wonderfully empowering to the GM—not in a "Ha ha, now I'll trounce the PCs" way, but in an "I can control the narrative a little bit, steering it more toward the story I want to create rather than relying on the dice" sort of way. Consider that old classic plot development in which the PCs get captured and must escape from the bad guys. In heroic fiction, this is such a staple that it would almost seem strange if it didn't happen. But in many roleplaying games, it's a nearly impossible turn of events—the PCs usually have too many ways to get out

of the bad guy's clutches even before they're captured. The dice have to be wildly against them. It virtually never happens. With GM intrusion, it could happen (again, in the context of the larger encounter, not as a single intrusion that results in the entire group of PCs being captured with little explanation or chance to react).

For example, let's say the PCs are surrounded by orcs. One character is badly injured—debilitated—and the rest are hurt. Some of the orcs produce a large weighted net. Rather than asking for a lot of rolls and figuring the mechanics for escape, the GM uses intrusion and says that the net goes over the PCs who are still on their feet. The rest of the orcs point spears menacingly. This is a pretty strong cue to the players that surrender is a good (and possibly the only) option. Some players won't take the hint, however, so another use of intrusion might allow the orcs to hit one of the trapped PCs on the head and render him unconscious while his friends struggle in the net. If the players still don't surrender, it's probably best to play out the rest of the encounter without more GM intrusions—using more would be heavy-handed by anyone's measure—although it's perfectly reasonable to rule that a character rendered debilitated is knocked unconscious, since the orcs are trying to take the PCs alive.

USING GM INTRUSION AS A RESOLUTION MECHANIC

This mechanic offers a way for the GM to determine how things happen in the game without leaving it all to random chance. Bad guys trying to smash down the door to the room where the PCs are holed up? The GM could roll a bunch of dice, compare the NPCs' stats to the door's stats, and so on, or he could wait until the most interesting time, have the bad guys break in, and award an experience point to the PC who tried his best to bar the door. The latter way is the Cypher System way. Intrusion is a task resolution tool for the GM. In other words, he doesn't base things on stats but on narrative choice. (Frankly, a lot of great GMs over the years—even in the very early days of the hobby—have run their games this way. Sometimes they rolled dice or pretended to roll dice, but they were really manipulating things.) This method frees the GM from worrying about mechanics and looking up stats and allows him to focus on the story.

This isn't cheating—it's the rules of the game. This rule simply replaces traditional dice rolling with good game mastering, logic, and intelligent storytelling. When a PC is climbing a burning rope, and everyone knows that it will break at some point, the game has a mechanism to ensure that it breaks at just the right time.

Variant: If you want more randomness in your game, or if you want your game to seem like more of a simulation, assign a flat percentage chance for whatever you're trying to resolve. For example, each round, the star troopers have a 20% chance to blast through the door—or, if you want the risk to escalate, a cumulative 20% chance to blast through the door. By not using GM intrusion, this method robs the PCs of a few XP, but when they see you rolling dice, it might help with their immersion. Alternatively, you can pretend to roll dice but really use GM intrusion, though this method seriously robs the characters of XP.

There's a better way. Announce your intrusion, but say that there's only a chance it will happen (state the percentage chance), and then roll the dice in plain view of everyone. If the intrusion occurs, award the XP as normal. This is likely the best of both worlds. However, it takes the narrative power out of your hands and gives it to the dice. Perhaps this method is best used only occasionally. If nothing else, it injects some variety and certainly some drama.

Remember that GM intrusions can occur at any time, not just during combat. Disrupting or changing a tense interaction with NPCs can have big repercussions.

USING (AND NOT ABUSING) GM INTRUSION

Too much of a good thing will make the game seem utterly unpredictable—even capricious. The ideal is to use about four GM intrusions per game session, depending on the length of the session, or about one intrusion per hour of game play. This is in addition to any intrusions that are triggered by players rolling a 1.

INTRUSION THROUGH PLAYER ROLLS

When a PC rolls a 1, handle the GM intrusion the same way that you'd handle an intrusion you initiated. The intrusion could mean the PC fumbles or botches whatever she was trying to do, but it could mean something else. Consider these alternatives:

- In combat, the PC's foe is not as hurt as she thought. Give the foe 5 extra points of health.
- In combat, the PC drops her guard, and the foe gets a free attack.
- In combat, reinforcements for the PC's foes show up.
- In combat (or any stressful situation), an ally decides to flee.
- In combat (or any stressful situation), an ally doesn't like the PCs as much as they thought. He steals from them or betrays them.
- Out of combat, the PC's pack falls open, or the sole of her shoe tears open.
- Out of combat, it begins to rain heavily.
- Out of combat, a surprise foe appears, and the scene turns into a combat.
- In an interaction, the GM introduces a surprising motive for the NPC. For example, the PCs are trying to bribe an official for information, and he reveals that what he really wants isn't money but for someone to rescue his kidnapped son.

This might not be true of your players, but many players rarely, if ever, spend XP to refuse an intrusion from the GM, but they regularly use XP to avoid an intrusion that comes from a bad roll. And there's nothing wrong with that. Some GMs might want to forbid using an XP to reroll a 1, but there's really no point—if you've got an idea for a good intrusion, you don't need to wait until a player rolls a 1 to use it.

GM INTRUSION THAT AFFECTS THE GROUP

The core of the idea behind GM intrusion is that the player being adversely affected gains an experience point. But what if the intrusion affects the whole group equally? What if the GM uses it to have an unstable device overload and explode, harming all the characters? In this case, if no PC is involved more than the others (for example, no single PC was frantically attempting to repair the device), the GM should give 1 XP to each character but not give any of them an extra XP to hand out to someone else.

However, this kind of group intrusion should be an exception, not the rule. GM intrusions are much more effective if they are more personal.

EXAMPLE GM INTRUSIONS

It's not a good idea to use the same events as GM intrusions over and over ("Dolmar dropped his sword *again*?"). Below are a number of different intrusions you can use.

BAD LUCK

Through no fault of the characters, something happens that is bad or at least complicating. For example:

- The floorboard beneath the PC gives way.
- The boat lists to starboard at just the wrong moment.
- A gust of wind blows the papers out of the character's hand.
- The buckle of the PC's pack snaps at an inopportune time.
- The NPC that the characters need to speak with is home sick today.
- A device (cypher or artifact) malfunctions or gives the user a jolt.

AN UNKNOWN COMPLICATION EMERGES

The situation was more complex (and therefore more interesting) than the PCs knew—perhaps even more than the GM knew, at least at the start. For example:

- A poisonous snake darts out from the tall grass and attacks.
- The box that holds the plans is trapped with a poison needle.
- The NPC that the PCs need to befriend doesn't speak their language.
- The NPC that the PCs try to bribe is allergic to the bottle of alcohol they offer.
- The PCs find the book they need, but the pages are so brittle that if they open it, it might crumble.

AN IMPENDING COMPLICATION EMERGES

GMs can use this type of intrusion as a resolution mechanic to determine NPC success or failure. Rather than rolling dice to see how long it takes an NPC to rewire a damaged force field generator, it happens at a time of the GM's choosing—ideally when it would be most interesting. For example:

- The goblin reinforcements finally get through the locked door.
- The ropes of the old rope bridge finally snap.

- The city guards show up.
- The unstable ceiling collapses.
- The NPC who holds a dagger to a character's throat and says "Don't move" cuts the PC when he does, in fact, move, putting him immediately at debilitated on the damage track.

OPPONENT LUCK OR SKILL

The PCs aren't the only ones with surprising tricks up their sleeves. For example:

- The PC's opponent uses a lightning-fast maneuver to dodge all attacks.
- The PC's opponent sees an opening and makes an additional, immediate attack.
- The NPC commander rallies her troops, and they all deal 2 additional points of damage for one round.
- The PC's opponent uses a cypher or similar device that produces just the right effect for the situation.
- A bit of the wall collapses in the middle of the fight, preventing the characters from chasing the fleeing NPC.

FUMBLES

Although you might not want every player roll of 1 to be a fumble, sometimes it could be just that. Alternatively, the GM could simply declare that a fumble has occurred. In either case, consider the following examples:

- In combat, the PC drops his weapon.
- In combat, the PC misses and strikes the wall, breaking or damaging his weapon.
- In combat, the NPC hits the PC harder than usual, inflicting 2 additional points of damage.
- In combat, the PC hits an ally by accident and inflicts regular damage.
- Out of combat, the PC drops or mishandles an important object or piece of equipment.
- In an interaction, the PC inadvertently or unknowingly says something offensive.

PARTIAL SUCCESS

GM intrusion doesn't have to mean that a PC has failed. For example:

- The PC disables the explosive device before it goes off, but if someone doesn't remain and hold the detonator, it will still explode.

- The PC creates the antidote, but it will turn the imbiber's flesh blue for the next few weeks.
- The PC jumps across the pit but accidentally knocks loose some stones from the edge, making the jump harder for her friend right behind her.

It's telling that in the Cypher System, the rules define "quite hurt" and "pretty far" very generally, intentionally leaving a lot up to the GM's storytelling abilities. A game with a less story-based approach would likely define such things far more precisely.

THE REST OF THE RULES

I'll say it again: the rules exist to be used as tools to shape the game, the story, and the experience. When you tell a player that the howling, bestial Cro-Magnon warriors at the top of the cliff throw heavy stones down on her character and she gets hurt, the rules give you a way to explain just how hurt.

One way to look at it is this: the GM is the sensory input for the player. The player can't know anything about what's going on in the fictional reality of the game unless the GM tells her. The rules, then, are one way to convey information to the players in a manner that is meaningful to everyone sitting at the table. The GM could say, "You're quite hurt," but the rules clarify how hurt she is. The GM could say, "You can hurl that spear pretty far," but the rules provide a definition of "pretty far" that helps keep things consistent, moderately realistic, and understandable so the GM doesn't have to repeat things over and over.

The rules do more than that, of course. They determine success or failure for PCs and NPCs. They help define what resources characters have to interact with the world (although the best resource is the players' ingenuity, and that isn't defined by the rules).

Needler, page 254

ADJUDICATING

A lot of what I'm talking about here is what people sometimes call "adjudicating." Adjudicating is basically the difference between a computer game and a game run by an actual, living human being. All a computer can do (as of yet) is follow the rules. But a human can use his sense of logic (we'll discuss that in detail below) to determine whether the rules make sense for a given situation, and he can do it on a case-by-case basis. Because there's a human GM using logic, the rules for how to play the Cypher System take up only a small part of this hefty book. If the rules had to cover every imaginable situation, well, this would be a very different book.

For example, imagine that the PCs encounter an assassin who tries to kill them with a needler loaded with poisoned needles. One of the PCs is heavily armored, so she takes no damage from the needles—not even close. That sort of sounds like the needles just bounced off her armor. Should the poison on a needle that can't penetrate a character's armor affect that character? Probably not. But that's not an actual rule. Well, why not make it a rule? Because then suddenly anyone wearing a leather jerkin can't be affected by poison needles. Should that be the case? No, because the thick leather doesn't protect every area on the PC's body. It's more complex than that. Could you devise a rule to cover both situations? Probably, but why bother? The GM can make a decision based on the situation. (She can also use GM intrusion and say that a needle hit where the armor didn't offer protection—GM intrusion really does solve a lot of these issues.)

Likewise, sometimes a character who falls off a high ledge should be stunned and lose his next turn. That isn't the rule, but it makes sense—sometimes. And the key word is *sometimes*. Because sometimes the situation or the context means you don't want that to happen, so you adjudicate.

A character falling from a 100-foot (30 m) ledge might take 10 points of damage. That's a lot, but a fresh character with a decent amount of Might can take that and keep going. Sometimes that's okay, but sometimes it stretches our suspension of disbelief. If a player reads the rules on how much damage is dealt by falling, he might even have his character jump off a high cliff deliberately, knowing that he can take it. So you adjudicate that he doesn't just lose his next turn, but the fall also knocks him down a step on the damage track. That's harsh, and the player will really feel it. But he should, and it will keep him from exploiting what might seem like a hole in the rules in a way that no real person would (and no one in a story would).

Remember, it's your job to use the rules to simulate the world, even if the world is a fictional place with all kinds of strangeness. You're not a slave to the rules—it's the other way around. If you come across a hole in the rules or something that doesn't make sense, don't shrug your shoulders and say, "Well, that's what the rules say (or don't say)." Fix it.

When talking about rules, sometimes people will toss around words like "game balance" or refer to rules as "broken." These concepts belong in games where players build characters using extensive rules and make a lot of choices and then pit those characters against specific challenges to see how they fare. In such a game, a challenge rated or designed poorly, or a character option that grants too much or too little power, can throw everything completely out of whack. Advancing and improving characters is the point of that kind of game, and the way that characters "win" is by overcoming challenges (often, by fighting). Because the Cypher System is not a game about matching PC builds against specific challenges, nor a game about advancing characters (at least not solely, and in any event, characters do not advance due to fights or overcoming challenges), these concepts really don't apply. If something seems broken, change it. If a PC ability is too powerful, make it less so. Do it either as part of the story, or—perhaps even better—just be upfront with the players. "Hey, guys, this new psychic power of Ray's is just too good. It's making every fight a pushover and that's not fun. So I'm going to tone down its effect. Sound okay?" An honest discussion with the players is often the best way to handle, well, just about any problem that crops up in a game. And if a player can't handle that kind of interaction, maybe you don't want him at your table anyway.

Logic

Running a game requires a lot of logic rather than a careful reading of the rules. For example, some things give characters a resistance to fire (almost always expressed as Armor). But there is no special rule for "fire damage" as opposed to "slicing damage" or "lightning damage." Instead, you use logic to determine whether the damage inflicted counts as fire. In these situations, there are only two times when your answer is wrong.

The first is when the answer breaks the players' suspension of disbelief. For example, something that makes a PC fire resistant should probably provide some protection against a heat-based weapon. If it doesn't, your answer will spoil the moment for the group.

The second wrong answer is when you're inconsistent. If you allow a PC's fireproof armor to give him some protection against lava one time but not the next, that's a problem—not only because it breaks the suspension of disbelief but also because it gives the players nothing to base their decisions on. Without predictable

While GMs always have notes that they put together before the game session, it's smart to have a lot of blank paper to scribble notes on during the game. You'll invariably have to make stuff up as you go, and later you might want to be able to remember what you did. Sometimes it will be a rules issue (remembering that it was a difficulty 4 jump to cross the pit, so that it will be consistent when the PCs come back that way again), and sometimes it will just be an NPC's name or some detail about them.

At any time, it's reasonable to switch one "condition" for another. Thus, if a PC moves one step down on the damage track as the result of someone attempting to knock him out, something equally dire happens instead. This could also be the case if someone tried to blind or deafen a PC, or anything else appropriate. Conversely, an effect that normally blinds a character could just move her one step down the damage track instead.

consistency, they can't make intelligent decisions.

The Cypher System rules are written with the assumption that the GM does not need to fall back on rules for everything, either for her own sake or as a defense against the players. "I'm going to run a long distance and jump on my big friend's back. On his action, he will run a long distance. So I can move twice as far in one round. There's no rule against that, right?" It's true that there isn't a rule against that, but it makes no sense. The GM's logic rules the day here.

GMs can encourage smart players to be ready with their actions, and to know enough about how actions work so that you don't have to ask if they're using Effort or tell them to make a roll. In a perfect world, when it's Michele's turn and you ask what she's doing, she says, "I'm going to try to climb the tree to get out of reach of the golem. I'm using a level of Effort, and I rolled a 14." That way, you can take the info and immediately tell her if she succeeded or not. This keeps play moving at a wonderfully brisk pace, and doesn't let talk of game mechanics bog things down.

You shouldn't need pedantic rules to defend against the players. You and the players should work together to create a logical, consistent, and believable world and story. Players who try to use the lack of pedantry in the rules to gain unrealistic and illogical advantages for their characters should revisit the basic concept of the Cypher System.

Further, the rules don't say things like, "The GM decides if the NPC knows the answer to the question, or if he will answer, or how he will answer." Of course that's the kind of thing you decide—that's your role. The rules don't state that you decide if something is logical and appropriate to the story or setting any more than they state that the player decides what actions his character will take. That's just the way the game works.

Does this put more pressure on the GM? Yes and no. It means that you need to make more judgment calls—more of the adjudication described above—which can be challenging if you're new at it. But being an arbiter of what seems appropriate and makes sense is something that we all do, all day long. Look at it this way: when you're watching a television show or a movie, at some point you might say, "That seems wrong," or "That seems unrealistic." There's no difference between doing that and using logic as a GM.

In the long run, relying on logic frees the GM. No longer saddled with hundreds (or thousands) of individual rules, compatibility issues, loopholes, and the like, you are free to move ahead with the story being told by the group. You can focus more on the narrative elements of the game than on the mechanical ones. To look at it a different way, in other games GMs sometimes spend a lot of time preparing, which is almost always rules-related stuff: creating NPC stat blocks, memorizing rules subsystems that will come into play, carefully balancing encounters, and so on. A Cypher System GM does very little of that. Prepping for the game means figuring out cool storylines, weird new devices or foes, and the best way to convey the atmosphere. The mechanical elements can be handled during the game, using logic at the table.

DICE ROLLING

Using the rules involves rolling dice. If the dice don't mean anything, then everything is predetermined, and it's no longer a game by any definition—just a story being told. So the dice need to matter. But that means that sometimes a PC will fail when she would succeed if it were a story, and vice versa. That's not a flaw; it's a feature. It's what makes roleplaying games so exciting. When we're watching an action movie, we know that in the third act the hero will defeat the villain at just the right moment. But in an RPG, maybe not. It's not so predictable. That's one of the things that makes them so special.

On the other hand, things like GM intrusions sometimes trump the die rolls to help the story move along in a direction that is (hopefully) best for the game. How do you manage it all?

As you describe the action or as the PCs move about the world, the vast majority of things that happen shouldn't involve dice. Walking around, buying things in a market, chatting with NPCs, crossing the wilderness, looking for an ancient ruin—these are not actions that normally require die rolls. However, it's easy to think of exceptions where rolls might be needed. How do you decide? There are two rules of thumb.

First, don't ask for a roll unless it seems like there should be a chance of failure and a chance of success. If a PC wants to shoot an arrow from his bow and hit the moon, there's no need to roll, because there's no chance for success. Likewise, if he wants to shoot that same arrow at a large building from 10 feet (3 m) away, there's no chance for failure. You and logic run the game, not the dice.

Second, if a creature (PC or NPC) or object is affected in a harmful way—or, in the case of a creature, in a way that he doesn't want to be affected, harmful or not—you need to involve a die roll. Whether the action is slashing with a blade, using deception to trick someone, intrusively reading an NPC's mind, breaking down a door, or applying poison, something is being harmed or affected in a way that it doesn't want to be, so a die roll is needed.

Thus, someone using a power to become invisible likely doesn't require a roll. It just works. There's really no chance of failure (unless the power comes from a faulty device or some other extraneous force is at work), and it doesn't directly affect anyone or anything other than the character becoming invisible. However, using a device to shape the emotions of another creature would require a die roll.

Of course, sometimes a character can use Effort to reduce the difficulty so there's no need to make a roll. But you, as the GM, can also waive the need for a roll. Consider an adept who uses her Flash ability on a bunch of level 1 rodents. Each has 3 health, and the PC needs to roll only 3 or higher to affect each one, but there are twenty-four rodents. You can simply say, "With a discharge of sudden energy, you incinerate the swarm of rodents, leaving little behind but scorch marks and the smell of burnt hair." This keeps things moving and prevents the game from coming to a dead stop while the player makes two dozen rolls. Frankly, most first-tier characters will find level 1 creatures merely a nuisance, so no drama is ruined when the adept takes them all out. Move on to another, greater challenge.

When you waive the need for a die roll, what you're effectively doing is making the action routine, so no roll is needed. In the case of the adept, you're reducing the difficulty by one step due to circumstances: the rodents just aren't that tough. That's not breaking the rules—that's using the rules. That's the way the game is meant to be played.

Flash, page 33

Flavor, page 50

Remember, most of the time, powers, abilities, devices, and so forth are written from the point of view of the characters. But the players make die rolls, not the GM. So, for example, if the circumstances call for an NPC to make a defense roll, that means a PC should make an attack roll instead.

Feel free to rename the types to anything you want or make them fit a player's character concept.

As an aside, this doesn't mean that the swarm of rodents is a bad encounter. It would be bad in a game where it takes an hour and a half to resolve a fight that was no real challenge. But in the Cypher System? Even if the adept doesn't blast every rodent, an encounter like that can be resolved in five minutes. Not every encounter needs to be life-or-death to be interesting. But we'll talk about designing encounters (and the related issue of pacing) later in this chapter.

USING CHARACTER TYPES TO DEFINE THE SETTING

Much more than in other Cypher System games like Numenera or The Strange, the types presented in chapter 5 of this book are meant to be tools for you to customize your game. Nothing helps define the specifics of the setting like the options that characters have at their disposal, just as nothing defines the setting of a novel like the main characters—who they are, what they know, and what they can do.

This means that you have all the freedom in the world to mix and match abilities, or predetermine ability choices. If, in your fantasy world, you have a character type that is a wizard who is a master of magic, it might be hard to imagine that character not being trained in magical lore. So you take the adept type, rename it "wizard," and make the Magic Training ability mandatory at first tier, leaving the player three rather than four choices for special abilities.

For a more in-depth example, consider the glaive from Numenera. The glaive is a warrior, but at first tier, the abilities Extra Edge and Practiced in Armor are predetermined for the type, ensuring that the glaive is the most physical of the types and reinforcing the idea that most of them wear armor (which is common in that setting). This leaves glaives with two ability choices at first tier. At second tier, they get one choice because all glaives get Skill With Attacks.

This emphasis is intended to reinforce (not limit) the setting and the character concept. In Numenera's setting, glaives are combatants, and most combatants wear armor and they all make attacks. A glaive who is not skilled in attacks makes no sense within the context of the setting.

The types can also be ad hoc rather than predetermined. Find out what the player's character concept is, and tailor the type to that concept, perhaps using flavor.

For example, if a player in a modern game wants to be a rock musician, use the speaker type but call it "musician" (all of the abilities will be music based rather than word based, but the effects remain the same). If a player in the same game wants to be a rebellious teen who sneaks out a lot, make her an explorer with lots of physical skills and abilities (perhaps add in stealth flavor) and call it "teenager." If she changes her mind and wants to be a scientist, she can still be an explorer, but focus the type on knowledge skills (perhaps add in skills and knowledge flavor) and call it "scientist."

Basically, the thing to remember is that types serve two purposes: to help define the setting, and to help fulfill the player's character concept. Descriptor and focus also help to do the latter, so GMs should feel free to make whatever changes or predetermined choices they see fit for the types offered in their game.

TYING ACTIONS TO STATS

Although the decision is open to your discretion, when a PC takes an action, it should be fairly obvious which stat is tied to that action. Physical actions that involve brute force or endurance use Might. Physical actions that involve quickness, coordination, or agility use Speed. Actions that involve intelligence, education, insight, willpower, or charm use Intellect.

In rare instances, you could allow a PC to use a different stat for a task. For example, a character might try to break down a door by examining it closely for flaws and thus use Intellect rather than Might. This kind of change is a good thing because it encourages player creativity. Just don't let it be abused by an exuberant or too-clever player. It's well within your purview to decide that the door has no flaws, or to rule that the character's attempt will take half an hour rather than one round. In other words, using a stat that is not the obvious choice should be the exception, not the rule.

THE FLOW OF INFORMATION

You are the eyes and ears of the players. They can't know anything about the world unless you tell them. Make sure that the information you provide is both precise and concise. (We'll discuss good description later in this chapter.) Be evocative, but not to the point that the players lose details in the language you use. Be open to answering their questions about the world around them.

Sometimes it's easy: a PC looks over the top of the hill, and you tell her what she sees. Other times things are hidden, or there's a chance that she misses something important—secret panels, cloaked assassins, creatures with natural camouflage, details of significance in a crowded marketplace, and so on. In these cases, perhaps a roll is involved. But it's odd to ask players to roll when they haven't taken any actions. It's within the bounds of the rules, but it can be jarring. There are different ways to handle the situation: you can call for a roll, compare levels, or use an intrusion.

GM Calls for Rolls: This is the most straightforward approach. It's always the best choice if a PC's action is to search, listen, or otherwise keep an eye out. If a PC is on watch while her comrades rest, call for an Intellect roll immediately and use the result if anything happens during the entire time she is guarding.

But what if the PC isn't actively looking? Let's say a pickpocket moves up behind her to lift a few coins, so you ask the player to make an Intellect roll with a difficulty equal to the pickpocket's level. (Arguably, she could make a Speed-based roll to see if she is quick enough to catch a glimpse—it's up to you.) Some PCs are skilled in perceiving, and that would come into play here. Success means that you tell the character what she sees, and failure means that she notices nothing. However, the player knows that she had to make a roll, so she knows that something was up. One way to keep players on their toes is to call for rolls when there is nothing to notice.

GM Compares Levels: You can take the player out of the equation (so as not to alert her suspicions) by comparing the PC's tier to the difficulty of the perceiving task. Ties go to the PC. You can still figure in skills and assets as bonuses to the PC's tier. So a third-tier character trained in perceiving will spot the level 4 predator cat stalking up behind him. This method is particularly good for determining simple results, such as whether the PC hears a river in the distance. That kind of thing isn't worth a roll, but for some reason, you might not want to give out the information automatically. This method also rewards a perceptive character, who will hear the noise before anyone else. Don't forget to increase the difficulty for distance in such a situation.

GM Intrudes: Rarely, you can keep things to yourself and spring the knowledge of what happened as a GM intrusion. If the PC discovers that her pocket is now empty of coins, that's certainly a complication. Sometimes the "discovery" itself is a complication—for example, the character notices a mugging going on in the alley as she walks by.

In addition, the GM is the source of knowledge about the part of the PCs' lives that doesn't take place in a game session. If a character used to be in the military and needs to know the name of her old unit commander, you need to give it to the player (or, better yet, let her come up with the name).

FAILURE TO NOTICE

Consider PCs missing a sensory detail very carefully. If there's a cool secret chamber in the ancient complex or an important clue under the table in the castle guardroom, maybe a perceptive PC should just find it (no roll required), particularly if she said she was looking. To do otherwise might mean submitting to the tyranny of the dice. Just because the PC rolled a 2, should the adventure come to a dead stop?

Well, in the first place, don't design a scenario that can come to a dead stop if the PCs botch one roll. There should always be multiple paths to success. In the second, consider your other options. Maybe the PCs will learn about the secret chamber later and they'll have to backtrack to find it. If the characters don't find the clue under the table, an NPC might—and then lord it over them with a show of superiority. If all else fails, as noted above, sometimes discovery is a complication, and you can simply foist it upon a PC through GM intrusion. In such a case, however, you might want to include a challenge. For example, the PC finds the secret door accidentally by leaning against the hidden control pad, which lets out the flying insectoid hunter-seekers guarding the chamber before the characters are ready for them.

A good rule of thumb is: players should always know why they are rolling. If you suddenly say, "Give me a roll" to see if they notice something, it's probably better either to act as if they noticed it and give them the information, or to proceed as if they didn't, and then spring a surprise on them via a GM intrusion. Of course, if a player says that he's looking around carefully, that's another story entirely.

On the other hand, perhaps in such a situation, the PCs didn't "earn" the discovery—if there was no roll, then no Effort was expended and no risks were taken. That's not good. Maybe the PCs just miss out this time. Maybe they should learn to be more observant.

In other words, the answer depends on the situation. Don't hesitate to vary things. It keeps the players guessing.

GRADUATED SUCCESS

Sometimes, a GM will break away from the traditional model that governs Cypher System task resolution and allow for a graduated success. With this method, she sets a difficulty as usual, but if the player succeeds at a difficulty at least one step higher, his success is better than normal. Likewise, if his roll indicates that he would have succeeded at one step (or more) lower, he might have a partial success.

For example, a PC tracking the bandits that robbed the train looks for tracks in the woods to see if any of them came down a certain path recently. Given the terrain and the weather, the GM decides that the difficulty is 4, so the target number is 12. The player rolls a 10. This isn't enough to accomplish the task that the PC set out to do, but since he would have succeeded if the difficulty had been 3, the GM decides that he still learns that something had come down the path recently—he just isn't certain if it was bandits. The reason is that if the PC had simply been looking for tracks of any kind, the GM would have set a difficulty of 3. Similarly, if the player had rolled a 17—a success at least one step higher—the GM would have said that not only did he find bandit tracks, but there were five of them, and their tracks show that they were burdened. In other words, the player would have received more information than he asked for.

In a situation where there are more results than simply success or failure, the GM can convey these results based on multiple difficulties. A player can state an action, and a GM can come up with not one difficulty but two, three, or more. For example, if the PCs try to persuade a merchant to give them information, the GM can predetermine that he gives them one minor bit of information if they succeed at a task with a difficulty of 2, a fair bit of information if they succeed at a task with a difficulty of 3, and everything he knows on the topic if they succeed at a task with a difficulty of 4. The players don't make three different rolls. They make one roll with a scaled, graduated success.

As a rule of thumb, reverse-engineer the situation. If the player rolls considerably higher or lower than the target number (more than 3 away), consider what a success at the difficulty he did overcome would have gained him. If creating a makeshift electronic key to open a sealed door has a target number of 18, what does the PC create if the player rolls 16? Perhaps the answer is nothing, but perhaps it is a makeshift key that works intermittently.

This system is rarely (if ever) used in combat or situations where something either works or doesn't. But when crafting an object, interacting with an NPC, or gaining information, it can be very useful. Of course, the GM is never required to use this model of task resolution—sometimes success or failure is all you need to know. Usually, graduated success involves going only one step higher or lower than the original difficulty, but the GM can be as flexible about that as she wishes.

Finally, sometimes a GM can offer a "consolation prize" for trying. Say a PC fears that a door has been rigged with a trap. He searches it but fails the roll. The GM might still reveal something about the door. "You don't find anything special, but you do note that the door appears quite sturdy and is locked." It's the kind of information the GM might give automatically (think of it as a difficulty of 0), but it softens the blow of failure. Some information is better than none, and it makes sense that the PC will learn at least something if he studies an object for a few minutes.

DEALING WITH CHARACTER ABILITIES

A lot of people might think that the Cypher System is a class-and-level game because it has things that are enough like classes (types) and levels (tiers) that it's easy to see the misconception. And that's fine.

But here's the real secret, just between you and me: it's not tiers, types, or any of that stuff that is the key to really understanding the system.

It's the cyphers.

The cyphers are the key to making the game work differently than other games. The Cypher System isn't about playing for years before a character is allowed to teleport, travel to other dimensions, lay waste to a dozen enemies at once, or create a mechanical automaton to do his bidding. He can do it right out of the gate if he has the right cypher.

This system works because both the GM and the player have a say over what cyphers a character has. It's not limiting—it's freeing.

The easiest way to design a good game is to limit—and strictly define—PC power. Characters of such-and-such a level (or whatever) can do this kind of thing but not that kind of thing. The GM knows that the characters aren't going to ruin everything because they can see into the past or create a nuclear explosion.

But that's not the only way to design a good game. What if you—the GM—decide that while it would not be so great if the PCs could see into the past (which would ruin the mystery of your scenario), it would be okay if they could blow up half the city? The Cypher System allows you to permit anything you feel is appropriate or interesting.

To put it another way (and to continue the ever-more-absurd examples), PCs who can solve every mystery and blow up every city probably end up making the game a pushover (and thus dull), but PCs who can solve one mystery or blow up one city won't ruin the campaign. Cyphers allow the characters to do amazing, cool, and fun things—just not reliably or consistently. Thus, although they potentially have access to great power from time to time, they have to use it wisely.

As the GM, it's important to remember the distinction between a character ability gained through type or focus, an ability or advantage gained through an artifact, and an ability gained through a cypher. The first two kinds of abilities will shape the way you expect the characters to behave, but

Exists Partially Out of Phase, page 122

Cyphers teach us as GMs to design different kinds of scenarios—ones in which if a player has something that can basically solve a single problem (defeat a foe, read a mind, bypass a barrier), the whole adventure isn't wrecked. There should always be more to the adventure than one linchpin encounter, obstacle, foe, or secret.

the cyphers won't. If a PC has the Exists Partially Out of Phase focus, she's going to be walking through walls all the time—it's what she does—so it shouldn't catch you off guard. In a way, you should "prepare" for it. I put that word in quotes because I don't mean that you nullify it. Don't put in a bunch of walls that she can't get through. That's no fun. Walking through walls is what she does, and if you take that away, she doesn't get to do anything. (Foiling her power every once in a while is fine because it might add to the challenge, but it should be the exception, not the rule.) By "preparing" for her ability, I mean don't expect a locked door to keep her out. Be ready when she sneaks into places most people can't go, and be ready to tell her what she finds.

But with cyphers, no preparation is necessary. First of all, most of them don't throw a wrench into anything—they just help the character deal with a situation in a faster way, giving her some healing, a temporary boost, or a one-use offensive power. Second, the PCs never end up with a cypher that you didn't give them, so you can have as much say over their cyphers as you want. And third (and perhaps most important), when a PC pulls out a detonation cypher and blows up the lead wagon in the caravan, completely changing the situation, that's part of the fun. You'll have to figure out on the fly what happens next, and so will the players. That's not ruining things—that's what is supposed to happen. Players surprising the GM is part of the game. Cyphers just make those surprises more frequent, and in ways as interesting as you're willing to allow.

We'll look at designing encounters later, but for now, remember this point: no single encounter is so important that you ever have to worry about the players "ruining" it. You hear those kinds of complaints all the time. "Her telepathic power totally ruined that interaction," or "The players came up with a great ambush and killed the main villain in one round, ruining the final encounter."

No. No, no, no. See the forest for the trees. Don't think about the game in terms of encounters. Think about it in terms of the adventure or the campaign. If a PC used a potent cypher to easily kill a powerful and important opponent, remember these three things:

1. She doesn't have that cypher anymore.
2. There will be more bad guys.
3. Combat's not the point of the game—it's merely an obstacle. If the players discover a way to overcome an obstacle more quickly than you expected, there's nothing wrong with that. They're not cheating, and the game's not broken. Just keep the story going. What happens next? What are the implications of what just happened?

CYPHERS

Although it's all right if players think of cyphers as equipment or treasure, the GM should look at them as character abilities. This means that it is incumbent upon the GM to make sure that players always have plenty of cyphers to use. In the course of their travels, the PCs should find that cyphers are extremely common. And since the PCs are limited in the number of cyphers they can carry, they will use the devices liberally.

Cyphers can be found by scavenging through old ruins. They can be found in the corpses of magical or technological foes. They can be found among the possessions of intelligent fallen opponents or the lairs of unintelligent creatures, either amid the bones of former meals or as shiny decorations in a nest. They can be found in villages, in the back of a merchant's cart that sells junk and scavenged parts. They are offered as rewards by people who are grateful for the PCs' help.

Some adventures will offer more cyphers than others. Still, as a rule of thumb, in any given adventure, a character should use at least as many cyphers as she can carry. This means she should find that number of cyphers in that same amount of time (give or take). Thus, you can simply add up the number of cyphers the PCs can carry, and on average, they should find at least that many cyphers in a given adventure.

ENCOURAGING PLAYER CREATIVITY

The Cypher System is a game that places more importance on creativity than on understanding the rules. The players should succeed not because they've chosen all the "right" options when creating their characters but because they come up with the best ideas when facing challenges. This means that for every challenge, there should be a straightforward solution (destroy the lightning-emitting turret to get into the tower) and a not-so-straightforward one (sneak up to the tower, find the power conduit to the turret, and sever it). It's not your responsibility as the GM to come up with both. The players will come up with the not-so-straightforward solutions. You just have to be willing to go with their ideas.

This doesn't mean you have to let them succeed if they try something weird. On the contrary, the not-so-straightforward solution might end up being as hard or harder than the straightforward one. But you have to be ready to adjudicate the idea no matter what. It's tempting to say that there's no way to find or sever the power conduit and the PCs have to destroy the turret the old-fashioned way (a combat encounter). In some situations, that might be appropriate—perhaps the conduit is simply not accessible to the PCs on the outside of the tower. But a GM has to be willing to say that sometimes it is possible and to adjudicate the details on the fly. If you don't, and you shut down the players' outside-the-box ideas, they will learn that the only thing to do is charge into the fray every time. That the obvious solution is the only possible solution. Eventually, this will make for boring play because things will seem repetitive and too tightly structured.

The best solution is not to develop preconceived notions of how the PCs might deal with the encounters in an adventure. If they're going to break into a tower, you can note that the tower has a few guards, a pressure-sensitive intruder alert system around the perimeter, and a lightning-emitting turret on the top. But you don't know if the PCs will fight the guards, bribe them, or sneak past them. You don't know how they're going to deal with the alert system and the turret. That's not the kind of thing you need to think about ahead of time, but you have to be ready when it comes up at the table. You should prepare for the most obvious situations—for example, predetermine the level of the turret and how much damage it does. But when a player states that his action is to look around for spots where the turret cannot strike because a wall blocks it or the angle prevents it, that's when you take a second to consider and (particularly if he rolls well on an Intellect action) maybe say, "Yes, as a matter of fact, there is a spot," even if no such thing had occurred to you before that moment.

If your players are typical, they will use combat-related cyphers liberally but hold onto their utility cyphers. A ray emitter or defensive shield will be used, but a suspensor belt or phasing module will linger longer on their character sheets.

As with everything else in the game, it's intentionally very easy for the GM to create new cyphers. Just think of the effect and how to express it as a game advantage. Two kinds of cyphers exist: those that allow the user to do something better, and those that allow the user to do something she couldn't do otherwise.

The first group includes everything that reduces the difficulty of a task (including defense tasks). The second group includes things that grant new abilities, such as flight, a new means of attack, the ability to see into the past, or any number of other powers.

A few more important notes about devising new cyphers:

- Cyphers should be single-use items. The PCs use them up and find new ones.
- Cyphers should be potent. A minor ability isn't worth the trouble. If an attack cypher isn't as good as a regular weapon, why bother with it?
- Cyphers shouldn't have drawbacks.
- Cyphers should be temporary. Typically, a power is used once. Abilities or advantages that have a duration last from ten minutes to twenty-four hours (at most).
- Cyphers can take any form. Just make it appropriate to the genre.

ARTIFACTS

In terms of the narrative, artifacts are a lot like cyphers, except that most are not one-use items. Mechanically, they serve a very different purpose. It's assumed that characters are exploring with some cyphers at their disposal. Artifacts, however, are added abilities that make characters broader, deeper, and often more powerful. They aren't assumed—they're extra.

You may wish to forbid the use of XP to reroll artifact depletion rolls. That's actually pretty reasonable.

The powers granted by artifacts are more like the abilities gained from a character's type or focus in that they change the way the PC is played overall. The difference is that almost all artifacts are temporary. They last longer than cyphers do, but because they have a depletion roll, any use could be their last.

Like cyphers, then, artifacts are a way for the GM to play a role in the development of the characters. Although armor, weapons, and the like are fine, special capabilities—such as long-range communication or travel—can really change the way the PCs interact with the world and how they deal with challenges. Some of these abilities enable the actions you want the PCs to take. For example, if you want them to have an underwater adventure, provide them with artifacts (or cyphers) that allow them to breathe underwater.

Also like cyphers, artifacts are simple for the GM to create. The only difference with artifacts is that you give them a depletion roll, using any numbers on 1d6, 1d10, 1d20, or 1d100. If you want the artifact to be used only a few times, give it a depletion roll of 1 in 1d6, 1 or 2 in 1d10, or even 1 or 2 in 1d6. If you want the PCs to use it over and over, a depletion roll of 1 in 1d100 more or less means that they can use it freely without worrying too much.

SKILLS AND OTHER ABILITIES

Sometimes, the rules speak directly to character creativity. For example, players can make up their own skills. It's possible to have a skill called "tightrope walking" that grants a character a better chance to walk across a tightrope, and another skill called "balance" that gives a character a better chance to walk across a tightrope and perform other balance actions as well. This might seem unequal at first, but the point is to let players create precisely the characters they want. Should you let a character create a skill called "doing things" that makes him better at everything? Of course not. The GM is the final arbiter not only of logic but also of the spirit of the rules, and having one or two single skills that cover every contingency is clearly not in the spirit.

It's important that players play the character they want. This concept is supported not only with the open-ended skill system but also with the ability to get an experience point advance to tailor a character further. Likewise, the GM should be open to allowing a player to make small modifications to refine her character. In many cases, particularly ones that don't involve stat Pools, Armor, damage inflicted, or the costs of Effort or special abilities, the answer from the GM should probably be, "Sure, why not?" If a PC ends up being really good at a particular skill—better than she "should" be—what's the harm? If Dave can swim incredibly well, how does that hurt the game in terms of the play experience or the story that develops? It doesn't. If Helen can pick practically any mundane lock she finds, why is that a bad thing? In fact, it's probably good for the game—there's likely something interesting on the other sides of those doors.

In a way, this is no different than adjudicating a not-so-straightforward solution to a challenge. Sometimes you have to say "No, that's not possible." But sometimes, if it makes sense, open yourself up to the possibility.

HANDLING NPCs

Nonplayer characters are people and creatures that live in the world alongside the PCs. They are just as much a part of the world as the PCs and should be portrayed just as realistically. NPCs are the main way to breathe life into the world, tell the stories the world has to tell, and portray the kind of game you want to run. Memorable NPCs can make or break a campaign.

NPCs shouldn't be "cannon fodder" because no one thinks of themselves that way. Real people value their lives. They shouldn't be idiots, easily fooled into doing things or acting in ways that no person ever would, simply because a die roll suggests it (unless they're not very bright or something more powerful—like mind control—is at work).

Think about real people that you know or characters from books, television, and movies. Base your NPCs' personalities on them. Make them as widely varying, as interesting, and as deep as those people.

Remember, too, that there are minor characters and major ones, just like in a book. The bandits who waylay the PCs are in the spotlight for only a few minutes at most and don't need a lot of development, but a major adversary or ally might get a lot of attention from the players and therefore deserves a lot from you. As with so many things related to being a good GM, consistency and believability are the keys to developing a good NPC.

NPC GAME STATS

NPCs should be easy to create. Most can simply be pegged at a level from 1 to 10 and you're done. Working on how to describe or portray them will take longer than working up their game stats.

Sometimes, though, you'll want to elaborate on the NPC's capabilities and tailor them to the concept. A level 4 NPC who is a computer genius might be level 5 or 6 in computer-related tasks. But don't simply make the NPC level 5 or 6 overall because then she'd also be better at combat, interactions, climbing, jumping, and everything else, and that doesn't fit your concept.

Use the NPCs in chapter 17 as good starting points or as examples for what you can do. But you're not limited by them. In fact, you're not limited in any way. The most important thing to remember about NPCs in the Cypher System is that they do not follow the same rules as PCs. They don't have descriptors, types, or foci. They don't have tiers or any of the same stats. They don't even roll dice.

NPCs work precisely as you (and the setting and story) need them to. If an NPC is the greatest swordsman in the land, you can give him obvious advantages with a sword in attack and defense, but you can go outside the box as well, allowing him to attack more than once per turn, attempt to disarm foes with a flick of his blade, and so on.

There are no hard-and-fast rules for creating an NPC who can be matched perfectly against the PCs in combat—it's not that kind of game, and that's not the purpose of NPCs. Instead, use the game's simple mechanics to portray the NPCs in the world and in your narrative so that they make sense and can do what you want them to do (and cannot do what you don't want them to do).

Like the player characters, NPCs often carry and use cyphers. Thus, any NPC could have virtually any capability at his disposal as a one-shot power. In theory, NPCs can heal themselves, create force fields, teleport, turn back time, hurt a foe with a sonic blast, or do anything else. An NPC might also use spells, possess mutant powers, or have biomechanical implants. You can lay out these cyphers and abilities when preparing for the game, or you can just go with the idea that certain NPCs can produce amazing and surprising effects and make them up as you go along—with some caveats.

If all NPCs can do whatever they want, whenever they want, that won't instill much believability in the players or give you much credibility as a GM. So keep the following things in mind.

Keep to the Level: NPCs should generally keep to their level parameters. Sure, you can

Although an NPC's level and stats are important, just as important are his appearance, the way he talks, and how he acts. If an NPC is going to be more than a simple, short-term foe (like a bandit), when you make your notes about things like his level and Armor, also note something about his appearance or personality. If an NPC is going to interact with the PCs for more than a minute, note at least two different things: he makes stupid jokes, he has a scar on his ear, he laughs too much, he talks very softly, he smells bad, and so on.

Because Cypher System games aren't just about combat and gaining power, the NPCs should be motivated by things beyond that. Love, lust, embarrassment, loyalty, revenge, familial ties, altruism, and curiosity are all great motivators.

give a tough NPC more health than his level might indicate, and the aforementioned great swordsman might attack and defend with his blade at higher than his normal level, but these are minor exceptions.

Explain Things However You Want: If you keep to the level parameters generally, you can express them in all sorts of interesting ways. For example, a level 5 NPC usually inflicts 5 points of damage. But that damage might come from waves of magnetic force that he can produce thanks to a nanotech virus that has taken over his body.

Wild Cards: You might give some NPCs—sorcerers, gadgeteers with many strange devices, and the like—a wild card ability that allows them to do interesting things like levitate, use telekinesis, construct objects of pure force, and so forth. You don't have to nail down these powers ahead of time. These rare NPCs can just do weird things. As long as you keep them reasonable most of the time, no one will bat an eye. (If every important foe has a force field, that will seem repetitious, dull, and unfair to the PCs.)

Chapter 9: Rules of the Game, page 188

Use GM Intrusions: Since a PC can produce all kinds of interesting, useful, and surprising effects thanks to cyphers, you can occasionally replicate this for an NPC by using GM intrusion to give him precisely the ability needed in the current situation. If the NPC has been poisoned, he pulls out a vial of antivenom. If a villain is cornered by the PCs, she activates a device on her belt that lets her phase down through the floor. If the foe is at the extreme edge of health, he injects himself with a temporary adrenaline boost that restores 15 points of health immediately.

NPCs AND DEATH

As explained in Chapter 9: Rules of the Game, NPCs have a health score rather than three stat Pools. When an NPC reaches 0 health, he is down. Whether that means dead, unconscious, or incapacitated depends on the circumstances as dictated by you and the players. Much of this can be based on logic. If the NPC is cut in half with a giant axe, he's probably dead. If he's mentally assaulted with a telepathic attack, he might be insane instead. If he's hit over the head with a club, well, that's your call.

It depends on the intentions of those who are fighting the NPC, too. PCs who want to knock out a foe rather than kill him can simply state that as their intention and describe their actions differently—using the flat of the blade, so to speak.

INTERACTIONS

Let's say the PCs want to learn more about a missing man, so they talk to his best friend. You and the players roleplay the conversation. The players are friendly and helpful and ask their questions with respect. Do you call for an Intellect roll (using the friend's level to determine the difficulty) to see if he will talk to them, or do you simply decide that he reacts to them well and gives them the information?

As another example, an old woman has watched over the entrance to an ancient ruin for years. She considers it a duty given to her by the gods and has never told anyone the secrets she knows. The PCs come along with some training in interactions, roll dice, and expect the woman to spill her guts. Does she tell them everything?

The answer to both questions is: it depends. In either situation, you're justified in ignoring the dice and mechanics and simply handling things through table conversation. That's what makes interaction encounters so interesting and so distinctive from, say, combat. You can't put aside the dice and act out the fight between the PCs and a giant, but you can roleplay a conversation. In such cases, you can portray the NPCs precisely as you want, in ways that seem fitting to their personalities, without worrying about die rolls. The best friend probably wants to help the PCs find his missing comrade. The old woman would never give her secrets to a band of smooth talkers that shows up on her doorstep one day. You can also ensure that the players get the information you want them to get—and don't get the information you don't want them to get.

On the other hand, sometimes using game mechanics is a better option. For example, a person who isn't particularly eloquent might want to play a character who's a smooth talker. You wouldn't require a player who's never held a sword in real life to prove that he's an adept combatant to win a fight in the game, so you should not force the player of a charming character to be, well, charming. The game mechanics can simulate those qualities.

And sometimes, you can use both approaches. You can let the conversation with the NPC play out around the table, and then call for rolls—not to determine whether the PCs succeed or fail at the interaction, but to get an idea of the degree of success. For example, if the characters have a good cover story for why the guards at the gate should let them pass, the roll might determine not whether the guards say yes (you can use logic for that) but whether the guards accompany the PCs beyond the gate. In a way, the die roll shapes an NPC's reaction. It's not an on/off switch but a general degree of the overall trust that the PCs earn.

GMs need to be fluid and flexible as they're running a game. Sometimes a strict mechanical approach is needed, and other times it's fine to just handwave the situation and keep the story moving. The important thing—particularly for newer GMs—isn't always knowing when to do which, but to remember that you have the freedom to experiment.

LANGUAGE

Careful readers will have noticed that there are no intricate rules for languages in the Cypher System, just a brief mention that you can become fluent in a new language rather than gain a skill. That's because for most people, language is more of a background or roleplaying feature than a mechanical one. You don't want to have to make a roll to speak, for example. Characters should begin the game knowing the language(s) that make the most sense for them.

Language is a special case, however, because some people won't want to deal with it. And that's fine. Some players and GMs will find it an interesting challenge to communicate with people or creatures who don't share a common language. Others will think it's an impediment to interaction with no real upside. You can handle the issue however you want.

NPC ALLIES

Because the players usually roll all the dice, NPCs who are not opponents raise unique issues in the Cypher System. If a character gains an NPC ally who accompanies the group, how are the ally's actions resolved?

Most of the time, the GM should decide what makes the most sense in the context of the situation and the NPC. If the characters climb up a steep slope and must make rolls to ascend, the NPC doesn't make a roll. Instead, the GM quickly considers whether he could climb it and goes from there. A fit, able ally should simply climb the slope. A feeble or overweight NPC will need assistance. In other words, the NPC doesn't face the challenge (that's what the PCs do)—he remains a part of the unfolding story. The old man the PCs must escort through dangerous mountains needs help climbing because that's part of the story of the adventure. His able-bodied son who also travels with the group does not need help because that wouldn't make much sense.

If the entire group is caught in a landslide later in that same adventure, the GM can do one of two things in regard to the NPCs. Either decide what happens to them as seems most logical or fitting (perhaps using GM intrusion, since what befalls the NPCs also affects the PCs), or have the players roll on behalf of the NPCs and treat them just like the player characters in every way possible.

Stagger means that if the creature strikes a foe, the target must make an immediate Might defense roll or lose its next turn.

CREATURES

Whenever possible, creatures should be handled like other NPCs. They don't follow the same rules as the player characters. If anything, they should have greater latitude in doing things that don't fit the normal mold. A many-armed beast should be able to attack multiple foes. A charging rhinolike animal ought to be able to move a considerable distance and attack as part of a single action.

Consider creature size very carefully. For those that are quick and hard to hit, increase the difficulty to attack them by one step. Large, strong creatures should be easier to hit, so decrease the difficulty to attack them by one step. However, you should freely give the stagger ability to anything twice as large as a human. This means that if the creature strikes a foe, the target must make an immediate Might defense roll or lose its next turn.

A creature's level is a general indicator of its toughness, combining aspects of power, defense, intelligence, speed, and more into one rating. In theory, a small creature with amazing powers or extremely deadly venom could be high level, and a huge beast that isn't very bright and isn't much of a fighter

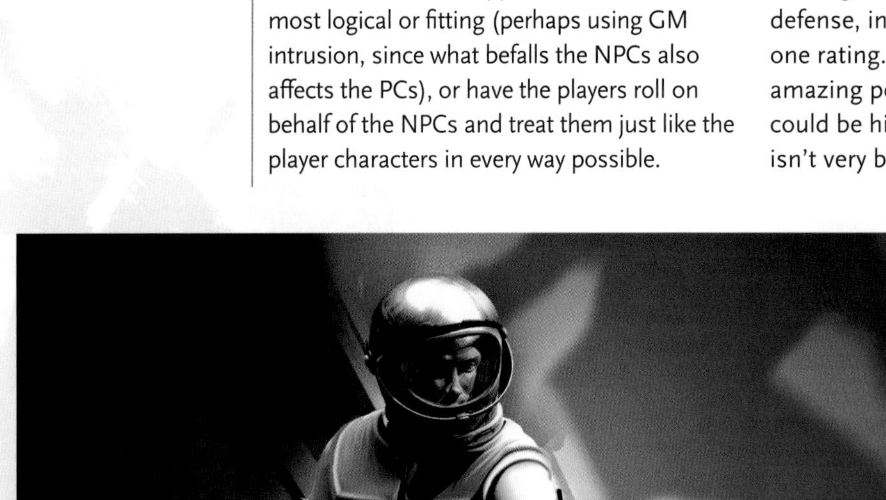

could be low level. But these examples go against type. Generally, smaller creatures have less health and are less terrifying in combat than larger ones.

The Cypher System has no system for building creatures. There is no rule that says a creature with a certain ability should be a given level, and there is no rule dictating how many abilities a creature of a given level should have. But keep the spirit of the system in mind. Lower-level creatures are less dangerous. A level 1 creature could be poisonous, but its venom should inflict a few points of damage at most. The venom of a level 6 creature, however, might knock a PC down a step on the damage track or put him into a coma if he fails a Might defense roll. A low-level creature might be able to fly, phase through objects, or teleport because these abilities make it more interesting but not necessarily more dangerous. The value of such abilities depends on the creature that uses them. In other words, a phasing rodent is not overly dangerous, but a phasing battle juggernaut is terrifying. Basic elements such as health, damage, and offensive or defensive powers (such as poison, paralysis, disintegration, immunity to attacks, and so on) need to be tied directly to level—higher-level creatures get better abilities and more of them.

TEACHING THE RULES

It's not really your job to teach the players the rules, yet it often falls upon the GM to do just that. Before beginning a game, encourage the players to read Chapter 3: How to Play the Cypher System to get an overview of the game. It won't take them long.

You'll probably also want to give them an overview of the setting you've created and the genre expectations that exist. Focus primarily on the kinds of characters a player can create and what they might do in the game. Once players understand who they are and what they'll do, the rest of the setting is just details they can discover as they go along.

The key to teaching someone the game is to start with the idea of die rolls and how they use the same mechanic no matter what a character tries to do. Then explain using Effort, which involves an introduction to the three stats. After that, a player is ready to start making a character. Taking a new player through the character-creation process gets him ready to play. Don't overload him with a lot of details beyond that. All of those can be picked up as needed in the course of play.

THE FIRST FEW SESSIONS

With any game, GMs should consider running it a little differently the first few times, and the Cypher System is no different. There are a few things a GM can expect with a table full of new players. First of all, they won't get the terminology and the jargon right—they'll use the terminology and jargon of the last game they played. And that's fine. But the GM should try to get it right because the players will follow her lead, and after a session or two, they'll start getting it right. If the GM always calls things by the wrong name, the players will, too. However, don't just spout jargon. Each time you use a new term for the first time, such as "damage track," "GM intrusion," or even "difficulty," explain what it means. Make sure everyone's on the same page, even with the basic stuff.

The players won't know what's easy and what's hard. Part of good Cypher System play is knowing when to use Effort and when to conserve, but beginning players will have no frame of reference. In this case, the best way to give them solid ground to stand on is to be fairly transparent. Tell them the target number for each task before they attempt an action. Guide them through the process. Remind them that they can use Effort if need be, although they probably won't forget. On the contrary, beginning players tend to use Effort on every roll. You can almost count on it. This means you can expect beginning characters to do very well in whatever they set out to do, but they'll have to rest more often because they'll deplete their stat Pools more quickly.

When referring to distance, feel free to use the terms "close" and "immediate" interchangeably. Use whatever sounds best in context. The adept might be "close" to the warrior, within "close range," or within "immediate distance."

Chapter 3: How to Play the Cypher System, page 7

RUNNING CYPHER SYSTEM COMBATS

Cypher System combats should be about something. There should be something interesting at stake. "Trying not to die" is an interesting stake, but it's not the only one. Combat can be fun and hopefully exciting in its own right, but it's not necessarily the focus. In other words, fighting through a long combat isn't the point, and finding a way to win a combat quickly through creative thought isn't cheating. In fact, it should be encouraged. Defeating the "big boss monster" easily should not be a letdown; it should be the result of smart, creative play. And Cypher System adventures shouldn't always have a climax involving a "big boss monster," anyway. The exciting end to the story could involve surviving a massive landslide, finding a way to shut down a dangerous machine, or convincing a tyrannical warlord to let the hostages go.

Encourage the players to describe their actions, not the mechanics involved. The game is more fun if a player says things like, "I leap up on the table and swing my sword down on the creature," instead of "I use my jump skill to get up on the table and get a one-step advantage on my attack roll."

The Cypher System is about discovery. Can you have discovery through combat?

Sure. Say the PCs are exploring an ancient complex and encounter a strange life form. The creature attacks, but during the fight, it telepathically says "Curious" and "Creature unknown" and "Protect the sanctum." It's telepathically talking to someone else, but the PCs "overhear." Although the combat is fairly standard, the PCs have discovered a new creature, and they know it's something that's never encountered a human before. There are more of them, somewhere, and there's some kind of sanctum. It's not just a fight. The PCs have learned something.

In a more standard setup, the combat is the obstacle that the PCs must overcome to reach the discovery, which again reinforces the idea that there is no right or wrong way to overcome the obstacle. Sneak past the foes or convince them to let the PCs pass—both are entirely valid.

Mechanically, combat in the Cypher System doesn't play out as it does in many games where damage whittles down a character's hit points or health score. This kind of slow attrition is less likely to happen in the Cypher System because the PCs will try to avoid getting hit. For example, many players will spend points from their Speed Pool to add Effort to their defense rolls to ensure that they don't get hit (and thus don't lose points from their Might Pool). Characters also have numerous abilities to add to their Speed defense rolls or reduce the difficulty of a Speed defense task. Last, and perhaps most significant, the most frequent use of experience points for rerolls will probably be defensive in nature. Players just don't like their characters to get hit.

There are two important aspects to this. The first is that it's the players' choice. They're in control of which points they lose and how many, so it feels different, even though the effect is largely the same—a slow loss of points over time. The second aspect is that, narratively, you don't have to explain and describe lots of minor wounds and scratches that eventually amount to something. In Cypher System combats, when PCs are struck, it's likely significant. Plus, so many creatures and foes have effects that paralyze, infect, poison, stun, and so on that the damage is not necessarily the interesting or significant part. That's why there are creatures whose attacks can move a PC down the damage track a step or two. It's not so much about the points of damage but the consequences of being hit at all.

CRAFTING STORIES

I keep saying over and over that the Cypher System is all about story—narrative. Your biggest job as the GM is to provide the impetus for stories in the game. The stories themselves arise out of gameplay, but they are started and guided by you. You provide the seed of the story and present the events as they unfold because of what the PCs and NPCs do.

Crafting a good story is a topic that could fill a book of this size. I highly recommend that interested GMs read books or articles aimed at fiction writers (many of which are available on the Internet) that provide advice on plot. For that matter, similar sources about characterization can help in the creation of NPCs, as well.

For now, remember these key concepts:

- Learn what motivates the players at your table. Exploration? Combat? Puzzle-solving? Interacting with NPCs? Cater to these desires.
- Learn what motivates the PCs that the players run. What are the characters' goals? What do they seek? Wealth? Curiosity? Power? Protecting others? Use these things to start your stories.
- Create stories that involve the PCs as directly as possible. If something bad is affecting people, have it affect the PCs or their loved ones, too. Rather than enticing them to strive to save a random farmer, get them to save a character's brother or best friend.
- Remember that the players are your co-storytellers, and that the PCs are the main characters of the story, so their decisions should have direct impact on what happens.
- Weave multiple stories together. Have the PCs learn about the beginning of one story while they're still embroiled in another.
- Vary your stories. Follow a combat-heavy exploration of an ancient ruin with an intrigue-filled adventure in a large city that involves a lot of interaction. Create one story that is a long quest but then follow it up with another that wraps up in a single game session.
- Vary the encounters within a story. Even in the middle of a series of battles, there's always room for exploration or interaction (and it breaks things up).
- Not every story needs to be about saving the world. Sometimes the smaller stories about helping one person can be the most interesting.
- Twists and unexpected events are wonderful and should be used often, but sometimes the biggest twist is to have things go exactly the way the players think they will.
- Don't get bogged down justifying, rationalizing, or explaining every detail. The players aren't supposed to understand everything.
- Stories that involve a lot of events the PCs are unaware of will end up making little sense to the players, and should probably be avoided.
- Base your stories on real human emotion. NPC villains can be driven by greed or power, but also by love, longing, curiosity, or even misguided altruism. Don't make your players just interact with the events—make them react to the emotions behind the events. Villains should inspire actual hate and anger. The loss of a valued ally should inspire actual sadness and loss.
- Occasionally, create stories that are sequels to your previous stories. The decisions that the players made in the past affect things in the present. Villains return for another try at reaching their goal, or perhaps just for revenge.

PACING

The key to running a great game as opposed to an adequate one is often the simple matter of pacing. Well, pacing is simple to describe, but it's not so simple to understand or implement. It comes with practice and a sort of developed intuition.

Pacing can mean many things. Let's briefly break them down.

I've seen bad pacing ruin more games than probably anything else. Keep things moving. Keep them interesting.

PACING WITHIN AN ENCOUNTER

Keep things moving. Don't let the action get bogged down by indecisive players, arguments about the rules, or irrelevant minutiae. Don't let the middle of an encounter get sidetracked by something that reminds a player (or worse, you) of a gaming story, a movie, or a funny thing on the Internet. There's time for all of that later, probably after the game session is over.

Don't let the end of the encounter drag out. When it's clear how things are going to turn out, and people might start to get bored, wrap it up. If the PCs were fighting two dozen giant rats and only three are left, there's nothing wrong with saying that those last three run away or that the PCs handily dispatch them. Wrap things up and move along.

PACING WITHIN A GAME SESSION

Have many different encounters in a session—some long, some short, some complex, some straightforward. One of the trickiest aspects of game session pacing is deciding what to play out and what to skip. For example, the PCs want to buy new gear with the money they were paid for a job. You could describe the town's market and roleplay each interaction with various merchants. You could even call for occasional rolls to see if the characters get good deals or not. Alternatively, you could say, "Okay, you guys buy whatever you want," and then move on. There are good cases to be made for both approaches, depending on the context. Maybe one of the PCs contracted a disease on the last mission and doesn't realize it until he is interacting with people in the market. Maybe a pickpocket in the mall attempts to steal from the PCs, or they notice a thief stealing from a store. Maybe the players like interacting with NPCs and enjoy your portrayal of minor characters. All of these are good reasons to play out a shopping encounter. But if there's no compelling reason, just advance through it.

Sometimes, you should do this even if one player wants to play out every moment of his character's life and describe everything in excruciating detail. Although you want everyone to be happy, you're in charge of pacing. If you must err, make the players struggle to keep up, rather than letting them be bored and wonder when you're going to get on with it. Thus, if there's no compelling reason against it, don't hesitate to advance time, even in large chunks. If the PCs finish a big scenario and some downtime makes sense, there's nothing wrong with announcing, "So, three weeks later, you hear that . . ." and starting the next storyline (as long as the players are content with it). Books and movies do this kind of thing all the time. Skip the boring bits.

In addition, feel free to intrude on player discussions for the purpose of moving things along. Sometimes players spin their wheels or plan and plan their next move, never accomplishing anything. You can intrude by throwing an encounter or a surprise their way ("A message arrives from the priests at the clave"), or you can simply say, "Let's move things along, guys."

Keep a clock handy so you can see how much time is left in the session. Never lose track of time. You want to end a session at a good point—a place where everyone can catch their breath, at a good cliffhanger, or as everything in a story wraps up so you can start anew next time. These are all fine stopping points, but you want to control which one you use. Next session, you'll have to start things up again, recap past events, and get everyone back into the swing of things.

Try to ensure that at the end of any session, the players can look back on what they did and feel like they accomplished something.

PACING WITHIN A STORY

This aspect of pacing goes back to researching how fiction writers handle story creation, and it's a huge subject, but consider the standard three-act structure as a good starting point. In act one, the problem is introduced. In act two, things get worse (or a new complication is introduced). In act three, things are resolved. There are many other ways to do it, but remember that the action needs to ebb and flow. You need downtime between the moments of action, horror, or high drama.

PACING WITHIN A CAMPAIGN

Mix short scenarios in with longer ones. Weave the plotlines together so that as one story ends, the PCs still have things to do. But don't be afraid of downtime. Let the characters have a week, a month, or longer here or there to live their normal lives before throwing them once again into the heart of danger. If a campaign takes a year of play time in the real world, you don't want it to take place in only three weeks of game time. That never feels right.

DESCRIPTION

Earlier, I recommended using description that was both precise and concise. Precision comes from avoiding relative terms like "big" or "small" or emotional words like "terrifying" because these words mean different things to different people. This

doesn't mean you have to specify the exact height of every structure the PCs find. But rather than describing a building as "a tall tower," consider saying "a tower at least five times the height of the trees around it."

Being concise is important, too. Go on too long with descriptions, and the players' minds will drift. Sometimes, what works best are short, declarative, evocative descriptions with pauses in between for player comments or questions.

DESCRIBING THE ACTION

Great roleplaying game sessions often involve immersion. Immersion comes from a sense of being truly caught up in the action and the fictional world. Just as when you read a great book or watch a well-made movie, playing an RPG can get you caught up in your own imagination. And best of all, you're sharing your imaginative escape with everyone else at the table. For immersion to work, you have to give great descriptions.

Cypher System combat, for example, is very simple and open-ended rather than precise, giving you lots of room to describe how characters move, how they attack, and how they avoid attacks. A successful Speed defense roll might mean dodging, blocking with a weapon, or ducking behind a pillar. A character who is struck in combat for 3 points of damage might have dodged the weapon attack but fallen backward onto a jagged and ruined control console.

The players should describe their actions, too. Encourage them to be creative in what they do and how they perform a task, whether it involves the way they attack, what they do to give themselves the best chance to make a difficult leap over a pit, or how they slip into a noble's study to steal the map they need.

Don't take any of this as a requirement. Long descriptions can be tedious as easily as they can be interesting. Sometimes the best way to serve the pacing of a combat encounter is to state whether an attack hit and how much damage is dealt and keep things moving. Vivid description is great, but it's not a valid excuse for you or a player to drag things out and destroy the pacing.

Combat, page 8

DESCRIBING THE WORLD

With so many different choices in the Cypher System, "the world" could mean a lot of different things. Here are a few thoughts about genres.

Fantasy, page 236

Fantasy: A fantasy setting can be a weird place, and describing it can be difficult. It's all right to fall back on clichés—castles, knights, dragons, and so forth. Keep in mind, however, that these concepts are so well worn that if you use them, either you need to be okay with the "generic" image that pops into the players' heads, or you need to be very specific about what makes this dragon different. (And if you have the time and inclination, by all means make your dragon or your knight different—the players will enjoy it and remember it.)

Horror, page 258

Don't hesitate to make your fantasy world grand and striking. If magic is prevalent in the world, have the Emperor's palace made of nothing but foes petrified by his pet basilisk. Have the cavalry mounted on six-winged birds rather than horses. Put the sorcerer's home on the other side of a magical portal found only in a waterfall at midnight.

When possible, stress the most interesting aspect of your description. For example, don't bother telling the PCs about the normal buildings in the city if the central tower is a hundred feet tall and topped with a huge red crystal.

Modern, page 244

Superheroes, page 266

Modern: If the setting is the modern world, use specific references when you can. The bad guys aren't in a car—they're in a Ford Explorer. The agency boss is wearing a blue Armani suit and offers you a glass of 18-year-old Glenfiddich.

On the other hand, since it's the real world, don't bother with description that's not needed. You don't need to detail every building the characters drive by, obviously—just the one they're going to. The rest is simply "downtown."

Science fiction, page 250

Science Fiction: As with fantasy, use clichés and tropes if they're handy. Refer to scenes from television and movies that would be familiar to the players.

Be wary of shorthand description and inappropriate comparisons. If the PCs see an alien vehicle flying through the air toward them and you describe it as "sort of like a flying car," they're going to picture a flying 21st-century sedan with tires, a steering wheel, and bumpers, and that's probably not the image you want in their heads. Instead, try to give them the gist of the vehicle. Saying something like "A large, dark vehicle—sharply angled and full of strange protrusions from all directions—suddenly rumbles toward you through the sky, blocking out the sun" puts a more evocative and weird image in the players' minds. It's better to be vague than incorrect or, worse, jarringly inappropriate.

If you must, use 21st-century terms or comparisons to describe things, but introduce them sparingly because they can break the mood very easily.

Horror: Description is vital in horror—both in what you say and in what you don't. Although precision is a good thing, pedantic, exhaustive detail is not. Even if that's what is needed to fully describe the monster or phenomenon, don't do it. Leave the players with an impression rather than an exact description. "A creature that looks like three black beetles, each the size of a mastiff, with too many legs and eyes" isn't a full description, but it's an impression. It gives the players something to picture, even if it's not precisely what you're picturing. It's weird and evocative, and that's important.

Superheroes: While the setting is ostensibly the modern world, everything in superhero games is usually bigger, bolder, and brighter. Strong characters are rippling with muscles. Important characters are usually good-looking—or hideously ugly. When a supervillain creates a device that will destroy a city, the machine *looks* dangerous. Things in this setting are rarely vague or subtle.

PREPARING FOR THE GAME SESSION

The Cypher System doesn't require you to spend hours carefully designing stats for NPCs (unless you want to). There aren't a lot of rules to memorize. It's not worth writing out elaborate descriptions of each encounter because if you let things proceed organically, many planned encounters might not be used. The rules of the Cypher System allow you to come up with a lot of the details as you go along, since you don't have to reference loads of books and stats during the game session.

To prepare for a session, you need to create only three things: a list of names, a brief outline, and a list of ideas.

1. A list of names appropriate to the setting

No matter how much you prepare, you'll end up creating some NPCs on the fly, so have a list of names to use when this happens. Leave room to write a quick note next to each name you use in case that NPC shows up in the game again.

2. A brief outline

The outline is an idea of where you think the story could go. Of course, the key word is *think*. You can't know for certain—the actions of the PCs will take things in unexpected directions. In truth, "outline" is probably not the right word. Think in terms of places the PCs might go, people or creatures they might interact with, and events that might occur. For example, let's say that in a fantasy campaign, the PCs enter a small village. You plan to start the session by having them hear about a local man named Barlis who disappeared mysteriously. Your notes might say:

- Barlis disappeared outside the flour mill where he worked. North of town.
- Barlis lived in a small, run-down house. Partner: Nillen—distraught and prone to drink.
- Flour mill: About a dozen workers. Boss: Vorriln. Witness: Vadda saw Barlis disappear right in front of her. Doesn't want to talk about it because she's heard about some kind of faerie curse that she thinks is involved (level 4 to get her to talk). Knows Barlis recently found a strange item—looked like a large silver coin with a horned skull on it.
- Pickpocket (level 3) attempts to steal from one PC while they're in town.
- Local priest: Rorich. Has seen small coins like the one Vadda describes, and says that they are symbols of a demonic cult. Sends PCs to a hermit that lives west of the village who knows more about the cult.

And so on.

Obviously, that's just the beginning, but you've covered a lot of the contingencies, assuming the PCs investigate Barlis's disappearance at all. Some of that material might not get used. The PCs might not go to his house—only to the mill and then to the priest. Maybe they won't go to the priest at all, and you'll need to have someone else direct them to the hermit. Or maybe the PCs will come up with a wholly unexpected path of investigation.

3. A list of ideas

Just like with the list of names, jot down a bunch of random ideas. These are things you can throw into the game at a moment's notice. They might be flavor, cool visuals, or important side plots. For example, in a horror game, your list might include:

- A music box from the 1800s with ornate but slightly macabre decoration, currently broken
- Man with one side of his face horribly burned long ago
- Graffiti painted on the side of a building: "I saw it. And worse, it saw me."
- Dogs constantly barking in the distance, and then silence
- A trail of blood that leads to a door that won't open

These are all ideas that you can sprinkle into the game when appropriate. You haven't tied them to a specific encounter, so you can insert them whenever you want. You might not use them all in the same adventure—they're just ideas.

Remember that anything you prepare that doesn't get used can always be recycled later. Never force the players into a situation just because you planned it out and are really fond of what you came up with. Save that cool idea and use it later.

HANDLING PLAYERS

Part of being a GM is "handling" players. This means a lot of things. For example, it's partially your job to make sure that everyone has a good time. You need to ensure that all the players get to do the kinds of things they like to do in games, and that no one is left out. If one player really likes combat and another enjoys NPC interaction, provide some of both. Before you can do that, you need to find out what the players want in the first place, so talk to them and learn their expectations.

Another big part of handling players is coping with disruptive players. Disruptive players can be the death of a game. They can hog all the attention, tell other players what to do, or challenge your rulings at every turn. A lot of GMs are tempted to deal with such players during the game by punishing them or giving them negative feedback. For example, they have the character get attacked more often, lose experience points, or suffer similar consequences. Resist this temptation. Instead, speak with the player person to person (not GM to player) outside of the game and explain that his behavior is causing problems. Be clear, direct, and firm, but also be friendly.

The bottom line, however, is don't play games with jerks. One disruptive, rude, or offensive player can ruin the whole group's fun.

A different problem player is one who just doesn't get the narrative focus of the Cypher System. These kinds of players tend to see all games as competitive enterprises, and they might try to "win" by exploiting what they see as holes in the rules to create and play an unbeatable character. Although part of many people's RPG experience is the fun of playing a powerful character, it shouldn't be the ultimate goal in the Cypher System because such a player will get frustrated and bored.

For example, a player might try to use the Energy Protection ability to protect against kinetic energy and then claim that he is immune to all attacks. He'll see this as a hole that he was smart enough to exploit, and he'll hold up the rules and say, "Show me where I'm wrong!"

Energy Protection, page 33

When a player does that, point him here: "You're wrong."

He's wrong because the Cypher System isn't a board game where the rules are like a puzzle to be solved or beaten. The rules exist to facilitate the story and portray the world. If there's a "hole" in the rules or a rule that would produce an illogical or unenjoyable result if followed to the letter, change it, redefine it, or just overrule it. It's that easy.

On the other hand, some players absolutely will get it. They'll understand that it's the spirit of the rules, not the letter, that's important. They'll get that the story being told is key. Rather than poring over the description of a power and trying to twist the words to an unintended meaning, they'll use their intelligence and creativity to figure out the best way to use the power to portray a character who fits the setting and is fun to play.

People who try to exploit the rules don't understand the Cypher System, but people who exploit the situations do. If a player is smart and creative enough to turn the tables on his foes in an unexpected way by using what's around him, allow it (if it makes sense). If the PCs find a pool of caustic fluid and lure their foes into it rather than fighting them in a straightforward manner, that's not cheating—that's awesome.

Be certain you don't accidentally penalize players for not doing the obvious or straightforward thing. Be generous with people who take nonstandard actions or who do something realistic (such as using their action to take stock of the situation rather than attack—grant them a step bonus). Don't make "attack" always the right choice. It's a creative game, so allow the players to be creative.

MATURE THEMES

Sometimes, it's appropriate to involve mature themes in Cypher System games. Sex, extreme violence, and other topics can certainly fit into the world. But each group must decide for themselves if such themes fit into their game. You should also prepare your stories with your specific players in mind. If one or more are very young or have issues with certain topics, avoid things that would be inappropriate. Also be aware that some topics, like overt sexuality, rape, and graphic violence might disturb players even when you aren't expecting it. It's always best to know for certain before allowing these topics into your game.

Think of it like the movie rating system. If you can tell the story that you want to tell

in a G or PG (or even PG-13) way, you're likely fine. If events unfold that will give your game an R rating or higher, it's best to talk with your players ahead of time. It's not a matter of good or bad, but a matter of appropriateness for the "audience" and giving people a heads-up ahead of time—just like movie ratings.

DESIGNING ENCOUNTERS

Encounters are to a game session what scenes are to a movie or a book. They're a way to break up the session, and the adventure at large, into smaller, more manageable chunks.

Sometimes it's more difficult to know where one encounter ends and another begins. For that reason, "encounter" is not always a useful or meaningful game term. It's only useful for you when you think about the scenes of your adventure. When the PCs talk to the temple priests, that's one encounter. After they do so, hopefully getting the information they need, they head off into the wilderness, where they have to cross a deep chasm—another encounter. When a dragon appears and attacks, that's another encounter, and so on.

Thus, not everything that happens is an encounter. Heading off into the wilderness, for example, probably involved gathering supplies, deciding on a route, and so on, but it isn't really an encounter. An encounter is when you, the GM, provide a lot of detail. You and the players interact a lot in an encounter. You might decide to subdivide everyone's actions into rounds to help keep track of who's doing what, when.

COMPLEX ENCOUNTERS

Encounters aren't just about combat. As mentioned above, talking to NPCs is an encounter. Dealing with a physical obstacle is an encounter. Figuring out how to use a complex machine is an encounter. The best encounters—the really memorable ones, in fact—involve multiple things happening at once. A fight on a boat racing down the rapids, for example, is an interesting encounter. An encounter where a couple of PCs must disable a bomb before it blows up the space station while the others fend off attacking star troopers is interesting too.

Sometimes an encounter can be intentionally designed with that goal. At least occasionally, you should take an idea you have for an encounter and then add something else that will make it even more interesting, exciting, or challenging. The possibilities are endless. Perhaps gravity functions differently than expected. A weird fungus gives off spores that alter perception. The encounter takes place inside a sentient machine that must be reasoned with and appeased while everything else is going on. An interdimensional effect makes all metal in the encounter temporarily cease to exist. And that's just for starters. Make things crazy and fun. Design encounters that are like nothing the players have ever experienced.

Sometimes, the term "adventure" gets just as messy as "encounter." Deciding where one adventure begins and another ends can be—and perhaps should be—difficult. "Adventure" is a useful term for published products, but for your own use, you might want to toss the concept out and just let one story or event flow into another naturally.

Sometimes encounters with multiple levels of action or weird complications arise out of the game itself. The PCs have to leap onto a moving platform to get down into the giant machine's interior conduit system, which is interesting, but the robots that they ran from earlier suddenly show up. You didn't plan for that ahead of time; it just happened because that's the way things went. And that's great.

GM intrusion, page 193

Finally, GM intrusions can bring about these kinds of encounters on the fly. The PCs have to repair a huge device at the heart of an ancient complex that is venting poisonous gas before they are all overcome. With a GM intrusion that occurs to you at the last moment, you let them know that the gas also weakens the structural integrity of metal, and the supports under the floor the PCs are standing on are buckling and will collapse at any moment.

BALANCING ENCOUNTERS

In the Cypher System, there is no concept of a "balanced encounter." There is no system for matching creatures of a particular level or tasks of a particular difficulty to characters of a particular tier. To some people, that might seem like a bad thing. But as I've written earlier, matching character builds to exacting challenges is not part of this game. It's about story. So whatever you want to happen next in the story is a fine encounter as long as it's fun. You're not denying the characters XP if you make things too easy or too difficult, because that's not how XP are earned. If things are too difficult for the PCs, they'll have to flee, come up with a new strategy, or try something else entirely. The only thing you have to do to maintain "balance" is set difficulty within that encounter accurately and consistently.

In a game like the Cypher System, if everyone's having fun, the game is balanced. Two things will unbalance the game in this context.

- One or more PCs are far more interesting than the others. Note that I said "more interesting," not "more powerful." If my character can do all kinds of cool things but can't destroy robots as efficiently as yours does, I still might have a whole lot of fun.
- The challenges the PCs face are routinely too easy or too difficult.

The first issue should be handled by the character creation rules. If there's a problem, it might be that poor choices were made or a player isn't taking full advantage of her options. If someone really doesn't enjoy playing her character, allow her to alter the PC or—perhaps better—create a new one.

The second issue is trickier. As previously stated, there is no formula that states that N number of level X NPCs are a good match for tier Y characters. However, when the game has four or five beginning characters, the following guidelines are generally true.

- Level 1 opponents will be nothing but a nuisance, even in sizable numbers (twelve to sixteen).
- Level 2 opponents will not be a challenge unless in numbers of twelve or more.
- Level 3 opponents will be an interesting challenge in numbers of four to eight.
- Level 4 opponents will be an interesting challenge in numbers of two or three.
- A single level 5 opponent might be an interesting challenge.
- A single level 6 opponent will be a serious challenge.
- A single level 7 or 8 opponent will likely win in a fight.
- A single level 9 or 10 opponent will win in a fight without breaking a sweat.

But let me caution you, and I can't stress this enough: it depends on the situation at hand. If the PCs are already worn down from prior encounters, or if they have the right cyphers, any of the expectations listed above can change. That's why there is no system for balancing encounters. Just keep in mind that beginning characters are pretty hardy and probably have some interesting resources, so you aren't likely to wipe out the group by accident. Character death is unlikely unless the PCs have already been through a number of other encounters and are worn down.

RESOLVING ENCOUNTERS

Don't plan for how an encounter will end. Let the game play determine that. This ensures that players have the proper level of input. You decide, for example, that if the PCs go into the tower, a gang of mutants inside will attack. However, you can't decide how that encounter will end. Maybe the PCs will be victorious. Maybe they won't. Maybe they'll flee, or maybe they'll bargain for their lives.

If you try to decide such things ahead of time, that's called railroading the game, and it puts the players in the role of observers rather than actors. Even if you try to plan out the results of an encounter ahead of time but then let the game play dictate them, you still might end up planning for a lot of outcomes that don't happen. In other words, if you base a whole plotline on the PCs fleeing the tower to get away from the mutants, but instead they manage to drive the mutants out instead, all your plans are wasted.

Plan for various possible outcomes, but don't predetermine them. Think of your story as having many possible plotlines, not just one.

CHALLENGING CHARACTERS

If the game has a balance problem, it's more likely due to players finding things too easy rather than too hard. If things are too hard, they should run away and find something else to do (or you should lighten up a bit). But if the characters in the group need a greater challenge, try one or more of the following options.

Damage Track: Sometimes a few points of damage aren't enough to scare a player. But a weapon or effect that immediately moves him one step down the damage track will terrify him. No matter how big a character's stat Pools are, no matter how much Armor he has, there are only three such steps to death.

Ongoing Damage: Poisons that inflict even a small amount of damage (1 or 2 points) every round until an antidote is found can be extremely deadly. Or consider this: one of the reasons that napalm is so terrible is that it clings to surfaces, including flesh. Imagine a weapon or effect that inflicts 5 points of fire damage every round and persists for eight rounds unless the characters can figure out a way to douse it.

Effects Other Than Damage: Attacks can blind, stun, grapple, paralyze, infect, hobble, or otherwise hinder a character without dealing any points of damage at all.

Effects That Harm Equipment: A PC's gear is often the source of his abilities. Destroying or nullifying cyphers or artifacts damages him just as surely as breaking his leg would—it limits a player's options, which really hurts.

Enemies Working in Concert: Although a group effectively acting as one is a special ability of some creatures, you could apply it to any creature you like. As a general rule, for every four creatures working together, treat them as one creature with a level equal to the highest of them plus 1, dealing a minimum of 2 additional points of damage. So a level 4 bandit who has three level 3 allies could team up and attack one foe as a level 5 NPC. That means their attack deals more damage and is harder to defend against. It also means less die rolling, so the combat moves along faster.

Beef up the Foes: You're in charge of the NPC stats. If they need more Armor, more health, or higher levels to be a challenge, simply make it so. It's easy and straightforward to give an NPC a "boost package" of four things:

- +10 health
- +1 to Armor
- 3 additional points of damage
- Attacks and defends as one level higher

Damage track, page 202

That should do the trick, but if necessary, give the boost package to the same NPC again.

Beef up the Obstacles: Include more exotic materials in doors and other barriers, which increase their level. Make physical challenges more difficult—the surfaces that need to be climbed are slippery, the waters that need to be swum are roiling, and other actions are hampered by strong winds. Don't beef up obstacles in this way too often, but remember that circumstances

Sometimes players will be unwilling to spend XP on anything other than character benefits, which in turn lead to advancing to new tiers. The truth is, spending XP on immediate or short-term gains very likely provides as much overall benefit. In other words, in the big picture, four crucial rerolls are probably about the same as acquiring a new skill. It will take some players a while to come to that conclusion, however.

Inability, page 63

such as weather are your tools for adjusting the difficulty of any action.

HIGHER-TIER CHARACTERS

Although characters start out quite capable, by the time they reach the fifth or sixth tier, they will be truly legendary. Both you and the players might find reaching the upper tiers more rewarding and satisfying if the journey unfolds more gradually, so you can slow down this progress if desired. To do this, starting at third or fourth tier, you can specify how the players can spend the experience points they earn. Requiring that some XP (as much as half) must be spent on immediate, short-term, or long-term advantages—rather than on character advancement—will slow down the progression through the upper tiers. But it won't take anything away from the play experience because spending XP on those advantages is fun and rewarding, too.

CHARACTER DEATH

Challenging characters is important. If there is no threat of failure—or at least the perceived threat of failure—it's hard for players to feel compelled by the story. Very often, the ultimate failure a PC might face is death. An adventurer's life is a dangerous one. But death is serious because it means the player can no longer play his character.

If a character dies, the easiest and most straightforward response is to have the player create a new character. Ideally, he will make a beginning character (which is the easiest to create), but if the other characters are third tier or higher, it will be more satisfying to let the player create his new character at an advanced tier.

However, keep in mind that a lower-tier character can operate effectively in the company of higher-tier characters. The differences are not so striking. If a player brings a new beginning character into a group of advanced characters, be particularly generous with XP to help the new character catch up to the others a bit.

Regardless, arrange the circumstances of the story so that you can bring in the new character in a logical fashion and as quickly as possible.

Not Quite Dead: There is an alternative for a player who really, really wants to keep playing the same character. Allow the PC to teeter on the brink of death but survive, saved by his companions or by sheer luck. He might recover but have serious injuries that result in a weakness, an inability, or some other drawback. The point is not to penalize the PC (although barely escaping death should have some repercussions) but to change the character in a memorable way.

AN EXAMPLE OF PLAY

Sometimes the best way to understand a game is to see it played. This section provides the next best thing: a script depicting a group playing through a Cypher System encounter in a science fiction space opera setting.

GAME MASTER: Just as the scanners indicated, you see the structure near the river. You note that its smooth walls are 40 feet high and faceted, almost like crystal. There's a small door on the side facing the river.

STEVE (playing a second-tier explorer named Catissan): Does it look like something a human might build?

GM: It's tough to know that without investigating further, but it does occur to you that the door seems designed for creatures both taller and narrower than you.

SASHA (playing a second-tier warrior named Viddo): This is where the Muggariks we're after went, then. They were tall and thin.

GM: Perhaps.

TONY (playing a second-tier adept named Irom): I walk up to the building.

SASHA: I cover him with my blaster rifle.

STEVE: I'm going to check around the door—search for anything strange or dangerous.

GM: Okay, Steve. That's going to be an Intellect task.

STEVE: I'm going to use a level of Effort. I have an Intellect Edge of 1, so it will cost me 2 points from my Pool.

The GM knows there's nothing to find at the doorway, but she muses for half a second as if pretending to figure out a target number.

GM: Roll.

STEVE: Rolled a 7.

GM: You don't find anything out of the ordinary. However, tracks on the ground indicate that a number of creatures go through this doorway on a regular basis, and their footprints are longer and narrower than a human's.

This bit of information is a "gimme." The characters had already figured out that this was made by the alien Muggariks.

SASHA: The Muggariks. We're at the right place.

TONY: I take out my light blaster and go inside.

STEVE (to Tony): Steady, there. We should go in as a team. (To GM) I go, too.

SASHA: I go in, too. They'll need me.

TONY: I've got my Ward to protect me. Don't forget, I've got cool psychic powers.

STEVE: Still, I'm going to take the lead.

GM: Okay.

SASHA: I'm following close, but keeping to the shadows and keeping quiet.

The GM knows that Sasha's Tough warrior is flavored with stealth, so her tactics are no surprise.

GM: The door opens, and it's quiet and dimly lit inside. The ceilings are high, and there's weird art on the walls that just looks like colored blobs to you.

STEVE: No guards? No alarm?

GM: Not that you perceive.

SASHA: I keep my eyes peeled.

TONY: I walk in farther and call out in my most charming voice, "Hey, fellas, it's us, the guys whose hyperdrive crystals you stole. We're just here to talk!"

SASHA: That never works.

STEVE: No, I think it's prudent. Maybe we can talk this through. We still don't know why they stole them.

GM: Well, there's no response to your entreaty. Eventually, you explore the structure's interiors and see what might be some sleeping chambers, a common area, and some storage, but no one's here.

TONY: And no sign of the crystals?

GM: Nope.

SASHA: Have we explored the whole place?

GM: There's one door near the back you haven't opened. It seems to be sealed.

STEVE: That must be it. I'll try to force it open.

GM: That's a Might roll.

STEVE: I roll a 13.

GM: It doesn't budge.

SASHA: Damn.

TONY: Is there a mechanical seal? Something I can tap into with my Machine Interface ability?

Tony's adept has tech flavoring. The GM calls his type a "psi-tech."

GM: Yes.

SASHA: Before he starts that process, I'm going to spend 3 Intellect points for an Insight.

The GM thinks for a moment.

GM: Okay. You know from having read about the Muggariks that their race has a powerful sense of claustrophobia. They hate feeling closed in or trapped, and can't stand locked doors.

STEVE: That explains the front door, but what's with this one?

TONY: Maybe we're not dealing with Muggariks after all.

SASHA: Back at the spaceport, we heard that guy talking about alien mind-control spiders or something.

TONY: That was quite a while ago, though. I don't know if that's involved.

STEVE: Still, if we see a Muggarik, let's not necessarily shoot to kill or anything. Maybe they're being controlled and aren't themselves.

GM (to TONY): Going to try to open the door?

TONY: Yes. I'm trained and Machine Interface reduces the task by another level. I won't bother with Effort at this point. I roll a 7.

GM: Good enough. You realize that it was kind of a jury-rigged seal. This door was never meant to be locked.

SASHA: Nice work. What's inside?

GM: It's dark, but you hear something moving around, out of sight.

TONY: "Hello?"

STEVE: He's not actually trained in social interaction—he just thinks he is. Any chance I can use my Good Advice ability from my Leads focus to help him if we start a dialogue? My Intellect Edge means that it doesn't actually cost me anything.

GM: Sure thing. But so far, Irom doesn't have anyone to talk to.

SASHA: I'll sneak ahead and see if I can figure out what's making the noise.

GM: Farther in, you see a tall, angular figure in a torn shipsuit. It has smooth reddish skin, and its back is to you.

TONY: That's a Muggarik!

STEVE: Don't shoot it, Sasha—remember what we said.

SASHA: I know. "Hey, you," I say.

GM: The alien figure turns around. In the dim light from the open doorway, you see that there's something covering its face—something alive with a number of squirming legs.

SASHA: I was right! Mind-control spiders!

STEVE: Let's try not to hurt the guy, just the thing on his face.

TONY: When did we start to care about the Muggariks so much? They stole our hyperdrive crystals.

STEVE: They were probably mind-controlled then, too.

GM: I need initiative rolls.

The Muggarik is a level 4 NPC. That means the target number to beat it in initiative (and just about anything else) is 12. It also means the Muggarik has 12 health and if it hits in combat, it will do 4 points of damage. The thing on its face is level 4 as well, but level 5 for Speed defense because it is so small.

STEVE: I got a 12.

TONY: 4.

SASHA: 8.

GM: Okay, Catissan goes first, but Irom and Viddo don't act until after the Muggarik.

STEVE: I run up and try to yank that thing off his face.

GM: It's not a big room, so it's just an immediate distance. You need to make an attack roll.

STEVE: Right. I'll use two levels of Effort. That will cost me 4 points, because I have a Might Edge of 1. I roll a 20!

GM: That not only hits, but you get the points back, too. Plus, you get a major effect.

STEVE: I want to grab the thing with all the legs and pull it off the Muggarik! Then I throw it on the ground, hoping Viddo will shoot it.

GM: Sounds like a reasonable major effect. You pull it off his face and toss it down. The Muggarik stumbles backward.

TONY: Nice one.

GM: The Muggarik seems dazed and incoherent. His face is pale. The smaller thing scuttles across the ground and leaps toward Catissan. Speed defense roll, please.

STEVE: Oh, no. I wish I had something to block it. A shield or something.

SASHA: We'll get you one for next time.

TONY: If there *is* a next time.

STEVE: I'm putting Effort into this roll too. Just one level. That costs 3 points because I don't have any Speed Edge. I roll a 12.

GM: The thing leaps toward your face, but you duck backward. It lands on the wall next to you and clings there.

TONY: I shoot it with my blaster on my turn. I . . . roll a 1. Crap.

GM: Okay. That's an intrusion. The Muggarik shakes off its condition and draws a long knife. It doesn't have a thing clutched to its face, but it's moving strangely.

SASHA: It's still controlled, maybe.

TONY: Just shoot him!

GM: It uses the knife to slash at Catissan.

STEVE: I don't use Effort for this Speed defense. I roll a 7.

GM: The knife slashes your arm. You take 4 points of damage. But you've got light armor, so you lose 3 points from your Might Pool.

TONY: Shoot him!

SASHA: I shoot my blaster rifle, but at the creepy thing on the wall. I use one level of Effort and roll a 14.

GM: It's small and fast, but that's a hit, thanks to putting Effort into it.

SASHA: I do 6 points of damage, plus 1 from my Masters Weaponry focus.

GM: Your blast sends some of its many legs flying across the room. Yellow fluid splatters across the wall. But it's still alive.

STEVE: Ew. Okay, my turn? I step back, keeping my eye on both of them, but wait to use my Good Advice ability to help Tony's attack on his turn.

GM: Okay. Both of them continue to attack you, Steve.

STEVE: I figured. It's costly, but I'm going to use a level of Effort on both Speed defense rolls. I roll a 16 against the spider-thing, but only a 4 against the Muggarik.

GM: The Muggarik cuts you with his knife again. That's 3 more points after you subtract your Armor.

STEVE: Ouch. I'm really hurting here, guys.

TONY: I shoot the spider-thing. Since Catissan's ability is reducing the level of difficulty, and I've got a light blaster that reduces it another, I'm going to use a level of Effort, but for damage. I roll a 17!

GM: That's a hit!

TONY: Okay, so the blaster does 2 points of damage, but my Effort makes that 5, and my 17 roll adds another 1, for a total of 6 points.

GM: Its blackened corpse slides down to the floor.

TONY: That's the way it's done, my friends.

SASHA: All right. What about the Muggarik?

GM: He stands utterly motionless for a moment and then falls to the ground.

SASHA: Aha! I was hoping that would happen. Kill the icky thing, and the mind control ends.

STEVE: Whenever it's my turn, I'm making a recovery roll.

GM: We don't need to pay attention to initiative at this point, although I guess it depends on what you guys do next.

STEVE: I got a 4 on my roll, and I add 2 points for my tier. I'm putting all those points back into my Might Pool.

SASHA: I check out the Muggarik.

GM: He's alive and conscious. His large black eyes don't seem to focus.

TONY: Ask him where our crystals are.

SASHA: I'm going to give him a minute first.

STEVE: Yeah, I help Viddo. We make him comfortable. We'll ask him about the crystals when he can talk.

TONY: I don't trust him. My blaster is still out.

GM: Eventually the Muggarik seems to recover a bit. He sees the two of you giving him some aid, but then he spots Irom's blaster pointed at him.

Normally, the Muggarik would be grateful, but the GM decides that it panics instead, so she slides two cards toward Steve—a GM intrusion. (The group uses cards to represent XP)

GM: The Muggarik's eyes grow wide, and he tries to get up and make a run for it.

SASHA: We should grab him.

STEVE: I try to calm him down. "Hey, friend. It's okay, we just got rid of that thing that was controlling you."

SASHA: Yeah, I try to help. I'm trained in pleasant social interactions, so I'll reduce the difficulty a step.

GM: Okay, make a roll.

STEVE: I'll use a level of Effort, too. That costs 3 points because I don't have any Intellect Edge. And I roll . . . a 2.

SASHA (sliding an XP card toward the GM): I'm going to spend an experience point to have Steve reroll that.

GM: Okay. Steve, roll again.

STEVE: Thank you, Sasha. I roll a 12 this time. That's better, at least.

GM: It's good enough. The Muggarik stops and calms down. Oh, and Steve, you still have an experience point to give to one of the other players.

STEVE: Right. I give it to Sasha, obviously, for helping me.

SASHA: Thanks.

TONY: "All right, dude. Where's our hyperdrive crystals? And where are the rest of your buddies?" And I'll holster my blaster.

GM: Now that he's calm, he clearly realizes that you saved him. Getting him to talk won't require a roll. He begins to tell you about the K-chiln in a strangely cracking voice. "They are horrible, awful, multilegged insectlike creatures that have taken control of many of my people. I do not know what I did while under their control, but I do recall a number of my friends leaving with some canisters holding crystals. They were headed for a starship at a landing platform in the woods." What do you do?

Part 5
BACK MATTER

INDEX

INDEX

CAMPAIGN DESIGN WORKSHEET

CAMPAIGN

GENRE

GM

TYPES AVAILABLE

TYPE	BASED ON	MODIFICATIONS

DESCRIPTORS AVAILABLE

- ☐ Appealing
- ☐ Brash
- ☐ Calm
- ☐ Charming
- ☐ Clever
- ☐ Clumsy
- ☐ Craven
- ☐ Creative
- ☐ Cruel
- ☐ Dishonorable
- ☐ Doomed
- ☐ Driven
- ☐ Empathic
- ☐ Exiled
- ☐ Fast
- ☐ Foolish
- ☐ Graceful
- ☐ Guarded
- ☐ Hardy
- ☐ Hideous
- ☐ Honorable
- ☐ Impulsive
- ☐ Inquisitive
- ☐ Intelligent
- ☐ Jovial
- ☐ Kind
- ☐ Learned
- ☐ Lucky
- ☐ Mad
- ☐ Mechanical
- ☐ Mysterious
- ☐ Mystical
- ☐ Naive
- ☐ Noble
- ☐ Perceptive
- ☐ Resilient
- ☐ Rugged
- ☐ Sharp-Eyed
- ☐ Skeptical
- ☐ Spiritual
- ☐ Stealthy
- ☐ Strong
- ☐ Strong-Willed
- ☐ Swift
- ☐ Tongue-Tied
- ☐ Tough
- ☐ Vengeful
- ☐ Virtuous
- ☐ Wealthy
- ☐ Weird

FOCI AVAILABLE

- ☐ Abides in Stone
- ☐ Awakens Dreams
- ☐ Battles Robots
- ☐ Bears a Halo of Fire
- ☐ Blazes With Radiance
- ☐ Builds Robots
- ☐ Calculates the Incalculable
- ☐ Carries a Quiver
- ☐ Casts Spells
- ☐ Channels Divine Blessings
- ☐ Commands Mental Powers
- ☐ Conducts Weird Science
- ☐ Consorts With the Dead
- ☐ Controls Beasts
- ☐ Controls Gravity
- ☐ Crafts Illusions
- ☐ Crafts Unique Objects
- ☐ Defends the Weak
- ☐ Doesn't Do Much
- ☐ Employs Magnetism
- ☐ Entertains
- ☐ Exists in Two Places at Once
- ☐ Exists Partially Out of Phase
- ☐ Explores Dark Places
- ☐ Explores Deep Waters
- ☐ Fights Dirty
- ☐ Fights With Panache
- ☐ Focuses Mind Over Matter
- ☐ Fuses Flesh and Steel
- ☐ Fuses Mind and Machine
- ☐ Grows to Towering Heights
- ☐ Howls at the Moon
- ☐ Hunts Nonhumans
- ☐ Hunts Outcasts
- ☐ Hunts With Great Skill
- ☐ Infiltrates
- ☐ Interprets the Law
- ☐ Is Idolized by Millions
- ☐ Is Licensed to Carry
- ☐ Leads
- ☐ Lives in the Wilderness
- ☐ Looks for Trouble
- ☐ Masters Defense
- ☐ Masters the Swarm
- ☐ Masters Weaponry
- ☐ Metes Out Justice
- ☐ Moves Like a Cat
- ☐ Moves Like the Wind
- ☐ Murders
- ☐ Needs No Weapon
- ☐ Never Says Die
- ☐ Operates Undercover
- ☐ Performs Feats of Strength
- ☐ Pilots Starcraft
- ☐ Rages
- ☐ Rides the Lightning
- ☐ Sees Beyond
- ☐ Separates Mind From Body
- ☐ Shepherds Spirits
- ☐ Siphons Power
- ☐ Slays Monsters
- ☐ Solves Mysteries
- ☐ Speaks for the Land
- ☐ Stands Like a Bastion
- ☐ Talks to Machines
- ☐ Throws With Deadly Accuracy
- ☐ Travels Through Time
- ☐ Wears a Sheen of Ice
- ☐ Wields Two Weapons at Once
- ☐ Works Miracles
- ☐ Works the Back Alleys
- ☐ Works the System
- ☐ Would Rather Be Reading

OTHER NOTES

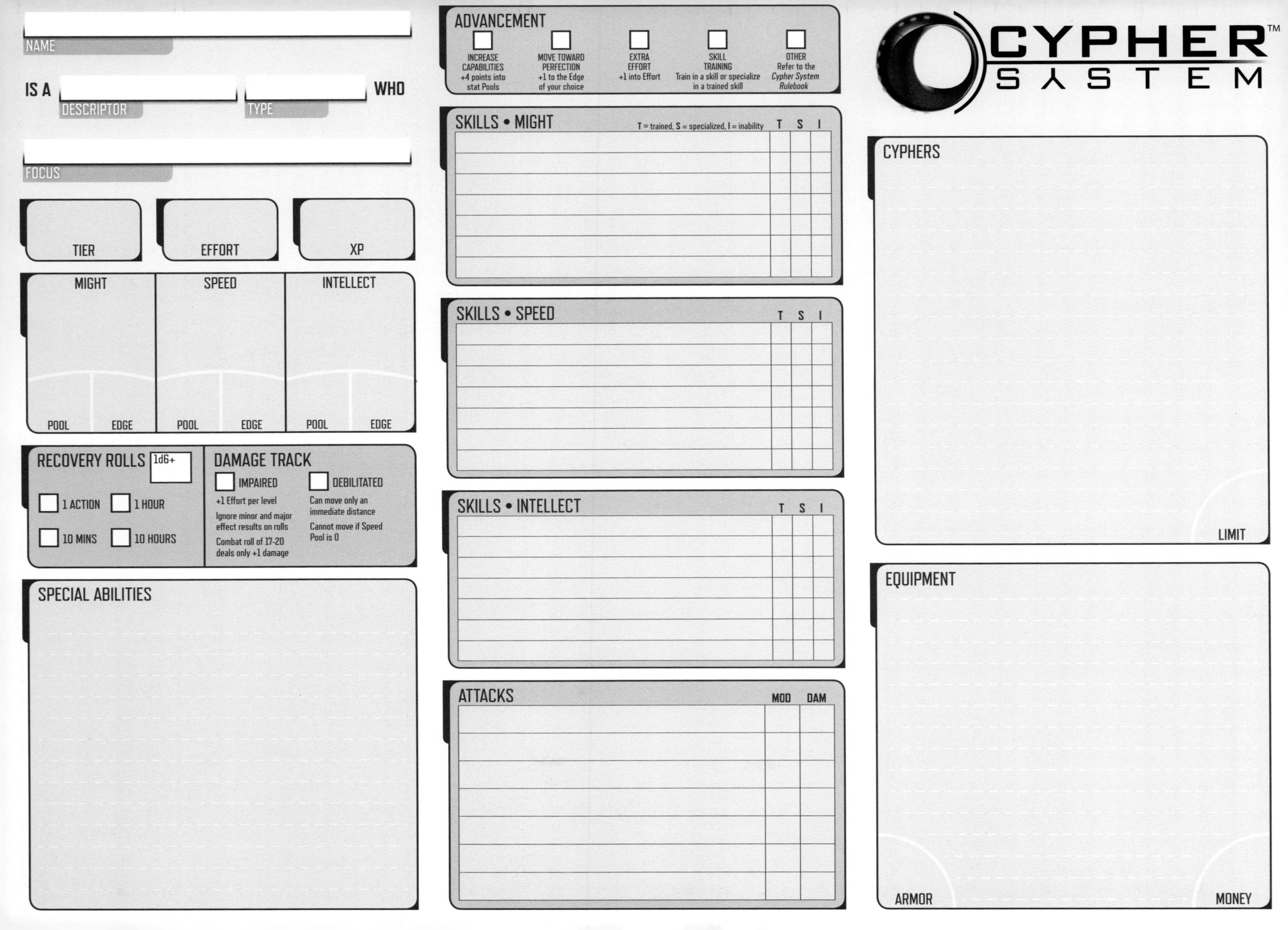

CYPHER SYSTEM™

NAME

IS A DESCRIPTOR TYPE WHO

FOCUS

TIER

EFFORT

XP

MIGHT		SPEED		INTELLECT	
POOL	EDGE	POOL	EDGE	POOL	EDGE

RECOVERY ROLLS 1d6+

☐ 1 ACTION ☐ 1 HOUR

☐ 10 MINS ☐ 10 HOURS

DAMAGE TRACK

☐ IMPAIRED

+1 Effort per level

Ignore minor and major effect results on rolls

Combat roll of 17-20 deals only +1 damage

☐ DEBILITATED

Can move only an immediate distance

Cannot move if Speed Pool is 0

SPECIAL ABILITIES

ADVANCEMENT

☐ INCREASE CAPABILITIES +4 points into stat Pools

☐ MOVE TOWARD PERFECTION +1 to the Edge of your choice

☐ EXTRA EFFORT +1 into Effort

☐ SKILL TRAINING Train in a skill or specialize in a trained skill

☐ OTHER Refer to the *Cypher System Rulebook*

SKILLS • MIGHT

T = trained, S = specialized, I = inability

	T	S	I

SKILLS • SPEED

	T	S	I

SKILLS • INTELLECT

	T	S	I

ATTACKS

	MOD	DAM

CYPHERS

LIMIT

EQUIPMENT

ARMOR

MONEY

BACKGROUND
NOTES
PORTRAIT